Contents

INSTRUCTOR'S ANNOTATED EDITION

Grassroots with Readings

The Writer's Workbook

Eighth Edition

INSTRUCTOR'S ANNOTATED EDITION

Grassroots with Readings

The Writer's Workbook

Eighth Edition

Susan Fawcett

Houghton Mifflin Company Boston New York

VP, Publisher: Patricia Coryell
Senior Sponsoring Editor: Lisa Kimball
Senior Development Editor: Judith Fifer
Editorial Assistant: Peter Mooney
Senior Project Editor: Cecilia Molinari
Editorial Assistant: Sean McGann
Senior Composition Buyer: Sarah L. Ambrose
Art and Design Manager: Gary Crespo
Senior Photo Editor: Jennifer Meyer Dare
Manufacturing Coordinator: Chuck Dutton
Senior Marketing Manager: Annamarie Rice
Senior Designer: Henry Rachlin

Cover image: © Brett Baunton/Getty Images

Acknowledgements appear on page 444.

Printed in the U.S.A.

Library of Congress Control Number: 2004115231

ISBN: 0-618-50855-4

1 2 3 4 5 6 7 8 9 – WEB – 08 07 06 05

The Eighth Edition of *Grassroots* is making a splash!!

"I love the changes and additions! I want to use the book right now!"

—Karen Sidwell,
St. Petersburg College

"I encourage my students to keep this book with them throughout their college days as a valuable resource in their subsequent college-credit writing projects. I also tell them that I plan to be buried with my copy of *Grassroots*."

—Chandler McRee,
Brevard Community College–Melbourne Campus

A new, colorful design and four-color photos ▶ enhance ***Grassroots***' clear, friendly pedagogy and provide a new focus on critical viewing—in addition to enhanced coverage of critical thinking.

"Students will respond to the visuals."

— Deborah Stallings,
Hinds Community College–Raymond Campus

Jennifer Lopez performs in San Juan, Puerto Rico.

PRACTICE 7 REVIEW

Now check your work in the preceding exercises or have it checked. Do you see any patterns in your errors? Do you tend to miss regular or irregular verbs? To help yourself learn, copy all four forms of each verb that you missed into your notebook in a chart like the one below. Use the chart to study.

Personal Review Chart

Simple	Present Tense (he, she, it)	Past Tense	Past Participle
go	goes	went	gone

PART D Using the Present Perfect Tense

The **present perfect tense** is composed of the present tense of *to have* (*has* or *have*) plus the past participle.

Present Perfect Tense

Singular	Plural
I *have* spoken	we *have* spoken
you *have* spoken	you *have* spoken
he / she / it } *has* spoken	they *have* spoken

◀ Critical thinking skills are further promoted with more third-person models and assignments, more collaborative problem-solving and revising, Web links for further study, and visuals for analysis.

UNIT 2

REVIEW

Proofreading and Revising

Proofread the following essay to eliminate all sentence fragments. Circle the number of every fragment. (You should find nine.) Then correct the fragments in any way you choose—by connecting them to a sentence before or after, by completing any incomplete verbs, and so on. Make your corrections above the lines.

Living Without Television

(1) What would you do without your television? (2) Every spring, millions of Americans answer this question for themselves. (3) By taking part in TV Turn-Off Week. (4) They find out that they can in fact lead enjoyable lives without watching TV. (5) Begun in 1995, TV Turn-Off Week now has motivated 24 million participants to spend seven full days. (6) Engaging in activities other than TV viewing. (7) Although many Turn-Off Week participants initially fear that they will be bored without their TVs. (8) They often rediscover the joys of reading, talking to family and friends, going for walks, exercising, and learning new skills like playing the guitar.

(9) Statistics help explain the power of TV Turn-Off Week. (10) Americans watch more than four hours of TV a day. (11) That's two full months each year. (12) Simply turning off the box leaves people with lots of time to do other things. (13) Nearly half of the U.S. population watches TV while eating dinner. (14) Instead of using that time to talk to other family members. (15) Because 56 percent of children have a television set in their bedrooms. (16) They tend to watch programs alone instead of doing homework, interacting with their parents and siblings, or exercising.

(17) Interestingly, the consequences of TV Turn-Off Week seem to be lasting. (18) Many past participants say that they have changed their viewing habits. (19) While a few people go so far as to get rid of their televisions. (20) Most report that they now watch fewer shows. (21) And are less likely to leave the TV sputtering as unwatched background noise. (22) Some move their televisions. (23) Taking them out of bedrooms and the family room. (24) Others cancel or reduce their cable or satellite services. (25) One major benefit is that individuals and families

prove to themselves that they can find other, more engaging things to do. (26) Many parents gain confidence about limiting their children's viewing time. (27) And more important, about teaching their children how and when to watch TV.

EXPLORING ONLINE

Turn off all TVs in your house for one week, keeping notes on any reactions or changes. Use these notes to write about the experience.

<http://tvturnoff.org/> Visit the website and read for ideas. See "Facts and Figures." Then use this information in a composition arguing for or against watching less TV.

328 CHAPTER 30

(1) Every spring and summer, storm chaser's spreads out across the Midwestern part of the United States known as Tornado Alley. (2) Armed with video cameras maps and radios. (3) These lovers of violent weather follows huge weather systems called supercells, which sometimes produces tornadoes. (4) On a good day, a storm chaser may find a supercell. (5) And get close enough to film the brief, destructive life of a tornado. (6) Some joins the storm-chasing tours offered every summer by universities or private companies. (7) Others learn what they can from Internet websites and sets off on their own to hunt tornadoes. (8) Storm chasing can be very dangerous. (9) A large tornado spins winds between 125 and 175 mph, tearing roofs off houses ripping limbs from trees, and overturning cars. (10) The greatest danger comes from airborne branches boards shingles and glass hurtling through the air like deadly weapons. (11) Even if a supercell don't spawn tornadoes. (12) It often produces winds over 50 mph, heavy rain, large hail, and intense lightning. (13) Most storm chasers avoids these risks by racing out of a tornados' path before it gets too close. (14) Despite or perhaps because of these dangers, dramatized in the 1996 movie *Twister*. (15) Storm chasing remains popular. (16) Fans claim that few things in life matches the thrill of discovering a tornado and witnessing the power of nature.

Storm chasers confront a deadly twister in Tornado Alley.
©Carsten Peter/National Geographic Magazine.

◀ **A new chapter, "Putting Your Proofreading Skills to Work," provides paragraphs and essays for students to practice proofreading skills and features a mix of errors that they will likely encounter in real-world writing situations.**

"I am greatly in favor of mixed-error proofreading exercises; such exercises are a better preparation for the reality of writing."

— Rebecca Smith Mann,
Guilford Technical Community College

Many new high-interest models and practices—plus 50% new readings—keep students engaged, while they hone their grammar skills. ▶

"The great strength of **Grassroots** *is its high-interest content."*

— Frederick L. DeNaples,
Bronx Community College

Look-Alikes/Sound-Alikes 367

CHAPTER REVIEW

Proofread this essay for look-alike/sound-alike errors. Write your corrections above the lines.

Rapper with a Difference

(1) If you're concept of hip-hop music is gang fights, drugs, the fast life, and negative views of women, than perhaps you haven't heard of Wyclef Jean. (2) Like many rappers, Jean is committed to making music with powerful lyrics and driving rhythms. (3) However, this Haitian-born former Fugee sends a very different message and lives a quiter lifestyle than many hip-hop artists do.

(4) Unlike some hip-hop music—named "gangsta rap" for it's glorification of violence—Jean's songs celebrate nonviolence and understanding. (5) For example, in his fourth solo album, *The Preacher's Son*, Jean shares his vision of a peaceful world were everyone gets along. (6) He believes that if people can set and talk, they can work though almost anything. (7) Wyclef pleads for an end to dangerous feuds between rappers, such as the clashes between 50 Cent and Ja Rule, Jay-Z and Nas, and the passed rivalry, kept alive in music, between Tupac Shakur and Notorious B.I.G., both gunned down in there prime.

(8) Jean also differs from other rappers in his calm lifestyle. (9) While many hip-hop celebrities live the high life, traveling with bodyguards and a posse of

Activist Wyclef Jean in concert
©2004 Getty Images.

More extensive ESL emphasis includes new **ESL Tips and Teaching Tips** in the Instructor's Annotated Edition, ESL websites and an appendix in the text, and websites with rich additional resources for both students and instructors. ▶

APPENDIX 2

Some Guidelines for Students of English as a Second Language

Count and Noncount Nouns

Count nouns refer to people, places, or things that are separate units. You can often point to them, and you can always count them.

Count Noun	Sample Sentence
computer	The writing lab has four *computers*.
dime	There are two *dimes* under your chair.
professor	All of my *professors* are at a conference today.
notebook	I carry three *notebooks* in my backpack.
child	Why is your *child* jumping on the table?

Noncount nouns refer to things that are wholes. You cannot count them separately. Noncount nouns may refer to ideas, feelings, and other things that you cannot see or touch. Noncount nouns may refer to food or beverages.

Noncount Noun	Sample Sentence
courage	It takes *courage* to study a new language.
equipment	The company sells office *equipment*.
happiness	We wish the bride and groom much *happiness*.
bread	Who will slice this loaf of *bread*?
meat	Do you eat *meat*, or are you a vegetarian?
coffee	The *coffee* turned cold as we talked.

ESL TIP
Suggest that students try practicing with flash cards, memorizing when necessary. Also refer them to online exercises like the crossword puzzle at <http://www.ccc.commnet.edu/grammar/quizzes/cross/cross_prep2.htm>.

ESL TIP
If ESL learners need more practice with prepositions, refer them to Writespace for *Grassroots* and to Error #3: Preposition Error in the "8 Common ESL Errors" on the *Grassroots* student website.

The preposition shows a relationship between the object of the preposition and some other word in the sentence. Below are some sentences with prepositional phrases:

(1) Ms. Kringell arrived *at noon*.
(2) A man *in a gray suit* bought three lottery tickets.
(3) The huge moving van sped through the tunnel.

- In sentence (1), the prepositional phrase *at noon* tells when Ms. Kringell arrived. It describes *arrived*.
- In sentence (2), the prepositional phrase *in a gray suit* describes how the man was dressed. It describes *man*.
- What is the prepositional phrase in sentence (3)? through the tunnel
  Which word does it describe? sped

PRACTICE 1

Underline the prepositional phrases in the following sentences.

1. Bill collected some interesting facts about human biology.
2. Human eyesight is sharpest at midday.
3. In extreme cold, shivering produces heat, which can save lives.

"The ESL material is probably the best addition to **Grassroots**."

— Stephen W. B. Rizzo, *Bevill State Community College*

displayed these paintings. (9) No major commercial gallery had showcased an African American artist before. (10) The *Migration Series* depicts southern blacks journeying north to find work after World War I. (11) The paintings show people searching for a better life. (12) Lawrence's work portrays the poverty and prejudice the migrants endured. (13) He also wanted viewers of his work "to experience the beauty of life." (14) During his long career, Lawrence painted many more energetic canvases and series. (15) His work reminds us that we are all migrants. (16) We are always on the move. (17) We are seeking something more.

EXPLORING ONLINE

See Lawrence's paintings at the Whitney Museum of Art online. <http://www.whitney.org/jacoblawrence/> Click on "Jacob Lawrence's Art." Describe your favorite painting to someone who has never seen it. More writing ideas appear under "Explore" and "Tell Your Own Story."

Brownstones, 1958, by Jacob Lawrence.
Courtesy of Clark Atlanta University.

EXPLORING ONLINE

<http://www.ccc.commnet.edu/grammar/quizzes/indep_clause_quiz.htm>
Interactive clause line-up: I.D. the independent or dependent clauses.

<http://web2.uvcs.uvic.ca/elc/studyzone/330/grammar/subcon.htm>
Explanation of subordination followed by interactive practice sets.

<http://college.hmco.com/devenglish> Visit the *Grassroots* 8/e Student Website for more exercises and quizzes.

◀ A new feature, ***Exploring Online***, at the end of every chapter and in selected practices, directs readers to selected websites that provide opportunities for further study and practice, including leading **Online Writing Lab (OWL)** sites.

Spotlight on Writing

Correct punctuation adds to the power of this writer's humorous look at a serious subject. If possible, read his paragraph aloud.

My daughter, Olivia, who just turned three, has an imaginary friend whose name is Charlie Ravioli. Olivia is growing up in Manhattan, and so Charlie Ravioli has a lot of local traits: he lives in an apartment "on Madison and Lexington," he dines on grilled chicken, fruit, and water, and having reached the age of seven and a half, he feels, or is thought, "old." But the most peculiarly local thing about Olivia's imaginary playmate is this: he is always too busy to play with her. She holds her toy cell phone up to her ear, and we hear her talk into it. "Ravioli? It's Olivia. . . It's Olivia. Come and play? OK. Call me. Bye." Then she snaps it shut and shakes her head. "I always get his machine," she says. Or she will say, "I spoke to Ravioli today." "Did you have fun?" my wife and I ask. "No. He was busy working. On a television" (leaving it up in the air if he repairs electronic devices or has his own talk show).

Adam Gopnik, "Bumping Into Mr. Ravioli," *The New Yorker*

- This writer describes his daughter's imaginary playmate as someone too busy to play! Why do you think Olivia has invented a playmate like Ravioli? Where did she learn about cell conversations, phone machines, and busy-ness?
- Does this paragraph point out a modern problem? If so, is it a big-city problem or a problem that exists in many places? What is the solution?

- ***Taking time to play***
- ***A time when "child's play" taught you something important***

"The explanation of the writing process and the grammar sections are top-notch."

— Crystal L. Echols,
Sinclair Community College

◀ ***Grassroots'*** **compelling pedagogy, engaging grammar practices, and assignments always bring the focus back to writing.** ▼

"One of the strongest features of this text is the ***Writers' Workshop*** *at the end of each unit and the following* ***Writing Assignments*** *page. The variety of suggested topics and points of view suggested for student writings I found* **IMPRESSIVE***. The writing assignments in the text are* **STRONG***…"*

— Norma Craig,
Miami Dade College

UNIT 4

WRITERS' WORKSHOP

Describe a Detour off the Main Highway

When a writer really cares about a subject, often the reader will care too. In your group or class, read this student's paragraph, aloud if possible. As you read, underline any words or details that strike you as vivid or powerful.

Sometimes detours off the main highway can bring wonderful surprises, and last week this happened to my husband and me. On the Fourth of July weekend, we decided to drive home the long way, taking the old dirt farm road. Pulling over to admire the afternoon light gleaming on a field of wet corn we saw a tiny farm stand under a tree. No one was in sight, but a card table covered with a red checked cloth held pints of tomatoes, jars of jam, and a handwritten price list. Next to these was a vase full of red poppies and tiny American flags. We bought tomatoes, leaving our money in the tin box stuffed with dollar bills. Driving home we both felt so happy—as if we had been given a great gift.

Kim Lee, student

1. How effective is Kim Lee's paragraph?

   ____ Clear topic sentence? ____ Rich supporting details?

   ____ Logical organization? ____ Effective conclusion?
2. Discuss your underlinings with one another, explaining as specifically as possible why a particular word or sentence is effective. For instance, the "red poppies and tiny American flags" are so exact that you can see them.
3. This student supports her topic sentence with a single *example*, one brief story told in detail. If you were to support the same topic sentence, what example from your own life might you use?
4. The concluding sentence tells the reader that she and her husband felt they had been given "a great gift." Do you think that the gift was being trusted to be honest?
5. Proofread for grammar and spelling. Do you notice any error patterns (two or more errors of the same type) that this student should watch out for?

About her writing process, Kim Lee says:

I wrote this paper in my usual way—I sort of plan, and then I freewrite on the subject. I like freewriting—I pick through it for certain words or details, but of course it is also a mess. From my freewriting I got "light gleaming on a field of wet corn" and the last sentence, about the gift.

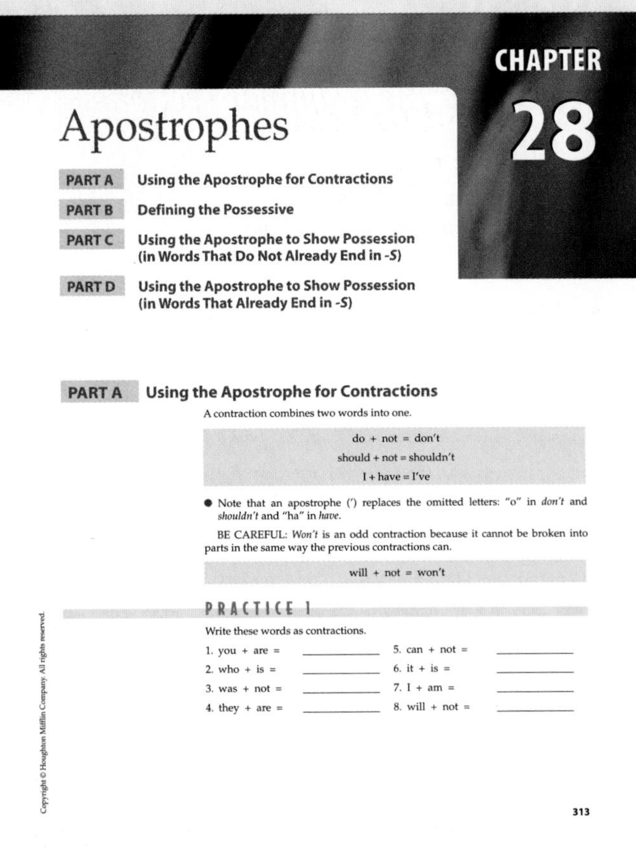
CHAPTER 28

Apostrophes

PART A Using the Apostrophe for Contractions

PART B Defining the Possessive

PART C Using the Apostrophe to Show Possession (in Words That Do Not Already End in *-S*)

PART D Using the Apostrophe to Show Possession (in Words That Already End in *-S*)

PART A Using the Apostrophe for Contractions

A contraction combines two words into one.

do + not = don't
should + not = shouldn't
I + have = I've

- Note that an apostrophe (') replaces the omitted letters: "o" in *don't* and *shouldn't* and "ha" in *have*.

BE CAREFUL: *Won't* is an odd contraction because it cannot be broken into parts in the same way the previous contractions can.

will + not = won't

PRACTICE 1

Write these words as contractions.

1. you + are =	________	5. can + not =	________
2. who + is =	________	6. it + is =	________
3. was + not =	________	7. I + am =	________
4. they + are =	________	8. will + not =	________

313

*"Another aspect of the text concept I find very appealing is her use of language that students can understand… Ms. Fawcett does not talk **down** to those to whom she writes; she talks **to them** not **at them.**"*

— Susan Warrington,
Phillips Community College of the University of Arkansas

◀ **Engaging chapter preview and review pedagogy enable students to *enjoy* mastering chapter content.** ▼

14 CHAPTER 2

You will soon find that ideas for writing will occur to you all day long. Before they slip away, capture them in words. Writing is like ice skating. You have to practice.

PRACTICE 7

Write in your journal for at least ten minutes three times a week.

At the end of each week, read what you have written. Underline striking passages, and mark interesting topics and ideas that you would like to explore further.

As you complete the exercises in this book and work on the writing assignments, try all four techniques—freewriting, brainstorming, clustering, and keeping a journal—and see which ones work best for you.

PRACTICE 8

From your journal, choose one or two passages that you might want to rewrite and allow others to read. Put a check beside each of those passages so that you can find them easily later. Underline the parts you like best. Can you already see ways you might rewrite and improve the writing?

CHAPTER HIGHLIGHTS

To get started and to discover your ideas, try these techniques.

- **Focused freewriting: freewriting for five or ten minutes about one topic**
- **Brainstorming: freely jotting many ideas about a topic**
- **Clustering: making word associations on paper**
- **Keeping a journal: writing regularly about things that interest and move you**

EXPLORING ONLINE

<http://uwc.tamu.edu/handouts/started/gs_freewriting.html> Peter Elbow shares ideas for using freewriting to become a better writer.

<http://depts.gallaudet.edu/englishworks/writing/prewriting.html> Review or print this handy chart of prewriting strategies.

<http://college.hmco.com/devenglish> For more exercises and quizzes on the Student Website, visit the link, click Developmental Writing, and find the home page for *Grassroots,* 8/e. Bookmark the site for future visits as you work through this book.

*"I would feel very comfortable assigning almost every exercise in **Grassroots**, which I cannot say without reservation about the other textbooks I've encountered."*

— Frederick L. DeNaples,
Bronx Community College

Better than ever! A full array of supplements provides busy instructors with all the materials they'll need to teach *and* gives students additional resources that will help them master the material.

- The **Instructor's Annotated Edition (IAE)** now includes marginal ESL and Teaching Tips.

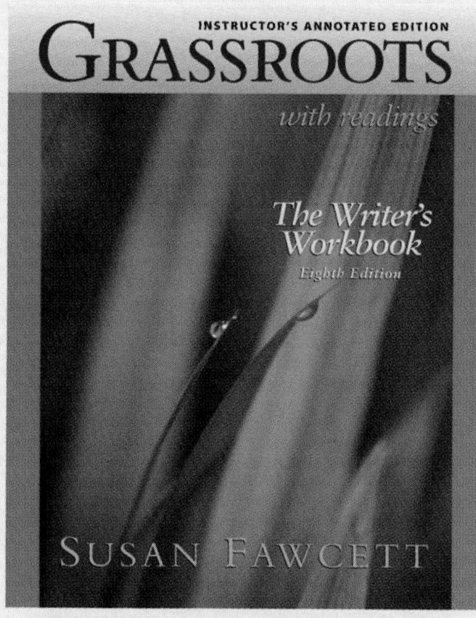

- The revised and expanded ***Grassroots* Test Bank** is available in three formats—in print, on the HM Testing CD-ROM, and on the Web.

- **NEW! PowerPoint slides** can be used to enhance classroom activities.

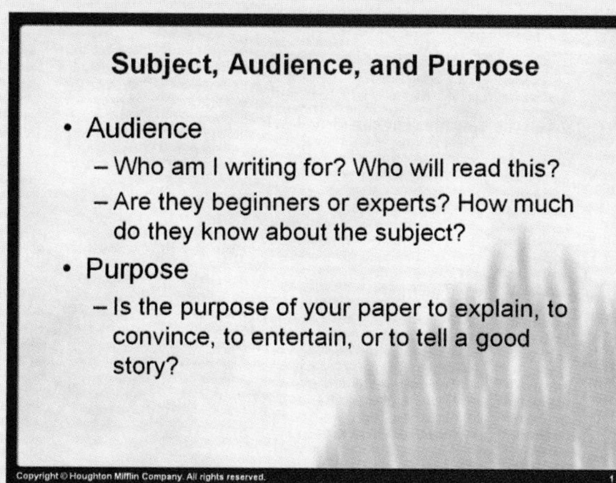

Subject, Audience, and Purpose
• Audience
– Who am I writing for? Who will read this?
– Are they beginners or experts? How much do they know about the subject?
• Purpose
– Is the purpose of your paper to explain, to convince, to entertain, or to tell a good story?
Copyright © Houghton Mifflin Company. All rights reserved.
1-5

- A more robust **Website** now includes many new resources for both students and instructors.

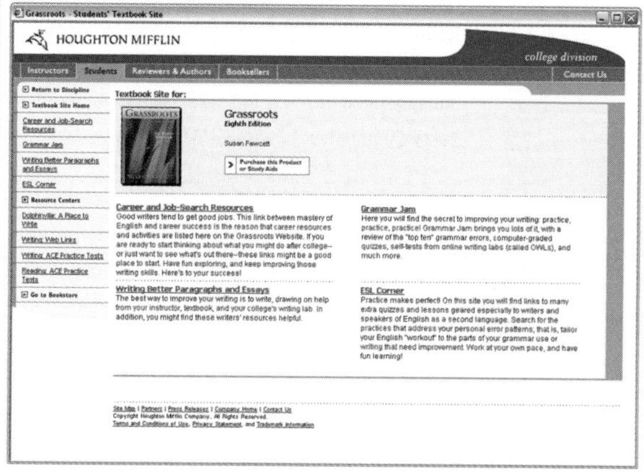

- The **Student Answer Key** provides answers to all objective exercises.

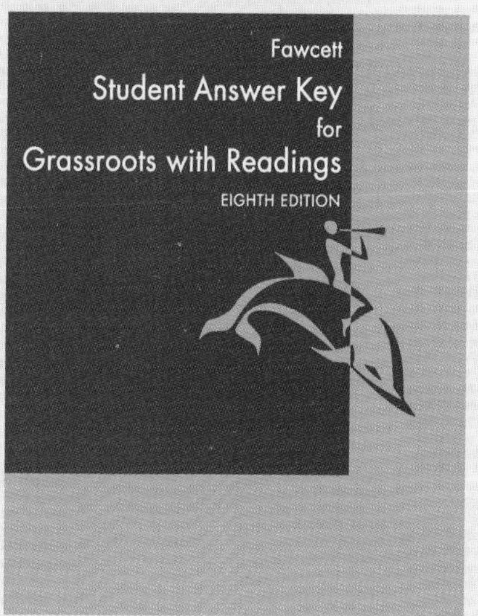

> *"I hope our developmental English program will continue to re-adopt* **Grassroots** *for a long time to come. It is so very accessible for our instructors and students alike."*
>
> —Chandler McRee,
> *Brevard Community College –Melbourne Campus*

New online technology!

WriteSpace, part of Houghton Mifflin's new Eduspace© online learning tool powered by Blackboard, provides hundreds of additional interactive high-interest practices and tests written specifically for Grassroots. WriteSpace offers immediate feedback for students and a course management system for instructors.

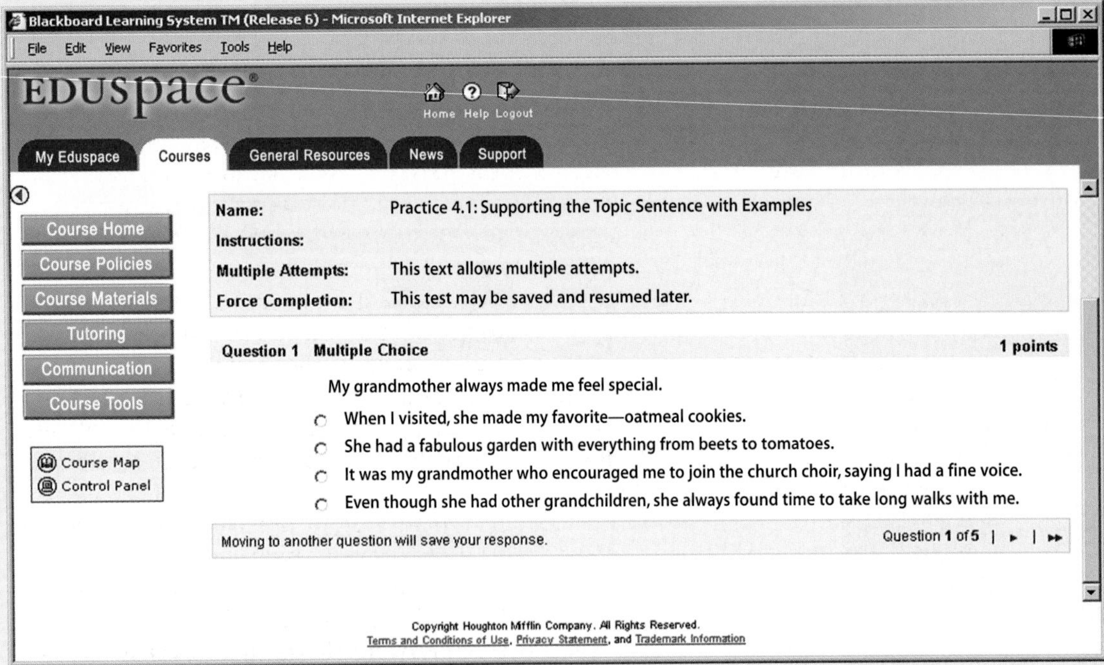

WriteSpace's password-protected website also gives students access to SMARTHINKING online tutoring, which connects them to experienced writing instructors for one-on-one writing assistance during peak hours.

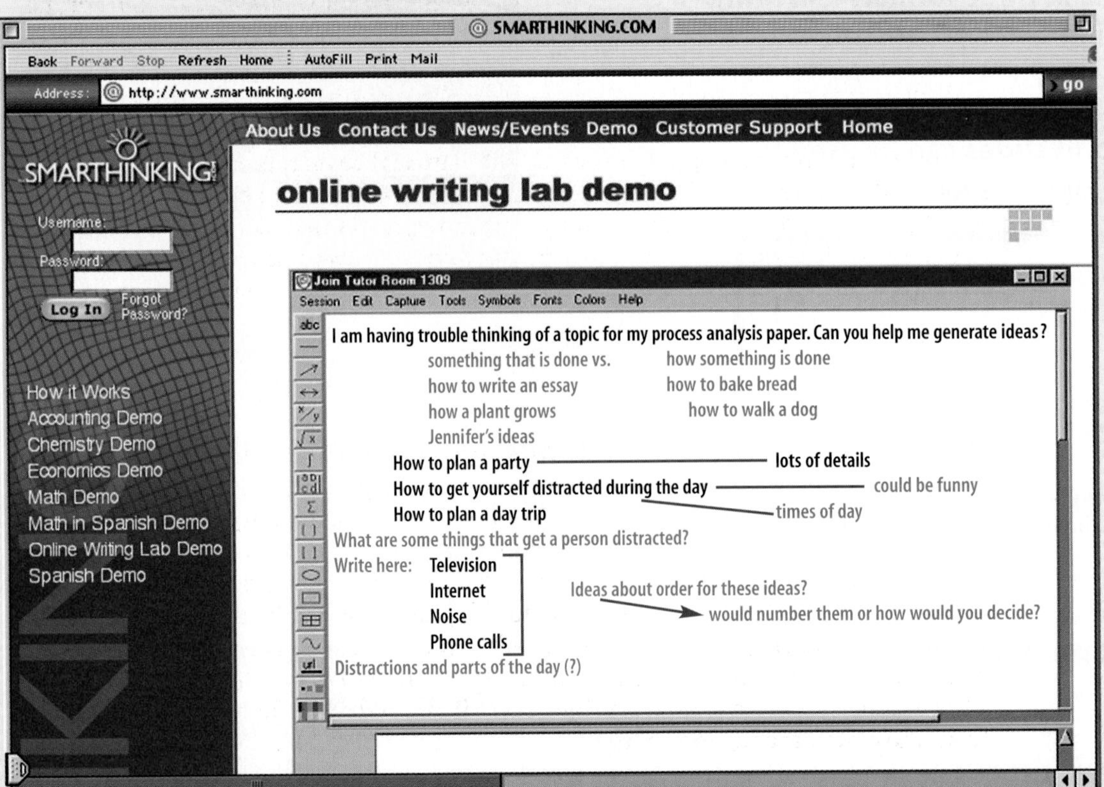

Preface

Grassroots with Readings grew out of my classroom experience at Bronx Community College of the City University of New York. It is designed for a range of students—native and nonnative; diverse in age, ethnicity, and background—who have not yet mastered the basic writing skills so necessary for success in college and most careers. Through its clear, paced lessons, inspiring student and professional models, and variety of high-interest practices and writing assignments, *Grassroots* has helped over one and a half million students become better writers.

I am excited about this sparkling new Eighth Edition. I have kept the carefully honed flow of grammar and writing lessons that prompt so many instructors and students to tell me that *Grassroots* keeps fulfilling its promise to help students improve their writing. However, I have thoroughly updated the text in light of the college and workplace challenges our students face in the twenty-first century and integrated features and emphases that better address contemporary realities. Notably, students must become not only competent writers but also critical thinkers and, increasingly, critical viewers as well. The addition of color enhances *Grassroots'* clear, friendly pedagogy and provides a new focus on critical viewing—with photographs, ads, paintings, and images from the World Wide Web. Because critical thinking skills are so vital for students at every level, I have embedded more thinking activities throughout the text. A new chapter on mixed-error proofreading helps students apply their skills to "real-world" tasks.

More nonnative students are entering basic writing classes than ever before—and most instructors are not trained in ESL but learn, as I did, flying by the seats of their pants. Therefore, I have added Teaching Tips and professionally vetted ESL Tips in the margins of the Instructor's Annotated Edition. These suggest classroom approaches and alert teachers to trouble spots and to ESL coverage integrated throughout the text.

Computer and Web resources are opening new avenues for faculty to improve their teaching and lighten their grading load and for students to learn more effectively. Thus, Web links or searches now appear in every chapter of this edition, guiding students to online practice or exploration and connecting with *Grassroots'* extensive new technology package. Finally, more than 25 percent of all practices and models have been replaced with fresh material to engage students and promote cultural literacy. Likewise, nearly half the readings have been replaced with strong contemporary selections. Minor improvements include a more engaging Chapter 1, strategic cuts where instructors told me coverage was beyond ample, and reformatting of some revising exercises so that students need not recopy.

Special Features of *Grassroots with Readings,* Eighth Edition

Full Color and Photographs. A four-color design and twenty-three color images now punctuate *Grassroots'* pedagogy. Every photo and painting was chosen to engage students and prompt them to pause, think more deeply, and connect with the material they have just read. For example, a photo of Frank Gehry's Disney Concert Hall lets students *see* why the adjacent paragraph claims his buildings are unique. Other images include a giant Galapagos tortoise, Aaron McGruder's comic-strip *Boondocks* characters, a public service ad from Adbusters, a painting by Carmen Lomos Garza, Julia Hill in the redwood she saved, the New York Public Library's grand reading room, Tony Hawk in flight, Lady Cowdiva from the Cow Parade, and more.

More Critical Thinking. To better foster college-level thinking skills, this edition contains fewer first-person narratives, more third-person models and assignments, and more level-appropriate thinking activities. Examples include more collaborative problem-solving and revising tasks, more provocative practice content, linked Internet sites, and visuals and humor to analyze.

New Mixed-Error Proofreading Chapter. A new Chapter 30, "Putting Your Proofreading Skills to Work," provides paragraphs and essays with a random, "real-world" mix of errors. Students test their proofreading skills while they learn about subjects like tornado chasers, police artist Jeanne Boylan, or a secret society promoting good deeds. This chapter works well for grammar review, proofreading practice, or assessment.

Integrated ESL Coverage. To better help nonnative writing students, marginal ESL Tips and general Teaching Tips appear in the Instructor's Annotated Edition. Written in partnership with an ESL expert who has twelve years of college teaching experience, these tips flag trouble spots or suggest class-tested ways to enhance the lesson and utilize the ESL coverage integrated throughout *Grassroots*. For instance, the text's verb coverage is more extensive than that of competing texts, anticipating the typical verb problems of nonnative as well as native students. Websites and the ESL Appendix offer students additional help and practice, as does the *ESL Corner* on *Grassroots'* Student Website.

New *Exploring Online* Feature. Selected websites throughout the text give students the option of further online study, practice, or discovery. For example, one or more top OWL (online writing lab) sites conclude every chapter. In addition, websites extend the reach of selected practices and readings on topics like Television Turn-off Week, goal setting, Barbie and body image, and the paintings of Jacob Lawrence. Links to every website in *Grassroots* can be found on the Student and Instructor Websites.

More than 25 percent New High-Interest Models and Practices. High-interest content is essential to *Grassroots'* success, keeping students engaged as they practice, modeling good writing and rhetorical modes, and promoting cultural literacy. The fifty-five new topics include robotics genius Dean Kamen, Latina crossover stars, job-search techniques, activist rapper Wyclef Jean, rude cell phone users, Habitat for Humanity, surfer Lisa Anderson, Surgeon General Richard Carmona, the advantages and disadvantages of online dating, and gratitude research.

Nearly 50 Percent New Reading Selections. Based on faculty and student ratings, Unit 9 has been extensively freshened with nine provocative contemporary readings on a broader range of themes. New are Julia Alvarez on learning English, Dave Barry on SUVs, Leonard Pitts Jr. on the dark side of the Internet, Ana Veciana-Suarez on lottery dreams and work, Jack Riemer on an unforgettable Itzhak Perlman concert, Firoozeh Dumas on her family's wacky immigrant experiences, Lauren Mehler on getting career insights from neighbors, and Norman M. Lobsenz on the power of childhood memories. Colman McCarthy's ideas for ending "peace illiteracy," with sample student annotations, now introduce the unit. Readers' favorite eleven selections from the last edition have been retained.

More Humor. Humor is a fine instructional tool. New humorous offerings include classified-ad bloopers, the Great American Mutt Show, Adam Gopnik on his daughter's imaginary playmate who is always too busy to play, and several *New Yorker* and Dilbert cartoons.

Other Improvements. Chapter 1 is now more engaging, with an advertisement to analyze, more stress on writing and success, and more humor. Throughout, some coverage has been trimmed and some revision exercises have been reformatted so that students need not recopy.

Extensive Technology and Ancillary Package

A loaded technology package and other useful ancillaries are now available on adoption of the text. Instructors have told us that the change they most wanted to see was more and better technology. We heard them. New to this edition are a number of exciting technology offerings designed or adapted specifically for use with *Grassroots*.

- **Instructor's Annotated Edition** with answers and new Teaching and ESL Tips.
- **New! WriteSpace for Grassroots.** WriteSpace, Houghton Mifflin's online learning tool powered by Blackboard, dynamically expands students' learning opportunities and instructors' teaching options. *WriteSpace for Grassroots* offers hundreds of interactive exercises and quizzes—many of them high-interest paragraphs and essays—all created for *Grassroots* and keyed to every part and chapter. Students get lots of extra practice, immediate feedback, and a score. Instructors praise WriteSpace's flexible course management system, with an online gradebook linked to the exercises (so that keeping track of student progress is easy); one convenient environment for course objectives, syllabi, and class information; and the chance to interact with students through live online hours, discussion boards, chat rooms, and an announcement center. Visit **<http://www.eduspace .com/>** for more information or to sign up for a demo.
- **SMARTHINKING™ online writing tutoring program** (which students can access on WriteSpace) links students to a Web-based writing center, staffed by experienced composition instructors. Students have four different kinds of support. *Live Help* provides access to 20 hours per week of real-time, one-on-one instruction from Sunday to Thursday, 9 p.m. to 1 a.m. Eastern Time. *Online Writing Lab* accepts unlimited paper submissions for expert review of grammar, punctuation, and syntax. *Questions Anytime* allows students to submit questions 24 hours a day, 7 days a week, for response by an e-structor within 24 hours. *Independent Study Resources* connects students around the clock to additional educational services, ranging from interactive websites to frequently asked questions.
- **Expanded and Revised Grassroots Test Bank,** now available electronically on the *HM Testing* CD-ROM, on the password-protected Instructor Website, or in paper format. In addition to revised and updated content throughout, Unit 1 now includes a rich selection of essay tests for every chapter, including material that makes use of visuals and tests critical thinking skills.
- **New! 120 PowerPoint Slides.** Keyed to *Grassroots*, these slides can be used to enhance classroom presentations or create handouts. They are available on the *HM Testing* CD-ROM with the electronic version of the Test Bank, or they can be downloaded from the Instructor Website.
- **Enriched Student Website.** Much expanded and more engaging, the *Grassroots'* Student Site has five resource areas: (1) *Grammar Jam* with many interactive ACE tests for self-study, 10 Most Common Errors and How to Correct Them, and useful interactive grammar sites; (2) *ESL Corner* with 15 ESL sites for study and graded practice and 8 Common ESL Errors and How to Correct Them; (3) *Writing Better Paragraphs and Essays* with printable checklists and peer feedback sheet, web links, and extra writing and revising help; (4) *Career and Job-Search Resources* with information, advice, links to tools like active verb lists for resume writers, and a list of careers that require writing skills; (5) Live links to every website in *Grassroots*.

- **New! Instructor Website.** This all-new site has six resource areas: (1) *Electronic Ancillaries for Grassroots* easily links the instructor to the new Test Bank in MS Word, PowerPoint slides, the Student Website, login for *WriteSpace for Grassroots*, and more; (2) *ESL Resources for Writing Instructors* with articles, tools, and ideas to enhance teaching of nonnative students; (3) *Grammar and Writing Links* with easy access to the many interactive links on the Student Site, plus live links to every website in the text; (4) *Creative Classroom Links* with some of the author's favorite assignments and course resources; (5) *Professional Organizations and Publications;* (6) *Shedding Light on Plagiarism* with insight and help from colleagues across the country.
- **New! HM Grammar CD-ROM** focuses on parts of speech, sentence problems, punctuation, mechanics, and spelling, with three to five exercises per topic.
- **Student Answer Key,** a paper resource with answers to all objective exercises.

Organization of the Text

The range of material and flexible format of *Grassroots with Readings* make this worktext and its much-expanded technology package adaptable to almost any teaching-learning situation: classroom, laboratory, or self-teaching. Each chapter is a self-contained lesson, so instructors may teach the chapters in any sequence that fits their course design. *Grassroots* is versatile enough to support many different approaches to basic writing instruction.

Acknowledgments

The author wishes to thank these reviewers whose thoughtful comments and suggestions helped strengthen this Eighth Edition.

Denise Bausch *Northern Virginia Community College*
Michelle J. Biferie *Palm Beach Community College*
Jessica Carroll *Miami-Dade College—Wolfson Campus*
Judy D. Covington *Trident Technical College*
Norma Craig *Miami-Dade College—Kendall Campus*
Frederick De Naples *Bronx Community College*
Shelly Dorsey *Pima Community College—Downtown Campus*
Crystal L. Echols *Sinclair Community College*
Janice Filer *Shelton State Community College*
Reginald Gerlica *Henry Ford Community College*
Peggy Harbers *Nashville State Community College*
Teresa S. Irvin *Columbus State University*
Debi Kirkland *Jackson State Community College*
John Lundquist *Golden West College*
Teri Maddox *Jackson State Community College*
Rebecca S. Mann *Guilford Technical Community College*
Peter Marcoux *El Camino College*
Chandler McRee *Brevard Community College*
Carol Miter *Riverside Community College—Norco Campus*
Betty Palmer Nelson *Volunteer State Community College*
Stephen Rizzo *Bevill State Community College*

Rebecca Samberg *Housatonic Community College*
Karen Sidwell *St. Petersburg College*
Deborah Stallings *Hinds Community College*
Doug Stuva *Iowa Western Community College*
Dennielle True *Manatee Community College*
Susan Warrington *Philllips Community College of the University of Arkansas*
Dornell L. Wolford *Wor-Wic Community College*

I am indebted to my editors at Houghton Mifflin, who worked hard to make this simply the best revision of *Grassroots* ever created. My deep thanks to Pat Coryell, Vice President and Publisher, for her special and much-appreciated support in making this book happen on time; Lisa Kimball, Senior Sponsoring Editor, who hit the grass running, brims with great ideas, and convinced me that using full color would not distract basic writers from their primary task; Judy Fifer, Senior Development Editor, whose competence and experience so enhance our team; Cecilia Molinari, Senior Project Editor, for guiding this beautiful baby into print; Janet Edmonds, wonderful techie and human being; and Peter Mooney, Editorial Associate, for his excellent and tireless work during a time of multiple transitions and crazy deadlines. I am grateful to Annamarie Rice, Marketing Manager, for graciously sharing her national perspectives and helping me think through some important issues.

The talented Ann Marie Radaskiewicz, my Development Editor for this project, has played a vital role researching, drafting, pulling ancillaries together, and brainstorming about *Grassroots* in cyberspace when we both should have been taking a break. Her professionalism and can-do cheer make working with her a delight. ESL expert Professor Nora Dawkins, Sr. Associate Professor of ESL at Miami-Dade Community College, North Campus, did a wonderful job suggesting ESL Tips for instructors and vetting tips I had created. The depth of her knowledge and the compactness with which she shared it will help many instructors better serve their nonnative and bilingual students. Dr. Frederick De Naples, Chair of English at Bronx Community College, CUNY, talked through pedagogical trends with me, suggested some great topics for this edition, and wrote several excellent practices. Susan Holtz tolerated my perfectionism, secured permissions, and alerted me to images I didn't know about. Dr. Karen Castellucci Cox provided a wonderful student paragraph for the Writers' Workshop as well as ideas that have affected my thinking.

Love and gratitude to the friends and family who supported me during the long days and nights of this revision, clipped articles or phoned with hot topics I might use, brought me flowers and goodies, and basically loved me anyway—especially Maggie Smith, Colleen Huff, Trisha Nelson, Bryan Hoffman, Sondra Zeidenstein, David Fawcett, Harriet Fawcett, and my husband, Richard Donovan.

I dedicate this Eighth Edition to the basic writing students in whose dreams I too believe.

S. F.

Suggestions to the Writing Instructor

Although most teachers of English agree that students learn to write by writing, effective course designs are probably as numerous and varied as good instructors. In the paragraphs that follow, I offer a few suggestions based on my own experience teaching basic writing to a mix of native and nonnative students.

Student Attitude and Motivation

A student's attitude toward writing can affect both motivation and performance. He or she must feel comfortable enough to write freely and to learn instead of trying to hide errors by writing as little as possible. Since basic writing students may bring to your classroom negative attitudes about English and about their own abilities, you may need to fight the "I can't write" attitude by helping students see that their reluctance is the cause of many writing problems rather than the result of them. Remember, too, that your own expectations will have an enormous impact on your students. Studies document what many teachers have long suspected: that the instructor's attitude and expectations are key factors in student learning. To help you help your students, ESL Tips and Teaching Tips are provided in the margins of your Instructor's Annotated Edition.

Creating a Writers' Community

Beware your own sense of grammatical urgency ("But I have so many errors to correct and only one short term to work miracles!"). The first weeks of any basic writing course can make or break student attitude and, thus, affect student progress. Establishing a collegial workshop atmosphere early will serve you well all term. For the first week, I make sure that my students write nearly every day, as they will all term. These writings might be short, get-acquainted exercises like having each student write for five minutes on his or her name—how it was chosen, whether the student likes it, and so forth. Samples of student writing (perhaps anonymous at the outset) are either read aloud by volunteers or reproduced for the class and then discussed. Here's the catch: *no grammar is marked for the full week*. Instead, we talk about the content of the papers or about what strikes us as "powerful writing." Further, the classroom rule is this: *we talk only about what is good in each paper*. If we don't like anything about a particular paper, we don't say anything. The result? Students open up, write regularly, learn that they can write something "good" and show it to a group without derision, and find that their own reactions to other people's writing have value. Meanwhile, the instructor has a chance to survey the grammatical needs of the class and to plan the term accordingly.

The second week, when discussion enlarges to include criticism and I begin marking errors in the papers, we all continue to emphasize what the student is doing right, not just what is wrong. For every error cited, we cite something positive as well—the sense of humor, the vivid example, the honesty of the writing. As the term progresses, groups or pairs of students can read, critique, and revise work, thus honing their skills. Such collaborative activities create a writers' community in the classroom and enhance learning. The Writers' Workshop at the end of each unit models this approach.

Writing Assignments

Beginning the term with frequent short compositions done in class will avoid the problem of students' getting stuck at home and giving up altogether or seeking outside help. Further, the communal experience of writing and reading papers in class will create a subtle but important dynamic as the term progresses. I use dyads, groups, and full-class discussions to hone writing and revising skills. Once the class begins to enjoy its work and to sense its own strength, at-home compositions will prove that there is no magic in the classroom that is responsible for success. Students will begin to see that the skills are *within them.*

Theme topics should be snappy enough to hold the attention of the class but difficult enough to provide a challenge, point to a new perspective, or foster a new skill. Developmental and ESL students generally write more easily about things they know best—their neighborhoods, families, friends, jobs, and college experiences. It is helpful to begin with these familiar sources of material and build toward more sophisticated assignments. Be sure to include third-person writing, critical thinking activities, analysis of visual images, and so forth. Our students need these skills in order to succeed in college and at work.

Aim for a variety of writing tasks. The assignments in the chapters and at the end of each unit of *Grassroots* will provide you with a wide range of interesting, level-appropriate writing tasks, a number of them collaborative. The prompts include letter writing, problem solving, interviewing a classmate, evaluating a grammar website, and, of course, many suggestions for writing about contemporary life and issues. Journals can provide regular writing practice, a sense of the power of personal expression, and a source of ideas for classroom papers. You may wish to base some writing assignments on the grammar lesson just covered so that students can apply what they have learned. For example, if you have just taught verb agreement, have the class visit the student lounge or ball field and describe in the present tense what is happening there. Additionally, *Grassroots'* high-interest practices, Web links, and visuals offer rich sources for discussion and writing. The reading selections in Unit 9 also model and inspire good writing.

Using High-Interest Practice Content for Thinking and Writing

Many of the high-interest paragraph- and essay-length exercises in *Grassroots* are intended to do double duty: to provide targeted skills practice and, if the instructor wishes, to spark class discussion, critical thinking, or writing. Portraits of intriguing people like Surgeon General Richard Carmona, Jane Goodall, activist rapper Wyclef Jean, J. K. Rowling, Nelson Mandela, Oprah, Tony Hawk, and celebrities recovering from addiction can shed light on achievers and the obstacles they overcome. Topics like TV Turn-Off Week, humor as a job asset, the Galapagos Islands, gratitude research, fast food, rude cell phone users, tornado chasers in the Midwest, alcohol and pregnancy, and Frank Gehry's unusual buildings are likely to elicit lively responses from students as they also provide grammar practice and promote cultural literacy. To encourage students to make mental connections, I have added a linked website, photo, cartoon, or writing suggestion after selected practices.

Using Collaborative Assignments Effectively

Collaborative work at this level must be carefully set up and supervised to be effective. For example, putting students in groups and asking them to edit one another's papers won't accomplish much if they don't know what to look for. My "writers' community" approach just described is one way to teach writing and editing principles to the whole class first and to establish "quality control." The Writers' Workshop that concludes each unit also provides closely guided discussion of student work as well as practical opportunities for peer editing. The end-of-chapter writing assignments include many that are collaborative, letting students interact while they apply the grammar skills they have been learning to their own writing. For peer editors, Chapter 3 includes a list of useful questions students can answer as they respond to a classmate's paper.

Assessment and Computer Support

The challenge of many basic writing courses is balance: of grammar work with writing assignments, of student motivation with high standards. The principle of balance applies to assessment as well. Besides marking papers, try other ways of letting students know where they stand. Frequent conferences, for example, keep students informed of their progress. Specific written comments on students' papers are helpful, especially if you focus on just two or three errors per paper. Peer evaluation can be a good feedback tool, provided that you guide students through the process first and supply detailed guidelines, however brief, as they read and respond to each other's work. A simple peer evaluation sheet might include such questions as these: *What is most effective about this paper? What is the main idea? What one change would most improve this paper?* To prepare students for the realities of writing final examinations, you might administer "mock finals" several times toward the end of the term. Grade these (or have a colleague do so) as if they were the actual finals; students will be highly motivated to correct any problems that might keep them from passing the course. *Grassroots'* new Chapter 30, in which students proofread for a random mix of errors, provides excellent "real-world" practice and review.

As teachers of basic writing, we may always fight the paper load, but help exists, especially from an array of computer and Web support for *Grassroots*. First, encourage your students to know their error patterns, review, and practice on their own, habits that will empower them as learners. A *Student Answer Key* is available; copy and distribute the answers for any practices or chapter parts you want your students to correct. New *Exploring Online* links in every chapter direct students to OWLs and other sites for self-paced interactive practice or instruction. The *Grassroots* Test Package (with chapter, unit, diagnostic, and mastery tests) is available in paper and online to save you grading time. Additional interactive ACE tests tailored to *Grassroots'* lessons are available on the Student Website, and a major new online resource—*WriteSpace for Grassroots*—provides a range of interactive writing and grammar quizzes for every text chapter. It is my hope that *Grassroots with Readings* plus its unified package of computerized practices and tests, classroom-management software, electronic grade book, and other tools will inspire you to create the most effective possible course for your students.

Notes on Using *GRASSROOTS*

Organization of *Grassroots*

The units in *Grassroots* reflect the major problem clusters encountered in composition classrooms: "Writing Forceful Paragraphs," "Writing Complete Sentences," "Using Verbs Effectively," "Joining Ideas Together," and so on. The order of units and chapters in *Grassroots* represents one possible way to organize a developmental English course—teaching paragraph writing first and building from there. Another instructor might see the sentence as central and will start the term with Chapter 6, "Subjects and Verbs." Someone else might begin with lessons in verb agreement. Obviously, your preferences and the needs of your students will determine the best shape of your course.

Grassroots is extremely versatile. Each unit is a sequence of self-contained chapters, so the book may be adapted to almost any course design. A careful look through the book will suggest possibilities. In addition, each unit begins and ends with writing-based features that place grammar study firmly in the context of the writing process. A two-page unit opener introduces material to be covered, using an interesting, well-written professional paragraph. These openers can provide a dynamic launch to instruction or, through their ideas and style, prompt discussion or writing. At the end of each unit are varied review practices, usually dealing with essays and other whole pieces of writing; a Writers' Workshop; and four high-interest writing assignments. The eight Writers' Workshops showcase inspiring student paragraphs or essays, each processed carefully with questions and followed by writing ideas. The Workshops make excellent full-class or collaborative activities, teaching the arts of peer editing and revision and inspiring students by example.

Whatever concepts you wish to stress, whatever the order of presentation, it is probably a good idea to assign some important chapters to the whole class and to go over the exercises together in class. This procedure familiarizes students with the text at the outset. Furthermore, students enjoy this activity because it affords them a chance to share not only "answers" but also creations—sentences and paragraphs.

Finally, *Grassroots* lends itself to tutorials and self-teaching. Individuals and small groups with special problems can complete appropriate chapters on their own.

Organization of Each Chapter

Each chapter is a self-contained lesson, short enough so that flagging concentration will not interfere with learning. Each stresses the development of writing skills rather than mere error correction. Points that frequently confuse students receive the most exact attention. The text assumes that the student brings very little prior knowledge to each task; it presents, step by logical step, the vocabulary and concepts necessary to the skill being taught, keeping explanations simple but accurate. For example, after the student learns to spot subjects in Chapter 6, he or she then practices distinguishing between singular and plural subjects, an ability vital to the rest of the lesson and one that cannot be presupposed. Similarly, the treatment of subject-verb agreement in Chapter 8 includes an exercise on transforming noun subjects into pronouns; only after completing this exercise does the student tackle sentences in which pronoun subjects appear.

In general, the exercises in each chapter move from the very elementary to the more demanding, repeating basic skills and building upon them. Because the exercises are varied in form and difficulty and often explore engaging or humorous topics, students will not be bored or be able simply to fill in right answers without really learning anything. Many exercises—often paragraph or essay length—require students to spot and correct particular errors, thus honing their proofreading and revising skills.

Each chapter in the book includes an *Exploring Online* feature, which directs students to the Internet for more exploration, research, or practice. Each chapter also includes *Chapter Highlights*, which summarize important points covered in the chapter and can be used by students as a brief review. Beginning with Unit 2, each chapter ends with two additional elements: a *Writing Assignment* and a *Chapter Review*. Often a collaborative effort, the Writing Assignment is a structured writing task that helps students think through the issues of audience and purpose. The Chapter Review is composed of paragraph- or essay-length practices that provide an opportunity for students to revise and proofread in context. New to the Eighth Edition are numerous colorful and interesting photographs and cartoons, which are chosen to provide additional practice with critical thinking.

Unit 1: Writing Forceful Paragraphs

Unit 1 consists of five chapters: "Exploring the Writing Process"; "Prewriting to Generate Ideas"; "Developing Effective Paragraphs"; "Improving Your Paragraphs," which presents more advanced material like illustration and coherence, and "Moving from Paragraph to Essay," a brief optional chapter that prepares students for later courses.

Chapter 1 introduces the writing process itself as well as subject, audience, and purpose. It contains a list of guidelines for submission of written college work, which the instructor can amend as desired. Chapter 2 presents four prewriting techniques, each illustrated with student examples: freewriting, brainstorming, clustering, and keeping a journal. I believe that journals work best if you periodically assign topics and let students know you will be collecting the journals at some point. Encourage your students to try all four prewriting techniques and discover what works best for them.

Chapter 3 guides the student through the process of writing simple paragraphs. I realize that the actual writing process may be messier than this chapter makes it appear, but the steps presented provide beginning writers with a reassuring way of writing basic paragraphs. Part A defines the paragraph and introduces the idea of the topic sentence. Part B shows the student how to turn a broad topic into a specific topic sentence, a step that many students have trouble with because they believe that a broad topic is easier to write about. You should stress that the topic sentence controls the paragraph and that limiting the topic will help students write more easily later. Students who have trouble writing the topic sentence should be encouraged to try brainstorming first to help focus the topic and then to compose the topic sentence.

Parts C, D, and E detail the generation and arrangement of ideas within the paragraph. Students usually enjoy Part C, "Generating Ideas for the Body of the Paragraph," which covers brainstorming. Those who have completed Chapter 2, "Prewriting to Generate Ideas," will see how freewriting, brainstorming, and clustering can be rich sources of details and examples that will later make the paragraph effective and interesting. In teaching this material, consider writing a sample topic sentence on the board and having the class brainstorm or freewrite ideas to develop it, select the best ideas, and then arrange them in some logical order.

Parts F and G guide students through the revision process, stressing revision for clear topic sentences, good support, basic transitions, and unity. Model first and revised drafts are given, showing revision techniques. A section on peer revision is included, with a specific and useful list of questions for students to answer if you ask them to respond to one another's written work. The more guidance peer editors are given, the more helpful the result. Attention is paid as well to proofreading, especially for omitted words.

Chapter 4 covers somewhat more difficult material: using examples, types of order, revising for exact and concise language, and turning assignments into paragraphs. If your students' level of preparedness is quite low, this full chapter may not be appropriate. Part A explains just what examples are and how they can be used to develop a paragraph. Many students have trouble understanding the relationship between a general statement and a specific example, but putting example topic sentences on the board—and having students suggest and evaluate examples that support them—is an excellent way to address this problem.

Part B explains time order, space order, and order of importance. Your students, like ours, will probably be inspired by the model paragraphs of space order and importance, both written by students. You may wish to go over the three kinds of order in class and then to assign an at-home paragraph, allowing each student to choose one kind of order. Later, have successful paragraphs read to the class.

Part D, "Turning Assignments into Paragraphs," helps students see the practical application of the writing instruction they receive in English class to other course work. Here they learn how to turn an exam question into a topic sentence and to plan their answer. Even if you do not assign the rest of Chapter 4, you may wish to assign Part D. Consider giving a "mock exam," using this material as the basis of a lesson: students love this kind of academic "basic training."

For instructors who wish to use it, Chapter 5, "Moving from Paragraph to Essay," briefly applies paragraph-writing skills to essay writing. It includes an actual student essay called "Tae Kwon Do" that will probably provoke interest and discussion. Instructors who teach short essays in this course will find that the four Writers' Workshops showcasing student essays and the many essay-based practices throughout the text work well with Chapter 5 to enrich basic essay instruction.

Unit 2: Writing Complete Sentences

This unit concerns itself with the basics of the complete sentence. Chapter 6, "Subjects and Verbs," provides students with practice in spotting and using these two essential parts of a sentence, thereby preparing them for the next chapter on fragments and for Chapter 8, "Present Tense," where the ability to recognize subjects and verbs is crucial. Part C, "Spotting Prepositional Phrases, " helps students find the real subject and not be confused by prepositional phrases that intervene between subject and verb. Since students often assume that a verb is necessarily a single word, Part F of Chapter 6 focuses on verbs of more than one word: this section can also be helpful in a discussion of compound tenses.

Chapter 7, "Avoiding Sentence Fragments," covers the three sentence fragment errors most common to developmental writing—the incomplete past participle, the incomplete progressive, and the subordinate clause written as an entire sentence. These problems are also covered in Chapters 10, 11, and 14. In Chapter 7, once students have corrected fragments by writing sentences with complete subjects and verbs, they proofread paragraphs for sentence fragments since fragments are most likely to appear in longer pieces of writing. Some instructors may wish to teach Chapter 25, "Parallelism," in conjunction with Unit 2: the principle of parallelism is fairly easy for students to master and helps them to develop a sense of balance and style in sentence writing.

Unit 3: Using Verbs Effectively

A large portion of this text is devoted to verbs because they present the most difficulties for developmental writing and ESL students. Many grammar handbooks cover only sophisticated problems in agreement, but Chapter 8, "Present Tense," concentrates on the third person singular ending, that elusive *-s* or *-es* that is so conspicuously absent from the themes of developmental writers. *To be, to have,* and *to do* are singled out for special attention: these verbs appear incorrectly so often on such a large number of papers that they deserve separate treatment. More subtle problems in agreement are explained in Part G.

Chapter 9, "Past Tense," stresses the student's ability to recognize the past tense and to form it by adding *-ed* or *-d* to regular verbs. Except for *to be*, which requires special work, students generally have less trouble with irregular verbs than with regular verbs in the past tense. This phenomenon may be due to the fact that the *-ed* or *-d* ending is often virtually absent from students' spoken vocabulary, but irregular verbs are easier to remember and more apt to be taught in the lower grades. In any case, it would be wise to reinforce the section on regular verbs with extra sentences or short themes written exclusively in the past tense. Beware: Students usually "catch on" to the *-ed* or *-d* quickly but then tend to return after a short time to their old habits. Periodic reviews and constant correction of themes can counteract this tendency.

Chapter 10, "The Past Participle in Action," is central to a multitude of problems for developmental and ESL writers and should be covered carefully and, whenever possible, in class. This chapter introduces the student to new tenses and time relationships; it shows the function of the past participle in the passive voice; and finally, it explains the use of the past participle form as an adjective. The greatest difficulty students face in understanding these areas is their assumption that the *-ed* or *-d* ending always signifies past tense.

Students also have trouble understanding the subtle differences between the perfect tenses and the other tenses. I have attempted to clarify these differences in the charts and examples provided in Parts D and E; however, my experience has been that a teacher's explanation is required in addition to the charts and examples. You may wish to skip the sections on present perfect tense and past perfect tense altogether and go straight to work on the passive voice and past participles as adjectives.

Chapter 11, "Progressive Tenses," explains the difference between the progressive tense and the simple present or past. This chapter will be of special value to nonnative writers of English who often overuse the progressive tenses. Part D reminds students to make progressive verb forms complete with the use of *to be* as a helper; this section may be combined with Chapter 7, "Avoiding Sentence Fragments."

Chapter 12, "Fixed-Form Helping Verbs and Verb Problems," begins with a discussion of the fixed form of the modal helping verbs and the simple form that their main verbs must take. This emphasis is necessary because students learning about verb endings sometimes develop a penchant for affixing *-es, -s, -ed*, or *-d* to the modals or to their main verbs.

Can, could, will, and *would* are singled out for special treatment; many students confuse the present and past tenses of these verbs and do not understand their conditional forms. Parts C and D, which deal with these problems, might be covered directly after Chapter 9, "Past Tense," while the difference between past and present is fresh in students' minds.

Part E, "Writing Infinitives," covers a common student error—putting endings on infinitives. This problem occurs when developmental or ESL writers attempt to make all verbs show tense or time. Part F, "Revising Double Negatives," could be assigned selectively to those students who use double negatives, although at times enough students require the explanation to warrant covering this part with the entire class.

Unit 4: Joining Ideas Together

This unit teaches the student six ways to combine simple ideas and create more complicated and interesting sentences. It builds upon the concept of the sentence expounded in Unit 2; the instructor may wish to combine material from this unit with the work on sentence fragments in Chapter 7, "Avoiding Sentence Fragments." Each chapter presents one method of joining ideas and highlights the correct punctuation necessary for that construction. A number of practices in this unit provide extra work in sentence combining. Please note the useful chart on page 210 and on the inside back cover; this chart provides a handy reference for students once they have learned these methods.

Chapters 13 to 15, "Coordination," "Subordination," and "Avoiding Run-Ons and Comma Splices," will probably be the best-thumbed chapters in this unit. Chapter 13, "Coordination," presents a compact explanation of the seven common coordinating conjunctions. Since many students do not really understand the precise meanings of these words, the chapter contains exercises that require the student to choose the conjunction that correctly expresses the relationship between paired ideas.

Chapter 14, "Subordination," is also reduced to essentials and gives the student a basic list of subordinating conjunctions. Special attention is paid to the order of main idea and subordinate idea and to punctuation, when to use a comma and when not to. This chapter may be used with Chapter 7, "Avoiding Sentence Fragments," for work on one kind of sentence fragment problem.

Chapter 15, "Avoiding Run-Ons and Comma Splices," defines these two errors and encourages students to use either coordination or subordination—discussed in the previous two chapters—to correct them. Here, as elsewhere in the book, I stress skill building rather than error correction. The Chapter Review provides students with paragraphs to proofread and revise so that they will be better able to transfer these skills to their own writing.

Chapter 16, "Semicolons and Conjunctive Adverbs," includes instruction on semicolons and the adverbial conjunctions. Many instructors of developmental English choose not to teach these two areas at all. However, those who do will find these lessons simplified and clear, teaching basic patterns, not all possible uses. In this spirit, only eight common conjunctive adverbs are introduced.

The student is given two other options for joining ideas together—Chapter 17, "Relative Pronouns," and Chapter 18, "-ING Modifiers." These two chapters, like Chapter 14, may be used with Chapter 7 to address the problem of sentence fragments.

Unit 5: Choosing the Right Noun, Pronoun, Adjective, Adverb, or Preposition

This unit zeroes in on five parts of speech. You may wish to assign these chapters individually to students or to entire classes needing work in certain areas, say, plural endings or possessive pronouns.

Chapter 19, "Nouns," a basic review, and Part F, "Demonstrative Adjectives," in Chapter 21, "Adjectives and Adverbs," provide the extensive practice in singular and plural formations that some students, ESL students in particular, need.

Chapter 20, "Pronouns," deals exhaustively with pronouns, a source of much bafflement, and clears up most of the confusion that students experience. Part A introduces the concept of the antecedent. Parts B through D explain the basics of pronoun-antecedent agreement: indefinite pronouns, collective nouns, and so forth. Part E deals with vague and redundant pronouns. Parts F, G, and H discuss case: often, however, choosing the correct case can be taught by ear without a great deal of drill in case forms and usage. Finally, Part I, "Using Pronouns with -SELF and -SELVES," can be covered at almost any time during the term since it is largely concerned with spelling.

Chapter 21, "Adjectives and Adverbs," differentiates between these two parts of speech. Practices here stress the formation of comparatives and superlatives, with special attention paid to *good* and *well*. Also included is work on the demonstratives *this/that* and *these/those.*

Chapter 22, "Prepositions," is a key chapter for ESL students. It demystifies *on, in*, and *like* and contains a chart of common phrases containing prepositions, which can present problems for nonnative speakers of English. Students requiring work with this part of speech can be assigned the chapter on an individual basis.

Unit 6: Revising for Consistency and Parallelism

The chapters in this unit can be taught together or used separately as follow-ups to earlier chapters. Chapter 23, "Consistent Tense," might be effectively taught after Chapters 8 and 9, on present and past tense verbs, because students often shift from present to past tense and from past to present. Similarly, Chapter 24, "Consistent Person," might be taught after Chapter 20, "Pronouns"; students often use singular, plural, and indefinite pronouns in a single paragraph without being aware of their lack of consistency. The paragraph practices at the end of each chapter provide exercises in proofreading and revising for consistency.

Chapter 25, "Parallelism," can be taught as early in the term as you feel your students can benefit from such a lesson. In fact, beginning writers are apt to understand parallelism rather easily. They perceive the balance, shape, and form in their sentences and are often able to eliminate problems like inconsistent tenses, incomplete verb forms, and poor transitions by applying the principles of parallelism.

Unit 7: Mastering Mechanics

This unit explains not only those marks of punctuation that frequently trouble students but also the rules of capitalization. Basic rules governing capitalization are briefly listed in Chapter 26; students proofread for and correct capitalization errors in practice sentences and in a practice essay.

The comma is a mark of punctuation that often bewilders students. Chapter 27 explains eight basic uses of the comma, each rule reinforced by a practice. Note that the correct use of the comma with coordinating and subordinating conjunctions, covered in Chapters 13 and 14, is reinforced in this chapter.

Chapter 28 explains the two basic uses of the apostrophe—contractions and possessives. Since students who misunderstand the apostrophe often add one when they form the plural of nouns, you may wish to refer them to Part A of Chapter 19, "Nouns." Additional work on commonly confused pairs of words—*it's* and *its*, *you're* and *your*—is found in Chapter 32, "Look-Alikes/Sound-Alikes."

Chapter 29 teaches the difference between direct and indirect quotations and how to punctuate them.

The new Chapter 30, "Putting Your Proofreading Skills to Work," gives students the chance to practice their proofreading skills on paragraphs and longer passages that include different kinds of errors.

Unit 8: Improving Your Spelling

Chapter 31, "Spelling," provides students with clear explanations of some basic spelling rules and their exceptions, each reinforced with lots of practice. It is best to teach this entire chapter slowly since the rules take time to digest and since spelling drills can quickly become tedious.

Parts A and B might be discussed early in the term so that students can begin to keep spelling lists, devise tricks for remembering difficult words, and get in the habit of using spell-check software. Part C is often a necessary preface to further work in spelling because many students are not really sure what vowels and consonants are. Since Parts D and E deal with the doubling of consonants, they might logically be discussed after Chapter 9, "Past Tense," and Chapter 11, "Progressive Tenses." The rules discussed in Parts G and H can likewise be related to lessons on present tense verbs, past tense verbs, and noun plurals.

Chapter 32, "Look-Alikes/Sound-Alikes," treats groups of words that writing students tend to confuse, like *to, too,* and *two*, or *where, were,* and *we're*. A simple explanation of each word in the group is given, followed by practice—an approach I have found to be effective in clearing up these errors. Assign these sections to individuals or to the class as the need arises.

Unit 9: Reading Selections and Quotation Bank

The twenty reading selections in *Grassroots with Readings* were chosen for their high-interest subjects, readability, and variety. The introduction, "Effective Reading: Strategies for the Writer," explains to the student some basic techniques of effective reading—previewing the selection, underlining main ideas, and so on—and provides a sample annotated reading. Difficult words within the readings are glossed on the bottom of the pages. Each reading is followed by four questions to stimulate class discussion or journal assignments and by three writing assignments.

The Quotation Bank contains more than seventy brief quotations. An admixture of the profound and the whimsical, these quotations may be used in a variety of ways. They can provide topics for discussion and written assignments. Students may wish to agree or disagree with a quotation, using their own experience to support their stand, or simply to read through the Quotation Bank, seeking inspiration or ideas. One of these quotations might start or augment a composition. You might tell your students about such volumes as *Bartlett's Familiar Quotations*, available in libraries and bookstores.

Appendix 1: Parts of Speech Review

Appendix 1 defines the eight parts of speech and provides examples of their use. It can serve as a review or as an introduction to the principles of grammar.

Appendix 2: Some Guidelines for Students of English as a Second Language

Appendix 2 covers some topics that are troublesome for ESL students. These include count and noncount nouns, verbs with gerunds and infinitives, and prepositions with gerunds. All sections have short exercises for student practice.

Notes on the Readings

Suggestions for Thematic Groupings

The reading selections are grouped below according to a variety of topics and themes; this list is not exhaustive, but it might inspire or assist you as you plan your course. Specific suggestions for teaching each reading follow.

American Culture

Education and Language

Friendship, Community, and Ethics

Gender Roles

Immigrant Experience

Mentors and Role Models

Overcoming Obstacles

Parents and Children

Work

Lauren Mehler, *For Career Insight, Try Talking to Neighbors*

Recent graduate Lauren Mehler shares the proactive steps she took to turn her anxiety about choosing the right career into useful information. As an intern at *CollegeJournal.com* (from the *Wall Street Journal*), Mehler had begun to conduct informational interviews with people whose jobs interested her. After each interview, she wrote up her findings, at first for herself and later for publication on the *CollegeJournal.com* site. This illustration essay explains, with three well-developed examples, Mehler's discovery that even neighbors can be a revealing source of job information. In addition, the author not only shares the useful tools of informational interviewing but also models the process of thinking through problems on paper. Your students might be interested to see how central writing is to Lauren's thinking and job-search process. If they want to read other articles by Mehler, they can scroll her titles at **http://www.collegejournal.com/search/index.asp.**

This essay provides an opportunity to discuss the factors that affect career choice. Although many of your students probably have decided that college is essential to a rewarding future, some may remain unsure about exactly what they want to do once they graduate. Ask students who have already identified a career goal to share *how* and *why* they chose this path. What advice would *they* give to people who are trying to choose a career? If any students have returned to college in order to upgrade their careers, ask what motivated them to make this change. The author writes that it is important to love one's work; what do your students think about this? What other factors are important? Having your students conduct and share the results of informational job interviews is an assignment sure to provoke interest.

Consider pairing Mehler's essay with Ana Veciana-Suarez's "You Can Take This Job and . . . Well, It Might Surprise You," which discusses the non-monetary benefits of work. Or have students read Mehler in conjunction with Daniel Meier's "One Man's Kids," Jack Riemer's "Playing a Violin with Three Strings," or Maya Angelou's "Mrs. Flowers"—all on people passionate about their work.

Jack Riemer, *Playing a Violin with Three Strings*

In this eloquent article, columnist Jack Riemer tells the story of an Itzhak Perlman concert that became not only a dazzling performance but also a powerful lesson in life. Riemer's precise description illuminates a seemingly unique situation—handicapped violinist faces an added handicap—but the tale soon becomes universal. Ask students to point out the author's most effective details. Have groups or the full class analyze the effects the author creates by spending the first several paragraphs on setting the scene. Ask what students can infer about Itzhak Perlman's personality and character from specific details. You might draw students' attention to Riemer's use of adjectives and adverbs, perhaps in conjunction with Chapter 21, "Adjectives and Adverbs." Many verbs, too, are vivid and exact, so you might teach this work with Part C of Chapter 4, "More Work on Revising: Exact and Concise Language."

Consider helping students to understand the story's *metaphoric* importance. Engaging them in a discussion of how a literal tale suggests symbolic or "transferable" meaning will give them valuable practice in critical thinking. Have students write briefly about a time when they "played a violin with three strings," and then have volunteers read their papers aloud. Use humor to steer any concrete thinkers ("But I don't play a violin") in the right direction.

This essay could be paired with others about the lessons of wise mentors—Leo Buscaglia's "Papa, the Teacher"; Maya Angelou's "Mrs Flowers"; Malcolm X's "Homemade Education"; or Lauren Mehler's "For Career Insight, Try Talking to Neighbors." Ask students to think critically about the mentors in their own lives. You might ask them to write about any lessons they have learned from others, especially those like Perlman who do not let obstacles of any kind stand in their way.

Maya Angelou, *Mrs. Flowers*

This selection from Angelou's autobiographical *I Know Why the Caged Bird Sings* describes the young Angelou's life-changing relationship with a neighbor who saw her specialness and invited her into the world of spoken poetry, from which she regained her speaking voice. (Earlier in the book, Angelou has described being raped by her mother's live-in friend Mr. Freeman, his mysterious murder after the trial, and her own self-imposed silence.) You might discuss Angelou's rich and evocative style: "My name was beautiful when she said it" (paragraph 7); "I said, "'Yes ma'am.' It was the least I could do, but it was the most also" (paragraph 29); "I was liked . . . for just being Marguerite Johnson" (paragraph 32). How do these sentences affect the reader? Do students have favorite lines?

This essay provides an opportunity to discuss the kinds of friendships or activities that help us through tough, even traumatic, times. Students might enjoy sharing such transformative relationships—either as the recipients or the givers of "gifts." Some of your students may have trouble speaking up, perhaps because of the way they speak or their accent. You could ask students if they think it is important to be able to speak up, in class and elsewhere, but you may hear only from those who vocalize easily. Consider instead asking the class to do a focused freewriting in response to the question "Where do you feel most and least comfortable speaking up?" If students exchange their freewritings, you could ask the "easy vocalizers" to read some of the responses aloud.

Consider pairing this selection with others dealing with voice: "Montgomery Alabama, 1955," in which Rosa Parks summons the courage to speak up for equal rights; "One Man's Kids," in which Daniel Meier selects which thoughts to express depending on his listeners; or "Four Directions," in which a daughter loses confidence when her mother withdraws support, vocal and otherwise.

Daniel Meier, *One Man's Kids*

For the *New York Times* "About Men" series, an elementary school teacher defends not only his nontraditional career but also his irregular use of traditionally "female" language. You might ask students what classroom details suggest that Meier is a gifted teacher. Meier soon takes the reader outside the classroom, first on a man-to-man job interview and then into a mixed social setting, thereby illuminating the linguistic relationship between gender and context.

Students who relish the opening paragraphs, so evocative of the dynamic chaos from which real learning emerges, may wish to share their grade-school experiences. Are students as familiar with the subtleties of job interviews? Why does Meier sense that he cannot respond frankly to the principal? Do students find the dinner-party schism plausible, where men have little to discuss with a male first-grade teacher but women have plenty? What about language? Don't men use the word *love*? Is it "female"?

Consider drawing students' attention to Meier's paragraphing, perhaps using it to augment Chapter 3, "Developing Effective Paragraphs." You might want to look at paragraphs 5 and 11 for topic sentences, paragraphs 6 and 8 for support, and paragraphs 2 through 4 for unity. Paragraph 6 can be used to cover all three aspects. Meier's essay can be grouped with Lauren Mehler's "For Career Insight, Try Talking to Neighbors" and Ana Veciana-Suarez's essay for a discussion about the nonfinancial benefits of work. A cluster of readings on stereotyping might include this one for male roles and Amy Tan's "Four Directions" and Anna Quindlen's "Barbie at 35" for female roles.

Dave Barry, *Another Road Hog with Too Much Oink*

In this humorous essay from the book *Dave Barry Is Not Taking This Sitting Down*, Barry explores America's obsession with large sport utility vehicles, or SUVs. Barry uses wit and irony to expose the absurdities of the super-sized SUVs that loom over other cars on the road today. You might begin by asking for a show of hands: Who owns (or wants to own) an SUV? Who craves that armored giant, the Humvee? Ask specifically why these students like SUVs. What image do they imagine these vehicles project? These questions will likely spark a lively debate between SUV owners and car owners about the virtues and vices of multiton vehicles. Do people really need vehicles this large? Why does Dave Barry think that they don't?

Barry's writing is a gold mine for discussing the elements of humor. You might start by asking students to talk about the humor of the first sentence. Is Barry being serious or sarcastic? How do they know? Barry is a master of *comic exaggeration*. Ask students to share their favorite examples and tell why they like them. Discuss passages that demonstrate Barry's talent for using *description* to create vivid and hilarious mental images, such as the series of images in paragraph 7. The word *irony* is a good one for students to know; you might define it as "speech or writing that says one thing but means the opposite." Have groups or individuals locate instances of *irony* in Barry's piece, such as the example developed in paragraphs 2 and 3.

This essay can segue into a discussion of American culture and character. Such a cluster of readings could include Anna Quindlen's "Barbie at 35," Firoozeh Dumas' "Hot Dogs and Wild Geese," and Liza Gross' "The Hidden Life of Bottled Water." The shadow side of consumer culture is explored in Leonard Pitts' "Anonymity Brings Out Our Dark Sides." On the other hand, essays by Milloy, Angelou, Parks, Meier, and others reveal the generosity, courage, and depth that runs through the American character as well.

Ana Veciana-Suarez, *You Can Take This Job and . . . Well, It Might Surprise You*

In this newspaper column, Ana Veciana-Suarez takes a serious look at a common fantasy: winning the lottery and quitting one's job. She moves from her own daydreams of winning to a serious reflection on the nonmonetary benefits of work. Some of your students may be among those who buy lottery tickets regularly; many have imagined what they would do if they won a large sum of money. Consider having students freewrite on this topic and then ask volunteers to read aloud. Try conducting a quick poll, asking which students would quit work if they suddenly won millions of dollars. Then help students weigh Ana Veciana-Suarez's arguments *against* quitting work, no matter how much cash is in the bank. Ask what your students get from work besides money. Are there other aspects of a job that are as important—or even more important?

Veciana-Suarez develops her ideas in a number of different ways, including using examples from the news, family anecdotes, personal experiences and observation, and statistics gathered from research. Additionally, you might wish to analyze her conversational style (first-person point of view, directly addressing the reader as "you," using asides in parenthesis, idioms like "isn't all that it's cracked up to be," and mainstreamed Yiddish slang (like *schlepped*). Students will likely enjoy discussing those written occasions when informality is or is *not* appropriate. Finally, ask the class to evaluate the author's occasional use of Spanish phrases in her English prose (as Julia Alvarez also does in the reading selection "My English").

Consider pairing this essay with others about work—Lauren Mehler's "For Career Insight, Try Talking to a Neighbor" and Daniel Meier's "One Man's Kids." Do your students think that Mehler and Meier would be likely to quit their jobs if they won the lottery? Have students think critically about whether these reading selections support Veciana-Suarez's ideas on the benefits of work.

Malcolm X, *A Homemade Education*

This essay stimulates keen interest in a major historical figure and readily leads to a discussion of Malcolm X's determination to obtain literacy in the bleakest of circumstances. The essay begins with an honest assessment of his stumbling attempts to write letters to his spiritual mentor and the contrast between his speaking and writing abilities. Now literate, he feels liberated to voice his ideas in writing with the same degree of success he has enjoyed in speaking. Most students will identify with Malcolm X's struggle to read and write effectively, although Malcolm X is set apart by his impressive determination in copying the dictionary. Ask your students how many would go to this length to improve their skills. What motivated Malcolm X? Did his incarceration make learning easier? Is the author exaggerating when he claims that reading freed him, even though he was in prison?

The essay provides an excellent lead-in to class discussions about learning to write and the motivation, means, and ongoing hard work this requires. Ask students what motivates them to learn—and to keep on when frustration occurs. Consider connecting this essay with a lesson in dictionary use or vocabulary building. Writing Assignments 1 and 3 address these topics with activities students will probably find engaging.

You might consider pairing this essay with Maya Angelou's "Mrs. Flowers" for a discussion of the not-so-obvious similarities between the written and spoken word. What motivates a writer and a speaker to express a thought? What stops each? Both "A Homemade Education" and "Mrs. Flowers" can be used in conjunction with the Unit 2 Writers' Workshop, "Discuss an Event That Influenced

You" or with the Unit 5 Writers' Workshop, "Tell How Someone Changed Your Life." This piece also works nicely with Leo Buscaglia's "Papa, the Teacher" or Julia Alvarez's "My English."

Anna Quindlen, *Barbie at 35*

In this selection, Barbie's birthday prompts not a celebration but the resurrection of a mother-daughter quarrel about Barbie's impact. Quindlen uses university research on self-image to convince her ten-year-old that Barbie is more harmful than a few ounces of molded plastic and nylon tresses would imply. "It's just a toy," the child counters. Is this true, or is Barbie a powerful "parody of the female form"? Ask the class whether this best-selling doll has helped cause an epidemic of eating disorders and breast implants. Female students might share their Barbie experiences, as either children or parents. Do any believe that Barbie's height, weight, and unusual curves made them despair about falling short, being heavy, or both? What views do your male students hold? Dismissive? Sympathetic? Barbie turned 45 in 2004. Is Quindlen's essay still relevant today?

Your class will likely eagerly debate whether the research cited—which concludes that black girls and women have healthier body images than white women—is valid. Note that in 1980, Mattel introduced the first African-American and Hispanic Barbie dolls, with many having been sold since. Do Barbies of color negatively affect children of color? Do your students' ratings of Barbie's influence vary with their race? The class might wish to conduct its own poll or other type of research—for example, studying how Barbie has and has not changed through the years. (See **<http://www.barbiecollectibles.com/collecting/barbiehistory/index.asp>** for photos and notes on Barbie's history.)

This essay works nicely with Amy Tan's "Four Directions," a fictional account of another mother-daughter contretemps. For a discussion of gender roles, Quindlen's essay can be paired with Daniel Meier's "One Man's Kids." Combining personal anecdote and research data, "Barbie at 35" also illustrates the more advanced Unit 7 Writers' Workshop, "Explain a Cause or an Effect."

Leo Buscaglia, *Papa, the Teacher*

What can parents do to inspire children with a respect for learning? Buscaglia gives one answer, using his father as an example. The author says that his father had "natural wisdom" and believed that the greatest sin was to go to bed as ignorant at night as one was on waking that morning. In great detail, using quotations, Buscaglia describes the family's dinner ritual. What do your students think of this ritual? Did it put needless pressure on the children? Does it sound too good to be true? If a child has no such parent to promote excellence, can he or she overcome this lack? How?

A quick review of focused freewriting, brainstorming, and clustering (Chapter 2) can start students on Writing Assignment 1, "Describe a typical dinnertime in your family as you were growing up." Writers might read aloud or describe what they've written. Because Buscaglia's piece leads naturally to discussing or writing about specific ways in which parents encourage children to learn (or discourage them from learning), it may be paired effectively with Amy Tan's "Four Directions," a more complex, fictional portrait of a parent who first supports and then sabotages her daughter's talent. "Papa, the Teacher" can also be grouped with other selections on teaching and learning, for example, Malcolm X's "A Homemade Education" and Daniel Meier's "One Man's Kids." For an exploration of mentors and role models, Buscaglia's essay can be clustered with Jack Riemer's "Playing a Violin with Three Strings," Rosa Parks's "Montgomery, Alabama, 1955," or Maya Angelou's "Mrs. Flowers."

Julia Alvarez, *My English*

In this autobiographical essay from her book *Something to Declare,* Julia Alvarez describes the process by which she made the English language her own after her family moved to the United States. If appropriate, you may want to ask immigrant students in your class to share anecdotes about mastering English and life in America. If your class does not include immigrants, help students relate to this selection by asking them to recall a time when they were or felt like outsiders. Did they suspect, like the author, that their knowledge or skills were inferior to those of the people who surrounded them? What did they do to begin to fit in and feel accepted by those who already belonged? You might enjoy discussing the dynamism of the English language with them, pointing out how new words are coined, introduced, or accepted through use. As more Spanish speakers enter the culture, more Spanish words, as well as "mix-up" or "Spanglish," a blend of English and Spanish, are gaining currency. You and your students might make use of the fascinating wordspy website (**<http://www.wordspy.com/>**), which defines new, often hilariously accurate, terms in common parlance.

Help students appreciate Alvarez's graceful style and talent for precise descriptions, such as the one of Sister Maria in paragraph 12. If you have time, guide students through her final, unifying image (paragraph 13), comparing the English language to snow and then to fluid waves. Ask students to analyze the effect of these comparisons. What is Alvarez saying about how becoming fluent in English affected her? How does the title of the essay, too, reflect this point? Metaphors are used well elsewhere, like the three interesting comparisons (paragraphs 6 and 7) that help readers understand the nature of Spanglish.

This narrative may be paired with Firoozeh Dumas' "Hot Dogs and Wild Geese" to explore the theme of cultural assimilation or taught in a cluster with Maya Angelou's "Mrs. Flowers," Daniel Meier's "One Man's Kids," and Dumas' essay for a discussion on the significance of language. American culture and what being "American" means are other themes that can be pursued.

Rosa Parks, *Montgomery, Alabama, 1955*

This autobiographical account captures a defining moment in U.S. history as it unfolds. While gently correcting other accounts, Parks reflects on her own actions and motivation. Students who recognize her name might connect it to the civil rights movement while others may need a quick review of race segregation in the twentieth-century South. In either case, students usually cheer Parks' plain refusal.

What motivated Parks? The bus driver? The other riders? How do students view Parks' refusal in view of the others' compliance? You might want to broaden the discussion to include students' experiences. Did anyone ever grow "tired" of what passes for accepted standards? Why did they dare to make a difference? Consider reading aloud the final paragraph, in which Parks writes that if she had had time to anticipate the consequences, she might have given up her seat. Is she downplaying her part in history or explaining how injustice long endured makes accidental heroes?

Rosa Parks' narrative provides an opportunity to discuss an important purpose of writing—to explore how a writer lives, thinks, feels. The discussion of writing as a personal record of history can lead to observations about how one writer's account can differ remarkably from another's while both are valid. Parks' account can be used with Chapter 1, Part B ("Subject, Audience, and Purpose"), and with the Unit 6 Writers' Workshop, "Shift Your Audience and Purpose," especially the second idea for writing: "Describe an important moment in history as if you were there." As autobiography, Parks' selection can also work well with Malcolm X's "A Homemade Education." For a discussion about how one individual can make a difference, you can discuss Parks' essay alongside Maya Angelou's "Mrs. Flowers"; Leo Buscaglia's "Papa, the Teacher"; Norman M. Lobsenz's "The Importance of Childhood Memories"; or even Leonard Pitts' "Anonymity Brings Out Our Dark Sides."

Norman M. Lobsenz, *The Importance of Childhood Memories*

According to Lobsenz, childhood memories largely mold our adult personalities: positive memories give us sources of strength to draw on in difficult times. You might ask students to freewrite about one of their most vivid memories from childhood. Then ask them to reread their writing, thinking critically about *why* they remember this event with such clarity. Was it positive or negative? What is the larger significance of the event in their lives? Volunteers can share their memories and findings, or you might collect the papers and read some randomly and anonymously. In addition, students who are parents may enjoy sharing their hopes and fears about what their own children will remember most as they grow up.

Direct students' attention to Lobsenz's use of examples from his own and others' experiences, including the narrative illustration in his opening. Does this story effectively capture our attention while letting us know what the piece is about? Which of the writer's examples do students find most moving? This essay can be taught together with Chapter 4, Part A ("More Work on Support: Examples"). The accompanying painting by Carmen Lomas Garza provides an excellent critical thinking opportunity; interpret the painting with the class to elicit its meaning.

Consider grouping this selection with others on parents and children: Leo Buscaglia's "Papa, The Teacher"; and Amy Tan's "Four Directions." Or pair this selection with Goleman's "Emotional Intelligence" or a lesson in cause-effect writing, drawing upon the Unit 7 Writers' Workshop, "Explain a Cause or an Effect."

Courtland Milloy, *The Gift*

Most students are inspired and provoked by this newspaper account of Jermaine Washington's gift to a friend of a kidney. His act is all the more amazing because his relationship with Michelle Stevens is platonic, and her own brothers and fiancé have refused to help her. The author, through quotations and scenes like the one in the barbershop (paragraph 1), underlines the bafflement that others felt at Washington's act.

Ask students what they would have done in his place. Why do they think he did it? What did he give up, and what did he get in return? Was it worth it? What are your students' views on organ donation? What happens to those who, unlike Michelle Stevens, fail to obtain the transplants needed to survive?

Paired with Leonard Pitts' "Anonymity Brings Out Our Dark Sides," this essay could spark an interesting discussion about what we do and do not owe to our fellow humans. Considering "The Gift" alongside Daniel Goleman's "Emotional Intelligence" might give rise to a discussion about Jermaine Washington's level of emotional intelligence. Milloy's essay can also be used in conjunction with the Unit 4 Writers' Workshop, "Describe a Detour off t he Main Highway."

Leonard Pitts, Jr., *Anonymity Brings Out Our Dark Sides*

This powerful essay about the shadow side of the Internet—an erosion of human compassion—should provide lively discussion among your students. How many students have ever communicated online with people they had never met face to face? Do they agree with the author that in cyberspace, "we tend to drop our masks and expose sides of ourselves we never knew were there" (paragraph 15)? Were your students shocked that Ripper's "friends" did nothing to help him? Why do they think that Ripper's friends, like those who witnessed Kitty Genovese's murder, chose not to get involved, even when they realized the seriousness of the situation? You might segue into a discussion of reality TV shows and Web-cams. Have groups or the class think critically about why so many people today want to turn themselves into entertainment by recording their daily activities or by agreeing to be filmed twenty-four hours a day on reality television shows. Why do so many others love to watch them? Finally, drugs and alcohol play a major role in Ripper's death—another theme that will reward discussion and writing .Note that the Chapter 8 Review practice, page 109, discusses the risk of online dating.

Help students understand Pitts' stand, opinions, and his support of them. What is his purpose in writing this essay? What is his attitude about his subject? Is he disgusted? outraged? sad? Does he willfully ignore the many examples of anonymous kindness in the world? Is it fair to make such pronouncements as "We forget to strive toward what we imagine ourselves to be" (paragraph 11) on the strength of just two examples (Ripper and Kitty Genovese)? Make sure that students consider the effect of Pitts' brief but moving concluding sentence.

You might contrast this essay with Courtland Milloy's "The Gift" or another that illustrates human compassion and noble sacrifice. Pitts' essay also can be paired with more critical views of modern American culture, such as Anna Quindlen's "Barbie at 35" and Dave Barry's "Another Road Hog with Too Much Oink."

Firoozeh Dumas, *Hot Dogs and Wild Geese*

Dumas' light-hearted, humorous essay recounts her family's linguistic and other challenges upon moving to America from Iran. Much of her humor derives from examples of the English words and idioms that confused the family—thus, her title—and goofily detailed descriptions of her parents' blunders in the New World. You might encourage your ESL students to share their own anecdotes, funny or otherwise, with the class; a group setting or an anonymous writing assignment might tempt shy students to share. Or, if you wish, broaden the discussion to include the students born in this country by having them talk or freewrite about the times which they themselves have felt like a "stranger in a strange land." Dumas comically addresses the serious issue of children being cast as translators for their parents. Some ESL students might identify with this role. What are some possible effects of such role reversal?

Dumas uses delightful details and memorable examples to bring her story to life. For example, she describes specific incidents to back up generalizations like "I always encouraged my mother to learn English, but her talents lay elsewhere" (paragraph 8). Her specifics (Tater Tots, Campbell's tomato soup, La-Z-Boy recliners) all help support her point about the process of cultural assimilation. Therefore, this essay can be used in conjunction with Chapter 4, particularly Part A,"More Work on Support: Examples"; Part C, "More Work on Revising: Exact and Concise Language"; or the Unit 3 Writers' Workshop, "Tell a Lively Story."

Consider pairing Dumas's work with Julia Alvarez's "My English," for both are immigrant tales, one wacky, one elegant. Both essays explore the process of cultural assimilation through—in large part—mastery of the English language. Or examine formal versus informal education, including the benefits and drawbacks of each, by clustering Dumas' essay with Malcolm X's "A Homemade Education," Maya Angelou's "Mrs. Flowers," and Leo Buscaglia's "Papa, the Teacher."

Shoba Narayan, *In This Arranged Marriage, Love Came Later*

This firsthand account of an arranged marriage is sure to provoke intense discussion. Narayan, an American-educated Indian journalist, explains her decision to let her family choose her husband and describes her subsequent journey within the marriage from open-mindedness to active dislike to love.

At first, most American students are appalled by the idea of not marrying for love. Ask them whether there are different kinds of love or whether love alone can meet the day-to-day requirements of marriage. The author mentions such factors as horoscopes that Indian families consider as they match mates. Would these provide at least as solid a partnership as romantic love? Some of your students may share firsthand knowledge of arranged marriages from their birth countries. Do they agree with the author that arranged marriages work only in the context of stable traditional societies and close family relationships?

You will need to explain such references as those to Giacometti, Munch, and Kandinsky, by which Narayan contrasts her artistic temperament with her husband's more practical nature. This article works well with Courtland Milloy's "The Gift"—about a young man who is moved to donate a kidney to his friend after her boyfriend and brothers refuse. It also works with the two other selections—Firoozeh Dumas' "Hot Dogs and Wild Geese" and Julia Alvarez's "My English"—that explore cultural differences. "In This Arranged Marriage, Love Came Later" can be used with the Unit 5 Writers' Workshop, "Tell How Someone Changed Your Life."

Liza Gross, *The Hidden Life of Bottled Water*

"Is bottled water better?" To reach a conclusion, Liza Gross investigates sources, ingredients, and containers. You may encounter a split reaction from your class: from some, enjoyment in learning about so familiar a subject; from others, fatigue from struggling with the scientific support ("endocrine disruptor"?). Because technical language confronts all college students, you might want to encourage the class not to become intimidated by the unfamiliar language. Remind them to use the definitions that are given and to rely on what they are learning: effective writing results from a main idea that is convincingly supported, optimally arranged, and precisely expressed. You might want to break the class into thirds, assigning each group the job of explaining a different aspect (sources, ingredients, containers) of "The Hidden Life of Bottled Water" to the class.

You might want students to discuss the following questions: What is their usual source for water? If they drink bottled water, why do they not rely on tap water? How can they learn whether a water supply is contaminated? What motivates consumers to spend $4 billion a year on a natural resource that is artificially processed? You might also want the class to discuss Gross' sources: Do they trust "a health and nutrition specialist at the University of Georgia"? the federal agencies? the independent foundation? How did Gross locate the supporters of her argument? Did she decide on her viewpoint and then hunt (or surf the Web) for sources of agreement? (You may want to point out that she doesn't offer any other points of view.)

This article could be effectively paired with Dave Barry's "Another Hog with Too Much Oink" for a discussion of Americans as consumers. You might also consider pairing "The Hidden Life of Bottled Water" with Anna Quindlen's "Barbie at 35," which also uses outside research for support.

Amy Tan, *Four Directions*

In this excerpt from *The Joy Luck Club,* Tan describes a young girl who loses confidence in herself—and consequently loses her skill as a chess player—because of her mother's withdrawal of support. Discuss with your class what has actually happened to this child. What stages does she go through before she finally gives up? What strategies does she use to try to get her mother back on her side? Why does the mother make such a complete about-face? Has she helped her daughter in the long run—or has she damaged her?

This excerpt begins with the words "I was ten years old" and ends with the words "I was fourteen." Ask why Tan brackets the section with this information about age. Students might enjoy discussing changes that took place in their own personalities between the ages of ten and fourteen. Did any of them lose their childhood confidence? Why? Are the pressures greater on girls or boys? Were any of them disillusioned by others?

This narrative might be clustered with other selections about self-image and cultural expectations: Maya Angelou's "Mrs. Flowers"; Anna Quindlen's "Barbie at 35"; and Rosa Parks' "Montgomery, Alabama, 1955." "Four Directions" can be used in conjunction with the Unit 7 Writers' Workshop, "Explain a Cause or an Effect," especially with the second writing idea, "Write about something important that you gave up and why you did so." You might also consider Tan's story in light of the ideas presented in Norman M. Lobsenz's "The Importance of Childhood Memories" and have students make predictions about the young chess player's future strengths and weaknesses.

Daniel Goleman, *Emotional Intelligence*

This article, based on the author's much discussed best-selling book, raises important questions about the nature of intelligence and its relationship to success. Your students may find the concepts and vocabulary in this piece challenging, but I believe the ideas explored here are worth the effort. The material lends itself nicely to both collaborative class activities and to exercises in critical thinking. Goleman names five qualities that constitute emotional intelligence. Discuss these one by one in class. An enjoyable exercise that encourages critical thinking is to have students cite, for each trait, two examples: one, a situation in which someone showed "emotional genius" and another in which someone showed "emotional ignorance."

A fertile area for class discussion and writing is the handling of anger. The author cautions against "ventilating." Of course, uncontrolled anger and violence loom large in American society, and many school programs are attempting to teach young people to be more emotionally intelligent through "conflict resolution" and other skills. Can these skills be taught in school if they are not taught in the home? Have groups of students think of constructive ways to handle anger or create a lesson on the subject for fifth-grade boys and girls. Make sure your students grasp the point of the marshmallow study Goleman refers to: the article makes a connection between the ability to resist a marshmallow in childhood and the impulse control that predicts success in school and work. Of course, having students assess their own emotional intelligence can be instructive.

Consider having students apply the concepts learned here to people and situations in other reading selections. For example, in "Papa, the Teacher," does the author's father draw on emotional intelligence as he teaches his children to love learning? What are his skills? In "The Gift," is the young man who donates his kidney emotionally intelligent or just crazy (as some of his neighbors think)? Does a lack of emotional intelligence contribute to the tragedy described in Leonard Pitts' "Anonymity Brings Out Our Dark Sides"? Consider as well having students discuss Goleman's self-help piece before undertaking the Unit 8 Writers' Workshop, "Examine Positive (or Negative) Values."

INSTRUCTOR'S ANNOTATED EDITION

Grassroots with Readings

The Writer's Workbook

Eighth Edition

UNIT 1

Writing Forceful Paragraphs

The goal of *Grassroots* is to make you a better writer, and Unit 1 is key to your success. In this unit, you will

- Learn the importance of subject, audience, and purpose
- Learn the parts of a good paragraph
- Practice the paragraph-writing process
- Learn how to revise and improve your paragraphs
- Apply these skills to exam questions and short essays

Spotlight on Writing

Here, writer Alice Walker recalls her mother's extraordinary talent. If possible, read the paragraph aloud.

My mother adorned with flowers whatever shabby house we were forced to live in, and not just your typical straggly country stand of zinnias, either. She planted ambitious gardens—and still does—with over fifty different varieties of plants that bloom profusely from early March until late November. Before she left home for the fields, she watered her flowers, chopped up the grass, and laid out new beds. When she returned from the fields she might divide clumps of bulbs, dig a cold pit, uproot and replant roses, or prune branches from her taller bushes or trees—until night came and it was too dark to see.

Alice Walker, "In Search of Our Mothers' Gardens"

- Ms. Walker's words bring to life her mother's passion for flowers. Are any details especially vivid? Why do you think Walker's mother worked so hard on her gardening?
- Words are powerful: they can make us remember, see, feel, or think in certain ways. Unit 1 will introduce you to the power of writing well.

- ***An activity that your parent or guardian passionately enjoyed***
- ***Someone who inspired you with her or his ambition or creativity***

CHAPTER

1

Exploring the Writing Process

Did you know that the most successful students and employees are people who write well? In fact, many good jobs today require excellent writing and communication skills in fields as varied as computer technology, health sciences, education, and social services.

The goal of this book is to help you become a better and more confident writer. You will realize that the ability to write well is not a magical talent that some people possess and others don't but rather a life skill that can be learned. I invite you now to make a decision to excel in this course. It will be one of the best investments you could ever make in yourself, your education, and your future. Let *Grassroots* be your guide, and enjoy the journey.

PART A The Writing Process

This chapter will give you an overview of the writing process, as well as some tips on how to approach your writing assignments in college. Many people have the mistaken idea that good writers just sit down and write a perfect paper or assignment from start to finish. In fact, experienced writers go through a **process** consisting of steps like these:

TEACHING TIP
Consider illustrating the recursive nature of the writing process by writing the three steps in a circle on the board and using arrows to show how a writer can move forward or backward from one step to the next.

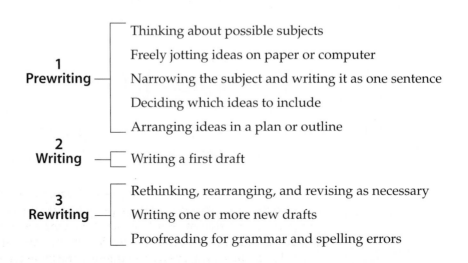

1 Prewriting
- Thinking about possible subjects
- Freely jotting ideas on paper or computer
- Narrowing the subject and writing it as one sentence
- Deciding which ideas to include
- Arranging ideas in a plan or outline

2 Writing
- Writing a first draft

3 Rewriting
- Rethinking, rearranging, and revising as necessary
- Writing one or more new drafts
- Proofreading for grammar and spelling errors

Writing is a personal and sometimes messy process. Writers don't all perform these steps in the same order, and they may have to go through some steps more than once. However, most writers **prewrite, write, rewrite**—and **proofread**. The rest of this unit and much of the book will show you how.

PRACTICE 1 SELF-ASSESSMENT

TEACHING TIP
Encourage students to perform similar self-assessments each time they receive feedback on their writing and to use self- and instructor-assessment to set personal goals in this course.

Choose something that you wrote recently for a class or for work and think about the *process* you followed in writing it. With a group of three or four classmates, or in your notebook, answer these questions:

1. Did I do any planning or prewriting—or did I just start writing the assignment?
2. How much time did I spend improving and revising my work?
3. Was I able to spot and correct my own grammar and spelling errors?
4. What one change in my writing process would most improve my writing? Taking more time for prewriting? Spending more time revising? Improving my grammar or spelling skills?

PRACTICE 2

TEACHING TIP
You might engage students in a discussion about the kinds of writing they already have done for college or work as well as the kinds of writing they expect to do in their future professions.

Bring in several newspaper help-wanted sections. In a group with four or five classmates, study the ads in career fields that interest you. Next, count the number of ads that stress writing and communication skills. Alternately, if you have Internet access, you could visit a job-search website like **<http://www.monster.com>** and perform the same exercise. Be prepared to present your findings to the class.

PART B Subject, Audience, and Purpose

As you begin a writing assignment, give some thought to your **subject, audience,** and **purpose**.

When your instructor assigns a broad **subject,** try to focus on one aspect that interests you. For example, suppose the broad subject is *music*, and you play the conga drums. You might focus on why you play them rather than some other instrument, or on what drumming means to you. Whenever possible, choose subjects you know and care about: observing your neighborhood come to life in the morning, riding a dirt bike, helping a child become more confident, learning more about your computer. Your answers to such questions will suggest promising writing ideas. Keep a list of the best ones.

ESL TIP
Studies show that it is harder to remember information exchanged orally in a second language; thus, for ESL students (and visual learners), writing on the board, working directly from pages in the text, and charts are useful memory aids.

To find or focus your subject, ask

- What special experience or knowledge do I have?
- What angers, saddens, or inspires me?
- What campus, job, or community problem do I have ideas about solving?
- What story in the news affected me recently?

How you approach your subject will depend on your **audience,** your readers. Are you writing for classmates, a professor, people who know about your subject, or people who do not? For instance, if you are writing about weight training, and your readers have never been inside a gym, you will approach your subject in a simple and basic way, perhaps stressing the benefits of weightlifting. An audience of bodybuilders, however, already knows these things; for them, you would write in more depth, perhaps focusing on how to develop one muscle group.

To focus on your audience, ask

- For whom am I writing? Who will read this?
- Are they beginners or experts? How much do they know about the subject?
- Do I think they will agree or disagree with my ideas?

Finally, keeping your **purpose** in mind helps you know what to write. Do you want to explain something to your readers, convince them that a certain point of view is correct, entertain them, or just tell a good story? If your purpose is to persuade parents to support having school uniforms, you can explain that uniforms lower clothing costs and may reduce student crime. However, if your purpose is to convince students that uniforms are a good idea, you might approach the subject differently, emphasizing how stylish the uniforms look or why students from other schools feel that uniforms improve their school atmosphere.

PRACTICE 3

List five subjects you might like to write about. Consider your audience and purpose. For whom are you writing? What do you want them to know about your subject? For ideas, reread the boxed questions.

TEACHING TIP
Developmental students may think they have nothing to write about. To help counter this myth, ask volunteers to share their answers to some of the boxed questions; do these help them complete Practice 3?

	Subject	Audience	Purpose
EXAMPLE: 1.	how to make a Greek salad	inexperienced cooks	to show how easy it is to make a great Greek salad
2.			
3.			
4.			
5.			

PRACTICE 4

With a group of three or four classmates, or on your own, jot down ideas for the following two writing tasks. Notice how your points and details differ, depending on your audience and purpose. (If you are not employed, write about a job with which you are familiar.)

TEACHING TIP
Use actual memoranda, letters of introduction, and other real-world documents to engage students and underscore the relevancy of effective writing.

1. For a new coworker, you plan to write a description of a typical day on your job. Your purpose is to help train this person, who will perform the same duties you do. Your supervisor will need to approve what you write.
2. For one of your closest friends, you plan to write a description of a typical day on your job. Your purpose is to make your friend laugh because he or she has been feeling down recently.

PRACTICE 5

TEACHING TIP
Print ads and cartoons are excellent tools to spark student interest and prompt critical thinking about subject, audience, and purpose.

Study the advertisement shown below and then answer these questions: What *subject* is the ad addressing? Who do you think is the target *audience*? What is the ad's intended *purpose*? In your view, how successful is the ad in achieving its purpose? Why or why not?

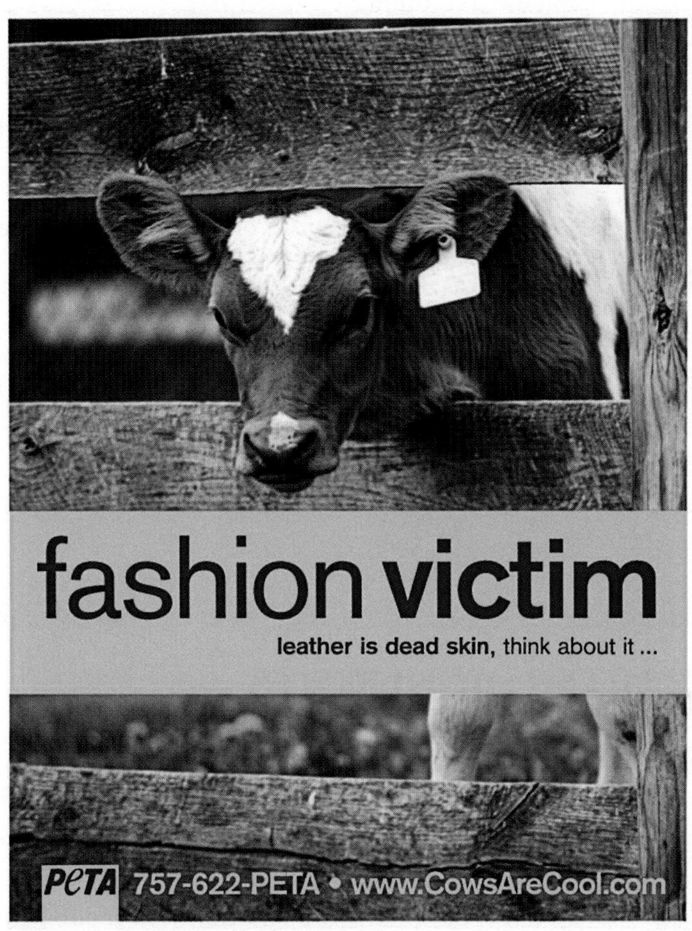

© 2004 People for the Ethical Treatment of Animals.

PRACTICE 6

ESL TIP
ESL students may require intensive instructor feedback at the beginning of a new task, assignment, or unit. Clarifying instructions can sometimes improve their performance on a task.

In a group with three or four classmates, read the following classified ads from real city newspapers around the country. The *subject* of each ad is a product or service that is for sale, the *audience* is the potential customer, and the *purpose* is to convince that customer to buy the product or service. How does each ad writer undercut his or her own purpose? How would you revise each ad so that it better achieves its apparent purpose?

1. Do you need a dramatic new look? Visit our plastered surgeons.
2. We do not tear your clothing with machinery. We do it carefully by hand.
3. Now is your chance to have your ears pierced and get an extra pair to take home free.
4. Tired of cleaning yourself? Let me do it.
5. Auto repair service. Try us once, and you'll never go anywhere again.

PART C Guidelines for Submitting Written Work

TEACHING TIP
Discuss with students the negative impression that messy or unattractive written work gives readers.

Learn your instructor's requirements for submitting written work, as these may vary from class to class. Here are some general guidelines. Write in any special instructions.

1. Choose sturdy white $8\frac{1}{2}$-by-11-inch paper, lined if you write by hand, plain if you use a computer.
2. Clearly write your name, the date, and any other required information, using the format requested by your instructor.
3. If you write by hand, do so neatly in black or dark blue ink.
4. Write on only one side of the paper.
5. Double-space if you write on a computer. Some instructors also want handwriting double-spaced.
6. Leave margins of at least one inch on all sides.
7. Number each page of your assignment, starting with page 2. Place the numbers at the top of each page, either centered or in the top right corner.

ESL TIP
Nonnative students may not understand the importance of speaking English whenever possible. Urge them to find a partner or study group with whom to practice speaking and writing English—other students truly dedicated to achieving success.

Other guidelines: ______________________________

____

____

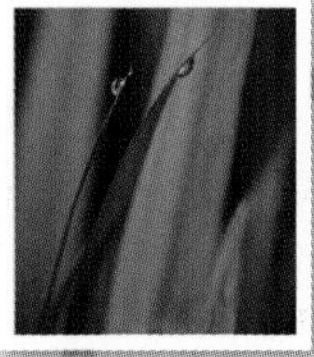

CHAPTER HIGHLIGHTS

Tips for Succeeding in This Course

- **Remember that writing is a process: prewriting, writing, and rewriting.**
- **Before you write, always be clear about your subject, audience, and purpose.**
- **Follow your instructor's guidelines for submitting written work.**
- **Practice.**

EXPLORING ONLINE

TEACHING TIP
More practice and assessment are available in the *Grassroots* Test Bank; linked ACE tests on the *Grassroots* student website; *WriteSpace for Grassroots*; and the Exploring Online links in this chapter.

Throughout this text, the Exploring Online feature will suggest ways that you can use the Internet to improve your writing and grammar skills. You will find that if you need extra writing help, online writing centers (called OWLs) can be a great resource. Many provide extra review or practice in areas in which you might need assistance. You will want to do some searching to find the best sites for your needs, but here are two excellent OWL sites to explore:

<http://owl.english.purdue.edu/> Purdue University.

<http://www.ccc.commnet.edu/grammar/> Capital Community College.

<http://college.hmco.com/devenglish> For more exercises and quizzes on the Student Website, visit the link, click Developmental Writing, and find the home page for *Grassroots,* 8/e. Bookmark the site for future visits as you work through this book.

CHAPTER 2

Prewriting to Generate Ideas

The author of this book used to teach ice skating. On the first day of class, her students practiced falling. Once they knew how to fall without fear, they were free to learn to skate.

Writing is much like ice skating: the more you practice, the better you get. If you are free to make mistakes, you'll want to practice, and you'll look forward to new writing challenges.

The problem is that many people avoid writing. Faced with an English composition or a report at work, they put it off and then scribble something at the last minute. Other people sit staring at the blank page or computer screen—writing a sentence, crossing it out, unable to get started. In this chapter, you will learn four useful prewriting techniques that will help you jump-start your writing process and generate lots of ideas: freewriting, brainstorming, clustering, and keeping a journal.

TEACHING TIP
Emphasize to students that freewriting and other prewriting techniques are tools for the *writer*—not meant to be shared with others; therefore, the writer can feel free to explore.

PART A Freewriting

Freewriting is a method many writers use to warm up and get ideas. Here are the guidelines: For five or ten full minutes, write without stopping. Don't worry about grammar or about writing complete sentences; just set a timer and go. If you get stuck, repeat or rhyme the last word you wrote, but keep writing nonstop until the timer sounds. Afterward, read what you have written, and underline any parts you like.

Freewriting is a wonderful way to let your ideas pour out without getting stuck by worrying too soon about correctness or "good writing." Sometimes freewriting produces nonsense, but often it provides interesting ideas for further thinking and writing. **Focused freewriting** can help you find subjects to write about.

TEACHING TIP
Mention to students that they can freewrite using a computer *or* paper and pencil, whichever method works best for them.

Focused Freewriting

In *focused freewriting,* you try to focus your thoughts on one subject as you freewrite. The subject can be one assigned by your instructor, one you choose, or one you discover in unfocused freewriting.

Here is one student's focused freewriting on the topic *someone who strongly influenced me.*

Thin, thinner, weak, weaker. You stopped cooking for yourself—forced yourself to choke down cans of nutrition. Your chest caved in; your bones stuck out. You never asked, Why me? With a weak laugh you asked, Why not me? I had a wonderful life, a great job, a good marriage while it lasted. Have beautiful kids. Your wife divorced you—couldn't stand to watch you die, couldn't stand to have her life fall apart the way your body was falling apart. I watched you stumble, trip over your own feet, sink, fall down. I held you up. Now I wonder which one of us was holding the other one up. I saw you shiver in your summer jacket because you didn't have the strength to put on your heavy coat. Bought you a feather-light winter jacket, saw your eyes fill with tears of pleasure and gratitude. You said they would find you at the bottom of the stairs. When they called to tell me we'd lost you, the news wasn't unexpected, but the pain came in huge waves. Heart gave out, they said. Your daughter found you crumpled at the foot of the stairs. How did you know? What else did you guess?

Daniel Corteau, student

TEACHING TIP
Research indicates that freewriting can be confusing to some students with learning disabilities. Instead, they need to *verbalize* ideas before writing. Suggest that they talk with a partner for two minutes before they start to write.

- This student later used his freewriting as the basis for an excellent paragraph.
- Underline any words or lines that you find especially striking or powerful. Be prepared to discuss your choices.
- How was the writer influenced by the man he describes?

PRACTICE 1

1. Set a timer for ten minutes, or have someone time you. Freewrite without stopping for the full ten minutes. Repeat or rhyme words if you get stuck, but keep writing! Don't let your pen or pencil leave the page or your fingers leave the keyboard.
2. When you finish, write down one or two words that describe how you feel while freewriting. ____________________
3. Now read your freewriting. Underline any words or lines you like—anything that strikes you as powerful, moving, funny, or important. If nothing strikes you, that's okay.

PRACTICE 2

Now choose one word or idea from your freewriting or from the following list. Focus your thoughts on it, and do a ten-minute focused freewriting. Try to stick to the topic, but don't worry too much about it. Just keep writing! When you finish, read and underline any striking lines or ideas.

1. home
2. a good student
3. the biggest lie
4. a dream
5. someone who influenced you
6. your experiences with writing
7. the smell of ____________
8. strength

PRACTICE 3

Try two more focused freewritings at home, each one ten minutes long. Do them at different times of the day when you have a few quiet moments. If possible, use a timer: set it for ten minutes, and then write fast until it rings. Later, read your freewritings, and underline any ideas or passages you might like to write more about.

PART B Brainstorming

Brainstorming means freely jotting ideas about a topic on paper or on a computer. As in freewriting, the purpose of brainstorming is to get as many ideas down as possible so that you will have something to work with later. Just write down everything that comes to mind about a topic—words and phrases, ideas, details, examples, little stories. Once you have brainstormed, read over your list, underlining any ideas you might want to develop further.

Here is one student's brainstorming list on *an interesting job:*

> midtown messenger
>
> frustrating but free
>
> I know the city backward and forward
>
> good bike needed
>
> fast, ever-changing, dangerous
>
> drivers hate messengers—we dart in and out of traffic
>
> old clothes don't get respect
>
> I wear the best Descent racing gear, a Giro helmet
>
> people respect you more
>
> I got tipped $100 for carrying a crystal vase from the showroom to Wall Street in 15 minutes
>
> other times I get stiffed
>
> lessons I've learned—controlling my temper
>
> having dignity
>
> staying calm no matter what—insane drivers, deadlines, rudeness
>
> weirdly, I like my job

ESL TIP
To draw out nonnative students who hesitate to share aloud, try the Anonymous Brainstorming Game, in which each student writes an idea related to the chosen topic (use pre-cut scraps of paper if you wish). Ideas are then chosen randomly and discussed by the class.

As he brainstormed, this writer produced many interesting facts and details about his job as a bicycle messenger, all in just a few minutes. He might want to underline the ideas that most interest him—perhaps the time he was tipped $100—and then brainstorm again for more details.

PRACTICE 4

Choose one of the following topics that interests you, and write it at the top of your page. Then brainstorm! Write anything that comes into your head about the topic. Let your ideas flow.

1. a singer or a musician
2. the future
3. an intriguing job
4. a story in the news
5. the best/worst class I've ever had
6. making a difference
7. a place to which I never want to return
8. a community problem

After you fill a page with your list, read it over, underlining the most interesting ideas. Draw arrows to connect related ideas. Do you find one idea that might be the subject of a paper?

PART C Clustering

Some writers find **clustering** or **mapping** an effective way to get ideas onto paper. To begin clustering, write one idea or topic—usually one word—in the center of your paper. Then let your mind make associations, and write those ideas down, branching out from the center. When one idea suggests other ideas, details, or examples, jot those around it in a cluster, like this:

TEACHING TIP
Clustering works especially well for generating sensory details about descriptive topics.

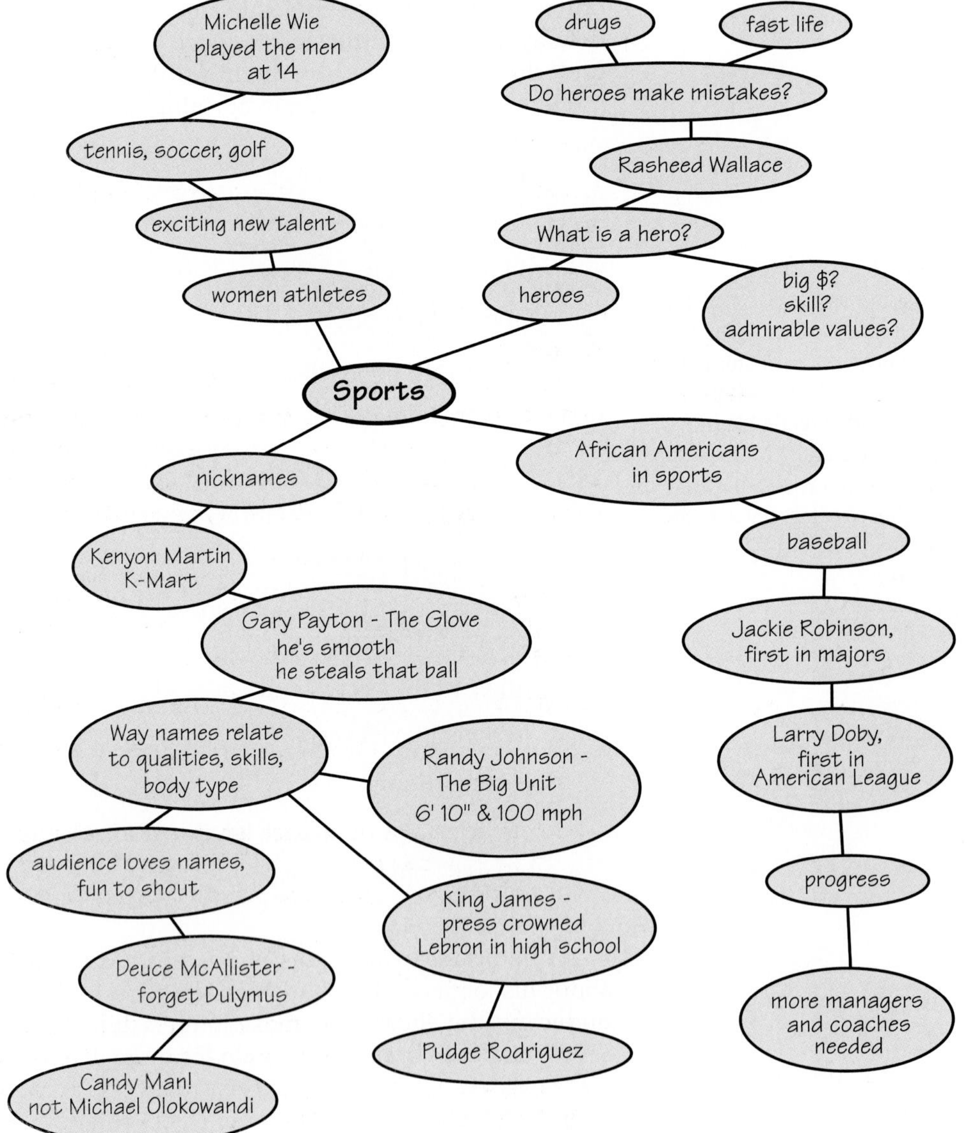

Once this student filled a page with clustered ideas about the word *sports*, his next step was choosing the cluster that most interested him and writing further. He might even have wanted to freewrite for more ideas.

PRACTICE 5

Read over the clustering map on page 12. If you were giving advice to the writer, which cluster or branch do you think would make the most interesting paper? Why?

PRACTICE 6

Choose one of these topics or another topic that interests you. Write it in the center of a piece of paper and then try clustering. Keep writing down associations until you have filled the page.

1. movies
2. a pet
3. a lesson
4. sports
5. my hometown
6. self-esteem
7. a relative
8. someone I don't understand

PART D Keeping a Journal

Keeping a **journal** is an excellent way to practice your writing skills and to discover ideas for future writing. Most of all, your journal is a place to record your private thoughts and important experiences. Open a journal file on your computer, or get yourself a special book with $8\frac{1}{2}$-by-11-inch lined paper. Every night, or several times a week, write for at least ten minutes in your journal.

What you write about will be limited only by your imagination. Here are some ideas:

TEACHING TIP
Ask students who are already in the habit of keeping a journal to share with the class the benefits of journaling.

- Write in detail about things that matter to you—family relationships, falling in (or out) of love, an experience at school or work, something important you just learned, something you did well.
- List your personal goals, and brainstorm possible steps toward achieving them.
- Write about problems you are having, and "think on paper" about ways to solve them.
- Comment on classroom instruction or assignments, and evaluate your learning progress. What needs work? What questions do you need to ask? Write out a study plan for yourself and refer to it regularly.
- Write down your responses to your reading—class assignments, newspaper items, magazine articles, websites that impress or anger you.
- Read through the quotations at the end of this book until you find one that strikes you. Then copy it into your journal, think about it, and write. For example, Agnes Repplier says, "It is not easy to find happiness in ourselves, and it is not possible to find it elsewhere." Do you agree with her?
- Be alert to interesting writing topics all around you. If possible, carry a notebook during the day for "fast sketches." Jot down moving or funny moments, people or things that catch your attention—an overworked waitress in a restaurant, a scene at the day-care center where you leave your child, a man trying to persuade an officer not to give him a parking ticket.

TEACHING TIP
Explain to students that although they may prefer one prewriting technique, they should try using several techniques if they need to generate more ideas about a topic.

You will soon find that ideas for writing will occur to you all day long. Before they slip away, capture them in words. Writing is like ice skating. You have to practice.

PRACTICE 7

Write in your journal for at least ten minutes three times a week.

At the end of each week, read what you have written. Underline striking passages, and mark interesting topics and ideas that you would like to explore further.

As you complete the exercises in this book and work on the writing assignments, try all four techniques—freewriting, brainstorming, clustering, and keeping a journal—and see which ones work best for you.

PRACTICE 8

From your journal, choose one or two passages that you might want to rewrite and allow others to read. Put a check beside each of those passages so that you can find them easily later. Underline the parts you like best. Can you already see ways you might rewrite and improve the writing?

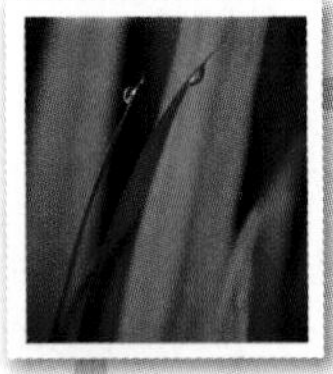

CHAPTER HIGHLIGHTS

To get started and to discover your ideas, try these techniques.

- **Focused freewriting: freewriting for five or ten minutes about one topic**
- **Brainstorming: freely jotting many ideas about a topic**
- **Clustering: making word associations on paper**
- **Keeping a journal: writing regularly about things that interest and move you**

EXPLORING ONLINE

TEACHING TIP
More practice and assessment are available in the *Grassroots* Test Bank; linked ACE tests on the *Grassroots* student website; *WriteSpace for Grassroots*; and the Exploring Online links in this chapter.

<http://uwc.tamu.edu/handouts/started/gs_freewriting.html> Peter Elbow shares ideas for using freewriting to become a better writer.

<http://depts.gallaudet.edu/englishworks/writing/prewriting.html> Review or print this handy chart of prewriting strategies.

<http://college.hmco.com/devenglish> For more exercises and quizzes on the Student Website, visit the link, click Developmental Writing, and find the home page for *Grassroots,* 8/e. Bookmark the site for future visits as you work through this book.

CHAPTER 3

Developing Effective Paragraphs

The **paragraph** is the basic unit of writing. This chapter will guide you through the process of writing paragraphs.

PART A Defining the Paragraph and the Topic Sentence

A *paragraph* is a group of related sentences that develop one main idea. Although a paragraph has no definite length, it is often four to twelve sentences long. A paragraph usually appears with other paragraphs in a longer piece of writing—an essay, a letter, or an article, for example.

A paragraph looks like this on the page:

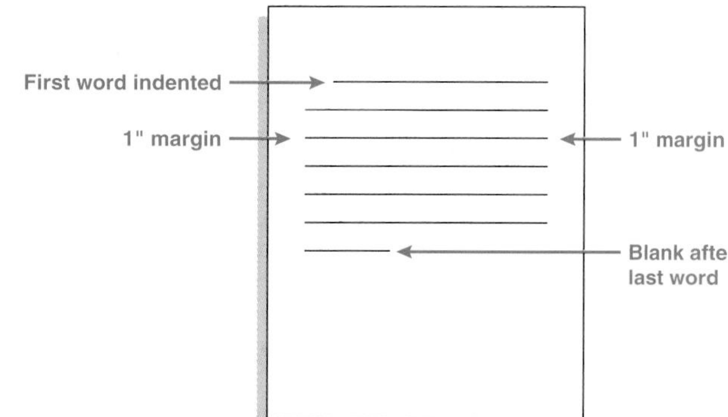

- Clearly **indent** the first word of every paragraph about 1 inch (five spaces on the computer).
- Extend every line of a paragraph as close to the right-hand margin as possible.
- However, if the last word of the paragraph comes before the end of the line, leave the rest of the line blank.

Topic Sentence and Body

TEACHING TIP
Review with students the concepts of *general* and *specific* before covering the information about the main idea and topic sentence.

Most paragraphs contain one main idea to which all the sentences relate. The **topic sentence** states this main idea. The **body** of the paragraph supports this main idea with specific details, facts, and examples.

> When I was growing up, my older brother Joe was the greatest person in my world. If anyone teased me about my braces or buckteeth, he fiercely defended me. When one boy insisted on calling me "Fang," Joe threatened to knock his teeth out. It worked—no more teasing. My brother always chose me to play on his baseball teams though I was a terrible hitter. Even after he got his driver's license, he didn't abandon me. Instead, every Sunday, the two of us went for a drive. We might stop for cheeseburgers, go to a computer showroom, drive past some girl's house, or just laugh and talk. It was one of childhood's mysteries that such a wonderful brother loved me.
>
> *Jeremiah Woolrich, student*

- The first sentence of this paragraph is the *topic sentence.* It states in a general way the main idea of the paragraph: that *Joe was the greatest person in my world.* Although the topic sentence can appear anywhere in the paragraph, it is often the first sentence.
- The rest of the paragraph, the *body,* fully explains this statement with details about braces and buckteeth, baseball teams, Sunday drives, cheeseburgers, and so forth.
- Note that the final sentence provides a brief conclusion so that the paragraph *feels* finished.

PRACTICE 1

ESL TIP
Because ways of organizing ideas and language vary from culture to culture, Practice 1 is very important.

Each group of sentences below can be arranged and written as a paragraph. Circle the letter of the sentence that would be the best topic sentence. REMEMBER: The topic sentence states the main idea of the entire paragraph and includes all the other ideas.

EXAMPLE: a. Speed-walking three times a week is part of my routine.

(b.) Staying healthy and fit is important to me.

c. Every night, I get at least seven hours of sleep.

d. I eat as many fresh fruits and vegetables as possible.

(Sentence b is more general than the other sentences; it would be the best topic sentence.)

1. a. Trained bomb-sniffing dogs have a nearly perfect record of separating real explosives from false alarms.
   b. Most air travelers love these dogs, prompting one police officer to say that people react to his Labrador retriever, Chili, as if she were Julia Roberts.
   (c.) Bomb-sniffing dogs have become an important and often-beloved security safeguard at airports.
   d. Because dogs are mobile—unlike machines—they can easily lead their handlers to the source of a problem.

TEACHING TIP
Practice 1 works well in class.

2. a. When his family moved to Los Angeles in 1974, ten-year-old Lenny won a place in the California Boys Choir and taught himself to play many instruments.
   b. As a teen, he studied music at the Berkeley Hills School and created the dramatic look for which he is now famous.
   c. Before he was ten, he had convinced his parents to take him to concerts by James Brown, Duke Ellington, and the Jackson 5.
   d. Lenny and his father produced his first album, *Let Love Rule,* which won him a Virgin Records contract and huge numbers of fans.
   (e.) A childhood love of performing music launched rocker and songwriter Lenny Kravitz on the path to stardom.
   f. As a toddler in Brooklyn, New York, Lenny made his own drum set out of pots and pans.

3. a. Physical courage allows soldiers or athletes to endure bodily pain or danger.
   b. Those with social courage dare to expose their deep feelings in order to build close relationships.
   c. Those rare people who stand up for their beliefs despite public pressure possess moral courage.
   d. Inventors and artists show creative courage when they break out of old ways of seeing and doing things.
   (e.) Psychologist Rollo May claimed that there are four different types of courage.

4. (a.) Many old toys and household objects are now collectors' items.
   b. A Barbie or Madame Alexander doll from the 1950s can bring more than $1,000.
   c. Old baseball cards are worth money to collectors.
   d. Fiesta china, made in the 1930s, has become popular again.

5. a. You should read the ingredients on every package of food you buy.
   b. Children should not eat mandelona, which is made from peanuts soaked in almond flavoring.
   c. Avoid buying food from bins that do not list ingredients.
   (d.) If your child is allergic to peanuts, you need to be constantly on the alert.
   e. In a restaurant, tongs may have been used to pick up items containing peanuts.

PART B Narrowing the Topic and Writing the Topic Sentence

The rest of this chapter will guide you through the process of writing paragraphs of your own. Here are the steps we will discuss:

1. Narrowing the topic and writing the topic sentence
2. Generating ideas for the body
3. Selecting and dropping ideas
4. Grouping ideas in a plan
5. Writing and revising the paragraph
6. Writing the final draft

Narrowing the Topic

TEACHING TIP
Students often need extra practice in recognizing topics that are too broad for a paragraph. List topics of varying levels of specificity on the board, or use students' own ideas from the prewriting exercises in Chapter 2. Then lead a discussion about which topics should be narrowed.

Often your first step as a writer will be **narrowing** a broad topic—one assigned by your instructor, one you have thought of yourself, or one suggested by a particular writing task, like a letter. That is, you must cut the topic down to size and choose one aspect that interests you.

Assume, for example, that you are asked to write a paragraph describing a person you know. The trick is to choose someone you would *like* to write about, someone who interests you and would probably also interest your audience of readers.

At this point, many writers find it helpful to think on paper by *brainstorming, freewriting,* or *clustering.** As you jot down or freely write ideas, ask yourself questions. Whom do I love, hate, or admire? Who is the funniest or most unusual person I know? Is there a family member or friend about whom others might like to read?

Suppose you choose to write about your friend Beverly. *Beverly* is too broad a topic for one paragraph. Therefore, you should limit your topic further, choosing just one of her qualities or acts. What is unusual about her? What might interest others? Perhaps what stands out in your mind is that Beverly is a determined person who doesn't let difficulties defeat her. You have now *narrowed* your broad topic to just *Beverly's determination.*

Writing the Topic Sentence

The **topic sentence** states your narrowed topic clearly in sentence form. It makes one point that the rest of your paragraph will support and explain. A topic sentence can be very simple *(Beverly is a determined person)*, or, better yet, it can state your attitude or point of view about the topic *(Beverly inspires admiration because she is so determined)*. A good topic sentence should be limited and complete.

Your topic sentence should be **limited.** It should make a point that is neither too broad nor too narrow to be supported in a paragraph. As a rule, the more specific and well-defined the topic sentence, the better the paragraph. Which of these topic sentences do you think will produce the best paragraph?

(1) My recent trip to Colorado was really bad.

(2) My recent trip to Colorado was disappointing because the weather ruined my camping plans.

- Topic sentence (1) is so broad that the paragraph could include almost anything.
- Topic sentence (2), on the other hand, is *limited* enough to provide the main idea for a good paragraph: how terrible weather ruined the writer's camping plans.

*Brainstorming is discussed further in Part C. Also see Chapter 2 for more information about prewriting.

(3) The Each-One-Reach-One tutoring program encourages academic excellence at Chester Elementary School.

(4) Tutoring programs can be found all over the country.

- Topic sentence (3) is limited enough to provide the main idea for a good paragraph. Reading this topic sentence, what do you expect the paragraph to include?

  It might explain ways in which the program encourages academic excellence at Chester.

- Topic sentence (4) lacks a limited point. Reading this sentence, someone cannot guess what the paragraph will be about.

In addition, the topic sentence must be a **complete sentence**; it must contain a subject and a verb and express a complete thought.* Do not confuse a topic with a topic sentence. For example, *the heroism of Christopher Reeve* cannot be a topic sentence because it is not a complete sentence. Here is one possible topic sentence: *Christopher Reeve's work with other spinal-cord injury patients makes him a true hero.*

For now, it is best to place your topic sentence at the beginning of the paragraph. After you have mastered this pattern, you can try variations. Placed first, the topic sentence clearly establishes the focus of your paragraph and helps grab the reader's attention. Wherever the topic sentence appears, all other sentences must relate to it and support it with specific details, facts, examples, arguments, and explanations. If necessary, you can revise the topic sentence later to make it more accurately match the paragraph you have written.

Caution: Do not begin a topic sentence with *This paragraph will be about . . .* or *I am going to write about . . .* These extra words contribute nothing. Instead, make your point directly. Make every word in the topic sentence count.

TEACHING TIP
An extremely common problem among new writers is awkwardly announcing the subject of their paper with "This paper will be about . . ." Emphasize the role of the topic sentence as stating a point of view about the subject, not announcing it.

PRACTICE 2

Put a check beside each topic sentence that is limited enough to be the topic sentence of a good paragraph. If you think a topic sentence is too broad, limit the topic according to your own interests; then write a new, specific topic sentence.

Sample answers

EXAMPLES:

✔ E-mail has changed my life in three ways.

Rewrite: ______________________________

I am going to write about cell phones.

Rewrite: Talking on a cell phone can distract drivers to the point of causing accidents.

✔ 1. Working in the complaint department taught me tolerance.

Rewrite: ______________________________

____

2. A subject I want to write about is money.

Rewrite: Saving money requires discipline but has unexpected rewards.

____

*For more work on writing complete sentences, see Chapters 6 and 7.

3. This paragraph will discuss food.

   Rewrite: It is hard to change some of the attitudes about food that we learn as children.

4. Some things about college have been great.

   Rewrite: Being able to set my own study schedule in college has improved my attitude toward studying.

✔5. Living in a one-room apartment forces a person to be organized.

   Rewrite: ______

PRACTICE 3

Here is a list of topics. Choose one that interests you from this list or from your own list in Chapter 1 on page 6. Narrow the topic, and write a topic sentence limited enough to provide the main idea for a good paragraph. Make sure that your topic sentence is a complete sentence.

A talented musician	An act of courage
Why get an education?	Advertising con jobs
AIDS	Clothing styles on campus

Narrowed topic: ______

Topic sentence: ______

PART C Generating Ideas for the Body of the Paragraph

ESL TIP
Many ESL and other students tend to overuse generalizations. Try the acronym FIRE (fact, incident, reason/result, explanation) to remind them to be specific.

Rich supporting detail is one key to effective writing. A good way to generate ideas for the body of a paragraph is by *brainstorming*, freely jotting down ideas. This important step may take just a few minutes, but it gets your ideas on paper and may pull ideas out of you that you didn't even know you had.

Freely jot down anything that might relate to your topic—details, examples, little stories. Don't worry at this point if some ideas don't seem to belong. For now, just keep jotting.

Here is a possible brainstorming list for the topic sentence *Beverly inspires admiration because she is so determined.*

TEACHING TIP
Create a paragraph with the class, honing a topic sentence, brainstorming, and selecting ideas for the body.

1. saved enough money for college
2. worked days, went to school nights
3. has beautiful brown eyes
4. nervous about learning to drive but didn't give up
5. failed road test twice—passed eventually
6. her favorite color—wine red

7. received degree in accounting
8. she is really admirable
9. with lots of will power, quit smoking
10. used to be a heavy smoker
11. married to Virgil
12. I like Virgil too
13. now a good driver
14. never got a ticket
15. hasn't touched another cigarette

As you saw in Part B, some writers also brainstorm or use other prewriting techniques *before* they write the topic sentence. Do what works best for you.

PRACTICE 4

Now choose the topic from Practice 2 or Practice 3 that most interests you. Write your limited topic sentence here.

Topic sentence: ______________________________

____

Next, brainstorm, freewrite, or cluster for specific ideas to develop a paragraph. On paper or on a computer, write anything that comes to you about your topic sentence. Just let ideas pour out—details, memories, facts. Try to fill at least one page.

PRACTICE 5

TEACHING TIP
Practice 5 is difficult for some students and might be best done in small groups.

Many writers adjust the topic sentence *after* they have finished drafting the paragraph. In a group of three or four classmates, study the body of each of the following paragraphs. Then, working together, write the most exact and interesting topic sentence you can. Answers will vary.

1. Topic sentence: Multiplex movie theaters have at least three advantages over smaller theaters.

The first advantage is the wide choice of movies. Most multiplexes have eight, twelve, or even twenty screens playing at once, so the moviegoer has a good chance of finding a movie that she or he actually wants to see. A second advantage of the multiplex is comfortable seating. Most multiplexes have large stadium seats that lean back like lounge chairs. Finally, the multiplex is a lively and pleasant place to be on Friday or Saturday night. In a college town, for example, the moviegoer is likely to run into friends and classmates, a definite plus—unless she or he hates crowds or wants to spend an evening hiding in the dark with a jumbo tub of popcorn. Some might long for the little movie houses of the past, but nostalgia can't outweigh the advantages of the multiplex.

2. Topic sentence: Winter mornings in Minnesota were bitterly cold but beautiful.

Frigid air would hit us in the eyes when we stepped out the door to catch the school bus. Even though our faces were wrapped in scarves and our heads covered with wool caps, the cold snatched our breath away. A thin layer of snow crunched loudly under our boots as we ran gasping out to the road. I knew that the famous Minnesota wind chill was pulling temperatures well below zero, but I tried not to think about that. Instead, I liked to see how everything in the yard was frozen motionless, even the blades of grass that shone like little glass knives.

Ari Henson, student

PART D Selecting and Dropping Ideas

This may be the easiest step in paragraph writing because all you have to do is to select those ideas that best support your topic sentence and drop those that do not. Also drop ideas that just repeat the topic sentence but add nothing new to the paragraph.

Here is the brainstorming list for the topic sentence *Beverly inspires admiration because she is so determined.* Which ideas would you drop? Why?

1. saved enough money for college
2. worked days, went to school nights
3. has beautiful brown eyes
4. nervous about learning to drive but didn't give up
5. failed road test twice—passed eventually
6. her favorite color—wine red
7. received degree in accounting
8. she is really admirable
9. with lots of will power, quit smoking
10. used to be a heavy smoker
11. married to Virgil
12. I like Virgil too
13. now a good driver
14. never got a ticket
15. hasn't touched another cigarette

You probably dropped ideas 3, 6, 11, and 12 because they do not relate to the topic. You also should have dropped idea 8 because it merely repeats the topic sentence.

PRACTICE 6

Now read through your own brainstorming list in Practice 4. Select the ideas that best support your topic sentence, and cross out those that do not. In addition, drop ideas that merely repeat the topic sentence. You should be able to give good reasons for keeping or dropping each idea in the list.

PART E Arranging Ideas in a Plan or an Outline

Next, choose an **order** in which to arrange your ideas. First, group together ideas that have something in common, that are related or alike in some way. Then decide which ideas should come first, which second, and so on. Many writers do this by numbering the ideas on their list.

Here is a plan for a paragraph about Beverly's determination.

TEACHING TIP
Organizing ideas is a key skill that many students lack. You might illustrate the process by "thinking aloud" as you reason out the best order of ideas for a paragraph. That is, model the mental process that writers go through when they plan.

Topic sentence: Beverly inspires admiration because she is so determined.

worked days, went to school nights
saved enough money for college
received degree in accounting

nervous about learning to drive but didn't give up
failed road test twice—passed eventually
now a good driver
never got a ticket

used to be a heavy smoker
with lots of will power, quit smoking
hasn't touched another cigarette

- How are the ideas in each group related? The first group of ideas deals with school, the second with driving, and the third with smoking.
- Does it make sense to discuss college first, driving second, and smoking last? Why? Yes, it makes sense. This may be the order of importance to the writer.

Keep in mind that there is more than one way to arrange ideas. As you group your own brainstorming list, think of what you want to say; then arrange ideas accordingly.*

PRACTICE 7

On paper or on a computer, make a plan or outline from your brainstormed list of ideas. First, group together related ideas. Then decide which ideas will come first, which second, and so on.

PART F Writing and Revising the Paragraph

Writing the First Draft

By now, you should have a clear plan or outline from which to write the first draft of your paragraph. The **first draft** should contain all the ideas you have decided

*For more work on choosing an order, see Chapter 4 , Part B.

to use, in the order in which you have chosen to present them. Writing on every other line will leave room for later changes.

Explain your ideas fully, including details that will interest or amuse the reader. If you are unsure about something, put a check in the margin and come back to it later, but avoid getting stuck on any one word, sentence, or idea. If possible, set the paper aside for several hours or several days; this step will help you read it later with a fresh eye.

PRACTICE 8

On paper or on a computer, write a first draft of the paragraph you have been working on.

Revising

Whether you are a beginning writer or a professional, you must **revise**—that is, rewrite what you have written in order to improve it. You might cross out and rewrite words or entire sentences. You might add, drop, or rearrange details.

As you revise, keep the reader in mind. Ask yourself these questions:

- Is my topic sentence clear?
- Can the reader easily follow my ideas?
- Is the order of ideas logical?
- Will this paragraph keep the reader interested?

In addition, revise your paragraph for *support* and for *unity*.

ESL TIP
Ask students to think about any differences between their native language and English that might cause problems as they write and revise in English.

Revising for Support

Make sure your paragraph contains excellent **support**—that is, specific details, facts, and examples that fully explain your topic sentence.

Avoid simply repeating the same idea in different words, especially the idea in the topic sentence. Repeated ideas are just padding, a sign that you need to brainstorm or freewrite again for new ideas. Which of the following two paragraphs contains the best and most interesting support?

A. Every Saturday morning, Fourteenth Street is alive with activity. From one end of the street to the other, people are out doing everything imaginable. Vendors sell many different items on the street, and storekeepers will do just about anything to get customers into their stores. They will use signs, and they will use music. There is a tremendous amount of activity on Fourteenth Street, and just watching it is enjoyable.

B. Every Saturday morning, Fourteenth Street is alive with activity. Vendors line the sidewalks, selling everything from DVD players to wigs. Trying to lure customers inside, the shops blast pop music into the street or hang brightly colored banners announcing "Grand Opening Sale" or "Everything Must Go." Shoppers jam the sidewalks, both serious bargain hunters and families just out for a stroll, munching chilidogs as they survey the merchandise. Here and there, a panhandler hustles for handouts, taking advantage of the Saturday crowd.

- The body of *paragraph A* contains vague and general statements, so the reader gets no clear picture of the activity on Fourteenth Street.

- The body of *paragraph B*, however, includes many specific *details* that clearly explain the topic sentence: *vendors selling everything from DVD players to wigs, shops blasting pop music, brightly colored banners.*
- What other details in paragraph B help you see just how Fourteenth Street is alive with activity?

serious bargain hunters

strolling families

chilidogs

a panhandler

PRACTICE 9

Check the following paragraphs for strong, specific support. Mark places that need more details or explanation, and cross out any weak or repeated words. Then revise and rewrite each paragraph *as if you had written it*, inventing and adding support when you need to. Answers will vary.

Paragraph A: Aunt Alethia was one of the most important people in my life. She had a strong influence on me. No matter how busy she was, she always had time for me. She paid attention to small things about me that no one else seemed to notice. When I was successful, she praised me. When I was feeling down, she gave me pep talks. She was truly wise and shared her wisdom with me. My aunt was a great person who had a major influence on my life.

Paragraph B: Just getting to school safely can be a challenge for many young people. Young as he is, my son has been robbed once and bullied on several occasions. The robbery was very frightening, for it involved a weapon. What was taken was a small thing, but it meant a lot to my son. It angers me that just getting to school is so dangerous. Something needs to be done.

Revising for Unity

TEACHING TIP
Stress to students that outlining first and then using the outline as a guide while writing will help prevent problems with unity.

While writing, you may sometimes drift away from your topic and include information that does not belong in the paragraph. It is important, therefore, to revise your paragraph for **unity;** that is, to drop any ideas or sentences that do not relate to the topic sentence.

This paragraph lacks unity:

> (1) Franklin Mars, a Minnesota candy maker, created many popular candy snacks. (2) Milky Way, his first bar, was an instant hit. (3) Snickers, which he introduced in 1930, also sold very well. (4) Milton Hershey developed the very first candy bar in 1894. (5) M&Ms were a later Mars creation, supposedly designed so that soldiers could enjoy a sugar boost without getting sticky trigger fingers.

- What is the topic sentence in this paragraph? sentence (1)
- Which sentence does *not* relate to the topic sentence? sentence (4)
- Sentence (4) has nothing to do with the main idea, that *Franklin Mars created many popular candy snacks.* Therefore, sentence (4) should be dropped.

PRACTICE 10

TEACHING TIP
Practice 10 is fun to do in class.

Check the following paragraphs for unity. If a paragraph is unified, write U in the blank. If it is not, write the number of the sentence that does not belong in the paragraph.

1. U (1) Families who nourish their children with words as well as food at dinner time produce better future readers. (2) Researchers at Harvard University studied the dinner conversations of sixty-eight families. (3) What they found was that parents who use a few new words in conversation with their three- and four-year-olds each night quickly build the children's vocabularies and their later reading skills. (4) The researchers point out that children can learn from eight to twenty-eight new words a day, so they need to be "fed" new words. (5) Excellent "big words" for preschoolers include *parachute, emerald, instrument,* and *education,* the researchers say.

2. 3 (1) Personalized license plates have become very popular. (2) These "vanity plates" allow car owners to express their sense of humor, marital status, pet peeves, or ethnic pride. (3) Of course, every car must display a plate on the rear bumper or in the back window. (4) Drivers have created messages such as ROCK ON, NT GUILTY, and (on a tow truck) ITZ GONE. (5) In some states, as many as one in seven autos has a personalized plate. (6) Recently, *Parade* magazine chose the nation's top ten vanity plates, including XQQSME on a Massachusetts plate, ULIV1S on an Arkansas plate, and on an SUV in Missouri, a message to be read in the rear-view mirror—TI-3VOM.

3. 5 (1) Swimming is excellent exercise. (2) Swimming vigorously for just twelve minutes provides aerobic benefits to the heart. (3) Unlike jogging and many other aerobic sports, however, swimming does not jolt the bones and muscles with sudden pressure. (4) Furthermore, the motions of swimming, such as reaching out in the crawl, stretch the muscles in a healthy, natural way. (5) Some swimmers wear goggles to keep chlorine or salt out of their eyes while others do not.

Peer Feedback for Revising

You may wish to show your first draft or read it aloud to a respected friend or classmate. Ask this person to give an honest reader response, not to rewrite your work. To elicit useful responses, ask specific questions of your own, or use the Peer Feedback Sheet on the following page. You may want to photocopy the sheet rather than write on it so that you can reuse it.

PRACTICE 11

Now read the first draft of your paragraph with a critical eye. Revise and rewrite it, checking especially for a clear topic sentence, strong support, and unity.

PRACTICE 12

Exchange *revised* paragraphs with a classmate. Ask specific questions or use the Peer Feedback Sheet.

When you *give* feedback, try to be as honest and specific as possible; saying a paper is "good," "nice," or "bad" doesn't really help the writer. When you *receive* feedback, think over your classmate's responses; do they ring true?

Now revise a second time, with the aim of writing a fine paragraph.

PEER FEEDBACK SHEET

To ____________________ From ____________________ Date ____________________

1. What I like about this piece of writing is ____

____

____

2. Your main point seems to be ____

____

____

3. These particular words or lines struck me as powerful.

Words or lines:	I like them because
____________________	____________________
____________________	____________________
____________________	____________________
____________________	____________________

4. Some things aren't clear to me. These lines or parts could be improved (meaning not clear; supporting points missing; order seems mixed up; writing not lively):

Lines or parts:	Need improving because
____________________	____________________
____________________	____________________
____________________	____________________
____________________	____________________

5. The one change you could make that would most improve this piece of writing is

____

____

____

PART G Writing the Final Draft

When you are satisfied with your revisions, recopy your paper. Be sure to include all your corrections, and write neatly and legibly—a carelessly scribbled paper seems to say that you don't care about your work.

The first draft of the paragraph about Beverly, with the writer's changes, and the revised final draft follow. Compare them.

First Draft with Revisions

(1) Beverly inspires admiration because she is so determined. (2) Although she could not afford to attend college right after high school, she worked [doing what? add details] to save money. (3) It took a long time [How long?! Better support needed—show her hard work!], but she got her degree. (4) She is now a good driver. (5) At first, she was very nervous about getting behind the wheel and even failed the road test twice, but she didn't quit. (6) [The third time,] ~~S~~she passed eventually. (7) Her husband, Virgil, loves to drive; he races cars on the weekend. [Drop Virgil—he doesn't belong] (8) Anyway, Beverly has never gotten a ticket. (9) A year ago, Beverly quit smoking. (10) For a while [how long??], she had a rough time, but she hasn't [too general—add details here] touched a cigarette. (11) Now she says that the urge to smoke has faded away. (12) She doesn't let difficulties [better conclusion needed] defeat her.

Guide the reader better from point to point! Choppy—

Final Draft

(1) Beverly inspires admiration because she is so determined. (2) Although she could not afford to attend college right after high school, she worked as a cashier to save money for tuition. (3) It took her five years working days and going to school nights, but she recently received a BS in accounting. (4) Thanks to this same determination, Beverly is now a good driver. (5) At first, she was very nervous about getting behind the wheel and even failed the road test twice, but she didn't give up. (6) The third time, she passed, and she has never gotten a ticket. (7) A year ago, Beverly quit smoking. (8) For a month or more, she chewed her nails and endless packs of gum, but she hasn't touched a cigarette. (9) Now she says that the urge to smoke has faded away. (10) When Beverly sets a goal for herself, she doesn't let difficulties defeat her.

- This paragraph provides good support for the topic sentence. The writer has made sentences (2) and (3) more specific by adding *as a cashier, for tuition, five years working days and going to school nights,* and *recently received a BS in accounting*.
- What other revisions did the writer make? How do these revisions improve the paragraph? The writer made sentence (6) more exact and combined it with sentence (8), dropped the sentence about Virgil, added details to sentence (10), and expanded sentence (12) to relate it to the topic sentence. The paragraph is now more unified and specific.

- *Transitional expressions* are words and phrases that guide the reader smoothly from point to point. In sentence (5) of the final draft, *at first* is a transitional expression showing time. What other transitional expressions of time are used?

  The third time, a year ago, for a month or more, now

- What phrase provides a transition from sentence (3) to (4)?

  Thanks to this same determination

- Note that the last sentence now provides a brief *conclusion* so that the paragraph *feels* finished.

Proofreading

TEACHING TIP
Suggest that your students begin keeping lists of their personal error patterns. This will make them better proofreaders. Returned papers, suggestions from you, the practices and links in this text and on both its Student and Instructor Websites will heighten students' grammatical self awareness.

Finally, carefully **proofread** your paper for grammatical and spelling errors, consulting your dictionary and this book as necessary. Errors in your writing will lower your grades in almost all college courses. Writing errors may also affect your job opportunities. Units 2 through 8 of this textbook will help you improve your grammar, punctuation, and spelling skills.

Some students find it useful to point to each word and say it softly. This method also helps them catch errors as well as any words they may have left out as they wrote, especially little words like *and, at, of,* and *on.*

In which of these sentences have words been omitted?

(1) Despite its faulty landing gear, the 777 managed land safely.

(2) Plans for the new gym were on display the library.

(3) Mr. Sampson winked at his reflection in the bathroom mirror.

ESL TIP
Urge your ESL students to use English-only reference materials as they proofread.

- Words are missing in sentences (1) and (2).
- Sentence (1) requires *to* before *land.*
- What word is omitted in sentence (2)? *in*
- Where should this word be placed? *after* display

PRACTICE 13

Proofread these sentences for omitted words. Add the necessary words above the lines. Some sentences may already be correct.

EXAMPLE: People were not always able ^to^ tell time accurately.

1. People used to guess the time ^of^ day by watching the sun move across the sky.
2. Sunrise and sunset were easy ^to^ recognize.
3. Recognizing noon ^was^ easy, too.
4. However, telling time by the position of ^the^ sun was very difficult at other times.
5. People noticed that shadows lengthened during the day.
6. They found it easier to tell time by looking at the shadows than by looking ^at^ the sun.

7. People stuck poles into the ground to ^tell time by the length of the shadows.
8. Those ^were the first shadow clocks, or sundials.
9. In 300 BC, ^a Chaldean astronomer invented a more accurate, bowl-shaped sundial.
10. Today, most sundials ^are decorative, but they can still be used to tell time.

PRACTICE 14

Proofread the final draft of your paragraph, checking for grammar or spelling errors and omitted words.

PRACTICE 15 WRITING AND REVISING PARAGRAPHS

The assignments that follow will give you practice in writing and revising basic paragraphs. In each assignment, aim for (1) a clear topic sentence and (2) sentences that fully support and explain the topic sentence. As you write, refer to the checklist in the Chapter Highlights on page 31.

Paragraph 1: Describe a public place. Reread paragraph B on page 24. Then choose a place in your neighborhood that is "alive with activity"—a park, street, restaurant, or club. In your topic sentence, name the place and say when it is most active; for example, "Every Saturday night, the Blue Dog Café is alive with activity." Begin by freewriting or by jotting down as many details about the scene as possible. Then describe the scene. Arrange your observations in a logical order. Revise for support, making sure that your details are so lively and interesting that your readers will see the place as clearly as you do.

Paragraph 2: Describe a portrait. Study this photograph of Eminem. Notice his eyes, facial expression, mouth, posture, tattoos, and other details. Now write a paragraph in which you describe this photo for someone who has not seen it. In your topic sentence, state one overall impression, feeling, or message that this portrait conveys. Support this impression with specific details. If you prefer, you may use

© MTV Networks Europe.

Google or another search engine to find an expressive photo of your favorite entertainer and describe that instead. Conclude your paragrapoh; don't just stop.

Paragraph 3: Create a holiday. Holidays honor important people, events, or ideas. If you could create a new holiday for your town or state, or for the country, what would that holiday be? In your topic sentence, name the holiday and tell exactly whom or what it honors. Then explain why this holiday is important, and discuss how it should be celebrated. Take a humorous approach if you wish. For instance, you might invent a national holiday in honor of the first time you got an A in English composition. As you revise, make sure you have arranged your ideas in a logical order. Proofread carefully.

Paragraph 4: Choose your time of day. Many people have a favorite time of day—the freshness of early morning, 5 p.m. when work ends, late at night when the children are asleep. In your topic sentence, name your favorite time of day. Then develop the paragraph by explaining why you look forward to this time and exactly how you spend it. Check your work for any omitted words.

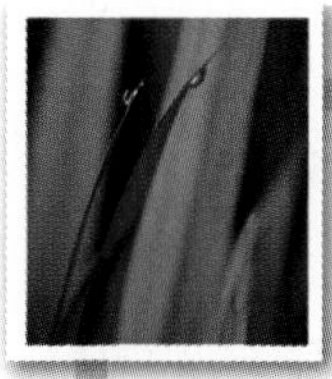

CHAPTER HIGHLIGHTS

Checklist for Writing an Effective Paragraph

- **Narrow the topic: Cut the topic down to one aspect that interests you and will probably interest your readers.**
- **Write the topic sentence. (You may wish to brainstorm or freewrite first.)**
- **Brainstorm, freewrite, or cluster ideas for the body: Write down anything and everything that might relate to your topic.**
- **Select and drop ideas: Select those ideas that relate to your topic and drop those that do not.**
- **Group together ideas that have something in common; then arrange the ideas in a plan.**
- **Write your first draft.**
- **Read what you have written, making any necessary corrections and additions. Revise for support and unity.**
- **Write the final draft of your paragraph neatly and legibly, making sure to indent the first word.**
- **Proofread for grammar, punctuation, spelling, and omitted words. Make neat corrections in ink.**

EXPLORING ONLINE

TEACHING TIP
More practice and assessment are available in the *Grassroots* Test Bank; linked ACE tests on the *Grassroots* student website; *WriteSpace for Grassroots*; and the Exploring Online links in this chapter.

<http://www.ccc.commnet.edu/grammar/paragraphs.htm> Review paragraph unity and topic sentences.

<http://college.hmco.com/devenglish> For more exercises and quizzes on the Student Website, visit the link, click Developmental Writing, and find the home page for *Grassroots*, 8/e. Bookmark the site for future visits as you work through this book.

CHAPTER 4

Improving Your Paragraphs

In Chapter 3, you practiced the steps of the paragraph-writing process. This chapter builds on that work. It explains several skills that can greatly improve your writing: using examples; achieving coherence; choosing exact, concise language; and turning assignments into paragraphs.

PART A More Work on Support: Examples

One effective way to make your writing specific is by using **examples**. Someone might write, "Divers in Monterey Bay can observe many beautiful fish. For instance, tiger-striped treefish are common." The first sentence makes a general statement about the beautiful fish in Monterey Bay. The second sentence gives a specific example of such fish: *tiger-striped treefish*.

Use one, two, or three well-chosen examples to develop a paragraph.

> Many of the computer industry's best innovators were young when they first achieved success. For example, David Filo and Jerry Yang were graduate students at Stanford when they realized that their hobby of listing the best pages on the World Wide Web might become a business. They created Yahoo!, a Web index now used by more than 500,000 people every day. Another youthful example is Marc Andreesen, who helped start the software company Netscape and designed one of the most popular computer programs ever, the Navigator. At age twenty-four, Andreesen suddenly had $58 million in the bank. A third young computer genius is Masayoshi Son. As a Berkeley undergraduate, he started importing the Space Invaders video game from his native Japan and made a small fortune. After graduation, at twenty-four, Son returned to Japan, started the Softbank company, and built a worldwide computer empire.

TEACHING TIP
Point out that knowing how to choose excellent examples to develop a point will serve students well in college and on the job.

- The writer begins this paragraph with a topic sentence about the youth of many computer innovators.

- What three examples does the writer provide as support?

Example 1: David Filo and Jerry Yang

Example 2: Marc Andreesen

Example 3: Masayoshi Son

- Note that the topic sentence and the examples make a rough plan for the paragraph.

TEACHING TIP
Transitional expressions to introduce details and support will be very helpful to both ESL and native students. Encourage them to keep personal lists with a variety of introductory expressions to use in their writing.

The simplest way to tell a reader that an example will follow is to say so, using a transitional expression: *For example, David Filo . . .*

Transitional Expressions to Introduce Examples

for example	for instance
to illustrate	another example

PRACTICE 1

Each example in a paragraph must clearly relate to and explain the topic sentence. Each of the following topic sentences is followed by several examples. Circle the letter of any example that does *not* clearly illustrate the topic sentence. Be prepared to explain your choices.

EXAMPLE: Some animals and insects camouflage themselves in interesting ways.

a. Snowshoe rabbits turn from brown to white in winter, thus blending into the snow.
b. The cheetah's spotted coat makes it hard to see in the dry African bush.
(c.) The bull alligator smashes its tail against the water and roars during mating season.
d. The walking stick is brown and irregular, much like the twigs among which this insect hides.

1. State troopers report that many people do dangerous and outrageous things while driving.
   a. One woman applied mascara, pressing her face close to the rear-view mirror as she drove 65 miles an hour.
   (b.) A woman shopped in a Detroit supermarket while wearing a Queen Elizabeth mask and a crown.
   c. Another man glanced up and down as he changed lanes, writing in a spiral notebook propped against the steering wheel.
   d. A man ate scrambled eggs with a fork—from a plate on his dashboard.

2. Major League baseball has seen a recent influx of talented players from Japan.
   a. The Seattle Mariners signed a skilled outfielder in 2001, Ichiro Suzuki of Japan's Pacific League.
   b. In 2003, the New York Yankees scored when they imported hitter Hideki Matsui.
   c. Pitcher Hideo Nomo of the Osaka Buffaloes signed with the Los Angeles Dodgers in 1995.
   (d.) Baseball has been played and loved for many years in Japan.

3. Mrs. Makarem is well loved in this community for her generous heart.
   a. Her door is always open to neighborhood children, who stop by for lemonade or advice.
   b. When the Padilla family had a fire, Mrs. Makarem collected clothes and blankets for them.
   c. "Hello, dear," she says with a smile to everyone she passes on the street.
   (d.) Born in Caracas, Venezuela, she has lived on Bay Road for thirty-two years.

4. A number of unusual, specialized scholarships are offered by colleges across the United States.
   a. North Carolina State University offers up to $7,000 to undergraduates with the last name of *Gatlin* or *Gatling*.
   (b.) The University of Vienna in Austria has funds for "noncommunist creative writers ages 22 to 35."
   c. Left-handed, financially needy students can get special scholarships at Juniata College in Pennsylvania.
   d. Wisconsin's Ripon College offers $1,500 to students with a 3.0 average who once were Badger Girls or Badger Boys.

5. English borrows words from many other languages.
   a. The Spanish *la reata* gives us *lariat*, "a rope."
   b. The expression *gung ho* comes from the Chinese *keng ho*, which literally means "more fire."
   (c.) *Diss* is a term meaning "disrespect."
   d. *Kimono* is the Japanese word for "thing for wearing."

PRACTICE 2

TEACHING TIP
Practice 2 works well as a group exercise. Have each group develop its own example to support the same statement; then share the examples and let the full class choose the most effective ones.

The secret of good illustration lies in well-chosen and well-written examples. Think of one example that illustrates each of the following general statements. Write out the example in sentence form—one to three sentences—as clearly and exactly as possible. Sample answers

1. Many films today have amazing special effects.
   Example: In *Independence Day*, for instance, a huge spaceship hovers over major cities.

2. Television programs have reached new lows in the past few years.
   Example: The wedding on *Who Wants to Marry a Multi-Millionaire?* made a mockery of marriage.

3. Dan is always buying strange gadgets.
   Example: On Tuesday, he bought a combination lint remover–beard brush; and on Thursday, he couldn't resist getting an automatic sauce-stirring device.

4. Even when she is very busy, Grace finds ways to exercise.
   Example: She sometimes walks up the stairs to her office on the twelfth floor.

5. Children often say surprising things.

   Example: My five-year-old niece Rachel once told me that God wears a blue nightshirt.

PRACTICE 3 WRITING ASSIGNMENT

Write a paragraph developed by examples. Make sure your topic sentence can be supported by examples. Prewrite and pick the best one to three examples to explain your topic sentence. Here are some ideas:

offensive "reality" television shows

great places to study on campus

ads that appeal to ________

disastrous wedding stories

PART B More Work on Arranging Ideas: Coherence

TEACHING TIP
The three types of order taught here give students useful options for ordering their ideas.

Every paragraph should have **coherence**. A paragraph *coheres*—holds together—when its ideas are arranged in a clear and logical order.

Sometimes the order of ideas will flow logically from your topic. However, three basic ways to organize ideas are **time order, space order,** and **order of importance.**

Time Order

Time order means arranging ideas chronologically, from present to past or from past to present. Careful use of time order helps to avoid such confusing writing as *Oops, I forgot to mention before that . . .*

Most instructions, histories, processes, and stories follow the logical order of time.

> The talent and drive of surfer Lisa Andersen quickly propelled her to the top of her sport. In 1983, thirteen-year-old Andersen paddled a friend's surfboard into the ocean off the coast of Florida's Ormond Beach, caught a breaking wave, and easily rode it to shore. Thrilled to discover this natural talent, she realized that she might have the potential to become a serious female surfer. Soon, in hopes of gaining a competitive edge, she began practicing only with her most skilled male counterparts. In 1987, this strategy paid off when she won the U.S. amateur women's surfing contest. Later that same year, Lisa turned professional; by 1992, she was winning major competitions and training for the world championship. Almost immediately, however, news that she was pregnant put any plans to win the 1993 championship on hold. Andersen says that although it cost her one year's title, the birth of her daughter Erica motivated her to go all the way to the top. In 1994, Lisa was crowned world surfing champion, a title she won again in 1995, 1996, and 1997. Today, the four-time winner is credited with inspiring a generation of young women to enter the once male-dominated world of surfing.

- The paragraph moves in time from Lisa Andersen's first surfing experience as a teenager to her world championship victories.
- Note how some transitional expressions—such as *in 1983, soon, later that same year, almost immediately,* and *today*—show time and connect the events in the paragraph.

Transitional Expressions to Show Time

first, second, third

then, next, finally

before, during, after

soon, the following month, the next year

PRACTICE 4

Arrange each set of sentences in time order, numbering them 1, 2, 3, and so on. Be prepared to explain your choices.

1. In eighty years, the T-shirt rose from simple underwear to fashion statement.

   2 During World War II, women factory workers started wearing T-shirts on the job.

   3 Hippies in the 1960s tie-dyed their T-shirts and wore them printed with messages.

   4 Now, five billion T-shirts are sold worldwide each year.

   1 The first American T-shirts were cotton underwear, worn home by soldiers returning from France after World War I.

2. The short life of Sadako Sasaki has inspired millions to value peace.

   1 Sadako was just two years old in 1945 when the atom bomb destroyed her city, Hiroshima.

   3 From her sickbed, Sadako set out to make 1,000 paper cranes, birds that, in Japan, symbolize long life and hope.

   4 Although she died before making 1,000, classmates finished her project and published a book of her letters.

   2 At age eleven, already a talented runner, she was crushed to learn that she had leukemia, caused by radiation from the bomb.

   5 Now, every year, the Folded Crane Club places 1,000 cranes at the foot of a statue of Sadako, honoring her wish that all children might enjoy peace and a long life.

3. Scientists who study the body's daily rhythms can suggest the ideal time of day for different activities.

   1 Taking vitamins with breakfast will help the body absorb them.

   4 Allergy medication should be taken just before bedtime to combat early-morning hay fever—usually the worst of the day.

   3 The best time to work out is 3 p.m. to 5 p.m., when strength, flexibility, and body temperature are greatest.

   2 Ideal naptime is 1 p.m. to 3 p.m., when body temperature falls, making sleep easier.

PRACTICE 5 WRITING ASSIGNMENT

Have you ever been through something that lasted only a few moments but was unforgettable—for example, a sports victory, an accident, or a kiss? Write a paragraph telling about such an event. As you prewrite, pick the highlights of the experience and arrange them in time order. As you write, try to capture the drama of what happened. Use transitional expressions of time to make the story flow smoothly.

Space Order

Space order means describing a person, a place, or a thing from top to bottom, from left to right, from foreground to background, and so on.

Space order is most often used in descriptions because it moves from detail to detail, like a camera's eye.

> When the city presses in on me, I return in my mind to my hometown in St. Mary, Jamaica. I am alone, high in the mango tree on our property on the hilltop. The wind is blowing hard as usual, making a scared noise as it passes through the lush vegetation. I look down at the coconut growth with its green flooring of banana plants. Beyond that is a wide valley and then the round hills. Farther out lies the sea, and I count the ships as they pass to and from the harbor while I relax on my special branch and eat mangoes.
>
> *Daniel Dawes, student*

- The writer describes this scene from his vantage point high in a tree. His description follows space order, moving from the plants below him, farther out to the valley and the hills, and then even farther, to the sea.
- Notice how *transitional expressions* indicating space—*beyond that, then,* and *farther out*—help the reader to follow and "see" the details.

Transitional Expressions to Show Space Order

to the left, in the center, to the right

behind, beside, in front of

next, beyond that, farther out

PRACTICE 6

Arrange each set of details according to space order, numbering them 1, 2, 3, and so on. Be prepared to explain your choices.

1. After the party, the living room was a mess.

 2 (3) greasy pizza boxes on the coffee table

 1 (4) empty soda cans on the floor

 4 (1) deflated balloons on the ceiling light

 3 (2) pictures hanging at odd angles on the wall

2. The nurse quietly strode into my aunt's hospital room.

3 (3) black and silver stethoscope draped around his neck

2 (4) crisp, white cotton pants and short-sleeved tunic

4 (2) reassuring smile

1 (5) blue paper covers on his shoes

5 (1) kind, dark brown eyes

3. The taxicab crawled through rush-hour traffic in the rain-drenched city.

3 (3) fare meter on the dashboard ticking relentlessly

1 (5) headlights barely piercing the stormy gray dusk

2 (4) windshield wipers losing their battle with the latest cloudburst

5 (1) back-seat passengers frantically checking their watches

4 (2) driver wishing hopelessly that he could be home watching the news

PRACTICE 7 WRITING ASSIGNMENT

Study this portrait of Dr. Mae Jemison, the first woman of color ever to soar into space. Notice her facial expression, posture, clothing, equipment, and other details. Then describe the photograph to someone who has never seen it. In your topic sentence, state one feeling, impression, or message that this picture conveys and then choose details that support this idea. Arrange these details in space order—from left to right, top to bottom, and so on. As you revise, make sure that your sentences flow clearly and smoothly.

To learn more about the life of this amazing astronaut, search Google or use your favorite search engine.

JSC Digital Image Collection/NASA

Gehry's Disney Concert Hall in Los Angeles
©Richard Cummins/CORBIS

Order of Importance

Order of importance means arranging your ideas from most to least important—or vice versa.

Frank Gehry is one of the greatest living architects. There are at least three reasons for his worldwide influence. Most important, Gehry has created new shapes for buildings, literally moving outside the boxes in which we often live and work. He has found ways to build walls that look like mountains, sails, and wings. In addition, Gehry uses new materials—or old materials in new ways. Going beyond plaster and wood, Gehry's buildings have rounded metal walls, curves made of glass, and stone in strange places. Third, because of its striking looks, a Gehry building can bring tourist dollars and international attention to a town or city. This happened when Gehry designed the now-famous Guggenheim Museum building in the little town of Bilbao, Spain. And like the latest blockbuster movie, the Disney Concert Hall in Los Angeles recently opened to rave reviews.

- The three reasons in this paragraph are discussed from the most important reason to the least important.
- Note that the words *most important, in addition,* and *third* help the reader move from one reason to another.

Sometimes you may wish to begin with the least important idea and build toward a climax at the end of the paragraph. Paragraphs arranged from the least important idea to the most important idea can have dramatic power.

Although my fourteen-year-old daughter learned a great deal from living with a Pennsylvania Amish family last summer, adjusting to their strict lifestyle was difficult for her. Kay admitted that the fresh food served on the farm was great, but she missed her diet colas. More difficult was the fact that she had to wear long dresses—no more jeans and baby tees. Still worse in her view were the hours. A suburban girl and self-confessed night person, my daughter had to get up at 5 a.m. to milk cows! By far the most difficult adjustment concerned boys. If an Amish woman is not married, she cannot spend time with males, and this rule now applied to Kay. Yes, she suffered and complained, but by summer's end, she was a different girl—more open-minded and proud of the fact that all these deprivations put her more in touch with herself.

Lucy Auletta, student

- The adjustment difficulties this writer's daughter had are arranged from least to most important. How many difficulties are discussed? ____four____
- Note how the words *more difficult, still worse,* and *by far the most difficult adjustment* help the reader move from one idea to the next.

TEACHING TIP
After students learn the three types of order, have each student choose one type of order and write a paragraph. Bring in the most successful examples of each type and ask authors to read them aloud.

Transitional Expressions to Show Importance

first, next, finally

more, most

less, least

PRACTICE 8

Arrange the ideas that develop each topic sentence in order of importance, numbering them 1, 2, and 3. Begin with the most important idea, or reverse the order if you think that a paragraph would be more effective if it began with the least important idea. Be prepared to explain your choices. Then, on a separate sheet of paper, write the ideas in a paragraph.

1. For three reasons, joining a serious study group is an excellent idea.

   __2 (2)__ A study group will expose you to new points of view and effective study habits.

   __3 (1)__ Joining a study group is a good way to make new friends.

   __1 (3)__ Statistics show that students who regularly attend a study group get better grades and are less likely to drop out of college.

2. Tigers should not be made to perform in stage shows.

   __3__ Forcing tigers to perform tricks and live in small cages is cruel to these beautiful wild cats.

   __1__ Because even well-trained tigers are dangerous wild animals, they pose a serious risk to the health and lives of people in the audience.

   __2__ These animals are a potential danger to their handlers as well, as the public learned when the world's most famous tiger trainer, Roy Horn, was attacked onstage in Las Vegas.

3. At 2 a.m., arriving on the scene of a rollover with injuries, the fire rescue team had to act quickly.

 ___2___ One team member lit flares and placed them on the road to warn other drivers to slow down.

 ___3___ On the ambulance radio, a team member called for "sanders" to drop sand on local roads, which were becoming slippery in the falling snow.

 ___1___ A lone woman, conscious with head injuries, was carefully moved from the driver's seat into the ambulance.

 ___4___ Someone held the woman's dog, who was shivering but seemed unhurt.

PRACTICE 9 WRITING ASSIGNMENT

Your college is offering free classes in photography, money management, or fitness for senior citizens in the area. Choose just one of these classes and write a paragraph encouraging local seniors to sign up. Discuss the three most important reasons why this class would benefit them, and arrange these reasons in order of importance—least to most important or most to least important, whichever you think would make a better paragraph. Don't forget to use transitional expressions. If you wish, use humor to win over your audience.

PART C More Work on Revising: Exact and Concise Language

Good writers do not settle for the first words that spill onto their paper or computer screen. Instead, they revise what they have written, replacing vague words with exact language and repetitious words with concise language.

Exact Language

As a rule, the more specific, detailed, and exact the language is, the better the writing. Which sentence in each of the following pairs contains the more vivid and exact language?

(1) The office was noisy.

(2) In the office, phones jangled, faxes whined, and copy machines hummed.

(3) What my tutor said made me feel good.

(4) When my tutor whispered, "Fine job," I felt like singing.

- Sentence (2) is more exact than sentence (1) because *phones jangled, faxes whined, and copy machines hummed* provide more vivid information than the general word *noisy*.
- What exact words does sentence (4) use to replace the general words *said* and *made me feel good*? whispered, "Fine job," I felt like singing.

You do not need a large vocabulary to write exactly and well, but you do need to work at finding the right words to fit each sentence.

PRACTICE 10

These sentences contain vague language. Revise each one, using vivid and exact language wherever possible. Sample answers

EXAMPLE: A man went through the crowd.

Revise: A man in a blue leather jacket pushed through the crowd.

1. An automobile went down the street.

   Revise: A late-model Infiniti roared down Maple Street.

2. This apartment has problems.

   Revise: This apartment has peeling paint and leaky water pipes.

3. When Allison comes home, her pet greets her.

   Revise: When Allison walks in the door, her cat meows and rubs up against her leg.

4. This magazine is interesting.

   Revise: This issue of *National Geographic* has beautiful photographs of wolves.

5. The expression on his face made me feel comfortable.

   Revise: His reassuring eyes and warm smile made me feel comfortable.

6. My job is fun.

   Revise: Selling toe rings and ear cuffs to enthusiastic teenagers lifts my spirits.

7. There was a big storm here last week.

   Revise: A freak electrical storm swept through Cleveland last week.

8. The emergency room has a lot of people in it.

   Revise: Crying children, people with broken bones, and busy nurses fill the emergency room.

TEACHING TIP
Review with students a list of common wordy expressions. For one such list, see **<http://owl.english.purdue.edu/handouts/general/gl_concise.html>**.

Concise Language

Concise writing never uses five or six words when two or three will do. It avoids repetitious and unnecessary words that add nothing to the meaning of a sentence. As you revise your writing, cross out unnecessary words and phrases.

Which sentence in each of the following pairs is more concise?

(1) Because of the fact that Larissa owns an antiques shop, she is always poking around in dusty attics.

(2) Because Larissa owns an antiques shop, she is always poking around in dusty attics.

(3) Mr. Tibbs entered a large, dark blue room.

(4) Mr. Tibbs entered a room that was large in size and dark blue in color.

- Sentences (2) and (3) are concise; sentences (1) and (4) are wordy.
- In sentence (1), *because of the fact that* is a wordy way of saying *because.*
- In sentence (4), *in size* and *in color* just repeat which ideas?

large and dark blue

Of course, conciseness does not mean writing short, choppy sentences. It does mean dropping unnecessary words and phrases.

PRACTICE 11

The following sentences are wordy. In a group with two or three others, make each sentence more concise by deleting unnecessary words. Write your revised sentences on the lines provided. Answers will vary.

EXAMPLE: Venice, an Italian city in Italy, is trying to reduce its huge number of visitors who go to see it.

Revise: Venice, a city in Italy, is trying to reduce its huge number of visitors.

1. For a great many hundreds of years, this beautiful city of such loveliness has been a major tourist attraction.

   Revise: For hundreds of years, this beautiful city has been a major tourist attraction.

2. The reasons why people go to Venice are because they want to see its priceless art and palaces, famous bridges, and canals that serve as streets.

   Revise: People go to Venice to see its priceless art and palaces, famous bridges, and canals that serve as streets.

3. At this time now, however, Venice is being destroyed by floods, by polluted air and water that are dirty, and by tourists who visit it.

   Revise: Now, however, Venice is being destroyed by floods, polluted air and water, and tourists.

4. Twelve million annual visitors invade Venice every year, and most of them are day-trippers who come only for the day and then go home.

   Revise: Twelve million visitors invade Venice every year, and most of them are day-trippers.

5. The day-trippers, who often bring their own drinks and sandwiches with them to eat, spend little money in town, thus contributing very little to the city's economy of money.

   Revise: The day-trippers, who often bring their own drinks and sandwiches, contribute very little to the city's economy.

6. However, they contribute enormously and in large amounts to the city of Venice's congestion, transportation, and sanitation nightmares.

   Revise: However, they contribute enormously to Venice's congestion, transportation, and sanitation nightmares.

7. Recently, the city tried to scare off day-trippers with a negative publicity campaign that gave bad publicity about the city.

   Revise: Recently, the city tried to scare off day-trippers with a negative publicity campaign.

8. Posters showed tourists being devoured and eaten by Venice's well-known and famous pigeons.

   Revise: Posters showed tourists being devoured by Venice's famous pigeons.

9. An immense giant toilet plunger became the symbol of a city that some say is the city that is the most romantic city in the world.

   Revise: A giant toilet plunger became the symbol of the most romantic city in the world.

10. Unfortunately, the bad publicity did not work or stop tourists from pouring into Venice, so city officials are trying a new plan—asking visitors to make reservations to visit the city on a particular day.

    Revise: Unfortunately, the bad publicity did not stop tourists from pouring into Venice, so city officials are trying a new plan—asking visitors to make reservations.

PRACTICE 12 REVIEW

TEACHING TIP
Practice 12 makes an amusing in-class activity and underscores the relevance of clear writing to everyday life and to business.

Following are statements from real accident reports collected by an insurance company. As you will see, these writers need help with more than their fenders!

In a group with four or five classmates, read each statement and try to understand what each writer *meant* to say. Then revise each statement so that it says, exactly and concisely, what the writer intended.

1. "The guy was all over the place. I had to swerve a number of times before I hit him."
2. "The telephone pole was approaching fast. I was attempting to swerve out of its path when it struck my front end."
3. "Coming home, I drove into the wrong house and collided with a tree I don't have."
4. "I was on my way to the doctor's with rear-end trouble when my universal joint gave way, causing me to have an accident."
5. "I was driving my car out of the driveway in the usual manner when it was struck by the other car in the same place it had been struck several times before."

PRACTICE 13 REVIEW

Choose a paragraph or paper you wrote recently. Read it with a fresh eye, checking for exact and concise language. Then rewrite it, eliminating all vague or wordy language.

PART D Turning Assignments into Paragraphs

In Chapter 3, Part B, you learned how to narrow down a broad topic and write a specific topic sentence. Sometimes, however, your assignment may take the form of a specific question, and your job may be to answer the question in one paragraph.

For example, this question asks you to take a stand on—for or against—a particular issue.

Are professional athletes overpaid?

You can often turn this kind of question into a topic sentence:

(1) Professional athletes are overpaid.

(2) Professional athletes are not overpaid.

(3) Professional athletes are sometimes overpaid.

- These three topic sentences take different points of view.
- The words *are, are not,* and *sometimes* make each writer's opinion clear.

Sometimes you will be asked to agree or disagree with a statement:

(4) Salary is the most important factor in job satisfaction. Agree or disagree.

- This is really a question in disguise: *Is salary the most important factor in job satisfaction?*

In the topic sentence, make your opinion clear and repeat key words.

(5) Salary is the most important factor in job satisfaction.

(6) Salary is not the most important factor in job satisfaction.

(7) Salary is only one among several important factors in job satisfaction.

- The words *is, is not,* and *is only one among several* make each writer's opinion clear.
- Note how the topic sentences repeat the key words from the statement—*salary, important factor, job satisfaction.*

Once you have written the topic sentence, follow the steps described in Chapter 2—freewriting, brainstorming, or clustering; selecting; grouping—and then write your paragraph. Be sure that all ideas in the paragraph support the opinion you have stated in the topic sentence.

PRACTICE 14

Here are four exam questions. Write one topic sentence to answer each of them. REMEMBER: Make your opinion clear in the topic sentence and repeat key words from the question. Answers will vary.

1. Should computer education be required in every public high school?

   Topic sentence: Computer education should be required in every public high school.

2. Would you advise your best friend to buy a new car or a used car?

   Topic sentence: A late-model used car can have all the advantages of a new car and save people a lot of money.

3. Is there too much bad news on television news programs?

   Topic sentence: There is too much bad news on television news programs.

4. How have your interests changed in the past five years?

   Topic sentence: I have become more interested in both local and national politics in the past five years.

PRACTICE 15

Imagine that your instructor has just written the exam questions from Practice 14 on the board. Choose the question that most interests you and write a paragraph answering that question. Prewrite, select, and arrange ideas before you compose your paragraph. Then read your work, making neat corrections in ink.

PRACTICE 16

Here are four statements. Agree or disagree, and write a topic sentence for each. Answers will vary.

1. All higher education should be free. Agree or disagree.

   Topic sentence: All high school graduates should be able to continue their higher education free of charge.

2. Expecting one's spouse to be perfect is the most important reason for the high divorce rate in the United States. Agree or disagree.

   Topic sentence: Expecting one's spouse to be perfect is one of the most important reasons for the high divorce rate in the United States.

3. Parents should give children money when they need it rather than give them an allowance. Agree or disagree.

   Topic sentence: Parents should give children an allowance so that they can learn how to handle money.

4. Silence is golden. Agree or disagree.

   Topic sentence: It is usually better to speak out on important issues than to remain silent.

PRACTICE 17

Choose the statement in Practice 16 that most interests you. Then write a paragraph in which you agree or disagree.

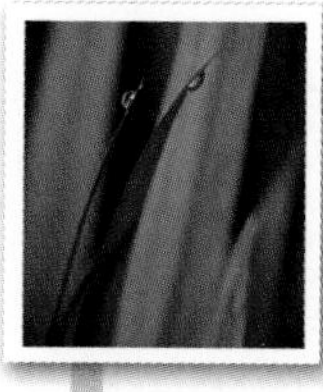

CHAPTER HIGHLIGHTS

To improve your writing, try these techniques:

- **Use well-chosen examples to develop a paragraph.**
- **Organize your ideas by time order.**
- **Organize your ideas by space order.**
- **Organize your ideas by order of importance, either from the most important to the least or from the least important to the most.**
- **Use language that is exact and concise.**
- **Turn assignment questions into topic sentences.**

EXPLORING ONLINE

TEACHING TIP
More practice and assessment are available in the *Grassroots* Test Bank; linked ACE tests on the *Grassroots* student website; *WriteSpace for Grassroots*; and the Exploring Online links in this chapter.

<http://writesite.cuny.edu/projects/keywords/example/hand2.html> Online process: Develop your idea with examples.

<http://lrs.ed.uiuc.edu/students/fwalters/coheres.html> Review coherence: Read sample paragraphs and check your skills.

<http://college.hmco.com/devenglish> For more exercises and quizzes on the Student Website, visit the link, click Developmental Writing, and find the home page for *Grassroots,* 8/e. Bookmark the site for future visits as you work through this book.

CHAPTER 5

Moving from Paragraph to Essay

PART A Defining the Essay and the Thesis Statement

PART B The Process of Writing an Essay

So far, you have written single paragraphs, but to succeed in college and at work, you will need to handle longer writing assignments as well. This chapter will help you apply your paragraph-writing skills to planning and writing short essays.

PART A Defining the Essay and the Thesis Statement

An **essay** is a group of paragraphs about one subject. In many ways, an essay is like a paragraph in longer, fuller form. Both have an introduction, a body, and a conclusion. Both explain one main idea with details, facts, and examples.

However, an essay is not just a padded paragraph. An essay is longer because it contains more ideas.

TEACHING TIP
You might want to explain to students the similarities in structure between paragraph and essay yet show how the essay differs in length and depth. Students often find this graphic very helpful. Mention that outlining becomes more important in essay writing.

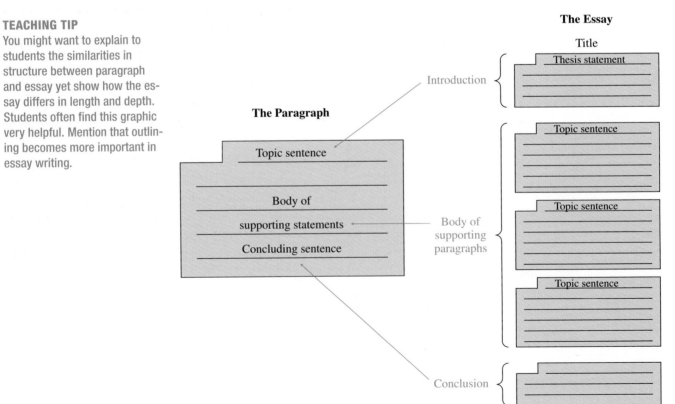

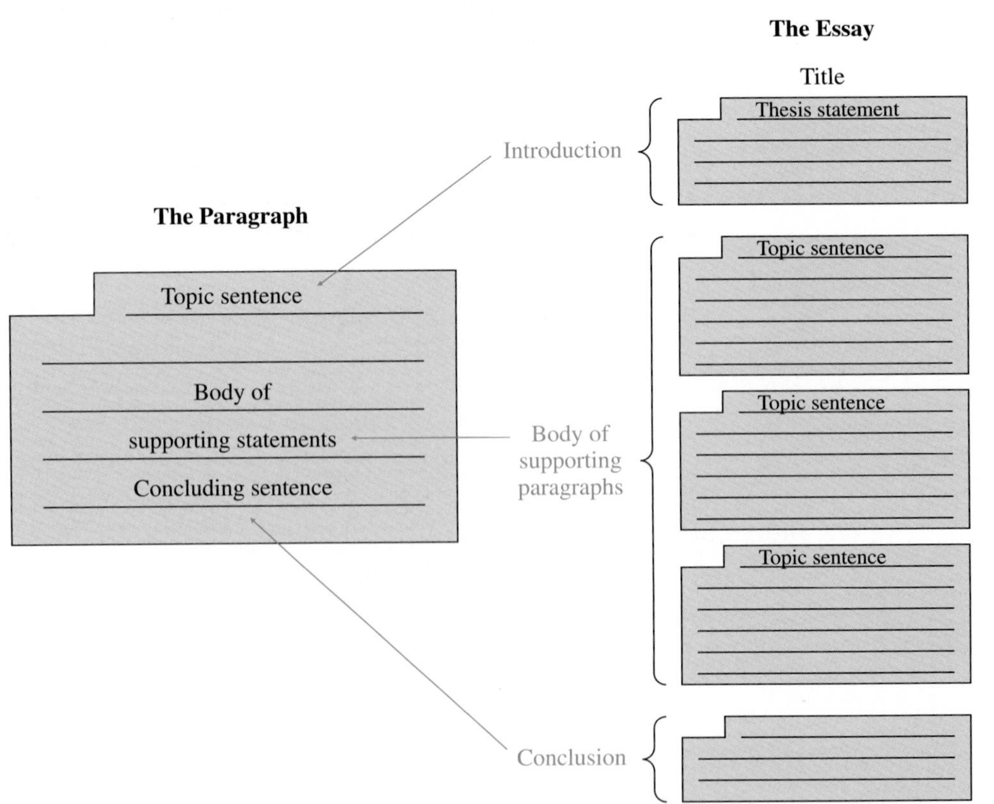

PRACTICE 2

Discuss with several classmates or write your answers to these questions.

TEACHING TIP
Discussing Ms. Williams' essay will likely engage your students. Questions like these hone their revising and writing skills.

1. Did Wineth Williams' introduction (paragraph 1) catch and hold your interest? Would this essay be just as good or better if it had no introduction but started right in with the thesis statement? Why or why not?
2. In paragraph (4), the writer says she now can "take care of business." Is this language appropriate for a college essay? Will readers know what this means?
3. Is the conclusion effective, or is it too short?
4. Williams' audience was her English class. Her purpose (though not directly stated in the essay) was to let people know some of the benefits that come from practicing tae kwon do. Did she achieve her purpose?
5. What did you like best about the essay? What, if anything, would you change?

PART B The Process of Writing an Essay

Whether you are writing a paragraph or an essay, the writing process is the same. Of course, writing an essay will probably take longer. In this section, you will practice these steps of the essay-writing process:

- Narrowing the subject and writing the thesis statement
- Generating ideas for the body of the essay
- Selecting and arranging ideas in a plan
- Writing and revising your essay

Narrowing the Subject and Writing the Thesis Statement

While an essay subject should be broader than a paragraph topic, a good essay subject also must be narrow enough to write about in detail. For example, the topic *jobs* is broad enough to fill a book. But the far narrower topic *driving a bulldozer at the town dump* could make a good essay. Remember to select or narrow your subject in light of your intended audience and purpose. Who are your readers, and what do you want your essay to achieve?

Writing the *thesis statement* forces you to narrow the topic further: *Driving a bulldozer for the Department of Highways was the best job I ever had.* That could be an intriguing thesis statement, but the writer could focus it even more: *For three reasons, driving a bulldozer for the Department of Highways was the best job I ever had.* The writer might discuss one reason in each of three paragraphs.

Here are two more examples of the narrowing process:

(1) Subject:	music
Narrowed subject:	Cuban singer Lucretia
Thesis statement:	In talent and style, Cuban singer Lucretia might be the next Celia Cruz.
(2) Subject:	pets
Narrowed subject:	Pains and pleasures of owning a parrot
Thesis statement:	Owning a parrot will enrich your life with noise, occasional chaos, and lots of laughs.

- On the basis of each thesis statement, what do you expect the essays to discuss?

  Writer 1 will show how Cuban singer Lucretia's talent and style might make her the next Celia Cruz. Writer 2 will discuss the noise, chaos, and laughs of parrot ownership.

Although the thesis statement must include all the ideas in the body of the essay, it should also be **clear** and **specific**. Which of these thesis statements is specific enough for a good essay?

(1) Three foolproof techniques will help you avoid disastrous first dates.

(2) NBA basketball is the most exciting sport in the world.

(3) Dr. Villarosa is a competent and caring physician.

TEACHING TIP
Provide students with additional thesis statements that are too broad or too vague, and demonstrate how they can be improved.

- Thesis statements (1) and (3) are both specific. From (1), a reader might expect to learn about the "three foolproof techniques," each one perhaps explained in a paragraph.
- On the basis of thesis statement (3), what supporting points might the essay discuss? 1. Dr. Villarosa's competence 2. his or her caring ways
- Thesis statement (2), however, is too broad for an essay—or even a book. It gives the reader (and writer) no direction.

PRACTICE 3

TEACHING TIP
Practice 3 works well as a group activity or as the basis of a class discussion.

Choose one of these topics for your own essay. Then narrow the topic and write a clear and specific thesis statement.

The benefits of a sport or practice

The most fascinating/boring/important job I ever had

Qualities of an excellent husband/wife/partner

Narrowed subject: ______________________________

____

Thesis statement: ______________________________

____

Generating Ideas for the Body of the Essay

Writers generate support for an essay just as they do for a paragraph—by prewriting to get as many interesting ideas as possible. Once you know your main point and have written a thesis statement, use your favorite prewriting method—freewriting, for example. If you feel stuck, change to brainstorming or clustering. Just keep writing.

PRACTICE 4

Now generate as many good ideas as possible to support your thesis statement. Fill at least one or two pages with ideas. As you work, try to imagine how many paragraphs your essay will contain and what each will include.

Selecting and Arranging Ideas in a Plan

TEACHING TIP
Tell students that a plan or outline is especially important in essay writing because the writer must organize much material.

Next, underline or mark the most interesting ideas that support your thesis statement. Cross out the rest.

Make a rough **plan** or **outline** that includes an introductory paragraph, two or three paragraphs for the body of the essay, and a brief conclusion. Choose a logical order to present your ideas. Which idea will come first, second, third?

For example, the bulldozer operator might explain why that job was "the best" with three reasons, arranged in this order: 1. *On the job, I learned to operate heavy equipment.* 2. *Working alone at the controls gave me time to think.* 3. *One bonus was occasionally finding interesting items beside the road.* This arrangement moves logically from physical skills to mental benefits to a surprising bonus.

PRACTICE 5

Read over your prewriting pages, selecting your best ideas and a logical order in which to present them. Make an outline or a plan that includes an introduction and a thesis statement; two or three supporting paragraphs, each with a clear topic sentence; and a brief conclusion.

Writing and Revising Your Essay

ESL TIP
Alert ESL students to the ESL Guidelines at the end of this text and to the excellent resources—quizzes and links—available online. Have them visit ESL Corner on the *Grassroots* student website and search the Web for help—for instance, **<http://a4esl.org/>**.

Drafting

Now write your first draft. Try to express your ideas clearly and fully. If a section seems weak or badly written, put a check in the margin and go on; you can come back to that section later, prewriting again if necessary for fresh ideas. Set aside your draft for an hour or a day.

Revising and Proofreading

Revising may be the most important step in the writing process. Reread your essay as if you were reading someone else's work, marking it up as you answer questions like these:

- Are my main idea and my thesis statement clear?
- Have I supported my thesis in a rich and convincing way?
- Does each paragraph in the body clearly explain the main idea?
- Does my essay have a logical order and good transitions?
- Are there any parts that don't belong or don't make sense?
- What one change would most improve my essay?*

You also might wish to ask a respected friend to read or listen to your essay, giving peer feedback before you revise.**

PRACTICE 6

Now read your first draft to see how you can improve it. Trust your instincts about what is alive and interesting and what is dull. Take your time. As you revise, try to make this the best paper you have ever written.

Finally, write a new draft of your essay, using the format preferred by your instructor. Proofread carefully, correcting any grammar or spelling errors.

---

* See Chapter 3, Part F, for more revising ideas.
** See Chapter 3, page 27, for a sample Peer Feedback Sheet.

PRACTICE 7

Exchange essays with a classmate. Write a one-paragraph evaluation of each other's work, saying as specifically as possible what you like about the essay and what might be improved. If you wish, use the Peer Feedback Sheet (page 27).

Possible Topics for Essays

1. The Best/Worst Class I Ever Had
2. Two Sure-fire Ways to Relax
3. Modern Dating
4. A Major Decision
5. Tips for the New Driver (College Student, NBA Draft Pick, Cell Phone User, and so forth)
6. A Valuable/Worthless Television Show
7. A Good Friend
8. Can Anger Be Used Constructively?
9. How I Fell in Love with Books (German Shepherds, Rock Climbing, Video Games, and so forth)
10. What Childhood Taught Me About Boys/Girls in Society

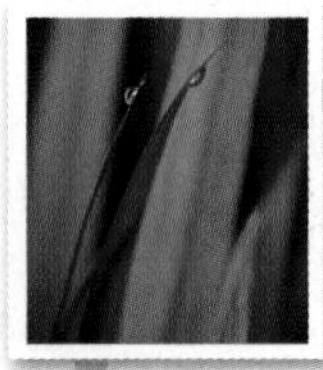

CHAPTER HIGHLIGHTS

Checklist for Writing an Effective Essay

- **Narrow the topic in light of your audience and purpose. Be sure you can discuss the topic fully in a short essay.**
- **Write a clear thesis statement. If you have trouble, freewrite or brainstorm first; then narrow the topic and write the thesis statement.**
- **Freewrite, brainstorm, or cluster to generate facts, details, and examples to support your thesis statement.**
- **Plan or outline your essay, choosing from two to three main ideas to support the thesis statement.**
- **Write a topic sentence that expresses each main idea.**
- **Decide on a logical order in which to present the paragraphs.**
- **Plan the body of each paragraph, using all you have learned about support and paragraph development.**
- **Write the first draft of your essay.**
- **Revise as necessary, checking your essay for support, unity, and coherence.**
- **Proofread carefully for grammar, punctuation, and spelling.**

TEACHING TIP
More practice and assessment are available in the *Grassroots* Test Bank; linked ACE tests on the *Grassroots* student website; *WriteSpace for Grassroots*; and the Exploring Online links in this chapter.

EXPLORING ONLINE

<http://www.powa.org/> Review the essay-writing process.

<http://college.hmco.com/devenglish> For more exercises and quizzes on the Student Website, visit the link, click Developmental Writing, and find the home page for *Grassroots*, 8/e. Bookmark the site for future visits as you work through this book.

TEACHING TIP
Introduce students to the POWA website and underscore the help available on the OWL sites given at the end of each chapter.

WRITING ASSIGNMENTS

As you complete each writing assignment, remember to perform these steps:

- Write a clear, complete topic (or thesis) sentence.
- Use freewriting, brainstorming, or clustering to generate ideas for the body of your paragraph or essay.
- Arrange your best ideas in a plan.
- Revise for support, unity, coherence, and exact language.
- Proofread for grammar, punctuation, and spelling errors.

Writing Assignment 1: *Discuss one requirement for a happy family life.* Complete this topic sentence: "A basic requirement for a happy family life is ________________." What do you believe a family should have? Is it something material, like a house or a certain amount of money? Is it related to the number or types of people in the family? Does it have to do with nonmaterial things, like communication or support? Begin by jotting down all the reasons why you would require this particular thing. Then choose the three most important reasons and arrange them in order of importance—either from the least to the most important or the reverse. Explain each reason, making clear to the reader why you feel as strongly as you do.

Writing Assignment 2: *Interview a classmate about an achievement.* Write about a time when your classmate achieved something important, like winning a sales prize at work, losing thirty pounds, or helping a friend through a bad time. To gather interesting facts and details, ask your classmate questions like these and take notes: *Is there one accomplishment of which you are very proud? Why was this achievement so important? Did it change the way you feel about yourself?* Keep asking questions until you feel you can give your reader a vivid sense of your classmate's triumph.

In your first sentence, state the person's achievement—for instance, *Getting her first A in English was a turning point in Jessica's life.* Then explain specifically why the achievement was so meaningful.

Writing Assignment 3: *Describe an annoying trait.* Choose someone you like or love and describe his or her most annoying habit or trait. In your topic sentence, name the trait. For instance, you might say, "My husband's most annoying trait is carelessness." Then give one to three examples explaining the topic sentence. Make your examples as specific as possible; be sure they support the topic sentence.

Writing Assignment 4: *Develop a paragraph with examples.* Below are topic sentences for possible paragraphs. Pick the topic sentence that most interests you and write a paragraph using one to three examples to explain the topic sentence. If you prefer, choose a quotation from the Quotation Bank at the end of this book and explain it with one or more examples.

a. A sense of humor can make difficult times easier to bear.

b. Mistakes can be great teachers.

c. Television commercials often insult my intelligence.

UNIT 1

REVIEW

Choosing a Topic Sentence

Each group of sentences could be unscrambled and written as a paragraph. Circle the letter of the sentence that would be the best topic sentence.

1. a. Rooftops and towers made eye-catching shapes against the winter sky.
   b. Far below, the faint sounds of slush and traffic were soothing.
   (c.) From the apartment-house roof, the urban scene was oddly relaxing.
   d. Stoplights changing color up and down the avenues created a rhythmic pattern invisible from the street.

2. a. Actor Andy Garcia and *CSI Miami* star Adam Rodriguez own homes in Miami.
   b. Mexican actress and singer Lucia Mendez resides there, as does Venezuelan soap opera star Jose Luis Rodriguez.
   c. Singers Ricky Martin and Enrique Iglesias call Miami home.
   (d.) In recent years, Miami has become the Hollywood of South America.

Selecting Ideas

Here is a topic sentence and a brainstormed list of possible ideas for a paragraph. Check "Keep" for ideas that best support the topic sentence and "Drop" for ideas that do not.

Topic sentence: Oprah Winfrey is a force for tremendous good in the United States.

Keep	Drop	
✓	___	1. on her TV show, often has experts who help people with relationships or finances
✓	___	2. through her book club, inspired millions to start reading and periodically introduces a vast audience to new and old authors
✓	___	3. proves that women don't need to be thin to be beautiful, popular, famous, and greatly loved
___	✓	4. was born in 1954 on a farm in Mississippi
___	✓	5. at age six was sent to Milwaukee; kept cockroaches in a jar as substitute for farm animals
✓	___	6. is a well-known example of someone who overcame many obstacles, including childhood abuse and racial prejudice
___	✓	7. another example of someone who has overcome abuse and prejudice is actress Halle Berry
___	✓	8. physical abuse by a former boyfriend caused Berry to lose 80 percent of her hearing in one ear
✓	___	9. Winfrey gives millions to causes such as helping South African children orphaned by AIDS
✓	___	10. her website and magazine encourage women to develop their spirituality and pursue personal goals

Examining a Paragraph

Read this paragraph and answer the questions.

(1) Students at some American colleges are learning a lot from trash by studying "garbology." (2) Wearing rubber gloves, they might sift through the local dump, counting and collecting treasures that they examine back at the laboratory. (3) First, they learn to look closely and to interpret what they see, thus reading the stories that trash tells. (4) More important, they learn the truth about what Americans buy, what they eat, and how they live. (5) Students at the University of Arizona, for instance, were surprised to find that low-income families in certain areas buy more educational toys for their children than nearby middle-income families. (6) Most important, students say that garbology courses can motivate them to be better citizens of planet Earth. (7) One young woman, for example, after seeing from hard evidence in her town's landfill how many people really recycled their glass, cans, and newspapers and how many cheated, organized an annual recycling awareness day.

1. Write the number of the topic sentence in the paragraph. 1
2. What kind of order does this writer use? order of importance
3. Students learn three things in garbology courses. (a) Write the numbers of the sentences stating these. (b) Which two ideas are supported by examples?

   (a) 3, 4, 6 (b) 4 and 6

WRITERS' WORKSHOP

Discuss Your Name

Good writers are masters of exact language and thoughtful observation. Read this student's paragraph about her name. Underline any words or details that strike you as well written, interesting, or powerful.

~~In this paragraph I will write about my name.~~ My name YuMing is made up of two Chinese characters that mean "the universe" and "the crow of a bird." This may seem like a strange name to an American, but in fact it has a special meaning for me. In ancient Chinese literature, there is a story about a bird that was owned by God. This bird was rumored to have the most beautiful voice in the universe. A greedy king wanted this bird, so he had it captured and placed in a big cage. He sat next to this cage day after day waiting for the bird to sing, but the bird stayed silent. After three years, the impatient king threw open the cage door and set the bird free. As the bird flew up toward the heavens, it made its first crow in three years. The sound shocked everyone in the kingdom because they realized the legend was true—they had never heard such a beautiful voice before! My parents told me that they gave me this name because they want me to be like the bird in the story. Though I may stay silent for a while as I establish myself in society, they hope that I will "crow" one day when it is the right time for me, and crow loudly so everyone in the universe can hear.

YuMing Lai, student

1. How effective is YuMing Lai's paragraph about the meaning of her name?

   __N__ Good topic sentence? __Y__ Rich supporting details?

   __Y__ Logical organization? __Y__ Effective conclusion?

2. Underline the words, details, or sentences you like best. Put a check beside anything that needs improvement.
3. Now discuss your underlinings with your group or class. Try to explain as exactly as you can why you like something. For example, in the last sentence, the way that the writer ties her parents' wish for her to the meaning of the story is moving and surprising.
4. Is YuMing's topic sentence as good as the rest of her paragraph? If not, how might you change it? No, she should drop the first sentence and begin with "My name YuMing . . . "

5. Did YuMing's thoughts about her name make you think about your own name? Do you like your name? Why or why not? Do you know why your parents chose it?

6. What order does this paragraph employ? time order

Writing and Revising Ideas

TEACHING TIP
Students will likely enjoy discussing and writing about their names. The Web link given affords an excellent opportunity for miniresearch and critical thinking about trends in boys' and girls' names through the years.

1. Write about the meaning of your name or the name of someone close to you.

2. Visit the government's website below listing the most popular baby names selected in the United States, year by year. Do you see any patterns? How popular is your name? Your parents' names?
<http://www.ssa.gov/OACT/babynames/>

For help with writing your paragraph, see Chapter 3 and Chapter 4, Parts B and C. As you revise, pay special attention to writing a clear, catchy topic sentence supported by interesting details.

TEACHING TIP
If you don't have time to reproduce good student writing for class discussion, you can use the Writers' Workshops at the end of each unit for group work and peer editing. This student's subject—the meaning of her name—makes a fine assignment. Refer students to the intriguing website mentioned in Writing and Revising Idea 2.

UNIT 2

Writing Complete Sentences

The sentence is the basic unit of all writing, so good writers must know how to write clear and correct sentences. In this unit, you will

- Learn to spot subjects and verbs
- Practice writing complete sentences
- Learn to avoid or correct any sentence fragments

Spotlight on Writing

Notice the way this writer uses strong, simple sentences to capture a moment with her grandfather, her *abuelo*. If possible, read the paragraph aloud.

My grandfather has misplaced his words again. He is trying to find my name in the kaleidoscope of images that his mind has become. His face brightens like a child's who has just remembered his lesson. He points to me and says my mother's name. I smile back and kiss him on the cheek. It doesn't matter what names he remembers anymore. Every day he is more confused, his memory slipping back a little further in time. Today he has no grandchildren yet. Tomorrow he will be a young man courting my grandmother again, quoting bits of poetry to her. In months to come, he will begin calling her Mama.

Judith Ortiz Cofer, "The Witch's Husband"

- How does the writer feel about her grandfather? Which sentences tell you this?
- Why do you think the writer arranges the last three sentences in the order that she does?

- ***A visit with a loved (or feared) relative***
- ***Your relationship with someone who has a disability***

CHAPTER

6 Subjects and Verbs

PART A Defining and Spotting Subjects

The sentence is the basic unit of all writing. To write well, you need to know how to write correct and effective sentences. A **sentence** is a group of words that expresses a complete thought about something or someone. It contains a **subject** and a **verb.**

(1) _______________ jumped over the black Buick, scaled the building, and finally reached the roof.

(2) _______________ needs a new coat of paint.

These sentences might be interesting, but they are incomplete.

- In sentence (1), *who* jumped, scaled, and reached? Spider-Man, Alicia Keys, the English teacher?
- Depending on *who* performed the action—jumping, scaling, or reaching—the sentence can be exciting, surprising, or strange.
- What is missing is the *who* word—the *subject*.
- In sentence (2), *what* needs a new coat of paint? The house, the car, the old rocking chair?
- What is missing is the *what* word—the *subject*.

ESL TIP
If you have many nonnative students, you might discuss possible differences between their language and English, such as word order or singulars and plurals, that might confuse them as they write sentences in English.

For a sentence to be complete, it must contain a *who* or *what* word—a *subject*. The subject tells you *who* or *what* does something or exists in a certain way.

The subject is often a *noun*, a word that names a person, place, or thing (such as *Alicia Keys, English teacher,* or *house*). However, a *pronoun* (*I, you, he, she, it, we,* or *they*) also can be the subject.*

*For more work on pronoun subjects, see Chapter 20, Part F.

PRACTICE 1

In each of these sentences, the subject (the *who* or *what* word) is missing. Fill in your own subject to make the sentence complete. Sample answers

EXAMPLE: A(n) ___fox___ dashed across the road.

1. The ___hockey puck___ skidded across the ice.
2. The ___student___ was eager to begin the semester.
3. Because of the crowd, the ___spy___ slipped out unnoticed.
4. For years, ___comic books___ piled up in the back of the closet.
5. The cheerful yellow ___wallpaper___ brightened Sheila's mood.
6. ___Papers___ and ___pencils___ were scattered all over the doctor's desk.
7. The ___singer___ believed that his ___voice___ would return someday.
8. The ___farmhouse___ was in bad shape. The ___ceiling___ was falling in, and the ___downstairs windows___ were all broken.

As you may have noticed, the subject can be a noun only, but it can also include *words that describe the noun* (such as *the, cheerful,* or *yellow*).

The noun or pronoun alone is called the *simple subject;* the noun or pronoun plus the words that describe it are called the *complete subject.*

(3) Three yellow roses grew near the path.

(4) A large box was delivered this morning.

- The simple subject of sentence (3) is the noun *roses.*
- The complete subject is *three yellow roses.*
- What is the simple subject of (4)? ___box___
- What is the complete subject of (4)? ___a large box___

PRACTICE 2

Circle the *simple* subject in each sentence. (A person's complete name—though more than one word—is considered a simple subject.)

EXAMPLE: Many (people) love scary films.

(1) (Dr. Leon Rappoport) studies the fear factor in movies. (2) (Humans) have always liked to explore their feelings of fear and anxiety, according to Rappoport. (3) Frightening (movies) allow them to master those emotions and work through them. (4) Other (psychologists) agree. (5) (People) like to be scared in the absence of any real danger. (6) Horror (films and stories) provide opportunities for such expe-

riences. (7) Also, some moviegoers like to explore their uncivilized, antisocial nature in safe settings. (8) Many teenagers, in particular, need to test their tolerance for threatening situations. (9) In addition, parents often declare horror movies inappropriate. (10) Therefore, adolescents want to see this forbidden entertainment more than ever.

PRACTICE 3

In these sentences, the complete subject has been omitted. You must decide where it belongs and fill in a complete subject (a *who* or *what* word along with any words that describe it). Write in any complete subject that makes sense.

ESL TIP
If ESL students repeat the subject with a pronoun—as in "My worried friend, *she* raced down the street"—refer them to Error #4: Repeated Subject in "8 Common ESL Errors," on the *Grassroots* student website.

EXAMPLE: Raced down the street.

My worried friend raced down the street.

1. Trained day and night for the big event.
   The gymnasts trained day and night for the big event.

2. Has a dynamic singing voice.
   Ricky Martin has a dynamic singing voice.

3. Landed in the cornfield.
   A small plane landed in the cornfield.

4. After the show, applauded and screamed for fifteen minutes.
   After the show, the crowd applauded and screamed for fifteen minutes.

5. Got out of the large gray van.
   Mr. Sandhurst got out of the large gray van.

PART B Spotting Singular and Plural Subjects

Besides being able to spot subjects in sentences, you need to know whether a subject is singular or plural.

ESL TIP
Remind ESL students of the importance of *pronouncing* plurals in English. Native Spanish speakers often do not pronounce the final *s*, so correcting pronunciation can improve their comprehension, verb agreement, and spelling.

(1) The man jogged around the park.

- The subject of this sentence is *the man.*
- Because *the man* is one person, the subject is *singular.*

Singular means only one of something.

(2) The man and his friend jogged around the park.

- The subject of sentence (2) is *the man and his friend.*
- Because *the man and his friend* refers to more than one person, the subject is *plural.*

Plural means more than one of something.

PRACTICE 4

Here is a list of possible subjects of sentences. If the subject is singular, put a check in the Singular column; if the subject is plural, put a check in the Plural column.

Possible Subjects	Singular (one)	Plural (more than one)
EXAMPLES: an elephant	✔	____
children	____	✔
1. our cousins	____	✔
2. a song and a dance	____	✔
3. Kansas	✔	____
4. their trophy	✔	____
5. women	____	✔
6. a rock star and her band	____	✔
7. his three pickup trucks	____	✔
8. salad dressing	✔	____

PRACTICE 5

TEACHING TIP
Many high-interest practice exercises can also be used as minireadings—useful for discussion, critical thinking, or topics to write about.

Circle the complete subjects in these sentences. Then, in the space at the right, write *S* if the subject is singular or *P* if the subject is plural.

EXAMPLE: (This young cartoonist) is getting national attention. S

1. (Aaron McGruder) was a student at the University of Maryland. S
2. (Comic books and hip hop music) intrigued him. P
3. To Aaron, (existing comics) did not capture racial diversity in a real way. P
4. (McGruder) decided to create a comic strip called *Boondocks*. S
5. (The characters) were African-American city kids in suburbia. P

Aaron McGruder and his characters

Boondocks © 2004 Aaron McGruder. Dist. by Universal Press Syndicate. Reprinted with permission. All Rights Reserved.

6. The strip appeared in the college's student paper, *The Diamondback*, in 1997. S
7. Rave reviews and a few angry letters poured in. P
8. A major music magazine soon began publishing *Boondocks* every day. S
9. Expanding racial dialogue by using humor is Aaron's goal. S
10. The daily strip, a book, and TV projects now keep him very busy. P

PART C Spotting Prepositional Phrases

TEACHING TIP
Part C anticipates and addresses a common problem: many basic writers confuse the object of a preposition with the subject of the sentence.

One group of words that may confuse you as you look for subjects is the prepositional phrase. A **prepositional phrase** contains a *preposition* (a word like *at, from, in,* or *of*) and its *object* (a *noun* or *pronoun*). Here are some prepositional phrases:*

Prepositional Phrase	= Preposition	+ Object
at work	at	work
behind her	behind	her
of the students	of	the students
on the blue table	on	the blue table

The object of a preposition *cannot* be the subject of a sentence. Therefore, crossing out prepositional phrases can help you find the real subject.

(1) On summer evenings, girls in white dresses stroll under the trees.
(2) ~~On summer evenings~~, girls ~~in white dresses~~ stroll ~~under the trees~~.
(3) ~~From dawn to dusk~~, we hiked.
(4) The president ~~of the college~~ will speak tonight.

- In sentence (1), you may have trouble spotting the subject. However, once the prepositional phrases are crossed out in (2), the subject, *girls,* is easy to see.
- Cross out the prepositional phrase in sentence (3). What is the subject of the sentence? we
- Cross out the prepositional phrase in sentence (4). What is the subject of the sentence? the president

ESL TIP
For more in-depth work on the meanings of prepositions and idiomatic phrases—often a problem for ESL students—see Chapter 22.

Here are some common prepositions you should know:

Common Prepositions

about	against	at
above	along	before
across	among	behind
after	around	beside

*For more work on prepositions, see Chapter 22.

between	into	to
by	like	toward
during	of	under
except	off	until
for	on	up
from	over	with
in	through(out)	without

PRACTICE 6

Cross out the prepositional phrase or phrases in each sentence. Then circle the *simple* subject of the sentence.

EXAMPLE: Millions ~~of people~~ walk ~~on the Appalachian Trail~~ each year.

1. That famous trail stretches ~~from Springer Mountain in Georgia to Mount Katahdin in Maine.~~
2. One quarter ~~of the trail~~ goes ~~through Virginia~~.
3. The majority ~~of walkers~~ hike ~~for one day~~.
4. ~~Of the four million trail users~~, two hundred people complete the entire trail every year.
5. ~~For most hikers~~, the trip ~~through fourteen states~~ takes four or five months.
6. ~~In the spring~~, many hardy souls begin their 2,158 mile-long journey.
7. These lovers ~~of the wilderness~~ must reach Mount Katahdin ~~before winter~~.
8. ~~On the trail~~, men and women battle heat, humidity, bugs, blisters, muscle sprains, and food and water shortages.
9. ~~After beautiful green scenery~~, the path becomes rocky and mountainous.
10. Hikers ~~in the White Mountains of New Hampshire~~ struggle ~~against high winds~~.
11. A pebble ~~from Georgia~~ is sometimes added ~~to the pile of stones at the top of Mount Katahdin~~.
12. ~~At the bottom of the mountain~~, the conquerors ~~of the Appalachian Trail~~ add their names ~~to the list of successful hikers~~.

TEACHING TIP
After students have completed Parts A, B, and C, they might highlight all subjects in a recent paragraph of their own, exchange work, and check each other's answers.

PART D Defining and Spotting Action Verbs

(1) The pears ________________ on the trees.

(2) Robert ________________ his customer's hand and ________________ her dog on the head.

These sentences tell you what or who the subject is—*the pears* and *Robert*—but not what each subject does.

- In sentence (1), what do the pears do? Do they *grow, ripen, rot, stink,* or *glow?*

- All these *action verbs* fit into the blank space in sentence (1), but the meaning of the sentence changes depending on which action verb you use.
- In sentence (2), what actions did Robert perform? He might have *shaken, ignored, kissed, patted,* or *scratched.*
- Depending on which verb you use, the meaning of the sentence changes.
- Some sentences, like sentence (2), contain two or more action verbs.

For a sentence to be complete, it must have a *verb*. An *action verb* tells what action the subject is performing.

PRACTICE 7

Fill in each blank with an action verb.

1. Shaquille O'Neal ____sailed____ through the air for a slam dunk.
2. An artist ____sketched____ the scene at the waterfront.
3. When the rooster ____crowed____, the dogs ____barked____.
4. A fierce wind ____raged____ and ____howled____.
5. The audience ____clapped____ while the conductor ____bowed____.
6. This new kitchen gadget ____chops____ and ____slices____ any vegetable you can imagine.
7. When the dentist ____broke____ his drill, Charlene ____cheered____.
8. Will Smith ____slides____ and ____glides____ across the stage.

PRACTICE 8

Circle the action verbs in these sentences. Some sentences contain more than one action verb.

(1) Sometimes the combination of talent and persistence (explodes) into well-deserved fame and fortune. (2) For almost a year, J. K. Rowling (survived) on public assistance in Edinburgh, Scotland. (3) Almost every day that year, she (brought) her baby to a coffee shop near their damp, unheated apartment. (4) In the warmth of the café, the divorced, unemployed mother (sat) and (wrote). (5) Almost at the end of her endurance, she finally (finished) her first book. (6) Today, Rowling's Harry Potter books (sell) hundreds of millions of copies in sixty languages. (7) Each book (tells) about Harry's adventures, both in the everyday world (the Muggles' world) and at a new grade level at Hogwarts School of Witchcraft and Wizardry. (8) The imaginative and very funny series about the courageous young wizard-in-training (attracts) and (enthralls) adults as well as children. (9) In fact, the *New York Times* (began) a children's bestseller list for the first time—after months of Harry Potter books in slots 1, 2, and 3 on the adult bestseller list!

PART E Defining and Spotting Linking Verbs

The verbs you have been examining so far show action, but a second kind of verb simply links the subject to words that describe or rename it.

(1) Aunt Claudia sometimes seems a little strange.

- The subject in this sentence is *Aunt Claudia,* but there is no action verb.
- Instead, *seems* links the subject, *Aunt Claudia,* with the descriptive words *a little strange.*

Aunt Claudia	seems	a little strange.
↓	↓	↓
subject	linking verb	descriptive words

(2) They are reporters for the newspaper.

- The subject is *they*. The word *reporters* renames the subject.
- What verb links the subject, *they,* with the word *reporters*? are

For a sentence to be complete, it must contain a *verb*. A *linking verb* links the subject with words that describe or rename that subject.

Here are some linking verbs you should know:

Common Linking Verbs

be (am, is, are, was, were)	look
act	seem
appear	smell
become	sound
feel	taste
get	

- The most common linking verbs are the forms of *to be,* but verbs of the senses, such as *feel, look,* and *smell,* also may be used as linking verbs.

PRACTICE 9

The subjects and descriptive words in these sentences are boxed. Circle the linking verbs.

1. Jerry sounds sleepy today.
2. Ronda always was the best debater on the team.
3. His brother often appeared relaxed and happy.
4. By evening, Harvey felt confident about the exam.
5. Mara and Maude became talent scouts.

PRACTICE 10

Circle the linking verbs in these sentences. Then underline the subject and the descriptive word or words in each sentence.

1. The sweet potato pie tastes delicious.
2. You usually seem energetic.
3. During the summer, she looks calm.
4. Under heavy snow, the new dome roof appeared sturdy.
5. Raphael is a gifted animal trainer.
6. Lately, I feel very competent at work.
7. Luz became a medical technician.
8. Yvonne acted surprised at her baby shower.

PART F Spotting Verbs of More Than One Word

All the verbs you have dealt with so far have been single words—*look, walked, saw, are, were,* and so on. However, many verbs consist of more than one word.

(1) Sarah is walking to work.

ESL TIP
Ask nonnative students how verbs in their language differ from verbs in English.

- The subject is *Sarah*. What is *Sarah* doing?
- Sarah is walking.
- *Walking* is the *main verb*. *Is* is the *helping verb*; without *is*, *walking* is not a complete verb.

(2) Should I have written sooner?

- The subject is *I*.
- *Should have written* is the *complete verb*.
- *Written* is the *main verb*. *Should* and *have* are the *helping verbs;* without *should have, written* is not a complete verb.

(3) Do you eat fish?

- What is the subject? ___you___
- What is the main verb? ___eat___
- What is the helping verb? ___do___

The *complete verb* in a sentence consists of all the helping verbs and the main verb.

PRACTICE 11

TEACHING TIP
Practices 11 and 12 make enjoyable full-class exercises.

ESL TIP
ESL students may be confused by the variety of verb forms and tenses in Practice 11. Be prepared to refer the students to the appropriate chapters in Unit 3 for explanations.

The blanks following each sentence tell you how many words make up the complete verb. Fill in the blanks with the complete verb; then circle the main verb.

EXAMPLE: Language researchers at the University of Arizona have been studying parrots.

have ______ been ______ (studying) ______

1. Dr. Irene Pepperberg has worked with Alex, an African Gray parrot, for years.

   has ______ (worked) ______

2. About one hundred words can be used by this intelligent bird.

   can ______ be ______ (used) ______

3. Alex is believed to understand the words, not just "parrot" sounds.

   is ______ (believed) ______

4. For example, from a tray of objects, Alex can select all the keys, all the wooden items, or all the blue items.

   can ______ (select) ______

5. Dr. Pepperberg might show Alex a fuzzy cloth ball.

   might ______ (show) ______

6. The bird will shout, "Wool!"

   will ______ (shout) ______

7. Alex has been practicing counting to six.

   has ______ been ______ (practicing) ______

8. Currently, he and the other parrots are learning letters and their sounds.

   are ______ (learning) ______

9. Can these birds really be taught to read?

   can ______ be ______ (taught) ______

10. Scientists in animal communication are excited by the possibility.

   are ______ (excited) ______

PRACTICE 12

Box the simple subject, circle the main verb, and underline any helping verbs in each of the following sentences.

EXAMPLE: Most [people] have (wondered) about the beginning of the universe.

1. [Scientists] have (developed) one theory.
2. According to this theory, the [universe] (began) with a huge explosion.
3. The [explosion] has been (named) the Big Bang.
4. First, all [matter] must have been (packed) into a tiny speck under enormous pressure.
5. Then, about 15 billion years ago, that [speck] (burst) with amazing force.

6. Everything in the universe has come from the original explosion.
7. In fact, the universe still is expanding from the Big Bang.
8. All of the planets and stars are moving away from each other at an even speed.
9. Will it expand forever?
10. Experts may be debating that question for a long time.

PRACTICE 13 WRITING ASSIGNMENT

Whether you have just graduated from high school or have worked for several years, the first year of college can be difficult. Imagine that you are writing to an incoming student who needs advice and encouragement. Pick one serious problem you had as a first-year student and explain how you coped with it. State the problem clearly. Use examples from your own experience or the experience of others to make your advice more vivid.

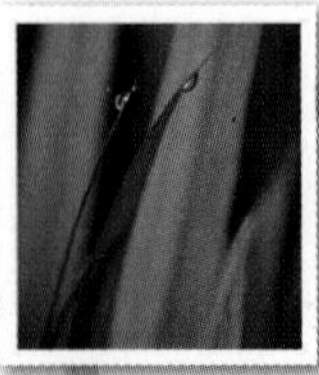

CHAPTER HIGHLIGHTS

- **A sentence contains a subject and a verb, and expresses a complete thought:**

  S V
  Jennifer swims every day.

  S V
  The two students have tutored in the writing lab.

- **An action verb tells what the subject is doing:**

  Toni Morrison *writes* novels.

- **A linking verb links the subject with words that describe or rename it:**

  Her novels *are* bestsellers.

- **Don't mistake the object of a prepositional phrase for a subject:**

  S PP
  The red car [in the showroom] is a Corvette.

  PP S
  [In my dream,] *a sailor and his parrot* were singing.

CHAPTER REVIEW

Circle the simple subjects, crossing out any confusing prepositional phrases. Then underline the complete verbs. If you have difficulty with this review, consider rereading the lesson.

Target Practice

(1) Successful people know an important secret about setting and reaching goals. (2) These high achievers break their goals down into smaller, more manageable steps or targets. (3) Hitting these targets one by one will lead them to the

TEACHING TIP
Goal setting, the subject of this chapter review, is an important skill for students to learn early in their college experience. You might use this topic as the basis of a class discussion, group work, or writing (see Writing Assignment 1, p. 83).

goal. (4) ~~On the other hand~~, huge goals overwhelm most people. (5) These might include graduating from college, becoming a bank president, or hitting forty home runs in one season.

(6) In order to break down a major goal into small steps, many achievers start by thinking backward. (7) Dillon's goal, ~~for example~~, was to lose twenty pounds by graduation. (8) In order to lose that much weight, Dillon decided to set smaller targets for himself. (9) His first target was to reduce his eating between meals. (10) No snacks would be allowed except an apple or other low-calorie fruit to calm a major craving. (11) Dillon's second target was to avoid going back for second helpings at any meal—no matter what. (12) Taking a walk every evening after dinner became his third target. (13) ~~At night~~, Dillon checked off the targets hit that day.

(14) Even high achievers do not complete a major goal, like losing a lot of weight, every day. (15) However, they feel satisfaction about moving forward, one small step at a time. (16) The photographer ~~at Dillon's graduation~~ captured his beaming smile. (17) ~~Under that cap and gown~~, Dillon's weight had dropped by twenty-two pounds.

EXPLORING ONLINE

TEACHING TIP
More practice and assessment are available in the *Grassroots* Test Bank; linked ACE tests on the *Grassroots* student website; *WriteSpace for Grassroots*; and the Exploring Online links in this chapter.

<http://www.ccc.commnet.edu/grammar/quizzes/subjector.htm> Interactive quiz: Identify the subjects.

<http://www.ccc.commnet.edu/grammar/quizzes/verbmaster.htm> Interactive quiz: Identify verbs of one or more words.

<http://college.hmco.com/devenglish> Visit the *Grassroots* 8/e Student Website for more exercises and quizzes.

CHAPTER

7

Avoiding Sentence Fragments

PART A Writing Sentences with Subjects and Verbs

Which of these groups of words is a sentence? Be prepared to explain your answers.

(1) People will bet on almost anything.
(2) For example, every winter the Nenana River in Alaska.
(3) Often make bets on the date of the breakup of the ice.
(4) Must guess the exact day and time of day.
(5) Recently, the lucky guess won $300,000.

TEACHING TIP
Students should know that sentence fragments are considered a serious and distracting error in college and the workplace. Ask, "Are fragments one of your personal error patterns?" What look like eight errors might be one error—fragments—repeated eight times!

- In (2), you probably wanted to know what the Nenana River *does*. The idea is not complete because there is no *verb*.
- In (3) and (4), you probably wanted to know *who* often makes bets on the date of the breakup of the ice and *who* must guess the exact day and time of day.

  The ideas are not complete. What is missing? the subjects
- But in sentences (1) and (5), you knew *who did what*. These ideas are complete.

  Why? They have a subject and a verb, and they express a complete thought.

Below is the same group of words written as complete sentences:

(1) People will bet on almost anything.
(2) For example, every winter the Nenana River in Alaska freezes.
(3) The townspeople often make bets on the date of the breakup of the ice.
(4) Someone must guess the exact day and time of day.
(5) Recently, the lucky guess won $300,000.

Every *sentence* must have both a subject and a verb—and must express a complete thought.

A *fragment* lacks either a subject or a complete verb—or does not express a complete thought.

PRACTICE 1

All of the following are *fragments;* they lack a subject, a verb, or both. Add a subject, a verb, or both in order to make the fragments into sentences. Answers will vary.

EXAMPLE: Raising onions in the backyard.
Rewrite: Charles is raising onions in the backyard.

1. Melts easily.
   Rewrite: On a hot day in Alabama, butter melts easily.
2. That couple on the street corner.
   Rewrite: That couple on the street corner just won the lottery.
3. One of the fans.
   Rewrite: One of the fans caught a fly ball.
4. Manages a Software City store.
   Rewrite: My next-door neighbor manages a Software City store.
5. The tip of her nose.
   Rewrite: The tip of her nose was red from the cold.
6. DVD players.
   Rewrite: DVD players are replacing VCRs in many homes.
7. Makes me nervous.
   Rewrite: Parking my car at the airport all week makes me nervous.
8. A person who likes to take risks.
   Rewrite: Edgardo is a person who likes to take risks.

PART B Writing Sentences with Complete Verbs

Do not be fooled by incomplete verbs.

(1) She leaving for the city.
(2) The students gone to the cafeteria for dessert.

- *Leaving* seems to be the verb in (1).
- *Gone* seems to be the verb in (2).

But . . .

- An *-ing* word like *leaving* is not by itself a verb.
- A word like *gone* is not by itself a verb.

(1) She { *is* / *was* } leaving for the city.

(2) The students { *have* / *had* } gone to the cafeteria for dessert.

- To be a verb, an *-ing* word (called a *present participle*) must be combined with some form of the verb *to be*.*

Helping Verb		Main Verb
am	were	
is	has been	jogging
are	have been	
was	had been	

- To be a verb, a word like *gone* (called a *past participle*) must be combined with some form of *to have* or *to be*.**

Helping Verb		Main Verb
am	have	
is	had	
are	has been	forgotten
was	have been	
were	had been	
has		

PRACTICE 2

All of the following are fragments; they have only a partial or an incomplete verb. Complete each verb in order to make these fragments into sentences. Answers will vary.

EXAMPLE: Both children grown tall this year.
Rewrite: Both children have grown tall this year.

1. The Australian winning the tennis match.
   Rewrite: The Australian is winning the tennis match.
2. Her parents gone to the movies.
   Rewrite: Her parents have gone to the movies.
3. Steve's letter published in the *Miami Herald*.
   Rewrite: Steve's letter was published in the *Miami Herald*.
4. My physics professor always forgetting the assignment.
   Rewrite: My physics professor is always forgetting the assignment.
5. This sari made of scarlet silk.
   Rewrite: This sari is made of scarlet silk.
6. For the past two years, Joan working at a computer company.
   Rewrite: For the past two years, Joan has been working at a computer company.
7. You ever been to Alaska?
   Rewrite: Have you ever been to Alaska?
8. Yesterday, Ed's wet gloves taken from the radiator.
   Rewrite: Yesterday, Ed's wet gloves were taken from the radiator.

*For a detailed explanation of present participles, see Chapter 11.
**For a detailed explanation of past participles, see Chapter 10.

PRACTICE 3

All of the following are fragments; they lack a subject, and they contain only a partial verb. Make these fragments into sentences by adding a subject and by completing the verb. Answers will vary.

EXAMPLE: Written by Ray Bradbury.
Rewrite: This science fiction thriller was written by Ray Bradbury.

1. Forgotten the password.
   Rewrite: The spy has forgotten the password.
2. Now running the copy center.
   Rewrite: Students are now running the copy center.
3. Making sculpture from old car parts.
   Rewrite: Jim is making sculpture from old car parts.
4. Been working at the state capitol building.
   Rewrite: My aunt has been working at the state capitol building.
5. Creeping along the windowsill.
   Rewrite: Two cats are creeping along the windowsill.
6. Driven that tractor for years.
   Rewrite: Phil Hamilton has driven that tractor for years.
7. Slept through the TV program.
   Rewrite: My sister and I slept through the TV program.
8. Been to a wrestling match.
   Rewrite: None of my friends had been to a wrestling match.

PRACTICE 4

Fragments are most likely to occur in paragraphs or longer pieces of writing. Proofread the paragraph below for fragments; check for missing subjects, missing verbs, or incomplete verbs. Circle the number of every fragment; then write your corrections above the lines. Answers will vary.

(1) On a routine day in 1946, a scientist at the Raytheon Company ^put^ his hand into his pants pocket for a candy bar. (2) The chocolate, however, ^was^ a messy, sticky mass of gunk. (3) Dr. Percy Spencer had been testing a magnetron tube. (4) Could the chocolate have melted from radiation leaking from the tube? (5) Spencer sent out for a bag of popcorn kernels. (6) ~~Put~~ ^He put^ the kernels near the tube. (7) Within minutes, corn ^was^ popping wildly onto the lab floor. (8) Within a short time, Raytheon ^was^ working on the development of the microwave oven. (9) Microwave cooking ^became^ the first new method of preparing food since the discovery of fire more than a million years ago. (10) ~~Was~~ ^It was^ the first cooking technique that did not directly or indirectly apply fire to food.

PART C Completing the Thought

TEACHING TIP
Many dependent clause fragments could be called "afterthoughts." This idea helps some students. Often, attaching such a fragment to the preceding sentence is the best method of correction.

ESL TIP
Many ESL students begin sentences with subordinators like *because* and *although*, so this type of fragment is a common problem. Some are copying the oral speech patterns they hear. Others come from language backgrounds, like Japanese, in which this construction is accepted written practice.

Can these ideas stand by themselves?

(1) Because oranges are rich in vitamin C.

(2) Although Sam is sleepy.

- These ideas have a subject and a verb (find them), but they cannot stand alone because you expect something else to follow.
- Because oranges are rich in vitamin C, then *what?* Should you *eat them, sell them,* or *make marmalade?*
- Although Sam is sleepy, *what will he do?* Will he *wash the dishes, walk the dog,* or *go to the gym?*

(1) Because oranges are rich in vitamin C, *I eat one every day.*

(2) Although Sam is sleepy, *he will work late tonight.*

- These sentences are now complete.
- Words like *because* and *although* make an idea incomplete unless another idea is added to complete the thought.*

PRACTICE 5

Make these fragments into sentences by adding some idea that completes the thought. Answers will vary.

EXAMPLE: Because I miss my family, I am going home for the weekend.

1. As May stepped off the elevator, she bumped into her old boyfriend.
2. If you are driving to Main Street, please take me with you.
3. While Kimi studied chemistry, Maurie did his math homework.
4. Because you believe in yourself, you will succeed.
5. Although spiders scare most people, I find them fascinating.
6. Unless the surgery is absolutely necessary, I do not want to have it.
7. Whenever I hear Macy Gray sing, I think of Billie Holiday.
8. Although these air conditioners are expensive to run, we have to keep them on all night.

Can these ideas stand by themselves?

(3) Graciela, who has a one-year-old daughter.

(4) A course that I will always remember.

- In each of these examples, you expect something else to follow. Graciela, who has a one-year-old daughter, *is doing what?* Does she *attend town meetings, knit sweaters,* or *fly planes?*

*For more work on this type of sentence, see Chapter 14.

- A course that I will always remember *is what?* The thought must be completed.

> (3) Graciela, who has a one-year-old daughter, *attends Gordon College.*
> (4) A course that I will always remember *is documentary filmmaking.*

- These sentences are now complete.*

PRACTICE 6

Make these fragments into sentences by completing the thought. Sample answers.

EXAMPLE: Kent, who is a good friend of mine, rarely writes to me.

1. The horoscopes that appear in the daily papers make me laugh.
2. Couples who never argue seem unreal.
3. Robert, who is a superb pole-vaulter, will compete in the Olympics.
4. Radio programs that ask listeners to call in are often very funny.
5. A person who has coped with a great loss often can help others.
6. My dog, which is the smartest animal alive, starts to bark five minutes before I arrive.
7. Libraries that are up-to-date offer e-mail and other Internet services.
8. The video that we watched last night was rented from Video Watch.
9. A person who becomes upset easily should never go into sales.
10. A country that I have always wanted to visit is Kenya.

PRACTICE 7

To each fragment, add a subject, a verb, or whatever is required to complete the thought. Sample answers.

1. Visiting the White House.
   Rewrite: Are they visiting the White House?
2. That digital clock blinking for hours.
   Rewrite: That digital clock has been blinking for hours.
3. People who can't say no to their children.
   Rewrite: People who can't say no to their children will probably regret not doing so.
4. Make tables from driftwood they find on the beach.
   Rewrite: Tanya and Jerry make tables from driftwood they find on the beach.
5. Over the roof and into the garden.
   Rewrite: The squirrel scampered over the roof and into the garden.
6. Raúl completed a culinary arts program, and now he a well-known chef.
   Rewrite: Raúl completed a culinary arts program, and now he is a well-known chef.
7. Chess, which is a difficult game to play.
   Rewrite: Six-year-old Eric loves chess, which is a difficult game to play.
8. Whenever Dolly starts to yodel.
   Rewrite: Whenever Dolly starts to yodel, her dog starts to howl.

---

*For more work on this type of sentence, see Chapter 17, Part A.

PRACTICE 8

Proofread the paragraph for fragments. Circle the number of every fragment, and then write your corrections above the lines.

(1) The Special Olympics is an international ~~program.~~ program that (2) ~~That~~ is held for mentally disabled children and adults. (3) Special Olympics athletes train and compete in regular ~~sports.~~ sports, which (4) ~~Which~~ include floor hockey, skiing, soccer, swimming, speed skating, and tennis. (5) The Special Olympics winter and summer international games are held every other year. (6) Although 150 countries participate in the world ~~games.~~ games, Special (7) ~~Special~~ Olympics are also held yearly at local and state levels. (8) Altogether, more than a million athletes participate. (9) Whereas Special Olympics competitors may not swim as fast or jump as high as Olympics ~~stars.~~ stars, they (10) ~~They~~ are very eager to do their best. (11) Their courage and accomplishments inspire ~~everyone.~~ everyone and (12) ~~And~~ change these athletes' lives forever.

PRACTICE 9 WRITING ASSIGNMENT

Working in a small group, choose one of the sentences below that could begin a short story.

1. As soon as Sean replaced the receiver, he knew he had to take action.
2. Suddenly, the bright blue sky turned dark.
3. No matter where she looked, Elena could not find her diary.

TEACHING TIP
Suggest that students try the "bottom-up" proofreading technique—reading the last sentence first, then the second to last, and so on until they reach the first sentence.

Next, each person in the group should write his or her own short story, starting with that sentence. First decide what type of story yours will be—science fiction, romance, action, comedy, murder mystery, and so on; perhaps each person will choose a different type. It may help you to imagine the story later becoming a TV show. As you write, be careful to avoid fragments, making sure each sentence has a subject and a complete verb—and expresses a complete thought.

Then exchange papers, checking each other's work for fragments. If time permits, read the papers aloud to the group. Are you surprised by the different ways in which that first sentence was developed?

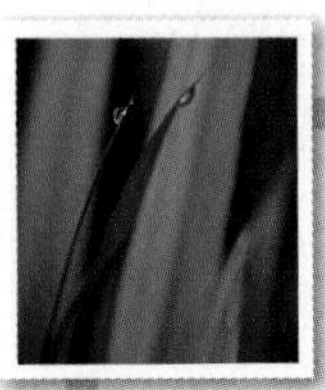

CHAPTER HIGHLIGHTS

A sentence fragment is an error because it lacks

- **a subject:** Was buying a gold ring. (*incorrect*)
  Diamond Jim was buying a gold ring. (*correct*)
- **a verb:** The basketball game Friday at noon. (*incorrect*)
  The basketball game *was played* Friday at noon. (*correct*)
- **a complete thought:** While Teresa was swimming. (*incorrect*)
  While Teresa was swimming, she lost a contact lens.(*correct*)

  The woman who bought your car. (*incorrect*)
  The woman who bought your car is walking down the highway. (*correct*)

CHAPTER REVIEW

Circle the number of each fragment. Correct it in any way that makes sense, changing it into a separate idea or adding it to another sentence.

A. (1) Steel drums [are] wonderful and unusual musical instruments. (2) Steel bands use them to perform calypso, jazz, ~~and~~ popular ~~music.~~ [music, and] (3) ~~And~~ even classical symphonies. (4) Steel drums were invented in ~~Trinidad.~~ [Trinidad, where] (5) ~~Where~~ they were made from the ends of discarded oil ~~drums.~~ [drums that] (6) ~~That~~ had been left by the British navy. (7) Although the first steel drums produced only ~~rhythm.~~ [rhythm, now] (8) ~~Now~~ they can be tuned to play up to five octaves. (9) Steel orchestras produce ~~music.~~ [music that] (10) ~~That~~ surrounds and delights listeners without the use of amplifiers. (11) The worldwide popularity of steel drums has been increasing steadily. (12) The Trinidad All Steel Percussion Orchestra was a smash ~~hit.~~ [hit when] (13) ~~When~~ it first performed in England a number of years ago. (14) Recently, the Northern Illinois University Steel Band has been thrilling audiences from the United States to Taiwan.

B. (1) Many people seem to forget all about good ~~manners.~~ [manners when] (2) ~~When~~ they use a cell phone. (3) They rudely allow the ringing phone to interrupt conversations, meetings, appointments, performances, and romantic dinner dates. (4) Some even answer calls in church or at ~~funerals.~~ [funerals and] (5) ~~And~~ then proceed to talk ~~loudly.~~ [loudly, forcing] (6) ~~Forcing~~ others to listen or wait for them to finish talking. (7) Public relations consultant Carol ~~Page,~~ [Page is] known as the "Miss Manners of Cell Phones." (8) She created ~~*cellmanners.com.*~~ [cellmanners.com, which] (9) ~~Which~~ is a website promoting cell phone courtesy and civility. (10) Page believes that in order to stop cell ~~rudeness.~~ [rudeness, we] (11) ~~We~~ should fix a "cell glare" on any cell phone user who is behaving badly. (12) If that doesn't ~~work.~~ [work,] (13) ~~We~~ [we] can interrupt and gently ask if the phone conversation might be postponed. (14) Setting a good example when you use your own cell phone [is] probably the best way to teach good cellular phone manners to others.

DILBERT reprinted by permission of United Feature Syndicate, Inc.

C. (1) Braille, which is a system of reading and writing now used by blind people all over the ~~world.~~ world, was (2) ~~Was~~ invented by a fifteen-year-old French boy. (3) In 1824, when Louis Braille entered a school for the blind in ~~Paris.~~ Paris, he (4) ~~He~~ found that the library had only fourteen books for the blind. (5) These books used a system that he and the other blind students found hard to use. (6) Most of them just gave up. (7) Louis Braille devoted himself to finding a better way. (8) Working with the French army method called ~~night-writing.~~ night-writing, he (9) ~~He~~ came up with a new system in 1829. (10) Although his classmates liked and used ~~Braille.~~ Braille, it was (11) ~~It~~ not widely accepted in England and the United States for another hundred years.

D. (1) Not all employers have a problem with employees who sleep on the job. (2) In fact, when workers get that after-lunch draggy ~~feeling.~~ feeling, some (3) ~~Some~~ employers encourage them to nap. (4) Sleep researchers believe that people have a natural tendency to fall ~~asleep.~~ asleep during (5) ~~During~~ the afternoon. (6) Short naps energize ~~workers.~~ workers (7) ~~And~~ and improve both safety and performance. (8) Of course, nappers always have found ways to catch a few winks. (9) They snooze at (or under) desks and in cars, closets, cafeterias, meeting rooms, and bathroom stalls. (10) Now, however, more and more companies ^are providing "relaxation rooms" and "nap nooks." (11) Camille and Bill Anthony, authors of *The Art of Napping at Work*, are even promoting a new holiday, National Workplace Napping Day. (12) Because it falls on the Monday after the end of daylight-saving ~~time.~~ time, employees (13) ~~Employees~~ can make up the lost hour of sleep by napping at work. (14) To learn more, read the Anthonys' ~~book.~~ book, (15) ~~Which~~ which includes chapters on napping places, napping policies, and the future of workplace napping!

EXPLORING ONLINE

TEACHING TIP
More practice and assessment are available in the *Grassroots* Test Bank; linked ACE tests on the *Grassroots* student website, *WriteSpace for Grassroots*; and the Exploring Online links in this chapter.

<http://owl.english.purdue.edu/handouts/grammar/g_fragEX1.html> Graded quiz: Can you find the fragments?

<http://www.ccc.commnet.edu/cgi-shl/quiz.pl/fragments_add2.htm> Interactive quiz: Find the correct sentence in each group.

<http://college.hmco.com/devenglish> Visit the *Grassroots* 8/e Student Website for more exercises and quizzes.

UNIT 2

WRITING ASSIGNMENTS

As you complete each writing assignment, remember to perform these steps:

- Write a clear, complete topic sentence.
- Use freewriting, brainstorming, or clustering to generate ideas for your paragraph, essay, or memo.
- Arrange your best ideas in a plan.
- Revise for support, unity, coherence, and exact language.
- Proofread for grammar, punctuation, and spelling errors.

Writing Assignment 1: *Plan to achieve a goal.* Did you know that nearly all successful people are good goal-planners? Choose a goal you would truly love to achieve, and write it down. Next, write down three to six smaller steps or targets that will lead you to your goal. Arrange these in time order. Have you left out any crucial steps? To inspire you and help you plan, reread "Target Practice" on page 72 or try out the interactive goal-planner from Paradise Valley Community College at **<http://www.pvc.maricopa.edu/advisement/goalplan.html>.**

Writing Assignment 2: *Describe your place in the family.* Your psychology professor has asked you to write a brief description of your place in the family—as an only child, the youngest child, the middle child, or the oldest child. Did your place provide you with special privileges or lay special responsibilities on you? For instance, youngest children may be babied; oldest children may be expected to act like parents. Did your place in the family have an effect on you as an adult? In your topic sentence, state what role your place in the family played in your development: *Being the ____________________ child in my family has made me* ____________________. Proofread for fragments.

Writing Assignment 3: *Write about someone who changed jobs.* Did you, someone you know, or someone you know about change jobs because of a new interest or love for something else? Describe the person's first job and feelings of job satisfaction (or lack of them). What happened to make the person want to make a job switch? How long did the switch take? Was it difficult or easy to accomplish? Describe the person's new job and feelings of job satisfaction (or lack of them). Proofread for fragments.

Writing Assignment 4: *Ask for a raise.* Compose a memo to a boss, real or imagined, persuading him or her to decide to raise your pay. In your first sentence, state that you are asking for an increase. Be specific: Note how the quality of your work, your extra hours, or any special projects you have been involved in have made the business run more smoothly or become more profitable. Do not sound vain, but do praise yourself honestly. Use the memo style shown here. Proofread for fragments.

MEMORANDUM

DATE: Today's date

TO: Your boss's name

FROM: Your name

SUBJECT: Salary Increase

UNIT 2

REVIEW

Proofreading and Revising

Proofread the following essay to eliminate all sentence fragments. Circle the number of every fragment. (You should find nine.) Then correct the fragments in any way you choose—by connecting them to a sentence before or after, by completing any incomplete verbs, and so on. Make your corrections above the lines.

Living Without Television

(1) What would you do without your television? (2) Every spring, millions of Americans answer this question for ~~themselves.~~ [themselves by] (3) ~~By~~ taking part in TV Turn-Off Week. (4) They find out that they can in fact lead enjoyable lives without watching TV. (5) Begun in 1995, TV Turn-Off Week now has motivated 24 million participants to spend seven full ~~days.~~ [days engaging] (6) ~~Engaging~~ in activities other than TV viewing. (7) Although many Turn-Off Week participants initially fear that they will be bored without their ~~TVs.~~ [TVs, they] (8) ~~They~~ often rediscover the joys of reading, talking to family and friends, going for walks, exercising, and learning new skills like playing the guitar.

(9) Statistics help explain the power of TV Turn-Off Week. (10) Americans watch more than four hours of TV a day. (11) That's two full months each year. (12) Simply turning off the box leaves people with lots of time to do other things. (13) Nearly half of the U.S. population watches TV while eating ~~dinner.~~ [dinner in-] (14) ~~Instead~~ [stead] of using that time to talk to other family members. (15) Because 56 percent of children have a television set in their ~~bedrooms.~~ [bedrooms, they] (16) ~~They~~ tend to watch programs alone instead of doing homework, interacting with their parents and siblings, or exercising.

(17) Interestingly, the consequences of TV Turn-Off Week seem to be lasting. (18) Many past participants say that they have changed their viewing habits. (19) While a few people go so far as to get rid of their ~~televisions.~~ [televisions, most] (20) ~~Most~~ report that they now watch fewer ~~shows.~~ [shows and] (21) ~~And~~ are less likely to leave the TV sputtering as unwatched background noise. (22) Some move their ~~televisions.~~ [televisions, taking] (23) ~~Taking~~ them out of bedrooms and the family room. (24) Others cancel or reduce their cable or satellite services. (25) One major benefit is that individuals and families

prove to themselves that they can find other, more engaging things to do. (26) Many parents gain confidence about limiting their children's viewing ~~time.~~ time (27) ~~And~~ and more important, about teaching their children how and when to watch TV.

EXPLORING ONLINE

Turn off all TVs in your house for one week, keeping notes on any reactions or changes. Use these notes to write about the experience.

<http://tvturnoff.org/> Visit the website and read for ideas. See "Facts and Figures." Then use this information in a composition arguing for or against watching less TV.

UNIT 2

WRITERS' WORKSHOP

Discuss an Event That Influenced You

Readers of a final draft can easily forget that they are reading the *end result* of someone else's writing process. The following paragraph is one student's response to the assignment *Write about an event in history that influenced you.*

In your class or group, read it aloud if possible. As you read, underline any words or lines that strike you as especially powerful.

> Though the Vietnam War ended almost before I was born, it changed my life. My earliest memory is of my ~~father. A~~ father, a grizzled Vietnam warrior who came back spat upon, with one less brother. He wore a big smile playing ball with my brother and me, but even then I felt the grin was a coverup. When the postwar reports were on, his face became despondent. What haunted his heart and mind, I could not know, but I tried in my childish way to reason with him. A simple "It'll be all right, Dad" would bring a bleak smirk to his face. When he was happy, I was happy. When he was down, I was down. Soon the fatherly horseplay stopped, and once-full bottles of liquor were empty. He was there in ~~body. Yet~~ body, yet not there. Finally, he was physically ~~gone. Either~~ gone, either working a sixty-hour week or out in the streets after a furious fight with my mother. Once they divorced, she moved us to another state. I never came to grips with the turmoil inside my father. I see him as an intricate puzzle, missing one piece. That piece is his humanity, tangled up in history and blown up by a C-19.
>
> *Brian Pereira, student*

1. How effective is Brian Pereira's paragraph?

   __Y__ Good topic sentence? __Y__ Rich supporting details?

   __Y__ Logical organization? __Y__ Effective conclusion?

2. Discuss your underlinings with the group or class. Did others underline the same parts? Explain why you feel particular words or details are effective. For instance, the strong words *bleak smirk* say so much about the father's hopeless mood and the distance between him and his young son.
3. The topic sentence says that the writer's life changed, yet the body of the paragraph speaks mostly about his troubled father. Does the body of the paragraph explain the topic sentence?
4. What order, if any, does this writer follow? Time order.
5. If you do not know what a "C-19" is in the last sentence, does that make the conclusion less effective for you?
6. Would you suggest any changes or revisions?

7. Proofread for grammar and spelling. Do you notice any error patterns (two or more errors of the same type) that this student should watch out for? Yes, sentence fragments.

Brian Pereira's fine paragraph was the end result of a difficult writing process. Pereira describes his process this way:

> The floor in my room looked like a writer's battleground of crumpled papers. Before this topic was assigned, I had not the slightest idea that this influence even existed, much less knew what it was. I thought hard, started a sentence or two, and threw a smashed paper down in disgust, over and over again. After hours, I realized it—the event in history that influenced me was Vietnam, even though I was too young to remember it! That became my topic sentence.

Writing and Revising Ideas

1. Discuss an event that influenced you.
2. Choose your best recent paper and describe your own writing process—what you did well and not so well.

For help with writing your paragraph, see Chapter 3 and Chapter 4, Part B (see "Time Order"). Give yourself plenty of time to revise. Stick with it, trying to write the best possible paper. Pay special attention to fully supporting your topic with interesting facts and details.

UNIT 3

Using Verbs Effectively

Every sentence contains at least one verb. Because verbs often are action words, they add interest and punch to any piece of writing. In this unit, you will

- Learn to use present, past, and other verb tenses correctly
- Learn when to add *-s* or *-ed*
- Recognize and use past participle forms
- Recognize *-ing* verbs, infinitives, and other special forms

Spotlight on Writing

Notice how vividly this writer describes the scene before him. His verbs are underlined.

Russell Thomas places the toe of his right sneaker one inch behind the three-point line. Inspecting the basket with a level gaze, he bends twice at the knees, raises the ball to shoot, then suddenly looks around. What is it? Has he spotted me, watching from the opposite end of the playground? No, something else is up. He is lifting his nose to the wind like a spaniel; he appears to be gauging air currents. Russell waits until the wind settles, bits of trash feathering lightly to the ground. Then he sends a twenty-five foot jump shot arcing through the soft summer twilight. It drops without a sound through the dead center of the bare iron rim. So does the next one. So does the one after that. Alone in the gathering dusk, Russell begins to work the perimeter against imaginary defenders, unspooling jump shots from all points.

Darcy Frey, *The Last Shot*

- Simple but well-chosen verbs help bring this description to life. Which verbs most effectively help you see and experience the scene?
- Do you think that the writer realistically captures this young athlete at practice? What, if anything, do you learn about Russell Thomas—his abilities, personality, even his loves—from reading this short passage?

- ***A person practicing or performing some sport, art, or task***
- ***A time when you watched or overheard someone in a public place***

CHAPTER

8

Present Tense (Agreement)

PART A Defining Agreement

ESL TIP
Many ESL students have trouble with verbs and verb tenses in English. You can tailor this comprehensive unit to your needs by assigning some chapters and parts to the full class and other parts selectively.

ESL TIP
In many languages—such as Chinese, Japanese, and Korean—subject-verb number agreement does not exist. Thus, ESL students may need extra help with the concept.

A subject and a present tense verb **agree** if you use the correct form of the verb with each subject. The chart below shows which form of the verb to use for each kind of pronoun subject (we discuss other kinds of subjects later).

Verbs in the Present Tense
(*example verb: to write*)

Singular			Plural		
	If the subject is ↓	the verb is ↓		If the subject is ↓	the verb is ↓
1st person:	I	write	1st person:	we	write
2nd person:	you	write	2nd person:	you	write
3rd person:	he / she / it	writes	3rd person:	they	write

PRACTICE 1

TEACHING TIP
Transformation exercises can be a mind gym for verbal flexibility. Supply a first person, present tense passage. Have students rewrite it or read it aloud, changing all subjects to *he* or *she* and making each verb agree.

Fill in the correct present tense form of the verb.

1. You *ask* questions.	1. He ___asks___ questions.
2. They *decide.*	2. She ___decides___.
3. I *remember.*	3. He ___remembers___.
4. They *wear* glasses.	4. She ___wears___ glasses.
5. We *hope* so.	5. He ___hopes___ so.
6. I *laugh* often.	6. She ___laughs___ often.
7. We *study* daily.	7. He ___studies___ daily.
8. He *amazes* me.	8. It ___amazes___ me.

Add *-s* or *-es* to a verb in the present tense only when the subject is *third person singular (he, she, it).*

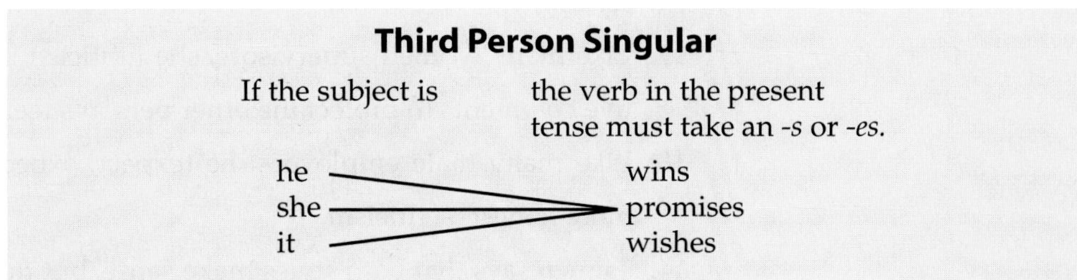

Third Person Singular
If the subject is
the verb in the present tense must take an -s or -es.
he
she
it
wins
promises
wishes

PRACTICE 2

Write the correct form of the verb in the space to the right of the pronoun subject.

EXAMPLE: **to see** I ___see___
they ___see___
she ___sees___

to find	**to ask**	**to go**
he ___finds___	I ___ask___	it ___goes___
they ___find___	she ___asks___	you ___go___
you ___find___	he ___asks___	we ___go___

to rest	**to hold**	**to select**
I ___rest___	it ___holds___	she ___selects___
they ___rest___	we ___hold___	he ___selects___
she ___rests___	you ___hold___	I ___select___

PRACTICE 3

First, underline the subject (always a pronoun) in each sentence below. Then circle the correct verb form. REMEMBER: If the subject of the sentence is *he, she,* or *it* (third person singular), the verb must end in *-s* or *-es* to agree with the subject.

1. According to researcher Deborah Tannen, we sometimes (fail, fails) to understand how men and women communicate on the job.

TEACHING TIP
Consider doing Practice 3 with the whole class or let smaller groups complete it, competing for the best verb-agreement score. Ask students whether Tannen's analysis is accurate or sexist.

2. When working together, they sometimes (differ, differs) in predictable ways.
3. In Tannen's book *Talking from 9 to 5: Women and Men at Work,* she (describe, describes) the following misunderstanding between Amy, a manager, and Donald, her employee.
4. She (read, reads) Donald's report and (find, finds) it unacceptable.
5. She (meet, meets) with him to discuss the necessary revisions.
6. To soften the blow, she (praise, praises) the report's strengths.
7. Then, she (go, goes) on to explain in detail the needed revisions.
8. The next day, he (submit, submits) a second draft with only tiny changes.
9. She (think, thinks) that Donald did not listen to her.
10. He (believe, believes) that Amy first liked his report, then changed her mind.
11. According to the author, they (represent, represents) different communication styles.
12. Like many women supervisors, she (criticize, criticizes) gently, adding positive comments to protect the other person's feelings.
13. Like many male employees, he (expect, expects) more direct—and to him, more honest—criticism.
14. Tannen says that both styles make sense, but they (cause, causes) confusion if not understood.
15. Stereotypes or truth? You (decide, decides) for yourself about the accuracy of Tannen's analysis.

PART B Troublesome Verb in the Present Tense: TO BE

A few present tense verbs are formed in special ways. The most common of these verbs is *to be.*

ESL TIP
A common ESL error is omitting the "be" verb in sentences (e.g., *He a student*) because some other languages do not require a verb in this instance.

Reference Chart: TO BE
(*present tense*)

Singular		Plural	
If the subject is ↓	the verb is ↓	If the subject is ↓	the verb is ↓
1st person: I	am	1st person: we	are
2nd person: you	are	2nd person: you	are
3rd person: he / she / it	is	3rd person: they	are

The chart on the following page also can be read like this:

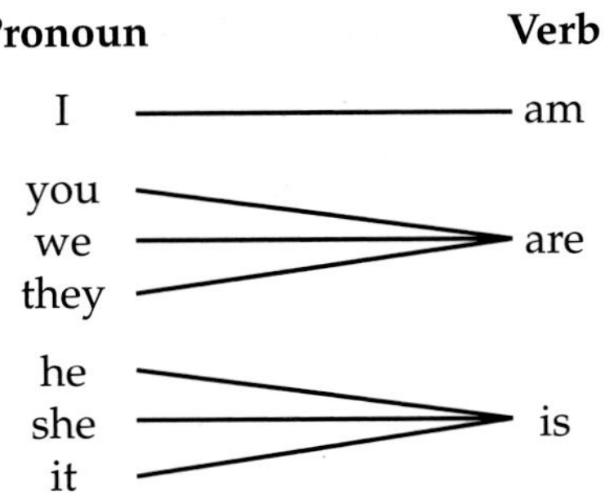

PRACTICE 4

Use the charts to fill in the present tense form of *to be* that agrees with the subject.

1. She ____is____ a member of the Olympic softball team.
2. We ____are____ both carpenters, but he ____is____ more skilled than I.
3. We ____are____ sorry about your accident; you ____are____ certainly unlucky with rollerblades.
4. They ____are____ salmon fishermen.
5. He ____is____ a drummer in the firefighters' band.
6. I ____am____ a secret jazz singer.
7. Because she ____is____ a native of Morocco, she ____is____ able to speak both Arabic and French.
8. I ____am____ too nervous to sleep because we ____are____ having an accounting exam tomorrow.
9. So you ____are____ the one we have heard so much about!
10. It ____is____ freezing outside, but she ____is____ opening all the windows.
11. Of course we ____are____ excited about the rodeo.
12. Try this seafood soup; it ____is____ delicious.
13. They ____are____ interpreters at the United Nations.
14. I ____am____ sure that she ____is____ a marine biologist.
15. If it ____is____ sunny tomorrow, we ____are____ going hot air ballooning.

PART C Troublesome Verb in the Present Tense: TO HAVE

Reference Chart: TO HAVE
(*present tense*)

Singular		Plural	
If the subject is ↓	the verb is ↓	If the subject is ↓	the verb is ↓
1st person: I	have	1st person: we	have
2nd person: you	have	2nd person: you	have
3rd person: he / she / it	has	3rd person: they	have

The chart on page 93 also can be read like this:

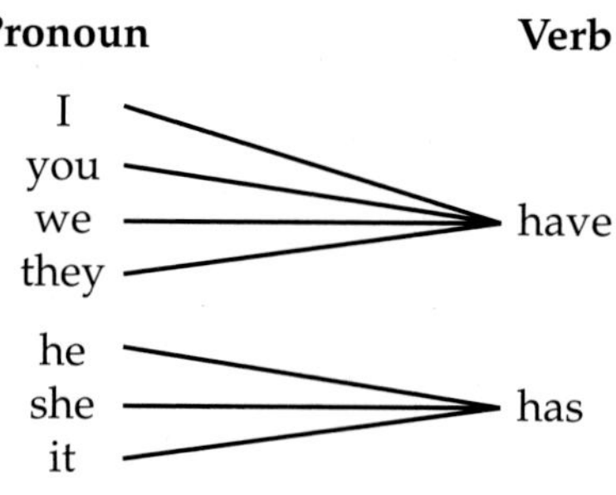

PRACTICE 5

Fill in the present tense form of *to have* that agrees with the subject. Use the charts.

1. He __has__ a cabin on Lake Superior.
2. You __have__ a wonderful sense of style.
3. We __have__ to taste these pickled mushrooms.
4. It __has__ to be spring because the cherry trees __have__ pink blossoms.
5. She __has__ the questions, and he __has__ the answers.
6. You __have__ a suspicious look on your face, and I __have__ to know why.
7. They __have__ plans to build a fence, but we __have__ plans to relax.
8. You __have__ one ruby earring, and she __has__ the other.
9. It __has__ to be repaired, and I __have__ just the person to do it for you.
10. If you __have__ $50, they __have__ an offer you can't refuse.

PART D Troublesome Verb in the Present Tense: TO DO (+ *NOT*)

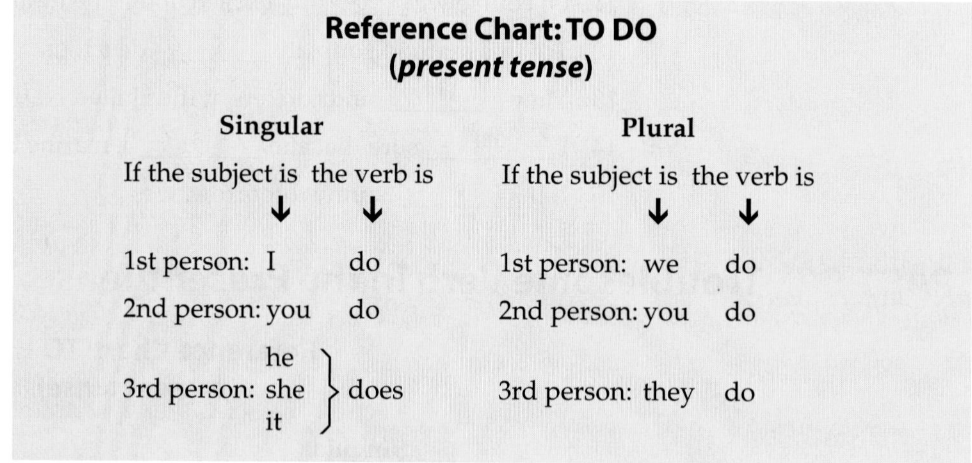

Reference Chart: TO DO
(*present tense*)

Singular		**Plural**	
If the subject is ↓	the verb is ↓	If the subject is ↓	the verb is ↓
1st person: I	do	1st person: we	do
2nd person: you	do	2nd person: you	do
3rd person: he / she / it	does	3rd person: they	do

The chart also can be read like this:

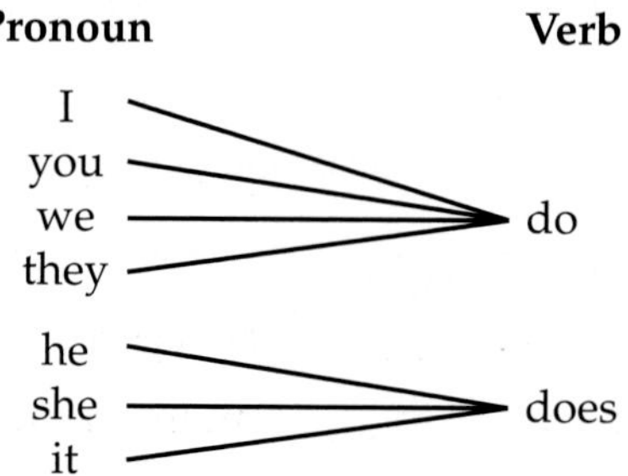

PRACTICE 6

Use the charts to fill in the correct present tense form of *to do.*

1. She always __does__ well in math courses.
2. I always __do__ badly under pressure.
3. It __does__ matter if you forget to vote.
4. They most certainly __do__ sell muscle shirts.
5. You __do__ the nicest things for people!
6. If you __do__ the dishes, I'll __do__ the laundry.
7. He __does__ seem sorry about forgetting your dog's birthday.
8. You sometimes __do__ surprise me.
9. __Do__ they dance the tarantella?
10. __Does__ she want to be a welder?

To Do + Not

Once you know how to use *do* and *does,* you are ready for *don't* and *doesn't.*

do + not = don't
does + not = doesn't

PRACTICE 7

In the Positive columns, fill in the correct form of *to do* (*do* or *does*) to agree with the pronoun. In the Negative columns, fill in the correct form of *to do* with the negative *not* (*don't* or *doesn't*).

Pronoun	Positive	Negative
1. he	does	doesn't
2. we	do	don't
3. I	do	don't
4. they	do	don't
5. she	does	doesn't
6. they	do	don't
7. it	does	doesn't
8. you	do	don't

PRACTICE 8

Fill in either *doesn't* or *don't* in each blank.

1. If they __don't__ turn down that music, I'm going to scream.
2. It just __doesn't__ make sense.
3. You __don't__ have to reply in writing.
4. He __doesn't__ always lock his door at night.
5. We __don't__ mind the rain.

6. If she ___doesn't___ stop calling collect, I ___don't___ want to talk to her.
7. He ___doesn't___ know the whole truth, and they ___don't___ want to know.
8. They ___don't___ want to miss *Larry King Live* tonight.
9. Although you ___don't___ like biking five miles a day to work, it ___doesn't___ do your health any harm.
10. When I ___don't___ try, I ___don't___ succeed.

PRACTICE 9 REVIEW

As you read this paragraph, fill in the correct present tense form of *be, have,* or *do* in each sentence. Make sure all your verbs agree with their subjects.

ESL TIP
To help ESL students improve their error recognition, ask them to read a paper aloud, stopping every time they see or hear an error. If students read past an error, you will know which errors they cannot yet identify.

(1) He ___has___ the expertise of a Tom Cruise or Angelina Jolie, but he ___is___ the real thing, not a movie hero performing fantasy stunts. (2) Right now, he ___is___ calm, even though he ___is___ ready to leap from the open door of a Navy aircraft. (3) On his back he ___has___ an oversized parachute capable of supporting both him and the extra hundred pounds of special equipment packed in his combat vest. (4) When he ___does___ hit the water, he ___is___ ready to face the real challenge: finding and defusing a bomb sixty feet under rough, murky seas. (5) He ___has___ a mission and a very tight time frame, and he ___does___ not want to let the enemy know he ___is___ there. (6) Swimming underwater in special scuba gear, he ___does___ not release any air bubbles to mark the water's surface. (7) Working in semidarkness, performing dangerous technical tasks, he quickly ___does___ the job. (8) However, unlike media heroes, he ___does___n't work alone. (9) He ___is___ a member of a highly trained team of Navy SEALs. (10) Among the most respected special forces in the world, they ___are___ commando divers ready for hazardous duty on sea, air, and land.

PART E Changing Subjects to Pronouns

So far, you have worked on pronouns as subjects (*I, you, he, she, it, we, they*) and on how to make verbs agree with them. Often, however, the subject of a sentence is not a pronoun but a noun—like *dog, banjo, Ms. Callas, José and Robert, swimming* (as in *Swimming keeps me fit*).

To be sure that your verb agrees with your subject, *mentally* change the subject into a pronoun and then select the correct form of the verb.

If the subject is	**it can be changed to the pronoun**
1. the speaker himself or herself →	I
2. masculine and singular (*Bill, one man*) →	he
3. feminine and singular (*Sondra, a woman*) →	she
4. neither masculine nor feminine and singular (a thing or an action) (*this pen, love, running*) →	it
5. a group that includes the speaker (I) (*the family and I*) →	we
6. a group of persons or things not including the speaker (*Jake and Wanda, several pens*) →	they
7. the person or persons spoken to →	you

PRACTICE 10

Change the subjects into pronouns. REMEMBER: If you add *I* to a group of people, the correct pronoun for the whole group is *we;* if you add *you* to a group, the correct pronoun for the whole group is *you.*

	Possible Subject	**Pronoun**
EXAMPLE:	Frank	he
	1. a huge moose	it
	2. a calculator and a checkbook	they
	3. Sheila	she
	4. my buddies and I	we
	5. you and the other actors	you
	6. the silk scarf	it
	7. Frank and Ted	they
	8. her son	he
	9. their power drill	it
	10. scuba diving	it

PRACTICE 11 REVIEW

Change each subject into a pronoun. Then circle the present tense verb that agrees with that subject. (Use the reference chart if you need to.)

EXAMPLES: Harry = ___he___ Harry (whistle, (whistles)).

Sam and I = ___we___ Sam and I ((walk,) walks).

1. Camilla = she
2. Their concert = it
3. You and Ron = you
4. The men and I = we
5. This blender = it
6. This beach = it
7. Our printer = it
8. Folk dancing = it
9. The museum and garden = they
10. Aunt Lil and I = we

1. Camilla (own, owns) a horse farm.
2. Their concert (is, are) sold out.
3. You and Ron (seem, seems) exhausted.
4. The men and I (repair, repairs) potholes.
5. This blender (grate, grates) cheese.
6. This beach (is, are) deserted.
7. Our printer (jam, jams) too often.
8. Folk dancing (is, are) our current passion.
9. The museum and garden (is, are) open.
10. Aunt Lil and I (like, likes) Swedish massages.

PART F Practice in Agreement

PRACTICE 12 REVIEW

TEACHING TIP
Practice 12 works well for in-class review. In addition, the content, photo, and Web link usually prompt vigorous discussion, critical thinking, and writing ideas.

Circle the correct verb in each sentence, making sure it agrees with its subject.

Selling Students—or Selling Them Out?

(1) (Does, Do) you believe that school (is, are) the one place free from commercials and advertisements? (2) Sadly, this (is, are) not true, according to Adbusters, a group concerned about commercialism in schools. (3) Many schools today (allows, allow) advertisers to address the captive audience of students through ads, lessons, and even textbooks. (4) Researchers (says, say) that all these tactics (builds, build) brand loyalty.

(5) Some schools (sells, sell) ad space for brand-name products—in the hallways, on the sides of school buses, or on bathroom walls. (6) YouthStream message boards (exists, exist) in 7,200 high school locker rooms nationwide. (7) Millions of American high school students (sees, see) the product advertisements on these boards each day.

(8) Furthermore, many teachers (uses, use) free lessons prepared by manufacturers. (9) For example, Kellogg (offers, offer) an art project in which students (makes, make) a sculpture from Rice Krispies cereal. (10) The Procter & Gamble company (has, have) an oral hygiene lesson with free samples of Crest toothpaste. (11) In one game, kids (figures, figure) out the number of chocolate chips in a Chips Ahoy cookie.

(12) Most people (thinks, think) that textbooks, at least, (is, are) free of ads. (13) However, some books (influences, influence) kids' buying behavior. (14) For instance, one company (publishes, publish) a sixth-grade math textbook with brand names mentioned in the equations. (15) The math problems (introduces, introduce) students to Burger King Whoppers, Nike shoes, and other products.

(16) Some adults (is, are) working to make schools commercial free. (17) Legislators in California (has, have) outlawed product placements in textbooks. (18) Activists (wants, want) to limit electronic advertising in schools. (19) The Adbusters group (publishes, publish) examples of brand-name brainwashing in schools and (encourages, encourage) citizens to protest. (20) Complaining to principals and school officials (helps, help) young minds stay focused on the Three R's, not shopping.

Adbusters' poster for commercial-free schools.

Reprinted by permission of Adbusters.

You can stare at ads in the bathroom and watch Channel 1 in class or . . . you can AIM HIGHER and make your school an ad-free zone.

EXPLORING ONLINE

<http://www.mediafamily.org/facts/facts_adsinschool_print.shtml> Are commercials in schools really so bad? Visit the website of the Institute on Media and the Family, and read the examples of in-school advertising. Then write a paper arguing for or against product advertisements in schools.

PRACTICE 13 REVIEW

In each blank, write the *present tense* form of one of the verbs from this list. Your sentences can be funny; just make sure that each verb agrees with each subject.

leap	spin	yip	woof	attend	win	compete
go	love	try	prance	wiggle	fly	encourage

(1) Dogs of every size and shape, their owners, and visitors all ___attend___ the Great American Mutt Show. (2) Sponsored by Tails in Need, the Mutt Show ___encourages___ people to adopt mixed-breed dogs instead of buying pure breeds. (3) Pooches ___compete___ in categories like Mostly Terrier, Most Misbehaved, Best Kisser, and Best Lap Dog Over 50 Pounds. (4) In one event, a shepherd mix named Top Gun ___leaps___ through the air to be crowned Best Jumper while a beagle named Jack ___spins___ his stumpy tail, energetically claiming the coveted trophy for Best Wag. (5) Four-legged hopefuls ___yip___ and ___woof___, trying to snag the award for Best Bark. (6) The proud winner of Best in Show ___goes___ home with a trophy designed by Michael Graves—a red fire hydrant topped by a golden bone.

PRACTICE 14 REVIEW

The sentences that follow have singular subjects and verbs. To gain skill in verb agreement, rewrite each sentence, changing the subject from *singular* to *plural*. Then make sure the verb agrees with the new subject. Keep all verbs in the present tense.

EXAMPLE: The train stops at Cold Spring.

Rewrite: The trains stop at Cold Spring.

1. The movie ticket costs too much.

   Rewrite: The movie tickets cost too much.

2. The pipeline carries oil from Alaska.

   Rewrite: The pipelines carry oil from Alaska.

3. A white horse grazes by the fence.

   Rewrite: White horses graze by the fence.

4. My brother knows American Sign Language.

   Rewrite: My brothers know American Sign Language.

5. The family needs good health insurance.

   Rewrite: The families need good health insurance.

6. The backup singer wears green contact lenses.

   Rewrite: The backup singers wear green contact lenses.

7. My niece wants an iguana.

   Rewrite: My nieces want an iguana.

8. A wave laps softly against the dock.

   Rewrite: Waves lap softly against the dock.

PRACTICE 15 REVIEW

The sentences that follow have plural subjects and verbs. Rewrite each sentence, changing the subject from *plural* to *singular*. Then make sure the verb agrees with the new subject. Keep all verbs in the present tense.

1. My cousins raise sheep.

   Rewrite: My cousin raises sheep.

2. The engines roar loudly.

   Rewrite: The engine roars loudly.

3. The students manage money wisely.

   Rewrite: The student manages money wisely.

4. The inmates watch *America's Most Wanted*.

   Rewrite: The inmate watches *America's Most Wanted.*

5. Overhead, seagulls ride on the wind.

   Rewrite: Overhead, a seagull rides on the wind.

6. Good card players know when to bluff.

   Rewrite: A good card player knows when to bluff.

7. On Saturday, the pharmacists stay late.

   Rewrite: On Saturday, the pharmacist stays late.

8. The jewels from Bangkok are on display.

   Rewrite: The jewel from Bangkok is on display.

PRACTICE 16 REVIEW

TEACHING TIP
Practice 16 makes an enjoyable class exercise. Ask a volunteer to read the paragraph aloud in the *present tense*, changing each verb on the spot. Ask another to repeat the exercise while the class listens for correct agreement.

Rewrite this paragraph in the present tense by changing the verbs. Write the present tense form of each verb above the lines. (Hint: You should change twenty-two verbs.)

watches whacks
(1) A six-month-old in a highchair watched intently as his father whacked golf
starts
balls into a net in the family garage. (2) When the baby started to walk, his
give drags
parents gave him a short putter, which he dragged around the house. (3) When he
is picks does
was nine months old, he carefully picked up the putter. (4) The child did an exact

imitation of his father's hip swivel, swung [swings], and sent [sends] the ball perfectly into the net. (5) Thunderstruck, the father and mother realized [realize] that they had [have] a golf genius on their hands. (6) From the age of eighteen months, the toddler practiced [practices] his pitch and putt strokes on a golf course. (7) At age three, on a TV show, the little boy exclaimed [exclaims] that he wanted [wants] to beat Jack Nicklaus some day. (8) In fact, he did [does] that at age twenty-one, winning the Masters with the lowest score in tournament history. (9) Suddenly, people all over the world knew [know] the name Tiger Woods. (10) At twenty-four, Tiger shattered [shatters] U.S. Open records by a twelve under par and a fifteen-stroke victory and tied [ties] Nicklaus's record of the lowest score ever in a U.S. Open. (11) His influence was [is] enormous. (12) Young people saw [see] golf as exciting, and the game had [has] thousands of new fans.

PART G Special Problems in Agreement

TEACHING TIP
The special problems in Part G are tricky for many students and may need extra explanation and practice.

So far, you have learned that if the subject of a sentence is third person singular (*he, she, it*) or a word that can be changed into *he, she,* or *it*, the verb takes *-s* or *-es* in the present tense.

In special cases, however, you will need to know more before you can make your verb agree with your subject.

Focusing on the Subject

(1) A box of chocolates sits on the table.

TEACHING TIP
If students erroneously make the verb agree with the object of the preposition in these constructions, remind them to cross out the intervening prepositional phrase and then verify agreement.

- *What* sits on the table?
- Don't be confused by the prepositional phrase before the verb—*of chocolates.*
- Just one *box* sits on the table.
- *A box* is the subject. *A box* takes the third person singular verb—*sits.*

A box (of chocolates) sits on the table.
↓ subject (*singular*) ↓ verb (*singular*)

(2) The children in the park play for hours.

- *Who* play for hours?
- Don't be confused by the prepositional phrase before the verb—*in the park.*
- *The children* play for hours.
- *The children* is the subject. *The children* takes the third person plural verb—*play.*

The children (in the park) play for hours.
subject
(plural)
verb
(plural)

(3) The purpose of the exercises is to improve your spelling.

- *What* is to improve your spelling?
- Don't be confused by the prepositional phrase before the verb—*of the exercises.*
- *The purpose* is to improve your spelling.
- *The purpose* is the subject. *The purpose* takes the third person singular verb—*is.*

The purpose (of the exercises) is to improve your spelling.
subject
(singular)
verb
(singular)

As you can see from these examples, sometimes what seems to be the subject is really not the subject. Prepositional phrases (groups of words beginning with *of, in, at,* and so on) *cannot* contain the subject of a sentence. One way to find the subject of a sentence that contains a prepositional phrase is to ask yourself *what makes sense as the subject.*

My friends from the old neighborhood often { visits / visit } me.

- Which makes sense as the subject of the sentence: *my friends* or *the old neighborhood?*

(a) My friends . . . visit me.

(b) The old neighborhood . . . visits me.

- Obviously, sentence (a) makes sense; it clearly expresses the intention of the writer.

PRACTICE 17

Now try these sentences. Cross out any confusing prepositional phrases and circle the correct verb.

1. The blue jays ~~in my yard~~ (squawk, squawks) loudly.
2. The traffic lights ~~along Clark Street~~ (blink, blinks) to a salsa beat.
3. The price ~~of the repairs~~ (seem, seems) high.
4. His popularity ~~with teenagers~~ (amaze, amazes) me.
5. The coffee stains ~~on his résumé~~ (show, shows) his carelessness.
6. The secret ~~to success~~ (is, are) often persistence.
7. The cause ~~of many illnesses~~ (is, are) poor diet.

8. The polar bear ~~in the zoo~~ (miss, misses) the Arctic.
9. My cousins ~~from Kenya~~ (run, runs) in marathons.
10. The laboratories ~~on the fifth floor~~ (has, have) new equipment.

Spotting Special Singular Subjects

Either of the students *Neither* of the students *Each* of the students *One* of the students *Every one* of the students	seems happy.

- *Either, neither, each, one,* and *every one* are the real subjects of these sentences.
- *Either, neither, each, one,* and *every one* are special singular subjects. They always take a singular verb.
- REMEMBER: The subject is never part of a prepositional phrase, so *the students* cannot be the subject.

PRACTICE 18

Circle the correct verb.

1. One of the forks (is, are) missing.
2. Each of my brothers (wear, wears) cinnamon after-shave lotion.
3. Each of us (carry, carries) a snakebite kit.
4. Neither of those excuses (sound, sounds) believable.
5. One of the taxi drivers (see, sees) us.
6. Either of the watches (cost, costs) about $30.
7. Neither of those cities (is, are) the capital of Brazil.
8. One of the butlers (commit, commits) the crime, but which one?
9. One of the desserts in front of you (do, does) not contain sugar.
10. Each of the cars (have, has) a CD player.

PRACTICE 19

On separate paper, write five sentences using the special singular subjects. Make sure your sentences are in the present tense.

Using THERE to Begin a Sentence

(1) *There* is a squirrel in the yard.

(2) *There* are two squirrels in the yard.

- Although sentences sometimes begin with *there, there* cannot be the subject of a sentence.
- Usually, the subject *follows* the verb in sentences that begin with *there.*

To find the real subject (so you will know how to make the verb agree), mentally drop the word *there* and rearrange the sentence to put the subject at the beginning.

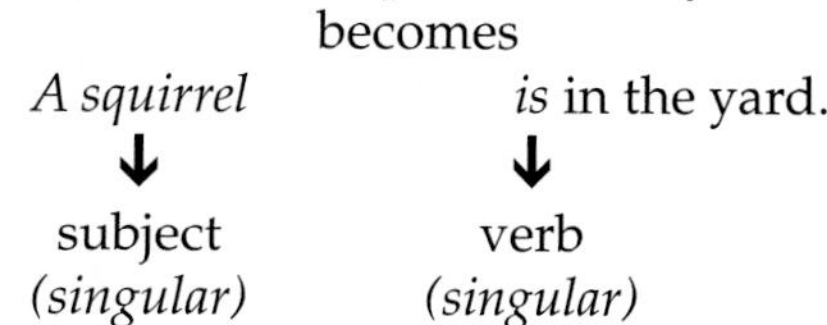
(1) There is a squirrel in the yard.
becomes
A squirrel
is in the yard.
subject
(singular)
verb
(singular)

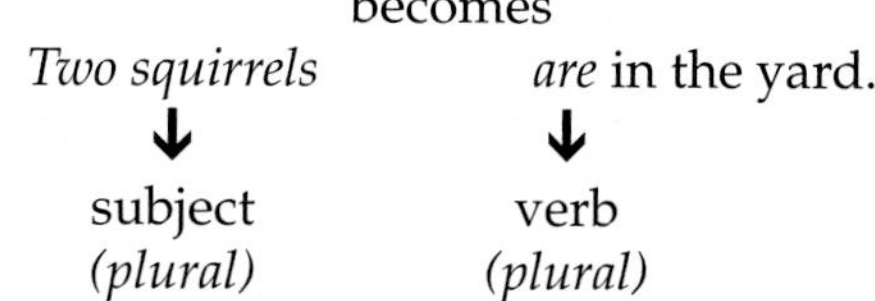
(2) There are two squirrels in the yard.
becomes
Two squirrels
are in the yard.
subject
(plural)
verb
(plural)

BE CAREFUL: Good writers avoid using *there* to begin a sentence. Whenever possible, they write more directly: *Two squirrels are in the yard.*

PRACTICE 20

In each sentence, mentally drop the word *there* and rearrange the sentence to put the subject at the beginning. Then circle the verb that agrees with the subject of the sentence. Answers to Practice 21 are above the lines.

A daycare center is on campus.
1. There (is, are) a daycare center on campus.

A scarecrow hangs near the barn.
2. There (is, are) a scarecrow near the barn.

Two scarecrows are near the barn.
3. There (is, are) two scarecrows near the barn.

One good reason to quit this job is my supervisor.
4. There (is, are) one good reason to quit this job—my supervisor.

Six customers are waiting ahead of you.
5. There (is, are) six customers ahead of you.

A water fountain is in the lounge.
6. There (is, are) a water fountain in the lounge.

A house and a barn stand in the wheat field.
7. There (is, are) a house and a barn in the wheat field.

Only two shopping days are left before my birthday.
8. There (is, are) only two shopping days left before my birthday.

Thousands of plant species grow in the rain forest.
9. There (is, are) thousands of plant species in the rain forest.

A single blue egg is in the nest over the kitchen door.
10. There (is, are) a single blue egg in the nest over the kitchen door.

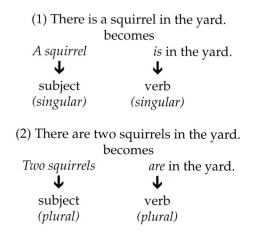

PRACTICE 21

On paper or on a computer, rewrite each sentence in Practice 20 so that it does not begin with *there is* or *there are*. (You may add or change a word or two if you like.) Sentences (1) and (2) are done for you. Answers to Practice 21 are above the lines in Practice 20. Answers will vary.

EXAMPLES: 1. A daycare center is on campus.
2. A scarecrow hangs near the barn.

Choosing the Correct Verb in Questions

(1) Where is Bob?

(2) Where are Bob and Lee?

(3) Why are they singing?

(4) Have you painted the hall yet?

- In questions, the subject usually *follows* the verb.
- In sentence (1), the subject is *Bob. Bob* takes the third person singular verb *is*.
- In sentence (2), the subject is *Bob and Lee. Bob and Lee* takes the third person plural verb *are*.
- What is the subject in sentence (3)? they What verb does it take? third person plural verb *are* + *singing*
- What is the subject in sentence (4)? you What verb does it take? second person plural verb *have* + *painted*

If you can't find the subject, mentally turn the question around:

(1) Bob is . . .

(2) Bob and Lee are . . .

PRACTICE 22

Circle the correct verb.

1. Where (is, are) my leather bomber jacket?
2. (Have, Has) our waiter gone to lunch?
3. How (is, are) your children enjoying summer camp?
4. Who (is, are) those people on the fire escape?
5. Which (is, are) your day off?
6. Why (do, does) she want to buy another motorcycle?
7. (Have, Has) you considered taking a cruise next year?
8. Where (is, are) Don's income tax forms?
9. (Have, Has) the groundhog raided the zucchini patch today?
10. Well, what (do, does) you know about that?

PRACTICE 23

On paper or on a computer, write five questions of your own. Make sure that your questions are in the present tense and that the verbs agree with the subjects.

Using WHO, WHICH, and THAT as Relative Pronouns

When you use a **relative pronoun**—*who, which,* or *that*—to introduce a dependent idea, make sure you choose the correct verb.*

(1) I know a woman *who* plays expert chess.

- Sentence (1) uses the singular verb *plays* because *who* relates or refers to *a woman* (singular).

(2) Suede coats, *which* stain easily, should not be worn in the rain.

- Sentence (2) uses the plural verb *stain* because *which* relates to the subject *suede coats* (plural).

(3) Computers *that* talk make me nervous.

- Sentence (3) uses the plural verb *talk* because *that* relates to what word?
  computers

PRACTICE 24

Write the word that the *who, which,* or *that* relates or refers to in the blank at the right; then circle the correct form of the verb.

EXAMPLE: I like people who (is, are) creative. people

1. My office has a robot that (fetch, fetches) the mail. robot
2. Never buy food in cans that (have, has) dents in them. cans
3. My husband, who (take, takes) marvelous photographs, won the Nikon Prize. husband
4. He likes women who (is, are) very ambitious. women
5. The old house, which (sit, sits) on a cliff above the sea, is called Balston Heights. house
6. Students who (love, loves) to read usually write well. students

*For work on relative pronouns, see Chapter 17.

7. I like a person who (think, thinks) for himself or herself. person
8. The only airline that (fly, flies) to Charlottesville is booked solid. airline
9. People who (live, lives) in glass houses should invest in blinds. people
10. Most students want jobs that (challenge, challenges) them. jobs

PRACTICE 25 REVIEW

Proofread the following paragraph for a variety of verb agreement errors. First underline all present tense verbs. Then correct any errors above the lines.

(1) Many people who love exciting theater admire admires Anna Deavere Smith. (2) She is well known for her thought-provoking plays. (3) Many of these dramas explore explores social conflicts in America, bringing important issues to life through the voices of different characters. (4) Smith's newest play, *House Arrest: First Edition*, probes probe the relationship between the media and the White House. (5) Politicians, journalists, and worried citizens, played by a variety of actors, all speak out. (6) In other shows, Smith brilliantly plays all the roles herself. (7) For example, one show, *Twilight: Los Angeles 1992,* examines examine the L.A. riots and the beatings of Rodney King and Reginald Denny. (8) Smith, who is African American, movingly expresses the feelings of white people, black people, Korean shopkeepers, angry rioters, and frightened citizens. (9) Once a shy and withdrawn child, Anna Deavere Smith works to open herself to the experiences of others. (10) She believes believe that both successful acting and successful democracy require requires us to grow in tolerance.

PRACTICE 26 WRITING ASSIGNMENT

In a group of three or four classmates, choose an area of the building or campus that contains some interesting action—the hallway, the cafeteria, or a playing field. Go there now and observe what you see, recording details and using verbs in the present tense. Choose as many good action verbs as you can. Keep observing and writing for ten minutes. Then head back to the classroom and write a first draft of a paragraph.

Next, exchange papers within your group. The reader should underline every verb, checking for verb agreement, and tell the writer what he or she liked about the writing and what could be improved.

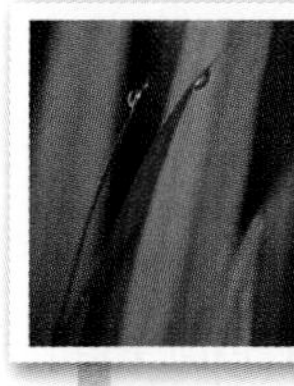

CHAPTER HIGHLIGHTS

- **A subject and a present tense verb must agree:**

  The light flickers. (*singular subject, singular verb*)

  The lights flicker. (*plural subject, plural verb*)

- **Only third person singular subjects (*he, she, it*) take verbs ending in *-s* or *-es*.**
- **Three troublesome present tense verbs are *to be, to have,* and *to do*.**
- **When a prepositional phrase comes between a subject and a verb, the verb must agree with the subject.**

  The *chairs* on the porch *are* painted white.

- **The subjects *either, neither, each, one,* and *every one* are always singular.**

  Neither of the mechanics *repairs* transmissions.

- **In a sentence beginning with *there is* or *there are*, the subject follows the verb.**

  There are three *oysters* on your plate.

- **In questions, the subject usually follows the verb.**

  Where are *Kimi and Fred?*

- **Relative pronouns (*who, which,* and *that*) refer to the word with which the verb must agree.**

  A *woman who* has children must manage time skillfully.

CHAPTER REVIEW

Proofread this essay carefully for verb agreement. First, underline all present tense verbs. Then correct each verb agreement error.

TEACHING TIP
This practice models the "advantages and disadvantages" approach—a paragraph or essay structure that students might try.

Advantages and Disadvantages of Online Dating

(1) Every month, about 40 million Americans visits [visit] online dating sites like Match.com and Matchmaker.com. (2) In fact, these sites now make more money than any other paid service on the Web. (3) Clearly, many people no longer feels [feel] embarrassed about using a dating service. (4) But are websites really good places to find a mate? (5) You decide. (6) There is [are] both advantages and disadvantages to cyberdating.

(7) Some busy people likes [like] the convenience of online dating and the chance to meet people at any time of day or night. (8) The Web makes a better meeting place than bars, they argue. (9) In addition, the sites allow individuals to search for mates with certain qualities or characteristics. (10) According to supporters of cyberdating, this method also encourage [encourages] people to get to know possible romantic partners better. (11) In cyberspace, they are less likely to be swept away by physical attraction alone.

(12) However, computer dating also have [has] dangers and drawbacks. (13) Online, many people tends [tend] to lie about their physical appearance, age, profession, or personality traits. (14) According to a recent study, about three out of ten people using online sites are married. (15) Others has [have] criminal backgrounds. (16) Therefore, safety remain [remains] a constant concern for cyberdaters. (17) Getting to know each other online takes more time. (18) Consequently, the online environment actually slow [slows] down the dating process instead of speeding it up.

EXPLORING ONLINE

TEACHING TIP
More practice and assessment are available in the *Grassroots* Test Bank; linked ACE tests on the *Grassroots* student website; *WriteSpace for Grassroots*; and the Exploring Online links in this chapter.

<http://depts.gallaudet.edu/englishworks/exercises/exgrammar/subver2.htm> Verb crossword puzzle: Change past tense verbs to present tense.

<http://www.ccc.commnet.edu/grammar/quizzes/svagr3.html> Interactive quiz: Choose the correct verbs in this essay about soccer.

<http://college.hmco.com/devenglish> Visit the *Grassroots* 8/e Student Website for more exercises and quizzes.

CHAPTER 9

Past Tense

PART A Regular Verbs in the Past Tense

Verbs in the past tense express actions that occurred in the past. The italicized words in the following sentences are verbs in the past tense.

ESL TIP
Verb tense can be a difficult concept for nonnative writers, requiring extra help and practice. Try using conversations or writings to elicit accounts of the past (e.g., *Where were you born? What was life like in your hometown?*), noting correct verbs.

(1) They *noticed* a dent in the fender.

(2) She *played* the guitar very well.

(3) For years I *studied* yoga.

- What ending do all these verbs take? *-d* or *-ed*
- In general, what ending do you add to put a verb in the past tense? *-d* or *-ed*
- Verbs that add *-d* or *-ed* to form the past tense are called *regular verbs*.

PRACTICE 1

TEACHING TIP
For students who don't pronounce or hear the *-ed* on regular verbs, these forms can be more problematic than irregulars. Help such students see that this is their error pattern.

Some of the verbs in these sentences are in the present tense; others are in the past tense. Circle the verb in each sentence. Write *present* in the column at the right if the verb is in the present tense; write *past* if the verb is in the past tense.

1. Ricardo (stroked) his beard. — past
2. Light (travels) 186,000 miles in a second. — present
3. They (donate) blood every six months. — present
4. Magellan (sailed) around the world. — past
5. The lake (looks) calm as glass. — present
6. Yesterday, Rover (buried) many bones. — past
7. Mount St. Helens (erupted) in 1980. — past
8. That chemical plant (pollutes) our water. — present
9. A robin (nested) in the mailbox. — past
10. He (owns) two exercise bikes. — present

PRACTICE 2

TEACHING TIP
Tense transformation exercises like this one increase verbal agility—and are fun. Try having a student read this or another present tense paragraph aloud to the class, changing all the verbs to past tense.

ESL TIP
The concept of verb tense and how to show it stymies some nonnative writers. For extra help, see Error #5: Wrong Verb Tense in the "8 Most Common ESL Errors" on the *Grassroots* student website.

Change the verbs in this paragraph to past tense by writing the past tense form above each italicized verb.

(1) Again this year, Carnival *transforms* [transformed] Rio de Janeiro, Brazil, into one of the most fantastic four-day parties on the planet. (2) On the Friday before Ash Wednesday, thousands of visitors *pour* [poured] into the city. (3) They *watch* [watched] all-night parades and *admire* [admired] the glittering costumes. (4) They *cheer,* [cheered] *sweat,* [sweated] and *dance* [danced] the samba. (5) Of course, preparation *starts* [started] long before. (6) For months, members of the samba schools (neighborhood dance clubs) *plan* [planned] their floats, *practice* [practiced] samba steps, and *stay* [stayed] up for nights making their costumes. (7) Using bright fabrics, sequins, feathers, and chains, both men and women *create* [created] spectacular outfits. (8) Each samba school *constructs* [constructed] a float that *features* [featured] a smoke-breathing dragon or a spouting waterfall. (9) During Carnival, judges *rate* [rated] the schools on costumes, dancing, and floats, and then they *award* [awarded] prizes. (10) Together, Brazilians and their visitors *share* [shared] great music, drink, food, fun, and the chance to go a little bit crazy.

As you can see from this exercise, many verbs form the past tense by adding either *-d* or *-ed*.

Furthermore, in the past tense, agreement is not a problem, except for the verb *to be*. This is because verbs in the past tense have only one form, no matter what the subject is.

PRACTICE 3

ESL TIP
Dictation, a traditional language-teaching technique, is gaining popularity with ESL teachers again. It is particularly helpful with past tense verb instruction.

The verbs have been omitted from this paragraph. Choose verbs from the list below and write a past tense form in each blank space. Do not use any of the verbs twice. Answers will vary.

arrive	cry	walk	help
install	climb	pound	learn
grab	hug	smile	work
paint	thank	shout	hurry

(1) Last month, Raoul and I ___helped___ to build a Habitat for Humanity house as part of our college's service learning program. (2) On the first day, we ___arrived___ at the construction site at dawn. (3) With three other volunteers, we ___grabbed___ our hammers and ___climbed___ onto the roof. (4) We ___pounded___ nails for hours while other volunteers ___installed___ the sheet rock walls. (5) For three weeks, we ___worked___ hard and ___learned___ a lot about plumbing, wiring, and interior finishes. (6) On our last day, the new homeowners ___cried___ with joy and ___thanked___ the whole crew.

PRACTICE 4

TEACHING TIP
You may wish to review spelling rules for adding *-d* or *-ed*: 1. If the verb ends in *e*, add *-d* (*lived, skated*); 2. If the verb ends in *y*, change the *y* to *i* and add *-ed* (*cried, applied*); 3. If the last two letters of the verb are a vowel plus a consonant (except *w* and *y*), double the consonant and add *-ed* (*tapped, committed*); 4. For all other verbs, add *-ed* (*picked, stayed, followed*).

Fill in the past tense of each verb.

1. Erik Weihenmayer, blinded at age thirteen, ___dreamed___ (dream) for years of climbing Mount Everest.
2. Mountaineers ___laughed___ (laugh) at the idea of a blind man scaling the world's tallest peak—a death trap of rock, wind, and cold.
3. But in 2001, Erik ___gathered___ (gather) a climbing team and ___started___ (start) the trek up Everest.
4. Before the climbers ___reached___ (reach) the first of several camps on the way to the top, Erik ___slipped___ (slip) into a crevasse, but he ___survived___ (survive).
5. When he finally ___stumbled___ (stumble) into the first camp, weak and dehydrated, Erik ___wondered___ (wonder) whether he had made a serious mistake.
6. Nevertheless, he and his teammates ___vowed___ (vow) to continue the climb.
7. The group ___battled___ (battle) upward through driving snow and icy winds.
8. Erik ___managed___ (manage) to keep up and even ___edged___ (edge) across the long, knife-blade ridge just below the peak, taking tiny steps and using his ice ax as an anchor.
9. Months after he began his journey, the blind mountaineer ___stepped___ (step) onto Everest's summit and ___stayed___ (stay) for ten minutes to savor his victory.
10. For many people around the world, this achievement ___symbolized___ (symbolize) the nearly unstoppable human power to reach a goal.

PART B Irregular Verbs in the Past Tense

Instead of adding *-d* or *-ed*, some verbs form the past tense in other ways.

ESL TIP
Irregular verbs can be a problem for ESL students and speakers of languages that do not include irregular verbs (e.g., Chinese). See also Error #6: Irregular Verb Errors, in the "8 Most Common ESL Errors" on the *Grassroots* student website.

(1) He *threw* a knuckle ball.

(2) She *gave* him a dollar.

(3) He *rode* from his farm into the town.

- The italicized words in these sentences are also verbs in the past tense.
- Do these verbs form the past tense by adding *-d* or *-ed?* ___no___
- *Threw, gave,* and *rode* are the past tense of verbs that do not add *-d* or *-ed* to form the past tense.
- Verbs that do not add *-d* or *-ed* to form the past tense are called *irregular verbs.*

TEACHING TIP
Tell students that many irregular verbs fall into one of three categories: 1. do not change (*cut/cut, hit/hit*); 2. change their vowel (*ride/rode, get/got, drink/drank*); 3. change completely (*teach/taught, think/thought*).

A chart listing common irregular verbs follows.

Reference Chart: Irregular Verbs

Simple Form	Past	Simple Form	Past
be	was, were	lose	lost
become	became	make	made
begin	began	mean	meant
blow	blew	meet	met
break	broke	pay	paid
bring	brought	put	put
build	built	quit	quit
burst	burst	read	read
buy	bought	ride	rode
catch	caught	ring	rang
choose	chose	rise	rose
come	came	run	ran
cut	cut	say	said
dive	dove (dived)	see	saw
do	did	seek	sought
draw	drew	sell	sold
drink	drank	send	sent
drive	drove	set	set
eat	ate	shake	shook
fall	fell	shine	shone (shined)
feed	fed	shrink	shrank (shrunk)
feel	felt	sing	sang
fight	fought	sit	sat
find	found	sleep	slept
fly	flew	speak	spoke
forget	forgot	spend	spent
forgive	forgave	spring	sprang
freeze	froze	stand	stood
get	got	steal	stole
give	gave	strike	struck
go	went	swim	swam
grow	grew	swing	swung
have	had	take	took
hear	heard	teach	taught
hide	hid	tear	tore
hold	held	tell	told
hurt	hurt	think	thought
keep	kept	throw	threw
know	knew	understand	understood
lay	laid	wake	woke
lead	led	wear	wore
leave	left	win	won
let	let	wind	wound
lie	lay	write	wrote

Learn the unfamiliar past tense forms by grouping together verbs that change from present tense to past tense in the same way. For example, some irregular verbs change *ow* in the present to *ew* in the past:

blow	blew	know	knew
grow	grew	throw	threw

Another group changes from *i* in the present to *a* in the past:

begin	began	sing	sang
drink	drank	spring	sprang
ring	rang	swim	swam

As you write, refer to the chart. If you are unsure of the past tense form of a verb that is not in the chart, check a dictionary. For example, if you look up the verb *go* in the dictionary, you will find an entry like this:

go \ went \ gone \ going

The first word listed is used to form the *present* tense of the verb (I *go,* he *goes,* and so on). The second word is the *past* tense (I *went,* he *went,* and so on). The third word is the *past participle (gone),* and the last word is the *present participle (going).*

Some dictionaries list different forms only for irregular verbs. If no past tense is listed, you know that the verb is regular and that its past tense ends in *-d* or *-ed.*

PRACTICE 5

Use the chart to fill in the correct form of the verb in the past tense.

1. Beryl Markham ____grew____ (grow) up in Kenya, East Africa.
2. As a child, this adventurer ____went____ (go) hunting with African tribesmen.
3. Once, while a lion attacked her, she ____lay____ (lie) still, thus saving her own life.
4. At age seventeen, she ____sought____ (seek) a license to train horses, becoming the first woman trainer in Kenya.
5. Her friend Tom Black ____taught____ (teach) her how to fly a small plane, the *D. H. Gipsy Moth.*
6. By her late twenties, she ____was____ (be) a licensed pilot.
7. As Africa's first female bush pilot, Markham regularly ____flew____ (fly) across East Africa, carrying supplies, mail, and passengers.
8. In 1936, she ____made____ (make) a solo flight across the Atlantic Ocean.
9. Despite poor flying conditions, fatigue, and low fuel, she ____kept____ (keep) her plane in the air for more than twenty hours.
10. Markham ____set____ (set) a record as the first woman to fly alone nonstop from England to Nova Scotia.
11. In 1942, she ____wrote____ (write) *West with the Night,* a book about her thrilling life.
12. This book ____became____ (become) a classic.

PRACTICE 6

Use the chart to fill in the correct past tense form of each verb.

How to Find a Great Job

(1) Emma ____began____ (begin) her job search in an organized way. (2) She ____thought____ (think) carefully about her interests and abilities. (3) She ____spent____ (spend) time in the library and ____read____ (read) books like

TEACHING TIP
Students enjoy discussing job-search techniques like these. Stress that lively verbs help get the job. Have students list action verbs for their respective résumés. For résumé verb lists, search "action verbs, résumés" online, or try **http://www.bc.edu/offices/careers/skills/resumes/verbs/**.

What Color Is Your Parachute? and *Job Hunting on the Internet*. (4) She also __did__ (do) online research about interesting professions at sites like Career Infonet (**http://www.acinet.org/acinet/**). (5) She __spoke__ (speak) to people with jobs that __had__ (have) special appeal for her.

(6) After Emma __understood__ (understand) her own skills and goals, she __wrote__ (write) a straightforward, one-page, error-free résumé. (7) Her clear objectives statement __told__ (tell) prospective employers about her job preferences. (8) After listing her educational experience, she __gave__ (give) her past employment, with the most recent job first. (9) She __chose__ (choose) lively action verbs like *calculated, filed, oversaw,* and *inspected* to describe her responsibilities at each job. (10) Her references __were__ (be) four people who __knew__ (know) her work well.

(11) At last, Emma __felt__ (feel) ready to answer newspaper ads, search for jobs online, and explore every lead she __got__ (get). (12) She __put__ (put) her résumé on the *monster.com* site so that hundreds of companies would see it. (13) Then, she __took__ (take) a friend's good suggestion that they interview each other to practice their skills. (14) A few days later, the phone __rang__ (ring), and Emma __made__ (make) preparations for her first job interview.

TEACHING TIP
Alert students to the *Career and Job-Search Resources* area of the *Grassroots* student website. Many links here stress the importance of English skills in careers.

PRACTICE 7

Look over the list of irregular verbs on page 114. Pick out the ten verbs that give you the most trouble and list them here.

Simple	Past	Simple	Past
________	________	________	________
________	________	________	________
________	________	________	________
________	________	________	________
________	________	________	________

Now, on paper or on a computer, write one paragraph using *all ten* verbs. Your paragraph may be humorous; just make sure your verbs are correct.

PART C Troublesome Verb in the Past Tense: TO BE

TEACHING TIP
In English, only *to be* changes in the past tense. Students might need extra help with *wasn't* and *weren't*—and the double whammy of agreement plus an apostrophe.

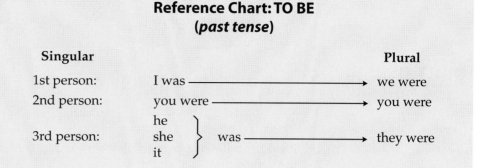

Reference Chart: TO BE
(*past tense*)

	Singular		**Plural**
1st person:	I was	→	we were
2nd person:	you were	→	you were
3rd person:	he / she / it } was	→	they were

- Note that the first and third person singular forms are the same—*was*.

PRACTICE 8

In each sentence, circle the correct past tense of the verb *to be*—either *was* or *were*.

1. Our instructor (was, were) a pilot and skydiver.
2. You always (was, were) a good friend.
3. Jorge Luis Borges (was, were) a great twentieth-century writer.
4. Why (was, were) they an hour early for the party?
5. I (was, were) seven when my sister (was, were) born.
6. Carmen (was, were) a Republican, but her cousins (was, were) Democrats.
7. The bride and groom (was, were) present, but where (was, were) the ring?
8. (Was, Were) you seasick on your new houseboat?
9. Either they (was, were) late, or she (was, were) early.
10. At this time last year, Sarni and I (was, were) in Egypt.

To Be + Not

Be careful of verb agreement if you use the past tense of *to be* with *not* as a contraction.

was + not = wasn't
were + not = weren't

PRACTICE 9

In each sentence, fill in the blank with either *wasn't* or *weren't*.

1. The printer cartridges ___weren't___ on sale.
2. That papaya ___wasn't___ cheap.
3. He ___wasn't___ happy about the opening of the nuclear power plant.
4. This fireplace ___wasn't___ built properly.
5. The parents ___weren't___ willing to tolerate drug dealers near the school.
6. That ___wasn't___ the point!

7. My pet lobster ___wasn't___ in the aquarium.
8. That history quiz ___wasn't___ so bad.
9. He and I liked each other, but we ___weren't___ able to agree about music.
10. Many young couples ___weren't___ able to afford homes.

PART D Review

PRACTICE 10 REVIEW

Read the following paragraph for meaning. Then write a different past tense verb in every blank. Sample answers

(1) In 1861, a French naturalist ___hiked___ through a dense jungle of Cambodia in Southeast Asia. (2) He ___came___ to a clearing and ___looked___ across the treetops. (3) He ___gasped___ in amazement. (4) Five enormous towers ___loomed___ above him. (5) With a pounding heart, he ___ran___ to the most gorgeous temple imaginable. (6) He ___climbed___ 250 feet to the top of the highest tower. (7) A huge abandoned city ___stretched___ for miles all around him. (8) Carvings of gods and goddesses ___decorated___ the palaces and monuments. (9) Unlike the ruins of Greece and Rome, every stone in these buildings ___was___ in place. (10) Local people ___called___ this marvelous lost city Angkor. (11) Five hundred years before, it had been the largest city in Asia. (12) Then for unknown reasons, its entire population ___disappeared___.

PRACTICE 11 REVIEW

Rewrite this paragraph, changing the verbs to the past tense.*

(1) Above the office where I work is a karate studio. (2) Every day as I go through my files, make out invoices, and write letters, I hear loud shrieks and crashes from the studio above me. (3) All day long, the walls tremble, the ceiling shakes, and little pieces of plaster fall like snow onto my desk. (4) Sometimes, the noise does not bother me; at other times, I wear earplugs. (5) If I am in a very bad mood, I stand on my desk and pound out reggae rhythms on the ceiling with my shoe. (6) However, I do appreciate one thing. (7) The job teaches me to concentrate, no matter what.

(1) Above the office where I worked was a karate studio. (2) Every day as I went through my files, made out invoices, and wrote letters, I heard loud shrieks and crashes from the studio above me. (3) All day long, the walls trembled, the ceiling shook, and little pieces of plaster fell like snow onto my desk. (4) Sometimes, the noise did not bother me; at other times, I wore

*See also Chapter 23, "Consistent Tense," for more practice.

earplugs. (5) If I was in a very bad mood, I stood on my desk and pounded out reggae rhythms on the ceiling with my shoe. (6) However, I did appreciate one thing. (7) The job taught me to concentrate, no matter what.

PRACTICE 12 WRITING ASSIGNMENT

With three or four classmates, invent a group fairy tale. Take five minutes to decide on a subject for your story. On a clean sheet of paper, the first student should write the first sentence—in the past tense, of course. Use vivid action verbs. Each student should write a sentence in turn until the fairy tale is finished.

Have a group member read your story aloud. As you listen, make sure the verbs are correct. Should any verbs be replaced with livelier ones?

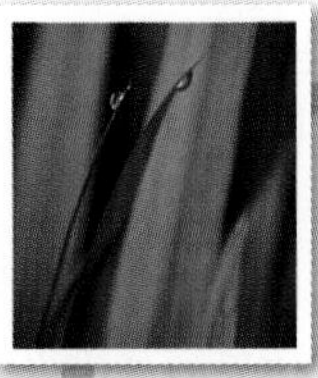

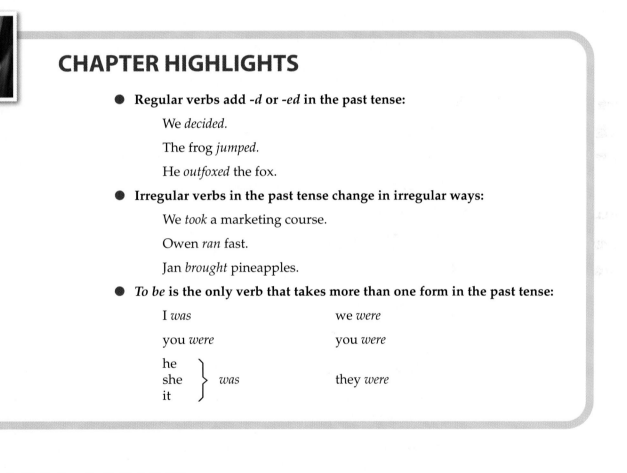

CHAPTER HIGHLIGHTS

- **Regular verbs add *-d* or *-ed* in the past tense:**

  We *decided.*

  The frog *jumped.*

  He *outfoxed* the fox.

- **Irregular verbs in the past tense change in irregular ways:**

  We *took* a marketing course.

  Owen *ran* fast.

  Jan *brought* pineapples.

- ***To be* is the only verb that takes more than one form in the past tense:**

I *was*	we *were*
you *were*	you *were*
he / she / it } *was*	they *were*

CHAPTER REVIEW

Fill in the past tense form of each verb in parentheses. Some verbs are regular; others are irregular.

Scientist and Hero

(1) Marie Curie ___led___ (lead) a heroic life. (2) Honored as one of the most brilliant scientists of the twentieth century, she also ___triumphed___ (triumph) over great hardship and loss.

(3) Born in Poland in 1867, Marie Curie ___began___ (begin) life as the daughter of a poor chemistry professor. (4) While a young woman, she ___postponed___ (postpone) her own studies and ___financed___ (finance) her older sister's medical education with the money she ___earned___ (earn) as a governess. (5) Then Curie's turn ___came___ (come). (6) She ___moved___ (move) to Paris in 1891 and ___became___ (become) the first woman to enroll in the Sorbonne, the greatest university in France. (7) For three years, she ___studied___ (study) hard and ___lived___ (live) in poverty. (8) Her work ___paid___ (pay) off. (9) The young scholar ___graduated___ (graduate) first in her class with a degree in physical science. (10) One year later, she ___completed___ (complete) another degree, in mathematics.

(11) The eleven years from 1895 to 1906 ___were___ (be) the happiest of her life. (12) She ___married___ (marry) Pierre Curie, a well-known scientist. (13) The devoted couple ___raised___ (raise) two daughters and ___worked___ (work) together every day on their research in radiation. (14) In 1898, Madame Curie ___found___ (find) two new radioactive elements. (15) One ___was___ (be) radium. (16) The other she ___called___ (call) polonium, after her native land. (17) In 1903, the Curies ___shared___ (share) the Nobel Prize in physics. (18) When the French Legion of Honor ___offered___ (offer) Pierre Curie membership, he ___refused___ (refuse) it because his wife ___was___ (be) left out.

(19) A truck ___struck___ (strike) and ___killed___ (kill) Pierre Curie in 1906. (20) This bitter blow ___drove___ (drive) Madame Curie further into her work. (21) She ___stepped___ (step) into Pierre Curie's professorship to become the first woman teacher at the Sorbonne. (22) Then, in 1911, she ___achieved___ (achieve) a second Nobel Prize, this one in chemistry.

(23) During World War I, the world-famous doctor ___risked___ (risk) her life driving an ambulance and treating soldiers at the battlefront. (24) Later, she ___established___ (establish) research centers in Paris and Warsaw, ___lectured___ (lecture) in many countries, and ___continued___ (continue) her studies. (25) Madame Curie ___died___ (die) in 1934 of cancer, caused by years of exposure to radioactivity.

EXPLORING ONLINE

TEACHING TIP
More practice and assessment are available in the *Grassroots* Test Bank; linked ACE tests on the *Grassroots* student website; *WriteSpace for Grassroots*; and the Exploring Online links in this chapter.

<http://chompchomp2.com/gbfree/irregular01/irregular01.htm> Interactive quiz: Choose the correct irregular verbs.

<http://www.ccc.commnet.edu/grammar/quizzes/chute.htm> Change present tense verbs to past in this passage from a famous book.

<http://college.hmco.com/devenglish> Visit the *Grassroots* 8/e Student Website for more exercises and quizzes.

CHAPTER 10

The Past Participle in Action

PART A Defining the Past Participle

Every verb has one form that can be combined with helping verbs like *has* and *have* to make verbs of more than one word. This form is called the **past participle.**

(1) She has solved the problem.

(2) I have solved the problem.

(3) He had solved the problem already.

- Each of these sentences contains a two-part verb. Circle the first part, or *helping verb,* in each sentence, and write each helping verb in the blanks that follow:

  (1) has

  (2) have

  (3) had

- Underline the second part, or *main verb,* in each sentence. This word, a form of the verb *to solve,* is the same in all three. Write it here: solved
- *Solved* is the past participle of *to solve.*

The past participle never changes, no matter what the subject is, no matter what the helping verb is.

PART B Past Participles of Regular Verbs

Fill in the past participle in each series below:

Present Tense	Past Tense	Helping Verb + Past Participle
(1) Beth dances.	(1) Beth danced.	(1) Beth has ___danced___.
(2) They decide.	(2) They decided.	(2) They have ___decided___.
(3) He jumps.	(3) He jumped.	(3) He has ___jumped___.

- Are the verbs *to dance, to decide,* and *to jump* regular or irregular? ___regular___ How do you know? ___The past tense ends in *-d* or *-ed.*___
- What ending does each verb take in the past tense? ___*-d* or *-ed*___
- Remember that any verb that forms its past tense by adding *-d* or *-ed* is a *regular* verb. What past participle ending does each verb take? ___*-d* or *-ed.*___

The past participle forms of regular verbs look exactly like the past tense forms. Both end in *-d* or *-ed*.

PRACTICE 1

The first sentence in each of these pairs contains a one-word verb in the past tense. Fill in the past participle of the same verb in the blank in the second sentence.

EXAMPLE: She designed jewelry all her life.

She has ___designed___ jewelry all her life.

1. Several students worked in the maternity ward.
   Several students have ___worked___ in the maternity ward.
2. The pot of soup boiled over.
   The pot of soup has ___boiled___ over.
3. The chick hatched.
   The chick has ___hatched___.
4. We congratulated Jorgé.
   We have ___congratulated___ Jorgé.
5. Nelson always studied in the bathtub.
   Nelson has always ___studied___ in the bathtub.
6. Many climbers scaled this mountain.
   Many climbers have ___scaled___ this mountain.
7. The landlord asked for a rent increase.
   The landlord has ___asked___ for a rent increase.

8. Sylvia located her long-lost cousin in New Jersey.
   Sylvia has ___located___ her long-lost cousin in New Jersey.
9. The satellite circled Jupiter.
   The satellite has ___circled___ Jupiter.
10. They signed petitions to save the seals.
    They have ___signed___ petitions to save the seals.

PRACTICE 2

Write the missing two-part verb in each of the following sentences. Use the helping verb *has* or *have* and the past participle of the verb written in parentheses.

EXAMPLE: ___Have___ you ever ___wished___ (to wish) for a new name?

1. Some of us ___have___ ___wanted___ (to want) new names at one time or another.
2. Many famous people ___have___ ___fulfilled___ (to fulfill) that desire.
3. Some ___have___ ___used___ (to use) only their first names.
4. Madonna Louise Ciccone ___has___ ___dropped___ (to drop) everything but *Madonna*.
5. Beyoncé Knowles ___has___ ___shortened___ (to shorten) her name to *Beyoncé*.
6. Other celebrities ___have___ ___retained___ (to retain) their last names and taken new first names.
7. For example, Eldrick Woods ___has___ ___turned___ (to turn) into Tiger Woods.
8. Replacing both her names, Dana Owens ___has___ ___transformed___ (to transform) herself into Queen Latifah.
9. Likewise, Marshall Bruce Mathers III ___has___ ___renamed___ (to rename) himself *Eminem*.
10. What new name would you ___have___ ___picked___ (to pick) for yourself?

PART C Past Participles of Irregular Verbs

TEACHING TIP
Students may want to use flash cards to review the past participle forms of irregular verbs. To find or create flash cards, try **<http://flashcardexchange.com/index.php>**.

ESL TIP
Some ESL teachers rely on memorization to teach irregular verb forms while others use only practice in context. A variety of approaches will address different learning and teaching styles.

Present Tense	Past Tense	Helping Verb + Past Participle
(1) He sees.	(1) He saw.	(1) He has seen.
(2) I take vitamins.	(2) I took vitamins.	(2) I have taken vitamins.
(3) We sing.	(3) We sang.	(3) We have sung.

- Are the verbs *to see, to take,* and *to sing* regular or irregular? ___irregular___
- Like all irregular verbs, *to see, to take,* and *to sing* do not add *-d* or *-ed* to show past tense.

- Most irregular verbs in the past tense are also irregular in the past participle—like *seen, taken,* and *sung*.
- Remember that past participles must be used with helping verbs.*

Because irregular verbs change their spelling in irregular ways, there are no easy rules to explain these changes. Here is a list of some common irregular verbs.

Reference Chart: Irregular Verbs

Simple Form	Past	Past Participle
be	was, were	been
become	became	become
begin	began	begun
blow	blew	blown
break	broke	broken
bring	brought	brought
build	built	built
burst	burst	burst
buy	bought	bought
catch	caught	caught
choose	chose	chosen
come	came	come
cut	cut	cut
dive	dove (dived)	dived
do	did	done
draw	drew	drawn
drink	drank	drunk
drive	drove	driven
eat	ate	eaten
fall	fell	fallen
feed	fed	fed
feel	felt	felt
fight	fought	fought
find	found	found
fly	flew	flown
forget	forgot	forgotten
forgive	forgave	forgiven
freeze	froze	frozen
get	got	gotten (got)
give	gave	given
go	went	gone
grow	grew	grown
have	had	had
hear	heard	heard
hide	hid	hidden
hold	held	held
hurt	hurt	hurt
keep	kept	kept
know	knew	known
lay	laid	laid
lead	led	led
leave	left	left
let	let	let
lie	lay	lain
lose	lost	lost

*For work on incomplete verbs, see Chapter 7, Part B.

Reference Chart: Irregular Verbs (*continued*)

Simple Form	Past	Past Participle
make	made	made
mean	meant	meant
meet	met	met
pay	paid	paid
put	put	put
quit	quit	quit
read	read	read
ride	rode	ridden
ring	rang	rung
rise	rose	risen
run	ran	run
say	said	said
see	saw	seen
seek	sought	sought
sell	sold	sold
send	sent	sent
set	set	set
shake	shook	shaken
shine	shone (shined)	shone (shined)
shrink	shrank (shrunk)	shrunk
sing	sang	sung
sit	sat	sat
sleep	slept	slept
speak	spoke	spoken
spend	spent	spent
spring	sprang	sprung
stand	stood	stood
steal	stole	stolen
strike	struck	struck
swim	swam	swum
swing	swung	swung
take	took	taken
teach	taught	taught
tear	tore	torn
tell	told	told
think	thought	thought
throw	threw	thrown
understand	understood	understood
wake	woke (waked)	woken (waked)
wear	wore	worn
win	won	won
wind	wound	wound
write	wrote	written

You already know many of these past participle forms. One way to learn the unfamiliar ones is to group together verbs that change from the present tense to the past tense to the past participle in the same way. For example, some irregular verbs change from *ow* in the present to *ew* in the past to *own* in the past participle.

blow	blew	blown
grow	grew	grown
know	knew	known
throw	threw	thrown

Another group changes from *i* in the present to *a* in the past to *u* in the past participle:

begin	began	begun
drink	drank	drunk
ring	rang	rung
sing	sang	sung
spring	sprang	sprung
swim	swam	swum

As you write, refer to the chart. If you are unsure of the past participle form of a verb that is not on the chart, check a dictionary. For example, if you look up the verb *see* in the dictionary, you will find an entry like this:

see \ saw \ seen \ seeing

The first word listed is the present tense form of the verb (*I see, she sees,* and so on). The second word listed is the past tense form (*I saw, she saw,* and so on). The third word is the past participle form (*I have seen, she has seen,* and so on), and the last word is the present participle form.

Some dictionaries list different forms only for irregular verbs. If no past tense or past participle form is listed, you know that the verb is regular and that its past participle ends in *-d* or *-ed*.

PRACTICE 3

The first sentence in each pair contains an irregular verb in the past tense. Fill in *has* or *have* plus the past participle of the same verb to complete the second sentence.

EXAMPLE: I ate too much.

I ___have___ ___eaten___ too much.

TEACHING TIP
For Practices 3 and 4, you might want to ask students to first circle the subject and ask whether it is singular or plural before choosing *has* or *have*.

1. The river rose over its banks.

   The river ___has___ ___risen___ over its banks.

2. She sold her 1956 Buick.

   She ___has___ ___sold___ her 1956 Buick.

3. For years, we sang in a barbershop quartet.

   For years, we ___have___ ___sung___ in a barbershop quartet.

4. Crime rates fell recently.

   Crime rates ___have___ ___fallen___ recently.

5. Ralph gave me a red satin bowling jacket.

   Ralph ___has___ ___given___ me a red satin bowling jacket.

6. They thought carefully about the problem.

   They ___have___ ___thought___ carefully about the problem.

7. I kept all your love letters.

   I ___have___ ___kept___ all your love letters.

8. The Joneses forgot to confirm the reservation.

   The Joneses ___have___ ___forgotten___ to confirm the reservation.

9. The pond froze solid.

   The pond ___has___ ___frozen___ solid.

10. The children knew about those caves for years.

    The children ___have___ ___known___ about those caves for years.

PRACTICE 4

Now you will be given only the first sentence with its one-word verb in the past tense. Rewrite the entire sentence, changing the verb to a two-word verb: *has* or *have* plus the past participle of the main verb.

EXAMPLE: He took his credit cards with him.

He has taken his credit cards with him.

1. They brought their Great Dane to the party.

   They have brought their Great Dane to the party.

2. T. J. drove a city bus for two years.

   T. J. has driven a city bus for two years.

3. She chose a Van Gogh poster for the hallway.

   She has chosen a Van Gogh poster for the hallway.

4. I saw a white fox near the barn.

   I have seen a white fox near the barn.

5. A tornado tore through the shopping center.

   A tornado has torn through the shopping center.

6. Margo became more self-confident.

   Margo has become more self-confident.

7. Councilman Gomez ran a fair campaign.

   Councilman Gomez has run a fair campaign.

8. The old barn stood there for years.

   The old barn has stood there for years.

9. Sam read about the islands of Fiji.

   Sam has read about the islands of Fiji.

10. Our conversations were very helpful.

    Our conversations have been very helpful.

PRACTICE 5 REVIEW

For each verb in the chart that follows, fill in the present tense (third person singular form), the past tense, and the past participle. BE CAREFUL: Some of the verbs are regular, and some are irregular.

Jennifer Lopez performs in San Juan, Puerto Rico.
© Getty Images.

PRACTICE 7 REVIEW

Now check your work in the preceding exercises or have it checked. Do you see any patterns in your errors? Do you tend to miss regular or irregular verbs? To help yourself learn, copy all four forms of each verb that you missed into your notebook in a chart like the one below. Use the chart to study.

Personal Review Chart

Simple	Present Tense (he, she, it)	Past Tense	Past Participle
go	goes	went	gone

PART D Using the Present Perfect Tense

The **present perfect tense** is composed of the present tense of *to have (has* or *have)* plus the past participle.

Present Perfect Tense

Singular	Plural
I *have* spoken	we *have* spoken
you *have* spoken	you *have* spoken
he / she / it } *has* spoken	they *have* spoken

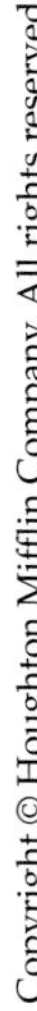

ESL TIP
The perfect tenses are not unique to English, but they are difficult for ESL students. Extra help and discussion of the differences between their native language and English may help.

Let us see how this tense is used.

(1) They *sang* together last Saturday.

(2) They *have sung* together for three years now.

- In sentence (1), the past tense verb *sang* tells us that they sang together on one occasion, Saturday, but are no longer singing together. The action began and ended in the past.
- In sentence (2), the present perfect verb *have sung* tells us something entirely different: that they have sung together in the past and *are still singing together now*.

(3) Janet *sat* on the beach for three hours.

(4) Valerie *has* just *sat* on the beach for three hours.

- Which woman is probably still sunburned? Valerie
- In sentence (3), Janet's action began and ended at some time in the past. Perhaps it was ten years ago that she sat on the beach.
- In (4), the present perfect verb *has sat* implies that although the action occurred in the past, it *has just happened,* and Valerie had better put some lotion on her sunburn *now.*
- Notice how the word *just* emphasizes that the action occurred very recently.

Use the *present perfect tense* to show either (1) that an action began in the past and has continued until now or (2) that an action has just happened.

ESL TIP
Tense sequence can be especially tricky for ESL learners. Using a tense sequence chart might help them. Try <http://www. ccc.commnet.edu/grammar/sequence.htm>

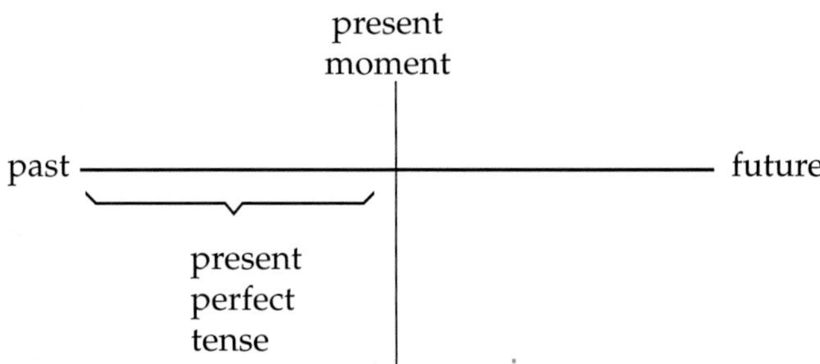

In writing about an action that began in the past and is still continuing, you will often use time words like *for* and *since.*

(5) We have watched the fireworks *for* three hours.

(6) John has sung in the choir *since* 2002.

In writing about an action that has just happened, you will often use words like *just, recently, already,* and *yet.*

(7) I have *just* finished the novel.

(8) They have *already* gone to the party.

PRACTICE 8

TEACHING TIP
Practice 8 works well in class. It promotes critical thinking, and students often are eager to discuss Kamen and the view he expresses in sentences 9 and 10.

Paying close attention to meaning, circle the verb that best completes each sentence.

EXAMPLE: Years ago, he (wanted, has wanted) to know how things worked. Since then, not much (changed, has changed).

1. Even as a young boy in New York City, Dean Kamen (loved, has loved) science and invention.
2. While just a teenager, he (got, has gotten) the job of automating the Times Square ball drop for New Year's Eve.
3. Since that time, Kamen (invented, has invented) many amazing machines, including a stair-climbing wheelchair, a robotic scooter, and a small dialysis machine.
4. For several years now, he (lived and worked, has lived and worked) in a huge, six-sided house in New Hampshire.
5. Inside and out, the house (began, has begun) to look like a fabulous science museum.
6. The collection (expanded, has expanded) to include helicopters, a steam engine, a special Humvee, and a wind turbine.
7. Some years ago, Kamen (decided, has decided) to encourage children to enter science careers.
8. In the 1990s, he (created, has created) FIRST—For Inspiration and Recognition of Science and Technology—to spark kids' interest in science and to sponsor robot-building contests.
9. In a recent speech, Kamen (said, has said), "Teenagers think they will become NBA stars and make millions, but their odds [of doing so] are less than 1 percent."
10. "However, many, many scientists and inventors (made, have made) big money and big contributions as well," he added. "Think about it."

PRACTICE 9

Fill in either the *past* tense or the *present perfect* tense form of each verb in parentheses.

(1) For the past two years, Angela Conti ___has spent___ (to spend) far too much money on clothes, restaurant meals, and gifts. (2) Like a growing number of college students, she ___has accumulated___ (to accumulate) thousands of dollars in credit card debt. (3) When Angela first ___arrived___ (to arrive) at college, she ___had___ (to have) one credit card. (4) But after credit card company representatives on campus ___offered___ (to offer) her free gifts to get more cards,

she ___opened___ (to open) three new accounts. (5) With all that "free money," Angela just ___started___ (to start) spending. (6) Now she admits that she ___has gotten___ (to get) herself into serious financial trouble. (7) Last week, she ___contacted___ (to contact) Consumer Credit Counseling Services for free help with her debt problem. (8) The counselor ___has helped___ (to help) her create a plan to stop using her cards, close all but one account, and start paying down her debt. (9) Since that meeting, Angela ___has felt___ (to feel) much better. (10) She ___has come___ (to come) to realize that she would rather have financial freedom and good credit than more "stuff."

PART E Using the Past Perfect Tense

The **past perfect tense** is composed of the past tense of *to have (had)* plus the past participle.

Past Perfect Tense

Singular	Plural
I *had* spoken	we *had* spoken
you *had* spoken	you *had* spoken
he / she / it } *had* spoken	they *had* spoken

Let us see how this tense is used.

(1) Because Bob *had broken* his leg, he *wore* a cast for six months.

- The actions in both parts of this sentence occurred entirely in the past, but one occurred before the other.
- At some time in the past, Bob *wore* (past tense) a cast on the leg that he *had broken* (past perfect tense) at some time before that.

When you are writing in the past tense, use the past perfect tense to show that something happened at an even earlier time.

TEACHING TIP

You might explain the past perfect tense as describing two actions in the past. The first action to occur will use a past perfect verb, and the second action to occur will use a simple past verb.

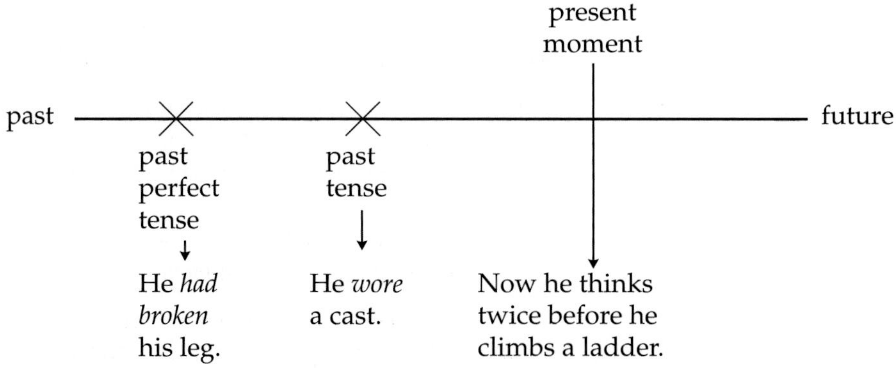

present moment

past — X — X — | — future

past perfect tense → He *had broken* his leg.

past tense → He *wore* a cast.

Now he thinks twice before he climbs a ladder.

As a general rule, the present perfect tense is used in relation to the present tense, and the past perfect tense is used in relation to the past tense. Read the following pairs of sentences and note the time relation.

(2) Sid *says* (present) he *has found* (present perfect) a good job.

(3) Sid *said* (past) he *had found* (past perfect) a good job.

(4) Grace *tells* (present) us she *has won* (present perfect) first prize.

(5) Grace *told* (past) us she *had won* (past perfect) first prize.

PRACTICE 10

Choose either the present perfect or the past perfect tense of the verb in parentheses to complete each sentence. Match present perfect tense with present tense and past perfect tense with past tense.

1. The newspaper reports that the dictator __has__ __left__ (to leave) the country.
2. The newspaper reported that the dictator __had__ __left__ (to leave) the country.
3. I plan to buy a red convertible; I __have__ __wanted__ (to want) a convertible for three years now.
4. Last year, I bought a red convertible; I __had__ __wanted__ (to want) a convertible for three years before that.
5. Mel __had__ __chosen__ (to choose) the steepest trail up the mountain; he was thoroughly worn out.
6. Mel __has__ __chosen__ (to choose) the steepest trail up the mountain; he is thoroughly worn out.
7. I am worried about my cat; she __has__ __drunk__ (to drink) bubble bath.
8. I was worried about my cat; she __had__ __drunk__ (to drink) bubble bath.
9. Sam told us that he __had__ __decided__ (to decide) to major in restaurant management.
10. Sam tells us that he __has__ __decided__ (to decide) to major in restaurant management.

PART F Using the Passive Voice

So far in this chapter, you have combined the past participle with forms of *to have.* But the past participle also can be used with forms of *to be (am, is, are, was, were).*

(1) That jam was made by Aunt Clara.

- The subject of the sentence is *that jam.* The verb has two parts: the helping verb *was* and the past participle *made.*
- Note that the subject, *that jam,* does not act but is acted on by the verb. *By Aunt Clara* tells us who performed the action.

That jam *was made* by Aunt Clara.

When the subject is acted on or receives the action, it is passive, and the verb *(to be + past participle)* **is in the** *passive voice.*

Now compare the passive voice with the active voice in these pairs of sentences:

TEACHING TIP
To help students improve their writing style, use these and other examples to show that passive voice sentences are often wordier than active voice sentences. Passive voice also allows for omission of the subject—desirable only when the subject is unknown or diplomacy is required (e.g., *The situation was mishandled*).

(2) **Passive voice:** Free gifts are given by the bank.

(3) **Active voice:** The bank gives free gifts.

(4) **Passive voice:** We were photographed by a tourist.

(5) **Active voice:** A tourist photographed us.

- In sentence (2), the subject, *free gifts,* is passive; it receives the action. In sentence (3), *the bank* is active; it performs the action.
- Note the difference between the passive verb *are given* and the active verb *gives.*
- However, the tense of both sentences is the same. The passive verb *are given* is in the present tense, and so is the active verb *gives.*
- Rewrite sentence (4) in the active voice. Be sure to keep the same verb tense in the new sentence.

Write in the passive voice only when you want to emphasize the receiver of the action rather than the doer. Usually, however, write in the active voice because sentences in the active voice are livelier and more direct.

PRACTICE 11

Underline the verb in each sentence. In the blank at the right, write *A* if the verb is written in the active voice and *P* if the verb is in the passive voice.

EXAMPLE: Nelson Mandela is respected worldwide as a leader. P

1. Nelson Mandela was born in South Africa on July 18, 1918, a member of the Xhosa tribe. P
2. Under the apartheid government, only whites, not the black majority, enjoyed basic rights. A
3. As a young lawyer, Mandela defended many black clients. A
4. They were charged with such crimes as "not owning land" or "living in the wrong area." P
5. Several times, Mandela was arrested for working with the African National Congress, a civil rights group. P
6. In 1961, he sadly gave up his lifelong belief in nonviolence. A
7. Training guerrilla fighters, he was imprisoned again, this time with a life sentence. P
8. Thirty years in jail did not break Mandela. A
9. Offered freedom to give up his beliefs, he said no. A
10. Finally released in 1990, this man became a symbol of hope for a new South Africa. A

11. In 1994, black and white South Africans lined up to vote in the first free elections. A

12. Gray-haired, iron-willed Nelson Mandela was elected president of his beloved country. P

PRACTICE 12

TEACHING TIP
If students need more practice converting sentences to active voice, have them rewrite the sentences in Practice 12, adding the missing subject where necessary.

In each sentence, underline both parts of the passive verb and circle the complete subject. Then draw an arrow from the verb to the word or words it acts on.

EXAMPLE: I was approached by Professor Martin.

1. The skaters were applauded vigorously by the crowd.
2. The corn is picked fresh every morning.
3. These flowered bowls were imported from Mexico.
4. Milos, my cat, was ignored by the mouse.
5. Hasty promises are often broken.
6. An antique train set was sold at the auction.
7. The speech was memorized by both actors.
8. Customers are lured into the store by loud music and bright signs.
9. Dutch is spoken on Curaçao.
10. Our quarrel was quickly forgotten.

PRACTICE 13

Whenever possible, write in the active, not the passive, voice. Rewrite each sentence, changing the verb from the passive to the active voice. Make all necessary verb and subject changes. Be sure to keep each sentence in the original tense.

EXAMPLE: Good medical care is deserved by all human beings.

All human beings deserve good medical care.

1. Doctors Without Borders was created by a small group of French doctors in 1971.

   A small group of French doctors created Doctors Without Borders in 1971.

2. Excellent health care was provided by them to people in poor or isolated regions.

   They provided excellent health care to people in poor or isolated regions.

3. Soon they were joined by volunteer doctors and nurses from all over the world.
   Soon volunteer doctors and nurses from all over the world joined them.

4. Today drugs and medical supplies are brought by the organization to people in need.
   Today the organization brings drugs and medical supplies to people in need.

5. Vaccinations are received by children in eighty countries.
   Children in eighty countries receive vaccinations.

6. Crumbling hospitals and clinics are restored by volunteers.
   Volunteers restore crumbling hospitals and clinics.

7. Victims of wars also are treated by the DWB staff.
   The DWB staff also treats victims of wars.

8. Information about humanitarian crises is gotten by the world.
   The world gets information about humanitarian crises.

9. Each year, thousands are given the gifts of health and life by these traveling experts.
   Each year, these traveling experts give the gifts of health and life to thousands.

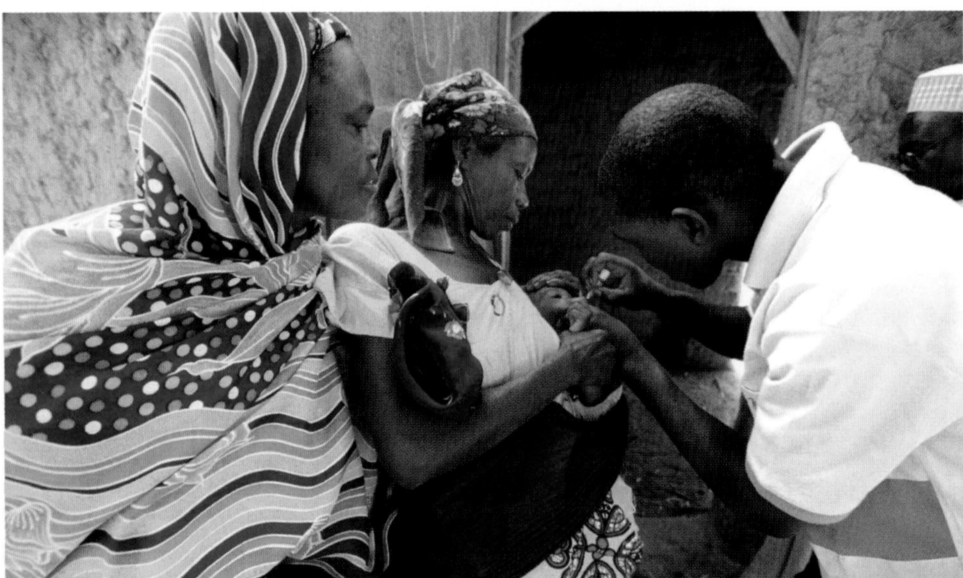

Visiting health workers fight polio in Niger.
© Getty Images.

PART G Using Past Participles as Adjectives

Sometimes the past participle is not a verb at all but an *adjective,* a word that describes a noun or pronoun.*

(1) Jay is *married.*

(2) The *broken* window looks terrible.

(3) Two *tired* students slept in the hall.

*For more work on adjectives, see Chapter 21.

ESL TIP
The use of participles as adjectives is often troublesome for ESL students. This concept might have to be reviewed throughout the term.

- In sentence (1), *married* is the past participle of the verb *to marry,* but here it is not a verb. Instead, it describes the subject, *Jay.*
- *Is* links the subject, *Jay,* with the descriptive word, *married.*
- In sentence (2), *broken* is the past participle form of *to break,* but it is used as an adjective to describe the noun *window.*
- In sentence (3), what past participle is an adjective? tired
- Which word does it describe? students

Past participles like *married, broken,* and *tired* are often used as adjectives.

Some form of the verb *to be* usually links descriptive past participles with the subjects they describe, but here are a few other common linking verbs that you learned in Chapter 6, Part E.

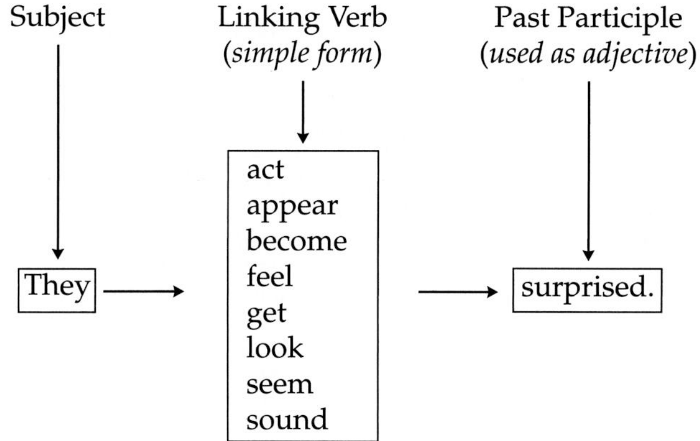

PRACTICE 14

Underline the linking verb in each sentence. Then circle the descriptive past participle or participles that complete the sentences.

EXAMPLES: The window was (polish, polished).

Harry seems very (worry, worried) these days.

1. This product is (guarantee, guaranteed) not to explode.
2. Nellie seems (qualify, qualified) for the job.
3. Your aunt appears (delight, delighted) to see you again.
4. After we read the chapter, we were still (confuse, confused).
5. The science laboratory is (air-condition, air-conditioned).
6. David feels (appreciate, appreciated) in his new job.
7. Did you know that one out of two American couples gets (divorce, divorced)?
8. We were (thrill, thrilled) to meet Venus and Serena Williams.
9. During the holidays, Paul feels (depress, depressed).
10. Are the potatoes (fry, fried), (bake, baked), or (boil, boiled)?

PRACTICE 15

Below is a list of verbs. Use the past participles of the verbs as adjectives to describe each noun in the exercise. Then use your adjective-noun combination in a sentence. Use a different past participle for each noun. Sample answers

bore	freeze	park	train
delight	hide	pollute	wear
dry	lose	tire	worry
embarrass	daze	toast	wrinkle

EXAMPLE: the ___dried___ fruit

We served the dried fruit for dessert.

1. a(n) ___worried___ man

   A worried man checked his e-mail every few minutes.

2. the ___hidden___ emeralds

   Charlie's Angels could not find the hidden emeralds.

3. these ___frozen___ muffins

   Please defrost these frozen muffins.

4. a(n) ___trained___ nurse

   A trained nurse must give the blood transfusion.

5. two ___embarrassed___ passengers

   Two embarrassed passengers searched for their train tickets.

PRACTICE 16

Proofread the following ad copy for past participle errors. First, underline all the past participles. Then make any corrections above the line.

(1) We are please [pleased] to introduce three automobiles this year, each one created by our experience [experienced] team of engineers. (2) Our racy new sport model, the Hormone, is guaranteed to provide adventure on the road. (3) It comes equip [equipped] with a powerful fuel-injected engine, steel-belt [belted] tires, and orange flames painted across the hood. (4) Growing families will prefer the Sesame ST. (5) Blue and modest on the outside, the Sesame ST's interior is make [made] for parents and children. (6) Its plastic upholstery is printed with yellow Big Bird designs. (7) Pop-out soda and hamburger holders come preinstall [preinstalled], and the sound system is program [programmed] for soft rock only, so your kids can't tune in to grunge, hard rock, or rap stations. (8) For the budget-minded car shopper, we offer the Chintz. (9) It comes equip [equipped] with a two-cylinder engine, steering wheel, and seats. (10) Recently, on *The Tonight Show with Jay Leno,* the Chintz was name [named] "the car that gives you less for less."

PRACTICE 17

Combine each pair of short sentences. First, find and underline the past participle. Then rewrite the two short sentences as one smooth sentence, using the past participle as an adjective.

EXAMPLE: The book is lost. It is worth $1,000.

The lost book is worth $1,000.

1. This rug has been dry-cleaned. It looks new.
   This dry-cleaned rug looks new.
2. His grades have fallen. He can bring them up.
   He can bring up his fallen grades.
3. The envelope was sealed. Harriet opened it.
   Harriet opened the sealed envelope.
4. The weather forecast was revised. It calls for sunshine.
   The revised weather forecast calls for sunshine.
5. These gold chains are overpriced. Do not buy them.
   Do not buy these overpriced gold chains.

PRACTICE 18

The sentences in the left column are in the present tense; those in the right column are in the past tense. If the sentence is shown in the present tense on the left, write the sentence in the past tense on the right, and vice versa. REMEMBER: Only the *linking verb*, never the past participle, changes to show tense.

EXAMPLES:

Smoking is forbidden.	Smoking was forbidden.
Lunches are served.	Lunches were served.

Present Tense	Past Tense
1. Your car is repaired.	1. Your car was repaired.
2. The store looks closed.	2. The store looked closed.
3. My feelings are hurt.	3. My feelings were hurt.
4. The seats are filled.	4. The seats were filled.
5. She is relaxed.	5. She was relaxed.
6. You seem qualified for the job.	6. You seemed qualified for the job.
7. He is supposed to meet us.*	7. He was supposed to meet us.
8. They are used to hard work.*	8. They were used to hard work.
9. It is written in longhand.	9. It was written in longhand.
10. You are expected at noon.	10. You were expected at noon.

*For more work on *supposed* and *used*, see Chapter 32, "Look-Alikes/Sound-Alikes."

PRACTICE 19 WRITING ASSIGNMENT

In a group of four or five classmates, write a wacky restaurant menu, using all the past participles that you can think of as adjectives: *steamed* fern roots, *fried* cherries, *caramel-coated* hamburgers, and so forth. Brainstorm. Get creative. Then arrange your menu in an order that makes sense (if that is the correct term for such a menu!).

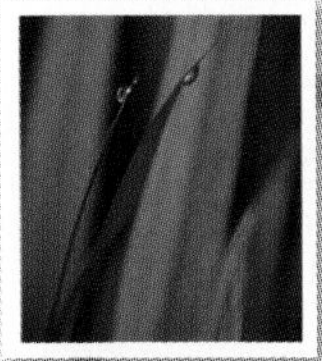

CHAPTER HIGHLIGHTS

- **Past participles of regular verbs add *-d* or *-ed*, just like their past tense forms:**

Present	Past	Past Participle
decide	decided	decided
jump	jumped	jumped

- **Past participles of irregular verbs change in irregular ways:**

Present	Past	Past Participle
bring	brought	brought
see	saw	seen
take	took	taken

- **Past participles can combine with *to have:***

  He *has edited* many articles for us. *(present perfect tense)*

  He *had edited* many articles for us. *(past perfect tense)*

- **Past participles can combine with *to be:***

  The report *was edited* by Mary. *(passive voice)*

- **Past participles can be used as adjectives:**

  The *edited* report arrived today. *(adjective)*

CHAPTER REVIEW

Proofread this student's essay for past participle errors. Correct each error above the line.

Three Ways to Be a Smarter Learner

(1) Once in a great while, a person is born with a photographic memory, allowing him or her to memorize a lot of information with almost no effort. (2) However, most of us have ~~struggle~~ struggled on our own to find the best ways to learn. (3) We have stayed up all night studying. (4) We have ~~mark~~ marked up our textbooks, highlighting and underlining like ~~skill~~ skilled tattoo artists. (5) Maybe, in frustration, we have even questioned our own intelligence. (6) Although everyone has his or her own learning style, three techniques have ~~make~~ made me and others better learners.

(7) The first technique is simple—sit at the front of the class! (8) A student who has ~~choose~~ chosen to sit up front is more likely to stay alert and ~~involve~~ involved than students at the back and sides. (9) By sitting away from windows or talkative friends, many students discover that they take a greater interest in the classroom subject and take better notes. (10) An extra benefit of sitting up front is that teachers are often ~~impress~~ impressed by students with whom they make eye contact, students whose behavior says, "I care about this class."

(11) Second, make a smart friend. (12) During the first week of class, exchange phone numbers with another front-row student. (13) You are looking for an intelligent, responsible classmate who seems committed to learning—not for a pizza buddy or a date. (14) Students who have ~~agree~~ agreed in advance to help each other can call if they miss a class. (15) What was ~~discuss~~ discussed that day? (16) Was homework ~~assign~~ assigned or a test announced? (17) Two students who "click" might want to become study partners, meeting regularly to review material and prepare for tests.

(18) Third, ask questions. (19) The student who has ~~sit~~ sat up front, made a study friend, and ~~pay~~ paid close attention in class should not be worried about asking the professor questions. (20) Learning a subject is like building a tower. (21) Each new level of understanding must be ~~build~~ built solidly on the level below. (22) If an important point or term is unclear, ask for help, in or after class.

(23) Students who use these techniques will be rewarded with ~~increase~~ increased understanding and better grades—even before they have ~~pull~~ pulled out their pastel highlighters.

Maurice Jabbar, student

EXPLORING ONLINE

TEACHING TIP
More practice and assessment are available in the *Grassroots* Test Bank; linked ACE tests on the *Grassroots* student website; *WriteSpace for Grassroots*; and the Exploring Online links in this chapter.

<http://www.ccc.commnet.edu/cgi-shl/par_quiz.pl/final-ed_add2.htm> Quiz with answers: Choose the past or past participle form.

<http://www.ccc.commnet.edu/grammar/quizzes/passive_quiz.htm> Interactive quiz: Revise these passive sentences. Make them active.

<http://college.hmco.com/devenglish> Visit the *Grassroots* 8/e Student Website for more exercises and quizzes.

CHAPTER 11

Progressive Tenses (*TO BE* + *-ING* Verb Form)

PART A Defining and Writing the Present Progressive Tense

Verbs in the *present progressive tense* have two parts: the present tense form of *to be (am, is, are)* plus the *-ing* (or present participle) form of the main verb.

Present Progressive Tense
(*example verb: to play*)

Singular	Plural
I am playing	we are playing
you are playing	you are playing
he / she / it } is playing	they are playing

Compare the present tense with the present progressive tense below.

(1) Larry works at the bookstore.

(2) Larry is working at the bookstore.

TEACHING TIP
Make sure students understand that the present progressive tense indicates ongoing or continuing action. Refer them to Part C for a more detailed explanation.

- Sentence (1) is in the present tense. Which word tells you this? works
- Sentence (2) is also in the present tense. Which word tells you this? is

- Note that the main verb in sentence (2), *working,* has no tense. Only the helping verb *is* shows tense.

PRACTICE 1

Change each one-word present tense verb in the left-hand column to a two-part present progressive verb in the right-hand column. Do this by filling in the missing helping verb (*am, is,* or *are*).

EXAMPLES:	I fly.	I __am__ flying.
	He wears my sweater.	He __is__ wearing my sweater.

Present Tense	Present Progressive Tense
1. Elsa and I set goals together.	1. Elsa and I __are__ setting goals together.
2. They eat quickly.	2. They __are__ eating quickly.
3. He plans the wedding.	3. He __is__ planning the wedding.
4. Our work begins to pay off.	4. Our work __is__ beginning to pay off.
5. We pose for the photographer.	5. We __are__ posing for the photographer.
6. Maryann smiles.	6. Maryann __is__ smiling.
7. Sal does his Elvis impression.	7. Sal __is__ doing his Elvis impression.
8. I speak Portuguese to Manuel.	8. I __am__ speaking Portuguese to Manuel.
9. My grandson gets silly.	9. My grandson __is__ getting silly.
10. You probably wonder why.	10. You __are__ probably wondering why.

REMEMBER: Every verb in the present progressive tense must have two parts: a helping verb (*am, is,* or *are*) and a main verb ending in *-ing*. The helping verb must agree with the subject.

PRACTICE 2

Below are sentences in the regular present tense. Rewrite each one in the present progressive tense by changing the verb to *am, is,* or *are* plus the *-ing* form of the main verb.

EXAMPLE: We play cards.
We are playing cards.

1. The telephone rings.
   The telephone is ringing.

2. Dexter wrestles with his math homework.
   Dexter is wrestling with his math homework.

3. James and Judy work in the emergency room.
   James and Judy are working in the emergency room.

4. I keep a journal of thoughts and observations.
   I am keeping a journal of thoughts and observations.

5. We polish all our old tools.
   We are polishing all our old tools.

PART B Defining and Writing the Past Progressive Tense

Verbs in the *past progressive tense* have two parts: the past tense form of *to be* (*was* or *were*) plus the *-ing* form of the main verb.

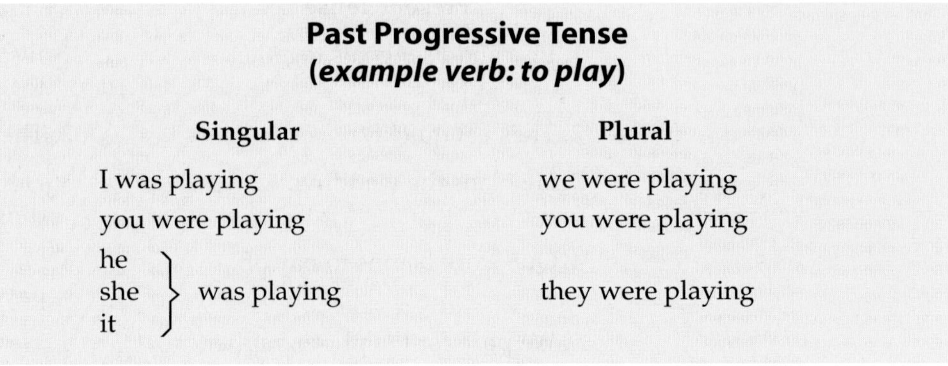

Past Progressive Tense
(*example verb: to play*)

Singular	Plural
I was playing	we were playing
you were playing	you were playing
he / she / it } was playing	they were playing

Compare the past tense with the past progressive tense below.

(1) Larry worked at the bookstore.

(2) Larry was working at the bookstore.

- Sentence (1) is in the past tense. Which word tells you this? worked
- Sentence (2) is also in the past tense. Which word tells you this? was
- Notice that the main verb in sentence (2), *working*, has no tense. Only the helping verb *was* shows tense.

PRACTICE 3

Change each one-word past tense verb in the left-hand column to a two-part past progressive verb in the right-hand column. Do this by filling in the missing helping verb (*was* or *were*).

EXAMPLES: I flew. — I was flying.
He wore my sweater. — He was wearing my sweater.

Past Tense	Past Progressive Tense
1. Elsa and I set goals together.	1. Elsa and I were setting goals together.
2. They ate quickly.	2. They were eating quickly.
3. He planned the wedding.	3. He was planning the wedding.
4. Our work began to pay off.	4. Our work was beginning to pay off.

5. We posed for the photographer.	5. We __were__ posing for the photographer.
6. Maryann smiled.	6. Maryann __was__ smiling.
7. Sal did his Elvis impression.	7. Sal __was__ doing his Elvis impression.
8. I spoke Portuguese to Manuel.	8. I __was__ speaking Portuguese to Manuel.
9. My grandson got silly.	9. My grandson __was__ getting silly.
10. You probably wondered why.	10. You __were__ probably wondering why.

PRACTICE 4

Below are sentences in the past tense. Rewrite each sentence in the past progressive tense by changing the verb to *was* or *were* plus the *-ing* form of the main verb.

EXAMPLE: You cooked dinner.
You were cooking dinner.

TEACHING TIP
For Practice 4, you might want to ask students to first circle the subject and then determine whether it is singular or plural before choosing *was* or *were*.

1. The two linebackers growled at each other.
   The two linebackers were growling at each other.
2. Leroy examined his bank receipt.
   Leroy was examining his bank receipt.
3. We watched the news.
   We were watching the news.
4. Marsha read the *Wall Street Journal*.
   Marsha was reading the *Wall Street Journal*.
5. He painted like a professional artist.
   He was painting like a professional artist.

PART C Using the Progressive Tenses

As you read these sentences, do you hear the differences in meaning?

(1) Lenore *plays* the piano.

(2) Dave *is playing* the piano.

- Which person is definitely at the keyboard right now?
- If you said Dave, you are right. He is *now in the process of playing* the piano. Lenore, on the other hand, *does* play the piano; she may also paint, write novels, and play center field, but we do not know from the sentence what she *is doing right now.*
- The present progressive verb *is playing* tells us that the action is *in progress.*

Here is another use of the present progressive tense:

(3) Tony *is coming* here later.

- The present progressive verb *is coming* shows *future* time: Tony is going to come here.

(4) Linda *washed* her hair last night.

(5) Linda *was washing* her hair when we arrived for the party.

- In sentence (4), *washed* implies a completed action.
- The past progressive verb in sentence (5) has a special meaning: that Linda was *in the process* of washing her hair when something else happened (we arrived).
- To say, "Linda *washed* her hair *when* we arrived for the party" means that first we arrived, and then Linda started washing her hair.

Writers in English use the progressive tenses *much less often* than the present tense and past tense. Use the progressive tense only when you want to emphasize that something is or was in the process of happening.

Use the *present progressive tense* (*am, is, are* + *-ing*) **to show that an action is in progress now or that it is going to occur in the future.**

Use the *past progressive tense* (*was, were* + *-ing*) **to show that an action was in progress at a certain time in the past.**

PRACTICE 5

Read each sentence carefully. Then circle the verb or verbs that best express the meaning of the sentence.

EXAMPLE: Right now, we (write, are writing) letters.

1. Thomas Edison (held, was holding) 1,093 patents.
2. Where is Ellen? She (drives, is driving) to Omaha.
3. Most mornings we (get, are getting) up at seven.
4. Believe it or not, I (thought, was thinking) about you when you phoned.
5. My dog Gourmand (eats, is eating) anything at all.
6. At this very moment, Gourmand (eats, is eating) the sports page.
7. Max (fried, was frying) onions when the smoke alarm (went, was going) off.
8. Please don't bother me now; I (study, am studying).
9. Newton (sat, was sitting) under a tree when he (discovered, was discovering) gravity.
10. The *Andrea Doria*, a huge pleasure ship, (sank, was sinking) on July 25, 1956.

PART D Avoiding Incomplete Progressives

Now that you can write both present and past progressive verbs, avoid mistakes like this one:

> We having fun. (*incomplete*)

- Can you see what is missing?
- All by itself, the *-ing* form *having* is not a verb. It has to have a helping verb.
- Because the helping verb is missing, *we having fun* has no time. It could mean *we are having fun* or *we were having fun.*
- *We having fun* is not a sentence. It is a fragment of a sentence.*

PRACTICE 6

Each group of words below is incomplete. Put an *X* over the exact spot where a word is missing. Then, in the Present Progressive column, write the word that would complete the sentence in the *present progressive tense.* In the Past Progressive column, write the word that would complete the sentence in the *past progressive tense.*

	Present Progressive	Past Progressive
EXAMPLE: He X having fun.	is	was
	(He is having fun)	(He was having fun.)
1. Fran and I X watching the sunrise.	are	were
2. You X taking a computer course.	are	were
3. A big log X floating down the river.	is	was
4. Her study skills X improving.	are	were
5. I X trying to give up caffeine.	am	was
6. Fights about money X getting me down.	are	were
7. Thick fog X blanketing the city.	is	was
8. That child X reading already.	is	was
9. Your pizza X getting cold.	is	was
10. They X discussing the terms of the new contract.	are	were

PRACTICE 7 WRITING ASSIGNMENT

Write a brief account that begins, "We are watching an amazing scene on TV. A man is trying to catch fish with his bare hands." Write four or five more sentences describing the unfolding action in the present progressive tense—as if the action is taking place right now. Then read over what you have written, checking the verbs.

Now rewrite the whole account in the past progressive tense. The new version will begin, "We were watching an amazing scene on TV. A man was trying to catch fish with his bare hands."

*For more on this type of fragment, see Chapter 7, Part B.

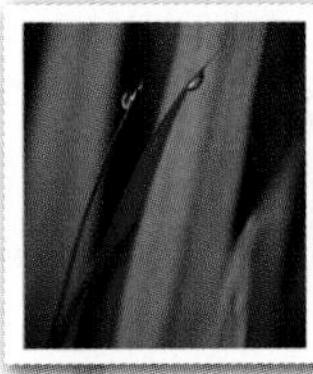

CHAPTER HIGHLIGHTS

- **The progressive tenses combine *to be* with the *-ing* verb form:**
  present progressive tense: I *am reading.* He *is reading.*
  past progressive tense: I *was reading.* He *was reading.*
- **The *-ing* verb form must have a helping verb to be complete:**
  She playing the tuba. *(incorrect)*
  She *is playing* the tuba. *(correct)*
- **The present progressive tense shows that an action is in progress now:**
  Aunt Belle *is waxing* her van.
- **The present progressive tense can also show that an action will take place in the future:**
  Later today, Aunt Belle *is driving* us to the movies.
- **The past progressive tense shows that an action was in progress at a certain time in the past:**
  Aunt Belle *was waxing* her van when she heard thunder.

CHAPTER REVIEW

Proofread this paragraph for incomplete progressive verbs. Write the missing verbs above the lines.

(1) Scientists ^are studying the role of human genes in everything from eye color and intelligence to the tendency to get heart disease. (2) Recently, a map of every gene in the human body—three billion elements in all—was completed by researchers of the Human Genome Project. (3) Scientists ^are using this new information to find the genes that cause certain diseases. (4) Already, the map ^is leading to cures and to other helpful discoveries, like finding bacteria that eat up oil spills and then die. (5) On the other hand, ethical problems ^are arising. (6) Some insurance companies ^are refusing to insure healthy people who carry certain genes. (7) In the future, will employers be allowed to use genetic tests the way some now use lie detectors or drug tests? (8) Will parents try to plan the physical traits or talents of their babies? (9) Because of questions like these, some people ^are calling genetic research a Pandora's box, not a magic bullet.

EXPLORING ONLINE

TEACHING TIP
More practice and assessment are available in the *Grassroots* Test Bank; linked ACE tests on the *Grassroots* student website; *WriteSpace for Grassroots*; and the Exploring Online links in this chapter.

<http://www.pacificnet.net/~sperling/quiz/past1.html> Interactive quiz: Practice using the progressive tense.

<http://college.hmco.com/devenglish> Visit the *Grassroots* 8/e Student Website for more exercises and quizzes.

CHAPTER 12

Fixed-Form Helping Verbs and Verb Problems

PART A Defining and Spotting the Fixed-Form Helping Verbs

You already know the common—and changeable—helping verbs: *to have, to do,* and *to be.* Here are some helping verbs that do not change:

Fixed-Form Helping Verbs

can	could
will	would
may	might
shall	should
must	

The fixed-form helping verbs do not change, no matter what the subject is. They always keep the same form.

PRACTICE 1

Fill in each blank with a fixed-form helping verb. Answers will vary.

1. You ___can___ do it!

TEACHING TIP
If your students need to review the meanings of these verbs, have them compare their answers to Practice 1 and discuss how meaning changes.

2. This ___must___ be the most exciting presidential debate ever held.
3. I ___will___ row while you watch for crocodiles.
4. Rico ___might___ go to medical school.
5. In South America, the elephant beetle ___may___ grow to twelve inches in length.
6. If the committee ___can___ meet today, we ___will___ have a new budget on time.
7. We ___should___ rotate the crops this season.
8. Violent films ___may___ cause children to act out violently.
9. You ___should___ have no difficulty finding a sales position.
10. Janice ___may___ teach users to do research on the Internet.

PART B Using the Fixed-Form Helping Verbs

(1) Al will stay with us this summer.

(2) Susan can shoot a rifle well.

- *Will* is the fixed-form helping verb in sentence (1). What main verb does it help? ___stay___
- *Can* is the fixed-form helping verb in sentence (2). What main verb does it help? ___shoot___
- Notice that *stay* and *shoot* are the simple forms of the verbs. They do not show tense by themselves.

When a verb has two parts—a fixed-form helping verb and a main verb—the main verb keeps its simple form.

PRACTICE 2

In the left column, each sentence contains a verb made up of some form of *to have* (the changeable helping verb) and a past participle (the main verb).

Each sentence in the right column contains a fixed-form helping verb and a blank. Write the form of the main verb from the left column that correctly completes each sentence.

	***Have* + Past Participle**	**Fixed-Form Helping Verb + Simple Form**
EXAMPLES:	I have talked to him.	I may ___talk___ to him.
	She has flown to Ireland.	She will ___fly___ to Ireland.
	1. Irena has written a song.	1. Irena must ___write___ a song.
	2. We have begun.	2. We can ___begin___ .
	3. Joy has visited Graceland.	3. Joy will ___visit___ Graceland.

4. He has slept all day.	4. He could __sleep__ all day.
5. I have run three miles.	5. I will __run__ three miles.
6. We have seen an eclipse.	6. We might __see__ an eclipse.
7. It has drizzled.	7. It may __drizzle__ .
8. Fred has gone on vacation.	8. Fred could __go__ on vacation.
9. Has he studied?	9. Should he __study__ ?
10. Della has been promoted.	10. Della might __be__ promoted.

PART C Using CAN and COULD

(1) He says that I *can* use any tools in his garage.

(2) He said that I *could* use any tools in his garage.

- What is the tense of sentence (1)? __present__
- What is the tense of sentence (2)? __past__
- What is the helping verb in (1)? __can__
- What is the helping verb in (2)? __could__
- As you can see, *could* may be used as the past tense of *can*.

Present tense: Today, I *can* touch my toes.

Past tense: Yesterday, I *could* touch my toes.

Can **means** *am/is/are able.* **It may be used to show present tense.**

Could **means** *was/were able* **when it is used to show the past tense of** *can.*

(3) If I went on a diet, I *could* touch my toes.

(4) Rod wishes he *could* touch his toes.

- In sentence (3), the speaker *could* touch his toes *if*. . . Touching his toes is a possibility, not a certainty.
- In sentence (4), Rod *wishes* he *could* touch his toes, but probably he cannot. Touching his toes is a wish, not a certainty.

Could **also means** *might be able,* **a possibility or a wish.**

PRACTICE 3

Fill in the present tense helper *can* or the past tense *could,* whichever is needed. To determine whether the sentence is present or past, look at the other verbs in the sentence or look for words like *now* and *yesterday*.

1. When I am rested, I ____can____ study for hours.
2. When I was rested, I ____could____ study for hours.
3. George insists that he ____can____ play the trumpet.
4. George insisted that he ____could____ play the trumpet.
5. A year ago, Zora ____could____ jog for only five minutes at a time.
6. Now Zora ____can____ jog for nearly an hour at a time.
7. If you're so smart, how come you ____can____ never find your own socks?
8. If you were so smart, how come you ____could____ never find your own socks?
9. When the air was clear, you ____could____ see the next town.
10. When the air is clear, you ____can____ see the next town.

PRACTICE 4

Circle either *can* or *could*.

1. Sue thinks that she (can, could) carry a tune.
2. Yesterday, we (can, could) not go to the town meeting.
3. I wish I (can, could) pitch like Pedro Martinez.
4. You should meet Tony: he (can, could) lift a two-hundred-pound weight.
5. Everyone I meet (can, could) do a cartwheel.
6. Until the party, everyone thought that Harry (can, could) cook.
7. She (can, could) ice skate better now than she (can, could) last year.
8. On the night that Smithers disappeared, the butler (can, could) not be found.
9. When my brother was younger, he (can, could) name every car on the road.
10. I hope that the snow leopards (can, could) survive in captivity.

PRACTICE 5

On separate paper, write five sentences using *can* to show present tense and five sentences using *could* to show past tense.

PART D Using WILL and WOULD

(1) You know you *will* do well in that class.

(2) You knew you *would* do well in that class.

- Sentence (1) says that *you know* now (present tense) that you *will* do well in the future. *Will* points to the future from the present.
- Sentence (2) says that *you knew* then (past tense) that you *would* do well after that. *Would* points to the future from the past.

Would **may be used as the past tense of** *will,* **just as** *could* **may be used as the past tense of** *can.*

(3) *If* you studied, you *would* pass physics.

(4) Juanita wishes she *would* get an A in French.

- In sentence (3), the speaker *would* pass physics *if* . . . Passing physics is a possibility, not a certainty.
- In sentence (4), Juanita *wishes* she *could* get an A, but this is a wish, not a certainty.

Would **can also express a possibility or a wish.**

PRACTICE 6

Fill in the present tense *will* or the past tense *would.*

1. The meteorologist predicts that it ___will___ snow on Friday.
2. The meteorologist predicted that it ___would___ snow on Friday.
3. Hernan said that he ___would___ move to Colorado.
4. Hernan says that he ___will___ move to Colorado.
5. Roberta thinks that she ___will___ receive financial aid.
6. Roberta thought that she ___would___ receive financial aid.
7. I ___will___ marry you if you propose to me.
8. Unless you stop adding salt, no one ___will___ want to eat that chili.
9. Hugo thinks that he ___will___ be a country and western star someday.
10. Because she wanted to tell her story, she said that she ___would___ write an autobiography.

PRACTICE 7

Circle either *will* or *would.*

1. You (will, would) find the right major once you start taking courses.
2. When the house is painted, you (will, would) see how lovely the old place looks.
3. Yolanda wishes that her neighbor (will, would) stop raising ostriches.
4. The instructor assumed that everyone (will, would) improve.
5. They insisted that they (will, would) pick up the check.
6. The whole town assumed that they (will, would) live happily ever after.
7. When we climb the tower, we (will, would) see for miles around.

8. If I had a million dollars, I (will, would) buy a big house on the ocean.
9. Your flight to Mars (will, would) board in fifteen minutes.
10. Because we hated waiting in long lines, we decided that we (will, would) shop somewhere else.

PART E Writing Infinitives

TEACHING TIP
Teach students that if *to* is followed immediately by a simple verb, it is part of an infinitive. If *to* is followed by a noun construction, it is a preposition.

Every verb can be written as an **infinitive.** An infinitive has two parts: *to* + the simple form of the verb—*to kiss, to gaze, to sing, to wonder, to help*. Never add endings to the infinitive form of a verb: no *-ed*, no *-s*, no *-ing*.

(1) Erin has *to take* a course in clinical dental hygiene.

(2) Neither dictionary seems *to contain* the words I need.

- In sentences (1) and (2), the infinitives are *to take* and *to contain.*
- *To* is followed by the simple form of the verb: *take, contain.*

Don't confuse an infinitive with the preposition *to* followed by a noun or a pronoun.

(3) Robert spoke *to Sam.*

(4) I gave the award *to her.*

ESL TIP
For extra help on infinitives, see Error #7: Wrong Verb Form After a Verb in the "8 Most Common ESL Errors" on the *Grassroots* student website.

- In sentences (3) and (4), the preposition *to* is followed by the noun *Sam* and the pronoun *her.*
- *To Sam* and *to her* are prepositional phrases, not infinitives.*

PRACTICE 8

Find the infinitives in the following sentences and write them in the blanks at the right.

	Infinitive
EXAMPLE: Many people don't realize how hard it is to write a funny essay.	to write
1. Our guests started to leave at midnight.	to leave
2. Barbara has decided to run for mayor.	to run
3. Hal has to get a *B* on his final exam, or he will not transfer to Wayne State.	to get
4. It is hard to think with that radio blaring!	to think
5. The man wanted to buy a silver watch to give to his son.	to buy, to give

*For more work on prepositions, see Chapter 6, Part C, and Chapter 22.

PRACTICE 9

Write an infinitive in each blank in the following sentences. Use any verb that makes sense. Remember that the infinitive is made up of *to* plus the simple form of the verb. Sample answers

1. They began ___to dance___ in the cafeteria.
2. Few people know how ___to skate___ well.
3. Would it be possible for us ___to meet___ again later?
4. He hopes ___to become___ an operating-room nurse.
5. It will be easy ___to learn___ ___to knit___.

PART F Revising Double Negatives

TEACHING TIP
Many students grew up speaking double negatives in their vernacular. Emphasize that these are red-flag errors in written as well as as spoken "workplace" English.

The most common **negatives** are *no, none, not, nowhere, no one, nobody, never,* and *nothing.*

The negative *not* is often joined to a verb to form a contraction: *can't, didn't, don't, hasn't, haven't,* and *won't,* for example.

However, a few negatives are difficult to spot. Read these sentences:

(1) There are hardly any beans left.

(2) By noon, we could scarcely see the mountains on the horizon.

- The negatives in these sentences are *hardly* and *scarcely.*
- They are negatives because they imply that there are *almost* no beans left and that we *almost couldn't* see the mountains.

Use only one negative in each idea. The **double negative** is an error you should avoid.

(3) **Double negative:** I *can't* eat *nothing.*

- There are two negatives in this sentence—*can't* and *nothing*—instead of one.
- Double negatives cancel each other out.

To revise a double negative, simply drop one of the negatives.

(4) **Revised:** I *can't* eat anything.

(5) **Revised:** I can eat *nothing.*

- In sentence (4), the negative *nothing* has been changed to the positive *anything.*
- In sentence (5), the negative *can't* has been changed to the positive *can.*

When you revise double negatives that include the words *hardly* and *scarcely,* keep those words and change the other negatives to positives.

(6) **Double negative:** They couldn't hardly finish their papers on time.

- The two negatives are *couldn't* and *hardly.*

(5) **Revised:** They could hardly finish their papers on time.

- Change *couldn't* to *could.*

PRACTICE 10

Revise the double negatives in the following sentences. Answers will vary.

EXAMPLE: I don't have no more homework to do.
Revised: I don't have any more homework to do.

1. I can't hardly wait for Christmas vacation.
   Revised: I can hardly wait for Christmas vacation.
2. Ms. Chandro hasn't never been to Los Angeles before.
   Revised: Ms. Chandro has never been to Los Angeles before.
3. Fido was so excited that he couldn't scarcely sit still.
   Revised: Fido was so excited that he could scarcely sit still.
4. Nat won't talk to nobody until he's finished studying.
   Revised: Nat won't talk to anybody until he's finished studying.
5. Yesterday's newspaper didn't contain no ads for large-screen television sets.
   Revised: Yesterday's newspaper didn't contain any ads for large-screen television sets.
6. Alice doesn't have no bathing suit with her.
   Revised: Alice doesn't have a bathing suit with her.
7. If Harold were smart, he wouldn't answer no one in that tone of voice.
   Revised: If Harold were smart, he wouldn't answer anyone in that tone of voice.
8. Kylie claimed that she hadn't never been to a rodeo before.
   Revised: Kylie claimed that she had never been to a rodeo before.
9. Some days, I can't seem to do nothing right.
   Revised: Some days, I can't seem to do anything right.
10. Umberto searched, but he couldn't find his gold bow tie nowhere.
    Revised: Umberto searched, but he couldn't find his gold bow tie anywhere.

PRACTICE 11 WRITING ASSIGNMENT

Review this chapter briefly. What part was most difficult for you? Write a paragraph in which you explain that difficult material to someone who is having the same trouble you had. Your purpose is to make the lesson crystal clear to him or her.

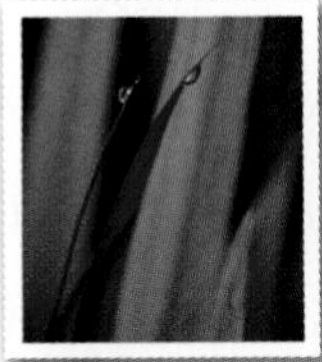

CHAPTER HIGHLIGHTS

- **Fixed-form verbs do not change, no matter what the subject is:**

  I *can.*

  He *can.*

  They *can.*

- **The main verb after a fixed-form helping verb keeps the simple form:**

  I will *sleep.*

  She might *sleep.*

  Sarita should *sleep.*

- **An infinitive has two parts, *to* + the simple form of a verb:**

  to drive

  to exclaim

  to read

- **Do not write double negatives:**

  I didn't order no soup. (*incorrect*)

  I didn't order any soup. (*correct*)

  They couldn't hardly see. (*incorrect*)

  They could hardly see. (*correct*)

CHAPTER REVIEW

Proofread the following essay for errors in fixed-form verbs, infinitives, and double negatives. Cross out each incorrect word and correct the error above the line.

Man of Honor

(1) According to public opinion polls, the most influential Hispanic American in the country is Edward James Olmos. (2) Olmos is someone who ~~couldn't~~ could never be happy promoting only himself. (3) He has tried to ~~setting~~ set an example for others through his choice of movie roles. (4) Olmos decided early in his career that he would not take ~~no~~ any parts in *Rambo*- and *Terminator*-style movies just to get rich. (5) Instead, he wanted his life work to be something that he and his descendants ~~will~~ would be proud of.

(6) As a result, his film projects have included *American Me*, an examination of gang members and life in prison. (7) Young people have told him that this film convinced them that they should not have ~~nothing~~ anything to do with gangs. (8) Olmos is

also famous for his portrayal of teacher Jaime Escalante in *Stand and Deliver*. (9) Other projects, from an anti–domestic violence documentary to a film about Brazilian political activist Chico Mendes called *The Burning Season*, aimed to ~~educating~~ educate the public.

(10) Olmos also hopes that he ~~would~~ will change lives through his community activism. (11) He gives antidrug speeches. (12) In addition, Olmos visits public schools and promotes projects that help Latinos. (13) For example, he cofounded and now codirects the Los Angeles Latino International Film Festival. (14) The actor also supports the Latino Book and Family Festival and oversees Latino Public Broadcasting. (15) Olmos knows from experience that one person ~~could~~ can make a difference.

EXPLORING ONLINE

TEACHING TIP
More practice and assessment are available in the *Grassroots* Test Bank; linked ACE tests on the *Grassroots* student website; *WriteSpace for Grassroots*; and the Exploring Online links in this chapter.

<http://depts.gallaudet.edu/englishworks/exercises/exgrammar/modal01.htm> Graded quiz: Help! Can you fix these verbs?

<http://www.bbc.co.uk/skillswise/words/grammar/texttypes/negatives/quiz.shtml> Double negatives game: Try all three levels.

<http://college.hmco.com/devenglish> Visit the *Grassroots* 8/e Student Website for more exercises and quizzes.

WRITING ASSIGNMENTS

As you complete each writing assignment, remember to perform these steps:

- Write a clear, complete topic sentence.
- Use freewriting, brainstorming, or clustering to generate ideas for the body of your paragraph, essay, or letter.
- Arrange your best ideas in a plan.
- Revise for support, unity, coherence, and exact language.
- Proofread for grammar, punctuation, and spelling errors.

Writing Assignment 1: *Describe a lively scene.* To practice choosing and using verbs, go where the action is—to a sports event, a busy store, a club, a public park, even woods or a field. Observe carefully as you take notes and freewrite. Capture specific sounds, sights, colors, actions, and smells. Then write a description of what takes place, using lively verbs. Choose either present or past tense and make sure to use that tense consistently throughout.

Writing Assignment 2: *Tell a family story.* Many of us heard family stories as we were growing up—how our great-grandmother escaped from Poland, how Uncle Chester took his sister for a joy ride in the Ford when he was six. Assume that you have been asked to write such a story for a scrapbook that will be given to your grandmother on her eightieth birthday. Choose a story that reveals something important about a member of your family. As you revise, make sure that all your verbs are correct.

Writing Assignment 3: *Describe the moments just before a big event.* Read paragraph A on page 162, which uses lively verbs to describe a runner's intense moments just before a race. This writer uses the present tense, as if the action is happening now. Describe the moments just before some important event—the birth of a child, the opening of an important letter, the arrival of a blind date, the verdict of a jury (or of the person to whom you just proposed). Decide whether present or past tense would be best and choose varied, interesting verbs. As you revise, make sure the verbs are correct.

Writing Assignment 4: *Write to Abby.* Think of a problem with love, marriage, parents, or school that might prompt you or someone you know to write to "Dear Abby." Then, as if you are the person with the problem, write a letter. In your first sentence, state the problem clearly. Then explain it. Remember, you are confused and don't know what to do. You want to give Abby enough information so that she can answer you wisely. Proofread your letter carefully. Don't let grammatical errors or incorrect verbs stand between you and happiness!

UNIT 3

REVIEW

Transforming

A. Rewrite this paragraph, changing every *I* to *she,* every *me* to *her,* and so forth. Keep all verbs in the present tense. Be sure all verbs agree with the new subjects and make any other necessary changes.

(1) The race is about to begin. (2) ~~My~~ Her heart pounds as ~~I peel~~ she peels off ~~my~~ her sweatpants and jacket and ~~drop~~ drops them on the grass. (3) ~~I step~~ She steps onto the new, all-weather track and ~~enter my~~ enters her assigned lane. (4) Next, ~~I check my~~ she checks her track shoes for loose laces. (5) By now, the athletes around ~~me~~ her are stretching backwards, forwards, and sideways. (6) ~~I extend~~ She extends one leg, then the other, and ~~bend~~ bends low, giving ~~my~~ her hamstrings a final stretch. (7) Although ~~I~~ she never ~~come~~ comes eye to eye with ~~my~~ her opponents, ~~I feel~~ she feels their readiness as they exhale loudly. (8) Their energy charges the air like electricity. (9) ~~I plant my~~ She plants her feet in the blocks. (10) Off to one side, a coach starts to speak. (11) ~~My~~ Her mind is flashing. (12) How will ~~my~~ her opponents kick off? (13) How will they start? (14) The seconds swell, thick and dreamlike. (15) The gun sounds.

Sheila Grant, student

B. Rewrite this paragraph, changing the verbs from present tense to past tense.

(1) It ~~is~~ was the morning of April 18, 1906. (2) Alfred Hunt ~~sleeps~~ slept peacefully in the Palace Hotel in San Francisco. (3) At 5:12, a violent jolt suddenly ~~shakes~~ shook his room and ~~sends~~ sent him rolling from bed. (4) The shaking ~~lasts~~ lasted for forty-five seconds. (5) During the calm of the next ten seconds, Hunt ~~staggers~~ staggered to the window. (6) Another tremor ~~rocks~~ rocked the city for twenty-five more seconds. (7) Hunt ~~watches~~ watched in terror. (8) The whole city ~~looks~~ looked like breaking waves. (9) Buildings ~~reel~~ reeled and ~~tumble~~ tumbled to the ground. (10) Then fires ~~break~~ broke out and ~~start~~ started to spread. (11) Hunt quickly ~~dresses, throws~~ dressed, threw open his door, and ~~runs~~ ran downstairs into the street. (12) Crowds of rushing people ~~block~~ blocked his path. (13) Some people ~~carry~~ carried screaming children while others ~~struggle~~ struggled under loads of furniture and other valuable objects. (14) It ~~takes~~ took Hunt four hours to push through the four blocks from his hotel to the safety of the Oakland ferry. (15) Later, he ~~will~~ would learn that the great San Francisco earthquake ~~has~~ had destroyed 520 city blocks and ~~has~~ had killed more than seven hundred people.

Proofreading

The following essay contains both past tense errors and past participle errors. First, proofread for verb errors, underlining all the incorrect verbs. Then correct the errors above the lines. (You should find a total of thirteen errors.)

TEACHING TIP
The subject of this practice—Goodall's work with chimps—and the Exploring Online links below can prompt discussion and miniresearch on endangered species and eco-topics.

Protector of the Chimps

(1) Jane Goodall has did [done] more than anyone else to understand the lives of chimpanzees. (2) Always an animal lover, Goodall was too poor to go to college to study animals. (3) She worked as a waitress until the age of twenty-five. (4) Then she fufilled a lifelong dream and gone [went] to East Africa. (5) There she was thrilled by the beauty of the land and the wild animals.

(6) In Africa, she meet [met] Louis Leakey, a famous naturalist. (7) Leakey recognize [recognized] Goodall's curiosity, energy, and passion for the natural world. (8) He hired her for a six-month study of the wild chimpanzees in a national park in Tanzania. (9) Despite malaria, primitive living conditions, and hostile wildlife, Goodall followed the activities of a group of chimps in the Gombe forest. (10) For months, she watch [watched] the chimps through binoculars. (11) She moved closer and closer until she eventually become [became] part of their lives. (12) Goodall named the chimps and recorded their daily activities. (13) She learned that chimps was [were] capable of feeling happiness, anger, and pain. (14) They formed complex societies with leaders, politics, and tribal wars. (15) One of her most important discoveries were [was] that chimps made and used tools. (16) Goodall expected to stay in Gombe for six months; instead she studied the chimps there for almost forty years. (17) Her studies lead [led] to a totally new understanding of chimps, and she became world famous.

(18) However, her life changed completely in 1986. (19) She attend [attended] a conference in Chicago, where she heard horrible stories about the fate of chimps outside Gombe. (20) She learned about the destruction of the forests and the wildlife of Africa. (21) From that day on, Goodall committed herself to education and conservation. (22) Since then, she has traveled, lectured, gave [given] interviews, and met with people. (23) She established both the Jane Goodall Institute and a young people's group, Roots & Shoots. (24) These worldwide organizations have already carry [carried] out many important conservation and educational projects. (25) The author of remarkable books and the subject of inspiring television specials, Jane Goodall is knowed [known] for her total commitment to chimps and to a healthy natural world.

EXPLORING ONLINE

<http://www.janegoodall.org>

<http://www.worldwildlife.org> Visit the Jane Goodall Institute or the World Wildlife Federation to learn more about endangered species.

WRITERS' WORKSHOP

Tell a Lively Story

A **narrative** tells a story. It presents the most important events in the story, usually in time order. Here, a student explains her main idea with a single example, a childhood narrative.

In your group or class, read this narrative essay aloud if possible. As you read, underline any words or details that strike you as vivid or powerful.

Happy in Butterfly Heaven

(1) When I was a child on our farm in South Carolina, my family always supported my expansive imagination. For example, one year, I had a favorite butterfly named Mr. Jonce Browne, and I named his wife Mrs. Sadie Caesar. I would play with them in the fields, flapping my arms and darting my head until I felt I had turned into a butterfly. One day I found Mr. Jonce Browne stiff and brittle in a spider web next to the barn. When I told Papa the tragic news, he said, "Give him a proper burial because Mrs. Sadie Caesar will be too busy taking care of her children."

(2) Mama gave me a wooden matchbox for a casket. Two of my sisters and three brothers made funeral arrangements. They dug a tiny grave, and we all picked wildflowers. My brother Emiza gave the eulogy from a milk crate. "We gather here today to put to rest a good butterfly papa." My sisters Gertrude and Jeanie jumped up and down flinging their arms and yelling, "Yes! He was a good papa!"

(3) The preacher started clapping his hands and flinging his arms. He rolled his eyes upward and raised his voice two octaves as he went on about the deceased's great qualities. "He never failed to bring home pretzels for his children!" I started waving my arms as I told how he always brought me balloons. "And yo-yos for me," my brother Jeff hollered.

(4) By this time, sweat was rolling down the preacher's face. He yelled and screamed, shaking his head. Spit was flying everywhere. Suddenly he squealed a high note that made my ears ring. My brother James started singing, "When the saints go marching in." We all sang as we covered the grave and put flowers on top. I felt assured that Mr. Jonce Browne was happy in butterfly heaven, knowing how much we all liked him.

Stelline Hill, student

1. How effective is Stelline Hill's essay?

   Y Clear thesis statement? Y Rich supporting details?

   Y Logical organization? Y Effective conclusion?

2. Underline the thesis statement (main idea sentence) for the whole essay. The rest of the paper—a childhood narrative—develops this idea.

3. How would you describe the writer's tone? Is she totally serious, or is she having some fun here? Do you find this subject appropriate for a college paper, or is it too childish?

4. On paper, as in life, this student shows a lively imagination. Discuss your underlinings with a group or with the class. How many of the words you liked are verbs or verb forms? Hill uses many different action verbs to help the reader see and hear the story, especially in paragraphs (3) and (4). Can you identify them?

5. Would you suggest any changes or revisions?

6. Proofread for grammar and spelling. Do you notice any error patterns (two or more errors of the same type) that this student should watch out for? No errors

Writing and Revising Ideas

1. Write a lively story about one way your family supported you (or failed to).

2. Use narration to develop this topic or thesis sentence: Country (or city) living has great advantages (or disadvantages).

For help writing your paragraph or essay, see Chapters 4 and 5. As you revise, make sure that your main idea is clear and that your paper explains it. To add punch to your writing as you revise, replace *is, was, has,* and *had* with action verbs whenever possible.

UNIT 4

Joining Ideas Together

Too many short, simple sentences can make your writing sound monotonous. This unit will show you five ways to create interesting sentences. In this unit, you will

- Join ideas through *coordination* and *subordination*
- Spot and correct run-ons or comma splices
- Use semicolons and conjunctive adverbs correctly
- Join ideas with *who*, *which*, and *that*
- Join ideas by using *-ing* modifiers

Spotlight on Writing

Here, writer Brent Staples uses several methods of joining ideas as he describes his first passionate kiss (at least, *he* was passionate). If possible, read the paragraph aloud.

I stepped outside and pulled the door closed behind me, and in one motion encircled her waist, pulled her to me, and whispered breathlessly that I loved her. There'd been no rehearsing this; the thought, deed, and word were one. "You do? You love me?" This amused her, but that didn't matter, I had passion enough for the two of us. When I closed in for the kiss, she turned away her lips and offered me her cheek. I kissed it feverishly and with great force. We stood locked this way until I came up for air. Then she peeled me from her and went inside for the flour.

Brent Staples, *Parallel Time*

- Brent Staples mixes simple sentences with sentences that join ideas in different ways. Sentences 1, 2, and 5, for example, combine ideas in ways you will learn in this unit.
- How do you think the writer now feels about this incident from his youth? Does his tone seem angry, frustrated, or amused? Which sentences tell you?

- ***Your first crush or romantic encounter***
- ***A time you discovered that a loved one's view of the relationship was very different from your view***

CHAPTER

13

Coordination

TEACHING TIP
The acronym FANBOYS is the tried-and-true mnemonic device for helping students remember the seven coordinating conjunctions.

As a writer, you will sometimes want to join short, choppy sentences to form longer sentences. One way to join two ideas is to use a comma and a **coordinating conjunction**.

(1) This car has many special features, and it costs less than $15,000.

(2) The television picture is blurred, but we will watch the football game anyway.

(3) She wants to practice her Italian, so she is going to Italy.

- Can you break sentence (1) into two complete and independent ideas or thoughts? What are they? Underline the subject and verb in each.
- Can you do the same with sentences (2) and (3)? Underline the subjects and verbs.
- In each sentence, circle the word that joins the two parts of the sentence together. What punctuation mark comes before that word?
- *And, but,* and *so* are called *coordinating conjunctions* because they coordinate, or join together, ideas. Other coordinating conjunctions are *for, nor, or,* and *yet*.

TEACHING TIP
Students often overuse the conjunction *and.* Encourage them to think critically about the exact *relationship* between two independent ideas before they select a conjunction.

To join two complete and independent ideas, use a coordinating conjunction preceded by a comma.

Now let's see just how coordinating conjunctions connect ideas:

Coordinating Conjunctions

and	*means*	in addition
but, yet	*mean*	in contrast
for	*means*	because
nor	*means*	not either
or	*means*	either, a choice
so	*means*	as a result

BE CAREFUL: *Then, also,* and *plus* are not coordinating conjunctions. By themselves, they cannot join two ideas.

> **Incorrect:** He studied, then he went to work.
>
> **Correct:** He studied, and then he went to work.

PRACTICE 1

Read these sentences for meaning. Then punctuate them correctly and fill in the coordinating conjunction that best expresses the relationship between the two complete thoughts. REMEMBER: Do you want to *add, contrast, give a reason, show a result,* or *indicate a choice*? Answers will vary.

1. Every year, thousands of people travel into Nevada's blistering Black Rock Desert __, for__ they want to participate in an amazing ritual.
2. They build and live in an experimental community called Black Rock City __, yet/but__ they tear it down completely just one week later.
3. The event is called the Burning Man Festival __, for__ on the final day, an eighty-foot-tall wooden figure of a man is set ablaze.
4. Each year there is a theme __, and/so__ past themes have included time, fertility, outer space, and belief.
5. Everyone is encouraged to contribute something related to the theme __, so__ participants experience artwork, costumes, foods, prayers, kite making, music, and other gifts from the heart.
6. People pay to get into the festival __, yet/but__ they then enter a volunteer and gift economy.
7. Commercial vendors are not allowed __, nor__ can the participants buy or sell anything using money.
8. People focus instead on giving something to the group __, for__ the festival encourages "radical self-expression."
9. The event began in 1986 as a small gathering of friends on a San Francisco beach __, but/yet__ today it has grown to include over 30,000 participants.
10. They might make the trip looking for a week-long party __, or__ they might be seeking a more satisfying way of life.

TEACHING TIP
After students complete Practice 1, consider discussing their answers as a class so that they can see which conjunctions work in a sentence and which don't.

EXPLORING ONLINE

<http://www.burningman.com> Would you make a pilgrimage to Black Rock for this festival? If not, write down three reasons why you wouldn't. If you would attend, write about what you would hope to gain from the experience and what you would contribute to the community.

PRACTICE 2

TEACHING TIP
Practice 2 works well in class.

Every one of these thoughts is complete by itself, but you can join them together to make more interesting sentences. Combine pairs of these thoughts, using *and, but, for, nor, or, so,* or *yet,* and write six new sentences on the lines that follow. Punctuate correctly.

babies need constant supervision

Rico overcame his disappointment

in the 1840s, American women began to fight for the right to vote

I will write my essay at home tonight

the ancient Chinese valued peaches

he decided to try again

they are the best Ping-Pong players on the block

you should never leave them by themselves

I will write it tomorrow in the computer lab

they did not win that right until 1920

they can't beat my cousin from Cleveland

they believed that eating peaches made a person immortal

1. Babies need constant supervision, so you should never leave them by themselves.
2. I will write my essay at home tonight, or I will write it tomorrow in the computer lab.
3. In the 1840s, American women began to fight for the right to vote, yet they did not win that right until 1920.
4. Rico overcame his disappointment, and he decided to try again.
5. They are the best Ping-Pong players on the block, but they can't beat my cousin from Cleveland.
6. The ancient Chinese valued peaches, for they believed that eating peaches made a person immortal.

PRACTICE 3

Finish these sentences by adding a second complete idea after the coordinating conjunction. Sample answers

1. She often interrupts me, but I try not to get upset.

2. Yuri has lived in the United States for ten years, so his English is quite good.

3. Len has been married three times, and now he's a widower.

4. I like owning a car, for it allows me to drive to the country on weekends.

5. I like owning a car, but I hate the repair bills.

PRACTICE 4

On paper or on a computer, write seven sentences of your own using each of the coordinating conjunctions—*and, but, for, nor, or, so,* and *yet*—to join two independent ideas. Punctuate correctly.

PRACTICE 5 WRITING ASSIGNMENT

Whether you are a teenager, a young adult, middle-aged, elderly, single, or part of a couple, there are characters in TV sitcoms who are supposed to represent you. Do these characters correctly portray the kind of person you are, or are you seeing one or more irritating exaggerations?

Write a letter of praise or complaint to a network that broadcasts one of these sitcoms. Make clear why you think a certain character does or does not correctly portray someone like you. Use examples and specific details. As you write, avoid choppy sentences by joining ideas with coordinating conjunctions.

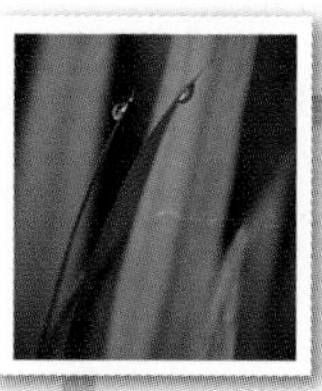

CHAPTER HIGHLIGHTS

- **A comma and a coordinating conjunction join two independent ideas:**

  The fans booed, *but* the umpire paid no attention.

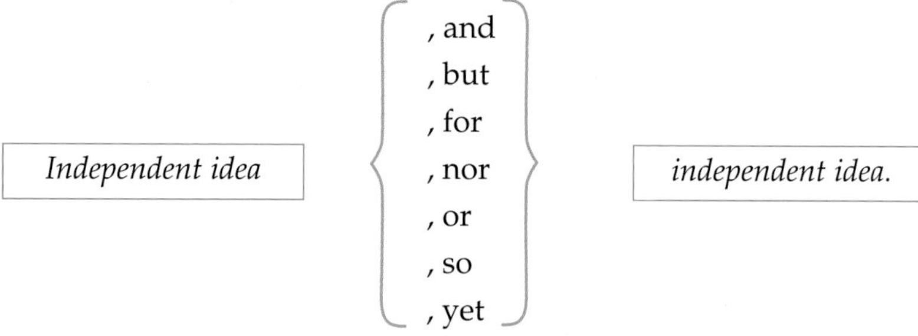

- **Note:** ***Then, also,*** **and** ***plus*** **are not coordinating conjunctions.**

CHAPTER REVIEW

TEACHING TIP
Have students apply what they have learned by looking for short, choppy sentences in a paragraph they have written and then revising, using coordinating conjunctions.

Read this paragraph of short, choppy sentences. Then rewrite it, using different coordinating conjunctions to combine some pairs of sentences. Keep some short sentences for variety. Copy your revised paragraph on a fresh sheet of paper. Punctuate with care. Answers will vary.

(1) In 1929, Alice Orr answered a want ad for bronco riders for a Wild West show. (2) She was hired ~~immediately~~ immediately, and her. (3) ~~Her~~ new job launched a remarkable career. (4) Orr became an international rodeo star. (5) She was an expert in every rodeo ~~event~~ event, but her. (6) ~~Her~~ specialty was saddle bronc riding. (7) That tough competition has since been dropped from women's ~~rodeos~~ rodeos, yet. (8) Orr won four world championships in it. (9) Orr was also concerned about working conditions for rodeo ~~competitors~~ competitors, so she. (10) ~~She~~ helped establish a professional rodeo association. (11) In the 1940s, Orr and her husband put on rodeos ~~themselves~~ themselves, and she. (12) ~~She~~ would demonstrate her world-famous saddle bronc riding. (13) Orr retired from rodeos in her ~~fifties~~ fifties, but she. (14) ~~She~~ did movie stunt work until she was eighty. (15) When Alice Orr died in 1995 at the age of 93, many people still remembered her as queen of the bronco riders.

EXPLORING ONLINE

TEACHING TIP
More practice and assessment are available in the *Grassroots* Test Bank; linked ACE tests on the *Grassroots* student website; *WriteSpace for Grassroots*; and the Exploring Online links in this chapter.

<http://www.ccc.commnet.edu/grammar/quizzes/nova/nova1.htm>
Interactive quiz: Place commas in sentences with coordinating conjunctions.

<http://aliscot.com/bigdog/joiners.htm> Coordination tips from Big Dog.

<http://college.hmco.com/devenglish> Visit the *Grassroots* 8/e Student Website for more exercises and quizzes.

CHAPTER 14

Subordination

PART A **Defining and Using Subordinating Conjunctions**

PART B **Punctuating Subordinating Conjunctions**

PART A Defining and Using Subordinating Conjunctions

TEACHING TIP
To begin a lesson on subordinating conjunctions, you might review with students the meanings of the terms *coordinate* and *subordinate*.

Another way to join ideas together is with a **subordinating conjunction**.

Read this paragraph:

> A great disaster happened in 1857. The SS *Central America* sank. This steamship was carrying six hundred wealthy passengers from California to New York. Many of them had recently struck gold. Battered by a storm, the ship began to flood. Many people on board bailed water. Others prayed and quieted the children. Thirty hours passed. A rescue boat arrived. Almost two hundred people were saved. The rest died. Later, many banks failed. Three tons of gold had gone down with the ship.

This could have been a good paragraph, but notice how dull the writing is because the sentences are short and choppy.

Here is the same paragraph rewritten to make it more interesting:

TEACHING TIP
Ask your students to describe the impression that short, choppy sentences give readers about the writer. (The effect can seem monotonous, unsophisticated, even childlike.)

> A great disaster happened in 1857 *when* the SS *Central America* sank. This steamship was carrying six hundred wealthy passengers from California to New York. Many of them had recently struck gold. Battered by a storm, the ship began to flood. Many people on board bailed water *while* others prayed and quieted the children. *After* thirty hours passed, a rescue boat arrived. Almost two hundred people were saved *although* the rest died. Later, many banks failed *because* three tons of gold had gone down with the ship.

- Note that the paragraph now reads more smoothly and is more interesting because the following words were used to join some of the choppy sentences: *when, while, after, although,* and *because*.
- *When, while, after, although,* and *because* are part of a large group of words called *subordinating conjunctions*. As you can see from the paragraph, these conjunctions join ideas.

BE CAREFUL: Once you add a *subordinating conjunction* to an idea, that idea can no longer stand alone as a complete and independent sentence. It has become a subordinate or dependent idea; it must rely on an independent idea to complete its meaning.*

---

*For more work on sentence fragments of this type, see Chapter 7, Part C.

(1) Because he is tired, he will take a nap.

(2) As I left the room, the waiter dropped a tray of desserts.

(3) If you know Spanish, will you translate the letter for me?

ESL TIP
ESL students tend to write dependent clause fragments. In some languages, like Japanese, freestanding dependent clauses are accepted as correct. Further, ESL students often duplicate English oral patterns, in which freestanding dependent clauses are common.

- Note that each of these ideas is dependent and must be followed by something else—a complete and independent thought.
- Sentence (1), for example, could be completed like this: Because he is tired, *he won't go out*.
- Add an independent idea to complete each dependent idea on the lines above.

Below is a partial list of subordinating conjunctions.

Common Subordinating Conjunctions

after	even though	when
although	if	whenever
as	since	where
as if	so that	whereas
as though	though	wherever
because	unless	whether
before	until	while

PRACTICE 1

TEACHING TIP
After students complete Practice 1, consider discussing the answers as a class so that students can see which conjunctions work in the sentence and which don't.

Read these sentences for meaning. Then fill in the subordinating conjunction that best expresses the relationship between the two ideas. Answers will vary.

1. __While__ the natural world is filled with exciting journeys, perhaps none is more amazing than the flight of monarch butterflies.
2. __Although__ monarchs are only five inches across and weigh only a fiftieth of an ounce, they travel thousands of miles: north to south and back again.
3. __When__ summer changes to fall, millions of these beautiful black-and-orange butterflies begin to migrate to warmer climates.
4. Monarchs have to migrate __because__ they need warm sunshine to stay alive.
5. The monarch butterflies that live west of the Rocky Mountains fly to the California coast __whereas__ those that live east of the Rockies go south.
6. For years, scientists wondered where eastern monarchs went __after__ they left Canada and the northern United States.
7. Researchers at the University of Toronto eventually began tagging the butterflies __before__ the monarchs migrated south.
8. Volunteers throughout the United States and Mexico would contact the university __whenever__ they saw a tagged monarch.

9. People continued to search ____until____ they finally tracked the butterflies to several sites in the forests of central Mexico.

10. At those sites, millions of butterflies cover the giant fir trees ____so that____ no green from the trees is visible.

11. ____Whenever____ the butterflies leave the trees to find water, they fill the sky, sometimes blocking out the sun completely.

12. ____As____ visitors from all over the world arrive at the monarch sanctuary in El Rosario, they marvel at the incredible beauty of this butterfly world.

13. Unfortunately, ____since____ an unusual cold spell in Mexico in 1995 killed up to 15 percent of the monarch population, monarchs have been in danger.

14. Another threat to their existence is logging ____because____ monarchs need the fir trees to keep themselves warm and dry.

15. Some experts have predicted that these wonderful butterflies will be extinct within twenty years ____if____ logging in the Mexican forests continues at recent levels.

PRACTICE 2

Now that you understand how subordinating conjunctions join thoughts together, try these sentences. Here you have to supply one idea. Make sure that the ideas you add have subjects and verbs. Sample answers

1. The cafeteria food improved when the college hired a new food manager.

2. Because Damon and Luis both love basketball, they often attend local games.

3. If the store won't refund his money, Adolph plans to get legal advice.

4. I was repairing the roof while Noah was ironing clothes.

5. Before you write that article, you should get all the facts.

PART B Punctuating Subordinating Conjunctions

As you may have noticed in the preceding exercises, some sentences with subordinating conjunctions use a comma while others do not. Here is how it's done.

(1) Because it rained very hard, we had to leave early.

(2) We had to leave early because it rained very hard.

- Sentence (1) has a comma because the dependent idea comes before the independent idea.

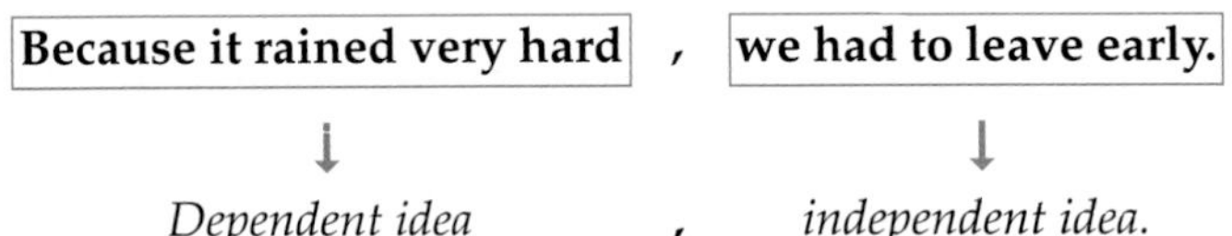
Because it rained very hard
,
we had to leave early.
Dependent idea
,
independent idea.

- Sentence (2) has no comma because the dependent idea follows the independent idea.

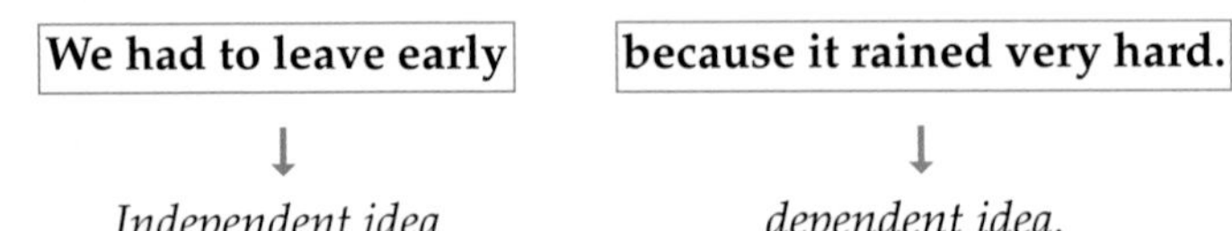
We had to leave early
because it rained very hard.
Independent idea
dependent idea.

Use a comma after a dependent idea; do not use a comma before a dependent idea.

PRACTICE 3

TEACHING TIP
Practice 3: Encourage students to locate and circle the subordinating conjunction first before deciding if the sentence needs a comma. Note that the practice's subject, fast food, can be a springboard for brisk discussion and for writing.

If a sentence is punctuated correctly, write C in the blank. If it is not, punctuate it correctly by adding a comma.

1. Whenever Americans get ~~hungry~~ hungry, they want to eat quickly. ___
2. When McDonald's opened in ~~1954~~ 1954, it started a trend that continues today. ___
3. Whether you are talking about pizza or ~~hamburgers~~ hamburgers, fast food is big business—earning more than $110 billion a year. ___
4. Fast food is appealing because it is cheap, tasty, and—of course—fast. C
5. While it has many ~~advantages~~ advantages, fast food also presents some health hazards. ___
6. Although the industry is ~~booming~~ booming, many people are worried about the amount of fat in fast foods. ___
7. Whereas some nutritionists recommend eating only thirty-five grams of fat a ~~day~~ day, you often eat more than that in just one fast-food meal. ___
8. If you order a Burger King Double Whopper with ~~cheese~~ cheese, you take in a whopping sixty-three grams of fat. ___
9. That goes up to sixty-seven fat grams whenever you devour a McDonald's Big Mac, large fries, and chocolate shake. C
10. Now some fast-food restaurants are claiming to serve low-fat items so that they can attract health-conscious customers. C
11. However, you still must pay attention to the ingredients~~, if~~ if you want to make sure that your meal is healthy. ___
12. For example, most grilled or roasted chicken sandwiches are relatively low in fat before they are slathered with mayonnaise and special sauces. C
13. Because just one tablespoon of mayonnaise or salad dressing contains eleven fat ~~grams~~ grams, these tasty toppings add gobs of extra fat and calories. ___
14. Although they might taste ~~delicious~~ delicious, cheese and cheese sauces also add surprising quantities of fat to a meal. ___

15. When you next order your favorite fast ~~food~~ food, don't forget to say, "Hold the sauce!" ___

©New Yorker Collection 1988 Tom Cheney from cartoonbank.com. All Rights Reserved.

PRACTICE 4

Combine each pair of sentences by using a subordinating conjunction. Write each combination two ways: once with the subordinating conjunction at the beginning of the sentence and once with the subordinating conjunction in the middle of the sentence. Punctuate correctly. Answers will vary.

EXAMPLE: Marriage exists in all societies.
Every culture has unique wedding customs.

Although marriage exists in all societies, every culture has unique wedding customs.

Every culture has unique wedding customs although marriage exists in all societies.

TEACHING TIP
Students might tend to use coordinating conjunctions in this exercise, so remind them to avoid using *for, and, nor, but, or, yet,* and *so* and to refer to the list of subordinating conjunctions on page 174 as they work.

1. Young couples in India marry.
The ceremony may last for days.

When young couples in India marry, the ceremony may last for days.

The ceremony may last for days when young couples in India marry.

ESL TIP
A common ESL error is to use both a subordinating and a coordinating conjunction in the same sentence (e.g., *Although it was raining, but she forgot her umbrella*). Remind students to check carefully for this overuse problem.

2. The wedding takes place at the bride's home.
   Everyone travels to the groom's home for more celebrating.
   After the wedding takes place at the bride's home, everyone travels to the groom's home for more celebrating.
   Everyone travels to the groom's home for more celebrating after the wedding takes place at the bride's home.

3. They are often included in Korean wedding processions.
   Ducks mate for life.
   Because ducks mate for life, they are often included in Korean wedding processions.
   Ducks are often included in Korean wedding processions because they mate for life.

4. Iroquois brides gave grain to their mothers-in-law.
   Mothers-in-law gave meat to the brides.
   Whereas Iroquois brides gave grain to their mothers-in-law, mothers-in-law gave meat to the brides.
   Iroquois brides gave grain to their mothers-in-law whereas mothers-in-law gave meat to the brides.

5. The food was exchanged.
   The bride and groom were considered married.
   When the food was exchanged, the bride and groom were considered married.
   The bride and groom were considered married when the food was exchanged.

6. The tradition went out of style.
   Finnish brides and grooms used to exchange wreaths.
   Until the tradition went out of style, Finnish brides and grooms used to exchange wreaths.
   Finnish brides and grooms used to exchange wreaths until the tradition went out of style.

7. The bride, groom, and bridal party dance special dances.
   A Zulu wedding is not complete.
   Unless the bride, groom, and bridal party dance special dances, a Zulu wedding is not complete.
   A Zulu wedding is not complete unless the bride, groom, and bridal party dance special dances.

8. The bride dances wildly and gloriously.
   She stabs at imaginary enemies with a knife.

   As the bride dances wildly and gloriously, she stabs at imaginary enemies with a knife.

   The bride stabs at imaginary enemies with a knife as she dances wildly and gloriously.

9. The wedding ring is a very old symbol.
   The elaborate wedding cake is even older.

   Although the wedding ring is a very old symbol, the elaborate wedding cake is even older.

   The wedding ring is a very old symbol although the elaborate wedding cake is even older.

10. The ring symbolizes the oneness of the new couple.
    The cake represents fertility.

    Whereas the ring symbolizes the oneness of the new couple, the cake represents fertility.

    The cake represents fertility whereas the ring symbolizes the oneness of the new couple.

PRACTICE 5

TEACHING TIP
For more practice, recommend that students try online practices and quizzes such as those found at **<http://a4esl.org/q/h/vm/conj02.html>.**

Now try writing sentences of your own. Fill in the blanks, being careful to punctuate correctly. Do not use a comma before a dependent idea.

1. ______________________________ because ______________________________.

2. Although ______________________________.

3. ______________________________ whenever ______________________________.

4. Unless ______________________________.

PRACTICE 6 WRITING ASSIGNMENT

Imagine that you are a teacher planning a lesson on courtesy for a class of young children. Use a personal experience, either positive or negative, to illustrate your point. Brainstorm, freewrite, or cluster to generate details for the lesson. Then write what—and how—you plan to teach. Keeping in mind that you are trying to reach young children, make sure that the significance of the experience you will describe is clear. Join ideas together with subordinating conjunctions, being careful about punctuation.

Form small groups to discuss one another's lessons. Which are most convincing? Why? Would children learn more from examples of good behavior or from examples of bad behavior?

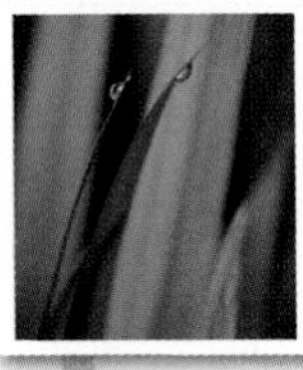

CHAPTER HIGHLIGHTS

- **A subordinating conjunction joins a dependent idea and an independent idea:**

  When I registered, all the math courses were closed.

  All the math courses were closed *when* I registered.

- **Use a comma after a dependent idea.**

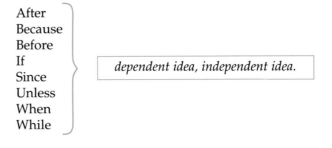

After / Because / Before / If / Since / Unless / When / While	*dependent idea, independent idea.*

- **Do not use a comma before a dependent idea.**

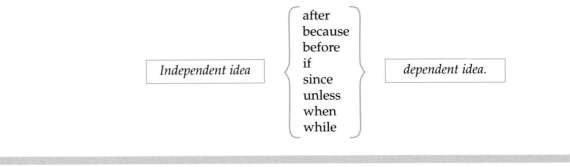

Independent idea	after / because / before / if / since / unless / when / while	*dependent idea.*

CHAPTER REVIEW

TEACHING TIP
After students try the Chapter Review on their own, consider reading aloud "before" and "after" versions of the paragraph so that students can hear how much smoother the revision sounds. Also, ask them whether the newly combined sentences help them understand the information better.

Read this paragraph of short, choppy sentences. Then revise it by making changes above the lines, using different subordinating conjunctions to combine pairs of sentences. Keep some short sentences for variety. Punctuate with care. Answers will vary.

(1) Jacob Lawrence was a great American painter, a powerful teller of stories
After young 1930, he
on canvas. ~~(2) Young~~ Jacob joined his mother in Harlem in ~~1930. (3) He~~ began to
paint the people around him. (4) Luckily, he found excellent art classes in ~~Harlem.~~
Harlem because the When he 23, he
~~(5) The~~ big art academies often excluded blacks then. ~~(6) He~~ was only ~~23. (7) He~~
gained fame for his sixty-picture *Migration Series*. (8) A New York gallery

displayed these ~~paintings. (9) No~~ paintings although no major commercial gallery had showcased an African American artist before. (10) The *Migration Series* depicts southern blacks journeying north to find work after World War I. (11) The paintings show people searching for a better life. ~~(12)~~ While Lawrence's work portrays the poverty and prejudice the migrants ~~endured. (13) He~~ endured, he also wanted viewers of his work "to experience the beauty of life." (14) During his long career, Lawrence painted many more energetic canvases and series. (15) His work reminds us that we are all ~~migrants.~~ migrants ~~(16) We~~ because we are always on the move. (17) We are seeking something more.

EXPLORING ONLINE

TEACHING TIP
Students can view excellent images of Lawrence's work on the Whitney Museum website, with ideas for both descriptive and storytelling assignments.

See Lawrence's paintings at the Whitney Museum of Art online. <http://www.whitney.org/jacoblawrence/> Click on "Jacob Lawrence's Art." Describe your favorite painting to someone who has never seen it. More writing ideas appear under "Explore" and "Tell Your Own Story."

Brownstones, 1958, by Jacob Lawrence.
Courtesy of Clark Atlanta University.

EXPLORING ONLINE

TEACHING TIP
More practice and assessment are available in the *Grassroots* Test Bank; linked ACE tests on the *Grassroots* student website; *WriteSpace for Grassroots*; and the Exploring Online links in this chapter.

<http://www.ccc.commnet.edu/grammar/quizzes/indep_clause_quiz.htm> Interactive clause line-up: I.D. the independent or dependent clauses.

<http://web2.uvcs.uvic.ca/elc/studyzone/330/grammar/subcon.htm> Explanation of subordination followed by interactive practice sets.

<http://college.hmco.com/devenglish> Visit the *Grassroots* 8/e Student Website for more exercises and quizzes.

CHAPTER

15

Avoiding Run-Ons and Comma Splices

TEACHING TIP
Stress to students that run-ons and comma splices are among the most common—and most serious—grammatical errors. By forcing readers to stop, back up, and try to figure out where one thought ends and another begins, these errors confuse and irritate the audience.

Now that you have had practice in joining ideas together, here are two errors to watch out for: the **run-on** and the **comma splice**.

Run-on: Herb talks too much nobody seems to mind.

- There are two complete ideas here: *Herb talks too much* and *nobody seems to mind*.
- A *run-on* incorrectly runs together two complete ideas without using a conjunction or punctuation.

Comma splice: Herb talks too much, nobody seems to mind.

- A *comma splice* incorrectly joins two complete ideas with a comma but no conjunction.

Here are three ways to correct a run-on and a comma splice.

TEACHING TIP
Chapter 16 covers semicolons, which can also be used to correct run-ons and comma splices.

1. **Write two separate sentences, making sure that each is complete.**

Herb talks too much. Nobody seems to mind.

2. **Use a comma and a coordinating conjunction (*and, but, for, nor, or, so, yet*).***

Herb talks too much, *but* nobody seems to mind.

3. **Use a subordinating conjunction (*for example, although, because, if, since,* or *when*).****

Although Herb talks too much, nobody seems to mind.

*For more work on coordinating conjunctions, see Chapter 13.
**For more work on subordinating conjunctions, see Chapter 14.

PRACTICE 1

Many of these sentences contain run-ons or comma splices. If a sentence is correct, write *C* in the right-hand column. If it contains a run-on or a comma splice, write either *RO* or *CS*. Then correct the error in any way you wish. Use each method at least once. Answers will vary.

TEACHING TIP
After students complete Practice 1, go over the answers in class so that you can demonstrate how to use all three revision methods for each sentence.

ESL TIP
ESL students often benefit from group activities, especially with a mix of native and ESL speakers. Try using Practice 1 as a pair or group activity. Ask the groups to present and explain each of their answers.

EXAMPLE:

Because a / ~~A~~ number of celebrities have admitted their ~~addictions~~ addictions, public awareness of addiction has increased. RO

1. Many famous people have struggled with alcoholism or drug ~~abuse~~ abuse, but some have overcome those problems. RO
2. Often politicians, athletes, and actors hide their addiction and their ~~recovery,~~ recovery because they do not want to risk ruining their careers. CS
3. Other celebrities are forced to go public in their battles with alcohol or drugs. C
4. A few feel that their struggles may help others, so they want to act as positive role models. CS
5. One such person was Betty Ford, a former First ~~Lady with~~ Lady. With her family's help, she became sober at age sixty. RO
6. ~~Her~~ Because her recovery was ~~successful~~ successful, she agreed to help several friends create a treatment center in Rancho Mirage, California. RO
7. At the Betty Ford Center, celebrities like Liz Taylor and Kelsey Grammer as well as everyday people receive support for their new way of life. C
8. Treatment centers now exist around the country, for the problem of addiction seems to be increasing, especially among the young. CS
9. For example, Drew Barrymore was famous at age six for her role in the film *E.T.*, but by age nine she was addicted to drugs and alcohol. CS
10. Forced into rehab at age thirteen, Drew was able to get her acting career back on track. C
11. ~~Actors~~ Although actors Charlie Sheen, Matthew Perry, and Ben Affleck likewise developed ~~addictions~~ addictions, getting treatment helped them stay on top in their profession. RO
12. Football legend Lawrence Taylor is one of many athletes who have gone through detox, but he claims that at last he has turned his life around. CS

13. Stardom seems to invite the risk of addiction; the Musician's Assistance Program has helped over 1,500 rock stars get straight. C

14. Alcohol and drugs might seem glamorous, especially to the young, ^yet they can destroy relationships, careers, and self-esteem. CS

15. ~~Millions~~ While millions of Americans are affected, when someone returns from addiction, his or her triumph can encourage others to seek help. CS

PRACTICE 2

Correct each run-on or comma splice in two ways. Be sure to punctuate correctly.
Answers will vary.

EXAMPLE:

Technology will change the way we shop will we like the new way?

a. Technology will change the way we shop. Will we like the new way?

b. Technology will change the way we shop, but will we like the new way?

1. For instance, you want to purchase a car, you may walk up to an outdoor booth.

a. For instance, when you want to purchase a car, you may walk up to an outdoor booth.

b. For instance, you want to purchase a car, so you may walk up to an outdoor booth.

2. You select the options on a computer screen, you press an order entry key.

a. After you select the options on a computer screen, you press an order entry key.

b. You select the options on a computer screen, and you press an order entry key.

3. A factory assembles your car it is later delivered to your local dealer.

a. A factory assembles your car, and it is later delivered to your local dealer.

b. A factory assembles your car. It is later delivered to your local dealer.

4. You go to a store to buy jeans, none are on the shelf.

   a. When you go to a store to buy jeans, none are on the shelf.

   b. You go to a store to buy jeans, but none are on the shelf.

5. Instead, you look at different styles onscreen you make your choice.

   a. Instead, as you look at different styles onscreen, you make your choice.

   b. Instead, you look at different styles onscreen, and you make your choice.

6. Taking measurements is not new now they can be taken by a three-dimensional camera.

   a. Although taking measurements is not new, now they can be taken by a three-dimensional camera.

   b. Taking measurements is not new, but now they can be taken by a three-dimensional camera.

7. Your measurements have been taken electronically your jeans will fit perfectly.

   a. Because your measurements have been taken electronically, your jeans will fit perfectly.

   b. Your measurements have been taken electronically, so your jeans will fit perfectly.

8. Your selection and measurements are transmitted to a factory your jeans are made to order.

   a. Your selection and measurements are transmitted to a factory. Your jeans are made to order.

   b. Your selection and measurements are transmitted to a factory, and your jeans are made to order.

9. You want to experiment with changing your hairstyle, a computer screen will show you with long, short, or differently colored hair.

   a. If you want to experiment with changing your hairstyle, a computer screen will show you with long, short, or differently colored hair.

   b. You want to experiment with changing your hairstyle. A computer screen will show you with long, short, or differently colored hair.

10. You can leave the way you came in you can leave with a new look.

    a. Although you can leave the way you came in, you can leave with a new look.

    b. You can leave the way you came in, or you can leave with a new look.

PRACTICE 3 WRITING ASSIGNMENT

On the first day of the term, teachers generally announce their rules: rules about how homework should be handed in or how many absences are allowed. This is your chance to think about rules that *students* might expect *instructors* to follow. In small groups, discuss what rules instructors should follow in order to help students learn. List at least five rules.

Then let each group member choose one rule to write about, using examples from his or her classroom experiences to explain why that rule is important. Finally, exchange papers with another group member and check each other's work for run-ons and comma splices.

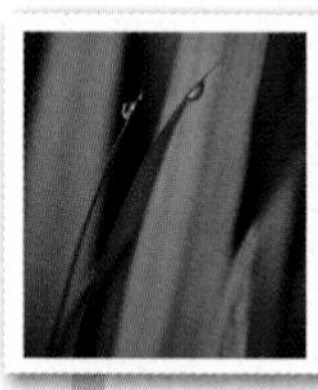

CHAPTER HIGHLIGHTS

Avoid run-ons and comma splices:

Her house faces the ocean the view is breathtaking. (*run-on*)

Her house faces the ocean, the view is breathtaking. (*comma splice*)

Use these techniques to avoid run-ons and comma splices.

- **Write two complete sentences:**

  Her house faces the ocean. The view is breathtaking.

- **Use a coordinating conjunction:**

  Her house faces the ocean, *so* the view is breathtaking.

- **Use a subordinating conjunction:**

  Because her house faces the ocean, the view is breathtaking.

CHAPTER REVIEW

Run-ons and comma splices are most likely to occur in paragraphs or longer pieces of writing. Proofread each paragraph for run-ons and comma splices. Correct them in any way that makes sense: Make two separate sentences, add a coordinating conjunction, or add a subordinating conjunction. Make your corrections above the lines. Punctuate with care. Answers will vary.

Tony Hawk airborne.
© 2000 Getty Images.

TEACHING TIP
Refer students to page 210 for a useful and graphic summary of five ways to join ideas. Many students have this page copied and keep it handy as they write.

A. (1) Skateboarder Tony Hawk has not only dramatically changed his sport, but he also has contributed to the popularity of all extreme sports. (2) The wholesome Hawk is responsible for cleaning up skateboarding's early reputation as the pastime of rebels and ~~hoodlums now~~ hoodlums. Now it's an acceptable, mainstream activity. (3) Hawk is also famous for defying the laws of physics to create amazing new aerial acrobatics. (4) In 1999, at the age of thirty-one, he was the first skater ever to complete a ~~900, this~~ 900. This is a 360-degree spin done two-and-a-half times in mid-air. (5) As a result, he is called "the Michael Jordan of skateboarding." (6) Today, although he has retired from competition, he performs in exhibitions all over the ~~country~~ country, and surveys of young people reveal that he is more popular than Shaquille O'Neal or Tiger Woods. (7) Hawk's fame has created a huge interest in skateboarding. (8) In 2001, 8.2 million Americans under the age of eighteen played baseball, but 10.6 million skateboarded. (9) Today, these young athletes roll into skate parks that have sprung up all over the country, thanks to Hawk's influence.

TEACHING TIP
Because run-ons and comma splices, like fragments, are most likely to occur in longer pieces of writing, proofreading exercises like these are especially important.

B. (1) Nearly one million people traveled to Graceland last ~~year it~~ year. It is the most visited home in America except for the White House. (2) In case you didn't know, Graceland was the home of rock-and-roll legend Elvis ~~Presley he~~ Presley. He bought it in 1957 at the age of twenty-two when he suddenly became rich and famous. (3) It was opened to the public in 1982, five years after Elvis died there. (4) The eighteen-room Memphis mansion was Elvis's home for twenty years, so visitors can see what was considered luxury living in the 1960s and 1970s. (5) Vinyl beanbag chairs, mirrored ceilings, and shag carpeting were high fashion then. (6) However, many visitors travel to the singer's home to honor the man rather than to see the house. (7) For some, a trip to Graceland has become a spiritual ~~experience during~~ experience. During Elvis Presley's "Death Week," tens of thousands arrive from all over the world to honor their idol.

C. (1) What do you do every night before you go to sleep and every morning when you wake up? (2) You probably brush your teeth, ^but most people in the United States did not start brushing their teeth until after the 1850s. (3) People living in the nineteenth century did not have ~~toothpaste,~~ toothpaste, so Dr. Washington Wentworth Sheffield developed a tooth-cleaning substance, which soon became widely available. (4) With the help of his son, this Connecticut dentist changed our daily habits by making the first ~~toothpaste it~~ toothpaste. It was called Dr. Sheffield's Creme Dentifrice. (5) ~~The~~ Because the product was not marketed cleverly enough, the idea of using toothpaste caught on slowly. (6) Then toothpaste was put into tin ~~tubes~~ tubes, and everyone wanted to try this new product. (7) Think of life without tubes of mint-flavored ~~toothpaste~~ toothpaste, and then thank Dr. Sheffield for his idea.

D. (1) The first semester of college is difficult for many students ^because they must take on many new responsibilities. (2) For instance, they must create their own schedules. (3) New students get to select their ~~courses in~~ courses. In addition, they have to decide when they will take them. (4) Students also must purchase their own ~~textbooks,~~ textbooks. ~~colleges~~ Colleges do not distribute textbooks each term as high schools do. (5) No bells ring to announce when classes begin and ~~end~~ end, yet students are supposed to arrive on time. (6) Furthermore, many professors do not call the ~~roll~~ roll, for they expect students to attend classes regularly and know the assignments. (7) Above all, new students must be self-disciplined. (8) No one stands over them telling them to do their homework or to visit the writing lab for extra ~~help, they~~ help. They must balance the temptation to have fun and the desire to build a successful future.

E. (1) Languages are disappearing in countries on every continent. (2) North America has two hundred Native American languages, ^but only about fifty now have more than a thousand speakers. (3) The Celtic languages of northwest Europe also have been declining for many generations. (4) However, the death of languages is most noticeable in isolated communities in Asia and Australia. (5) A different language is spoken in each tiny ~~community sometimes~~ community. Sometimes only ten people speak it.

(6) In such small communities, a whole language can die if one village perishes. When (7) Westerners explored a rain forest in Venezuela in the ~~1960s~~ 1960s, they carried a flu virus into a tiny community. (8) The virus killed all the villagers, and their language disappeared with them. (9) However, most languages fade out when a smaller community comes into close contact with a larger, more powerful ~~one,~~ one. ~~people~~ People begin to use the "more important" language. (10) A language that gives better access to education, jobs, and new technology usually prevails over a native mother tongue.

(11) According to scholars who study languages, almost half of the world's 6,500 languages are in danger of extinction. (12) That statistic represents more than the loss of specific ~~languages,~~ languages because every language represents a way of looking at the world. (13) Whenever a language disappears, we lose a unique point of view. (14) No other language can really take its place.

EXPLORING ONLINE

TEACHING TIP
More practice and assessment are available in the *Grassroots* Test Bank; linked ACE tests on the *Grassroots* student website; *WriteSpace for Grassroots*; and the Exploring Online links in this chapter.

<http://chompchomp2.com/gbfree/csfs01/csfs01.htm> Interactive quiz-contest: Find comma splices or run-ons (called fused sentences here).

<http://www.ccc.commnet.edu/grammar/quizzes/nova/nova4.htm> Interactive quiz: Find and fix the run-ons in these sentences.

<http://college.hmco.com/devenglish> Visit the *Grassroots* 8/e Student Website for more exercises and quizzes.

CHAPTER 16

Semicolons and Conjunctive Adverbs

PART A Defining and Using Semicolons

TEACHING TIP
Students may have a tendency to use semicolons inappropriately. You might want to emphasize that there are only *two* uses for the semicolon: 1) to separate two sentences, and 2) to separate items in a series that contains internal commas.

So far you have learned to join ideas together in two ways.

Coordinating conjunctions *(and, but, for, nor, or, so, yet)* can join ideas:

(1) This is the worst food we have ever tasted, *so* we will never eat in this restaurant again.

Subordinating conjunctions (for example, *although, as, because, if,* and *when*) can join ideas:

(2) *Because* this is the worst food we have ever tasted, we will never eat in this restaurant again.

Another way to join ideas is with a **semicolon:**

ESL TIP
Few languages use the semicolon as English does. ESL students may be helped by a preliminary discussion of how punctuation is used in their native languages.

(3) This is the worst food we have ever tasted; we will never eat in this restaurant again.

A *semicolon* joins two related independent ideas without a conjunction; do not capitalize the first word after a semicolon.

Use the semicolon for variety. In general, use no more than one or two semicolons in a paragraph.

PRACTICE 1

Each independent idea below is the first half of a sentence. Add a semicolon and a second complete idea, one that can stand alone. Sample answers

EXAMPLE: Ken was a cashier at Food City *; now he manages the store.*

TEACHING TIP
Stress to students that semicolons connect only *related* ideas. If two ideas do not have a close relationship (such as a cause and an effect, a comparison of two like things, a time order relationship, etc.), they probably should be separated with a period.

1. My cat spotted a mouse ; both of them ran in opposite directions.

2. The garage became an art studio ; it was filled with canvases and old magazines for collage images.

3. Beatrice has an unlisted phone number ; I have it programmed into my phone.

4. I felt sure someone had been in the room ; my coat was not where I had left it.

5. Roslyn's first car had a stick shift ; her second one has an automatic transmission.

BE CAREFUL: Do not use a semicolon between a dependent idea and an independent idea.

> Although he is never at home, he is not difficult to reach at the office.

- You cannot use a semicolon in this sentence because the first idea *(although he is never at home)* cannot stand alone.
- The word *although* requires that another idea be added in order to make a complete sentence.

PRACTICE 2

Which of these ideas can be followed by a semicolon and an independent thought? Check them (✓).

TEACHING TIP
Ask students to explain why the clauses in 1, 3, 8, and 9 are dependent. They should be able to identify the subordinating conjunctions as the reason.

1. When Molly peered over the counter _____
2. The library has installed new computers ✓
3. After he finishes cleaning the fish _____
4. She suddenly started to laugh ✓
5. My answer is simple ✓
6. I cannot find my car keys ✓
7. The rain poured down in buckets ✓
8. Before the health fair is over _____
9. Unless you arrive early _____
10. Because you understand, I feel better ✓

Now copy the sentences you have checked, add a semicolon, and complete each sentence with a second independent idea. You should have checked sentences 2, 4, 5, 6, 7, and 10. Sample answers

2. The library has installed new computers; we can find information faster now.

4. She suddenly started to laugh; her dog had switched on the light.

5. My answer is simple; I will not go.

6. I cannot find my car keys; I have looked everywhere.

7. The rain poured down in buckets; everyone left the stands.

10. Because you understand, I feel better; I am ready to try again.

PRACTICE 3

Proofread for incorrect semicolons or capital letters. Make your corrections above the lines.

(1) The Swiss Army knife is carried in the pockets and purses of millions of travelers, campers, and just plain folks. (2) Numerous useful gadgets are folded into its famous red handle; ~~These~~ these include knife blades, tweezers, scissors, toothpick, screwdriver, bottle opener, fish scaler, and magnifying glass. (3) Because the knife contains many ~~tools;~~ tools, it is also carried by explorers, mountain climbers, and astronauts. (4) Lives have been saved by the Swiss Army knife. (5) It once opened the iced-up oxygen system of someone climbing Mount Everest; ~~It~~ it saved the lives of scientists stranded on an island who used the tiny saw on the knife to cut branches for a fire. (6) The handy Swiss Army knife was created for Swiss soldiers in ~~1891; and~~ 1891 and soon became popular all over the world. (7) It comes in many models and ~~colors many~~ colors; many people prefer the classic original. (8) The Swiss Army knife deserves its reputation for beautiful design and usefulness; a red one is on permanent display in New York's famous Museum of Modern Art.

PART B Defining and Using Conjunctive Adverbs

Another excellent method of joining ideas is to use a semicolon and a special kind of adverb. This special adverb is called a **conjunctive adverb** because it is part *conjunction* and part *adverb*.

TEACHING TIP
Point out to students that using conjunctive adverbs correctly will significantly increase the sophistication of their writing.

(1) (a) He received an *A* on his term paper; *furthermore,*
(b) the instructor exempted him from the final.

- *Furthermore* adds idea (b) to idea (a).
- The sentence might have been written, "He received an *A* on his term paper, *and* the instructor exempted him from the final."
- However, *furthermore* is stronger and more emphatic.
- Note the punctuation.

TEACHING TIP
Use sets of closely related sentences to demonstrate how the lack of a conjunctive adverb forces readers to discern the relationship between the two ideas on their own. Thus, readers are more likely to miss the connection or to misunderstand it.

(2) (a) Luzette has never studied finance; *however,*
(b) she plays the stock market like a pro.

- *However* contrasts ideas (a) and (b).
- The sentence might have been written, "Luzette has never studied finance, *but* she plays the stock market like a pro."
- However, the word *however* is stronger and more emphatic.
- Note the punctuation.

(3) (a) The complete dictionary weighs thirty pounds; *therefore,*
(b) I bring my pocket edition to school.

- *Therefore* shows that idea (a) is the cause of idea (b).
- The sentence might have been written, "*Because* the complete dictionary weights thirty pounds, I bring my pocket edition to school."
- However, *therefore* is stronger and more emphatic.
- Note the punctuation.

A *conjunctive adverb* may be used with a semicolon only when both ideas are independent and can stand alone.

Here are some common conjunctive adverbs and their meanings:

Common Conjunctive Adverbs

consequently	*means*	as a result
furthermore	*means*	in addition
however	*means*	in contrast
instead	*means*	in place of
meanwhile	*means*	at the same time
nevertheless	*means*	in contrast
otherwise	*means*	as an alternative
therefore	*means*	for that reason

Conjunctive adverbs are also called **transitional expressions**. They help the reader see the transitions, or changes in meaning, from one idea to the next.

PRACTICE 4

Add an idea after each conjunctive adverb. The idea you add must make sense in terms of the entire sentence, so keep in mind the meaning of each conjunctive adverb. If necessary, refer to the chart. Sample answers

TEACHING TIP
After students complete Practice 4, have them share their answers with a group or with the whole class.

EXAMPLE: Several students had questions about the final; therefore, they stayed after class to chat with the instructor.

1. Aunt Bessie did a handstand; meanwhile, Uncle Sid pole-vaulted over the fence.
2. Anna says whatever is on her mind; consequently, she sometimes offends people.
3. I refuse to wear those red cowboy boots again; furthermore, I won't wear the ten-gallon hat.
4. Travis is a good role model; otherwise, his little son might not be so polite.
5. Kim wanted to volunteer at the hospital; however, she couldn't find time to take the training course for volunteers.
6. My mother carried two bulky pieces of luggage off the plane; furthermore, she had her coat and a tennis racket under her arm.
7. I have many chores to do today; nevertheless, I will take time to shoot some baskets.
8. The gas gauge on my car does not work properly; therefore, I record my mileage every time I fill the gas tank.

PART C Punctuating Conjunctive Adverbs

Notice the punctuation pattern:

> Complete idea; conjunctive adverb, complete idea.

- The conjunctive adverb is preceded by a semicolon.
- It is followed by a comma.

PRACTICE 5

Punctuate these sentences correctly.

1. Many people think that art is serious rather than ~~fun however~~ fun; however, they might change their minds if they could see a Cow Parade.

TEACHING TIP
Since the first Chicago Cow Parade, animal statue parades have sprung up across the country. Decorated pigs in Cincinnati, fish in New Orleans, porpoises in Key West, and moose in Toronto are just a few examples.

2. For this public art event, a city's artists decorate identical, life-size sculptures of ~~cows consequently~~ cows; consequently, each cow becomes a humorous artistic work.
3. In the Chicago and New York Cow Parades, the finished art objects were anything but dull and ~~reserved instead~~ reserved; instead, they were wildly creative.
4. Each artist picked a character or idea to ~~portray furthermore;~~ portray; furthermore, he or she gave that special bovine a fitting name.
5. For example, one cow was painted with stars and stripes to resemble our country's ~~flag consequently~~ flag; consequently, its name was "Americow the Beautiful."
6. Dark-eyed "Cowapatra" was decorated like the Queen of the ~~Nile meanwhile~~ Nile; meanwhile, "Moozart" wore the red velvet coat and white wig of that famous composer.
7. "Prima Cowlerina" posed in a pink tutu and four toe shoes, and "Cownt Dracula" had ~~fangs therefore~~ fangs; therefore, even blasé city dwellers paused to admire them.
8. Many cows were decorated with a famous work of ~~art consequently~~ art; consequently, they had names like "Picowso," "Mootisse," or "Vincent Van Cogh."
9. People seem to love meeting a plaster cow dressed in hip hop clothing or covered with gumdrops on a city ~~street meanwhile~~ street; meanwhile, urban work and play can go on as usual.
10. Each event concludes with an auction of the cows to benefit ~~charity therefore~~ charity; therefore, a Cow Parade not only brings art to the public but also raises money for a good cause.

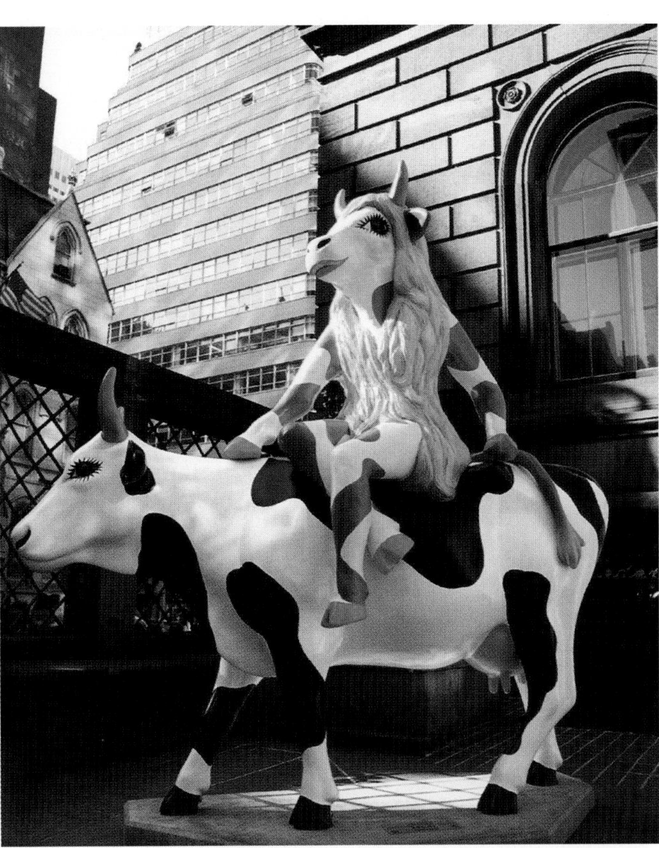

Lady Cowdiva,
New York Cow Parade.

Courtesy Cow Parade Holdings Corp.

PRACTICE 6

Combine each set of sentences into one, using a conjunctive adverb. Choose a conjunctive adverb that expresses the relationship between the two ideas. Punctuate with care. Answers will vary.

1. (a) Marilyn fell asleep on the train.
   (b) She missed her stop.
   Combination: Marilyn fell asleep on the train; therefore, she missed her stop.

2. (a) Last night Channel 20 televised a special about gorillas.
   (b) I did not get home in time to see it.
   Combination: Last night Channel 20 televised a special about gorillas; however, I did not get home in time to see it.

3. (a) Roberta writes to her nephew every month.
   (b) She sends a gift with every letter.
   Combination: Roberta writes to her nephew every month; furthermore, she sends a gift with every letter.

4. (a) It takes me almost an hour to get to school each morning.
   (b) The scenery makes the drive a pleasure.
   Combination: It takes me almost an hour to get to school each morning; nevertheless, the scenery makes the drive a pleasure.

5. (a) Luke missed work on Monday.
   (b) He did not proofread the quarterly report.
   Combination: Luke missed work on Monday; consequently, he did not proofread the quarterly report.

BE CAREFUL: Never use a semicolon and a conjunctive adverb when the conjunctive adverb does not join two independent ideas.

(1) *However,* I don't climb mountains.
(2) I don't *however,* climb mountains.
(3) I don't climb mountains, *however*.

- Why aren't semicolons used in sentences (1), (2), and (3)?
- These sentences contain only one independent idea; therefore, a semicolon cannot be used.

Never use a semicolon to join two ideas if one of the ideas is subordinate to the other.

(4) If I climbed mountains, *however*, I would hike in the Rockies.

- Are the two ideas in sentence (4) independent?
- *If I climbed mountains* cannot stand alone as an independent idea; therefore, a semicolon cannot be used.

PRACTICE 7 WRITING ASSIGNMENTS

Many people find that certain situations make them nervous or anxious—for example, giving a speech or meeting strangers at a social gathering. Have you ever conquered such an anxiety yourself or even learned to cope with it successfully?

Write to someone who has the same fear you have had; encourage him or her with your success story, explaining how you managed the anxiety. Describe what steps you took.

Use one or two semicolons and at least one conjunctive adverb in your paper. Make sure that you are joining together two independent ideas.

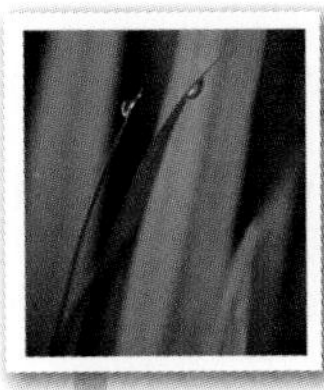

CHAPTER HIGHLIGHTS

- **A semicolon joins two independent ideas:**

  I like hiking; she prefers fishing.

- **Do not capitalize the first word after a semicolon.**

Independent idea	;	*independent idea.*

- **A semicolon and a conjunctive adverb join two independent ideas:**

  We can't go rowing now; *however,* we can go on Sunday.

  Lou earned an 83 on the exam; *therefore,* he passed physics.

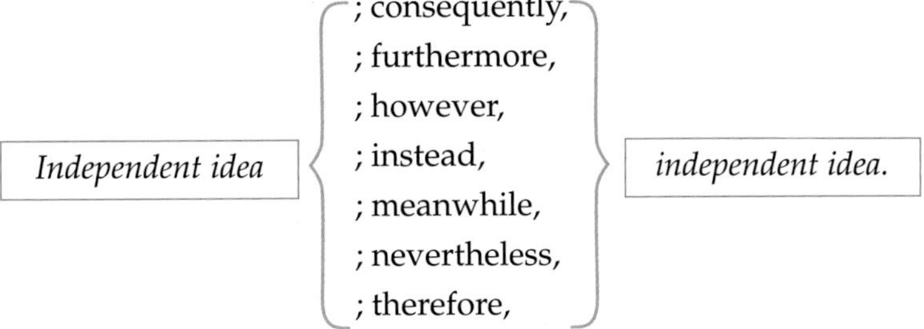

Independent idea { ; consequently, ; furthermore, ; however, ; instead, ; meanwhile, ; nevertheless, ; therefore, } *independent idea.*

- **Use a semicolon *only* when the conjunctive adverb joins two independent ideas:**

  I wasn't sorry; however, I apologized. *(two independent ideas)*

  I apologized, however. *(one independent idea)*

  If you wanted to go, however, you should have said so. *(one dependent idea + one independent idea)*

CHAPTER REVIEW

Proofread the following paragraph for semicolon errors, conjunctive adverb errors, and punctuation errors. Correct each error above the line.

(1) Perhaps you have seen a sleek circular symbol consisting of two connected teardrop shapes, one white and one black. (2) This is the Chinese symbol of Yin Yang. (3) According to ancient Chinese philosophy, we live in a world of opposites; consequently, ~~opposites consequently~~ the world contains female and male, dark and light, cold and hot, yin and yang. (4) Yin and yang represent contrasting life forces; however, ~~forces however~~ the symbol shows us a harmony of opposites that underlies the universe. (5) On the one hand, yin is any force that is feminine, soft, receptive, hidden, cool, and dark; thus, ~~dark, thus;~~ the dark part of the symbol represents yin. (6) Yang, on the other hand, describes any force that is masculine, hard, aggressive, open, hot, and light; ~~light,~~ therefore, the light part of the symbol represents yang. (7) However, the Yin Yang symbol also contains a dot of black in the white area and a dot of white in the black area. (8) These dots remind us that nothing is simply black or white; ~~white~~ everything contains an element of the opposing force. (9) For example, all people are a mix of yin and yang qualities, whatever their gender. (10) The whole symbol seems to say that we know pleasure because we have felt pain, beauty because we have seen ugliness, and love because we have known its opposite.

EXPLORING ONLINE

TEACHING TIP
More practice and assessment are available in the *Grassroots* Test Bank; linked ACE tests on the *Grassroots* student website; *WriteSpace for Grassroots*; and the Exploring Online links in this chapter.

<http://owl.english.purdue.edu/handouts/grammar/g_commacompEX1.html>
Paper-and-pencil quiz: Does each sentence require a comma or a semicolon?

<http://www.ccc.commnet.edu/cgi-shl/quiz.pl/run-ons_add1.htm>
Interactive quiz: Click the sentence that corrects the run-on or comma splice.

<http://college.hmco.com/devenglish> Visit the *Grassroots* 8/e Student Website for more exercises and quizzes.

CHAPTER 17

Relative Pronouns

PART A Defining and Using Relative Pronouns

PART B Punctuating Ideas Introduced by WHO, WHICH, or THAT

PART A Defining and Using Relative Pronouns

ESL TIP
For ESL students and visual learners, color coding can help show how relative clauses can be embedded in the main sentence or independent clause.

To add variety to your writing, you sometimes may wish to use **relative pronouns** to combine two sentences.

(1) My grandfather is eighty years old.

(2) He collects stamps.

- Sentences (1) and (2) are grammatically correct.
- They are so short, however, that you may wish to combine them.

(3) My grandfather, who is eighty years old, collects stamps.

- Sentence (3) is a combination of (1) and (2).
- *Who* has replaced *he*, the subject of sentence (2). *Who* introduces the rest of the idea, *is eighty years old*.
- *Who* is called a *relative pronoun* because it *relates* "is eighty years old" to "my grandfather."*

TEACHING TIP
You may want to take a moment to review with students what they learned about correcting fragments in Chapter 7, Part C. Point out that the sentences they corrected when they completed Practice 6 (p. 79) are all relative pronoun clause fragments.

BE CAREFUL: An idea introduced by a relative pronoun cannot stand alone as a complete and independent sentence. It is dependent; it needs an independent idea (like "My grandfather collects stamps") to complete its meaning.

Here are some more combinations:

(4) He gives great singing lessons.

(5) All his pupils love them.

(6) He gives great singing lessons, *which* all his pupils love.

*For work on subject-verb agreement with relative pronouns, see Chapter 8, Part G.

(7) I have a large dining room.

(8) It can seat twenty people.

(9) I have a large dining room *that* can seat twenty people.

- As you can see, *which* and *that* also can be used as relative pronouns.
- In sentence (6), what does *which* relate or refer to? great singing lessons
- In sentence (9), what does *that* relate or refer to? a large dining room

ESL TIP
ESL students face formidable challenges with relative clauses. In English and most European languages, the relative clause *follows* the noun being modified, but in several languages (e.g., Japanese, Chinese, and Korean), the relative clause *precedes* the noun being modified.

When *who, which,* and *that* are used as relative pronouns, they usually come directly after the words they relate to.

My father, who . . .

. . . singing lessons, which . . .

. . . dining room that . . .

BE CAREFUL: *Who, which,* and *that* cannot be used interchangeably.

Who **refers to people.**

Which **refers to things.**

That **refers to people or things.**

PRACTICE 1

TEACHING TIP
Sentence combining exercises like Practice 1 are an excellent way for students to practice writing more sophisticated sentences. For more sentence combining practice, students can try the interactive, computer-graded exercises at **<http://www.ccc.commnet.edu/grammar/combining_skills.htm>**.

Combine each set of sentences into one sentence. Make sure to use *who, which,* and *that* correctly.

EXAMPLE: a. The garden is beginning to sprout.
b. I planted it last week.

Combination: The garden that I planted last week is beginning to sprout.

1. a. My uncle is giving me diving lessons.
   b. He was a state champion.

   Combination: My uncle, who was a state champion, is giving me diving lessons.

2. a. Our marriage ceremony was quick and sweet.
   b. It made our nervous parents happy.

   Combination: Our marriage ceremony, which was quick and sweet, made our nervous parents happy.

3. a. The manatee is a sea mammal.
   b. It lives along the Florida coast.

   Combination: The manatee is a sea mammal that lives along the Florida coast.

4. a. Donna bought a new backpack.
   b. The backpack has thickly padded straps.

   Combination: Donna bought a new backpack that has thickly padded straps.

5. a. This walking tour has thirty-two stops.
   b. It is a challenge to complete.

   Combination: This walking tour, which has thirty-two stops, is a challenge to complete.

ESL TIP
Spanish does not distinguish between personal *(who)* and impersonal *(which, that)* pronouns. Furthermore, a relative pronoun cannot be omitted in Spanish, as it has been in the sentence *The girls we saw looked so happy.*

6. a. Hockey is a fast-moving game.
   b. It often becomes violent.

   Combination: Hockey, which is a fast-moving game, often becomes violent.

7. a. Andrew Jackson was the seventh U.S. president.
   b. He was born in South Carolina.

   Combination: Andrew Jackson, who was born in South Carolina, was the seventh U.S. president.

8. a. At the beach, I always use sunscreen.
   b. It prevents burns and lessens the danger of skin cancer.

   Combination: At the beach, I always use sunscreen, which prevents burns and lessens the danger of skin cancer.

PART B Punctuating Ideas Introduced by WHO, WHICH, or THAT

Ideas introduced by relative pronouns can be one of two types, either **restrictive** or **nonrestrictive**. Punctuating them must be done carefully.

Restrictive

Never eat peaches *that are* green.

TEACHING TIP
A caution for students: improper punctuation of relative pronoun clauses can create fragments, and wrong placement can create dangling or misplaced modifiers.

- A *relative clause* has (1) a subject that is a relative pronoun and (2) a verb.
- What is the relative clause in the sentence in the box? that are green
- Can you leave out *that are green* and still keep the basic meaning of the sentence?
- No! You are not saying *don't eat peaches*; you are saying don't eat *certain kinds* of peaches—*green* ones.
- Therefore, *that are green* is *restrictive*; it restricts the meaning of the sentence.

A *restrictive clause* is not set off by commas; it is necessary to the meaning of the sentence.

Nonrestrictive

My guitar, *which is a Martin*, was given to me as a gift.

TEACHING TIP
Students will need to memorize that the pronoun *that* is not used with a comma and the pronoun *which* is.

- In this sentence, the relative clause is which is a Martin.
- Can you leave out *which is a Martin* and still keep the basic meaning of the sentence?
- Yes! *Which is a Martin* merely adds a fact. It does not change the basic idea of the sentence, which is *my guitar was given to me as a gift.*
- Therefore, *which is a Martin* is *nonrestrictive;* it does not restrict or change the meaning of the sentence.

A *nonrestrictive clause* is set off by commas; it is not necessary to the meaning of the sentence.

Note: *Which* is often used as a nonrestrictive relative pronoun.

PRACTICE 2

Punctuate correctly. Write a *C* next to each correct sentence.

1. People who need help are often embarrassed to ask for it. C
2. Ovens that clean themselves are the best kind. C
3. Paint that contains lead can be dangerous to children. C
4. The ~~anaconda~~ anaconda, which is the largest snake in the ~~world~~ world, can weigh 550 pounds. ___
5. Edward's ~~watch~~ watch, which tells the time and the ~~date~~ date, was a gift from his wife. ___
6. ~~Carol~~ Carol, who is a flight ~~attendant~~ attendant, has just left for Pakistan.
7. Joel ~~Upton~~ Upton, who is a dean of ~~students~~ students, usually sings in the yearly talent show. ___
8. Exercise that causes severe exhaustion is dangerous. C

PRACTICE 3

Complete each sentence by completing the relative clause. Sample answers

EXAMPLE: Boxing is a sport that upsets me.

1. My aunt, who doesn't even like animals, rescued a cat last week.
2. A family that works as a team can solve its problems.
3. I never vote for candidates who promise too much.
4. This T-shirt, which lists all of Shakespeare's history plays, was a gift.
5. Paris, which has wonderful restaurants, is an exciting city to visit.

6. James, who wants to be a pilot, just enlisted in the Air Force.

7. I cannot resist stores that have bargain basements.

8. This company, which manufactures sportswear, provides health benefits and retirement plans for employees.

PRACTICE 4

On paper or on a computer, write four sentences using restrictive relative clauses and four using nonrestrictive relative clauses. Punctuate with care.

PRACTICE 5 WRITING ASSIGNMENT

In a small group, discuss a change that you would like to see made in your neighborhood—an additional traffic light or more police patrols. Your task is to write a flier that will convince neighbors that this change is important; your purpose is to win them over to your side. The flier might note, for instance, that a child was killed at a certain intersection or that you know of several burglaries that could have been prevented.

Each member of the group should write his or her own flier, including one or two sentences with relative pronouns and correct punctuation. Then read the fliers aloud; decide which are effective and why. Be prepared to defend your choices. Finally, exchange papers with a partner and check for the correct use of relative pronouns.

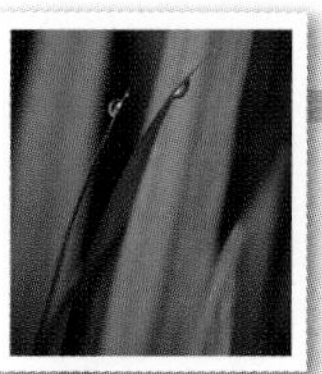

CHAPTER HIGHLIGHTS

- **Relative pronouns (*who, which,* and *that*) can join two independent ideas:**

  We met Krizia Stone, *who* runs an advertising agency.

  Last night, I had a hamburger *that* was too rare.

  My favorite radio station, *which* is WQDF, plays mostly jazz.

- **Restrictive relative clauses change the meaning of the sentence. They are not set off by commas:**

  The uncle *who is helping me through college* lives in Texas.

  The car *that we saw Ned driving* was not his.

- **Nonrestrictive relative clauses do not change the meaning of the sentence. They are set off by commas:**

  My uncle, *who lives in Texas,* owns a supermarket.

  Ned's car, *which is a 1992 Mazda,* was at the repair shop.

CHAPTER REVIEW

Proofread the following paragraph for relative pronoun errors and punctuation errors. Correct each error above the line.

(1) Charles Anderson is best known as the trainer of the Tuskegee ~~Airmen~~ Airmen, who were the first African-American combat pilots. (2) During a time when African Americans were prevented from becoming pilots, Anderson was fascinated by planes. (3) He learned about flying from books. (4) At age twenty-two, he bought a used ~~plane which,~~ plane, which became his teacher. (5) Eventually he met ~~someone,~~ someone who helped him become an expert flyer. (6) Battling against discrimination, Anderson became the first African American to earn an air transport pilot's license. (7) He and another pilot made the first round-trip flight across America by black Americans. (8) In 1939, Anderson started a civilian pilot training program at Tuskegee Institute in Alabama. (9) One day Eleanor Roosevelt, ~~which~~ who was First Lady at the ~~time~~ time, insisted on flying with him. (10) Soon afterward, Tuskegee Institute was chosen by the Army Air Corps for a special program. (11) ~~Anderson~~ Anderson, who was chief flight ~~instructor~~ instructor, gave America's first African American World War II pilots their initial training. (12) During the war, the Tuskegee Airmen showed great skill and ~~heroism~~ heroism, which were later recognized by an extraordinary number of honors and awards.

EXPLORING ONLINE

TEACHING TIP
More practice and assessment are available in the *Grassroots* Test Bank; linked ACE tests on the *Grassroots* student website; *WriteSpace for Grassroots*; and the Exploring Online links in this chapter.

<http://www.ccc.commnet.edu/grammar/quizzes/which_quiz.htm> Interactive quiz: Choose *who, which,* or *that*.

<http://www.dailygrammar.com/256to260.shtml> Graded quiz: Combine sentences with *who, which,* or *that* (here called adjective) clauses.

<http://college.hmco.com/devenglish> Visit the *Grassroots* 8/e Student Website for more exercises and quizzes.

CHAPTER 18

-ING Modifiers

PART A Using -ING Modifiers

PART B Avoiding Confusing Modifiers

PART A Using -ING Modifiers

Another way to join ideas together is with an **-ing modifier**, or **present participle**.

ESL TIP
ESL learners may be more likely to misplace phrases and clauses because of differences in word order between English and their native languages. These errors often occur more frequently when students think in their native language and then try to translate a thought into English.

(1) Beth was learning to ski. She broke her ankle.

(2) Learning to ski, Beth broke her ankle.

- It seems that *while* Beth was learning to ski, she had an accident. Sentence (2) emphasizes this time relationship and also joins two short sentences in one longer one.
- In sentence (2), *learning* without its helping verb, *was,* is not a verb. Instead, *learning to ski* refers to or modifies *Beth,* the subject of the new sentence.

Learning to ski, Beth broke her ankle.

- Note that a comma follows the introductory *-ing* modifier, setting it off from the independent idea.

PRACTICE 1

Combine the two sentences in each pair, using the *-ing* modifier to connect them. Drop unnecessary words. Draw an arrow from the *-ing* word to the word or words to which it refers.

EXAMPLE: Tom was standing on the deck. He waved good-bye to his family.

Standing on the deck, Tom waved good-bye to his family.

1. Kyla was searching for change. She found her lost earring.

Searching for change, Kyla found her lost earring.

2. The children worked all evening. They completed the jigsaw puzzle.

   Working all evening, the children completed the jigsaw puzzle.

3. They were hiking cross-country. They made many new friends.

   Hiking cross-country, they made many new friends.

4. She was visiting Santa Fe. She decided to move there.

   Visiting Santa Fe, she decided to move there.

5. You are loading your camera. You spot a grease mark on the lens.

   Loading your camera, you spot a grease mark on the lens.

6. Seth was mumbling to himself. He named the fifty states.

   Mumbling to himself, Seth named the fifty states.

7. Judge Smithers was pounding his gavel. He called a recess.

   Pounding his gavel, Judge Smithers called a recess.

8. The masons built the wall carefully. They were lifting huge rocks and cementing them in place.

   Lifting huge rocks and cementing them in place, the masons built the wall carefully.

PART B Avoiding Confusing Modifiers

TEACHING TIP
In addition to creating misplaced or dangling modifiers with *–ing* phrases, students are also likely to create fragments by punctuating these phrases as independent sentences.

Be sure that your *-ing* modifiers say what you mean!

(1) Hanging by the toe from the dresser drawer, Joe found his sock.

- Probably the writer did not mean that Joe spent time hanging by his toe. What, then, was hanging by the toe from the dresser drawer?
- *Hanging* refers to the *sock*, of course, but the order of the sentence does not show this. We can clear up the confusion by turning the ideas around.

Joe found his sock hanging by the toe from the dresser drawer.

Read your sentences in the previous exercise to make sure the order of the ideas is clear, not confusing.

(2) Visiting my cousin, our house was robbed.

- Does the writer mean that *our house* was visiting my cousin? To whom or what, then, does *visiting my cousin* refer?
- *Visiting* seems to refer to *I*, but there is no *I* in the sentence. To clear up the confusion, we would have to add or change words.

Visiting my cousin, I learned that our house was robbed.

PRACTICE 2

TEACHING TIP
Misplaced and confusing modifiers may be a new notion for many students, and learning to fix them will add clarity to their writing. The unintentional humor in Practice 2 makes it an excellent one to do with the full class.

Rewrite the following sentences to clarify any confusing *-ing* modifiers.

1. Biking and walking daily, Cheryl's commuting costs were cut.

   Rewrite: Biking and walking daily, Cheryl cut her commuting costs.

2. Leaping from tree to tree, Professor Fernandez spotted a monkey.

   Rewrite: Professor Fernandez spotted a monkey leaping from tree to tree.

3. Painting for three hours straight, the bathroom and the hallway were finished by Theresa.

   Rewrite: Painting for three hours straight, Theresa finished the bathroom and the hallway.

4. My son spotted our dog playing soccer in the schoolyard.

   Rewrite: Playing soccer in the schoolyard, my son spotted our dog.

5. Lying in the driveway, Tonya discovered her calculus textbook.

   Rewrite: Tonya discovered her calculus textbook lying in the driveway.

PRACTICE 3

On paper or on a computer, write three sentences of your own, using *-ing* modifiers to join ideas.

PRACTICE 4 WRITING ASSIGNMENT

Some people feel that much popular music degrades women and encourages drug abuse and violence. Others feel that popular songs expose many of the social ills we suffer from today. What do you think?

Prepare to take part in a debate to defend or criticize popular music. Your job is to convince the other side that your view is correct. Use specific song titles and artists as examples to support your argument. Use one or two *-ing* modifiers to join ideas together. Remember to punctuate correctly.

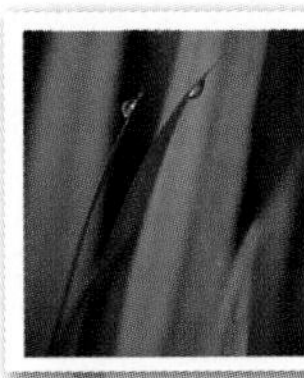

CHAPTER HIGHLIGHTS

- **An *-ing* modifier can join two ideas:**

  (1) Sol was cooking dinner.

  (2) He started a small fire.

  (1) + (2) *Cooking* dinner, Sol started a small fire.

- **Avoid confusing modifiers:**

  I finally found my cat riding my bike. *(incorrect)*

  Riding my bike, I finally found my cat. *(correct)*

CHAPTER REVIEW

Proofread the following paragraph for comma errors and confusing modifiers. Correct each error above the line.

(1) What happened in the shed behind Patrick O'Leary's house to start the Great Chicago Fire of 1871? (2) No one knows for sure. (3) ~~Smoking in the shed,~~ Some ~~some~~ people say the fire was started by careless ~~boys.~~ boys smoking in the shed. (4) In another story, poker-playing youngsters accidentally kicked over an oil lamp. (5) However, the blame usually is placed on Mrs. O'Leary's cow. (6) At 8:45 p.m., swinging a lantern at her side, ~~side~~ Mrs. O'Leary went out to milk the unruly cow. (7) Switching its tail, the ~~The~~ cow tipped the lantern. ~~lantern switching its tail.~~ (8) Recalling the incident, ~~incident~~ Mrs. Nellie Hayes branded the cow theory "nonsense." (9) In fact, she said that the O'Learys' neighbors were having a party on the hot night of October 7. (10) Looking for some fresh milk, ~~milk~~ a thirsty guest walked into the shed and dropped a lighted candle along the way. (11) Whatever happened, the fire was the greatest calamity of nineteenth-century America. (12) Killing three hundred people and destroying more than three square miles of buildings, it ~~buildings it~~ left ninety thousand people homeless.

EXPLORING ONLINE

TEACHING TIP
More practice and assessment are available in the *Grassroots* Test Bank; linked ACE tests on the *Grassroots* student website; *WriteSpace for Grassroots*; and the Exploring Online links in this chapter.

<http://www.uhv.edu/ac/grammar/dangling.html>
Are your modifiers misplaced? Review and put these modifiers in their correct places.

<http://college.hmco.com/devenglish> Visit the *Grassroots* 8/e Student Website for more exercises and quizzes.

WRITING ASSIGNMENTS

As you complete each writing assignment, remember to perform these steps:

- Write a clear, complete topic sentence.
- Use freewriting, brainstorming, or clustering to generate ideas for the body of your paragraph, essay, or letter.
- Arrange your best ideas in a plan.
- Revise for support, unity, coherence, and exact language.
- Proofread for grammar, punctuation, and spelling errors.

Writing Assignment 1: *Be a witness.* You have just witnessed a fender-bender involving a car and an ice cream truck. No one was hurt, but the insurance company has asked you to write an eyewitness report. First, visualize the accident and how it occurred. Then jot down as many details as possible to make your description of the accident as vivid as possible. Use subordinating conjunctions that indicate time (*when, as, before, while,* and so on) to show the order of events. Use as many techniques for joining ideas as you can, being careful about punctuation. Proofread for run-ons and comma splices.

Writing Assignment 2: *Discuss the advantages of pet ownership.* Many studies show that pets reduce stress, make us laugh, or otherwise improve our lives. Do you agree, or do you think that the disadvantages of pets outweigh their advantages? State your opinion in your topic sentence and then develop your paragraph with at least three supporting points. Including details about specific pets you have owned or observed will make your writing more interesting or humorous. No run-ons or comma splices, please.

Writing Assignment 3: *Evaluate so-called reality TV shows.* A newspaper has asked readers to respond to the question "Has reality television gone too far?" Think about the latest reality programs—*Survivor, Fear Factor,* and similar shows in which contestants are often humiliated and forced to do bizarre things. State whether reality TV has, or has not, gone too far. Then explain why you feel this way, using vivid details and examples from one or more programs to support your point. Use as many techniques for joining ideas as you can; proofread for run-ons and comma splices.

Writing Assignment 4: *React to a quotation.* From the "Work and Success" section of the Quotation Bank at the end of this book, choose a quotation that you strongly agree or disagree with. For instance, is it true that "most of us are looking for a calling, not a job" or that "money is like manure"? In your first sentence, repeat the entire quotation, explaining whether you do or do not agree with it. Then brainstorm, freewrite, or cluster to generate examples and facts supporting your view. Use your own or other people's experiences to strengthen your argument. Use as many techniques for joining ideas as you can. Proofread for run-ons and comma splices.

UNIT 4

REVIEW

Five Useful Ways to Join Ideas

In this unit, you have combined simple sentences by means of a **coordinating conjunction,** a **subordinating conjunction,** a **semicolon,** and a **semicolon** and **conjunctive adverb**. Here is a review chart of the sentence patterns discussed in this unit.

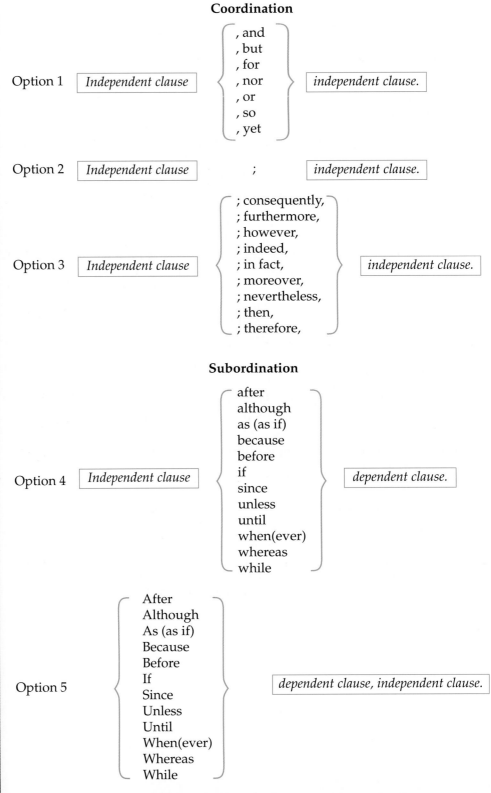

Coordination

Option 1 *Independent clause* { , and / , but / , for / , nor / , or / , so / , yet } *independent clause.*

Option 2 *Independent clause* ; *independent clause.*

Option 3 *Independent clause* { ; consequently, / ; furthermore, / ; however, / ; indeed, / ; in fact, / ; moreover, / ; nevertheless, / ; then, / ; therefore, } *independent clause.*

Subordination

Option 4 *Independent clause* { after / although / as (as if) / because / before / if / since / unless / until / when(ever) / whereas / while } *dependent clause.*

Option 5 { After / Although / As (as if) / Because / Before / If / Since / Unless / Until / When(ever) / Whereas / While } *dependent clause, independent clause.*

Proofreading

I have changed the student composition below so that it contains run-ons, comma splices, and misused semicolons. Proofread for these errors. Then correct them above the lines in any way you choose. (You should find eight errors.)
Answers will vary.

Managing Time in College

(1) When I started college, time was a problem. (2) I was always desperately reading an assignment just before class or racing to get to work on time. (3) The stress became too much. (4) It took a ~~while~~ while, but now I know how to manage my time. (5) The secret of my success is flexible planning.

(6) At the beginning of each semester, I mark a calendar with all the due dates for the ~~term these~~ term. These include deadlines for assignments, papers, and tests. (7) I also write in social events and ~~obligations, therefore;~~ obligations; therefore, I know at a glance when I need extra time during the next few months.

(8) Next, I make out a model weekly study schedule. (9) First, I block in the hours when I have to sleep, eat, work, go to class, and tend to my ~~family then~~ family. Then I decide what time I will devote to study and relaxation. (10) Finally, I fill in the times I will study each subject, making sure I plan at least one hour of study time for each hour of class time. (11) Generally, I plan some time just before or after a ~~class that~~ class. That way I can prepare for a class or review my notes right after a lecture.

(12) In reality, I don't follow this schedule ~~rigidly,~~ rigidly; I vary it according to the demands of the week and day. (13) In addition, I spend more time on my harder subjects and less time on the easy ones. (14) I also try to study my harder subjects in the ~~morning;~~ morning when I am most awake.

(15) I find that by setting up a model schedule but keeping it flexible, I can accomplish all I have to do with little worry. (16) This system may not help ~~everyone,~~ everyone; however, it has certainly worked for me.

Jesse Rose, student

Combining

Read each pair of sentences below to determine the relationship between them. Then join each pair in *two* different ways, using the conjunctions shown. Punctuate correctly. Answers will vary.

1. The tide had not yet come in.
   We went swimming.

   (although) Although the tide had not yet come in, we went swimming.

   (but) The tide had not yet come in, but we went swimming.

2. Michael enjoys drinking coffee.
   He needs to limit his caffeine intake.

   (yet) Michael enjoys drinking coffee, yet he needs to limit his caffeine intake.

   (nevertheless) Michael enjoys drinking coffee; nevertheless, he needs to limit his caffeine intake.

3. Alexis plays the trumpet very well.
   She hopes to have her own band someday.

   (and) Alexis plays the trumpet very well, and she hopes to have her own band someday.

   (furthermore) Alexis plays the trumpet very well; furthermore, she hopes to have her own band someday.

4. The lecture starts in five minutes.
   We had better get to our seats.

   (because) Because the lecture starts in five minutes, we had better get to our seats.

   (so) The lecture starts in five minutes, so we had better get to our seats.

5. He knows how to make money.
   He doesn't want to start another company.

   (although) Although he knows how to make money, he doesn't want to start another company.

   (however) He knows how to make money; however, he doesn't want to start another company.

Revising

Read through this essay of short, choppy sentences. Then revise it, combining some sentences. Use one coordinating conjunction, one subordinating conjunction, and any other ways you have learned to join ideas together. Keep some short sentences for variety. Make your corrections above the lines, and punctuate with care. Answers will vary.

Start Now!

(1) You may be young, but you ~~young.~~ (2) ~~You~~ are never too young to save money. (3) Save as much as you can, and start ~~can.~~ (4) ~~Start~~ as early as you can. (5) Invest your money well. (6) Compound interest earns money on your investment; moreover, it ~~investment.~~ (7) ~~It~~ also earns money on the interest you earn.

(8) Start investing at an early age; you ~~age.~~ (9) ~~You~~ will see amazing results. (10) Perhaps you'd like to have a million dollars by the age of sixty-five. (11) Look at the difference in the money you would have to put away, depending on the age at which you get started. (12) If you ~~You~~ start at age twenty, you ~~twenty.~~ (13) ~~You~~ would need to invest $1,391 a year to reach your goal. (14) You could start at age thirty, but you ~~thirty.~~ (15) ~~You~~ would then need to invest $3,690 a year. (16) If you ~~You~~ wait until age forty, you ~~forty.~~ (17) ~~You~~ would need to invest $10,168 a year. (18) Starting at age fifty is not too late; however, you ~~late.~~ (19) ~~You~~ would have to save $31,474 a year to reach your goal. (20) You can see the advantage of starting at a young age.

(21) We can look at the power of compound interest from another perspective. (22) Let's imagine that you've saved $1,000 a year from age twenty until age thirty. (23) Your total investment would be $10,000. (24) If you ~~You~~ received 10 percent interest on your investment, you ~~investment.~~ (25) ~~You~~ would now have a total of $15,937. (26) Your interest earnings would be $5,937. (27) You let the total amount sit in the bank, continuing to earn interest, and you ~~interest.~~ (28) ~~You~~ don't add another dime to that amount. (29) By age sixty-five, you'd have $447,869. (30) That's a total of $437,869 in interest! (31) Now you can see why it's never too early to start saving!

Adapted from Cheryl Richardson, *Take Time for Your Life*

WRITERS' WORKSHOP

Describe a Detour off the Main Highway

When a writer really cares about a subject, often the reader will care too. In your group or class, read this student's paragraph, aloud if possible. As you read, underline any words or details that strike you as vivid or powerful.

> Sometimes detours off the main highway can bring wonderful surprises, and last week this happened to my husband and me. On the Fourth of July weekend, we decided to drive home the long way, taking the old dirt farm road. Pulling over to admire the afternoon light gleaming on a field of wet ~~corn~~ corn, we saw a tiny farm stand under a tree. No one was in sight, but a card table covered with a red checked cloth held pints of tomatoes, jars of jam, and a handwritten price list. Next to these was a vase full of red poppies and tiny American flags. We bought tomatoes, leaving our money in the tin box stuffed with dollar bills. Driving ~~home~~ home, we both felt so happy—as if we had been given a great gift.
>
> *Kim Lee, student*

1. How effective is Kim Lee's paragraph?

   __Y__ Clear topic sentence? __Y__ Rich supporting details?

   __Y__ Logical organization? __Y__ Effective conclusion?

2. Discuss your underlinings with one another, explaining as specifically as possible why a particular word or sentence is effective. For instance, the "red poppies and tiny American flags" are so exact that you can see them.
3. This student supports her topic sentence with a single *example*, one brief story told in detail. If you were to support the same topic sentence, what example from your own life might you use?
4. The concluding sentence tells the reader that she and her husband felt they had been given "a great gift." Do you think that the gift was being trusted to be honest?
5. Proofread for grammar and spelling. Do you notice any error patterns (two or more errors of the same type) that this student should watch out for? She omits the comma when she begins a sentence with an *-ing* modifer.

> About her writing process, Kim Lee says:
>
> I wrote this paper in my usual way—I sort of plan, and then I freewrite on the subject. I like freewriting—I pick through it for certain words or details, but of course it is also a mess. From my freewriting I got "light gleaming on a field of wet corn" and the last sentence, about the gift.

Writing and Revising Ideas

1. Develop the topic sentence "Sometimes detours off the main highway can bring wonderful [disturbing] surprises."

2. Write about a time when you were trusted or distrusted by a stranger. What effect did this have on you?

As you plan your paragraph, try to angle the subject toward something that interests *you*—chances are, it will interest your readers too. Consider using one good example to develop your paragraph. As you revise, make sure that the body of your paragraph perfectly fits the topic sentence.

UNIT

5

Choosing the Right Noun, Pronoun, Adjective, Adverb, or Preposition

Choosing the right *form* of many words in English can be tricky. This unit will help you avoid some common errors. In this unit, you will

- Learn about singular and plural nouns
- Choose correct pronouns
- Use adjectives and adverbs correctly
- Choose the right prepositions

Spotlight on Writing

Here, two researchers set forth new findings about happiness. If possible, read the paragraph aloud.

TEACHING TIP
What makes a person happy? The subject and clear organization of points in this paragraph will likely engage your students. To prompt critical thinking, have them apply one or more of the four traits to themselves or another.

In study after study, four traits characterize happy people. First, especially in individualistic Western cultures, they like themselves. They have high self-esteem and usually believe themselves to be more ethical, more intelligent, less prejudiced, better able to get along with others, and healthier than the average person. Second, happy people typically feel personal control. Those with little or no control over their lives—such as prisoners, nursing home patients, severely impoverished groups or individuals, and citizens in totalitarian regimes—suffer lower morale and worse health. Third, happy people are usually optimistic. Fourth, most happy people are extroverted. Although one might expect that introverts would live more happily in the serenity of their less stressed . . . lives, extroverts are happier—whether alone or with others.

David G. Myers and Ed Diener, "The Pursuit of Happiness," *Scientific American*

- This well-organized paragraph tells us that happy people think they are "more *ethical*, more *intelligent*, less *prejudiced*, better *able* . . . , and *healthier* . . ." Do you know why these words—adjectives—are correct as written?
- If you don't know the meaning of the words extrovert and introvert, look them up. Which refers to you?

- ***Analyze how happy you are, based on the four traits mentioned above.***
- ***Describe an extrovert or an introvert you have observed.***

CHAPTER

19 Nouns

PART A Defining Singular and Plural

A **noun** names a person, a place, a thing, or an idea. Nouns may be singular or plural.

Singular **means one.** *Plural* **means more than one.**

TEACHING TIP
Many students will know some or all of the material in this chapter, so you may wish to assign topics selectively.

Singular	Plural
a reporter	the reporters
a pear	the pears
the couch	the couches

- Nouns usually add *-s* or *-es* to form the plural.

  Some nouns form their plurals in other ways. Here is a partial list:

Singular	Plural
child	children
foot	feet
goose	geese
man	men
mouse	mice
tooth	teeth
woman	women

ESL TIP
ESL students in particular have trouble with English noun forms and articles. Urge them to memorize any tricky rules and do extra practice.

- Many nouns ending in *-f* or *-fe* change their endings to *-ves* in the plural:

ESL TIP
Some ESL writers add *-s* to noncount words (e.g., *homeworks, furnitures*). Refer them to Error #1: Count or Noncount Noun Errors in the "8 Common ESL Errors" on the *Grassroots* student website. See also the Purdue OWL at **<http://owl.english.purdue.edu/handouts/esl/eslcount.html>**.

Singular	Plural
half	halves
knife	knives
leaf	leaves
life	lives
scarf	scarves
shelf	shelves
wife	wives
wolf	wolves

- Add *-es* to most nouns that end in *o*.

echo + *es* = echoes	potato + *es* = potatoes
hero + *es* = heroes	veto + *es* = vetoes

Here are some exceptions to memorize:

pianos	solos
radios	sopranos

Other nouns do not change at all to form the plural. Below is a partial list:

Singular	Plural
deer	deer
fish	fish
moose	moose
sheep	sheep

Hyphenated nouns usually form plurals by adding *-s* or *-es* to the first word:

Singular	Plural
brother-in-law	brothers-in-law
maid-of-honor	maids-of-honor
mother-to-be	mothers-to-be
runner-up	runners-up

If you are ever unsure about the plural of a noun, check a dictionary. For example, if you look up the noun *woman* in the dictionary, you will find an entry like this:

woman / women

The first word listed, *woman,* is the singular form of the noun; the second word, *women,* is the plural. Some dictionaries list the plural form of a noun only if the plural is unusual. If no plural is listed, the noun probably adds *-s* or *-es*.

PRACTICE 1

Make the following nouns plural.* If you are not sure of a particular plural, check the charts on the previous pages.

ESL TIP
Visual reinforcement is especially useful to ESL learners; try using flash cards to help students master noun forms. Prepare cards with the singular form of a word on one side and the plural on the other. To find or create flash cards online, try <http:/flashcardexchange.com/index. php>.

Singular	Plural	Singular	Plural
1. notebook	notebooks	11. brother-in-law	brothers-in-law
2. hero	heroes	12. technician	tehnicians
3. man	men	13. shelf	shelves
4. half	halves	14. potato	potatoes
5. bridge	bridges	15. mouse	mice
6. deer	deer	16. child	children
7. runner-up	runners-up	17. flight	flights
8. woman	women	18. wife	wives
9. radio	radios	19. place	places
10. tooth	teeth	20. maid-of-honor	maids-of-honor

REMEMBER: Do not add an *-s* **to words that form plurals by changing an internal letter or letters. For example, the plural of** *man* **is** *men,* **not** *mens;* **the plural of** *woman* **is** *women,* **not** *womens;* **the plural of** *foot* **is** *feet,* **not** *feets.*

PRACTICE 2

Proofread the following paragraph for incorrect plural nouns. Cross out the errors and correct them above the lines.

TEACHING TIP
Have students do the "mini-research" assignment suggested in Exploring Online (page 221), and then write a detailed paragraph about a park of their choice. Volunteers can read aloud as classmates listen for correct noun forms.

(1) Many ~~peoples~~ people consider Glacier National Park the jewel of the National Park System. (2) Its many mountains, glaciers, waterfalls, blue-green ~~lake~~ lakes, and amazing ~~wildlifes~~ wildlife are in the remote Rocky Mountains in the northwest corner of Montana. (3) Several ~~road~~ roads take visitors into the park, especially Going-to-the-Sun Road, which clings to the mountainside and offers spectacular, stomach-churning views. (4) At Logan Pass— 6,646 ~~foot~~ feet high—the road crosses the Continental Divide. (5) From this line along the spine of the ~~Rocky~~ Rockies, all ~~river~~ rivers flow either west to the Pacific Ocean, south to the Gulf, or east. (6) Because Glacier is truly a wilderness park, it is best seen by hikers, not drivers. (7) Most men, ~~woman~~ women, and ~~childs~~ children who hike the park's 700 miles of trails come prepared—with hats, long-sleeved shirts, and on their ~~feets~~ feet, proper hiking shoes. (8) Their ~~equipments~~ equipment includes bottled water and, just in case, bear spray. (9) Glacier has a large population of grizzly bears, which can weigh up to 1,400 pounds, have four-inch claws, and dislike surprises. (10) Besides grizzlies, one might glimpse mountain

*For help with spelling, see Chapter 31.

lions, ~~wolfs~~ wolves, black ~~bear~~ bears, white mountain goats, moose, bighorn ~~sheeps~~ sheep, elk, and many smaller mammals. (11) Salmon, ~~trouts~~ trout, and other ~~fishs~~ fish swim the ice-cold rivers and lakes. (12) ~~Scientist~~ Scientists worry that the glaciers are melting too quickly, but Glacier Park remains a treasure.

EXPLORING ONLINE

<http://www.nps.gov/parks.html> Visit the National Park Service website. Click on the long list of parks that the public can visit and select one (Glacier National Park or some other) that you might like to learn about. Read, explore, and jot down any writing—or travel—ideas.

PART B Signal Words: Singular and Plural

TEACHING TIP
Once your students do an exercise or two, you might wish to review relevant spelling rules, e.g., for words that end in *-y*, drop the *-y* and add *-ies* (*victory, victories*).

A *signal word* **tells you whether a singular or a plural noun usually follows.**
These **signal words** tell you that a singular noun usually follows:

Signal Words

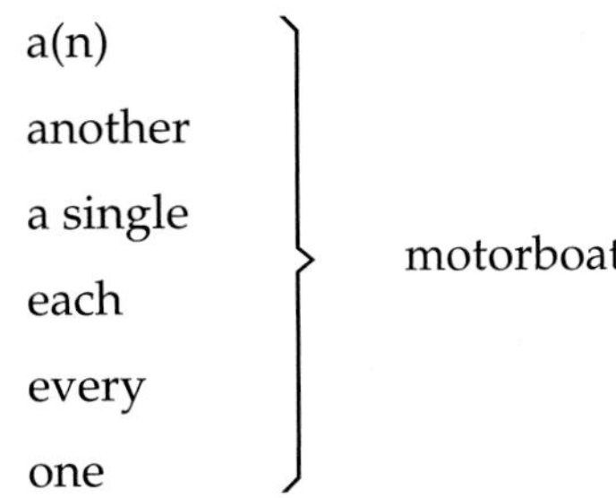

a(n)
another
a single
each
every
one
} motorboat

These signal words tell you that a *plural noun* usually follows:

ESL TIP
ESL students need to be careful about using words in English that resemble words in other languages but mean something different—e.g., the French *librairie* means *bookstore* in English.

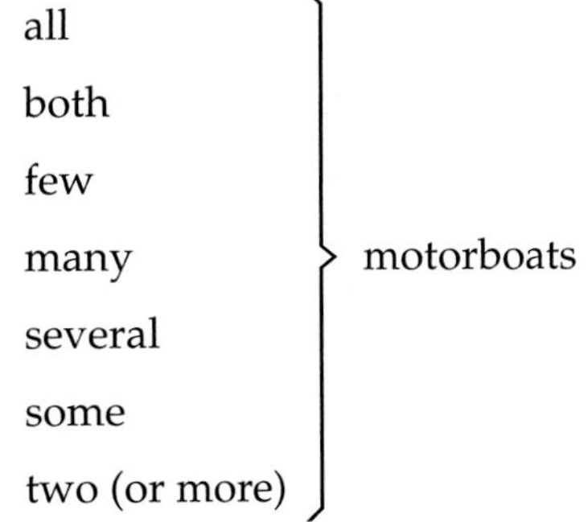

all
both
few
many
several
some
two (or more)
} motorboats

PRACTICE 3

In the blank following each signal word, write either a singular or a plural noun. Use as many different nouns as you can think of. Sample answers

EXAMPLES: a single stamp
most fabrics

1. a(n) map
2. some suitcases
3. few words
4. nine pens
5. one carton
6. all ticket holders

7. each moment
8. another tent
9. a single governor
10. every family
11. both situations
12. many countries

PRACTICE 4

Read the following essay for incorrect singular or plural nouns following signal words. Cross out the errors and correct them above the lines.

The Best Medicine

(1) Many ~~researcher~~ researchers believe that laughter is good for people's health. (2) In fact, some ~~doctor~~ doctors have concluded that laughter actually helps patients heal faster. (3) To put this theory into practice, several ~~hospital~~ hospitals have introduced humor routines into their treatment programs. (4) One ~~programs~~ program is a children's clown care unit that operates in seven New York City hospitals. (5) Thirty-five ~~clown~~ clowns from the Big Apple Circus go to the hospitals three times every ~~weeks~~ week. (6) Few ~~child~~ children can keep from laughing at the "rubber chicken soup" and "red nose transplant" routines.

(7) Although the program hasn't been studied scientifically, many ~~observer~~ observers have witnessed its positive effects. (8) However, some ~~specialist~~ specialists are conducting strictly scientific research on health and laughter. (9) One study, carried out at Loma Linda University in California, has shown the positive effects of laughter on the immune system. (10) Another ~~tests~~ test, done at the College of William and Mary in Virginia, has confirmed the California findings. (11) Other studies in progress are suggesting that all physiological ~~system~~ systems may be affected positively by laughter. (12) Finally, research also is backing up a ~~claims~~ claim made by Norman Cousins, author of the book *Anatomy of an Illness*. (13) While he was fighting a life-threatening ~~diseases~~ disease, Cousins maintained that hearty laughter took away his pain. (14) Several recent ~~study~~ studies have shown that pain does become less intense when the sufferer responds to comedy.

PRACTICE 5

On paper or on a computer, write three sentences using signal words that require singular nouns. Then write three sentences using signal words that require plural nouns.

PART C Signal Words with OF

Many signal words are followed by *of* . . . or *of the* . . . Usually, these signal words are followed by a *plural* noun (or a collective noun) because you are really talking about one or more from a larger group.*

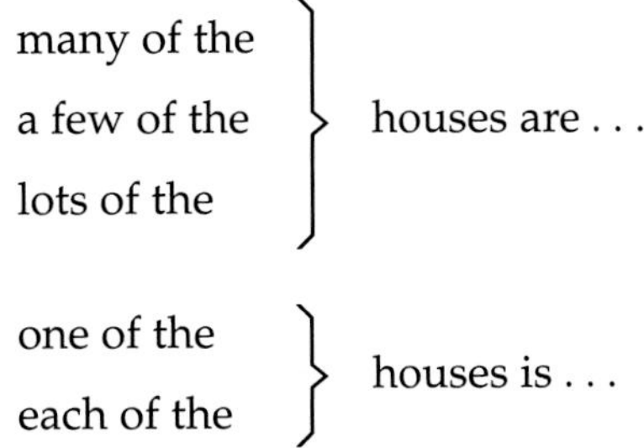

many of the / a few of the / lots of the } houses are . . .

one of the / each of the } houses is . . .

TEACHING TIP
The constructions in Part C confuse many students and can lead to both noun and verb-agreement errors. Remind students to cross out the prepositional phrase in order to find the subject and determine its number.

BE CAREFUL: The signal words *one of the* and *each of the* are followed by a *plural* noun, but the verb is *singular* because only the signal word (*one, each*) is the real subject.**

(1) *One* of the apples *is* spoiled.

(2) *Each* of the trees *grows* quickly.

- In sentence (1), *one* is the subject, not *apples*.
- In sentence (2), *each* is the subject, not *trees*.

PRACTICE 6

Fill in your own nouns in the following sentences. Use a different noun in each sentence. Sample answers

1. Many of the ____students____ enrolled in Chemistry 202.
2. Larry lost one of his ____sandals____ at the beach.
3. This is one of the ____suggestions____ that everyone liked.
4. Each of the ____protesters____ carried a sign.
5. You are one of the few ____parents____ who can do somersaults.
6. Few of the ____whales____ produced calves.

PRACTICE 7

Use a different noun in each sentence. Write five sentences using signal words with *of*.

EXAMPLE: (many of those . . .) ____I planted many of those flowers myself.____

1. (one of my . . .) ________________________________

____

*For more work on collective nouns, see Chapter 20, Part C.
**For more work on this type of construction, see Chapter 8, Part G.

2. (many of the . . .) ____

____

3. (lots of the . . .) ____

____

4. (each of these . . .) ____

____

5. (a few of your . . .) ____

____

PRACTICE 8

Read the following essay for correct plural nouns after signal words with *of*. Cross out the errors and correct them above the lines.

The Fender Sound

(1) If you are a fan of popular music or blues, the guitar sound you have been listening to was created by Leo Fender. (2) Leo Fender invented the modern amplified guitar, the instrument of choice for many of today's pop ~~star~~ stars. (3) The instrument that Fender introduced in the 1940s had an incredible sound—clear, crisp, and clean. (4) Buddy Holly, the Beatles, Jimi Hendrix, and B. B. King were just a few of the ~~performer~~ performers who bought and loved a Fender guitar.

(5) Unfortunately, by the time Fender sold his invention to CBS, the famous Fender guitars had declined in quality and were selling very poorly. (6) William Schultz, who worked for CBS at the time, felt that he could turn things around; however, few of the ~~musician~~ musicians who had played the original Fenders believed he could succeed. (7) He did.

(8) The Telecaster and the Stratocaster have become two of the most famous instruments in music history. (9) Approximately 335,000 are sold a year; each of these ~~instrument~~ instruments is considered a classic. (10) The next time you attend a concert, listen for the Fender sound.

PRACTICE 9 WRITING ASSIGNMENT

For some families, shopping—whether for food, clothing, or a computer—is a delightful group outing, a time to be together and share. For other families, it is an ordeal, a time of great stress, with arguments about what to purchase and how much to spend.

Describe a particularly enjoyable or awful family shopping experience. Your first sentence might read, "Shopping for ____________________ was (is) a(n) ____________________ experience." Explain what made it so good or so bad:

Was it what you were shopping for or where you were shopping? Were there arguments? Why?

Check your work for the correct use of singular and plural nouns. Be especially careful of nouns that follow signal words.

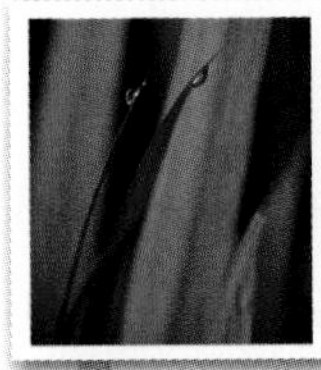

CHAPTER HIGHLIGHTS

- **Most plural nouns are formed by adding *-s* or *-es* to the singular noun:**

  job/jobs   watch/watches

- **Some plurals are formed in other ways:**

  child/children   woman/women   wolf/wolves

- **Some nouns ending in *o* add *-es*; others add *-s*:**

  echo/echoes   solo/solos

- **Some nouns have identical singular and plural forms:**

  fish/fish   equipment/equipment

- **Hyphenated nouns usually add *-s* or *-es* to the first word:**

  father-in-law/fathers-in-law

- **Signal words, with and without *of*, indicate whether a singular or a plural noun usually follows:**

  another musician   *many of the* musicians

CHAPTER REVIEW

Proofread the following essay for incorrect singular and plural nouns. Cross out the errors and correct them above the lines.

The Effects of Alcohol on Pregnancy

(1) All ~~mother-to-bes~~ mothers-to-be who drink alcohol run the risk of harming an innocent ~~children~~ child. (2) When a pregnant ~~women~~ woman takes a drink, the alcohol goes straight from her bloodstream into the bloodstream of her child. (3) When she has several ~~drink~~ drinks, the blood-alcohol level of her child rises as high as her own.

(4) Newborns can be harmed by alcohol in many ~~way~~ ways. (5) Some ~~infant~~ infants are born addicted to alcohol. (6) Other children are born mentally retarded. (7) In fact, most ~~doctor~~ doctors believe that exposure to alcohol before birth is one of the major ~~cause~~ causes of mental retardation. (8) In the worst cases, babies are born with a disease called fetal alcohol syndrome. (9) These unfortunate children not only are mentally re-

tarded but also can have many physical ~~deformity~~ deformities as well. (10) In milder cases, the children's problems don't show up until they go to school. (11) For instance, they may have poor memories and short attention spans. (12) Later, they may have trouble holding a ~~jobs~~ job.

(13) Too many young ~~life~~ lives have been ruined before birth because of alcohol consumption. (14) All unborn ~~child~~ children need and deserve a chance to have a healthy, normal ~~futures~~ future. (15) If you are a ~~women~~ woman who is expecting a baby, stop drinking alcohol now!

EXPLORING ONLINE

TEACHING TIP
If your students have computer access, Exploring Online, link 2, is unusual and fun: a painting and "noun hunt."

TEACHING TIP
More practice and assessment are available in the *Grassroots* Test Bank; linked ACE tests on the *Grassroots* student website; *WriteSpace for Grassroots*; and at the Exploring Online links in this chapter.

<http://a4esl.org/q/h/vf004-bp.html> Interactive quiz: Click on the correct singular or plural.

<http://www.ccc.commnet.edu/grammar/noun_exercise2.htm> Art Class! Study Bruegel's famous painting and hunt for nouns.

<http://college.hmco.com/devenglish/> Visit the *Grassroots* 8/e Student Website for more exercises and quizzes.

CHAPTER 20

Pronouns

PART A Defining Pronouns and Antecedents

Pronouns take the place of or refer to nouns or other pronouns. The word or words that a pronoun refers to are called the **antecedent** of the pronoun.

(1) *Bob* said that *he* was tired.

- *He* refers to *Bob.*
- *Bob* is the antecedent of *he.*

ESL TIP
Pronoun forms do not usually present a learning hardship to ESL students because the English pronoun system is far simpler than that of many other languages.

(2) *Sonia* left early, but I did not see *her* until later.

- *Her* refers to *Sonia.*
- *Sonia* is the antecedent of *her.*

(3) *Robert and Tyrone* have been good friends ever since *their* college days.

- *Their* refers to *Robert and Tyrone.*
- *Robert and Tyrone* is the antecedent of *their.*

A pronoun must agree with its antecedent. In sentence (1), the antecedent *Bob* requires the singular, masculine pronoun *he.* In sentence (2), the antecedent *Sonia* requires the singular, feminine pronoun *her.* In sentence (3), the antecedent *Robert and Tyrone* requires the plural pronoun *their.*

PRACTICE 1

In each of the following sentences, circle the pronoun. In the columns on the right, write the pronoun and its antecedent as shown in the example.

EXAMPLE:

	Pronoun	Antecedent
Susan B. Anthony promoted women's rights before (they) were popular.	they	rights
1. Susan B. Anthony deserves praise for (her) accomplishments.	her	Susan B. Anthony
2. Anthony became involved in the antislavery movement because of (her) principles.	her	Anthony
3. She helped President Lincoln develop (his) plans to free the slaves during the Civil War.	his	President Lincoln
4. Eventually, Anthony realized that women wouldn't be fully protected by law until (they) could vote.	they	women
5. When Anthony voted in the presidential election of 1872, (she) was arrested.	she	Anthony
6. She was found guilty and given a $100 fine, but she refused to pay (it).	it	fine
7. The judge did not sentence Anthony to jail because a sentence would have given (her) grounds for an appeal.	her	Anthony
8. If the Supreme Court had heard her appeal, (it) might have ruled that women had the right to vote.	it	Supreme Court
9. Audiences in England and Germany showed (their) appreciation of Anthony's work with standing ovations.	their	audiences
10. Unfortunately, women in the United States had to wait until 1920 before (they) could legally vote.	they	women

PRACTICE 2

Read this paragraph for meaning; then circle each pronoun you find and write its antecedent above the pronoun.

(1) In 1935, a Hungarian journalist got tired of the ink blotches (his) [journalist] fountain pen made. (2) So László Biro and (his) [Biro] brother developed a pen with a rolling ball at

the point. (3) It [pen] wrote without making blotches. (4) Their [Biro and his brother] pen wasn't the first ballpoint, but it was the first one that worked well. (5) The new pens got a big boost during World War II. (6) Pilots needed a pen they [pilots] could use at high altitudes. (7) Only ballpoints did the job. (8) In 1945, a department store in New York City introduced these pens to its [department store] shoppers. (9) The store sold ten thousand ballpoints the first day. (10) They [ballpoints] cost $12.50 each! (11) Today, people buy almost two *billion* ballpoints a year, for as little as ten cents apiece.

PART B Referring to Indefinite Pronouns

TEACHING TIP
Challenge students to memorize the list of singular indefinite pronouns. In groups or as a class, invent a mnemonic device to help remember them.

Indefinite pronouns do not point to a specific person.

anybody
anyone
each
everybody
everyone
no one
nobody
somebody
someone

Indefinite pronouns are usually *singular*. A pronoun that refers to an indefinite pronoun should also be singular.

TEACHING TIP
Explain to students that although we might not make our subjects and pronouns agree in casual conversation, we must do so in writing. Students have particular trouble with the special cases covered in Parts B, C, and D—and with Part E on vague or repeated pronouns.

(1) *Everyone* should do what *he* or *she* can to help.

- *Everyone* is a singular antecedent and must be used with the singular pronoun *he* or *she*.

(2) *Each* wanted to read *his* or *her* composition aloud.

- *Each* is a singular antecedent and must be used with the singular pronoun *his* or *her*.

(3) If *someone* smiles at you, give *him* or *her* a smile in return.

- *Someone* is a singular antecedent and must be used with the singular pronoun *him* or *her*.

In the past, writers used *he, his,* or *him* to refer to both men and women. Now, however, many writers use *he or she, his or her,* or *him or her.* Of course, if *everyone* is a woman, use *she* or *her;* if *everyone* is a man, use *he, his,* or *him.**

Someone left *her* purse in the classroom.

Someone left *his* wallet on the bus.

Someone left *his or her* glasses on the back seat.

*For more work on pronoun reference, see Chapter 24, "Consistent Person."

TEACHING TIP
Students are usually intrigued to discuss the modern consensus that using only *he, his,* or *him* when referring to both genders is considered sexist. It's better to switch to plural rather than risk offending someone.

It is often best to avoid the repetition of *his or her* and *he or she* by changing the indefinite pronoun to a plural.

(4) *Everyone* in the club agreed to pay *his or her* dues on time.

or

(5) The club *members* agreed to pay *their* dues on time.

PRACTICE 3

Fill in the blanks with the correct pronouns. Then write the antecedent of each pronoun in the column on the right.

Antecedent

EXAMPLE: Everyone should do ___his or her___ best. ___everyone___

1. The average citizen does not take ___his or her___ right to vote seriously enough. ___citizen___

TEACHING TIP
Encourage your students to practice making pronouns and antecedents agree, even in casual conversation. Mastering pronoun agreement in speech will help make it an automatic habit when writing.

2. If a person chooses a career in accounting, ___he or she___ must enjoy working with numbers. ___person___
3. Each player gave ___her___ best in the women's basketball finals. ___player___
4. Anyone can learn to do research on the Internet if ___he or she___ will put the time into it. ___anyone___
5. Fred and Nina always do ___their___ housecleaning on Tuesday. ___Fred and Nina___
6. Someone left ___his or her___ fingerprints on the windshield. ___someone___
7. The sales managers asked me to attend ___their___ meeting tomorrow. ___managers___
8. Everyone should see ___his or her___ dentist at least once a year. ___everyone___
9. Nobody wanted to waste ___his or her___ money on a singing stapler. ___nobody___
10. Everybody is welcome to try ___his or her___ luck in the lottery. ___everybody___

PRACTICE 4

Some of the following sentences contain errors in pronoun reference. Revise the incorrect sentences. Write a C in the blank next to each correct sentence.

EXAMPLE: Everyone must provide ~~their~~ his or her lunch. ___

1. Somebody left ~~their~~ his or her bag of popcorn on the seat. ___
2. A child should not carry heavy items in his or her backpack. ___C___

3. Everybody can take ~~their~~ his or her choice of two dishes from column A and one from column B. ___
4. No one works harder at ~~their~~ his or her paramedic job than my brother-in-law. ___
5. Each state has ~~their~~ its own flag. ___
6. Anyone can conquer his or her fear of speaking in public. C

PRACTICE 5

On paper or on a computer, write three sentences using indefinite pronouns as antecedents.

PART C Referring to Collective Nouns

Collective nouns imply more than one person but are generally considered *singular.* Here is a partial list:

Common Collective Nouns

board	family	panel
class	flock	school
college	government	society
committee	group	team
company	jury	tribe

TEACHING TIP
You might craft a lesson on pronoun and verb agreement with collective nouns by using a list of the fascinating nouns for groups of animals (e.g., *a lounge of lizards, a shiver of sharks*). Try **<http://rinkworks.com/words/collective.shtml>.**

(1) The *jury* meets early today because *it* must decide on a verdict.

- *Jury* is a singular antecedent and is used with the singular pronoun *it.*

(2) *Society* must protect *its* members from violence.

- *Society* is a singular antecedent and is always used with the singular pronoun *it.*
- Use *it* or *its* when referring to collective nouns.
- Use *they* or *their* only when referring to collective nouns in the plural (*schools, companies,* and so forth).

PRACTICE 6

Write the correct pronoun in the blank. Then write the antecedent of the pronoun in the column on the right.

Antecedent

EXAMPLE: The committee sent ___its___ best recommendations to the president of the college. ___committee___

1. Wanda's company will have ___its___ annual picnic next week. ___company___

2. The two teams picked up ___their___ gloves and bats and walked off the field. ___teams___
3. My high school class will soon have ___its___ tenth reunion. ___class___
4. The city is doing ___its___ best to build a new stadium. ___city___
5. Many soap operas thrive on ___their___ viewers' enjoyment of "a good cry." ___soap operas___
6. Each band has ___its___ guitar player and drummer. ___band___
7. The panel made ___its___ report public. ___panel___
8. This college plans to train ___its___ student teachers in classroom management. ___college___

PRACTICE 7

Some of the following sentences contain errors in pronoun reference. Cross out the incorrect pronoun and write the correct pronoun above the line. Write a *C* in the blank next to each correct sentence.

EXAMPLES: The committee will present ~~their~~ its report today. ___

The jury has reached its verdict. ___C___

1. The computer company retrains ~~their~~ its employees for new jobs. ___
2. Central Technical College wants to double ~~their~~ its enrollment by 2008. ___
3. That rock group has changed ~~their~~ its name for the third time. ___
4. The plumbing crew did its best to finish by 4 a.m. ___C___
5. The gas company plans to move ~~their~~ its headquarters again. ___
6. The Robinson family held its yearly reunion last week. ___C___

PRACTICE 8

On paper or on a computer, write three sentences using collective nouns as antecedents.

PART D Referring to Special Singular Constructions

each of . . . either of . . . every one of . . . neither of . . . one of . . .	Each of these constructions is *singular*. Pronouns that refer to them must also be singular.

(1) *Each* of the women did *her* work.

- *Each* is a singular antecedent and is used with the singular pronoun *her.*
- Do not be confused by the prepositional phrase *of the women.*

TEACHING TIP
In Chapter 8, "Present Tense (Agreement)," students learned to cross out prepositional phrases between the subject and verb. Suggest that they continue this practice here to make sure that the verb agrees with these special singular constructions.

(2) *Neither* of the men finished *his* meal.

- *Neither* is a singular antecedent and is used with the singular pronoun *his.*
- Do not be confused by the prepositional phrase *of the men.*

(3) *One* of the bottles is missing from *its* place.

- *One* is a singular antecedent and is used with the singular pronoun *its.*
- Do not be confused by the prepositional phrase *of the bottles.**

PRACTICE 9

Fill in the blanks with the correct pronouns. Then write the antecedent of each pronoun in the column on the right.

	Antecedent
EXAMPLE: Each of my nephews did ___his___ homework.	each
1. One of the hikers filled ___his or her___ canteen.	one
2. Every one of the women scored high on ___her___ entrance examination.	every one
3. Each of the puzzles has ___its___ own solution.	each
4. Either of them should be able to learn ___his or her___ lines before opening night.	either
5. One of my brothers does not have a radio in ___his___ car.	one
6. Neither of the dental technicians has had ___his or her___ lunch yet.	neither
7. Every one of the children sat still when ___his or her___ photograph was taken.	every one
8. Lin Li and her mother opened ___their___ boutique in 1998.	Lin Li and her mother

*For more work on these special constructions, see Chapter 8, Part G.

PRACTICE 10

Some of the following sentences contain errors in pronoun reference. Cross out the incorrect pronoun and write the correct pronoun above it. Write a *C* in the blank next to each correct sentence.

EXAMPLE: One of my uncles made ~~their~~ his opinion known. ___

1. One of the women at the hardware counter hasn't made ~~their~~ her purchase yet. ___
2. Each of the birds has ~~their~~ its distinctive mating ritual. ___
3. Most public speakers rehearse their speeches beforehand. C
4. I hope that neither of the men will change ~~their~~ his vote. ___
5. Both supermarkets now carry Superfizz Carrot Juice for their health-conscious customers. C
6. Neither of the women bought ~~their~~ her toe ring at Toes R Us. ___
7. One of the televisions was still in its box. C
8. Each of my grandchildren has ~~their~~ his or her own bedroom. ___

PRACTICE 11

On paper or on a computer, write three sentences that use the special singular constructions as antecedents.

PART E Avoiding Vague and Repetitious Pronouns

Vague Pronouns

Be sure that all pronouns *clearly* refer to their antecedents. Be especially careful of the pronouns *they* and *it*. If *they* or *it* does not refer to a *specific* antecedent, change *they* or *it* to the exact word you have in mind.

(1) **Vague pronoun:** At registration, they said I should take Math 101.

(2) **Revised:** At registration, an adviser said I should take Math 101.

- In sentence (1), who is *they?* The pronoun *they* does not clearly refer to an antecedent.
- In sentence (2), the vague *they* has been replaced by *an adviser.*

(3) **Vague pronoun:** On the beach, it says that no swimming is allowed.

(4) **Revised:** On the beach, a sign says that no swimming is allowed.

- In sentence (3), what is *it?* The pronoun *it* does not clearly refer to an antecedent.
- In sentence (4), the vague *it* has been replaced by *a sign.*

Repetitious Pronouns

Don't repeat a pronoun directly after its antecedent. Use *either* the pronoun *or* the antecedent—not both.

ESL TIP
Some ESL students tend to double the subject, writing both the subject and a pronoun. Refer them to Error #4: Repeated Subject in the "8 Common ESL Errors" on the *Grassroots* student website.

(1) **Repetitious pronoun:** The doctor, she said that my daughter is in perfect health.

- The pronoun *she* unnecessarily repeats the antecedent *doctor,* which is right before it.

(2) **Revised:** *The doctor* said that my daughter is in perfect health.

or

She said that my daughter is in perfect health.

- Use either *the doctor* or *she,* not both.

PRACTICE 12

Rewrite the sentences that contain vague or repetitious pronouns. If a sentence is correct, write *C.*

EXAMPLE: Dyslexia, it is a learning disorder that makes reading difficult.

Revised: Dyslexia is a learning disorder that makes reading difficult.

1. Many dyslexic persons, they have achieved success in their chosen professions.

   Revised: Many dyslexic persons have achieved success in their chosen professions.

2. For example, Albert Einstein, he was dyslexic.

   Revised: For example, Albert Einstein was dyslexic.

TEACHING TIP
Doing Practice 12 in class provides an opportunity for students to hone both their critical thinking and their revising skills.

3. In his biography, it says that he couldn't interpret written words the way others could.

   Revised: His biography says that he couldn't interpret written words the way others could.

4. At his elementary school, they claimed that he was a slow learner.

   Revised: His elementary school teachers claimed that he was a slow learner.

5. However, this slow learner, he changed the way science looked at time and space.

   Revised: However, this slow learner changed the way science looked at time and space.

6. Even politics has had its share of dyslexic leaders.

   Revised: C

7. American history, it teaches us that President Woodrow Wilson and Vice President Nelson Rockefeller, they were both dyslexic.

   Revised: American history teaches us that President Woodrow Wilson and Vice President Nelson Rockefeller were both dyslexic.

8. Authors can have this problem too; the well-known mystery writer Agatha Christie, she had trouble reading.

   Revised: Authors can have this problem too; the well-known mystery writer Agatha Christie had trouble reading.

9. Finally, in several magazines, they report that both Tom Cruise and Cher are dyslexic.

   Revised: Finally, several magazines report that both Tom Cruise and Cher are dyslexic.

10. Cher, she wasn't able to read until she was eighteen years old.

    Revised: Cher wasn't able to read until she was eighteen years old.

PART F Using Pronouns as Subjects, Objects, and Possessives

Pronouns have different forms, depending on how they are used in a sentence. Pronouns can be *subjects* or *objects* or *possessives.* They can be in the *subjective case, objective case,* or *possessive case.*

Pronouns as Subjects

A pronoun can be the *subject* of a sentence:

(1) *He* loves the summer months.

(2) By noon, *they* had reached the top of the hill.

- In sentences (1) and (2), the pronouns *he* and *they* are subjects.

Pronouns as Objects

A pronoun can be the *object* of a verb:

(1) Graciela kissed *him.*

(2) Sheila moved *it* to the corner.

- In sentence (1), the pronoun *him* tells whom Graciela kissed.
- In sentence (2), the pronoun *it* tells what Sheila moved.
- These objects answer the questions *kissed whom?* and *moved what?*

A pronoun can also be the *object* of a preposition, a word like *to, for,* or *at.**

(3) The umpire stood between *us.*

(4) Near *them,* the children played.

- In sentences (3) and (4), the pronouns *us* and *them* are the objects of the prepositions *between* and *near.*

Sometimes the prepositions *to* and *for* are understood, usually after words like *give, send, tell,* and *bring.*

(5) I gave *her* the latest sports magazine.

(6) Carver bought *him* a cowboy hat.

- In sentence (5), the preposition *to* is understood before the pronoun *her:* I gave *to* her . . .
- In sentence (6), the preposition *for* is understood before the pronoun *him:* Carver bought *for* him . . .

Pronouns That Show Possession

ESL TIP
Although most languages have a way of signaling possession, they don't all regard the same nouns as "possessable." In Spanish, one refers to parts of the body using the definite article whereas in English, we use a possessive form. One would say, in Spanish, *I have broken the leg.*

A pronoun can show *possession* or ownership.

(1) Bill took *his* report and left.

(2) The climbers spotted *their* gear on the slope.

- In sentences (1) and (2), the pronouns *his* and *their* show that Bill owns *his* report and that the climbers own *their* gear.

The chart below can help you review all the pronouns discussed in this part.

Pronoun Case Chart

	Singular Pronouns			Plural Pronouns		
	Subjective	**Objective**	**Possessive**	**Subjective**	**Objective**	**Possessive**
1st person:	I	me	my (mine)	we	us	our (ours)
2nd person:	you	you	your (yours)	you	you	your (yours)
3rd person:	he	him	his	they	them	their (theirs)
	she	her	her (hers)			
	it	it	its			

ESL TIP
Having students write sentences using each of the pronoun cases listed in the chart will help them identify any personal error patterns. Some students keep a copy of this chart handy as they write.

*See the list of prepositions on page 259.

PRACTICE 13

In the sentences below, underline the pronouns. Then, over each pronoun, write an *S* if the pronoun is in the subjective case, an *O* if it is in the objective case, and a *P* if it is in the possessive case.

Kiowa Dancer performing at a powwow
Peoria Journal Star/AP/Wide World.

EXAMPLE: Native American dancing has special significance for us. (*O*)

1. My brother Shadow Hawk and I represent our Kiowa tribe at many powwows, competing in the men's traditional dance category.
2. We wear costume pieces handed down to us from previous generations.
3. Each dancer wears a warrior's feather headdress, called a *roach*, and an impressive bustle of feathers tied to his back.
4. Because the bustles are made of sacred eagle feathers, spectators stand and remove their hats to show their reverence.
5. The steady drumbeat provides its rhythm for our movements.
6. This dance evolved from old forms of war dances, so we use it now to act out the story of a battle or a hunt.
7. Shadow Hawk interprets his story one way, and I interpret mine differently, so our movements are individually creative.

8. But we both begin by crouching low to the ground, looking for the tracks of the animal or the enemy.

9. The tempo of the drum increases, and he and I speed up our footwork to dramatize stalking our prey.

10. Acting out the dramatic final challenge means a lot to me because I can express with my movements the bravery, dignity, and pride that I feel.

PART G Choosing the Correct Case after AND or OR

When nouns or pronouns are joined by *and* or *or,* be careful to use the correct pronoun case after the *and* or the *or.*

(1) **Incorrect:** *Bob* and *her* have to leave soon.

- In sentence (1), the pronoun *her* should be in the *subjective case* because it is part of the subject of the sentence.

(2) **Revised:** *Bob* and *she* have to leave soon.

- Change *her* to *she.*

(3) **Incorrect:** The dean congratulated *Charles* and *I.*

TEACHING TIP
Many people wrongly substitute *I* for *me* because they think it sounds more formal; thus, they assume that it must be correct.

- In sentence (3), the pronoun *I* should be in the *objective case* because it is the object of the verb *congratulated.*
- The dean congratulated *whom?* The dean congratulated *me.*

(4) **Revised:** The dean congratulated *Charles* and *me.*

- Change *I* to *me.*

(5) **Incorrect:** Is that letter for *them* or *he?*

- In sentence (5), both objects of the preposition *for* must be in the *objective case.* What should *he* be changed to? ___him___

One simple way to make sure that you have the right pronoun case is to leave out the *and* or the *or*, and the word before it. You probably would not write these sentences:

(6) **Incorrect:** *Her* have to leave soon.

(7) **Incorrect:** The dean congratulated *I.*

(8) **Incorrect:** Is that letter for *he?*

These sentences look and sound strange, and you would know that they have to be corrected.

PRACTICE 14

TEACHING TIP
Crossing out the noun half of a compound construction is a good way to choose the correct case: e.g., *~~Frieda and~~ I dance; join ~~Frieda and~~ me.*

Circle the correct pronoun in the parentheses. If the pronoun is a *subject*, use the *subjective case*. If the pronoun is the *object* of a verb or a preposition, use the *objective case*.

1. Frieda and (I, me) were born in Bogotá, Colombia.
2. My brother gave Kylee and (I, me) a ride to the subway.
3. For (we, us), a swim in the ocean on a hot day is one of life's greatest joys.
4. If it were up to Angelo and (she, her), they would spend all their time searching for out-of-print LPs.
5. Our lab instructor expects Dan and (I, me) to hand in our report today.
6. I'm going to the movies tonight with Yolanda and (she, her).
7. The foreman chose Ellen and (he, him).
8. Between you and (I, me), I don't like spinach.
9. Robert and (he, him) have decided to go to Rocky Mountain National Park with Jacinto and (I, me).
10. Either (he, him) or (she, her) must work overtime.

PRACTICE 15

Revise the sentences in which the pronouns are in the wrong case. Write a C in the blank next to each sentence that is correct.

1. Annie and ~~me~~ I enjoy going to the gym every day. ___
2. ~~Her~~ She and ~~me~~ I have tried every class, from kickboxing to spinning. ___
3. Between you and ~~I~~ me, I favor hydroboxing, or kickboxing in water. ___
4. ~~Us~~ We and our friends also use the pool for water aerobics. ___
5. On cold days, however, they and I prefer step classes to keep warm. C
6. Stationary cycling sometimes feels boring to Annie and ~~I~~ me. ___
7. On the other hand, it is a good time for ~~she~~ her and ~~I~~ me to daydream. ___
8. Annie favors body pump classes, but I think she likes the instructor. C
9. I am not sure whether ~~him~~ he or weightlifting makes her sweat so much. ___
10. Talking while we work out gives her and me mouth and jaw exercise too. C

PART H Choosing the Correct Case in Comparisons

Pronouns in comparisons usually follow *than* or *as*.

(1) Ferdinand is taller *than* I.

(2) These guidelines help you as much *as* me.

- In sentence (1), the comparison is completed with a pronoun in the subjective case, *I*.
- In sentence (2), the comparison is completed with a pronoun in the objective case, *me*.

(1) Ferdinand is taller than I . . . (am tall).

(2) These guidelines help you as much as . . . (they help) . . . me.

- A comparison is really a kind of shorthand that omits repetitious words.

By completing the comparison mentally, you can choose the correct case for the pronoun.

BE CAREFUL: The case of the pronoun you place after *than* or *as* can change the meaning of the sentence.

(3) Diana likes Tom more than *I* . . . (more than *I* like him).

or

(4) Diana likes Tom more than *me* . . . (more than she likes *me*).

- Sentence (3) says that Diana likes Tom more than I like Tom.
- Sentence (4) says that Diana likes Tom more than she likes me.*

PRACTICE 16

Circle the correct pronoun in these comparisons.

TEACHING TIP
Students will be able to "hear" the correct pronoun better if they supply the missing words of a comparison (see examples on page 241). Ask them to add these words and then determine the correct pronoun case.

1. You study more often than (I, me).
2. The movie scared us more than it did (he, him).
3. Diego eats dinner earlier than (I, me).
4. She ran a better campaign for the local school board than (he, him).
5. Stan cannot memorize vocabulary words faster than (he, him).
6. The ringing of a telephone disturbs her more than it disturbs (they, them).
7. They may think they are sharper than (she, her), but wait until they tangle with her and find out the truth.
8. I hate doing laundry more than (they, them).
9. Sometimes our children are more mature than (we, us).
10. Remembering birthdays seems easier for me than for (he, him).

*For more work on comparisons, see Chapter 21, Part C.

PRACTICE 17

Revise only those sentences in which the pronoun after the comparison is in the wrong case. Write a C in the blank next to each correct sentence.

1. Ben learned to operate this program more slowly than ~~us~~ we. ___
2. Jean can sing Haitian folk songs better than ~~me~~ I. ___
3. Nobody, but nobody, can whistle louder than she. C
4. Sarah was surprised that Joyce paid more than ~~her~~ she for a ticket. ___
5. In a crisis, you can reach us sooner than you can reach them. C
6. Before switching jobs, I wanted to know if Rose would be as good a supervisor as ~~him~~ he. ___
7. The night shift suits her better than ~~I~~ me. ___
8. Antoinette is six feet tall; no one on the loading dock is taller than ~~her~~ she. ___

PRACTICE 18

On paper or on a computer, write three sentences using comparisons that are completed with pronouns. Choose each pronoun case carefully.

PART I Using Pronouns with *-SELF* and *-SELVES*

Pronouns with *-self* and *-selves* are used in two ways.

(1) José admired *himself* in the mirror.

- In sentence (1), José did something to *himself;* he admired *himself.* In this sentence, *himself* is called a **reflexive pronoun.**

(2) The teacher *herself* thought the test was too difficult.

- In sentence (2), *herself* emphasizes the fact that the teacher—much to her surprise—found the test too hard. In this sentence, *herself* is called an **intensive pronoun.**

This chart will help you choose the right reflexive or intensive pronoun.

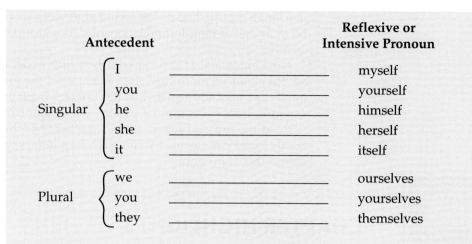

	Antecedent		Reflexive or Intensive Pronoun
Singular	I	______	myself
	you	______	yourself
	he	______	himself
	she	______	herself
	it	______	itself
Plural	we	______	ourselves
	you	______	yourselves
	they	______	themselves

Note that in the plural *-self* is changed to *-selves.*

TEACHING TIP
Students may have heard the word *theirselves* in casual conversation. Point out that it's neither a reflexive nor an intensive pronoun—nor even a real word!

PRACTICE 19

Write the correct reflexive or intensive pronoun in each sentence. Be careful to match the pronoun with the antecedent. Answers will vary.

EXAMPLES: I should have stopped ___myself___.

Roberta ___herself___ made this bracelet.

1. We built all the cabinets ___ourselves___.
2. He ___himself___ was surprised to discover that he had a green thumb.
3. Did you give ___yourselves___ a party after you graduated?
4. Rick, look at ___yourself___ in the mirror!
5. Don't bother; Don and André will hang the pictures ___themselves___.
6. The trainer ___herself___ was amazed at the progress the athletes had made.
7. Sonia found ___herself___ in a difficult situation.
8. These new lamps turn ___themselves___ on and off.
9. The oven cleans ___itself___.
10. Because he snores loudly, he wakes ___himself___ up several times each night.

PRACTICE 20

On paper or on a computer, write three sentences, using either a reflexive or an intensive pronoun in each.

PRACTICE 21 WRITING ASSIGNMENT

In a small group, discuss the factors that seem absolutely necessary for a successful marriage or long-term relationship. As a group, brainstorm for four or five key factors.

Now imagine that a friend with very little experience has asked you for written advice about relationships. Each member of the group should choose just one of the factors and write a letter to this person. Explain in detail why this factor—for example, honesty or mutual respect—is so important to a good relationship.

Read the finished letters to one another. Which letters give the best advice or are the most convincing? Why? Exchange letters with a partner, checking for the correct use of pronouns.

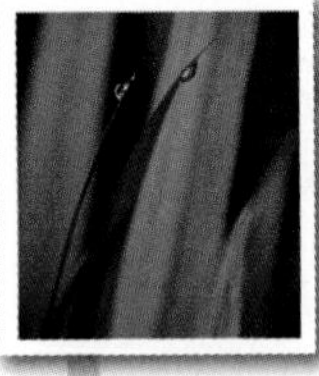

CHAPTER HIGHLIGHTS

- **A pronoun takes the place of or refers to a noun or another pronoun:**

  Louise said that *she* would leave work early.

- **The word that a pronoun refers to is its antecedent:**

  I have chosen *my* seat for the concert.
  (*I* is the antecedent of *my*.)

- **A pronoun that refers to an indefinite pronoun or a collective noun should be singular:**

  Everyone had cleared the papers off *his* or *her* desk.

  The *committee* will give *its* report Friday.

- **A pronoun after *and* or *or* is usually in the subjective or objective case:**

  Dr. Smythe and *she* always work as a team. *(subjective)*

  The bus driver wouldn't give the map to Ms. Tallon or *me*. *(objective)*

- **Pronouns in comparisons usually follow *than* or *as*:**

  Frank likes Sally more than *I*.
  (*subjective:* . . . more than I like Sally)

  Frank likes Sally more than *me*.
  (*objective:* . . . more than he likes me)

- **A pronoun ending in *-self* (singular) or *-selves* (plural) may be used as a reflexive or an intensive pronoun. A reflexive pronoun shows that someone did something to himself or to herself; an intensive pronoun is used for emphasis:**

  On his trip, Martin bought nothing for *himself*.

  The musicians *themselves* were almost late for the street fair.

CHAPTER REVIEW

Proofread the following essay for pronoun errors. Cross out any incorrect, vague, or repetitious pronouns and make your corrections above the lines. Use nouns to replace vague pronouns.

A New Beginning

(1) Martha Andrews, ~~she~~ was a good student in high school. (2) After graduation, she found a job as a bank teller in order to save money for college. (3) She liked her job because she knew her regular customers and enjoyed handling ~~his or her~~ their business. (4) When she was nineteen, Patrick Kelvin, another teller, and ~~her~~ she fell in love and married. (5) By the time she was twenty-two, she had become the mother of three children. (6) Martha's plans for college faded.

(7) As her fortieth birthday approached, Martha began thinking about going to college to study accounting; however, she had many fears. (8) Would she remember how to study after so many years? (9) Would the younger students be smarter than ~~her~~ she? (10) Would she feel out of place with them? (11) Worst of all, her husband, ~~he~~ worried that Martha would neglect him. (12) He thought that everyone who went to college forgot ~~their~~ his or her family. (13) He also feared that Martha would be more successful than ~~him~~ he.

(14) One of Martha's children, who attended college ~~hisself~~ himself, encouraged her. (15) With his help, Martha got the courage to visit Middleton College. (16) In the admissions office, ~~they~~ an advisor told her that older students were valued at Middleton. (17) Older students often enriched classes because ~~he or she~~ they brought a wealth of life experiences with them. (18) Martha also learned that the college had a special program to help ~~their~~ its older students adjust to school.

(19) Martha enrolled in college the next fall. (20) To their credit, ~~her~~ she and her husband soon realized that they had made the right decision.

EXPLORING ONLINE

TEACHING TIP
More practice and assessment are available in the *Grassroots* Test Bank; linked ACE tests on the *Grassroots* student website; *WriteSpace for Grassroots*; and at the Exploring Online links in this chapter.

<http://www.ccc.commnet.edu/cgi-shl/quiz.pl/pronouns_add2.htm>
Interactive quizzes: Choose the correct pronoun or verb.

<http://www.powa.org/edit/problem.html#Pronoun/AntecedentAgreement>
Click "pronoun antecedent agreement" for review and a graded quiz

<http://college.hmco.com/devenglish/> Visit the *Grassroots* 8/e Student Website for more exercises and quizzes.

CHAPTER 21

Adjectives and Adverbs

PART A Defining and Writing Adjectives and Adverbs

Adjectives and adverbs are two kinds of descriptive words. An **adjective** describes a noun or a pronoun. It tells *which one, what kind,* or *how many.*

ESL TIP
ESL learners may need extra work on the proper order for two or more adjectives. Refer them to Error #8: Wrong Order of Adjectives in the "8 Common ESL Errors" on the *Grassroots* student website.

(1) The *red* coat belongs to me.

(2) He looks *healthy.*

- In sentence (1), the adjective *red* describes the noun *coat.*
- In sentence (2), the adjective *healthy* describes the pronoun *he.*

An **adverb** describes a verb, an adjective, or another adverb. Adverbs often end in *-ly.* They tell *how, to what extent, why, when,* or *where.*

(3) Laura sings *loudly.*

(4) My biology instructor is *extremely* short.

(5) Lift this box *very* carefully.

- In sentence (3), *loudly* describes the verb *sings.* How does Laura sing? She sings *loudly.*

- In sentence (4), *extremely* describes the adjective *short.* How short is the instructor? *Extremely* short.
- In sentence (5), *very* describes the adverb *carefully.* How carefully should you lift the box? *Very* carefully.

PRACTICE 1

Complete each sentence with an appropriate adjective from the list below. Answers will vary.

funny	orange	sarcastic	energetic
old	tired	bitter	little

1. Janet is ___energetic___.
2. He often wears a(n) ___orange___ baseball cap.
3. ___Sarcastic___ remarks will be his downfall.
4. My daughter collects ___old___ movie posters.
5. This coffee tastes ___bitter___.

PRACTICE 2

Complete each sentence with an appropriate adverb from the list below. Answers will vary.

quietly	loudly	wildly	convincingly
madly	quickly	constantly	happily

1. The waiter ___quickly___ cleaned the table.
2. Mr. Huff whistles ___constantly___.
3. The lawyer spoke ___convincingly___.
4. They charged ___madly___ down the long hallway.
5. ___Quietly___, he entered the rear door of the church.

Many adjectives can be changed into adverbs by adding an *-ly* ending. For example, *glad* becomes *gladly, thoughtful* becomes *thoughtfully,* and *wise* becomes *wisely.*

Be especially careful of the adjectives and adverbs in this list; they are easily confused.

Adjective	Adverb	Adjective	Adverb
awful	awfully	quiet	quietly
bad	badly	real	really
poor	poorly	sure	surely
quick	quickly		

(6) This chair is a *real* antique.

(7) She has a *really* bad sprain.

- In sentence (6), *real* is an adjective describing the noun *antique.*

- In sentence (7), *really* is an adverb describing the adjective *bad*. How bad is the sprain? The sprain is *really* bad.

PRACTICE 3

Change each adjective in the left-hand column into its adverb form.*

EXAMPLE: You are polite. You answer politely.

Adjective	Adverb
1. She is honest.	1. She responds honestly.
2. They are loud.	2. They sing loudly.
3. It is easy.	3. It turns easily.
4. We are careful.	4. We decide carefully.
5. He is creative.	5. He thinks creatively.
6. She was quick.	6. She acted quickly.
7. It is perfect.	7. It fits perfectly.
8. It is real.	8. It is really hot.
9. He is eager.	9. He waited eagerly.
10. We are joyful.	10. We watch joyfully.

PRACTICE 4

TEACHING TIP
Practice 4 is an engaging full-class activity. It not only sharpens students' skill with adjectives and adverbs but also enhances their cultural literacy by teaching them about an important ecosystem.

Circle the adjective or adverb form of the word in parentheses.

EXAMPLE: Lovers of nature argue (passionate, passionately) that we must protect the Galapagos Islands.

1. These (remote, remotely) islands lie in the Pacific Ocean six hundred miles off the coast of Ecuador.
2. They are (actual, actually) just piles of volcanic lava.
3. Nevertheless, they are home to (abundant, abundantly) wildlife.
4. For centuries, the Galapagos Islands remained (complete, completely) isolated and undisturbed by humans.
5. As a result, some (rare, rarely) animal species developed there.
6. For example, giant tortoises up to six feet long from head to tail lumber (slow, slowly) across the hills and beaches.
7. The world's only swimming iguanas (lazy, lazily) sun themselves on jet-black rocks.
8. The islands are also home to many (amazing, amazingly) birds.
9. Blue-footed boobies waddle (comic, comically) over the boulders.
10. Flightless cormorants, who live only in the Galapagos, dive (graceful, gracefully) into the sea, searching for eel and octopus.
11. Tiny Galapagos penguins, the only ones north of the equator, hop (easy, easily) into and out of the ocean.

*If you have questions about spelling, see Chapter 31, Part E.

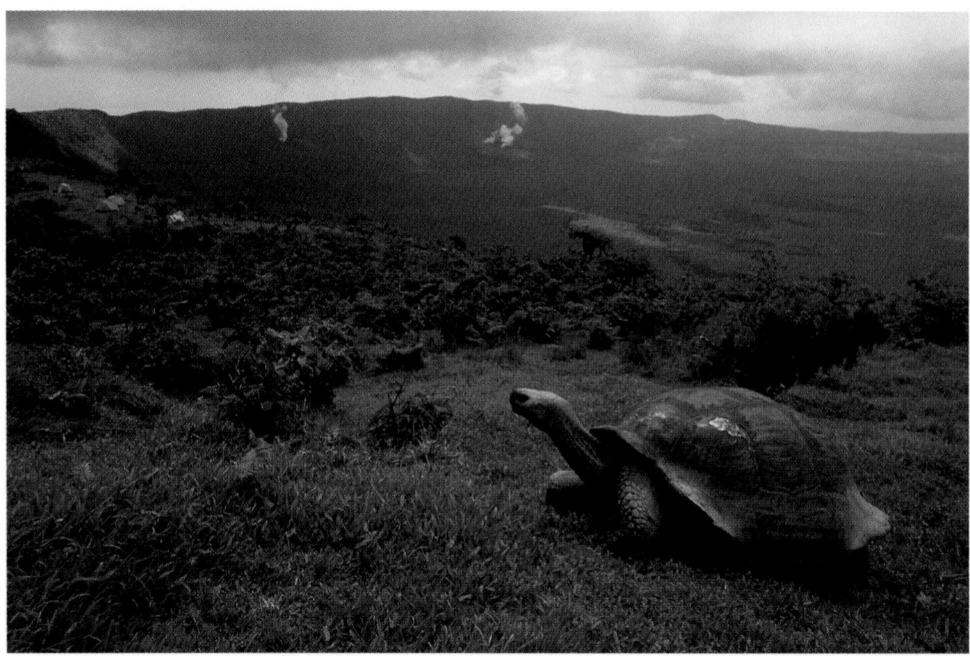

Giant Galapagos Islands Tortoise
©Craig Lovell/CORBIS.

12. During his voyage of 1831, Charles Darwin visited the Galapagos Islands and gathered evidence to support his (famous, famously) theory of natural selection.
13. Today, the islands are still the (perfect, perfectly) place for scientists to conduct research.
14. Ecotourists, too, are drawn to the (spectacular, spectacularly) scenery and (fabulous, fabulously) animals.
15. If we tread very (gentle, gently) on this fragile ecosystem, we might preserve it for future generations.

EXPLORING ONLINE

On Google or your favorite search engine, look up "Galapagos, animals, birds" or "Galapagos, Darwin's voyage" to see pictures and learn more about these islands.

PRACTICE 5

On paper or on a computer, write sentences using the following adjectives and adverbs: *quick/quickly, bad/badly, glad/gladly, real/really, easy/easily.*

EXAMPLES: *(cheerful)* You are cheerful this morning.
(cheerfully) You make breakfast cheerfully.

PART B A Troublesome Pair: GOOD/WELL

Unlike most adjectives, *good* does not add *-ly* to become an adverb; it changes to *well.*

TEACHING TIP
The error most commonly made is using *good* in place of *well* (as in *Julian plays ball very good*). Point out that although we might hear this in casual speech, it is a red flag error in writing. Before students complete Practice 6, you might suggest that they name the missing word's part of speech *before* they choose *good* or *well.*

(1) **Adjective:** Peter is a *good* student.

(2) **Adverb:** He writes *well.*

- In sentence (1), the adjective *good* describes or modifies *student.*
- In sentence (2), the adverb *well* describes or modifies *writes.*

Note, however, that *well* can be used as an adjective to mean *in good health*—for example, *He felt well after his long vacation.*

PRACTICE 6

Write either *good* or *well* in each sentence.

EXAMPLE: Charles plays ball very ____well____.

1. Lorelle is a ____good____ pilot.
2. She handles a plane ____well____.
3. How ____well____ do you understand virtual reality?
4. Pam knows my bad habits very ____well____.
5. It is a ____good____ thing we ran into each other.
6. Brian works ____well____ with other people.
7. How ____well____ or how badly did you do at the tryouts?
8. Were the cherry tarts ____good____ or tasteless?
9. Denzel Washington is not just a ____good____ actor; he's a great one.
10. These plants don't grow very ____well____ in the sunlight.
11. Carole doesn't look as though she takes ____good____ care of herself.
12. He asked ____good____ questions at the meeting, and she answered them ____well____.

PART C Writing Comparatives

TEACHING TIP
Consider combining Parts B and C with a spelling review (e.g., rules about doubling the final consonant or adding *-er* and *-est* to words ending in *-y*).

(1) John is *tall.*

(2) John is *taller* than Mike.

- Sentence (1) describes John with the adjective *tall,* but sentence (2) *compares* John and Mike in terms of how tall they are: John is the *taller* of the two.

Taller **is called the** *comparative* **of** *tall.*

Use the comparative when you want to compare two people or things.

TEACHING TIP
An activity likely to engage students is an analysis of adjectives, comparatives, and superlatives in advertising. Bring in print ads or have students do so. Locate and discuss the use of adjectives. Groups might wish to write ads for a product they use—or for one they invent.

To Form Comparatives

Add *-er* to adjectives and adverbs that have *one syllable:**

short	shorter
fast	faster
thin	thinner

Place the word *more* before adjectives and adverbs that have *two or more syllables:*

foolish	more foolish
rotten	more rotten
happily	more happily

PRACTICE 7

Write the comparative form of each word. Either add *-er* to the word or write *more* before it. Never add both *-er* and *more!*

EXAMPLES: ________ fresh er________

more________ willing ________

1. ________ fast er________
2. more________ interesting ________
3. more________ hopeful ________
4. ________ sweet er________
5. ________ thick er________
6. more________ modern ________
7. more________ valuable ________
8. ________ cold er________

Here is one important exception to the rule that two-syllable words use *more* to form the comparative:

To show the comparative of two-syllable adjectives ending in *-y*, change the *y* to *i* and add *-er.***

cloudy	cloudier
sunny	sunnier

PRACTICE 8

Write the comparative form of each adjective.

EXAMPLE: happy happier________

1. shiny shinier________
2. friendly friendlier________
3. lazy lazier________
4. easy easier________
5. fancy fancier________
6. lucky luckier________
7. lively livelier________
8. crazy crazier________

---

*For questions about spelling, see Chapter 31, Part D.
**For questions about spelling, see Chapter 31, Part G.

PRACTICE 9

The following incorrect sentences use both *more* and *-er*. Decide which one is correct and write your revised sentences on the lines provided.

REMEMBER: Write comparatives with either *more* or *-er*—not both!

EXAMPLES: Jan is more younger than her brother.

Jan is younger than her brother.

I feel more comfortabler in this chair than on the couch.

I feel more comfortable in this chair than on the couch.

1. Her new boss is more fussier than her previous one.

   Her new boss is fussier than her previous one.

2. The trail was more rockier than we expected.

   The trail was rockier than we expected.

3. The people in my new neighborhood are more friendlier than those in my old one.

   The people in my new neighborhood are friendlier than those in my old one.

4. Magda has a more cheerfuler personality than her sister.

   Magda has a more cheerful personality than her sister.

5. I have never seen a more duller TV program than this one.

   I have never seen a duller TV program than this one.

6. The audience at this theater is more noisier than usual.

   The audience at this theater is noisier than usual.

7. His jacket is more newer than Rudy's.

   His jacket is newer than Rudy's.

8. If today is more warmer than yesterday, we'll picnic on the lawn.

   If today is warmer than yesterday, we'll picnic on the lawn.

PRACTICE 10

On paper or on a computer, write sentences using the comparative form of the following adjectives or adverbs: *dark, cloudy, fortunate, slowly, wet.*

EXAMPLE: (*funny*) This play is funnier than the one we saw last week.

PART D Writing Superlatives

(1) Tim is the *tallest* player on the team.

(2) Juan was voted the *most useful* player.

- In sentence (1), Tim is not just *tall* or *taller than* someone else; he is the *tallest* of all the players on the team.
- In sentence (2), Juan was voted the *most useful* of all the players.

***Tallest* and *most useful* are called *superlatives*.**

Use the superlative when you wish to compare more than two people or things.

To Form Superlatives

Add *-est* to adjectives and adverbs of *one syllable:*

short shortest

Place the word *most* before adjectives and adverbs that have *two or more syllables:*

foolish most foolish

Exception: With two-syllable adjectives ending in *-y*, change the *y* to *i* and add *-est*.*

happy happiest

PRACTICE 11

Write the superlative form of each word. Either add *-est* to the word or write *most* before it; do not do both.

EXAMPLES: ________ tall est________

most________ ridiculous ________

1. ________ loud est________
2. most________ colorful ________
3. ________ brave est________
4. ________ strong est________
5. most________ brilliant ________
6. ________ wild est________
7. most________ practical ________
8. most________ frightening ________
9. ________ green est________
10. ________ hazy haziest________

PRACTICE 12

The following incorrect sentences use both *most* and *-est*. Decide which one is correct and write your revised sentences on the lines provided.

REMEMBER: Write superlatives with either *most* or *-est*—not both!

EXAMPLES: Jane is the most youngest of my three children.

Jane is the youngest of my three children.

He is the most skillfulest guitarist in the band.

He is the most skillful guitarist in the band.

1. My nephew is the most thoughtfulest teenager I know.
   My nephew is the most thoughtful teenager I know.
2. Mercury is the most closest planet to the sun.
   Mercury is the closest planet to the sun.
3. This baby makes the most oddest gurgling noises we have ever heard.
   This baby makes the oddest gurgling noises we have ever heard.

*For questions about spelling, see Chapter 31, Part 6.

4. Jackie always makes us laugh, but she is most funniest when she hasn't had enough sleep.
   Jackie always makes us laugh, but she is funniest when she hasn't had enough sleep.

5. When I finally started college, I was the most eagerest student on campus.
   When I finally started college, I was the most eager student on campus.

6. Ms. Dross raises the most strangest reptiles in her basement.
   Ms. Dross raises the strangest reptiles in her basement.

7. This peach is the most ripest in the basket.
   This peach is the ripest in the basket.

8. He thinks that the most successfulest people are just lucky.
   He thinks that the most successful people are just lucky.

PART E Troublesome Comparatives and Superlatives

These comparatives and superlatives are some of the trickiest you will learn:

TEACHING TIP
Students who use *worse* in place of *worst* might not hear the difference in pronunciation between the two words. Have groups create sentences using both words to reinforce their understanding of the difference.

		Comparative	**Superlative**
Adjective:	good	better	best
Adverb:	well	better	best
Adjective:	bad	worse	worst
Adverb:	badly	worse	worst

PRACTICE 13

Fill in the correct comparative or superlative form of the word in parentheses. REMEMBER: *Better* and *worse* compare *two* persons or things. *Best* and *worst* compare three or more persons or things.

EXAMPLES: Is this report ___better___ (good) than my last one?
(Here two reports are compared.)

It was the ___worst___ (bad) movie I have ever seen.
(Of *all* movies, it was the *most* awful.)

1. He likes jogging ___better___ (well) than running.
2. I like country and western music ___best___ (well) of all.
3. Bob's motorcycle rides ___worse___ (bad) now than it did last week.
4. That is the ___worst___ (bad) joke Molly has ever told!
5. The volleyball team played ___worse___ (badly) than it did last year.
6. He plays the piano ___better___ (well) than he plays the guitar.
7. The traffic is ___worse___ (bad) on Fridays than on Mondays.
8. That was the ___worst___ (bad) cold I have had in years.
9. Sales are ___better___ (good) this year than last.

10. Do you take this person for ___better___ (good) or for ___worse___ (bad)?

PART F Demonstrative Adjectives: THIS/THAT and THESE/THOSE

This, that, these, and *those* are called **demonstrative adjectives** because they point out, or demonstrate, which noun is meant.

(1) I don't trust *that* wobbly front wheel.

(2) *Those* toys are not as safe as their makers claim.

ESL TIP
Pronunciation can lead to errors in word choice. For example, Spanish speakers might pronounce the word *this* as "theese." Caution students not to let the ear fool them!

- In sentence (1), *that* points to a particular wheel, the wobbly front one.
- In sentence (2), *those* points to a particular group of toys.

Demonstrative adjectives are the only adjectives that change to show singular and plural:

Singular	Plural
this book	these books
that book	those books

This and *that* are used before singular nouns; *these* and *those* are used before plural nouns.

PRACTICE 14

In each sentence, circle the correct form of the demonstrative adjective in parentheses.

1. (This, These) corn flakes taste like cardboard.
2. Mr. Lathorpe is sure (this, these) address is correct.
3. You can find (that, those) maps in the reference room.
4. Can you catch (that, those) waiter's eye?
5. I can't imagine what (that, those) gadgets are for.
6. We prefer (this, these) tennis court to (that, those) one.
7. The learning center is in (that, those) gray building.
8. (These, This) biography tells the story of Charles Curtis, the first Native American elected to the Senate.

PRACTICE 15 WRITING ASSIGNMENT

Sports figures and entertainers can be excellent role models. Sometimes, though, they can set bad examples and teach the wrong lessons. For example, some athletes and entertainers have been convicted of drug possession, spousal abuse, or assault.

Assume that you are concerned that your child or sibling is being negatively influenced by one of these figures. Write a "fan letter" to this person explaining the bad influence he or she is having on young people—in particular, on your child or sibling. Convince him or her that being in the spotlight is a serious responsibility and that a positive change in behavior could help many young fans.

Brainstorm, freewrite, or cluster to generate ideas and examples to support your concern. Check your letter for the correct use of adjectives and adverbs.

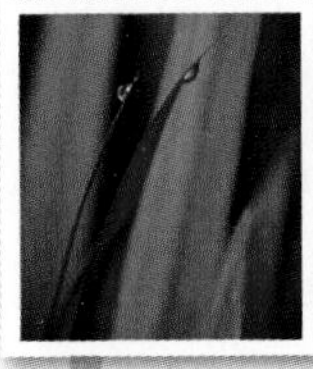

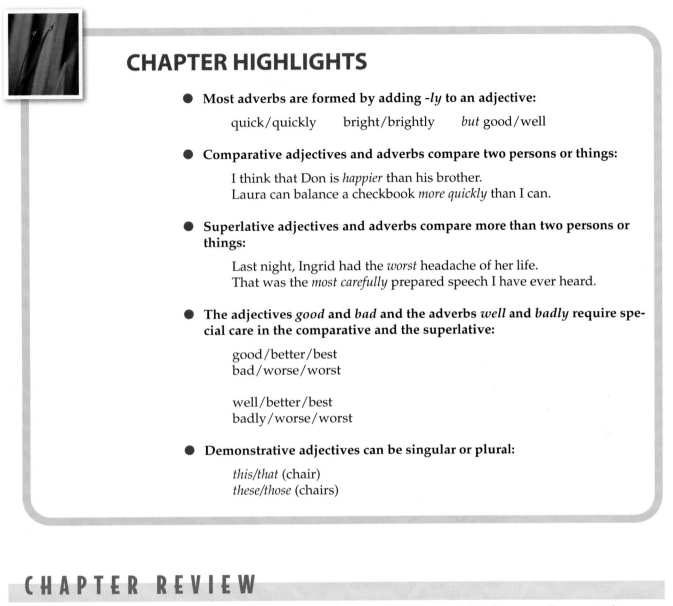

CHAPTER HIGHLIGHTS

- **Most adverbs are formed by adding *-ly* to an adjective:**

  quick/quickly   bright/brightly   *but* good/well

- **Comparative adjectives and adverbs compare two persons or things:**

  I think that Don is *happier* than his brother.
  Laura can balance a checkbook *more quickly* than I can.

- **Superlative adjectives and adverbs compare more than two persons or things:**

  Last night, Ingrid had the *worst* headache of her life.
  That was the *most carefully* prepared speech I have ever heard.

- **The adjectives *good* and *bad* and the adverbs *well* and *badly* require special care in the comparative and the superlative:**

  good/better/best
  bad/worse/worst

  well/better/best
  badly/worse/worst

- **Demonstrative adjectives can be singular or plural:**

  this/that (chair)
  these/those (chairs)

CHAPTER REVIEW

Proofread these paragraphs for adjective and adverb errors. Cross out the errors and correct them above the lines.

A. (1) The most ~~famousest~~ famous comet, Halley's comet, appears ~~regular~~ regularly every seventy-six years. (2) This mass of gas and dust has caused panic and fear because its appearance has often coincided with the ~~baddest~~ worst events in history. (3) During the Middle Ages, people believed that Halley's comet was a ~~surely~~ sure omen of destruction. (4) The ~~most silly~~ silliest notions about Halley's comet came about during its 1910 appearance when people bought pills and bottled oxygen to protect themselves. (5) Although that sounds ~~real~~ really foolish, they believed that poisonous gas was contained in the comet's ~~brilliantly~~ brilliant tail. (6) Despite the ~~most wildest~~ wildest superstitions, Halley's comet has given us ~~more better~~ better information about comets and our solar system.

B. (1) One of the ~~real~~ really inspirational stories of recent years is the story of Lance Armstrong. (2) In 1993, Armstrong became the World Cycling champion. (3) In 1999, he won the 2,287-mile Tour de France, the world's ~~most greatest~~ greatest bike race. (4) Between those two events, however, he won something that was even more ~~importanter~~ important.

(5) In 1996, Lance Armstrong was diagnosed with testicular cancer. (6) The cancer spread to his brain, abdomen, and lungs. (7) He was given only a 40 percent chance of surviving and even ~~worser~~ worse odds of ever returning to biking. (8) According to his doctors, however, he approached his cancer with the same skills he used for competitive sports: discipline, persistence, sacrifice. (9) Armstrong ~~courageous~~ courageously went through brain surgery and incredibly painful chemotherapy, but he also continued training. (10) Two years later, he became only the second American to win the twenty-one-day Tour de France. (11) ~~More stronger~~ Stronger than ever, Armstrong finished seven minutes and thirty-seven seconds ahead of his ~~most nearest~~ nearest competitor. (12) Astonishingly enough, he went on to win the Tour de France the following year and an Olympic bronze medal in 2000.

(13) Although some people believe that cancer is the ~~worstest~~ worst thing that can happen, Armstrong maintains that cancer is the ~~most best~~ best thing that ever happened to him. (14) In his book, *It's Not about the Bike,* he writes that without ~~those~~ that disease he would not have married or had a child. (15) When you face death, he says, your focus becomes really clear.

EXPLORING ONLINE

TEACHING TIP
More practice and assessment are available in the *Grassroots* Test Bank; linked ACE tests on the *Grassroots* student website; *WriteSpace for Grassroots*; and at the Exploring Online links in this chapter.

<http://www.dailygrammar.com/066to070.shtml> Five tests with answers: Choose the correct adjective or adverb.

<http://depts.gallaudet.edu/esl/compsuperl.htm> Practice with hints and answers: Write the correct comparatives or superlatives.

<http://college.hmco.com/devenglish/> Visit the *Grassroots* 8/e Student Website for more exercises and quizzes.

CHAPTER 22

Prepositions

PART A Defining and Working with Prepositional Phrases

A **preposition** is a word like *at, from, in,* or *of.* Below is a partial list of common prepositions:*

TEACHING TIP
Illustrate prepositions with simple drawings—a wavy line showing the ocean surface or a horizon line with house and tree. Demonstrate *above, below, inside, beside, across, under,* and *toward.*

ESL TIP
English prepositions often confuse nonnative students, even those who are highly proficient in English. One reason is that some languages (e.g., German, Russian, and Latin) use inflections to perform the work of prepositions. Another reason is the variability of preposition use.

Common Prepositions

about	beside	off
above	between	on
across	by	over
after	during	through
against	except	to
along	for	toward
among	from	under
around	in	until
at	into	up
before	like	with
behind	of	without

A preposition is usually followed by a noun or pronoun. The noun or pronoun is called the **object** of the preposition. Together, the preposition and its object are called a **prepositional phrase.**

Here are some prepositional phrases:

Prepositional Phrase	=	Preposition	+	Object
after the movie		after		the movie
at Kean College		at		Kean College
beside them		beside		them
between you and me		between		you and me

*For more work on prepositions, see Chapter 6, Part C.

ESL TIP
Suggest that students try practicing with flash cards, memorizing when necessary. Also refer them to online exercises like the crossword puzzle at <http://www.ccc.commnet.edu/grammar/quizzes/cross/cross_prep2.htm>.

The preposition shows a relationship between the object of the preposition and some other word in the sentence. Below are some sentences with prepositional phrases:

(1) Ms. Kringell arrived *at noon.*

(2) A man *in a gray suit* bought three lottery tickets.

(3) The huge moving van sped through the tunnel.

ESL TIP
If ESL learners need more practice with prepositions, refer them to Writespace for *Grassroots* and to Error #3: Preposition Error in the "8 Common ESL Errors" on the *Grassroots* student website.

- In sentence (1), the prepositional phrase *at noon* tells when Ms. Kringell arrived. It describes *arrived.*
- In sentence (2), the prepositional phrase *in a gray suit* describes how the man was dressed. It describes *man.*
- What is the prepositional phrase in sentence (3)? ___through the tunnel___

  Which word does it describe? ___sped___

PRACTICE 1

Underline the prepositional phrases in the following sentences.

1. Bill collected some interesting facts about human biology.
2. Human eyesight is sharpest at midday.
3. In extreme cold, shivering produces heat, which can save lives.
4. A pound of body weight equals 3,500 calories.
5. Each of us has a distinguishing odor.
6. Fingernails grow fastest in summer.
7. One of every ten people is left-handed.
8. The human body contains approximately ten pints of blood.
9. Beards grow more rapidly than any other hair on the human body.
10. Most people with an extra rib are men.

PART B Troublesome Prepositions: IN, ON, and LIKE

IN/ON for Time

Use *in* before seasons of the year, before months not followed by specific dates, and before years that do not include specific dates.

(1) *In the summer,* some of us like to lie around in the sun.

(2) No classes will meet *in January.*

(3) Rona was a student at Centerville Business School *in 2004.*

Use *on* before days of the week, before holidays, and before months if a date follows.

(4) *On Thursday,* the gym was closed for renovations.

(5) The city looked deserted *on Christmas Eve.*

(6) We hope to arrive in Burlington *on October 3.*

IN/ON for Place

In means *inside of.*

(1) My grandmother slept *in the spare bedroom.*

(2) The exchange student spent the summer *in Sweden.*

On means *on top of* or *at a particular place.*

(3) The spinach pie *on the table* is for tonight's book discussion group meeting.

(4) Dr. Helfman lives *on Marblehead Road.*

LIKE

Like is a preposition that means *similar to.* Therefore, it is followed by an object (usually a noun or a pronoun).

(1) *Like you,* I prefer watching films on DVD rather than going to a crowded movie theater.

Do not confuse *like* with *as* or *as if. As* and *as if* are subordinating conjunctions.* They are followed by a subject and a verb.

(2) *As the instructions explain,* insert flap B into slit B before folding the bottom in half.

(3) Robert sometimes acts *as if he has never made a mistake.*

PRACTICE 2

Fill in the correct prepositions in the following sentences. Be especially careful when using *in, on,* and *like.*

1. To celebrate America's one hundredth birthday, ___on___ July 4, 1876, the French decided to give a special statue ___to___ their "sister country."
2. Sculptor Frederic-Auguste Bartholdi sailed ___to___ America, seeking support ___for___ the ambitious project.

*For more work on subordinating conjunctions, see Chapter 14.

3. Bartholdi was awed __by__ America's vastness as he traveled __through__ redwood forests, __across__ prairies, and __over__ mountains.

4. __In__ Egypt he had seen huge monuments __like__ the pyramids and the Sphinx, and he wanted to honor liberty __with__ a structure as majestic as those.

TEACHING TIP
Practice 2 works well as a group activity. Exploring Online can serve as a miniresearch activity for your students.

5. His monument would be so big that visitors would be able to walk __into__ it and climb __up__ a staircase __to__ its top.

6. Funded __by__ the French, Bartholdi finally built his statue __of__ a woman raising her torch __toward__ the sky.

7. __After__ many delays, a newspaper urged American citizens to help pay for the statue's base; money poured __in__ , and the base was erected __on__ Bedloe's Island __in__ New York Harbor.

8. The Statue of Liberty was not shipped __from__ France __to__ America __until__ 1885, and then it took six months to mount her on the foundation.

9. One million people and hundreds of ships gathered __in__ the rain and fog to see the statue unveiled __on__ October 28, 1886.

10. Today, Lady Liberty still rises 305 feet __above__ the harbor, lighting the darkness __with__ her torch and symbolizing freedom __around__ the globe.

EXPLORING ONLINE

To learn more, look up "Statue of Liberty" on your favorite search engine. Can you answer these questions? 1. What famous person designed the metal skeleton, or scaffolding, that holds up Lady Liberty? 2. In how many pieces was the Statue of Liberty shipped from France? 1. Auguste Eiffel, who designed the Eiffel Tower. 2. 350 pieces.

PART C Prepositions in Common Expressions

Prepositions often are combined with other words to form certain expressions—groups of words, or phrases, in common use. These expressions can sometimes be confusing. Below is a list of some troublesome expressions. If you are in doubt about others, consult a dictionary.

Common Expressions with Prepositions

Expression	Example
acquainted with	He became *acquainted with* his duties.
addicted to	I am *addicted to* chocolate.
agree on (a plan)	They finally *agreed on* a sales strategy.
agree to (another's proposal)	Did she *agree to* their demands?
angry about or at (a thing)	The subway riders are *angry about* (or *at*) the delays.
angry with (a person)	The manager seems *angry with* Jake.

Common Expressions with Prepositions (*continued*)

apply for (a position)	You should *apply for* this job.
approve of	Does he *approve of* the proposed budget?
consist of	The plot *consisted of* both murder and intrigue.
contrast with	The red lettering *contrasts* nicely *with* the gray stationery.
convenient for	Is Friday *convenient for* you?
correspond with (write)	My daughter *corresponds with* a pen pal in India.
deal with	How do you *deal with* friends who always want to borrow your notes?
depend on	He *depends on* your advice.
differ from (something)	A diesel engine *differs from* a gasoline engine.
differ with (a person)	On that point, I *differ with* the medical technician.
different from	His account of the accident is *different from* hers.
displeased with	She is *displeased with* all the publicity.
fond of	We are all *fond of* Sam's grandmother.
grateful for (something)	Jim was *grateful for* the two test review sessions.
grateful to (someone)	We are *grateful to* the plumber for repairing the leak on Sunday.
identical with	This watch is *identical with* hers.
interested in	George is *interested in* modern art.
interfere with	Does the party *interfere with* your study plans?
object to	She *objects to* the increase in the state sales tax.
protect against	This vaccine *protects* people *against* the flu.
reason with	Don't *reason with* a hungry pit bull.
reply to	Did the newspaper editor *reply to* your letter?
responsible for	Omar is *responsible for* marketing.
shocked at	We were *shocked at* the damage to the buildings.
similar to	That popular song is *similar to* another one I know.
specialize in	The shop *specializes in* clothing for large men.
succeed in	Gandhi *succeeded in* freeing India from British rule.
take advantage of	Let's *take advantage of* that two-for-one paperback book sale.
worry about	I no longer *worry about* my manager's moods.

ESL TIP
Remind students that these expressions are best memorized.

PRACTICE 3

Circle the correct expressions in these sentences.

1. The amazing career of Albert Goodwill Spalding (consisted of, consisted in) baseball and business success.
2. At first, his mother did not (approve in, approve of) his playing professional ball.
3. Spalding obeyed his mother and (applied for, applied to) a "regular" job.
4. Eventually (displeased with, displeased at) the work he found, Spalding signed up with the Boston Red Stockings in 1871.
5. Over the next five years, the Boston team came to (depend on, depend with) his unusual underhand pitching style.
6. In fact, he was the first pitcher ever to (succeed in, succeed on) winning two hundred games.
7. Spalding soon became more (interested in, interested with) designing baseballs than in playing.
8. Pitchers were (grateful for, grateful to) him for marketing the ball he had designed for his own pitching use; it became the official ball of the National League.
9. Spalding became (fond for, fond of) designing other kinds of balls; for example, he designed the first basketball.
10. He also (dealt on, dealt with) the problem of what to use as goals in this new ball game.
11. He (took advantage of, took advantage for) peach baskets, and the new game was called basketball.
12. By the 1890s, Spalding had been (responsible for, responsible to) developing one of the world's largest sporting goods companies.

PRACTICE 4 WRITING ASSIGNMENT

A friend or relative of yours has come to spend a holiday week in your city. He or she has never been there before and wants advice on sightseeing. In complete sentences, write directions for one day's sightseeing. Make sure to explain why you think this person would enjoy visiting each particular spot.

Organize your directions according to time order: that is, what to do first, second, and so on. Use transitional expressions like *then, after,* and *while* to indicate time order. Be especially careful when using the prepositions *in* and *on*. Try to work in a few of the expressions listed in Part B.

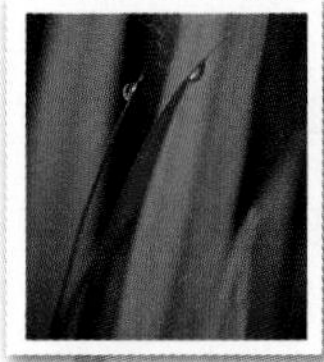

CHAPTER HIGHLIGHTS

- **Prepositions are words like *at, from, in,* and *of.* A prepositional phrase contains a preposition and its object:**

  The tree *beneath my window* has lost its leaves.

- **Be careful of the prepositions *in, on,* and *like:***

  I expect to graduate *in* June.
  I expect to graduate *on* June 10.

  The Packards live *in* Tacoma.
  The Packards live *on* Farnsworth Avenue.

  Like my father, I am a Dodgers fan.

- **Prepositions are often combined with other words to form fixed phrases:**

  convenient for, different from, reason with

CHAPTER REVIEW

Proofread this essay for preposition errors. Cross out the errors and correct them above the lines.

Listening for Life Among the Stars

(1) ~~On~~ In the film *Contact*, actress Jodie Foster plays a scientist searching for intelligent life ~~at~~ in the universe. (2) Foster's character is not real. (3) However, she is very similar ~~of~~ to Dr. Jill Tarter, research director at SETI, the Search for Extraterrestrial Intelligence Institute. (4) Dr. Tarter and her team listen for radio signals sent ~~off~~ from outer space because such signals might prove that life exists among the stars.

(5) Dr. Tarter earned her degrees ~~across~~ in engineering and physics ~~upon~~ in the 1960s and 1970s. (6) After completing her education, she worked for the space agency. (7) Then she heard ~~off~~ of a new program specializing ~~on~~ in the search for life ~~at~~ in space. (8) Dr. Tarter was greatly interested ~~of~~ in this exciting program. (9) Since then, she has spent more hours gazing ~~onto~~ into a telescope than anyone else ~~under~~ on the planet.

(10) To scan even bigger areas of space, Dr. Tarter led the development of the Allen Telescope Array ~~on~~ in California. (11) This group of telescopes searches twenty-four hours a day for communications from deep space. (12) Dr. Tarter is also raising funds ~~for~~ to build a radio telescope ten times more powerful than any used today. (13) She hopes that soon astronauts will install a radio telescope ~~in~~ on the moon. (14) Dr. Tarter maintains a sense of humor ~~around~~ about her unusual career. (15) When people tease her ~~of~~ about her search of "little green men," she laughingly replies ~~at~~ to these skeptics that she might find "big blue women" instead.

EXPLORING ONLINE

TEACHING TIP
More practice and assessment are available in the *Grassroots* Test Bank; linked ACE tests on the *Grassroots* student website; *WriteSpace for Grassroots*; and at the Exploring Online links in this chapter.

<http://a4esl.org/q/h/vm/prepos01.html> Interactive quiz: Select the right prepositions for each sentence.

<http://www.ruthvilmi.net/hut/help/grammar_help/beatrix_test.html> Quiz: Queen Beatrice visits Finland; help her with prepositions.

<http://college.hmco.com/devenglish/> Visit the *Grassroots* 8/e Student Website for more exercises and quizzes.

UNIT 5

WRITING ASSIGNMENTS

As you complete each writing assignment, remember to perform these steps:

- Write a clear, complete topic sentence.
- Use freewriting, brainstorming, or clustering to generate ideas for the body of your paragraph, essay, or speech.
- Arrange your best ideas in a plan.
- Revise for support, unity, coherence, and exact language.
- Proofread for grammar, punctuation, and spelling errors.

Writing Assignment 1: *Explain your job.* Explain what you do—your duties and responsibilities—to someone who knows nothing about your kind of work but is interested in it. In your first sentence, sum up the work you do. Then name the equipment you use and tell how you spend an average working day. Explain the rewards and drawbacks of your job. Finally, proofread for the correct use of nouns, pronouns, adjectives, adverbs, and prepositions.

Writing Assignment 2: *Give an award.* When we think of awards, we generally think of awards for the most home runs or the highest grade average. However, Cal Ripken Jr. of the Baltimore Orioles became famous because he played in a record number of consecutive games. In other words, his award was for *showing up,* for *being there,* for *constancy.* Write a speech for an awards dinner in honor of someone who deserves recognition for this kind of constancy. Perhaps your parents deserve the award, or your spouse, or the law enforcement officer on the beat in your neighborhood. Be specific in explaining why this person deserves the award. You might try a humorous approach. Proofread your speech for the correct use of nouns, pronouns, adjectives, adverbs, and prepositions.

Writing Assignment 3: *Discuss your future.* Imagine yourself ten years from now; how will your life be different? Pick one major way in which you expect it will have changed. You may want to choose a difference in your income, your marital status, your idea of success, or anything else that is important to you. Your first sentence should state this expected change. Then explain why this change will be important to you. Proofread for the correct use of nouns, pronouns, adjectives, adverbs, and prepositions.

Writing Assignment 4: *Respond to a natural setting.* Have you ever felt especially connected to the natural world? Did a special place (a specific mountain, forest, garden, beach, body of water, and so on) or a specific experience (a particular incident while you were camping, hiking, biking, skiing, and so on) make you feel that way? If so, describe the experience, including the setting. Explain how or why your response was different from your usual one. Proofread for the correct use of nouns, pronouns, adjectives, adverbs, and prepositions.

REVIEW

Proofreading

Proofread the following essay for the incorrect use of nouns, pronouns, adjectives, adverbs, and prepositions. Cross out errors and correct them above the lines. (You should find twenty-six errors.)

The Last Frontier

(1) When the government of Brazil opened the Amazon rain forest for settlement ~~on~~ in the 1970s, ~~they~~ it created the last frontier on earth. (2) Many concerned ~~man~~ men and ~~woman~~ women everywhere now fear that the move has been a ~~disasters~~ disaster for the land and for the people.

(3) The ~~most large~~ largest rain forest in the world, the Amazon rain forest has been hit ~~real~~ really hard. (4) The government built highways to make it ~~more easy~~ easier for poor people to get to the land, but the roads also made investors interested ~~to~~ in the forest. (5) Lumber companies chopped down millions of ~~tree~~ trees. (6) Ranchers and settlers ~~theirselves~~ themselves burned the forest to make room for cattle and crops. (7) All ~~this~~ these activities have taken their toll: in one area, which is the size of Colorado, three-quarters of the rain forest has already been destroyed. (8) Many kinds of plants and animals have been lost forever.

(9) ~~As~~ Like the rain forest itself, the Indians who live ~~they~~ there are threatened by this wholesale destruction. (10) Ranchers, miners, loggers, and settlers have moved onto Indian lands. (11) Contact with the outside world has changed the Indians' traditional way of life. (12) A few Indian ~~tribe~~ tribes have made economic and political gains; however, many tribes have totally disappeared.

(13) Many of the ~~settler~~ settlers are not doing very ~~good~~ well either. (14) People have poured into the region too ~~rapid~~ rapidly, and the government is unable to provide the needed services. (15) Small villages have become crowded cities, diseases (especially malaria) have spread, and lawlessness is common. (16) ~~Worse~~ Worst of all, the soil beneath the rain forest is not fertile. (17) After a few years, the settlers' ~~land, it~~ land is worthless. (18) As the settlers go into debt, businesses take advantage ~~for~~ of the situation by buying land ~~quick~~ quickly and exploiting it ~~bad~~ badly.

(19) Can the situation in the rain forest improve? (20) Although the Brazilian government has been trying to preserve ~~those~~ that forest, thousands of fires are still set every year to clear land for cattle grazing, planting, and building. (21) On the more hopeful side, however, scientists have discovered fruits in the rain forest that are ~~extreme~~ extremely high in vitamins and proteins. (22) Those fruits would be much better crops for the rain forest than the corn, rice, and beans that farmers are growing now. (23) The world watches ~~nervous~~ nervously. (24) Will the Earth's ~~preciousest~~ most precious rain forest survive?

Transforming

Change the subject of this paragraph from singular (the Saint Bernard) to plural (Saint Bernards), changing every *the dog* to *dogs,* every *it* to *they,* and so forth. Make all necessary verb and other changes. Write your revisions above the lines.

(1) ~~The Saint Bernard is a~~ Saint Bernards are legendary ~~dog~~ dogs famous for ~~its~~ their many acts of bravery. (2) Bred in the wild mountains of Switzerland, ~~it~~ they can find paths in the worst snowstorms, smell human beings buried in snow, and detect avalanches before they occur. (3) ~~This~~ These powerful yet sensitive ~~creature works~~ creatures work in rescue patrols. (4) When ~~a Saint Bernard finds~~ Saint Bernards find a hurt traveler, ~~it lies~~ they lie down next to the sufferer to keep him or her warm and ~~licks~~ lick the person's face to restore consciousness. (5) ~~Another dog goes~~ Other dogs go back to headquarters to sound the alarm and guide a rescue party to the scene. (6) In all, ~~the Saint Bernard has~~ Saint Bernards have saved more than two thousand lives. (7) Oddly enough, though ~~this dog has~~ these dogs have been known for about three hundred years, ~~the Saint Bernard~~ Saint Bernards did not get ~~its~~ their name until about a hundred years ago. (8) ~~The Saint Bernard was~~ Saint Bernards were named for a shelter in the Swiss Alps. (9) Monks of the shelter of Saint Bernard used ~~this dog~~ these dogs in rescue patrols.

WRITERS' WORKSHOP

Tell How Someone Changed Your Life

Strong writing flows clearly from point to point so that a reader can follow easily. In your class or group, read this essay, aloud if possible. As you read, pay special attention to organization.

Stephanie

(1) There are many people who are important to me. However, the most important person is Stephanie. Stephanie is my daughter. She has changed my life completely. She has changed my life in a positive way.

(2) Stephanie is only five years old, but she has taught me the value of education. When I found out that I was pregnant, my life changed in a positive way. Before I got pregnant, I didn't like school. I went to school just to please my mom, but I wasn't learning anything. When I found out that I was pregnant, I changed my mind about education. I wanted to give my baby the best of this world. I knew that without a good education, I wasn't going anywhere, so I decided to get my life together.

(3) Stephanie taught me not to give up. I remember when she was trying to walk, and she fell down. She didn't stop but kept on going until she learned how to walk.

(4) In conclusion, you can learn a lot from babies. I learned not to give up. Stephanie is the most important person in the whole world to me. She has changed me in the past, and she will continue to change me in the future.

Claudia Huezo, student

1. How effective is this essay?

   __Y__ Clear thesis statement? __N__ Good support?

   __Y__ Logical organization? __Y__ Effective conclusion?

2. Claudia Huezo has organized her essay very well: introduction and thesis statement, two supporting paragraphs, conclusion. Is the main idea of each supporting paragraph clear? Does each have a good topic sentence?

3. Is each supporting paragraph developed with enough facts and details? If not, what advice would you give the writer for revising, especially for reworking paragraph (3)? Aim for less repetition and more fresh facts and details.

4. This student has picked a wonderful subject and writes clearly—two excellent qualities. However, did you find any places where short, choppy, or repetitious sentences could be improved?

TEACHING TIP
This student's essay is moving and real, yet it is inadequately developed, especially in paragraph 3. In class, lead a peer critique to help students identify the problems. Then have them revise with details and examples as if the paper were their own.

If so, point out one or two places where Huezo might cross out or rewrite repetitious language (where she says the same thing twice in the same words). Point out one or two places where she might combine short sentences for variety. *

5. Proofread for grammar and spelling. Do you spot any error patterns this student should watch out for? No grammar errors.

Writing and Revising Ideas

1. Tell how someone changed your life.
2. Discuss two reasons why education is (is not) important.

Before you write, plan or outline your paragraph or essay so that it will be clearly organized (see Chapter 3, Part E, and Chapter 4, Part B). As you revise, pay special attention to the order of ideas and to clear, concise writing without needless repetition (see Chapter 4, Part C).

*Cross out paragraph 2, sentence 2, and paragraph 4, sentence 2. Combine paragraph 1, sentences 2 and 3. Combine paragraph 1, sentences 4 and 5.

UNIT 6

Revising for Consistency and Parallelism

This unit will teach you some easy but effective ways to add style to your writing. In this unit, you will

- Make sure your verbs and pronouns are consistent
- Use a secret weapon of many writers—parallel structure
- Vary the lengths and types of your sentences

Spotlight on Writing

This writer uses balanced sentences to make her point about date rape. If possible, read her paragraph aloud.

Women charge that date rape is the hidden crime; men complain it is hard to prevent a crime they can't define. Women say it isn't taken seriously; men say it is a concept invented by women who like to tease but not take the consequences. Women say the date-rape debate is the first time the nation has talked frankly about sex; men say it is women's unconscious reaction to the excesses of the sexual revolution. Meanwhile, men and women argue among themselves about the "gray area" that surrounds the whole murky arena of sexual relations, and there is no consensus in sight.

Nancy Gibbs, "When Is It Rape?" *Time*

TEACHING TIP
Your students probably will have lots to say about this well-crafted paragraph on date rape. Gibbs uses parallelism to present two contrasting views.

- This writer presents the differing ideas of many men and women by balancing their points of view in sentence after sentence, a technique you will learn in this unit.
- Note that she increases the force of the paragraph by placing the topic sentence last.

- ***Date rape***
- ***Another issue on which men and women may disagree***

CHAPTER

23 Consistent Tense

Consistent tense means using the same verb tense whenever possible within a sentence or paragraph. As you write and revise, avoid shifting from one tense to another—for example, from present to past—without a good reason for doing so.

ESL TIP
Nonnative writers may need extra work on avoiding tense shifts and on verb tenses in general. Refer them to Error #5: Wrong Verb Tense in the "8 Common ESL Errors" on the *Grassroots* student website.

(1) **Inconsistent tense:**	We *were* seven miles from shore. Suddenly, the sky *turns* dark.
(2) **Consistent tense:**	We *were* seven miles from shore. Suddenly, the sky *turned* dark.
(3) **Consistent tense:**	We *are* seven miles from shore. Suddenly, the sky *turns* dark.

TEACHING TIP
Help the class think critically about cases in which present or past tense would be more effective (e.g., present to show that events are ongoing).

- The sentences in (1) begin in the past tense with the verb *were* but then shift into the present tense with the verb *turns*. The tenses are inconsistent because both actions are occurring at the same time.
- The sentences in (2) are consistent. Both verbs, *were* and *turned,* are in the past tense.
- The sentences in (3) are also consistent. Both verbs, *are* and *turns,* are in the present tense.

Of course, you should use different verb tenses in a sentence or paragraph if they convey the meaning you want to convey.

(4) Two years ago, I *wanted* to be a chef, but now I *am studying* forestry.

- The verbs in sentence (4) accurately show the time relationship: In the past, I *wanted* to be a chef, but now I *am studying* forestry.

As you proofread your papers for tense consistency, ask yourself: Have I unthinkingly moved from one tense to another, from past to present, or from present to past?

PRACTICE 1

TEACHING TIP
Tell the class to beware of tense shifts in narrative writing. As writers relive past events in their minds, they may shift from past to present verbs.

Underline the verbs in these sentences. Then correct any inconsistencies above the line. Answers will vary.

EXAMPLE: As soon as I get [got] out of bed, I did fifty pushups.

or

As soon as I get out of bed, I did [do] fifty pushups.

1. We were walking near the lake when a large moose appears [appeared] just ahead.
2. When Bill asks [asked] the time, the cab driver told him it was after six.
3. The woman on the red bicycle was delivering newspapers while she is enjoying [was] the morning sunshine.
4. Dr. Choi smiled and welcomes [welcomed] the next patient.
5. The Oklahoma prairie stretches for miles, flat and rusty red. Here and there, an oil rig broke [breaks] the monotony.
6. They were strolling down Main Street when the lights go [went] out.
7. My cousins questioned me for hours about my trip. I describe [described] the flight, my impressions of Paris, and every meal I ate.
8. We started cheering as he approaches [approached] the finish line.
9. If Terry takes short naps during the day, she didn't [doesn't] feel tired in the evening.
10. Yesterday, we find [found] the book we need [needed] online. We ordered it immediately.

PRACTICE 2 WRITING ASSIGNMENT

TEACHING TIP
Ask students to color-code the verb tenses in their compositions with highlighters. This graphic presentation may enhance their awareness of a tense-shifting problem.

Suppose that you have been asked for written advice on what makes a successful family. Your adult child, an inexperienced friend, or a sibling has asked you to write down some words of wisdom on what makes a family work. Using your own family as an example, write your suggestions for making family life as nurturing, cooperative, and joyful as possible. You may draw on your family's experience to give examples of pitfalls to avoid or of positive behaviors and attitudes.

Revise for consistent tense.

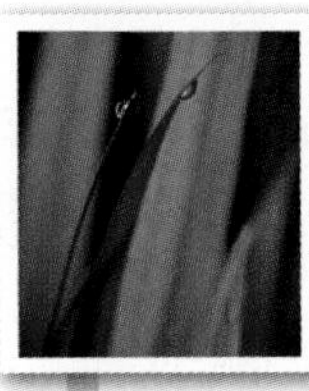

CHAPTER HIGHLIGHTS

- **In general, use the same verb tense within a sentence or a paragraph:**

  She *sings* beautifully, and the audience *listens* intently.

  or

  She *sang* beautifully, and the audience *listened* intently.

- **However, at times different verb tenses are required because of meaning:**

  He *is* not *working* now, but he *spent* sixty hours behind the counter last week.

CHAPTER REVIEW

TEACHING TIP
Chapter Review: If your students have learned types of order in Chapter 4, ask groups to identify the pattern of organization in each paragraph—A, order of importance; B, time order; C, illustration (examples).

Read each of these paragraphs for consistent tense. Correct any inconsistencies by changing the tense of the verbs. Write your corrections above the lines.

A. (1) Self-confidence is vital to success both in childhood and in adulthood. (2) With self-confidence, children ~~knew~~ know that they are worthwhile and that they have important goals. (3) Parents can teach their children self-confidence in several ways. (4) First, children ~~needed~~ need praise. (5) When they ~~drew~~ draw, for example, parents can tell them how beautiful their drawings are. (6) The praise lets them know they ~~had~~ have talents that other people admire. (7) Second, children ~~required~~ require exposure to many different experiences. (8) They soon ~~found~~ find that they need not be afraid to try new things. (9) They ~~realized~~ realize that they can succeed as well at chess as they do at basketball. (10) They ~~discovered~~ discover that a trip to a museum to examine medieval armor is fascinating or that they enjoy taking a class in pottery. (11) Finally, it ~~was~~ is very important to treat children individually. (12) Sensitive parents ~~did~~ do not compare their children's successes or failures with those of their brothers or sisters, relatives, or friends. (13) Of course, parents should inform children if their behavior or performance in school needs improvement. (14) Parents ~~helped~~ help children do better, however, by showing them how much they have accomplished so far and by suggesting how much they can and will accomplish in the future.

B. (1) Last summer, we visited one of the world's oddest museums, the home of someone who never existed. (2) Early one afternoon, we walked along the real Baker Street in London, England. (3) Suddenly, it ~~looms~~ loomed in front of us: number 221B, Mrs. Hudson's boarding house, home of the famous but fictitious detective Sherlock Holmes. (4) Once inside the perfect reproduction of Holmes' rooms, we ~~are~~ were astonished to find all of Holmes' belongings, including his violin, his walking stick, and his chemistry set. (5) We ~~learn~~ learned that the founders of the museum had searched the country for Victorian objects and furniture like those in the Holmes stories. (6) They ~~succeed~~ succeeded beyond any Sherlock Holmes fan's wildest dreams. (7) They ~~locate~~ located a Persian slipper like the one in which Holmes' stored pipe tobacco. (8) They even ~~uncover~~ uncovered a gold and emerald tie pin like the one Queen Victoria gave Holmes. (9) The museum also had quarters for Holmes' friend and assistant, Dr. Watson. (10) For him, the founders ~~buy~~ bought nineteenth-century medical supplies and surgical instruments. (11) After we ~~return~~ returned home that summer, I reread several Sherlock Holmes stories. (12) In my mind's eye, I ~~see~~ saw Holmes' rooms and belongings more vividly than ever before. (13) Of course, Holmes would have predicted that. (14) "Elementary," he would have said.

C. (1) Almost every major city in the world has a subway system. (2) Underground trains speed through complex networks of tunnels and ~~carried~~ carry millions of passengers every day.

(3) Subway systems sometimes differ because of their locations. (4) In Mexico City, for example, subway cars ~~traveled~~ travel through suspended tunnels capable of absorbing earthquake shocks. (5) Residents of Haifa, Israel, use an unusually short, straight subway that ~~ran~~ runs up and down inside a mountain. (6) The train ~~brought~~ brings people from Haifa's lower port city up—a thousand feet—to the upper residential city. (7) In Hong Kong, the world's first completely air-conditioned subway system ~~offered~~ offers relief from extremely hot and humid outdoor temperatures. (8) Cities like San Francisco, of course, expand the definition of subway to cover underwater as well as underground transportation. (9) The San Francisco Bay Area Rapid Transit (BART) system ~~included~~ includes several miles of track under San Francisco Bay.

(10) Some subway systems are famous for their artwork. (11) With paintings and walls of precious marble, many Moscow subway stations ~~looked~~ look like museums. (12) Several stations in Stockholm, Sweden, ~~seemed~~ seem like elegant caverns because of granite carvings and rock in its natural state. (13) With colorful designs and all kinds of special effects, subway stations from Montreal to Tokyo ~~resembled~~ resemble modern art galleries.

(14) Subways, therefore, ~~did~~ do more than provide an efficient means of public transportation. (15) They are creative solutions to special problems as well as expressions of art and culture.

EXPLORING ONLINE

TEACHING TIP
More practice and assessment are available in the *Grassroots* Test Bank; linked ACE tests on the *Grassroots* student website; *WriteSpace for Grassroots*; and at the Exploring Online links in this chapter.

<http://owl.english.purdue.edu/handouts/grammar/g_tensecEX1.html> Here are three exercises in tense consistency. Hone your skills.

<http://college.hmco.com/devenglish/> Visit the *Grassroots* 8/e Student Website for more exercises and quizzes.

CHAPTER 24

Consistent Person

TEACHING TIP
You might want to explain how the three "persons," or points of view, differ. First person is informal and is not welcomed in some courses and most workplaces. Second person usually should be avoided except in "how-to" writing. Third person is often the best choice for academic writing.

Consistent person means using the same person or personal pronoun throughout a sentence or a paragraph. As you write and revise, avoid confusing shifts from one person to another. For example, don't shift from *first person (I, we)* or *third person (he, she, it, they)* to *second person (you).**

(1) **Inconsistent person:**	College *students* soon see that *you* are on *your* own.
(2) **Consistent person:**	College *students* soon see that *they* are on *their* own.
(3) **Consistent person:**	In college, *you* soon see that *you* are on *your* own.

- Sentence (1) shifts from the third person plural *students* to the second person *you* and *your.*
- Sentence (2) uses the third person plural consistently. *They* and *their* now clearly refer to *students.*
- Sentence (3) is also consistent, using the second person *you* and *your* throughout.

PRACTICE 1

TEACHING TIP
Discuss with students why the pronoun *he* should not be used to refer to a noun that could be masculine or feminine. The writer should choose either *he or she* or *they*—and then be consistent.

Correct any inconsistencies of person in these sentences. If necessary, change the verbs to make them agree with any new subjects. Make your corrections above the lines.

EXAMPLE: Each hiker should bring ~~your~~ *his or her* own lunch.

1. Belkys treats me like family when I visit her. She always makes ~~you~~ *me* feel at home.

*For more work on pronouns, see Chapter 20.

2. I love to go dancing. ~~You~~ I can exercise, work off tension, and have fun, all at the same time.

TEACHING TIP
If your students need to review pronoun agreement, refer them to Chapter 20 for more help and practice.

3. If a person has gone to a large high school, ~~you~~ he or she may find a small college a welcome change.
4. When Lee and I drive to work at 6 a.m., ~~you~~ we see the city waking up.
5. Every mechanic should make sure ~~they have~~ he or she has a good set of tools.
6. People who want to buy cars today are often stopped by high prices. ~~You~~ They aren't sure how to get the most for ~~your~~ their money.
7. Do each of you have ~~his or her~~ your own e-mail address?
8. Many people mistakenly think that ~~your~~ their vote doesn't really count.
9. A teacher's attitude affects the performance of ~~their~~ his or her students.
10. It took me three years to decide to enroll in college; in many ways, ~~you~~ I really didn't know what ~~you~~ I wanted to do when ~~you~~ I finished high school.

PRACTICE 2 WRITING ASSIGNMENT

In small groups, write as many endings as you can think of for this sentence: "You can (cannot) tell much about a person by . . ." You might write, "the way he or she dresses," "the way he or she styles his or her hair," or "the kind of movies he or she likes." Each group member should write down every sentence.

Then let each group member choose one sentence and write a short paragraph supporting it. Use people in the news or friends as examples to prove your point. As you write, be careful to use the first, second, or third person correctly. When everyone is finished, exchange papers, checking each other's work for consistent person.

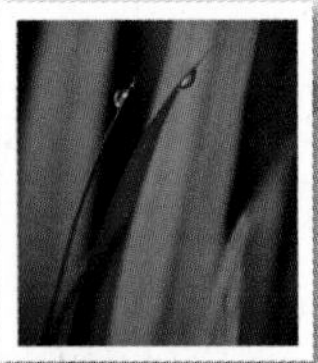

CHAPTER HIGHLIGHTS

- **Use the same personal pronoun throughout a sentence or a paragraph:**

  When *you* apply for a driver's license, *you* may have to take a written test and a driving test.

  When a *person* applies for a driver's license, *he or she* may have to take a written test and a driving test.

CHAPTER REVIEW

Correct the inconsistencies of person in these paragraphs. Then make any other necessary changes. Write your corrections above the lines.

A. (1) When exam time comes, do you become anxious because you aren't sure how to study for tests? (2) ~~They~~ You may have done all the work for ~~their~~ your courses, but you still don't feel prepared. (3) Fortunately, ~~he~~ you can do some things to make taking tests easier. (4) ~~They~~ You can look through the textbook and review the material ~~one has~~ you have underlined. (5) You might read the notes you have taken in class and highlight or underline main points. (6) ~~A person~~ You can think about some questions the professor may ask and then try writing answers. (7) Sometimes, ~~they~~ you can find other people from your class and form a study group to compare class notes. (8) The night before a test, ~~they~~ you shouldn't drink too much coffee. (9) ~~They~~ You should get a good night's sleep so that your mind will be as sharp for the exam as your pencil.

B. (1) The sport of mountain biking began in northern California in the 1970s. (2) Some experienced cyclists began using ~~his or her~~ their old one-speed fat-tire bikes to explore dirt roads and trails. (3) ~~You~~ They began by getting car rides up one of the mountains and pedaling their bikes down. (4) Then they began cycling farther up the mountain until ~~he and she~~ they were pedaling to the top. (5) Those cyclists eventually started designing bikes to fit ~~our~~ their sport. (6) By the end of the 1970s, road bike manufacturers decided ~~you~~ they would join the action. (7) By the mid-1980s, mountain biking had become a national craze, and sales of mountain bikes were exceeding sales of road bikes.

(8) Today, mountain bikers pay about $1,000 for bikes that have everything ~~we~~ they need for riding on rough trails: front-wheel shock absorbers, twenty-four gears that shift easily, a lightweight frame, flexible wheels, and even a full suspension frame. (9) Cyclists ride ~~your~~ their bikes everywhere; some of their favorite places are South Dakota's Badlands, Colorado's ski resorts, and Utah's Canyonlands National Park. (10) ~~You~~ They compete in mountain bike races all over the world. (11) To top this off, in 1996 some of ~~you~~ them competed in the first Olympic mountain bike race, outside Atlanta, Georgia. (12) The course, which had tightly spaced

trees and large rocks, included steep climbs and sharp descents with surprise jumps. (13) What were those early "inventors" thinking as ~~he and she~~ they watched that first Olympic race?

EXPLORING ONLINE

TEACHING TIP
More practice and assessment are available in the *Grassroots* Test Bank; linked ACE tests on the *Grassroots* student website; *WriteSpace for Grassroots*; and at the Exploring Online links in this chapter.

<http://www.powa.org/edit/problem.html> Click on "shift in person." Review and do Activity 4.16: Rewrite the paragraph in consistent first person (*I* or *we*) and then in third person (*he/she* or *they*).

<http://college.hmco.com/devenglish/> Visit the *Grassroots* 8/e Student Website for more exercises and quizzes.

CHAPTER 25

Parallelism

PART A Writing Parallel Constructions

Which sentence in each pair sounds better to you?

(1) Jennie is an artist, spends time at athletics, and flies planes.

(2) Jennie is *an artist, an athlete,* and *a pilot.*

(3) He slowed down and came sliding. The winning run was scored.

(4) He *slowed* down, *slid,* and *scored* the winning run.

TEACHING TIP
Most students are completely unaware of the concept of parallelism. Explain that, once grasped and put to use, parallel structures add sophistication and grace to one's writing.

- Do sentences (2) and (4) sound smoother and clearer than sentences (1) and (3)?
- Sentences (2) and (4) balance similar words or phrases to show similar ideas.

This technique is called *parallelism* **or** *parallel structure.* **The italicized parts of (2) and (4) are** *parallel.* **When you use parallelism, you repeat similar grammatical constructions in order to express similar ideas.**

- In sentence (2), can you see how *an artist, an athlete,* and *a pilot* are parallel? All three words in the series are singular nouns.
- In sentence (4), can you see how *slowed, slid,* and *scored* are parallel? All three words in the series are verbs in the past tense.

Now let's look at two more pairs of sentences. Note which sentence in each pair contains parallelism.

(5) The car was big, had beauty, and it cost a lot.

(6) The car was *big, beautiful,* and *expensive.*

(7) They raced across the roof, and the fire escape is where they came down.

(8) They raced *across the roof* and *down the fire escape.*

- In sentence (6), how are *big, beautiful,* and *expensive* parallel words?

  All three words are adjectives.

- In sentence (8), how are *across the roof* and *down the fire escape* parallel phrases?
  Both are prepositional phrases.

Certain special constructions require parallel structure:

(9) The room is *both* light *and* cheery.
(10) You *either* love geometry *or* hate it.
(11) Tanya *not only* plays the guitar *but also* sings.
(12) Richard would *rather* fight *than* quit.

ESL TIP
The regularity and predictability of parallel structures makes the concept fairly easy for ESL students to learn.

Each of these constructions has two parts:

both . . . and	not only . . . but also
(n)either . . . (n)or	rather . . . than . . .

The words, phrases, or clauses following each part must be parallel:

light . . . cheery	plays . . . sings
love . . . hate	fight . . . quit

Parallelism is an excellent way to add smoothness and power to your writing. Use it in pairs or in a series of ideas, balancing a noun with a noun, an *-ing* verb with an *-ing* verb, a prepositional phrase with a prepositional phrase, and so on.

PRACTICE 1

Circle the element that is *not* parallel in each list.

EXAMPLE: blue
red
(colored like rust)
purple

TEACHING TIP
Suggest that students read this chapter's examples and exercise items aloud so that they can better "hear" the parallel and nonparallel structures.

1. rowing
   jogging
   (runner)
   lifting weights
2. (my four dogs)
   out the door
   across the yard
   under the fence
3. (painting the kitchen)
   cans of paint
   several brushes
   one roller
4. persistent
   strong-willed
   (work)
   optimistic
5. opening his mouth to speak
   (toward the audience)
   smiling with anticipation
   leaning against the table
6. music shops
   clothing stores
   (buying a birthday present)
   electronics shops
7. (dressed for the office)
   laptop computer
   leather briefcase
   cellular phone
8. We shop for fruits at the market.
   We buy enough food to last a week.
   (We are baking a cake tonight.)
   We cook special meals often.

PRACTICE 2

Rewrite each sentence, using parallelism to accent the similar ideas.

EXAMPLE: Do you believe that gratitude and feeling happy are related?
Rewrite: *Do you believe that gratitude and happiness are related?*

TEACHING TIP
Caution students to avoid wordiness when correcting parallelism errors. Ask which sentence is clearer and more concise: *1. Do you believe that having gratitude and feeling happy are related?* or *2. Do you believe that gratitude and happiness are related?* Sentence 2 is concise.

1. Many people believe that they will be happy once they have money, they are famous, married to a spouse, or working at a good job.

   Rewrite: Many people believe that they will be happy once they have money, fame, a spouse or a good job.

2. Psychologist Martin Seligman found that gratitude is a key ingredient of happiness, and the "gratitude visit" was his invention.

   Rewrite: Psychologist Martin Seligman found that gratitude is a key ingredient of happiness and invented the "gratitude visit."

3. First, you think of a person who was truly helpful to you, and then a "gratitude letter" is written by you to that person.

   Rewrite: First, you think of a person who was truly helpful to you, and then you write a "gratitude letter" to that person.

4. In this letter, explain sincerely and with specifics why you are grateful.

   Rewrite: In this letter, explain sincerely and specifically why you are grateful.

5. Then visit this person and reading your letter aloud.

   Rewrite: Then visit this person and read your letter aloud.

6. According to Seligman, the ritual is moving, powerful, and there is a lot of emotion.

   Rewrite: According to Seligman, the ritual is moving, powerful, and emotional.

7. Seligman says people feel happier if they focus on the positive aspects of the past rather than being negative.

   Rewrite: Seligman says people feel happier if they focus on the positive aspects of the past rather than on the negative.

TEACHING TIP
Writing Assignment 1 on page 289 follows up on this practice, asking students to make and write about gratitude visits. The task is likely to provoke students' interest, critical thinking, and discussions.

8. Gratitude visits, he believes, increase how intense, the length, and the frequency of positive memories.

   Rewrite: Gratitude visits, he believes, increase the intensity, the length, and the frequency of positive memories.

9. In addition, they tend to inspire the receivers of thanks to become giving of thanks.

   Rewrite: In addition, they tend to inspire the receivers of thanks to become givers of thanks.

10. One gratitude visit leads to another, creating a chain of appreciation and also to make everyone feel more content.

    Rewrite: One gratitude visit leads to another, creating a chain of appreciation and contentment for everyone.

PRACTICE 3

Fill in the blanks in each sentence with parallel words or phrases of your own. Be creative. Take care that your sentences make sense and that your parallels are truly parallel. Sample answers.

EXAMPLE: I feel ___rested___ and ___happy___.

1. Ethan's favorite colors are ___yellow___ and ___green___.
2. The day of the storm, we ___sat by the window___, and they ___played cards___.
3. Her attitude was strange. She acted as if ___she was always right___ and as if ___everyone else was always wrong___.
4. I like people who ___love to hike___ and who ___love to sing___.
5. Some married couples ___spend most of their time together___ while others ___pursue separate interests___.
6. Harold ___flies a plane___, but I just ___fly my kite___.
7. To finish this project, work ___through the day___ and ___into the night___.
8. ___Playing the piano___ and ___lying on the beach___ relax me.
9. We found ___delicate shells___, ___smooth stones___, and ___broken glass___ on the beach.
10. They might want to ___paint the walls___ or to ___wallpaper the room___.

TEACHING TIP
Have students compare their answers to Practice 3 and help each other identify any inconsistent structures.

PART B Using Parallelism for Special Effects

By rearranging the order of a parallel series, you can sometimes add a little drama or humor to your sentences. Which of these two sentences is more dramatic?

(1) Bharati is a wife, a mother, and a black belt in karate.

(2) Bharati is a wife, a black belt in karate, and a mother.

- If you chose sentence (1), you are right. Sentence (1) saves the most surprising item—*a black belt in karate*—for last.

- Sentence (2), on the other hand, does not build suspense but gives away the surprise in the middle.

You can also use parallelism to set up your readers' expectations and then surprise them with humor.

TEACHING TIP
Students are often intrigued to learn that good orators—and good writers—use parallelism to help the audience follow their ideas. If you can, bring in Martin Luther King's "I Have a Dream" speech or Abraham Lincoln's "Gettysburg Address." Let students find and analyze uses of parallelism.

(3) Mike Hardware was the kind of private eye who didn't know the meaning of the word *fear*, who could laugh in the face of danger and spit in the eye of death—in short, a moron with suicidal tendencies.

- Clever use of parallelism made this sentence a winner in the Bulwer-Lytton Contest. Every year, contestants make each other laugh by inventing the first sentence of a bad novel.

PRACTICE 4

On paper or on a computer, write five sentences of your own, using parallel structure. In one or two of your sentences, arrange the parallel elements to build toward a dramatic or humorous conclusion. For ideas, look at Practice 3, but create your own sentences.

PRACTICE 5 WRITING ASSIGNMENT

Write a one-paragraph newspaper advertisement to rent or sell your house or apartment. Using complete sentences, let the reader know the number of rooms, their size, and their appearance, and explain why someone would be happy there. Emphasize your home's good points, such as "lots of light" or "closet space galore," but don't hide the flaws. If possible, minimize them while still being honest.

You may want to begin with a general description such as "This apartment is a plant lover's dream." Be careful, though: if you describe only the good features or exaggerate, readers may think, "It's too good to be true." Use parallel structure to help your sentences read more smoothly.

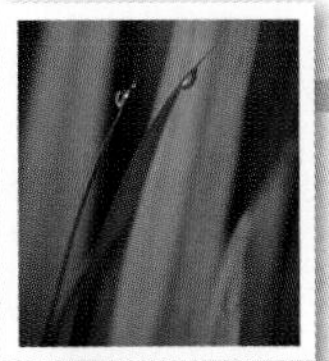

CHAPTER HIGHLIGHTS

- **Parallelism balances similar words or phrases to express similar ideas:**

  He left the gym *tired, sweaty,* and *satisfied.*

  Tami not only *finished the exam in record time* but also *answered the question for extra credit.*

  To celebrate his success, Roger *took in a show, went to a dance,* and *ate a late dinner.*

CHAPTER REVIEW

TEACHING TIP
Read "before" and "after" versions of the Chapter Review passage aloud so that students can hear both the faulty and the correct parallelism.

This essay contains both correct and faulty parallel constructions. Revise the faulty parallelism. Write your corrections above the lines.

Chinese Medicine in the United States

(1) When diplomatic relations between the United States and mainland China were restored in 1972, acupuncture was one import that sparked America's imagination and interest. ~~made people interested~~. (2) In the United States today, the most popular form of Chinese medicine is acupuncture.

(3) Acupuncture involves the insertion of thin, sterile, ~~made of~~ stainless steel needles at specific points on the body. (4) Chinese medical science believes that the *chi,* or life force, can be redirected by inserting and manipulating ~~by the manipulation of~~ these needles. (5) They are inserted to just below the skin and are either removed quickly or left ~~leave them~~ in for up to forty minutes. (6) In addition, the acupuncturist can twirl them, heat them, or charge ~~charging~~ them with a mild electrical current. (7) Acupuncture can reduce pain for those suffering from allergies, arthritis, backache, or ~~with a~~ toothache. (8) It also has helped in cases of chronic substance abuse, anxiety, and depression. ~~for depressed people~~.

(9) Chinese medicine has grown in popularity and importance ~~become important~~ in America. (10) Thirty-five schools in the United States teach Chinese acupuncture. (11) Forty-four states have passed laws that regulate or license ~~for licensing~~ the practice of acupuncture. (12) Since 1974, the government has authorized several studies of acupuncture's effectiveness and reliability ~~how reliable it is~~. (13) Although research has failed to explain how acupuncture works, it has confirmed that it does work. (14) The studies also suggest that acupuncture should continue to be tested and used ~~using it~~.

EXPLORING ONLINE

TEACHING TIP
More practice and assessment are available in the *Grassroots* Test Bank; linked ACE tests on the *Grassroots* student website; *WriteSpace for Grassroots*; and at the Exploring Online links in this chapter.

<http://www.ccc.commnet.edu/cgi-shl/quiz.pl/parallelism_quiz.htm>
Interactive quiz: Click on the sentence that uses parallelism correctly.

<http://www.ccc.commnet.edu/grammar/quizzes/niu/niu10.htm>
Interactive quiz: Which sentence in each group has parallelism errors?

<http://college.hmco.com/devenglish/> Visit the *Grassroots* 8/e Student Website for more exercises and quizzes.

UNIT

6

WRITING ASSIGNMENTS

As you complete each writing assignment, remember to perform these steps:

- Write a clear, complete topic sentence.
- Use freewriting, brainstorming, or clustering to generate ideas for the body of your paragraph, essay, or speech.
- Arrange your best ideas in a plan.
- Revise for support, unity, coherence, and exact language.
- Proofread for grammar, punctuation, and spelling errors.

Writing Assignment 1: *Pay a gratitude visit.* Experts like Dr. Martin Seligman claim that people who let themselves feel and express gratitude are happier than people who do not. Do your own research. 1. Pick a person who has been kind or helpful to you but whom you have never properly thanked. 2. Write a letter to this person, discussing specifically, in concrete terms, why you feel grateful to him or her. 3. Arrange a visit to the object of your gratitude and—in person—read your letter aloud. 4. Then write a one-paragraph report on how the two of you felt about the experience. Are the experts right? Revise for consistent tense and person; use parallelism to make your sentences read smoothly.

Writing Assignment 2: *Review a restaurant.* You have been asked to review the food, service, and atmosphere at a local restaurant. Your review will appear in a local newspaper and will have an impact on the success or failure of this eating establishment. Tell what you ordered, how it tasted, and why you would or would not recommend this dish. Note the service: was it slow, efficient, courteous, rude, or generally satisfactory? Is the restaurant one in which customers can easily carry on a conversation, or is there too much noise? Is the lighting good or poor? Include as much specific detail as you can. Revise for consistent tense and person.

Writing Assignment 3: *Take a stand on date rape.* In a group with classmates, read aloud and discuss Nancy Gibbs's powerful paragraph on date rape on page 273. Do you agree with her that the sexes often have different views on this topic? Do you know someone who has experienced date rape or anyone who has been accused of it? On your own, jot down ideas and narrow the subject to one aspect that interests you. Plan and write a paragraph or short essay. Revise carefully for consistency and parallelism.

Writing Assignment 4: *Evaluate a textbook.* A publisher has asked you to evaluate this textbook, *Grassroots,* or a text you use in a different course. The publisher wants an honest evaluation so that the new edition can be even better than the present one. Rate the textbook on clarity and organization: that is, does it explain the subject matter well, and does one chapter naturally follow from another? You also might want to consider whether the material is shown in a way that is pleasing to the eye. Most important, does the book help you learn? Revise for consistent tense and person; use parallelism to make your sentences read smoothly.

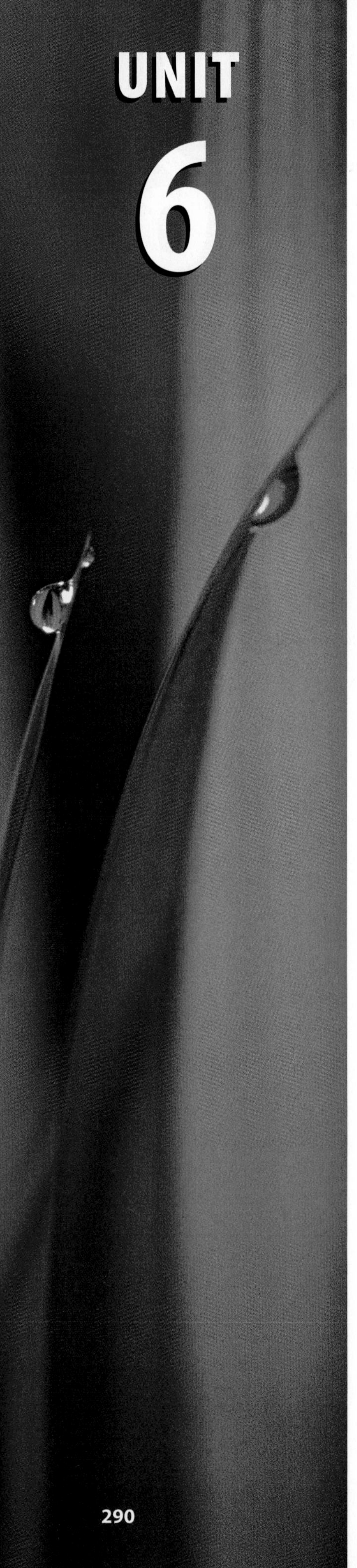

UNIT 6 REVIEW

Proofreading

A. We have changed this student's composition so that it contains inconsistent tenses and faulty parallelism. Proofread for these errors, and correct them above the lines. (You should find eleven errors.)

Inspiration

(1) When I was a freshman in high school, I ~~have~~ had a serious problem with English. (2) All day long, my head was filled with ideas for compositions, but when I arrived in English class, my mind ~~goes~~ went blank. (3) I feared that my teacher thought I was just another lazy student. (4) In fact, I almost gave up; thank goodness, I didn't!

(5) Then, by the strangest twist of fate, I ~~find~~ found out why my mind ~~goes~~ went blank and why my compositions were never finished. (6) One day, the English class moved from the basement to the third floor of the building. (7) The moment I stepped into the new room and ~~the window was seen~~ saw the window, I ~~know~~ knew what had bothered me all semester—no light, no fresh air, and ~~the fact that there wasn't a sense of~~ no space. (8) I ~~select~~ selected a seat near the window and looked over my shoulder at the tall oak tree that stretched past the third-floor window. (9) When I ~~pick~~ picked up my pen, the writing began to flow. (10) If I ran out of things to say, I just ~~glance~~ glanced over my shoulder at the tree and at the sky—and I ~~would be~~ was inspired to continue my essay.

Chistopher Moore, student

B. Proofread the following essay for inconsistent person and faulty parallelism. Correct the errors above the lines. (You should find eleven errors.)

Opening Up the Workplace

(1) New technology is helping people with disabilities enter the workforce in record numbers. (2) With the latest products, blind workers can see a computer screen, and deaf workers can ~~be hearing~~ hear a telephone call. (3) People who cannot speak can talk to others. (4) People can operate a computer even if ~~your~~ their fingers cannot type. (5) Pitney Bowes, Toshiba, Apple Computer, and other companies are creating a workforce revolution with "assistive technology."

(6) For example, if workers cannot move their arms or legs, ~~he or she~~ they can use an eye-gaze program. (7) They can direct a laser beam to points on ~~his or her~~ their computer screen just by *looking* at control keys. (8) The laser sets off commands for the computer to follow. (9) Users need only keep their head still and ~~controlling one eye is also necessary~~ control one eye.

(10) Some computers display information in Braille for blind people or ~~the print is~~ in extremely large print for those with vision problems. (11) Some software programs convert written text into speech so that blind workers can hear it. (12) Other products convert speech into written text so that deaf workers can see it.

(13) Assistive technology will also benefit the country's aging workforce. (14) Experts estimate that nearly two-thirds of the population will eventually suffer partial or ~~it may be~~ total hearing loss. (15) Glaucoma and ~~getting~~ cataracts will threaten vision. (16) Stroke victims may find ~~ourselves~~ themselves unable to communicate or ~~functioning~~ function independently. (17) The new technology will bring people into the workforce and ~~kept~~ keep them there.

WRITERS' WORKSHOP

Shift Your Audience and Purpose

Playing with the idea of audience and purpose can produce some interesting writing—such as writing to your car to persuade it to keep running until finals are over. Likewise, writing as if you are someone else can be a learning experience.

In your class or group, read this unusual essay, aloud if possible.

A Fly's-Eye View of My Apartment

(1) Hey, are you guys ready? Today is Armageddon!* When you enter this door, remember, you're not getting out alive. She's a pretty tough lady. Oh, and don't forget to eat all you can. The kids are always dropping crumbs. You can make it through the night if you stay on the ceilings. Whatever you do, stay out of the peach room that is always humid. Once the door is shut, you're trapped. Try not to be noticed on the cabinets in the room where the smells come from. There is nothing interesting in the room with the big screen, but the room with the large bed can be rather stimulating if you stay on the walls.

(2) She won't get tired of us until about 6 p.m.; that is usually around dinnertime. She switches around, using different swatters, so you never really know what to look for. When you hear the gospel music, start looking out. She gets an enormous amount of energy from this music, and her swats are accurate, which means they're deadly. It kills me how she becomes so baffled about how we get in since she has screens on the windows. Little does she know that it's every time she opens the front door.

(3) Well, I think she's ready to leave for work. I hear the lock. To a good life, fellows. See you in heaven—and remember to give her hell!

Tanya Peck, student

1. How effective is Tanya Peck's paragraph?

   __Y__ Interesting subject? __Y__ Good supporting details?

   __Y__ Logical organization? __Y__ Effective conclusion?

2. This writer cleverly plays with the notions of speaker, audience, and purpose. Who is Peck pretending to be as she writes? Whom is she addressing and for what purpose? She is a fly addressing flies about to enter Peck's apartment.

*Armageddon: a final battle between forces of good and evil.

3. The writer/speaker refers to the "pretty tough lady" of the house. Who is that lady? How do you know?

4. Peck divides her essay into two main paragraphs and a brief conclusion. Because of her unusual subject, the paragraphs do not have topic sentences. However, does each paragraph have a clear main idea? What is the main idea of paragraph (1)? of paragraph (2)? (1) a guide to the rooms (2) advice about the homeowner

5. Underline any details or sentences that you especially liked—for example, in paragraph (2), the clever idea that the fly realizes that gospel music (for some mysterious reason) energizes the woman with the swatter. Can you identify the rooms described in paragraph (1)?

6. The essay concludes by playing with the terms *heaven* and *hell.* Do you find this effective—or offensive? Are these words connected to *Armageddon* in the introduction? How?

7. Proofread for any grammar or spelling errors. No errors

Writing and Revising Ideas

1. Write a _____________'s-eye view (dog, cat, flea, canary, goldfish, ant, roach) of your home.

2. Describe an important moment in history as if you were there.

Before you write, read about audience and purpose in Chapter 1. Prewrite and plan to get an engaging subject. As you revise, pay special attention to keeping a consistent point of view; really try to imagine what that person (or other creature) would say in those circumstances.

UNIT 7

Mastering Mechanics

Even the best ideas may lose their impact if the writer doesn't know how to capitalize and punctuate correctly. In this unit, you will

- Learn when—and when not—to capitalize
- Recognize when—and when not—to use commas
- Find out how to use apostrophes
- Learn how to quote the words of others in your writing

Spotlight on Writing

Correct punctuation adds to the power of this writer's humorous look at a serious subject. If possible, read his paragraph aloud.

My daughter, Olivia, who just turned three, has an imaginary friend whose name is Charlie Ravioli. Olivia is growing up in Manhattan, and so Charlie Ravioli has a lot of local traits: he lives in an apartment "on Madison and Lexington," he dines on grilled chicken, fruit, and water, and having reached the age of seven and a half, he feels, or is thought, "old." But the most peculiarly local thing about Olivia's imaginary playmate is this: he is always too busy to play with her. She holds her toy cell phone up to her ear, and we hear her talk into it. "Ravioli? It's Olivia. . . It's Olivia. Come and play? OK. Call me. Bye." Then she snaps it shut and shakes her head. "I always get his machine," she says. Or she will say, "I spoke to Ravioli today." "Did you have fun?" my wife and I ask. "No. He was busy working. On a television" (leaving it up in the air if he repairs electronic devices or has his own talk show).

Adam Gopnik, "Bumping Into Mr. Ravioli," *The New Yorker*

- This writer describes his daughter's imaginary playmate as someone too busy to play! Why do you think Olivia has invented a playmate like Ravioli? Where did she learn about cell conversations, phone machines, and busy-ness?
- Does this paragraph point out a modern problem? If so, is it a big-city problem or a problem that exists in many places? What is the solution?

- ***Taking time to play***
- ***A time when "child's play" taught you something important***

CHAPTER

26 Capitalization

Here are the basic rules of capitalization:

TEACHING TIP
You might want to explain to students that although *African American* and *Caucasian* are capitalized, the words *black* and *white* usually are not.

1. nationality, race, language, religion —Capitalize→ American, African American, French, Latino, Protestant, Jewish, Catholic, Muslim, Buddhist, and so forth

- This group is *always capitalized.*

2. names of persons, countries, states, cities, places, streets, bodies of water, and so forth

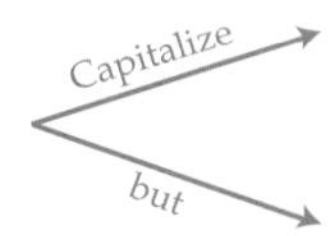

Capitalize: Bill Morse, New Zealand, Texas, Denver, Golden Gate Bridge, Jones Street, Pacific Ocean, and so forth

but: a person, a country, a large state, a city, a bridge, an ocean, and so forth

TEACHING TIP
You may wish to begin this lesson by reviewing with students the distinction between proper nouns/adjectives and common nouns/adjectives. Note that rules 2–11 are arranged so as to show this distinction.

- If you name a specific person, state, city, street, or body of water, *capitalize;* if you don't, use small letters.

3. buildings, organizations, institutions

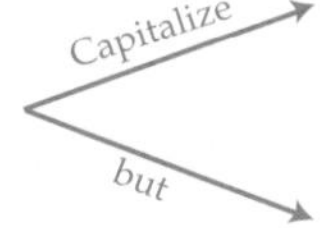

Capitalize: Art Institute of Chicago, Apollo Theater, National Council of La Raza, Johnson City Library, Smithson University, and so forth

but: a museum, a famous theater, an activist group, a library, an old school, and so forth

- If you name a specific building, group, or institution, *capitalize;* if you don't, use small letters.

4. historical events, periods, documents

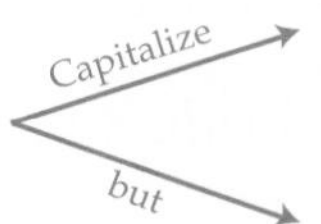

Capitalize: the Spanish-American War, the Renaissance, the Constitution, and so forth

but: a terrible war, a new charter, and so forth

ESL TIP
Many ESL students do not understand the importance of capitalization. Native Spanish speakers may need to review the rules regarding nationalities in order to avoid errors like this one: *My american friends are very interesting.*

- If you name a specific historical event, period, or document, *capitalize;* if you don't, use small letters.

5. months, days, holidays

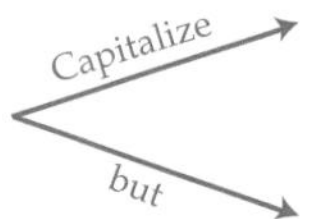

June, Monday, the Fourth of July, and so forth

summer, fall, winter, spring

- *Always capitalize* months, days, and holidays; use small letters for the seasons.

6. professional and civil titles

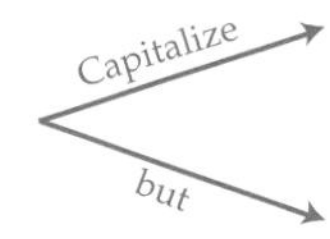

Dr. Smith, Professor Greenstein, Judge Alvarez, and so forth

the doctor, the professor, the judge, and so forth

- If you name the doctor, judge, and so forth, *capitalize;* if you don't, use small letters.

7. family names

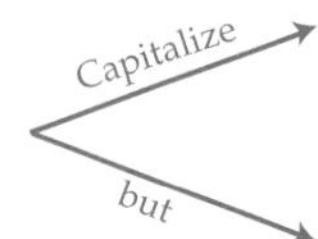

Uncle Xavier, Grandmother Stein, Cousin Emma, Mother, Grandfather, and so forth

an uncle, the grandmother, our cousin, my mother, and so forth

- If you name a relative or use *Mother, Father, Grandmother,* or *Grandfather* as a name, *capitalize;* however, if one of these words is preceded by the word *a, an,* or *the,* a possessive pronoun, or an adjective, use a small letter.

TEACHING TIP
People are still debating whether to capitalize certain words associated with the Internet. Most dictionaries capitalize *Internet, World Wide Web,* and *Web page,* but the words *e-mail* and *online* are never capitalized.

8. brand names

Greaso hair oil, Quick drafting ink, and so forth

- *Capitalize* the brand name but not the type of product.

9. geographic locations

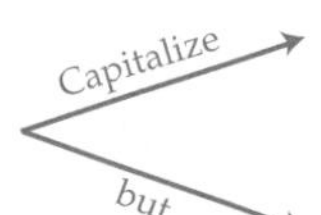

the East, the Northwest, the South, and so forth

east on the boulevard

- If you mean a geographic location, *capitalize;* if you mean a direction, use small letters.

TEACHING TIP
Urge students to use uppercase and lowercase letters (rather than all capitals) in *all* written work, including e-mail messages. Text written in all caps not only is hard to read but also seems to shout at the reader. Using good writing and well-chosen words is the best way to hold the readers' attention.

10. academic subjects

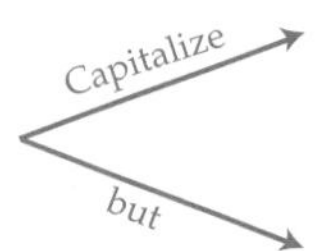

Mathematics 51, Sociology 11, English Literature 210, and so forth

a tough mathematics course, an A in sociology, a course in English literature, and so forth

- If you use the course number, *capitalize;* if you don't, use small letters. However, always capitalize languages and countries.

11. titles of books, poems, plays, films	Capitalize →	*Pride and Prejudice,* "Ode to a Bat," *Fences, Women on the Edge of a Nervous Breakdown,* and so forth

- *Capitalize* the first letter of words in titles except for *a, an,* and *the;* prepositions; and coordinating conjunctions. However, always capitalize the first letter of the *first* and *last* words of the title.

PRACTICE 1

Capitalize where necessary.

EXAMPLE: Dr. richard carmona went from high school dropout to surgeon general of the united states.

1. Richard carmona grew up in a poor puerto rican family in harlem, new york.
2. He started skipping classes in middle school and dropped out of dewitt clinton high school at age seventeen.
3. Carmona worked at dull, low-paying jobs until a conversation with a young man on leave from the u.s. army changed his life.
4. This soldier inspired him to join the military in 1967, and Carmona soon found himself working as a medic in vietnam.
5. He joined the green berets, earning two purple hearts for his brave service.
6. Carmona returned to america determined to become a doctor, so he enrolled at bronx community college.
7. He says that he owes his career to that college and to several of its professors—including michael steuerman and richard kor, who inspired him to succeed.
8. Carmona went on to earn degrees in biology and chemistry; he attended medical school at the university of california, graduating first in his class in three years instead of four.
9. Even after becoming a trauma surgeon and professor at the university of arizona, he continued to use his military training and knowledge of special operations.
10. This crime-fighting doctor joined the S.W.A.T. team for the pima county sheriff's department in 1986.
11. Carmona made headlines in 1992 when he dangled out of a helicopter to rescue a person stranded on the side of a cliff, an event that inspired a television movie.

ESL TIP
Here is an engaging activity that might prompt shy ESL students to share. Ask all students to write a brief autobiography—with people, places, pets, and dates capitalized correctly. Then have volunteers read their work aloud as class members learn about each other and listen for words that should be capped.

12. In 1999, he stopped at a traffic accident in tucson, arizona; saw a hostage taker holding a woman at gunpoint; and shot the suspect.
    T A

13. Less than a year after the terrorist attacks of september 11, 2001, president george w. bush selected dr. carmona for the country's top medical post, noting his knowledge of law enforcement, bioterrorism, and emergency preparedness.
    S P G W. B D C

14. The second latino to be named to the u.s. post, surgeon general Carmona thanked the president in both spanish and english.
    L U.S. S G S E

15. Senator john mccain said in the u.s. congress that carmona is "the embodiment of the american dream."
    J M C U.S. C C A

PRACTICE 2 WRITING ASSIGNMENT

Is your vacation usually a disaster or a success? Describe a particularly memorable vacation—either bad or good—in which you learned something about how to plan or enjoy a vacation.

In your first sentence, tell what you learned. Explain what went right and what went wrong. Be sure to name the places you visited and the sights you saw. You will probably want to arrange events in time order. Proofread for correct capitalization.

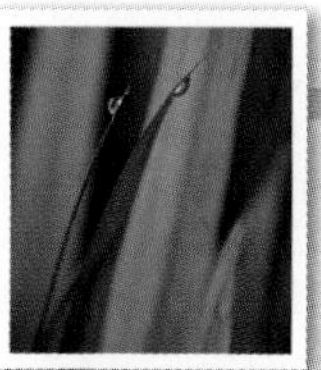

CHAPTER HIGHLIGHTS

- **Capitalize nationalities, languages, races, and religions:**
  Asian, French, Caucasian, Baptist
- **Capitalize specific countries, states, cities, organizations, and buildings:**
  Belgium, Utah, Akron, United Nations, the White House
- **Capitalize months, days, and holidays, but not seasons:**
  November, Friday, Labor Day, summer
- **Capitalize professional titles only when a person is named:**
  Mayor Gomez, the mayor, Superintendent Alicia Morgan
- **Capitalize brand names, but not the type of product:**
  Dawn dishwashing detergent
- **Capitalize geographic locations, but not directions:**
  the West, west of the city
- **Capitalize academic subjects only when they are followed by a course number:**
  History 583, psychology
- **Capitalize titles of books, poems, plays, and films:**
  House on Mango Street, "The Raven," *Rent*, *The Perfect Storm*

CHAPTER REVIEW

Proofread the following essay for errors in capitalization; correct the errors above the lines.

The Strange Career of Deborah Sampson

(1) Few Soldiers have had a stranger army career than Deborah Sampson. (2) Sampson disguised herself as a man so that she could fight in the revolutionary war. (3) Born on december 17, 1760, she spent her early years in a Town near plymouth, massachusetts. (4) Her Father left his large family, however, and went to sea when Sampson was seven years old. (5) After living with a Cousin and then with the widow of a Minister, sampson became a servant in a wealthy family.

(6) Household tasks and hard outdoor work built up her physical strength. (7) She was taller than the average Man and more muscular than the average Woman. (8) Therefore, she was able to disguise herself successfully. (9) Sampson enlisted in the continental army on may 20, 1782, under the name of robert shurtleff.

(10) Sampson fought in several Battles and was wounded at least twice. (11) One story says that she took a bullet out of her own leg with a penknife to avoid seeing a Doctor. (12) However, after the surrender of the british, Sampson's regiment was sent to philadelphia, where she was hospitalized with a high fever and lost consciousness. (13) At the Hospital, dr. Barnabas Binney made the discovery that ended Sampson's army life. (14) She was honorably discharged by general henry knox at west point on october 28, 1783.

(15) Officially female again, Sampson returned to Massachusetts and eventually married a Farmer named benjamin gannett. (16) The story of Sampson's adventures spread; in 1797, a book titled *the female review* was published about her. (17) When Sampson decided to earn money by telling her own story, she became the first american woman to be paid as a Public Speaker. (18) She gave her first talk at the federal street theatre in boston in march 1802 and toured until september. (19) Her health was poor, however, and she could not continue her appearances.

(20) In 1804, paul [P] revere [R], who was a neighbor of the gannetts [G], wrote to a member of the united [U] states [S] congress [C]. (21) He asked for a pension for this Soldier [s] who had never been paid and was still suffering from her war wounds. (22) Congress granted deborah [D] sampson [S] gannett [G] a pension of four dollars a month.

(23) Deborah Sampson died in sharon [S], Massachusetts, in april [A] 1827. (24) Her story inspired the People [p] of her own time and continues to inspire People [p] today. (25) Two plays have been written about her: *she [S] was [W] there [T]* and *portrait [P] of deborah [D].* (26) On veterans [V] day [D] in 1989, a life-size bronze statue was dedicated in front of the sharon [S] public [P] library [L] to honor her.

EXPLORING ONLINE

TEACHING TIP
More practice and assessment are available in the *Grassroots* Test Bank; linked ACE tests on the *Grassroots* student website; *WriteSpace for Grassroots*; and at the Exploring Online links in this chapter.

<http://www.ccc.commnet.edu/cgi-shl/par_numberless_quiz.pl/caps_quiz.htm> Interactive quiz: Capitalize as needed.

<http://www.dailygrammar.com/311to315.shtml> Four short quizzes: Practice your capitalization skills.

<http://college.hmco.com/devenglish/> Visit the *Grassroots* 8/e Student Website for more exercises and quizzes.

CHAPTER

27

Commas

TEACHING TIP
The comma is an often-misused mark, but only because students have not memorized the rules that govern comma usage. Point out that eight basic rules will serve writers well—all covered in this chapter.

The comma is a pause. It gives your reader a chance to stop for a moment to think about where your sentence has been and where it is going, and to prepare to read on.

Although this chapter will cover some basic uses of the comma, always keep this generalization in mind: If there is no reason for a comma, leave it out!

PART A Commas after Items in a Series

(1) I like apples, oranges, and pears.

- What three things do I like? apples, oranges, and pears

Use commas to separate three or more items in a series.

TEACHING TIP
Students may have been taught that the final comma preceding the conjunction is optional. Encourage them always to insert that last comma to avoid possible confusion or misreading.

(2) We will walk through the park, take in a film, and visit a friend.

- What three things will we do? walk through the park, take in a film, and visit a friend

(3) She loves to explore new ~~cultures~~ cultures, sample different ~~foods~~ foods, and learn foreign languages.

- In sentence (3), what are the items in the series?

explore new cultures, sample different foods,

and learn foreign languages

- Punctuate sentence (3).

However, if you want to join three or more items with *and* or *or* between the items, do not use commas.

(4) She plays tennis *and* golf *and* softball.

- Note that commas are not used in sentence (4).

PRACTICE 1

Punctuate these sentences correctly.

1. I can't find my ~~shoes~~ shoes, my ~~socks~~ socks, or my hat!
2. ~~Sylvia Eric~~ Sylvia, Eric, and James have just completed a course in welding.
3. Over lunch, they discussed new ~~accounts~~ accounts, marketing ~~strategy~~ strategy, and motherhood.
4. Frank is in ~~Florida~~ Florida, Bob is in ~~Brazil~~ Brazil, and I am in the bathtub.
5. On Sunday, we repaired the ~~porch~~ porch, cleaned the ~~basement~~ basement, and shingled the roof.
6. The exhibit will include ~~photographs diaries~~ photographs, diaries, and love letters.
7. ~~Spinning kickboxing~~ Spinning, kickboxing, and Tai Chi have become very popular recently.
8. Paula hung her coat on the ~~hook~~ hook, Henry draped his jacket over her ~~coat~~ coat, and Sonia threw her scarf on top of the pile.

PRACTICE 2

On paper or on a computer, write three sentences, each containing three or more items in a series. Punctuate them correctly.

PART B Commas after Introductory Phrases

TEACHING TIP
Students who overuse commas, "sprinkling" them throughout their writing, may claim they have been taught to use a comma "to avoid confusion" or wherever they "hear a pause." Stress that the secret of correct comma usage is memorizing and practicing the eight comma rules.

(1) By the end of the season, our local basketball team will have won thirty games straight.

- *By the end of the season* introduces the sentence.

An introductory phrase is usually followed by a comma.

(2) On Thursday we left for Hawaii.

However, a very short introductory phrase, like the one in sentence (2), need not be followed by a comma.

PRACTICE 3

Punctuate these sentences correctly. One sentence is already punctuated correctly.

1. During the ~~rainstorm~~ rainstorm, we huddled in a doorway.
2. Every Saturday at 9 ~~p.m.~~ p.m., she carries her telescope to the roof.
3. After their last ~~trip~~ trip, Fred and Nita decided on separate vacations.
4. The first woman was appointed to the U.S. Supreme Court in 1981.
5. By the light of the ~~moon~~ moon, we could make out a dim figure.
6. During the coffee ~~break~~ break, George reviewed his psychology homework.
7. In the deep end of the ~~pool~~ pool, he found three silver dollars.
8. In almost no ~~time~~ time, they had changed the tire.

PRACTICE 4

On paper or on a computer, write three sentences using introductory phrases. Punctuate them correctly.

PART C Commas for Direct Address

(1) Bob, you must leave now.

(2) You must, Bob, leave now.

(3) You must leave now, Bob.

(4) Don't be surprised, old buddy, if I pay you a visit very soon.

- In sentences (1), (2), and (3), *Bob* is the person spoken to; he is being *addressed directly*.
- In sentence (4), *old buddy* is being *addressed directly*.

The person addressed directly is set off by commas wherever the direct address appears in the sentence.

PRACTICE 5

Circle the person or persons directly addressed, and punctuate the sentences correctly.

1. I am happy to inform you, (Mr. Forbes), that you are the father of twins.
2. We expect to return on Monday, (Miguel).
3. It appears, (my friend), that you have won two tickets to the opera.
4. Get out of my roast, (you mangy old dog).
5. (Tom), it's probably best that you sell the old car at a loss.

6. If I were you, Hilda, I would wait to make the phone call until we are off the highway.
7. Bruce, it's time you learned to operate the lawn mower!
8. I am pleased to announce, ladies and gentlemen, that Madonna is our surprise guest tonight.

PRACTICE 6

On paper or on a computer, write three sentences using direct address. Punctuate them correctly.

PART D Commas to Set Off Appositives

(1) The Rialto, a new theater, is on Tenth Street.

- *A new theater* describes *the Rialto.*

(2) An elderly man, my grandfather walks a mile every day.

- What group of words describes *my grandfather?* an elderly man

(3) They bought a new painting, a rather beautiful landscape.

- What group of words describes *a new painting?*
  a rather beautiful landscape

- *A new theater, an elderly man,* and *a rather beautiful landscape* are called *appositives.*

An *appositive* is usually a group of words that renames a noun or pronoun and gives more information about it. The appositive can appear at the beginning, middle, or end of a sentence. An appositive is usually set off by commas.

PRACTICE 7

Circle the appositive, and punctuate the sentences correctly.

1. That door, the one with the X on it, leads backstage.
2. A short man, he decided not to pick a fight with the basketball player.
3. Hassim, my friend from Morocco, will be staying with me this week.
4. My nephew wants to go to Mama's Indoor Arcade, a very noisy place.
5. George Eliot, a nineteenth-century novelist, was a woman named Mary Ann Evans.
6. A very close race, the election for mayor wasn't decided until 2 a.m.
7. On the Fourth of July, my favorite holiday, my high school friends get together for an all-day barbecue.
8. Dr. Simpson, a specialist in ethnic music, always travels with a tape recorder.

PRACTICE 8

On paper or on a computer, write three sentences using appositives. Punctuate them correctly.

PART E Commas for Parenthetical Expressions

(1) By the way, I think that you're beautiful.

(2) I think, by the way, that you're beautiful.

(3) I think that you're beautiful, by the way.

TEACHING TIP
You may want to remind students that nonrestrictive relative clauses, covered in Part B of Chapter 17, are a type of parenthetical expression that requires commas.

- *By the way* modifies or qualifies the entire sentence or idea.
- It is called a **parenthetical expression** because it is a side remark, something that could be placed in parentheses: *(By the way) I think that you're beautiful.*

Set off a parenthetical expression with commas.

Below is a partial list of parenthetical expressions:

TEACHING TIP
Commas in direct quotations are covered in Chapter 29.

as a matter of fact	in fact
believe me	it seems to me
I am sure	it would seem
I assure you	to tell the truth

PRACTICE 9

Circle the parenthetical expressions in the sentences below; then punctuate them correctly.

1. Believe me, Sonia has studied hard for her driver's test.
2. He possesses, it would seem, an uncanny gift for gab.
3. It was, I assure you, an accident.
4. To tell the truth, I just put a treadmill in your basement.
5. Her supervisor, by the way, will never admit when he is wrong.
6. A well-prepared résumé, as a matter of fact, can help you get a job.
7. He is, in fact, a black belt.
8. To begin with, you need a new carburetor.

PRACTICE 10

On paper or on a computer, write three sentences using parenthetical expressions. Punctuate them correctly.

PART F Commas for Dates

(1) I arrived on Monday, March 20, 2004, and found that I was in the wrong city.

- Note that commas separate the different parts of the date.
- Note that a comma follows the last item in the date.

(2) She saw him on Wednesday and spoke with him.

However, a one-word date *(Wednesday* or *1995)* preceded by a preposition *(in, on, near,* or *from,* for example) is not followed by a comma unless there is some other reason for it.

PRACTICE 11

Punctuate these sentences correctly. Not every sentence requires additional punctuation.

1. By ~~Tuesday~~ Tuesday, October ~~6~~ 6, he had outlined the whole history text.
2. ~~Thursday~~ Thursday, May ~~8~~ 8, is Hereford's birthday.
3. She was born on January ~~9 1985~~ 9, 1985, in a small New England town.
4. He was born on July ~~4 1976~~ 4, 1976, the two-hundredth anniversary of the Declaration of Independence.
5. Do you think we will have finished the yearbook by May?
6. On January ~~24 1848~~ 24, 1848, James Wilson Marshall found gold in California.
7. My aunt is staying with us from Tuesday to Friday.
8. Charles Schulz's final *Peanuts* comic strip was scheduled for February ~~13 2000~~ 13, 2000, the day on which he died.

PRACTICE 12

On paper or on a computer, write three sentences using dates. Punctuate them correctly.

PART G Commas for Addresses

(1) We just moved from 11 Landow Street, Wilton, Connecticut, to 73 James Street, Charleston, West Virginia.

- Commas separate different parts of an address.

- A comma generally follows the last item in an address, usually a state *(Connecticut)*.

> (2) Julio Smith *from* Queens was made district sales manager.

However, a one-word address preceded by a preposition (*in, on, at, near,* or *from,* for example) is not followed by a comma unless there is another reason for it.

> (3) Julio Smith, Queens, was made district sales manager.

Commas are required to set off a one-word address if the preposition before the address is omitted.

PRACTICE 13

Punctuate these sentences correctly. Not every sentence requires additional punctuation.

1. Their address is 6 Great Ormond ~~Street London~~ Street, London, England.
2. ~~Seattle Washington~~ Seattle, Washington, faces the Cascade Mountains.
3. That package must be sent to 30 West Overland ~~Street Phoenix~~ Street, Phoenix, Arizona.
4. We parked on Marble Lane, across the street from the bowling alley.
5. His father now lives in ~~Waco Texas~~ Waco, Texas, but his sister has never left Vermont.
6. How far is ~~Kansas City Kansas~~ Kansas City, Kansas, from ~~Independence~~ Independence, Missouri?
7. The old watch factory at 43 North Oak ~~Street Scranton Pennsylvania~~ Street, Scranton, Pennsylvania, has been condemned by the building inspector.
8. Foster's ~~Stationery~~ Stationery, 483 Heebers ~~Street Plainview~~ Street, Plainview, sells special calligraphy pens.

PRACTICE 14

On paper or on a computer, write three sentences using addresses. Punctuate them correctly.

PART H Commas for Coordination and Subordination

Chapters 13 and 14 cover the use of commas with coordinating and subordinating conjunctions. Below is a brief review.

> (1) Enzio enjoys most kinds of music, but heavy metal gives him a headache.
>
> (2) Although the weather bureau had predicted rain, the day turned out bright and sunny.
>
> (3) The day turned out bright and sunny although the weather bureau had predicted rain.

- In sentence (1), a comma precedes the coordinating conjunction *but*, which joins together two independent ideas.
- In sentence (2), a comma follows the dependent idea because it precedes the independent idea.
- Sentence (3) does not require a comma because the independent idea precedes the subordinate one.

Use a comma before coordinating conjunctions—*and, but, for, nor, or, so,* or *yet*—that join two independent ideas.

Use a comma after a dependent idea only when the dependent idea precedes the independent one; do not use a comma if the dependent idea follows the independent one.

PRACTICE 15

Punctuate correctly. Not every sentence requires additional punctuation.

EXAMPLE: Because scrapped cars create millions of tons of ~~waste~~ *waste,* recycling auto parts has become an important issue.

1. Today new cars are made from many old ~~parts~~ parts, and manufacturers are trying to increase the use of recycled materials from old cars.
2. Scrapped cars can be easily recycled because they consist mostly of metals.
3. After these cars are ~~crushed~~ crushed, magnets draw the metals out of them.
4. However, the big problem in recycling cars is the plastic they contain.
5. Although plastic can be ~~recycled~~ recycled, the average car contains about twenty different kinds of plastic.
6. Separating the different types of plastic takes much ~~time~~ time, but companies are developing ways to speed up the process.
7. Still, new cars need to be made differently before recycling can truly succeed.
8. Their parts should detach ~~easily~~ easily, and they should be made of plastics and metals that can be separated from each other.
9. As we develop more markets for the recycled auto ~~parts~~ parts, new cars may soon be 90 percent recycled and recyclable.
10. Our environment will ~~benefit~~ benefit, and brand-new cars will really be more than fifty years old!

TEACHING TIP

Consider illustrating the importance of commas by bringing in a passage *without* any (Exploring Online, on page 312, provides two such passages). Have your students find sentences that are confusing or changed in meaning because of the absence of commas.

PRACTICE 16

On paper or on a computer, write three sentences, one with a coordinating conjunction, one beginning with a subordinating conjunction, and one with the subordinating conjunction in the middle.

PRACTICE 17 WRITING ASSIGNMENT

We live in what is often called the age of invention because of rapid advances in technology, communication, and medicine. Which modern invention has meant the most to you *personally,* and why? You might choose something as common as disposable diapers or as sophisticated as a special feature of a personal computer.

In the first sentence, name the invention. Then, as specifically as possible, discuss why it means so much to you. Proofread for the correct use of commas.

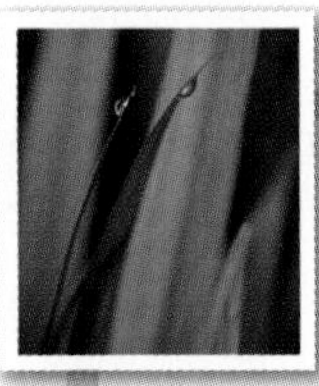

CHAPTER HIGHLIGHTS

- **Commas separate three or more items in a series:**

  He bought a ball, a bat, and a fielder's glove.

- **Unless it is very short, an introductory phrase is followed by a comma:**

  By the end of January, I'll be in Australia.

- **Commas set off the name of a person directly addressed:**

  I think, Aunt Betty, that your latest novel is a winner.

- **Commas set off appositives:**

  My boss, the last person in line in the cafeteria, often forgets to eat lunch.

- **Commas set off parenthetical expressions:**

  My wife, by the way, went to school with your sister.

- **Commas separate the parts of a date or an address, except for a one-word date or address preceded by a preposition:**

  On April 1, 1997, I was in a terrible blizzard.

  I live at 48 Trent Street, Randolph, Michigan.

  She works in Tucson as a plumber.

- **A comma precedes a coordinating conjunction that joins two independent ideas:**

  We had planned to see a movie together, but we couldn't agree on one.

- **If a dependent idea precedes the independent idea, it is followed by a comma; if the independent idea comes first, it is not followed by a comma:**

  Although I still have work to do, my project will be ready on time.

  My project will be ready on time although I still have work to do.

CHAPTER REVIEW

TEACHING TIP
This Chapter Review makes an interesting in-class activity likely to spark discussion about the power of one person to make a difference. Ask the class why Julia gave up so much for a single tree. Was she misguided?

Proofread the following essay for comma errors—either missing commas or commas used incorrectly. Correct the errors above the lines.

Treetop Crusader

(1) On December 18, ~~1999~~ 1999, Julia Butterfly Hill's feet touched ground for the first time in more than two years. (2) She had just climbed down from the ~~top,~~ top of an ancient tree in Humboldt ~~County~~ County, California. (3) The ~~tree~~ tree, a thousand-year-old ~~redwood~~ redwood, was named Luna. (4) Hill had climbed 180 feet up Luna on December ~~10~~ 10, ~~1997~~ 1997, for what she thought would be a protest of two or three weeks.

(5) Hill's action was intended to stop Pacific ~~Lumber~~ Lumber, a division of the Maxxam ~~Corporation~~ Corporation, from cutting down old-growth forests. (6) The area immediately next to ~~Luna, had~~ Luna had already been stripped of trees. (7) Because nothing was left to hold the soil to the ~~mountain~~ mountain, a huge part of the hill had slid into the town of ~~Stafford~~ Stafford, California. (8) Many homes had been destroyed.

(9) During her long tree-sit, Hill endured incredible hardships. (10) For more than two ~~years~~ years, she lived on a tiny platform eighteen stories off the ground. (11) El Niño storms almost destroyed her with ferocious ~~winds~~ winds, razor-sharp ~~rain~~ rain, and numbing cold. (12) She once wore two pairs of ~~socks booties~~ socks, booties, two pairs of thermal ski ~~pants~~ pants, two thermal ~~shirts~~ shirts, a wool ~~sweater~~ sweater, two ~~windbreakers~~ windbreakers, a ~~raincoat gloves~~ raincoat, gloves, and two hats to keep from freezing to death during a storm. (13) In addition to enduring nature's ~~hardships~~ hardships, Hill withstood life-threatening torment from the logging company. (14) She was harassed by ~~helicopters~~ helicopters, various ~~sieges~~ sieges, and interference with receiving supplies. (15) Of ~~course~~ course, she also endured ~~loneliness~~ loneliness, sometimes paralyzing ~~fear~~ fear, and always deep sorrow for the destruction around her.

(16) Only twenty-three at the beginning of her ~~tree-sit~~ tree-sit, Hill eventually became both world famous and very knowledgeable about ancient forests. (17) At the top of ~~Luna~~ Luna, she would use a cell ~~phone~~ phone, a ~~pager~~ pager, and a daily engagement planner. (18) She was trying to protect the tree ~~itself~~ itself, to slow down all logging in the ~~area~~ area, and to raise public awareness. (19) She gave hundreds of phone interviews and answered hundreds of letters.

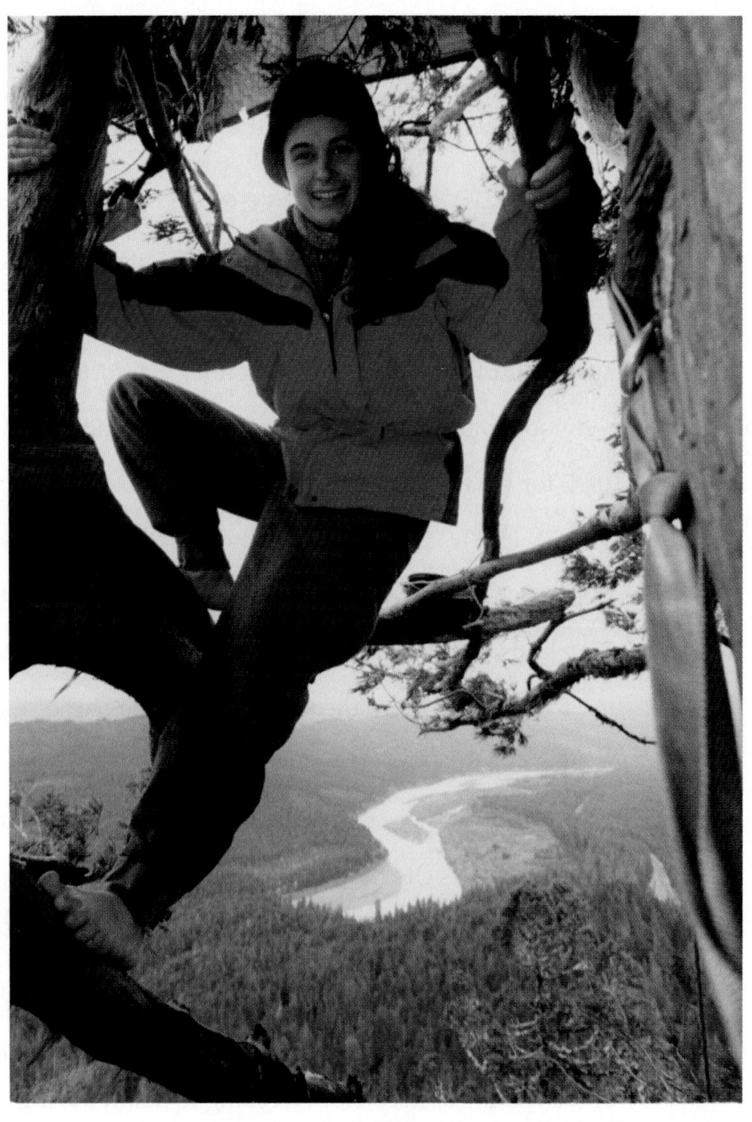

Julia Hill and Luna
©Shaun Walker.

(20) Hill's action was dramatically successful; Luna was eventually saved from destruction. (21) When Hill returned to normal ~~life~~ life, she wrote a ~~book~~ book, *The Legacy of Luna: The Story of a Tree, a Woman, and the Struggle to Save the Redwoods.* (22) Julia Butterfly Hill is now a ~~writer~~ writer, a ~~poet~~ poet, and an activist. (23) She is a frequent speaker at environmental ~~conferences~~ conferences, she helped found the Circle of Life Foundation for preserving all ~~life~~ life, and she has received many honors and awards.

EXPLORING ONLINE

TEACHING TIP
More practice and assessment are available in the *Grassroots* Test Bank; linked ACE tests on the *Grassroots* student website; *WriteSpace for Grassroots*; and at the Exploring Online links in this chapter.

<http://owl.english.purdue.edu/handouts/interact/g_commaessEX1.html> Interactive quiz: Where have all the commas gone?

<http://www.ccc.commnet.edu/grammar/quizzes/comma_quiz.htm> Interactive quiz: Add commas to this essay about basketball and score!

<http://college.hmco.com/devenglish/> Visit the *Grassroots* 8/e Student Website for more exercises and quizzes.

CHAPTER 28

Apostrophes

PART A Using the Apostrophe for Contractions

A contraction combines two words into one.

do + not = don't

should + not = shouldn't

I + have = I've

TEACHING TIP
Students should understand that the apostrophe has just two uses: 1) to form a contraction, and 2) to indicate possession. A writer should be able to justify every apostrophe with one of these two rules.

- Note that an apostrophe (') replaces the omitted letters: "o" in *don't* and *shouldn't* and "ha" in *have*.

BE CAREFUL: *Won't* is an odd contraction because it cannot be broken into parts in the same way the previous contractions can.

will + not = won't

PRACTICE 1

TEACHING TIP
You might take a few moments to have students think critically about the effect of contractions in writing. (They create an informal tone often inappropriate for formal academic assignments and workplace documents.)

Write these words as contractions.

1. you + are = you're
2. who + is = who's
3. was + not = wasn't
4. they + are = they're
5. can + not = can't
6. it + is = it's
7. I + am = I'm
8. will + not = won't

TEACHING TIP
It's/its, they're/their/there, you're/your, and *who's/whose* are some of the most often-confused words in the English language. Take a few moments to cover the differences and perhaps have the class write sentences to demonstrate their mastery.

PRACTICE 2

Insert the missing apostrophes in these contractions.

1. ~~Wont~~ Won't you go with us?
2. ~~Whats~~ What's in the locked box?
3. ~~Ive~~ I've called home twice.
4. ~~Youre~~ You're gorgeous.
5. ~~Whos~~ Who's appearing at the Blue Bongo?
6. ~~Arent~~ Aren't we early?
7. Now ~~were~~ we're in trouble
8. They just ~~cant~~ can't agree.
9. ~~Its~~ It's too early to leave.
10. ~~Lets~~ Let's have lunch now.
11. ~~Didnt~~ Didn't he mention his name?
12. She ~~doesnt~~ doesn't like rock; they ~~dont~~ don't like classical music.

PRACTICE 3

On paper or a computer, write five sentences using an apostrophe in a contraction.

PART B Defining the Possessive

A *possessive* is a word that shows that someone or something owns someone or something else.

PRACTICE 4

In the following phrases, who owns what?

EXAMPLE: "The hat of the man" means the man owns the hat.

1. "The camera of Judson" means Judson owns the camera.
2. "The hopes of the people" means the people have hopes.
3. "The thought of the woman" means the woman owns the thought.
4. "The trophies of the home team" means the home team owns trophies.
5. "The ideas of that man" means that man has ideas.

PART C Using the Apostrophe to Show Possession (in Words That Do Not Already End in *-S*)

ESL TIP
ESL students will need extra help with apostrophes because this mark is not used in Spanish, and it is used differently in French than it is in English. In both Spanish and French, possession is shown with the prepositions *of* or *by* (e.g., *The car of Maria is blue*), and contractions rarely exist.

(1) the hands of my father	becomes	(2) my father's hands

- In phrase (1), who owns what? My father owns the hands.
- In phrase (1), what is the *owner word?* father
- How does the owner word show possession in phrase (2)?
  Father ends in *'s*
- Note that what is owned, *hands,* follows the owner word.

If the *owner word* (possessive) does not end in *-s,* add an apostrophe and an *-s* to show possession.

PRACTICE 5

Change these phrases into possessives with an apostrophe and an *-s*. (Note that the owner words do not already end in *-s*.)

EXAMPLE: the friend of my cousin = my cousin's friend

1. the eyes of Rona = Rona's eyes
2. the voice of the coach = the coach's voice
3. the ark of Noah = Noah's ark
4. the technology of tomorrow = tomorrow's technology
5. the jacket of someone = someone's jacket

PRACTICE 6

Add an apostrophe and an *-s* to show possession in these phrases.

1. Judy's ~~Judy~~ briefcase
2. the diver's ~~diver~~ tanks
3. Murphy's ~~Murphy~~ Law
4. Bill's ~~Bill~~ decision
5. somebody's ~~somebody~~ umbrella
6. everyone's ~~everyone~~ dreams
7. your daughter's ~~daughter~~ sandwich
8. last month's ~~month~~ prices
9. that woman's ~~woman~~ talent
10. anyone's ~~anyone~~ guess

PRACTICE 7

On paper or on a computer, write five sentences. In each, use an apostrophe and an *-s* to show ownership. Use owner words that do not already end in *-s*.

PART D Using the Apostrophe to Show Possession (in Words That Already End in *-S*)

(1) the uniforms of the pilots becomes (2) the pilots' uniforms

- In phrase (1), who owns what? The pilots own the uniforms.
- In phrase (1), what is the *owner word*? pilots
- How does the owner word show possession in phrase (2)? Pilots ends in '.
- Note that what is owned, *uniforms*, follows the owner word.

If the *owner word* (possessive) ends in *-s*, add an apostrophe after the *-s* to show possession.*

*Some writers add an *'s* to one-syllable proper names that end in *-s*: *James's book.*

PRACTICE 8

Change these phrases into possessives with an apostrophe. (Note that the owner words already end in -*s*.)

EXAMPLE: the helmets of the players = *the players' helmets*

1. the farm of my grandparents = my grandparents' farm
2. the kindness of my neighbors = my neighbors' kindness
3. the dunk shots of the basketball players = the basketball players' dunk shots
4. the music of The Smashing Pumpkins = The Smashing Pumpkins' music
5. the trainer of the horses = the horses' trainer

PRACTICE 9

Add either *'s* or *'* to show possession in these phrases. BE CAREFUL: Some of the owner words end in -*s* and some do not.

1. the ~~models~~ models' faces
2. the ~~model~~ model's face
3. the ~~pilot~~ pilot's safety record
4. the ~~children~~ children's room
5. the ~~runner~~ runner's time
6. ~~Boris~~ Boris'/Boris's radio
7. my ~~niece~~ niece's CDs
8. your ~~parents~~ parents' anniversary
9. the ~~men~~ men's locker room
10. three ~~students~~ students' exams
11. several ~~contestants~~ contestants' answers
12. Mr. ~~Jones~~ Jones'/Jones's band

PRACTICE 10

Rewrite each of the following pairs of short sentences as *one* sentence by using a possessive.

EXAMPLE: Joan has a friend. The friend comes from Chile.
Joan's friend comes from Chile.

1. Rusty has a motorcycle. The motorcycle needs new brakes.
   Rusty's motorcycle needs new brakes.
2. Nurse Johnson had evidence. The evidence proved that the doctor was not careless.
   Nurse Johnson's evidence proved that the doctor was not careless.
3. Ahmad has a salary. The salary barely keeps him in peanut butter.
   Ahmad's salary barely keeps him in peanut butter.
4. Lee has a job. His job in the Complaint Department keeps him on his toes.
   Lee's job in the Complaint Department keeps him on his toes.
5. José has a bad cold. It makes it hard for him to sleep.
   José's bad cold makes it hard for him to sleep.
6. Jessie told a joke. The joke did not make us laugh.
   Jessie's joke did not make us laugh.

7. John Adams had a son. His son was the first president's son to also become president of the United States.

   John Adams' son was the first president's son to also become president of the United States.

8. My sisters have a daycare center. The daycare center is open seven days a week.

   My sisters' daycare center is open seven days a week.

9. The twins have a goal. Their goal is to learn synchronized swimming.

   The twins' goal is to learn synchronized swimming.

10. Darren has a thank-you note. The thank-you note says it all.

    Darren's thank-you note says it all.

TEACHING TIP
You might enjoy telling students about a British society formed to protect the "much-abused" apostrophe: <http://www.apostrophe.fsnet.co.uk/>.

PRACTICE 11

On paper or on a computer, write six sentences that use an apostrophe to show ownership—three using owner words that do not end in *-s* and three using owner words that do end in *-s*.

BE CAREFUL: Apostrophes show possession by nouns. As the following chart indicates, possessive pronouns do not have apostrophes.

TEACHING TIP
Many students confuse plurals and possessives—e.g., incorrectly adding an *-'s* at the end of a noun to form a plural. Take a few minutes to underscore the difference. Refer students to the graded *S* practice in Exploring Online.

Possessive Pronouns

Singular	Plural
my book, mine	our book, ours
your book, yours	your book, yours
his book, his	their book, theirs
her book, hers	
its book, its	

Do not confuse *its* (possessive pronoun) with *it's* (contraction for *it is* or *it has*) or *your* (possessive pronoun) with *you're* (contraction for *you are*).*

REMEMBER: Use apostrophes for contractions and possessive nouns only. Do not use apostrophes for plural nouns (*four marbles*), verbs (*he hopes*), or possessive pronouns (*his, hers, yours, its*).

PRACTICE 12 WRITING ASSIGNMENT

Assume that you are writing to apply for a position as a teacher's aide. You want to convince the school principal that you would be a good teacher, and you decide to do this by describing a time when you taught a young child—your own child, a younger sibling, or a friend's child—to do something new.

In your topic sentence, briefly state who the child was and what you taught him or her. What made you want to teach this child? Was the experience easier or harder than you expected? How did you feel afterward? Proofread for the correct use of apostrophes.

*See Chapter 32 for work on words that look and sound alike.

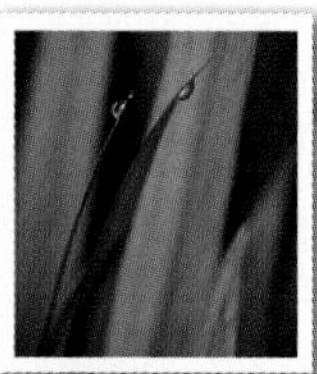

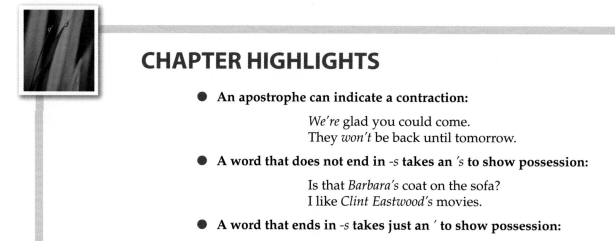

CHAPTER HIGHLIGHTS

- **An apostrophe can indicate a contraction:**

  We're glad you could come.
  They *won't* be back until tomorrow.

- **A word that does not end in *-s* takes an *'s* to show possession:**

  Is that *Barbara's* coat on the sofa?
  I like *Clint Eastwood's* movies.

- **A word that ends in *-s* takes just an *'* to show possession:**

  That store sells *ladies'* hats with feathers.
  I depend on my *friends'* advice.

CHAPTER REVIEW

Proofread this essay for apostrophe errors—missing apostrophes and apostrophes used incorrectly. Correct the errors above the lines.

The Magic Fastener

(1) ~~Its~~ It's hard to remember the world without Velcro. (2) Shoelaces had to be tied; ~~jackets'~~ jackets had to be zipped and ~~did'nt~~ didn't make so much noise when they were loosened. (3) We have a Swiss ~~engineers'~~ engineer's curiosity to thank for ~~todays~~ today's changes.

(4) On a hunting trip in 1948, Georges de Mestral became intrigued by the seedpods that clung to his clothing. (5) He knew that they ~~we're~~ were hitching rides to new territory by fastening onto him, but he ~~could'nt~~ couldn't tell how they were doing it. (6) He examined the seedpods to find that their tiny hooks were catching onto the threads of his jacket. (7) The idea of Velcro was born, but the actual product ~~wasnt~~ wasn't developed overnight. (8) It took eight more ~~years'~~ years before Georges de ~~Mestrals~~ Mestral's invention was ready for the market. (9) Today, Velcro is used on clothing, on space suits, and even in artificial hearts. (10) Velcro can not only help keep a skier warm but can also save a ~~persons'~~ person's life.

EXPLORING ONLINE

TEACHING TIP
More practice and assessment are available in the *Grassroots* Test Bank; linked ACE tests on the *Grassroots* student website; *WriteSpace for Grassroots*; and at the Exploring Online links in this chapter.

<http://owl.english.purdue.edu/handouts/interact/g_apostEX1.html>
Interactive quizzes: Choose the correct word for the sentence.

<http://depts.gallaudet.edu/englishworks/exercises/exgrammar/GUPets2.htm>
"Gallaudet Pets—graded *S* practice:" Choose singular, plural, or possessive.

<http://college.hmco.com/devenglish/> Visit the *Grassroots* 8/e Student Website for more exercises and quizzes.

CHAPTER 29

Direct and Indirect Quotations

PART A Defining Direct and Indirect Quotations

ESL TIP
Direct and indirect quotations challenge ESL students of all levels because presenting the words or ideas of others is not as strictly controlled in some languages as it is in English. Further, the shifting of verb tenses in reported speech is problematic, and paraphrasing can lead to wordiness or awkward meaning. Reinforcement may be needed throughout the term.

(1) John said that he was going.

(2) John said, "I am going."

- Which sentence gives the *exact words* of the speaker, John?
  sentence (2)
- Why is sentence (2) called a *direct quotation?*
  It gives the speaker's exact words.
- Why is sentence (1) called an *indirect quotation?*
  It reports the speaker's words without giving his exact words.
- Note that the word *that* introduces the *indirect quotation.*

PRACTICE 1

Write *D* in the blank at the right if the sentence uses a *direct quotation.* Write *I* in the blank at the right if the sentence uses an *indirect quotation.*

1. She said that she was thirsty. I
2. Rita asked, "Which is my laptop?" D
3. Ruth insisted that one turkey would feed the whole family. I
4. The students shouted, "Get out of the building! It's on fire!" D
5. "This is silly," she said, sighing. D
6. I suggested that Rod's future was in the catering business. I

PART B Punctuating Simple Direct Quotations

Note the punctuation:

(1) Rafael whispered, "I'll always love you."

TEACHING TIP
Explore with students some ways in which quotations can improve their writing in college courses and at work. Quotations can enliven a narrative or provide expert testimony to support a main idea.

- Put a comma before the direct quotation.
- Put quotation marks around the speaker's exact words.
- Capitalize the first word of the direct quotation.
- Put the period *inside* the end quotation marks.

Of course, the direct quotation may come first in the sentence:

(2) "I'll always love you," Rafael whispered.

- List the rules for a direct quotation written like the sentence above:

  Put quotation marks around the speaker's exact words.

  Capitalize the first word of the direct quotation.

  Put the comma inside the end quotation marks.

PRACTICE 2

Rewrite these simple direct quotations, punctuating them correctly.

1. He yelled answer the phone!
   Rewrite: He yelled, "Answer the phone!"
2. The usher called no more seats in front.
   Rewrite: The usher called, "No more seats in front."
3. My back aches she repeated dejectedly.
   Rewrite: "My back aches," she repeated dejectedly.
4. Examining the inside cover, Bob said, this book was printed in 1879.
   Rewrite: Examining the inside cover, Bob said, "This book was printed in 1879."
5. A bug is doing the backstroke in my soup the man said.
   Rewrite: "A bug is doing the backstroke in my soup," the man said.

PART C Punctuating Split Quotations

Sometimes one sentence of direct quotation is split into two parts:

(1) "Because it is 2 a.m.," he said, "you had better go."

- *He said* is set off by commas.
- The second part of the quotation—*you had better go*—begins with a small letter because it is part of one directly quoted sentence.

(2) "Because it is 2 a.m. . . . you had better go."

A direct quotation can also be broken into separate sentences:

(3) "It is a long ride to San Francisco," he said. "We should leave early."

- Because the second part of the quotation is a separate sentence, it begins with a capital letter.
- Note the period after *said.*

BE CAREFUL: If you break a direct quotation into separate sentences, be sure that both parts of the quotation are complete sentences.

PRACTICE 3

Rewrite these split direct quotations, punctuating them correctly.

1. Before the guests arrive she said let's relax.

   Rewrite: "Before the guests arrive," she said, "let's relax."

2. Don't drive so fast he begged I get nervous.

   Rewrite: "Don't drive so fast," he begged. "I get nervous."

3. Although Mort is out shellfishing Fran said his hip boots are on the porch.

   Rewrite: "Although Mort is out shellfishing," Fran said, "his hip boots are on the porch."

4. Being the youngest in the family she said has its advantages.

   Rewrite: "Being the youngest in the family," she said, "has its advantages."

5. This catalog is fantastic the clerk said and you can have it for free.

   Rewrite: "This catalog is fantastic," the clerk said, "and you can have it for free."

PRACTICE 4

On paper or on a computer, write three sentences using split quotations.

PART D Ending Direct Quotations

TEACHING TIP
Remind students that quotation marks are always used in pairs. When they proofread and edit their work, they should verify that they provided the end quotation mark.

A sentence can end in any of three ways:

- with a period (.)
- with a question mark (?)
- with an exclamation point (!)

The period is *always* placed inside the end quotation marks:

(1) He said, "My car cost five thousand dollars."

The question mark and the exclamation point go before or after the quotation marks—depending on the sense of the sentence.

(2) He asked, "Where are you?"

(3) Did he say, "I am thirty-two years old"?

(4) She yelled, "Help!"

- The question mark in sentence (2) is placed before the end quotation marks because the direct quotation is a question.
- The question mark in sentence (3) is placed after the end quotation marks because the direct quotation itself *is not a question.*

Note that sentence (2) can be reversed:

(5) "Where are you?" he asked.

- Can you list the rules for the exclamation point used in sentence (4)?

Place the exclamation point inside the end quotation marks.

Place the quotation marks around the speaker's exact words.

Note that sentence (4) can be reversed:

(6) "Help!" she yelled.

PRACTICE 5

Rewrite these direct quotations, punctuating them correctly.

1. Barbara asked is that your Humvee.

   Rewrite: Barbara asked, "Is that your Humvee?"

2. Did Shenoya make the team he inquired.

   Rewrite: "Did Shenoya make the team?" he inquired.

3. Be careful with that mirror she begged the movers.

   Rewrite: "Be careful with that mirror!" she begged the movers.

4. The truck driver shouted give me a break.

   Rewrite: The truck driver shouted, "Give me a break!"

5. Did she say I wouldn't give my social security number to that telemarketer.

   Rewrite: Did she say, "I wouldn't give my social security number to that telemarketer"?

PRACTICE 6 WRITING ASSIGNMENT

Write a note to someone with whom you have had an argument. Your goal is to get back on friendly terms with this person. In your first sentence, state this goal, asking for his or her open-minded attention. Then tell him or her why you think a misunderstanding occurred and explain how you think conflict might be avoided in the future. Refer to the original argument by using both direct and indirect quotations. Check for the correct use of quotation marks; be careful with *all* punctuation.

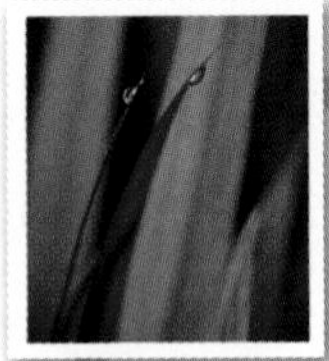

CHAPTER HIGHLIGHTS

- **A direct quotation requires quotation marks:**

  Benjamin Franklin said, "There never was a good war or a bad peace."

- **Both parts of a split quotation require quotation marks:**

  "It isn't fair," she argued, "for us to lose the money for the after-school programs."

- **When a direct quotation is split into separate sentences, begin the second sentence with a capital letter:**

  "It's late," he said. "Let's leave in the morning."

- **Always place the period inside the end quotation marks:**

  He said, "Sometimes I talk too much."

- **A question mark or an exclamation point can be placed before or after the end quotation marks, depending on the meaning of the sentence:**

  She asked, "Where were you when we needed you?"

  Did she say, "Joe looks younger without his beard"?

CHAPTER REVIEW

Proofread this essay for direct and indirect quotations. Punctuate the quotations correctly and make any other necessary changes above the lines.

Satchel Paige

(1) Some people say that the great pitcher Leroy Paige was called Satchel because of his big feet. (2) Paige himself ~~said I~~ said, "I got the nickname as a boy in Mobile before my feet ~~grew.~~ grew." (3) He earned money by carrying bags, called satchels, at the railroad station. (4) ~~I~~ "I figured out a way to make more money by carrying several bags at a time on a ~~pole~~ pole," he said. (5) Other boys began shouting at him that he looked like a satchel tree. (6) The name stuck.

(7) Unfortunately, for most of Paige's long pitching career, major league baseball excluded African-American players. (8) However, Satchel Paige pitched impressively in the black leagues and in tours against white teams. (9) In 1934, he won a thirteen-inning, one-to-nothing pitching duel against the white pitcher Dizzy Dean and a team of major league all-stars. (10) ~~My~~ "My fast ~~ball~~ ball," admitted ~~Dean~~ Dean, ~~looks~~ "looks like a change of pace alongside of that little bullet old Satchel shoots up to the ~~plate!~~ plate!"

(11) After Jackie Robinson broke the major league color barrier in 1948, Satchel Paige took his windmill windup to the Cleveland Indians. (12) He became the oldest rookie in major league history. (13) Some people said that he was too old, but his record proved them wrong. (14) His plaque in the Baseball Hall of Fame ~~reads he~~ reads, “He helped pitch the Cleveland Indians to the 1948 ~~pennant.~~ pennant.”

(15) Satchel Paige pitched off and on until he was sixty years old. (16) When people asked how he stayed young, he gave them his famous rules. (17) Everyone remembers the last one. (18) ~~Don't~~ “Don't look ~~back~~ back,” he said. (19) ~~Something~~ “Something might be gaining on ~~you.~~ you.”

EXPLORING ONLINE

TEACHING TIP
More practice and assessment are available in the *Grassroots* Test Bank; linked ACE tests on the *Grassroots* student website; *WriteSpace for Grassroots*; and at the Exploring Online links in this chapter.

<http://www.dailygrammar.com/371to375.shtml> Practice with answers: Place quotation marks and capitalize correctly.

<http://www.ccc.commnet.edu/grammar/quizzes/quotes_quiz.htm> Challenging interactive quiz: Think hard and punctuate.

<http://college.hmco.com/devenglish/> Visit the *Grassroots* 8/e Student Website for more exercises and quizzes.

CHAPTER

30

Putting Your Proofreading Skills to Work

TEACHING TIP
Lead a discussion about the effect that error-filled written work has on the reader, especially in academic and professional settings.

Proofreading is the important final step in the writing process. After you have planned and written a paragraph or an essay, you must **proofread,** carefully checking each sentence for correct grammar, punctuation, and capitalization. Proofreading means applying everything you have learned in Units 2 through 7. Is every sentence complete? Do all your verbs agree with their subjects? Have you mistakenly written any comma splices or sentence fragments?

This chapter gives you the opportunity to practice proofreading skills in real-world situations. As you proofread the paragraphs and essays that follow, you must look for any—and every—kind of error, just as you would in the real world of college or work. The first five practices tell you what kinds of errors to look for. If you have trouble, go back to the chapters listed and review the material. The final practices, however, give you no clues at all, so you must put your proofreading skills to the real-world test.

PRACTICE 1

TEACHING TIP
By now, your students should have learned their individual *error patterns* and know to proofread extra carefully for these. Make sure this is the case. Remember: one error repeated ten times looks like ten errors!

Proofread this paragraph, correcting any errors above the lines. (You should find seventeen individual errors.) To review, see these chapters:

Chapter 10	past participle verb errors
Chapter 15	run-on sentences and comma splices
Chapter 19	errors in forming plural nouns
Chapter 22	preposition errors

(1) Bono is an unusual superstar. (2) Instead of going ~~in~~ [on] shopping ~~spree~~ [sprees] and polishing his ego, he travels the world, using his fame to empower others. (3) Bono was born Paul Hewson ~~at~~ [in] Ireland. (4) Young friends there nicknamed him *Bonovox*, which means "good voice" in Latin. (5) The *vox* was ~~dropped, *bono*~~ [dropped, but *bono*] stuck. (6) Bono became the lead singer of the Irish rock band U2. (7) Using music to send

TEACHING TIP
Consider having students work in groups on the first few practices. They will talk about the errors as they identify them, thus reinforcing learning and boosting their confidence. Or turn one or more of the practices into a game. The first team to find and correct all of the errors wins.

a message of love and peace, U2 has ~~sell~~ sold more than 100 million ~~album~~ albums worldwide and has won fourteen Grammy Awards. (8) Yet perhaps Bono's greatest influence is not the sound of his voice crooning U2 songs ~~under~~ inside the heads of fans. (9) Rather, it is his work for human beings ~~on~~ in need. (10) Bono has ~~use~~ used his celebrity to turn the media's attention to Africa, where the lives of millions are being ~~destroy~~ destroyed by AIDS and starvation. (11) Frightening numbers of African ~~child~~ children are already AIDS ~~orphans, social~~ orphans; social structures in Africa are breaking down. (12) Bono urges the United States and other nations to relieve the crippling debt of African nations, one of the ~~factor~~ factors that keeps them unable to afford AIDS drugs and prevention programs. (13) He has ~~work~~ worked with former President Clinton, Oprah, and others to make the love he sings about become reality. (14) Bono has received many ~~award~~ awards for this humanitarian ~~work he~~ work; he was even ~~nominate~~ nominated for the Nobel Peace Prize.

PRACTICE 2

ESL TIP
A popular ESL proofreading technique is to ask students to check their work *from the end*, starting with the last sentence, proceeding to the next-to-the-last sentence, and so on to the first sentence. This process requires students to slow down and proof their work carefully.

Proofread this paragraph, correcting any errors above the lines. (You should find fifteen individual errors.) To review, see these chapters:

Chapter 7	sentence fragments
Chapter 9	past tense errors
Chapter 23	tense consistency
Chapter 26	capitalization errors

(1) Flying is so ~~common.~~ common (2) ~~That~~ that many people take it for granted. (3) They often see jets, helicopters, and airplanes in the sky and give them little thought. (4) However, what would people ~~think.~~ think (5) ~~If~~ if they ~~seen~~ saw a human being flying through the air? (6) In ~~july~~ July, 2003, Felix ~~baumgartner~~ Baumgartner ~~flied~~ flew across the ~~english~~ English Channel without using an engine, something that had never been done before. (7) His amazing flight ~~begun~~ began high above ~~England.~~ England (8) ~~When~~ when he jumped from an airplane at 30,000 feet. (9) He ~~is~~ was wearing a parachute, of course, but his other piece of special equipment was a six-foot-wide wing strapped to his back. (10) Even though he was falling very quickly, the wing let him fly forward at 220 miles per hour. (11) He ~~needs~~ needed to fly twenty-two miles to get to France, and he arrived over that country with 4,000 feet remaining. (12) After using the wing to slow himself ~~down.~~ down, (13) ~~He~~ he opened his parachute and landed. (14) The entire flight ~~lasts~~ lasted just six minutes. (15) People who want to experience this kind of flying can use the ~~Skyray.~~ Skyray, (16) ~~Which~~ which is similar to the special wing Baumgartner used to fly across the English ~~channel~~ Channel. (17) Of course, to use this wing, you have to wear a

parachute and jump out of an airplane. (18) Nevertheless, Skyray is bringing humans closer to the dream of flying like eagles.

PRACTICE 3

TEACHING TIP
Remind students that although programs like Microsoft Word can help them identify spelling and some grammatical errors in their papers, computers are far from foolproof. Proofreading is still the job of every writer.

Proofread this paragraph, correcting any errors above the lines. (You should find sixteen individual errors.) To review, see these chapters:

Chapter 7	sentence fragments
Chapter 10	past participle verb errors
Chapter 15	run-ons and comma splices
Chapters 19 and 28	plural and possessive errors

(1) Christiane Amanpour is one of the most respected foreign correspondents in the world, but she calls herself an "accidental ~~journalist."~~ journalist" (2) ~~Because~~ because she never intended to become one. (3) Her native Iran had no freedom of the ~~press, journalism~~ press, so journalism did not interest her. (4) Christiane attended high school in England. (5) Then the revolution in Iran brought chaos to her family, her ~~fathers~~ father's money was ~~froze,~~ frozen, and the ~~families fund~~ family's funds were very tight. (6) ~~Christianes'~~ Christiane's sister dropped out of journalism college in ~~London, Christiane~~ London, and Christiane took her place for the sole reason of saving the tuition money. (7) Soon she was ~~hook~~ hooked on reporting. (8) After graduating from the University of Rhode Island, she applied for a job at a new cable ~~station.~~ station (9) ~~Called~~ called CNN. (10) She longed to write news ~~story's~~ stories and go overseas but was ~~mock~~ mocked by her boss, who said she didn't have the right looks and that her name was difficult to pronounce. (11) Amanpour worked hard and hid her frustration with doing routine ~~task.~~ tasks (12) ~~Like~~ like bringing people coffee. (13) Every time a new job opened at CNN, she applied for it. (14) Her big break was being ~~send~~ sent to Germany and the Gulf War. (15) With ~~gunfires~~ gunfire and rockets around her, she reported the news with intelligence and heart. (16) Today Amanpour says it is not so bad that some people "always try to knock your dreams." (17) This gives you the chance, she believes, to prove that you are strong enough to keep going.

PRACTICE 4

Proofread this paragraph, correcting any errors above the lines. (You should find twenty individual errors.) To review, see these chapters:

Chapter 7	sentence fragments
Chapter 8	subject/verb agreement errors
Chapter 27	comma errors
Chapter 28	apostrophe errors

TEACHING TIP
Urge students to review the errors they fail to identify in this chapter's practices. Suggest that they either return to relevant chapters or complete additional online exercises such as those in the Guide to Grammar and Writing website at **<http://www.ccc.commnet.edu/grammar/index.htm>**.

(1) Every spring and summer, storm ~~chaser's~~ chasers ~~spreads~~ spread out across the Midwestern part of the United States known as Tornado Alley. (2) Armed with video ~~cameras~~ cameras, ~~maps~~ maps, and ~~radios.~~ radios, (3) ~~These~~ these lovers of violent weather ~~follows~~ follow huge weather systems called supercells, which sometimes ~~produces~~ produce tornadoes. (4) On a good day, a storm chaser may find a ~~supercell.~~ supercell (5) ~~And~~ and get close enough to film the brief, destructive life of a tornado. (6) Some ~~joins~~ join the storm-chasing tours offered every summer by universities or private companies. (7) Others learn what they can from Internet websites and ~~sets~~ set off on their own to hunt tornadoes. (8) Storm chasing can be very dangerous. (9) A large tornado spins winds between 125 and 175 mph, tearing roofs off ~~houses~~ houses, ripping limbs from trees, and overturning cars. (10) The greatest danger comes from airborne ~~branches~~ branches, ~~boards~~ boards, ~~shingles~~ shingles, and glass hurtling through the air like deadly weapons. (11) Even if a supercell ~~don't~~ doesn't spawn ~~tornadoes.~~ tornadoes, (12) ~~It~~ it often produces winds over 50 mph, heavy rain, large hail, and intense lightning. (13) Most storm chasers ~~avoids~~ avoid these risks by racing out of a ~~tornados'~~ tornado's path before it gets too close. (14) Despite or perhaps because of these dangers, dramatized in the 1996 movie ~~*Twister.*~~ *Twister,* (15) ~~Storm~~ storm chasing remains popular. (16) Fans claim that few things in life ~~matches~~ match the thrill of discovering a tornado and witnessing the power of nature.

Storm chasers confront a deadly twister in Tornado Alley.
©Carsten Peter/National Geographic Magazine.

PRACTICE 5

Proofread this paragraph, correcting any errors above the lines. (You should find seventeen individual errors.) To review, see these chapters:

Chapter 20	pronoun agreement errors
Chapter 21	adjective/adverb errors
Chapter 26	capitalization errors
Chapter 27	comma errors

(1) A secret society called SSSSH is gaining agents across the country. (2) To become a secret agent, one must simply perform a ~~well~~ good deed for someone else without taking credit for it or letting ~~them~~ him or her know who did it. (3) The group was inspired by a young Ohioan named ~~hal reichle~~ Hal Reichle (pronounced "Rike-el"), a graduate of ~~hiram college~~ Hiram College, who had a habit of ~~quiet~~ quietly helping people. (4) After Hal's death in a helicopter crash during the ~~gulf War~~ Gulf War, some friends started paying tribute to the fallen soldier by "pulling Reichles." (5) That is, they would do small or large good deeds, leaving only a card that said, "You are the recipient of an ~~anonymously~~ anonymous good deed done in the name of Hal Reichle." (6) The group called ~~themselves~~ itself SSSSH, or Secret Society of Serendipitous* Service to Hal. (7) After several newspapers wrote about the secret society, school children and people in other states began to pull Reichles ~~theirselves.~~ themselves. (8) If an agent wants to report, ~~they~~ he or she can write about the deed performed—without a signature or return address, of course—to Hal Reichle, P.O. Box ~~375 Hiram ohio~~ 375, Hiram, Ohio 44234. (9) A friend of Hal's ~~whom~~ who claimed to know only that SSSSH exists but nothing more said that the goal of the organization is a simple one: increasing goodness in the world.

PRACTICE 6

Proofread this essay, correcting any errors above the lines.

Crime-Fighting Artist

(1) Jeanne Boylan helps capture ~~Americas~~ America's most wanted ~~criminals~~ criminals, but she's not a police officer or a detective. (2) Instead, she is an artist who draws the faces of suspects, ~~base~~ based only on her gentle conversations with ~~victim's~~ victims and eyewitnesses. (3) Her portraits are so lifelike and accurate that she has ~~became~~ become famous for drawing nearly mirror images of criminals. (4) Boylan's sketches often ~~leads~~ lead to arrests. (5) She drew the Unabomber in his sunglasses and hooded sweatshirt, the kid-

*serendipitous: unexpectedly lucky

Boylan's sketch (left) led to the arrest of the Unabomber, Ted Kaczynski.

(left) AP/Wide World, (right) FBI/AP/Wide World.

napper-murderer of twelve-year-old Polly Klaas, and Timothy ~~McVeigh.~~ McVeigh, (6) ~~Who~~ who bombed Oklahoma City's Federal Building. (7) Once doubtful, FBI officials and police now ~~calls~~ call on Boylan in almost every major case.

(8) Boylan decided to become a sketch artist after she was the victim of a crime. (9) The police, following standard procedure, asked her to describe her attackers' ~~faces,~~ faces; then they showed her mug shots of ~~criminals.~~ criminals, (10) ~~Hoping~~ hoping that she would recognize the suspects. (11) Boylan sensed that this was the wrong approach to help her mind remember. (12) She realized that the ~~authorities~~ authorities' leading questions—questions like "Did he have a moustache? Was he wearing glasses?"—clutter the victim's mind with details that might not be true. (13) At the same time, the subconscious mind is trying to avoid reliving a traumatic ~~experience~~ experience; consequently, memories easily become distorted.

(14) Boylan developed a very different method for coaxing images from victims and witnesses. (15) What distinguishes hers from others, she says, is that she *listens.* (16) She takes her ~~time.~~ time, (17) ~~Talking~~ talking for hours with eyewitnesses to a crime. (18) She does not pressure them to recall the color of a suspect's eyes or ~~what~~ the shape of his nose ~~was~~. (19) Instead, she asks about their daily lives and interests, here and there asking non-leading questions about what they saw. (20) Slowly and ~~careful,~~ carefully, she guides people back through their confusion and pain to the moment when they ~~seen~~ saw or felt something that they desperately want to forget. (21) She asks them to describe whole shapes, forms, and textures rather than specific

details. (22) She sometimes gives children Play-Doh to mold as they explore their memories. (23) As they draw closer and closer to the terrifying images seared into their ~~minds.~~ minds, (24) Boylan watches, listens, and ~~sketching.~~ sketches. (25) "What people see," she says, "is evidence as fragile and valuable as a fingerprint. (26) And it should be protected with as much care."

(27) Many have claimed that Boylan's method, a blend of art, psychology, and human compassion, ~~are~~ is a unique gift. (28) Boylan insists, though, that her technique can be ~~teach.~~ taught. (29) "What I do is no great ~~mystery~~ mystery," she says. (30) "It has to do with allowing someone the freedom and the time to remember. (31) It has to do with the human heart."

PRACTICE 7

Proofread this essay, correcting any errors above the lines.

Quiet, Please!

(1) America is loud. (2) Horns and sirens ~~pierces~~ pierce the ~~air, car~~ air; car stereos pump out loud music. (3) Cell phones ~~rings,~~ ring, shriek, or ~~trumpets~~ trumpet the owner's noise of choice. (4) Construction ~~equipments~~ equipment, lawnmowers, and leaf blowers buzz and roar into the public space. (5) Restaurant and movie theater ~~manager's~~ managers often seem to link loudness with cultural cool. (6) Sounds are measured in decibels, with the human voice measuring about 60 ~~decibels,~~ decibels; the sound of a car is about 80 decibels. (7) According to the U.S. Environmental Protection Agency, 70 decibels is a safe daily average. (8) Here is the problem: the level of noise that many of us hear every day ~~are~~ is far above this.

(9) The sound of a food blender, for example, measures 90 decibels. (10) Many leaf ~~blower~~ blowers exceed 115 decibels, and a jet taking off is 120 decibels of ear-blasting noise. (11) All of this racket ~~are~~ is taking ~~it's~~ its toll on us both physically and ~~in psychological ways.~~ psychologically. (12) According to the American Speech-Language-Hearing Association (ASHA), 28 million U.S. citizens have already ~~suffer~~ suffered hearing loss from too much noise. (13) Furthermore, loud noise raises blood ~~pressure~~ pressure, increases stress hormone levels, and deprives us of sleep. (14) Noise pollution also increases aggression and even violence and harms concentration and learning. (15) One study found that New ~~york~~ York children in classrooms that faced the train tracks were almost a year behind children taught in ~~more quieter~~ quieter parts of the same school.

(16) In Europe, noise pollution has been taken ~~serious~~ seriously for years. (17) Now in the United States, organizations like the Noise Pollution Clearinghouse ~~is~~ are trying to raise awareness of the problem and promote solutions. (18) Members of this organization ~~believes~~ believe that just as smoke or toxins in the air are not acceptable, neither is loud noise. (19) They are working for new ~~laws.~~ laws (20) ~~To~~ to enforce our right to peace and quiet.

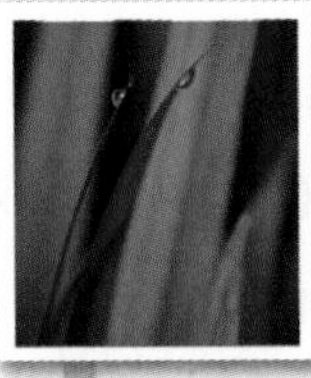

CHAPTER HIGHLIGHTS

- **Know your error patterns.** ***Most writers don't make hundreds of errors; they make the same few errors over and over again!*** By now, you should know the kinds of errors you tend to make. This knowledge is an important tool for improving your writing and your college performance. Do you tend to write fragments or leave the *–ed*s off certain verbs? Then pay special attention to these problems as you proofread.
- **Know where to find help.** Find expert help for erasing your error patterns in this book, at the Web links listed at the end of each chapter, and on the *Grassroots* student website. You can also search the OWLs you have bookmarked or type your search words—for example, "comma splices, explanation, practice"—into a search engine like Google. In addition, visit your college's writing lab to discover what writing help is offered there.

EXPLORING ONLINE

TEACHING TIP
More practice and assessment are available in the *Grassroots* Test Bank; linked ACE tests on the *Grassroots* student website; *WriteSpace for Grassroots*; and at the Exploring Online links in this chapter.

<http://owl.english.purdue.edu/handouts/general/gl_edit.html> Proofreading guide

<http://depts.gallaudet.edu/englishworks/writing/proofread.html> Punctuation and grammar review

<http://college.hmco.com/devenglish/> Visit the *Grassroots* 8/e Student Website for more exercises and quizzes.

WRITING ASSIGNMENTS

As you complete each writing assignment, remember to perform these steps:

- Write a clear, complete topic sentence.
- Use freewriting, brainstorming, or clustering to generate ideas for the body of your paragraph, essay, letter, or commercial.
- Arrange your best ideas in a plan.
- Revise for support, unity, coherence, and exact language.
- Proofread for grammar, punctuation, and spelling errors.

Writing Assignment 1: *Discuss an unusual friendship.* Have you ever had or witnessed a truly unusual friendship—for instance, between two people many years apart in age, between people from different social worlds who bonded because of a shared hobby or problem, or between a human being and an animal? Select one such unusual friendship and capture its essence in writing. How did the friendship start? What do you think bonded the two friends? Be as specific as possible so that the reader will understand this special relationship. Proofread carefully for correct use of capitals, commas, apostrophes, and quotation marks.

Writing Assignment 2: *Write a letter to compliment or to complain.* Write a letter to a store manager or a dean, to praise an especially helpful salesperson or a particularly good teacher. If you are not feeling complimentary, write the opposite: a letter of complaint about a salesperson or an instructor. State your compliment or complaint, describing what occurred and explaining why you are pleased or displeased. Remember, how well your letter is written will contribute to the impression you make. Proofread carefully for the correct use of capitals, commas, apostrophes, and quotation marks.

Writing Assignment 3: *Revise a quotation.* Pick a quotation from the Quotation Bank at the end of this book, and alter it to express something new. For example, you might want to change "Insanity is hereditary—you get it from your children" to "Insanity is learned—you get it from going to school." Be as serious or as humorous as you would like. Prove that your quotation is valid, arguing from your own or others' experience. Proofread carefully for the correct use of capitals, commas, apostrophes, and quotation marks.

Writing Assignment 4: *Create a print ad.* You and several classmates considering careers in advertising have been asked to create a print ad for a magazine, newspaper, or billboard. You must sell one product or idea of your choice—anything from a brand of jeans to a cell phone to a good cause, like recycling or becoming a foster parent. Your goal is to capture people's attention with a strong picture and then persuade them with a few well-chosen words. Sketch and draft your ad; don't let punctuation errors get in the way of your message. For online help step by step, visit this website: **<http://adbusters.org/spoofads/printad/>.**

REVIEW

Proofreading

A. Proofread the following business letter for incorrect or missing capitals, commas, apostrophes, and quotation marks. Correct all errors above the lines. (You should find thirty-one individual errors.)

Somers Street
99 ~~somers street~~
Ohio
Northfield, ~~ohio~~ 44056
January,
~~january~~ 11, 2005

Weird Walt's
~~weird walts~~ Discount Store
Office
Main ~~office~~
Akron,
~~akron,~~ Ohio 44313

Sir
Dear ~~sir~~ or Madam:

January 5, 2005,
On ~~january 5, 2005~~ I ordered a Panasonic forty-two-inch plasma flat panel
Avenue, Medina,
television with a remote control from your store at 1101 Lakeland ~~avenue medina~~
Ohio.
~~ohio.~~ The model number is TH42PX20UP. When your delivery man brought the
set to my home yesterday, he seemed impatient. He urged me to sign before I had
box, unpack it,
a chance to open the ~~box unpack it~~ or examine the equipment. In fact, he said,
buddy, I've I'm
"Listen, ~~buddy Ive~~ got five more deliveries, and ~~Im~~ out of here whether you open
not." dismay,
the box or ~~not.~~ To my ~~dismay~~ I later discovered that the hand-held remote control
was missing.

Panasonic
Please send me this remote control immediately. I purchased this ~~panasonic~~ in
Bowl
time to use it at my Super-~~bowl~~ party. Obviously, my friends and I need the re-
now, Walt's
mote control. For years ~~now~~ I have been a loyal customer of Weird ~~Walts~~ and will
Thank
appreciate your prompt attention to this matter. ~~thank~~ you.

yours,
Sincerely ~~your's,~~

Rainford
Milton ~~rainford~~

B. Proofread the following essay for incorrect or missing capitals, commas, apostrophes, and quotation marks. Correct the errors above the lines. (You should find thirty-eight individual errors.)

The Liberator of South America

(1) One day in ~~1805~~ 1805, Simón Bolívar made a vow. (2) He vowed that he ~~wouldnt~~ wouldn't rest until South America was free from ~~spanish~~ Spanish oppression. (3) This promise changed his life and Latin American ~~history~~ history. (4) ~~Bolívar~~ Bolívar, surprisingly ~~enough~~ enough, spent the first twenty-two years of his life as a rich aristocrat. (5) When he died at ~~fifty-seven~~ fifty-seven, he was known as the ~~george~~ George Washington of ~~south america.~~ South America.

(6) Bolívar was born in ~~caracas, Venezuela~~ Caracas, Venezuela, on July ~~24~~ 24, 1783. (7) ~~after~~ After he became an orphan at the age of ~~nine~~ nine, his uncle provided him with a ~~tutor~~ tutor, Simón ~~Rodriguez~~ Rodriguez. (8) A fierce ~~patriot~~ patriot, Rodriguez wanted South ~~American's~~ Americans to rule themselves. (9) ~~However~~ However, young Simón Bolívar ~~was'nt~~ wasn't very interested in his ~~tutors~~ tutor's ideas about independence. (10) ~~Bolívars~~ Bolívar's uncle sent Simón to ~~europe~~ Europe to help further the young ~~mans~~ man's education. (11) ~~during~~ During his travels in Spain, Bolívar realized that Latin America was destined to be independent of Spain.

(12) Bolívar returned to Venezuela and joined those fighting Spain. (13) His troops were ~~defeated~~ defeated, but Bolívar would not admit to failure. (14) In a famous letter that he wrote in 1814, he declared, ~~"the~~ "The bonds that unite us to Spain have been ~~cut".~~ cut." (15) Finally, the tide turned against Spain. (16) The ~~spaniards~~ Spaniards were driven out of ~~Colombia Venezuela Ecuador~~ Colombia, Venezuela, Ecuador, Peru, and ~~Bolivia~~ Bolivia. (17) Bolívar, leader of much of South ~~America~~ America, wanted to unite the people under one government. (18) His idea may have been a good ~~one~~ one, yet each area preferred to become a separate nation. (19) Although his plan for a united country ~~failed~~ failed, Bolívar is still remembered as South ~~Americas~~ America's greatest hero.

UNIT 7

WRITERS' WORKSHOP

Explain a Cause or an Effect

Examining causes and effects is a useful skill, both in college and at work. This student's thoughtful essay looks at the effects of school pressure to "speak like an American." In your group or class, read it aloud if possible. As you read, pay attention to the causes and effects he describes.

In America, Speak Like an American

(1) Many teachers tell immigrant students to lose their accents and "speak like an American." They mean well. They want the children to succeed. However, this can also encourage children to be ashamed of who they are and give up their heritage.

(2) When I was in fourth grade, I was sent to a class for "speech imperfections." Apparently, I had a Spanish accent. The class wasn't so ~~bad, it~~ bad. It taught us to say "chair" instead of "shair" and "school" instead of "eschool." It was so important for me to please the teacher, I did practically everything she asked. She told us things like "The bums on the street have ~~accents, that's~~ accents. That's why they're not working." I abandoned my roots and my culture and embraced "America." I learned about Stonewall Jackson and William Shakespeare. Soon Ponce de León and Gonzalo de Barca were just memories at the back of my mind. I listened to country music and rock because this was "American."

(3) I can't remember when it happened, but suddenly I found myself listening to Spanish love songs. They were great! They were so sincere, ^and the lyrics were beautiful. While turning the radio dial one day, I stopped at a Hispanic radio station. It was playing salsa. Holy smokes, I thought to myself. All the instruments were synchronized so tightly. The horn section kept accenting the singer's lines. All of a sudden, my hips started swaying, my feet started tapping, and I stood up. And then the horror. I couldn't dance to this ~~music, I~~ music. I had never learned how. There I was, a Puerto Rican boy, listening to Puerto Rican music, but unable to dance the typical Puerto Rican way.

(4) Anger flared through me as I remembered my fourth grade teacher. I was also upset with my ~~parents, in~~ parents. In their zeal to have me excel, they kept

TEACHING TIP
This well-crafted and beautifully detailed student essay (to which I added five comma splices for instructional purposes) usually inspires students and elicits their own sharing of experiences. The essay models cause and effect.

me from my roots as a first-generation Hispanic American. But that was years ago. I have searched for my Latin heritage. I've found beautiful music, wonderful literature, and great foods. I now associate with "my people" as well as with everyone else, and I am learning the joys of being Sam Rodriguez, Puerto Rican.

Sam Rodriguez, student

1. How effective is Sam Rodriguez's essay?

   __Y__ Clear main idea? __Y__ Good supporting details?

   __Y__ Logical organization? __Y__ Effective conclusion?

2. Does the essay have a *thesis statement*, one sentence that states the main idea of the entire essay? Which sentence is it? Paragraph 1, sentence 4

3. In paragraph (2), the writer says that he "abandoned [his] roots." In his view, what caused him to do this?

4. Underline the lines and ideas you find especially effective and share them with your group or class. Try to understand exactly why you like a word or sentence. For example, in paragraph (3), we can almost experience the first time the writer really *hears* salsa—the instruments, the horns accenting the singer's lines, his tapping feet and swaying hips.

5. As the writer gets older, he realizes he has lost too much of his heritage. At first he is angry (short-term effect), but what long-term effect does this new understanding have on him?

6. What order does this writer follow throughout the essay? Time order

7. This fine essay is finished and ready to go, but the student makes the same punctuation error five different times. Can you spot and correct the error pattern that he needs to watch out for? Five comma splices

Writing and Revising Ideas

1. What does it mean to "become American"?

2. Write about something important that you gave up and explain why you did so.

Plan carefully, outlining your paragraph or essay before you write. State your main idea clearly and plan your supporting ideas or paragraphs. As you revise, pay special attention to clear organization and convincing, detailed support.

UNIT 8

Improving Your Spelling

Some people are naturally better spellers than others, but anyone can *become* a better speller. In this unit, you will

- Master six basic spelling rules
- Learn to avoid common look-alike/sound-alike errors

Spotlight on Writing

No spelling errors mar this writer's memory of summer mornings years ago. If possible, read the paragraph aloud.

Summer, when I was a boy in Brooklyn, was a string of intimacies, a sum of small knowings, and almost none of them cost money. Nobody ever figured out a way to charge us for morning, and morning then was the beginning of everything. I was an altar boy in the years after the war, up in the morning before most other people for the long walk to the church on the hill. And I would watch the sun rise in Prospect Park—first a rumor, then a heightened light, something unseen and immense melting the hard early darkness; then suddenly there was a molten ball, screened by the trees, about to climb to a scalding noon. The sun would dry the dew on the grass of the park, soften the tar, bake the rooftops, brown us on the beaches, make us sweat, force us out of the tight small flats of the tenements.

Pete Hamill, "Spaldeen Summers"

- Through his choice and arrangement of words, this writer helps us see and feel the park at sunrise. He also has avoided the six most common types of spelling errors. The underlined words are all spelled correctly. If you don't know why, read on.

- ***Morning in a particular place (a desert, a suburb, an all-night bar, a mountaintop, and so forth)***
- ***An experience of "awe" or wonder***

CHAPTER 31

Spelling

PART A Suggestions for Improving Your Spelling

ESL TIP
To ESL students in particular, English spelling is difficult and unpredictable. Point out that many other languages have more regular spelling rules than English does.

TEACHING TIP
You may want to model for students exactly how to look up an unfamiliar word in the dictionary, especially when you don't know how to spell it. Talk aloud as you think through finding a word like *rhyme.*

One important ingredient of good writing is accurate spelling. No matter how interesting your ideas are, your writing will not be effective if your spelling is incorrect.

Tips for Improving Your Spelling

1. **Look closely at the words on the page.** Use any tricks you can to remember the right spelling. For example, "The *a*'s in *separate* are separated by an *r*," or "*Dessert* has two *s*'s because you want two *desserts*."
2. **Use a dictionary.** Even professional writers frequently check spelling in a dictionary. As you write, underline the words you are not sure of and look them up when you write your final draft. If locating words in the dictionary is a real problem for you, consider a "poor speller's dictionary." Ask your professor to recommend one.
3. **Use a spell checker.** If you write on a computer, make a habit of using the spell checker. See Part B for tips and cautions about spell checkers.
4. **Keep a list of the words you misspell.** Look over your list whenever you can and keep it handy as you write.
5. **Look over corrected papers for misspelled words** (often marked *sp*). Add these words to your list. Practice writing each word three or four times.

ESL TIP
Encourage nonnative students to invest in a good ESL dictionary. The latest versions include a CD-ROM and website with spelling, vocabulary, and grammar activities.

6. **Test yourself.** Have a friend dictate words from your list or from this chapter or use flash cards; computerized flash cards can be helpful.
7. **Review the basic spelling rules explained in this chapter.** Take time to learn the material; don't rush through the entire chapter all at once.
8. **Study the spelling list on page 349,** and test yourself on those words.
9. **Read through Chapter 32, "Look-Alikes/Sound-Alikes,"** for commonly confused words (*their, there,* and *they're,* for instance). The practices in that chapter will help you eliminate some common spelling errors from your writing.

PART B Computer Spell Checkers

TEACHING TIP
Suggest that students who save their papers as electronic files get in the habit of using an online dictionary—like <www.dictionary.com>—to check their spelling during the proofreading phase of the writing process.

If you write on a computer, always run the spell checker as part of your proofreading process. A spell checker picks up certain spelling errors and gives you alternatives for correcting them. Your program might also highlight misspelled words as you write. If your spell checker does not highlight misspellings as you write, run the program after you have made all your corrections. If you have introduced a new error, the program will let you know.

What a spell checker cannot do is *think*. If you have written one correctly spelled word instead of another—*if* for *it,* for example—the spell checker cannot bring that error to your attention. If you have written *then* for *than,* the spell checker cannot help.* To find such errors, you must always proofread your paper *after* running the spell checker.

PRACTICE 1

In a small group, read this poem, which "passed" every spell check. Correct the errors that the spell checker missed and write them above the lines.

I have checker,
~~Eye halve~~ a spelling ~~check her,~~

PC.
It came with my ~~pea see.~~

marks for review,
It clearly ~~marques four~~ my ~~revue,~~

Mistakes I cannot see.
~~Miss steaks~~ eye ~~kin knot~~ sea.

through
I've run this poem ~~threw~~ it.

sure you're pleased to know.
I'm ~~shore your please too no.~~

It's its way.
~~Its~~ letter perfect in ~~it's weigh.~~

told so.
My checker ~~tolled~~ me ~~sew.~~

PART C Spotting Vowels and Consonants

To learn some basic spelling rules, you must know the difference between vowels and consonants. See the chart on the following page.

*For questions about words that sound the same but are spelled differently, check Chapter 32, "Look-Alikes/Sound-Alikes."

ESL TIP
You may need to review the English vowel sounds for ESL learners, for differences in pronunciations can lead to misspellings. In some languages, such as Spanish, a long *i* is often pronounced *ee*, so the word *ship* can sound like *sheep*.

The **vowels** are *a, e, i, o,* and *u.*

The **consonants** are *b, c, d, f, g, h, j, k, l, m, n, p, q, r, s, t, v, w, x,* and *z.*

The letter *y* can be either a vowel or a consonant, depending on its sound:

happy	shy
young	yawn

- In both *happy* and *shy, y* is a vowel because it has a vowel sound: an *ee* sound in *happy* and an *i* sound in *shy*.
- In both *young* and *yawn, y* is a consonant becauses it has the consonant sound of *y*.

PRACTICE 2

Write *V* for vowel or *C* for consonant in the space over each letter. Be careful of the *y*.

EXAMPLE:
C C V C C V
s t a r r y

1. C C V C V
t h e r e

2. C V C C
j u m p

3. C V C V
r e l y

4. C V C C
y a m s

5. C V C C V C
h i d d e n

6. C V C C V C
s i l v e r

PART D Doubling the Final Consonant (in Words of One Syllable)

When you add a suffix or ending that begins with a vowel (like *-ed, -ing, -er, -est*) to a word of one syllable, double the final consonant *if* the last three letters of the word are consonant-vowel-consonant, or *cvc*.

TEACHING TIP
Point out that, for some words, failing to double the consonant correctly creates a word with a different sound and meaning (e.g., *hoped/hopped, riper/ripper, staring/starring*). Ask your students to think of other similar pairs.

mop + ed = mopped	swim + ing = swimming
burn + er = burner	thin + est = thinnest

- *Mop, swim,* and *thin* all end in *cvc;* therefore, the final consonants are doubled.
- *Burn* does not end in *cvc;* therefore, the final consonant is not doubled.

PRACTICE 3

Which of the following words double the final consonant? Check to see whether the word ends in *cvc*. Double the final consonant if necessary; then add the suffixes *-ed* and *-ing*.

	Word	Last Three Letters	-ed	-ing
EXAMPLES:	drop	cvc	dropped	dropping
	boil	vvc	boiled	boiling
	1. plan	cvc	planned	planning
	2. brag	cvc	bragged	bragging

3. dip	cvc	dipped	dipping
4. sail	vvc	sailed	sailing
5. stop	cvc	stopped	stopping

PRACTICE 4

Which of the following words double the final consonant? Check for *cvc*. Then add the suffixes *-er* or *-est*.

	Word	Last Three Letters	-er	-est
EXAMPLES:	hot	cvc	hotter	hottest
	cool	vvc	cooler	coolest
	1. tall	vcc	taller	tallest
	2. short	vcc	shorter	shortest
	3. fat	cvc	fatter	fattest
	4. slim	cvc	slimmer	slimmest
	5. wet	cvc	wetter	wettest
	6. quick	vcc	quicker	quickest

PART E Doubling the Final Consonant (in Words of More Than One Syllable)

TEACHING TIP
Review with students what *suffixes* and *stressed syllables* are.

When you add a suffix that begins with a vowel to a word of more than one syllable, double the final consonant *if*

(1) the last three letters of the word are *cvc, and*

(2) the accent or stress is on the *last* syllable.

TEACHING TIP
Have students come up with their own examples in order to reinforce their knowledge of the rule.

begin + ing = beginning
patrol + ed = patrolled

- *Begin* and *patrol* both end in *cvc.*
- In both words, the stress is on the last syllable: *be-gin´, pa-trol´.* (Pronounce the words aloud and listen for the correct stress.)
- Therefore, *beginning* and *patrolled* double the final consonant.

gossip + ing = gossiping
visit + ed = visited

- *Gossip* and *visit* both end in *cvc.*
- However, the stress is *not* on the last syllable: *gos´-sip, vis´-it.*
- Therefore, *gossiping* and *visited* do not double the final consonant.

PRACTICE 5

Which of the following words double the final consonant? First, check for *cvc*. Then check for the final stress and add the suffixes *-ed* and *-ing*.

	Word	Last Three Letters	-ed	-ing
EXAMPLES:	repel	cvc	repelled	repelling
	enlist	vcc	enlisted	enlisting
	1. occur	cvc	occurred	occurring
	2. happen	cvc	happened	happening
	3. polish	vcc	polished	polishing
	4. commit	cvc	committed	committing
	5. offer	cvc	offered	offering
	6. prefer	cvc	preferred	preferring
	7. exit	cvc	exited	exiting
	8. travel	cvc	traveled	traveling
	9. wonder	cvc	wondered	wondering
	10. omit	cvc	omitted	omitting

TEACHING TIP
Encourage students to say the words in Practice 5 aloud so they can hear the stressed syllable.

PRACTICE 6

Which words in parentheses double the final consonant? First, check for *cvc*. Then add the suffixes *-ed* and *-ing*. In words of two or more syllables, check for the final stress.

Martial Artist Jackie Chan

(1) Jackie Chan, the martial arts film star and director, worked (work + ed) long and hard for his success in movies. (2) When he was a child, his parents enrolled (enroll + ed) him in the Peking Opera Academy. (3) Unlike Western opera, Chinese opera is more like a circus that features acrobats, jugglers, and contortionists. (4) Throughout his film career, Chan has depended (depend + ed) on the tumbling and gymnastic skills he learned at the academy. (5) When he graduated, however, Chinese opera was out of fashion, and he was compelled (compel + ed) to take a job performing (perform + ing) stunts in martial arts films. (6) He obtained (obtain + ed) small parts in two of Bruce Lee's films and much larger parts in many other, unsuccessful pictures.

(7) Following Lee's death, a producer hoped (hope + ed) that Jackie Chan would be the new Bruce Lee and signed him to a multipicture contract. (8) After

more unsuccessful films, Chan admitted (admit + ed) to himself that he was getting (get + ing) nowhere. (9) He considered retiring (retire + ing) from the movies. (10) By a stroke of luck, another producer asked (ask + ed) him to star in the martial arts comedy *Snake in the Eagle's Shadow.* (11) Instead of trying to turn Chan into a poor copy of Bruce Lee, this producer permitted (permit + ed) him to create a comic underdog character. (12) The film was a huge success in Asia, and audiences demanded (demand + ed) more martial arts films starring (star + ing) the comically gifted Chan.

(13) Once Chan was a hit in the Far East, he planned (plan + ed) his break into the American film industry. (14) After he had a worldwide crossover hit with *Rumble in the Bronx* in 1994, Chan stopped (stop + ed) making films in Asia and announced that he preferred (prefer + ed) Hollywood. (15) Since then, films like *Rush Hour, Shanghai Noon, Shanghai Knights,* and *The Medallion* have drawn huge audiences with the winning (win + ing) combination of laughs and astonishing (astonish + ing) moves. (16) In fact, Chan has been proclaimed (proclaim + ed) "a human special effect."

PART F Dropping or Keeping the Final *E*

TEACHING TIP
The rules for keeping or dropping the final *e* should be memorized.

When you add a suffix that begins with a vowel (like *-able, -ence,* or *-ing*), drop the final *e*.

When you add a suffix that begins with a consonant (like *-less, -ment,* or *-ly*), keep the final *e*.

write + ing = writing   pure + ity = purity

- *Writing* and *purity* both drop the final *e* because the suffixes *-ing* and *-ity* begin with vowels.

hope + less = hopeless   advertise + ment = advertisement

- *Hopeless* and *advertisement* keep the final *e* because the suffixes *-less* and *-ment* begin with consonants.

TEACHING TIP
Ask students to explain how each of the exceptions deviates from the rules.

Here are some exceptions to memorize:

argument	courageous	knowledgeable	simply
awful	judgment	manageable	truly

PRACTICE 7

Add the suffix shown to each word.

EXAMPLES: come + ing = coming

rude + ness = rudeness

1. blame + less = blameless
2. guide + ance = guidance
3. debate + ing = debating
4. motive + ation = motivation
5. sincere + ly = sincerely
6. desire + able = desirable
7. argue + ment = argument
8. home + less = homeless
9. response + ible = responsible
10. rejoice + ing = rejoicing
11. awe + ful = awful
12. manage + er = manager
13. judge + ment = judgment
14. fame + ous = famous
15. grieve + ance = grievance
16. arrange + ing = arranging

PART G Changing or Keeping the Final *Y*

When you add a suffix to a word that ends in *-y*, change the *y* to *i* if the letter before the *y* is a consonant.

Keep the final *y* if the letter before the *y* is a vowel.

happy + ness = happiness   delay + ed = delayed

- The *y* in *happiness* is changed to *i* because the letter before the *y* is a consonant, *p*.
- However, the *y* in *delayed* is not changed to *i* because the letter before it is a vowel, *a*.

When you add *-ing* to words ending in *y*, always keep the *y*.

copy + ing = copying   delay + ing = delaying

Here are some exceptions to memorize:

day + ly = daily   pay + ed = paid

lay + ed = laid   say + ed = said

When the final *y* is changed to *i*, add *-es* instead of *-s*.

TEACHING TIP
Practicing with flash cards may help students learn to apply the rules more consistently.

fly + es = flies   candy + es = candies

marry + es = marries   story + es = stories

PRACTICE 8

Add the suffix shown to each of the following words.

EXAMPLES: vary + ed = varied

buy + er = buyer

1. cry + ed = cried
2. mercy + ful = merciful
3. worry + ing = worrying
4. say + ed = said
5. juicy + er = juicier
6. enjoy + able = enjoyable
7. clumsy + ness = clumsiness
8. wealthy + est = wealthiest
9. day + ly = daily
10. merry + ly = merrily

PRACTICE 9

Add the suffixes in parentheses to each word.

1. lively (er) livelier
   (est) liveliest
   (ness) liveliness
2. beauty (fy) beautify
   (ful) beautiful
   (es) beauties
3. healthy (er) healthier
   (est) healthiest
   (ly) healthily
4. study (es) studies
   (ous) studious
   (ing) studying
5. busy (ness) business
   (er) busier
   (est) busiest
6. try (es) tries
   (ed) tried
   (al) trial

PRACTICE 10

Add the suffix shown to each word in parentheses. Write the correctly spelled word in each blank.

Winter Blues

(1) Although Kim tried (try + ed) to ignore her feelings, she always felt hungrier (hungry + er), sleepier (sleep + er), angrier (angry + er), and lonelier (lonely + er) during the winter months. (2) As part of her denial (deny + al), she went about her business (busy + ness) as usual, but she knew that she no longer found life as pleasurable (pleasure + able) as before.

(3) Then one day she read a fascinating (fascinate + ing) magazine article about a medical condition called *seasonal affective disorder*, or *SAD*. (4) Kim immediately (immediate + ly) saw the similarities (similarity + es) between her yearly mood changes and the symptoms that people with SAD displayed (display + ed). (5) She learned that winter SAD is a kind of

depression triggered primarily (primary + ly) by lack of exposure (expose + ure) to light—by insufficient sunshine, inadequate indoor light at home or work, or even by mercilessly (mercy + lessly) cloudy weather.

(6) Happily (Happy + ly), Kim discovered that three or four kinds of treatment are available. (7) The most severe cases—people who sleep more than fourteen hours a day and still feel fatigued (fatigue + ed), for example—are usually cured by light therapy given in a clinic or at home under a doctor's care. (8) Taking medication, exercising (exercise + ing), or changing (change + ing) one's diet often bring noticeable (notice + able) relief. (9) Kim did some research on the Web and found a list of SAD clinics, guidance (guide + ance), and support. (10) Attending a light-therapy clinic near her home, she soon experienced her healthiest (healthy + est) winter in years.

PART H Choosing *IE* or *EI*

Write *i* before *e*, except after *c*, or in any *ay* sound like *neighbor*:

niece, believe, conceive, weigh

TEACHING TIP
Tell students that the "*i* before *e*" rule does not apply in words in which the *i* and *e* are pronounced as two sounds (like *science*) instead of one (as in *brief*).

- *Niece* and *believe* are spelled *ie*.
- *Conceive* is spelled *ei* because of the preceding *c*.
- *Weigh* is spelled *ei* because of its *ay* sound.

However, words with a *shen* sound are spelled with an *ie* after the *c*: *ancient, conscience, efficient, sufficient*.

Here are some exceptions to memorize:

either	height	seize	their
foreign	neither	society	weird

PRACTICE 11

Pronounce each word out loud. Then fill in the blanks with either *ie* or *ei*.

1. f i e ld	6. s e i ze	11. effic i e nt
2. w e i ght	7. rec e i ve	12. v e i n
3. n e i ther	8. br i e f	13. th e i r
4. w e i rd	9. h e i ght	14. for e i gn
5. ch i e f	10. ach i e ve	15. cash i e r

PART I Commonly Misspelled Words

Below is a list of commonly misspelled words. They are words that you probably use daily in speaking and writing. Each word has a trouble spot, the part of the word that is often spelled incorrectly. The trouble spot is in bold type.

Two tricks to help you learn these words are (1) to copy each word twice, underlining the trouble spot, and (2) to copy the words on flash cards and have someone else test you. If possible, consult this list while or after you write.

TEACHING TIP
Tell students that imprecise pronunciation can translate into spelling errors. Those who habitually say "probly" and "accidently," for example, are less likely to spell those words *probably* and *accidentally*.

1. a**c**ross
2. a**dd**ress
3. ans**w**er
4. arg**u**ment
5. a**thl**ete
6. begi**nn**ing
7. beha**vi**or
8. cal**e**nd**a**r
9. car**eer**
10. cons**cie**nce
11. crow**ded**
12. defi**ni**te
13. d**es**cribe
14. desp**er**ate
15. di**ffe**rent
16. dis**app**oint
17. disa**pp**rove
18. do**es**n't
19. eig**hth**
20. emba**rr**ass
21. envir**on**ment
22. exa**gg**erate
23. fam**ili**ar
24. fina**lly**
25. gove**rn**ment
26. gramm**a**r
27. hei**gh**t
28. **ill**egal
29. immed**iate**ly
30. impor**tant**
31. in**teg**ration
32. in**tell**igent
33. int**ere**st
34. int**er**fere
35. jew**el**ry
36. jud**gm**ent
37. knowle**d**ge
38. maint**ain**
39. math**e**matics
40. me**a**nt
41. ne**ce**ssary
42. nerv**ous**
43. o**cc**asion
44. opin**ion**
45. opt**i**mist
46. partic**u**lar
47. **per**form
48. **per**haps
49. perso**nn**el
50. po**ss**e**ss**
51. po**ss**ible
52. **pre**fer
53. pre**jud**ice
54. privil**ege**
55. pro**bab**ly
56. **psy**cholo**gy**
57. p**ur**sue
58. ref**er**ence
59. **rhy**th**m**
60. ridic**ul**ous
61. sep**ara**te
62. sim**ilar**
63. **sin**ce
64. sp**ee**ch
65. stren**gth**
66. su**cc**ess
67. **sur**prise
68. t**au**ght
69. temper**a**ture
70. th**orou**gh
71. though**t**
72. tire**d**
73. unt**il**
74. wei**ght**
75. wri**tt**en

TEACHING TIP
Encourage students to keep a list of personal problem words in their notebooks and to review the correct spellings frequently.

Personal Spelling List

In your notebook, keep a list of words that *you* misspell. Add words to your list from corrected papers and from the exercises in this chapter. First, copy each word as you misspelled it, underlining the trouble spot; then write the word correctly. Use the following form. Study your list often.

ESL TIP
Periodically, ask pairs of students—an ESL student and a native speaker—to quiz each other on the words in their personal spelling lists.

	As I Wrote It	Correct Spelling
1.	dissapointed	disappointed
2.		
3.		

PRACTICE 12 WRITING ASSIGNMENT

Success can be defined in many different ways. In a small group, discuss what the term *success* means to you. Is it a rewarding career, a happy family life, lots of money?

Now pick the definition that most appeals to you and write a paragraph explaining what success is. You may wish to use people in the news or friends to support your main idea. Proofread your work for accurate spelling, especially the words covered in this chapter. Finally, exchange papers and read each other's work. Did your partner catch any spelling errors that you missed?

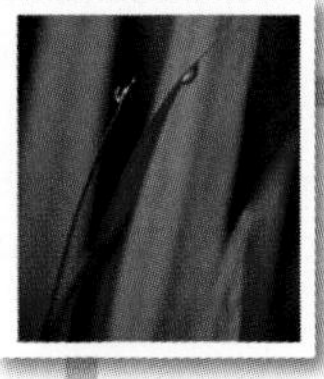

CHAPTER HIGHLIGHTS

- **Double the final consonant in one-syllable words that end in *cvc*:**

  hop/hopped   swim/swimming

- **Double the final consonant in words of more than one syllable if they end in *cvc* and if the stress is on the last syllable:**

  begin/beginning   prefer/preferred

- **Keep the final *e* when adding a suffix that begins with a consonant:**

  hope/hopeful   time/timely

- **Drop the final *e* when adding a suffix that begins with a vowel:**

  hope/hoping   time/timer

- **Keep the final *y* when adding a suffix if the letter before the *y* is a vowel:**

  buy/buying   delay/delayed

- **Change the *y* to *i* when adding a suffix if the letter before the *y* is a consonant:**

  snappy/snappiest   pity/pitiful

- **Write *i* before *e*, except after *c*, or in any *ay* sound like *neighbor*:**

  believe, niece, *but* receive, weigh

- **Remember that there are exceptions to all of these rules. Check a dictionary whenever you are uncertain.**

CHAPTER REVIEW

Proofread this essay for spelling errors. Correct the errors above the lines.

A Precious Resource

(1) Many people have pleasant ~~memorys~~ memories of ~~recieving~~ receiving their first library card or ~~chooseing~~ choosing books for the first time at a local public library. (2) Widely recognized as a priceless resource, the public library is defined just as you might expect: a collection of books and other materials supported by the public for public use.

(3) Several New England towns claim the honor of ~~contributeing~~ contributing the first public money for a library. (4) However, the first such library of meaningful size and influence—the first ~~fameous~~ famous public library—originated in Boston, Massachu-

setts, in 1854. (5) The Boston Public Library, with its useful ~~refrence~~ reference collection and its policy of ~~circulateing~~ circulating popular books, set the pattern for all public ~~librarys~~ libraries ultimately created in the United States and Canada. (6) By the end of the nineteenth century, many state ~~goverments~~ governments were ~~begining~~ beginning to raise taxes to support libraries. (7) They ~~beleived~~ believed that public libraries had an extremely ~~importent~~ important role to play in helping people pursue ~~knowlege~~ knowledge and continue ~~thier~~ their education. (8) Although public ~~libaries~~ libraries today have much the same goal, they now offer a ~~truely~~ truly ~~admireable~~ admirable number of resources and services. (9) These include story hours for children, book discussion clubs for adults, ~~intresting~~ interesting lectures, art exhibits, literacy classes, and most recently, computer training and ~~guideance~~ guidance.

TEACHING TIP
Tell your students about the interactive spelling quizzes at <http://www.ccc.commnet.edu/grammar/spelling.htm>.

(10) Technology, of course, has transformed the management of the public library as well as the way the library is used. (11) The ~~bigest~~ biggest changes—today's computerized catalogs, searchable databases, and Internet access—would ~~definately~~ definitely have gone beyond the wildest dreams of even the most ~~commited~~ committed early public ~~libary~~ library supporters.

New York Public Library, the Main Reading Room

(8/30/02) Fred R. Conrad/The New York Times.

EXPLORING ONLINE

TEACHING TIP
More practice and assessment are available in the *Grassroots* Test Bank; linked ACE tests on the *Grassroots* student website; *WriteSpace for Grassroots*; and at the Exploring Online links in this chapter.

<http://www.ccc.commnet.edu/cgi-shl/quiz20.pl/spelling_quiz3.htm>
Interactive quiz: Add endings to these words.

<http://owl.english.purdue.edu/handouts/interact/g_spelieEX1.html>
Is that *ei* or *ie*?

<http://college.hmco.com/devenglish/> Visit the *Grassroots* 8/e Student Website for more exercises and quizzes.

CHAPTER

32

Look-Alikes/ Sound-Alikes

ESL TIP
Look-alikes and sound-alikes present ongoing problems for ESL students. Remind them that all writers consult reference materials when in doubt.

A/An/And

1. ***A* is used before a word beginning with a consonant or a consonant sound.**

   a man   *a* house   *a* union (the *u* in *union* is pronounced like the consonant *y*)

2. ***An* is used before a word beginning with a vowel *(a, e, i, o, u)* or a silent *h*.**

   an igloo   *an* apple   *an* hour (the *h* in *hour* is silent)

3. ***And* joins words or ideas together.**

   Edward *and* Brad are taking the same biology class.

   He is very honest, *and* most people respect him.

PRACTICE 1

Fill in *a, an,* or *and.*

1. Don Miller has used each summer vacation to try out ___a___ different career choice.
2. Last summer, he worked in ___a___ law office, filling in for ___an___ administrative assistant on leave.
3. One lawyer was impressed by how carefully Don worked ___and___ suggested that Don consider ___a___ law career.
4. Don returned to school in the fall ___and___ talked to his adviser about becoming ___a___ paralegal.
5. ___A___ paralegal investigates the facts of cases, prepares documents, ___and___ does other background work for lawyers.
6. With his adviser's help, Don found ___a___ course of study to prepare for this career.
7. Next summer, he hopes to work for ___a___ public interest law firm ___and___ to learn about environmental law.
8. He is happy to have found ___an___ interesting career ___and___ looks forward to making ___a___ difference.

TEACHING AND ESL TIP
This unit can be a springboard for work on vocabulary building. Urge students to make use of online resources like Pop-up Lexicon, a year of new words: <http://www.ccc.commnet.edu/grammar/definition_list.htm> and ESL vocabulary links: <http://depts.gallaudet.edu/englishworks/reading/main/vocabulary.htm>.

Accept/Except

1. ***Accept* means "to receive."**

   Please *accept* my apologies. I *accepted* his offer of help.

2. ***Except* means "other than" or "excluding."**

   Everyone *except* Ron thinks it's a good idea.

PRACTICE 2

TEACHING TIP
To give students more practice with look-alikes/sound-alikes, you might ask them to write sentences using the words they confuse.

Fill in forms of *accept* or *except*.

1. Did Steve ___accept___ the collect call from his brother?
2. Mr. Francis will ___accept___ the package in the mailroom.
3. All of our friends attended the wedding ___except___ Meg.
4. The athlete proudly ___accepted___ his award.
5. Every toddler ___except___ my daughter enjoyed the piñata party.
6. ___Except___ for Jean, we all had tickets for the movie.
7. The tornado left every building standing ___except___ for the barn.
8. Everyone ___except___ Ranjan was willing to ___accept___ the committee's decision.

Been/Being

1. ***Been* is the past participle form of *to be*. *Been* is usually used after the helping verb *have, has,* or *had*.**

   I *have been* to that restaurant before.

   She *has been* in Akron for ten years.

2. ***Being* is the *-ing* form of *to be*. *Being* is usually used after the helping verbs *is, are, am, was,* and *were*.**

   They *are being* helped by the salesperson.

   Rhonda *is being* courageous and independent.

PRACTICE 3

Fill in *been* or *being*.

1. The children have ___been___ restless all day.
2. What good films are ___being___ shown on television tonight?
3. We have ___been___ walking in circles!
4. I haven't ___been___ in such a good mood for a week.
5. This building is ___being___ turned into a community center.
6. His last offer has ___been___ on my mind all day.
7. Which elevator is ___being___ inspected now?
8. Because you are ___being___ honest with me, I will admit that I have ___been___ in love with you for years.

Buy/By

1. *Buy* means "to purchase."

She *buys* new furniture every five years.

2. *By* means "near," "before," or "by means of."

He walked right *by* and didn't say hello.

By sunset, we had finished the harvest.

We prefer traveling *by* bus.

PRACTICE 4

Fill in *buy* or *by*.

1. Did you ___buy___ that computer, or did you rent it?
2. These tracks on the trail were made ___by___ a deer.
3. He stood ___by___ the cash register and waited his turn to ___buy___ a cheeseburger.
4. She finds it hard to walk ___by___ a bookstore without going in to browse.
5. It's better to stick with your budget than to ___buy___ that ten-seater couch.
6. Please answer this letter ___by___ October 10.
7. Pat trudged through the storm to ___buy___ a Sunday paper.
8. The dishes ___by___ the sink need to be put away.

Fine/Find

1. *Fine* means "good" or "well." It can also mean "a penalty."

He wrote a *fine* analysis of the short story.

She paid a $10 *fine*.

2. *Find* means "to locate."

I can't *find* my red suspenders.

PRACTICE 5

Fill in *fine* or *find*.

1. The library charges a large ___fine___ for overdue videotapes.
2. As soon as we ___find___ your lost suitcase, we'll send it to you.
3. Can you ___find___ me one of these in an extra-large size?
4. Harold made a ___fine___ impression on the assistant buyer.
5. By tonight, I will be feeling ___fine___ .
6. My father gave me good advice: "When you ___find___ good friends, stick with them."

TEACHING TIP
Alert students to the exhaustive "Notorious Confusables" bank of explanations, examples, and interactive quizzes: **<http://www.ccc.commnet.edu/grammar/notorious.htm>**.

It's/Its

1. *It's* is a contraction of *it is* or *it has*. If you cannot substitute *it is* or *it has* in the sentence, you cannot use *it's*.

It's a ten-minute walk to my house. *It's* been a nice party.

2. *Its* is a possessive and shows ownership.

The bear cub rolled playfully on *its* side.

Industry must do *its* share to curb inflation.

PRACTICE 6

Fill in *it's* or *its.*

1. If ___it's___ not too much trouble, drop the package off on your way home.
2. ___It's___ been hard for him to accept the fact that he can no longer play ball.
3. The *Daily News* reporter was lucky because the jury reached ___its___ verdict just before her deadline.
4. ___It's___ been a long time since I had a real vacation.
5. ___It's___ a chocolate cake with your social security number in pink frosting.
6. My family is at ___its___ best when there is work to be done.
7. ___It's___ impossible to open this window.
8. Although I hate shoveling the walk, I am happy ___it's___ been a good year for winter sports.
9. ___It's___ sad to see that seagull huddled in the sand.
10. If ___it's___ not flying, perhaps ___its___ wing is hurt.

Know/Knew/No/New

1. *Know* means "to have knowledge or understanding." *Knew* is the past tense of the verb *to know.*

Carl *knows* he has to finish by 6 p.m.

The police officer *knew* the quickest route to the pier.

2. *No* is a negative.

He is *no* longer dean of academic affairs.

3. *New* means "fresh" or "recent."

I like your *new* belt.

PRACTICE 7

Fill in *know, knew, no,* or *new.*

1. We will need ___new___ wiring to handle those powerful air conditioners.
2. She didn't ___know___ the lid was loose.
3. I ___know___ I need to find ___new___ jokes because no one laughs when I tell my old ones.
4. Because she ___knew___ the answer, she won a pool table and a popcorn machine.
5. Because you really ___know___ the ___new___ material, why don't you take the final early?
6. Charlene thinks there's ___no___ way we can do it, but I ___know___ we'll be speaking Italian by June.

7. Arnold knew that he shouldn't have eaten that third dessert.
8. We have no way of knowing how well you scored on the civil service examination.
9. He didn't know whether the used equipment came with a guarantee.
10. I wish I knew then what I know now.

Lose/Loose

1. *Lose* means "to misplace" or "not to win."

Be careful not to *lose* your way on those back roads.

George hates to *lose* at cards.

2. *Loose* means "ill fitting" or "too large."

That's not my size; it's *loose* on me.

PRACTICE 8

Fill in *lose* or *loose.*

1. Because the plug is loose in the socket, the television keeps blinking on and off.
2. A professional team has to learn how to win and how to lose gracefully.
3. If Irene doesn't tighten that loose hubcap, she will lose it.
4. I like wearing loose clothing in the summer.
5. Before these pants shrank in the dryer, they were too loose .
6. Act now, or you will lose your opportunity to get that promotion.
7. She won't lose those mittens again because I've clipped them onto her jacket.
8. I'm surprised you didn't lose those loose quarters.

Mine/Mind

1. *Mine* is a possessive and shows ownership.

This is your umbrella, but where is *mine*?

2. *Mind* means "intelligence." It can also be a verb meaning "to object" or "to pay attention to."

What's on your *mind*? I don't *mind* if you come late.

PRACTICE 9

Fill in *mine* or *mind.*

1. Her road test is tomorrow; mine was yesterday.
2. Will Doris mind if we spend the evening talking about our days in boot camp?
3. Sherlock put his mind to work and solved the mystery.
4. Please mind your manners when we meet the king.
5. Please don't interrupt us; we really mind when someone breaks our train of thought.

6. My ___mind___ is made up; I want to switch my major from accounting to marketing.
7. Don't ___mind___ him; he always snores in public.
8. "That toy is ___mine___," whined Tim, "and I *do* ___mind___ if you take it!"

ESL TIP
Many ESL students need vocabulary-development work, consider independent study assignments focusing on prefixes, roots, and suffixes. Also refer them to *ESL Corner* on the *Grassroots* Student Website for resources online.

Past/Passed

1. ***Past* is that which has already occurred; it is over with.**

   His *past* work has been satisfactory.

   Never let the *past* interfere with your hopes for the future.

2. ***Passed* is the past tense of the verb *to pass.***

   She *passed* by and nodded hello.

PRACTICE 10

Fill in *past* or *passed.*

1. He asked for the butter, but I absentmindedly ___passed___ him the mayonnaise.
2. Forget about failures in the ___past___ and look forward to success in the future.
3. The police car caught up to the truck that had ___passed___ every other car on the road.
4. I have ___passed___ this same corner every Saturday morning for a year.
5. Wasn't that woman who just ___passed___ us on a motorcycle your Aunt Sally?
6. In the ___past___, Frieda and Carolyn used to talk on the phone once a week.
7. Your ___past___ attendance record was perfect.
8. Don knew he had ___passed___ the test, but he had never received such a high grade in the ___past___.

Quiet/Quit/Quite

1. ***Quiet* means "silent, still."**

   The woods are *quiet* tonight.

2. ***Quit* means "to give up" or "to stop doing something."**

   Last year, I *quit* smoking.

3. ***Quite* means "very" or "exactly."**

   She was *quite* tired after playing soccer for two hours.

   That's not *quite* right.

PRACTICE 11

Fill in *quiet, quit,* or *quite.*

1. When it comes to expressing her feelings, Tonya is ___quite___ vocal.
2. I can't concentrate when my apartment is too ___quiet___.
3. Selling belly chains can be ___quite___ amusing.
4. Please be ___quiet___; I'm trying to listen to the news.

5. If she ___quits___ now, she will risk losing her vacation pay.
6. Dwight asked the crew to be absolutely ___quiet___ while the magicians performed.
7. Don't ___quit___ when the going gets rough; just increase your efforts and succeed.
8. I have the general idea, but I don't ___quite___ understand all the details.
9. This usually ___quiet___ library is now ___quite___ noisy.
10. She ___quit___ whistling when people in the line began to stare at her.

Rise/Raise

1. ***Rise* means "to get up by one's own power." The past tense of *rise* is *rose.* The past participle of *rise* is *risen.***

   The sun *rises* at 6 a.m.

   Daniel *rose* early yesterday.

   He *has risen* from the table.

2. ***Raise* means "to lift an object" or "to grow or increase." The past tense of *raise* is *raised.* The past participle of *raise* is *raised.***

   Raise your right hand.

   She *raised* the banner over her head.

   We *have raised* $1,000.

PRACTICE 12

Fill in forms of *rise* or *raise.*

1. When the moon ___rises___, we'll be able to see the path better.
2. During the meeting, she ___raised___ the possibility of a strike.
3. The jet ___rose___ off the runway and roared into the clouds.
4. Bud would like to ___rise___ early, but usually he wakes, turns over, and goes back to sleep.
5. Can you ___raise___ corn in this soil?
6. He couldn't ___rise___ from his chair because of the chewing gum stuck to his pants.
7. My boss has unexpectedly ___raised___ my salary.
8. I felt foolish when I accidentally ___raised___ my voice in the quiet concert hall.
9. The loaves of homemade bread have ___risen___.
10. He ___rose___ to his feet and shuffled out the door.

Sit/Set

TEACHING TIP
Students who speak certain regional or ethnic dialects are more likely to confuse words that they pronounce incorrectly (e.g., in the South, *sit* may be pronounced "set").

1. ***Sit* means "to seat oneself." The past tense of *sit* is *sat.* The past participle of *sit* is *sat.***

   Sit up straight!

   He *sat* down on the porch and fell asleep.

   She has *sat* reading that book all day.

2. *Set* means "to place" or "to put something down." The past tense of *set* is *set*. The past participle of *set* is *set*.

Don't *set* your books on the dining room table.

She *set* the package down and walked off without it.

He had *set* the pot on the stove.

PRACTICE 13

Fill in forms of *sit* or *set*.

1. Marcy ___set___ her glasses on the seat next to her.
2. Please ___sit___ there; the dentist will see you in ten minutes.
3. ___Set___ the cans of paint in the corner, please.
4. My grandfather always ___sits/sat___ in that overstuffed, red-and-blue plaid chair.
5. Please ___set___ that box of clothes by the door.
6. ___Sit___ down, and let me ___set___ this Hawaiian feast before you.
7. I would have ___set___ your bracelet on the counter, but I was afraid someone might walk off with it.
8. We have always ___sat___ in the first row, but tonight I want to ___sit___ at the back of the auditorium.

Suppose/Supposed

1. *Suppose* means "to assume" or "to guess." The past tense of *suppose* is *supposed*. The past participle of *suppose* is *supposed*.

Brad *supposes* that the teacher will give him an *A*.

We all *supposed* she would win first prize.

I had *supposed* Dan would win.

2. *Supposed* means "should have"; it is followed by *to*.

He is *supposed* to meet us after class.

You were *supposed* to wash and wax the car.

REMEMBER: When you mean *ought* or *should*, always use the *-ed* ending—*supposed*.

PRACTICE 14

Fill in *suppose* or *supposed*.

1. How do you ___suppose___ he will get himself out of this mess?
2. My father-in-law was ___supposed___ to arrive last night.
3. I ___suppose___ I'll find my car keys in my other pants.
4. Why do you ___suppose___ that cereal is so expensive?
5. You are not ___supposed___ to open the presents until your birthday.
6. Diane was ___supposed___ to check the bus schedule.

7. Where do you ___suppose___ he bought that gold lamé shirt?
8. What are we ___supposed___ to do with these three-by-five-inch cards?
9. Frank ___supposed___ that Meredith would meet him for dinner.
10. I ___suppose___ Ron is willing to shovel the snow this time.

Their/There/They're

TEACHING TIP
For fresh course ideas, links, and resources, explore the *Grassroots* Instructor Website—in particular, *Creative Classroom Links* (see Language Humor, English in the Real World, and Vocabulary activities), *Grammar and Writing Links*, and *ESL Resources for Writing Instructors.*

1. ***Their* is a possessive pronoun and shows ownership.**

   They couldn't find *their* wigs. *Their* children are charming.

2. ***There* indicates a location.**

   I wouldn't go *there* again. Put the lumber down *there*.

3. ***There* is also a way of introducing a thought.**

   There is a fly in my soup.

   There are two ways to approach this problem.

4. ***They're* is a contraction: *they* + *are* = *they're*. If you cannot substitute *they are* in the sentence, you cannot use *they're*.**

   They're the best poems I have read in a long time.

   If *they're* coming, count me in.

PRACTICE 15

Fill in *their, there,* or *they're.*

1. If you move over ___there___, I can get everyone into the picture.
2. ___There___ are three ways to mix paint, all of which are messy.
3. If ___they're___ here, we can set out the food.
4. That is ___their___ hot air balloon way up ___there___.
5. ___They're___ preparing for a hot, sticky summer.
6. Is ___there___ a faster route to Topeka?
7. ___They're___ never on time when it comes to paying ___their___ cell phone bills.
8. ___Their___ products contain no sugar and no preservatives.
9. Is ___there___ a wrench in the toolbox?
10. Because ___they're___ so quiet, I suppose ___they're___ asleep.

Then/Than

1. ***Then* means "next" or "at that time."**

   First, we went to the theater, and *then* we went for pizza.

   I was a heavyweight boxer *then*.

2. ***Than* is used in a comparison.**

   She is a better student *than* I.

PRACTICE 16

Fill in *then* or *than.*

1. Carlos works harder ___than___ anyone else in this office.
2. San Francisco has colder winters ___than___ San Diego.
3. Get your first paycheck; ___then___ think about moving into your own apartment.
4. It's often better to forgive someone ___than___ to carry a grudge.
5. If you receive straight *A*'s this semester, will you ___then___ apply for a scholarship?
6. You asked me a question and ___then___ interrupted me before I could answer.
7. This red convertible gets more miles to the gallon ___than___ any other car on the lot.
8. Now I'm ready for marriage; ___then___, I was confused.

Threw/Through

1. ***Threw* is the past tense of the verb *to throw.***

   Charleen *threw* the ball into the bleachers.

2. ***Through* means "in one side and out the other" or "finished."**

   He burst *through* the front door laughing.

   If you are *through* eating, we can leave.

PRACTICE 17

Fill in *threw* or *through.*

1. I went ___through___ my notes, but I couldn't find any reference to Guatemala.
2. He ___threw___ the pillow on the floor and plopped down in front of the television.
3. Gail ___threw___ her raincoat over her head and ran out into the storm.
4. You go ___through___ that door to get to the dean's office.
5. If you are ___through___ with that reference material, I would like to take a look at it.
6. We can always see ___through___ their tricks.

To/Too/Two

1. ***To* means "toward."**

   We are going *to* the stadium.

2. ***To* can also be combined with a verb to form an infinitive.**

   Where do you want *to go* for lunch?

3. ***Too* means "also" or "very."**

   Roberto is going to the theater *too.* They were *too* bored to stay awake.

4. ***Two* is the number 2.**

   Ms. Palmer will teach *two* new accounting courses this term.

PRACTICE 18

Fill in *to, too,* or *two.*

1. If you want __to__ enroll in college this fall, you will need __two__ letters of recommendation.
2. It will be __too__ awkward __to__ leave the dinner before the dessert is served.
3. He likes __to__ sing at parties __too__ .
4. It's __too__ early __to__ go __to__ the theater.
5. That dance step may be __too__ advanced for me right now.
6. Belkys and I have __to__ design __two__ outfits by Friday if we want __to__ enter the fashion competition.
7. We traveled __to__ the Grand Canyon __to__ try white-water rafting.
8. It's __too__ much trouble to make my own salad dressing.
9. She __too__ likes __to__ watch professional wrestling.
10. We saw __two__ undercover agents talking quietly __to__ the bartender.

Use/Used

1. ***Use* means "to make use of." The past tense of *use* is *used.* The past participle of *use* is *used.***

   Why do you *use* a Palm Pilot?

   He *used* the wrong paint in the bathroom.

   I have *used* that brand of toothpaste myself.

2. ***Used* means "in the habit of" or "accustomed"; it is followed by *to.***

   I am not *used to* getting up at 4 a.m. They got *used to* the good life.

REMEMBER: When you mean *in the habit of* or *accustomed,* always use the *-ed* ending—*used.*

PRACTICE 19

Fill in *use* or *used.*

1. Terry is __used__ to long bus rides.
2. It may take a few days to get __used__ to this high altitude.
3. Do you know how to __use__ a digital camera?
4. Vera hopes to get __used__ to her grumpy father-in-law.
5. Carlotta and Roland still __use__ the laundromat on the corner.
6. We __used__ the self-service pump; the gas was cheaper.
7. Feel free to __use__ my telephone if you need to make a call.
8. You'll get __used__ to it.
9. My grandmother does not __use__ her e-mail account because she has never gotten __used__ to it.
10. Never get __used__ to failure; always expect success.

Weather/Whether

1. ***Weather* refers to atmospheric conditions.**

   In June, the *weather* in Spain is lovely.

2. ***Whether* implies a question.**

   Whether you pass is up to you.

PRACTICE 20

Fill in *weather* or *whether.*

1. Rainy weather makes me lazy.
2. Be sure to tell the employment agency whether you plan to take the job.
3. You never know whether Celia will be happy or sad.
4. Good weather always brings joggers to the park.
5. Flopsy didn't know whether to eat the carrot or the lettuce first.
6. Please check to see whether the printer needs a new ink cartridge.
7. The real estate agent must know by 10 a.m. whether you intend to rent the house.
8. Whether the weather cooperates or not, we're going to the beach.

Where/Were/We're

1. ***Where* implies place or location.**

   Where have you been all day? Home is *where* you hang your hat.

2. ***Were* is the past tense of *are*.**

   We *were* on our way when the hurricane hit.

3. ***We're* is a contraction: *we* + *are* = *we're*. If you cannot substitute *we are* in the sentence, you cannot use *we're*.**

   We're going to leave now. Because *we're* in the city, let's go to the galleries.

PRACTICE 21

Fill in *where, were,* or *we're.*

1. The desk was emptied, but we're not sure who did it.
2. Where did you put the remote control?
3. Ted and Gloria were childhood sweethearts.
4. When you were in South America, where did your poodles stay?
5. Virginia is not where I was born.
6. The librarians were very helpful in showing us where to find the latest information.
7. Were you surprised to learn that we're commercial fishermen?

8. The clouds ___were___ blocking the sun in exactly the spot ___where___ we ___were___ sitting.
9. Everyone needs a peaceful hideaway, a place ___where___ he or she can be absolutely alone.
10. ___Where___ ___we're___ going, sir, is a question ___we're___ not about to answer.

Whose/Who's

1. *Whose* implies ownership and possession.

Whose term paper is that?

2. *Who's* is a contraction of *who is* or *who has*. If you cannot substitute *who is* or *who has*, you cannot use *who's*.

Who's knocking at the window?

Who's seen my new felt hat with the green bows?

PRACTICE 22

Fill in *whose* or *who's*.

1. ___Who's___ ready for an adventure?
2. ___Whose___ CDs are scattered all over the floor?
3. We found a puppy in the vacant lot, but we don't know ___whose___ it is.
4. ___Who's___ that playing the saxophone?
5. He's a physician ___whose___ diagnosis can be trusted.
6. Grace admires the late Marian Anderson, ___whose___ singing always moved her.
7. I'm not sure ___who's___ coming and ___who's___ not.
8. ___Who's___ been eating all the chocolate chip cookies?

Your/You're

1. *Your* is a possessive and shows ownership.

Your knowledge is astonishing!

2. *You're* is a contraction: *you* + *are* = *you're*. If you cannot substitute *you are* in the sentence, you cannot use *you're*.

You're the nicest person I know.

PRACTICE 23

Fill in *your* or *you're*.

1. Is that ___your___ iPod or mine?
2. If ___you're___ tired, take a nap.
3. Does ___your___ daughter like her new telescope?
4. I hope ___your___ teammates haven't forgotten the code words.
5. If ___you're___ in a rush, we can mail ___your___ scarves to you.

6. ___Your___ foreman was just transferred.
7. Please keep ___your___ Saint Bernard out of my rose garden.
8. ___You're___ in charge of ___your___ finances from now on.
9. When ___you're___ optimistic about life, everything seems to go right.
10. Let me have ___your___ order by Thursday; if it's late, ___you're___ not likely to receive the merchandise in time for the holidays.

PRACTICE 24 WRITING ASSIGNMENT

Look back through this chapter and make a list of the look-alikes that most confuse you. List at least five pairs or clusters of words. Then use them all correctly in a paper about a problem on your campus or in your neighborhood (such as a lack of public parks or playgrounds, too much drug or alcohol use, or a gulf between computer haves and have-nots). Try to use every word on your look-alikes list and proofread to make sure you have spelled everything correctly.

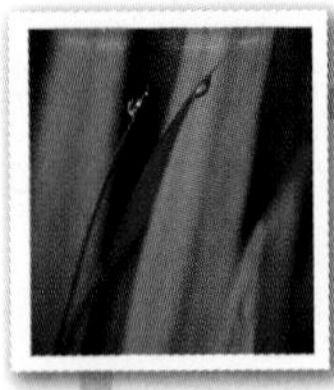

CHAPTER HIGHLIGHTS

Some words look and sound alike. Below are a few of them:

- **it's/its**

  It's the neatest room I ever saw.
  Everything is in *its* place.

- **their/they're/there**

  They found *their* work easy.
  They're the best actors I have ever seen.
  Put the lumber down *there.*

- **then/than**

  I was a heavyweight boxer *then.*
  He is a better cook *than* I.

- **to/too/two**

  We are going *to* the stadium.
  No one is *too* old to learn.
  I bought *two* hats yesterday.

- **whose/who's**

  Whose Italian dictionary is this?
  I'm not sure *who's* leaving early.

- **your/you're**

  Is *your* aunt the famous mystery writer?
  You're due for a promotion and a big raise.

CHAPTER REVIEW

Proofread this essay for look-alike/sound-alike errors. Write your corrections above the lines.

TEACHING TIP
The Chapter Review and its intriguing subject—Wyclef Jean—make this an effective exercise to discuss in class and one about which students may wish to write. Additionally, this essay models the comparison/contrast pattern.

Rapper with a Difference

(1) If ~~you're~~ your concept of hip-hop music is gang fights, drugs, the fast life, and negative views of women, ~~than~~ then perhaps you haven't heard of Wyclef Jean. (2) Like many rappers, Jean is committed to making music with powerful lyrics and driving rhythms. (3) However, this Haitian-born former Fugee sends a very different message and lives a ~~quiter~~ quieter lifestyle than many hip-hop artists do.

(4) Unlike some hip-hop music—named "gangsta rap" for ~~it's~~ its glorification of violence—Jean's songs celebrate nonviolence and understanding. (5) For example, in his fourth solo album, *The Preacher's Son*, Jean shares his vision of a peaceful world ~~were~~ where everyone gets along. (6) He believes that if people can ~~set~~ sit and talk, they can work ~~though~~ through almost anything. (7) Wyclef pleads for an end to dangerous feuds between rappers, such as the clashes between 50 Cent and Ja Rule, Jay-Z and Nas, and the ~~passed~~ past rivalry, kept alive in music, between Tupac Shakur and Notorious B.I.G., both gunned down in ~~there~~ their prime.

(8) Jean also differs from other rappers in his calm lifestyle. (9) While many hip-hop celebrities live the high life, traveling with bodyguards and a posse of

Activist Wyclef Jean in concert
©2004 Getty Images.

companions, the down-to-earth Jean insists on strolling the streets by himself. (10) He says he does not want to become disconnected from reality ~~buy~~ by cutting himself off from it. (11) So ~~its~~ it's not unusual to see Jean standing on a street corner talking with a homeless person or bonding with a young thug who tried to rob him moments before.

(12) Now Jean is ~~been~~ being seen as a role model by a new generation of hip-hop artists and fans. (13) One of his passions is Clef's Kids, an after-school music program, for music is a vehicle to his higher goal of changing the world. (14) Jean's preacher father, now deceased, ~~use~~ used to urge him to study theology, ~~too~~ to which Jean replied, "I am just a messenger in a different way."

EXPLORING ONLINE

TEACHING TIP
More practice and assessment are available in the *Grassroots* Test Bank; linked ACE tests on the *Grassroots* student website; *WriteSpace for Grassroots*; and at the Exploring Online links in this chapter.

<http://www.ccc.commnet.edu/cgi-shl/quiz.pl/spelling_add1.htm> Interactive quiz: Choose the correctly spelled word.

<http://owl.english.purdue.edu/handouts/interact/g_spelhomoEX1.html> Interactive quiz: Choose the correctly spelled word.

<http://a4esl.org/q/h/homonyms.html> Practice sound-alikes, like *night/knight*, that may confuse ESL students.

<http://college.hmco.com/devenglish/> Visit the *Grassroots* 8/e Student Website for more exercises and quizzes.

WRITING ASSIGNMENTS

As you complete each writing assignment, remember to perform these steps:

- Write a clear, complete topic sentence.
- Use freewriting, brainstorming, or clustering to generate ideas for the body of your paragraph, essay, letter, or review.
- Arrange your best ideas in a plan.
- Revise for support, unity, coherence, and exact language.
- Proofread for grammar, punctuation, and spelling errors.

Writing Assignment 1: *Take a stand.* Some experts believe that teaching children to play an instrument and to perform in a band or orchestra provides the young people with valuable life skills. For example, experts claim that practicing an instrument teaches a child discipline and that playing in a band teaches him or her team skills. Write a paper in which you take a stand for or against having a strong music program in your local schools. Present at least three reasons why each child should have the opportunity to learn an instrument—or three reasons why this would be a waste of time. Don't let spelling errors weaken your writing.

Writing Assignment 2: *Solve a problem.* You have identified what you consider to be a problem in your place of employment. When you go to your supervisor, you are asked to write up your concerns and to suggest a solution. Begin first by describing the problem and then by giving background information, including what you suspect are the causes of the problem. Then give suggestions for solving it. End with some guidelines for evaluating the success of the changes. In your concluding sentence, thank your supervisor for his or her consideration of your letter. Don't let typos or mistaken look-alikes/sound-alikes detract from your ideas. Proofread for accurate spelling!

Writing Assignment 3: *Review a movie.* Your college newspaper has asked you to review a movie. Pick a popular film that you especially liked or disliked. In your first sentence, name the film and state whether or not you recommend it. Explain your evaluation by discussing two or three specific reasons for your reactions to the picture. Describe as much of the film as is necessary to make your point, but do not retell the plot. Proofread for accurate spelling.

Writing Assignment 4: *Describe a family custom.* Most families have customs that they perform together. These customs often help strengthen the bond that the members of the family feel toward each other. A custom might be eating Sunday dinner together, going to religious services, celebrating holidays in a special way, or even holding a family council to discuss difficulties and concerns. Write about a custom in your family that is especially meaningful. Of what value has this custom been to you or other members of the family? Proofread for accurate spelling.

REVIEW

Proofreading

The following essay contains a number of spelling and look-alike/sound-alike errors. First, underline the misspelled or misused words. Then write each correctly spelled word above the line. (You should find twenty-eight errors.)

Nature's Weed Whackers

(1) If you raise goats mostly for milk and wool, you might be intrested [interested] in this new idea. (2) Your goats can earn a liveing [living] just buy [by] eating! (3) Parks, citys, [cities,] and other businesses are now using goats in three seperate [separate] but similer [similar] ways. (4) Goats are reduceing [reducing] forest fires, clearing overgrown feilds, [fields,] and protecting native plants—all threw [through] eating.

(5) Goats like nothing better then [than] chomping on tons of weeds and branchs. [branches.] (6) They are lawnmowers with legs, and, unlike human workers, they don't mind thorns or poisonous plants. (7) They scale steep hills easily an [and] get into places were [where] mowers can't go. (8) They work without the noise of chain saws. (9) Finaly, [Finally,] goats fertilize the land as they work.

(10) When goats reduce the vegetation in an area, they greatly reduce the intensity of fires. (11) If grasses are three feet tall, they create a fifteen-foot-high fire wall that moves at fifteen miles an hour. (12) If grasses are only too inchs [two inches] tall, they create a one-foot fire wall that moves at three miles an hour.

(13) Goats have been hired to eat foriegn [foreign] weeds and plants that have no natural enemys. [enemies.] (14) These plants, which were brought from other countrys, [countries,] are completely takeing [taking] over the native plants of some areas. (15) The use of goats avoids the nesessity [necessity] for using poisonous herbicides or for cuting [cutting] and triming [trimming] by hand.

(16) However, unless goats are managed carefuly, [carefully] they can turn the thickest forest or countryside into a desert. (17) If you accept this importent [important] new work for youre [your] goats, you must prevent them from purforming [performing] their job to [too] well!

WRITERS' WORKSHOP

Examine Positive (or Negative) Values

One good way to develop a paragraph or essay is by supporting the topic sentence or the thesis statement with three points. A student uses this approach in the following essay. In your group or class, read her work, aloud if possible.

Villa Avenue

(1) The values I learned growing up on Villa Avenue in the Bronx have guided me through thirty-five years and three children. Villa Avenue taught me the importance of having a friendly environment, playing together, and helping people.

(2) Villa Avenue was a three-block, friendly environment. I grew up on the middle block. The other ones were called "up the block" and "down the block." Mary's Candy Store was up the block. It had a candy counter and soda fountain on the left and on the right a jukebox that played three songs for twenty-five cents. My friends and I would buy candy, hang out, and listen to the Beatles and other music of the sixties. A little down from Mary's on the corner was Joey's Deli. When you walked into Joey's, different aromas would welcome you to a world of Italian delicacies. Fresh mozzarella in water always sat on the counter, with salami, pepperoni, and imported provolone cheese hanging above. On Sundays at Joey's, my father would buy us a black-and-white cookie for a weekly treat.

(3) On Villa Avenue, everyone helped everyone else. Everybody's doors were open, so if I had to go to the bathroom or needed a drink of water, I could go to a dozen different apartments. If my parents had to go somewhere, they would leave me with a friend. When people on the block got sick, others went to the store for them, cleaned for them, watched their kids, and made sure they had food to eat. If someone died, everyone mourned and pitched in to help with arrangements. When I reflect on those days, I realize that the way the mothers looked out for each other's children is like your modern-day play group. The difference is that our play area was "the block."

(4) The whole street was our playground. We would play curb ball at the intersection. One corner was home plate, and the other ones were the bases. Down the block where the street was wide, we would play Johnny

on the Pony with ten to fifteen kids. On summer nights, it was kick the can or hide and seek. Summer days we spent under an open fire hydrant. Everyone would be in the water, including moms and dads. Sometimes the teenagers would go to my Uncle Angelo's house and get a wine barrel to put over the hydrant. With the top and bottom of the barrel off, the water would shoot twenty to thirty feet in the air and come down on us like a waterfall.

Loretta M. Carney, student

1. How effective is Loretta Carney's essay?

   __Y__ Clear main idea? __Y__ Good supporting details?

   __Y/N__ Logical organization? (see #3 below) __N__ Effective conclusion?

2. What is the main idea of the essay? Can you find the thesis statement, one sentence that states this main idea? Sentence 2
3. The writer states that Villa Avenue taught her three values. What are they? Are these clearly explained in paragraphs 2, 3, and 4? Are they discussed in the same order in which the thesis statement presents them? If not, what change would you suggest? No, change thesis to match body or vice versa: friendliness, playfulness, helpfulness.
4. Does this essay *conclude* or just stop? What suggestions would you make to the writer for a more effective conclusion? Add a conclusion.
5. Proofread Carney's essay. Do you see any error patterns that she should watch out for? No

Writing and Revising Ideas

1. Describe a place or person that taught you positive (or negative) values.
2. Do places like Villa Avenue exist anymore? Explain why you do or do not think so.

See Chapter 5 for help with planning and writing. You might wish to present your topic with three supporting points, the way Loretta Carney does. As you revise, pay close attention to writing a good thesis sentence and supporting paragraphs that contain clear, detailed explanations.

UNIT 9

Reading Selections and Quotation Bank

Unit 9 contains three parts:

- **Effective Reading: Strategies for the Writer**
  This introduction to the readings section gives tips on how to get the most out of your reading.
- **The Readings**
  Here you will find twenty readings on a range of interesting subjects. Discussion questions and writing assignments follow each reading.
- **Quotation Bank**
  This section contains seventy-four brief quotations for you to read and enjoy, be inspired by, and use in your writing.

Reading Selections

Effective Reading Strategies for the Writer

The reading selections that follow were chosen to interest you, inspire you, and make you think. Many deal with issues you face at college, at work, or at home. Your instructor may ask you to read a selection and be prepared to discuss it in class or to write a composition or journal entry about it. The more carefully you read these selections, the better you will be able to think, talk, and write about them. Below are eight strategies that can help you become a more active and effective reader.

1. **Preview the reading selection.** Before you begin to read, scan the whole article to get a sense of the author's main idea and supporting points. First read the title, headnote, and any subtitles; next, quickly read the first and last paragraphs. This should give you a fairly clear idea of the author's subject and point of view. Finally, skim the whole selection, looking for the main supporting ideas. Previewing will increase your enjoyment and understanding as you read.

2. **Underline important ideas.** It is easy to forget what you have read, even though you have recently read it. Underlining or highlighting what you consider the main ideas will help you later to remember and discuss what you have read. Some students number the main points in order to understand the development of the author's ideas.

3. **Write your reactions in the margins.** If you strongly agree or disagree with an idea, write *yes* or *no* next to it. Record other questions and comments also, as if you were having a conversation with the author. Writing assignments will often ask you to respond to a particular idea or situation in a selection. Having already noted your reactions in the margins will help you focus your thinking and your writing.

4. **Prepare questions.** You will occasionally come across material that you cannot follow. Reread the passage. If you still have questions, place a question mark in the margin to remind you to ask a classmate or the instructor for an explanation.

5. **Circle unfamiliar words.** If you come across a new word that makes it difficult to follow what the author is saying, look it up immediately, jot the definition in the margin, and go back to reading. If, however, you can sense the meaning from the context—how the word fits the sentence—just circle it and, when you have finished the selection, consult a dictionary.

6. **Note effective or powerful writing.** If a particular line strikes you as especially important or moving, underline or highlight it. You may wish later to quote it in your written assignment. Be selective, however, in what you mark. *Too much* annotation can make it hard to focus on what is important when you discuss the selection in class or write about it.

7. **Vary your pace.** Some selections can be read quickly because you already know a great deal about the subject or because you find the material simple and direct. Other selections may require you to read slowly, pausing between sentences. Guard against the tendency to skim when the going gets tough: more difficult material will usually reward your extra time and attention.

8. **Reread.** If you expect to discuss or write about a selection, one reading is usually not enough. Budget your time so you will be able to give the selection a second or third reading. You will be amazed at how much more you can get

from the selection as you reread. You may understand ideas that were unclear the first time around. In addition, you may notice significant new points and details: perhaps you will change your mind about ideas you originally agreed or disagreed with. Rereading will help you discuss and write more intelligently and will increase your reading enjoyment.

The following essay has been marked by a student. Your own responses to this essay would, of course, be different. Examining how this essay was annotated may help you annotate other selections in this book and read more effectively in your other courses.

Like painting by numbers?

Needed: Teaching Peace Literacy by Numbers

COLMAN MCCARTHY

Catchy first sentence.

mired = stuck
sinkhole = a pit in the ground

Imagine you knew of a faraway country where citizens insisted 2 + 2 = 9 or 10 x 10 = 6. This was a nation of otherwise intelligent people recognized globally for their achievements in everything from politics to athletics. It's just that nearly everyone was mired in a deep sinkhole of ignorance about math.

This "country" is a very crazy place!

Social costs were large. Taxes couldn't be collected because few could fill in the forms with correct addition or subtraction, and no one at the IRS could tell the difference. Workers never knew the amounts of their next paychecks. At sporting events, winners and losers were never known because the score couldn't be kept.

eccentrics = people who act strangely
reformers = people who work for change
Where is this essay going?

When you inquired, you were told math wasn't taught in the schools. A few citizens picked it up on their own, but they were a minority and tended to be eccentrics anyway. Reformers were rare. No politicians ever ran for office on a pledge to get math courses in schools. Teachers who tried to get across the idea that 2 + 2 = 4 were reported to the school board as radicals.

Main Idea
Yes! This is so true!
Wow, peace illiterates are like math illiterates. Strong comparison!

That's about where we are regarding the teaching of nonviolent conflict resolution and peacemaking. We don't know because we weren't taught: not us adults yesterday or our kids today. As a logical result, we are *peace illiterates*, all but helpless to deal with conflicts in families, schools, neighborhoods, or among governments in any way except the failed methods of fists, guns, armies, and threats.

effects of peace illiteracy

The effects of ignorance—peace illiteracy—is a land awash in violence. No social problem is deadlier or more costly. Most U.S. cities saw record rates of homicide in the 1980s and 1990s. A violent crime is committed every 17 seconds. The leading cause of injury among American women is being beaten by a man at home. The United States sells weapons to 142 of the planet's 180 governments. More than 100,000 weapons are brought into schools every day.

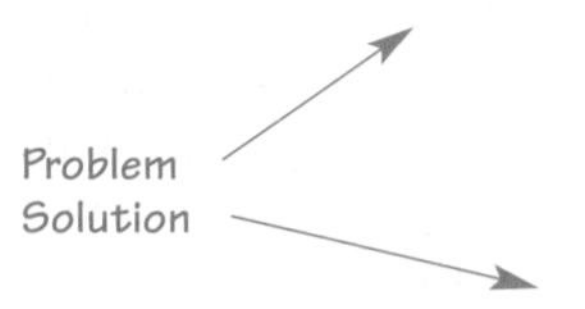

Those figures—and more—are routinely cited to describe the bind we are in. What's the solution?

Gee, another government office? I think parents have to teach peace skills at home.

I propose a modest but potentially powerful one: an office of peace education in the Department of Education. An assistant secretary for peace education would bring a federal presence where one is needed. Only a few of the nation's 78,000 elementary or 28,000 high schools have courses in conflict resolution, something that is needed at all grade levels.

Look up these peace foundations on Google!

An office of peace education would be a resource for school boards, administrators, teachers, students, and parents who request help either to begin or expand the necessary courses. One of its services would be curriculum development. It would coordinate the successful programs that are now working in all parts of the country, from those of the Oregon Peace Institute in many of that state's schools to teacher-training workshops in Florida, organized by the Peace Education Foundation of Miami.

He ties his idea back into the country without math...

Courses in peacemaking and conflict resolution are similar to those in, say, math. Starting in first grade, society prepares kids for some of life's problems that a knowledge of math might solve. We know, too, that children in first grade will go through life facing other problems: conflicts in human, social, and political relationships. Yet we have children in school for years and teach them little or nothing about nonviolent ways of settling these conflicts.

Very true.

And then we call the cops, social workers, psychiatrists, judges, jailers, and delinquency experts when homicides, spouse and child abuse, violent crime, and war continue. We graduate peace illiterates and wonder why violence engulfs us.

Author is so right describing problem, but is this the best solution? Not sure

A federal office of peace education, if allowed to be innovative, could be decisive in turning the country away from the vise of violence that grips it. It would affirm all those now in the schools teaching mediation, conflict resolution, theories in peacemaking, or alternatives to violence. It would be an overdue message from the Department of Education to those teachers of change: "You're onto something. Peacemaking can be taught."

Good conclusion

For Career Insight, Try Talking to Neighbors*

LAUREN MEHLER
(Provided by CollegeJournal.com)

Rutgers University student Lauren Mehler had no idea what she wanted to do when she graduated from college, so she decided to stop worrying and start taking action. This and ten other essays about her job search were published on *collegejournal.com*, sponsored by the *Wall Street Journal*. If you have doubts about your own career path, you might wish to try her pro-active approach. It worked. Mehler graduated in 2004 and found a good job.

"While I vegged out in front of a sitcom, that unease about my post-graduation life morphed into a two-ton weight."

Like many college students, I've been lost in a sea of tests, lectures, and assignments and had put my search for a career path on the back burner. How could I focus on my future when I could barely keep up with the present? I decided I needed a break from school and took a mini-vacation home on a recent weekend. While I vegged out in front of a sitcom, that vague fog of unease about my post-graduation life crept up and slowly morphed[1] into a two-ton weight. Then it dawned on me that I was literally next door to a previously untapped resource for career direction: my neighbors. 1

Over the past several months, I've been asking people I know about their careers in the hopes of finding one for myself. Since the start of my senior year, in fact, I've made it my personal mission to explore options by conducting "informational interviews" with just about anyone whose occupation piques[2] my interest. My hope is that I'll somehow get a clue about what to do after I graduate in May. 2

Abandoning the TV, I went to work. I had never called my neighbors just to talk to them. Our conversations have always been limited to: "Can we borrow an egg?" or "I'll watch him for a couple of hours." This was different, and I didn't know how to broach[3] the subject of an interview. I decided just to pick up the phone and call. I made some small talk, inquiring about their child's present grade and commenting on the bad weather. Then I made my pitch: "Would you 3

1. morphed:transformed
2. piques: provokes, arouses
3. broach: bring up

talk with me about your career?" I called other neighbors. Without making too much effort, I was invited to several homes to talk about careers, my future plans, 4
and the inevitable bumps in the road.

The Art World

Jennifer, 44, a freelance medical editor, invited me over for tea. While she makes a good living, what most interested me about her was her volunteer work. She sells tickets, answers phones, and does other hands-on work at the Whitney 5
Museum of Modern Art in New York City. She'd been an art history major in college, but marriage, among other life events, had changed her direction. Volunteering at the museum has allowed her to go back to something she loves.

To me, working in a museum had always seemed romantic; it seems to be about selecting artwork, guiding tour groups and scoring major coups in the art market. I study art history on my own and thought perhaps I could leverage[4] my knowledge into a museum career. Talking to Jennifer was a reality check. I was disheartened to hear that the art world involves an amazing amount of politick- 6
ing,[5] handshaking and bureaucracy[6] that sometimes runs counter to a museum's mission. And it seems that a love of art isn't enough; business knowledge is also essential. Hmm, business courses, anyone?

Still, Jennifer offered me a ray of hope. She explained that volunteering can help you get a foot in the door and try out a career without commitment. What's more, you can volunteer at any age. Granted, you can only do this when you have 7
another source of income. But it might be possible for me to intern part time and work part time after graduation so I could fully explore this or other fields. This was an option I hadn't considered.

The other valuable insight I gleaned from Jennifer was the need to be passionate about your work. She'd fallen into editing soon after graduation, but took to it quickly. She loves the challenge of deciphering[7] concepts she doesn't know much about and taking such new understandings home at the end of the day. I often worry about being bored in a career. Listening to Jen made one of my vague no- 8
tions more concrete: While her tasks remain the same—reading, making corrections—she stays excited because of the changing subject matter, which adds that needed "oomph."

The more I talk to people about their careers, the more I see that getting that 9
"oomph" from work is a necessity, not a fleeing hope.

The Government

My neighbor, Ron, 55, is an environmental engineer, and I didn't expect to relate to him at all because his field seemed too technical to me. But I instantly became interested when I learned he once worked for the state government, an 10
avenue I'd considered. Ron worked for the government primarily because it paid his way through graduate school. Do they still offer this benefit to government employees? If so, sign me up.

Tuition payments aside, Ron cautioned that people who like to make rapid decisions and work independently may not like government work. The pace of the work itself is slow, making the line at the state Division of Motor Vehicles look quick, he quipped. Ultimately, he left the job because of too much red tape. I was taken aback. I began to wonder whether I should nix government employers right off the bat. I'm impatient and waiting to get something done would be agonizing for me. Then I realized I was making a huge assumption about a career path I knew next to nothing about, so I resolved to do more research and talk to more people before making a decision. My assuming days are over.

---

4. leverage: use to gain an advantage
5. politicking: activities for the purpose of gaining power, career advancement, etc.
6. bureaucracy: maze of departments and red tape in an organization
7. deciphering: figuring out

Ron also told me he'd worked in Washington, D.C., for an environmental-consulting firm, living there part-time and commuting back to New Jersey to be with his wife. But the commute put too much stress on their relationship, and so he quit for another job closer to his home. I have so much trouble making decisions solely for me that I can barely fathom[8] evaluating the effect of a job decision on a relationship. No more looking at brides' magazines for the time being. 11

The Law

My final interview that weekend was with Debbie, 36, a lawyer with the New Jersey State Department's Division of Law. She defends the state against lawsuits over pensions. Initially, this didn't strike me as very exciting. But my parents have been pushing me toward law school, so I wanted to hear more about it. 12

Her work seemed clear-cut, until I learned the size of her caseload. Debbie had decided to work in the public sector partly because it required working fewer hours than at a private law firm and she wanted to have time for a family. Her caseload though is so large, she said, that she only has about three days to spend on each case and must work on weekends. I wonder if all the lawyers in her division work this hard. 13

Landing a government position in her field usually requires having an "in," which could be a networking referral or a prior position in government, she added. She'd found an internship with the state department. She was subsequently hired in the pension area, though there are dozens of offices for different legal specialties. Who knew there were so many types of attorneys? I decided that television definitely has narrowed my perceptions of what lawyers do in the real world. 14

Yet could any lawyer do her best work given Debbie's caseload? Debbie assured me that regardless of the hours, she loves her job. Since I expect to spend most of my waking hours at work, loving what I do is becoming essential to me. 15

A common theme that ran through each of my neighbors' stories is how their marriages have influenced their career decisions. Until very recently, I'd been thinking only of my own career aspirations. Now I see that having a spouse or children can affect my choices. I wonder if my friends with marriage plans have considered the future compromises they may have to make. I'm 21 years old; I don't want to compromise right now. I mulled over[9] this insight as much as I pondered Debbie's workload. 16

By the end of the weekend, I felt a lot less knowledgeable, but more determined to figure out the working world. So far, I've been brushing law aside, but I realized I don't know much about the field. Before I dismiss it altogether, I should know what I'm talking about. In fact, I need to think about my future career not only as it will fulfill my professional goals, but also as it will shape the other aspects of my life. For now, I'll take comfort in knowing I still have classes to attend and don't have to make all these decisions today.[10] 17

Discussion and Writing Questions

1. Can you identify with the author's "vague fog of unease about my post-graduation life" (paragraph 1)? What questions or worries do you have about your future career? Have you taken any steps to answer them?

2. Lauren Mehler's article explores an "untapped resource for career direction"—her neighbors. What examples does she present to develop her main idea? Choose one of Mehler's neighbors and explain what she learned from that person.

8. fathom: understand
9. mulled over: thought about carefully
10. After graduating and job hunting for six months, Lauren accepted a marketing position in Minneapolis.

3. The author decides that getting "oomph" from and even loving her work are very important (paragraphs 7 and 8). Do you agree? What aspects of the career you have chosen (or a career you are considering) would bring "oomph" into your life?
4. From your own or others' experiences, share examples of the ways that a spouse or children can affect one's career path. These effects might be negative, positive, or both.

Writing Assignments

1. Conduct an informational interview. Choose one person (or more) whose job interests you (a neighbor, co-worker, or college contact). Arrange a meeting, and come prepared with written questions and an open mind. What would you like to know about that person's career? Write up your findings in detail. (For advice, look up "conducting informational interviews" on Google or another search engine.)
2. Describe an activity that you engage in just because you love it. This might be singing full-blast while driving, playing chess in the park, or volunteering to read to children at the library. Try to capture in words exactly what you love about this activity and how it feeds your soul.
3. What is the best career advice you have ever received? Write a composition that begins by setting the scene, telling what this advice was, who gave it, and whether or not you welcomed it at the time. Then explain how this guidance has helped you.

Playing a Violin with Three Strings

JACK RIEMER

When Jack Riemer attended a concert by the famous violinist Itzhak Perlman, he and the rest of the audience felt lucky just to hear one of Perlman's dazzling musical performances. But then the unexpected happened. In this article for the *Houston Chronicle,* Riemer tells the story.

On November 18, 1995, Itzhak Perlman, the violinist, came on stage to give a concert at Avery Fisher Hall at Lincoln Center in New York City. Anyone who has ever been to a Perlman concert knows that getting on stage is no small achievement for him. 1

He was stricken with polio[1] as a child, and so he has braces on both legs and walks with the aid of two crutches. To see him walk across the stage one step at a time, painfully and slowly, is an unforgettable sight. He walks painfully, yet majestically,[2] until he reaches his chair. Then he sits down, slowly, puts his crutches on the floor, undoes the clasps on his legs, tucks one foot back and extends the other foot forward. Then he bends down and picks up the violin, puts it under his chin, nods to the conductor and proceeds to play. 2

By now, audience members are used to this ritual. They sit quietly while he makes his way across the stage to his chair. They remain reverently[3] silent while he undoes the clasps on his legs. They wait until he is ready to play. 3

But this time, something went wrong. Just as he finished the first few bars, one of the strings on his violin broke. We could hear it snap—it went off like gunfire 4

---

1. polio: a viral disease that disabled or killed many people until a polio vaccine was created in 1955
2. majestically: with greatness and dignity
3. reverently: with feelings of awe and respect

Itzhak Perlman in concert
AP/Wide World

across the room. There was no mistaking what that sound meant. There was no mistaking what he had to do. People who were there that night thought to themselves: "We figured that he would have to get up, put on the clasps again, pick up the crutches and limp his way off stage— to either find another violin or else find another string for this one."

"We could hear it snap—it went off like gunfire across the room. There was no mistaking what that sound meant."

5 But he didn't. Instead, he waited a moment, closed his eyes and then he played with such passion and such power and such purity as we had never heard before. Of course, anyone knows that it is impossible to play a symphonic[4] work with just three strings. I know that, and you know that, but that night Itzhak Perlman refused to know that. We could see him modulating,[5] changing, recomposing the piece in his head. At one point, it sounded like he was de-tuning the strings to get new sounds from them that they had never made before.

6 When he finished, there was an awesome silence in the room. And then people rose and cheered. There was an extraordinary outburst of applause from every corner of the auditorium. We were all on our feet, screaming and cheering, doing everything we could to show how much we appreciated what he had done.

7 He smiled, wiped the sweat from his brow, raised his bow to quiet us, and then he said, not boastfully, but in a quiet, pensive,[6] reverent tone, "You know, sometimes it is the artist's task to find out how much music he can still make with what he has left."

8 What a powerful line that is. It has stayed in my mind ever since I heard it. And who knows? Perhaps that is the definition of life—not just for artists but for all of us. Perhaps our task in this shaky, fast-changing, bewildering world in which we live is to make music, at first with all that we have, and then, when that is no longer possible, to make music with what we have left.

4. symphonic: meant for a large musical orchestra
5. modulating: adjusting or adapting
6. pensive: deeply thoughtful

Discussion and Writing Questions

1. The first three paragraphs vividly describe Perlman as he walks onto the stage, sits, and prepares to play. What words or details especially capture the process? Why do you think that the author devotes so many words to this description?

2. Why do you think the author compares the violin string's snapping to "gunfire" (paragraph 4)? What do the concert goers expect to happen next? Why are they so amazed when instead Perlman improvises—when he changes the music in his head to fit his new situation?

3. Can you draw any conclusions about Perlman's personality or character from the description of his physical appearance, actions, and words? What does this man seem to believe is important?

4. In paragraph 8, what do you think Riemer means when he writes that perhaps Perlman's words apply to all of us—that our task "is to make music, at first with all that we have, and then, when that is no longer possible, to make music with what we have left"? Does this relate to you or to anyone you know?

Writing Assignments

1. Sometimes things that go wrong can lead us down new—and better—paths. Itzhak Perlman, for example, gave one of his most amazing performances after a violin string broke. Write about someone who has turned a loss, an illness, or a disability into a strength.

2. Discuss a memorable musical concert or performance that you attended—any kind of music, any number of performers. Think of an opening that will capture your readers' attention, perhaps describing in detail, as Riemer does, how the performer(s) came onstage. Then try to capture in words what made the performance so unforgettable.

3. Write about a time when you (or someone else) had to improvise under pressure. Think of a situation that did not go as you had planned—during work, college, or leisure time. What happened, and what did you do in response? Would you behave differently today?

Mrs. Flowers

MAYA ANGELOU

Maya Angelou (born Marguerite Johnson) is one of America's best-loved poets and the author of *I Know Why the Caged Bird Sings.* In this book, her life story, she tells of being raped when she was eight years old. Her response to the traumatic experience was to stop speaking. In this selection, Angelou describes the woman who eventually threw her a "life line."

For nearly a year, I sopped around the house, the Store, the school and the church, like an old biscuit, dirty and inedible. Then I met, or rather got to know, the lady who threw me my first life line. 1

Mrs. Bertha Flowers was the aristocrat of Black Stamps. She had the grace of control to appear warm in the coldest weather, and on the Arkansas summer days it seemed she had a private breeze which swirled around, cooling her. She was thin without the taut[1] look of wiry people, and her printed voile[2] dresses and 2

1. taut: tight, tense
2. voile: a light, semi-sheer fabric

Girl in the Garden by Romare Bearden

Virginia Museum of Fine Arts, Richmond. Gift of Dr. Howard A. Parvan. Photo Katherine Wetzel © Virginia Museum of Fine Arts.

flowered hats were as right for her as denim overalls for a farmer. She was our side's answer to the richest white woman in town.

Her skin was a rich black that would have peeled like a plum if snagged, but 3
then no one would have thought of getting close enough to Mrs. Flowers to ruffle her dress, let alone snag her skin. She didn't encourage familiarity. She wore gloves too.

I don't think I ever saw Mrs. Flowers laugh, but she smiled often. A slow 4
widening of her thin black lips to show even, small white teeth, then the slow effortless closing. When she chose to smile on me, I always wanted to thank her. The action was so graceful and inclusively benign.[3]

She was one of the few gentlewomen I have ever known, and has remained 5
throughout my life the measure of what a human being can be. . . .

One summer afternoon, sweet-milk fresh in my memory, she stopped at the 6
Store to buy provisions. Another Negro woman of her health and age would have been expected to carry the paper sacks home in one hand but Momma said, "Sister Flowers, I'll send Bailey up to your house with these things."

She smiled that slow dragging smile, "Thank you, Mrs. Henderson. I'd prefer 7
Marguerite though." My name was beautiful when she said it. "I've been meaning to talk to her, anyway." They gave each other age-group looks.

Momma said, "Well, that's all right then. Sister, go and change your dress. You 8
going to Sister Flowers's." . . .

There was a little path beside the rocky road, and Mrs. Flowers walked in front 9
swinging her arms and picking her way over the stones.

She said, without turning her head, to me, "I hear you're doing very good 10
school work, Marguerite, but that it's all written. The teachers report that they have trouble getting you to talk in class." We passed the triangular farm on our left and the path widened to allow us to walk together. I hung back in the separate unasked and unanswerable questions.

3. benign: kind, gentle

11 “Come and walk along with me, Marguerite.” I couldn't have refused even if I wanted to. She pronounced my name so nicely. Or more correctly, she spoke each word with such clarity that I was certain a foreigner who didn't understand English could have understood her.

12 “Now no one is going to make you talk—possibly no one can. But bear in mind, language is man's way of communicating with his fellow man and it is language alone which separates him from the lower animals.” That was a totally new idea to me, and I would need time to think about it.

13 “Your grandmother says you read a lot. Every chance you get. That's good, but not good enough. Words mean more than what is set down on paper. It takes the human voice to infuse[4] them with the shades of deeper meaning.”

14 I memorized the part about the human voice infusing words. It seemed so valid and poetic.

15 She said she was going to give me some books and that I not only must read them. I must read them aloud. She suggested that I try to make a sentence sound in as many different ways as possible.

> ***“I was liked, and what a difference it made. I was respected not as Mrs. Henderson's grandchild or Bailey's sister but for just being Marguerite Johnson.”***

16 “I'll accept no excuse if you return a book to me that has been badly handled.” My imagination boggled at the punishment I would deserve if in fact I did abuse a book of Mrs. Flowers's. Death would be too kind and brief.

17 The odors in the house surprised me. Somehow I had never connected Mrs. Flowers with food or eating or any other common experience of common people. There must have been an outhouse, too, but my mind never recorded it.

18 The sweet scent of vanilla had met us as she opened the door.

19 ”I made tea cookies this morning. You see, I had planned to invite you for cookies and lemonade so we could have this little chat. The lemonade is in the icebox.”

20 It followed that Mrs. Flowers would have ice on an ordinary day, when most families in our town bought ice late on Saturdays only a few times during the summer to be used in the wooden ice-cream freezers.

21 She took the bags from me and disappeared through the kitchen door. I looked around the room that I had never in my wildest fantasies imagined I would see. Browned photographs leered or threatened from the walls and the white, freshly done curtains pushed against themselves and against the wind. I wanted to gobble up the room entire and take it to Bailey, who would help me analyze and enjoy it.

22 “Have a seat, Marguerite. Over there by the table.” She carried a platter covered with a tea towel. Although she warned that she hadn't tried her hand at baking sweets for some time, I was certain that like everything else about her the cookies would be perfect.

23 They were flat round wafers, slightly browned on the edges and butter-yellow in the center. With the cold lemonade they were sufficient for childhood's lifelong diet. Remembering my manners, I took nice little lady-like bites off the edges. She said she had made them expressly for me and that she had a few in the kitchen that I could take home to my brother. So I jammed one whole cake in my mouth and the rough crumbs scratched the insides of my jaws, and if I hadn't had to swallow, it would have been a dream come true.

24 As I ate she began the first of what we later called “my lessons in living.” She said that I must always be intolerant of ignorance but understanding of illiteracy. That some people, unable to go to school, were more educated and even more intelligent than college professors. She encouraged me to listen carefully to what country people called mother wit. That in those homely sayings was couched the collective[5] wisdom of generations.

25 When I finished the cookies she brushed off the table and brought a thick, small book from the bookcase. I had read *A Tale of Two Cities* and found it up to my

4. infuse: to fill or penetrate
5. collective: gathered from a group

standards as a romantic novel. She opened the first page and I heard poetry for the first time in my life.

"It was the best of times and the worst of times . . . " Her voice slid in and curved down through and over the words. She was nearly singing. I wanted to look at the pages. Were they the same that I had read? Or were there notes, music, lined on the pages, as in a hymn book? Her sounds began cascading[6] gently. I knew from listening to a thousand preachers that she was nearing the end of her reading, and I hadn't really heard, heard to understand, a single word. 26

"How do you like that?" 27

It occurred to me that she expected a response. The sweet vanilla flavor was still on my tongue and her reading was a wonder in my ears. I had to speak. 28

I said, "Yes ma'am." It was the least I could do, but it was the most also. 29

"There's one more thing. Take this book of poems and memorize one for me. Next time you pay me a visit, I want you to recite." 30

I have tried often to search behind the sophistication of years for the enchantment I so easily found in those gifts. The essence escapes but its aura[7] remains. To be allowed, no, invited, into the private lives of strangers, and to share their joys and fears, was a chance to exchange the Southern bitter wormwood[8] for . . . a hot cup of tea and milk with Oliver Twist.[9] 31

I was liked, and what a difference it made. I was respected not as Mrs. Henderson's grandchild or Bailey's sister but for just being Marguerite Johnson. 32

Childhood's logic never asks to be proved (all conclusions are absolute). I didn't question why Mrs. Flowers had singled me out for attention, nor did it occur to me that Momma might have asked her to give me a little talking to. All I cared about was that she had made tea cookies for *me* and read to *me* from her favorite book. It was enough to prove that she liked me. 33

Discussion and Writing Questions

1. Angelou vividly describes Mrs. Flowers' appearance and style (paragraphs 2–5). What kind of woman is Mrs. Flowers? What words and details convey this impression?

2. What strategies does Mrs. Flowers use to reach out to Marguerite?

3. What does Marguerite's first "lesson in living" include (paragraph 24)? Do you think such a lesson could really help a young person live better or differently?

4. In paragraph 31, the author speaks of her enchantment at receiving gifts from Mrs. Flowers. Just what gifts did Mrs. Flowers give her? Which do you consider the most important gift?

Writing Assignments

1. Has anyone ever thrown you a life line when you were in trouble? Describe the problem or hurt facing you and just what this person did to reach out. What "gifts" did he or she offer you (attention, advice, and so forth)? Were you able to receive them?

   If you prefer, write about a time when you helped someone else. What seemed to be weighing this person down? How were you able to help?

2. Mrs. Flowers read aloud so musically that Marguerite "heard poetry for the first time in [her] life." Has someone ever shared a love—of a sport, gardening,

6. cascading: falling like a waterfall
7. aura: a special quality or air around something or someone
8. wormwood: something harsh or embittering
9. Oliver Twist: a character from a novel by Charles Dickens

or history, for example—so strongly that you were changed? What happened and how were you changed?

3. Many people have trouble speaking up—in class, at social gatherings, even to one other person. Can you express your thoughts and feelings as freely as you would like in most situations? What opens you up, and what shuts you up?

One Man's Kids

DANIEL MEIER

A first-grade teacher describes his workday and reflects on his career—a career that crosses traditional gender boundaries. Daniel Meier raises questions for all of us to consider.

I teach first-graders. I live in a world of skinned knees, double-knotted shoelaces, riddles that I've heard a dozen times, stale birthday cakes, hurt feelings, wandering stories, and one lost shoe ("and if you don't find it my mother'll kill me"). My work is dominated by six-year-olds. 1

It's 10:45, the middle of snack, and I'm helping Emily open her milk carton. She has already tried the other end without success, and now there's so much paint and ink on the carton from her fingers that I'm not sure she should drink it at all. But I open it. Then I turn to help Scott clean up some milk he has just spilled onto Rebecca's whale crossword puzzle. 2

While I wipe my milk- and paint-covered hands, Jenny wants to know if I've seen that funny book about penguins that I read in class. As I hunt for it in a messy pile of books, Jason wants to know if there is a new seating arrangement for lunch tables. I find the book, turn to answer Jason, then face Maya, who is fast approaching with a new knock-knock joke. After what seems like the tenth "Who's there?" I laugh and Maya is pleased. 3

"In teaching, the inner rewards come from without."

Then Andrew wants to know how to spell "flukes"[1] for his crossword. As I get to "u," I give a hand signal for Sarah to take away the snack. But just as Sarah is almost out the door, two children complain that "we haven't even had ours yet." I stop the snack mid-flight, complying with their request for graham crackers. I then return to Andrew, noticing that he has put "flu" for 9 Down, rather than 9 Across. It's now 10:50. 4

My work is not traditional male work. It's not a singular[2] pursuit. There is not a large pile of paper to get through or one deal to transact. I don't have one area of expertise or knowledge. I don't have the singular power over language of a lawyer, the physical force of a construction worker, the command over fellow workers of a surgeon, the wheeling and dealing transactions of a businessman. My energy is not spent in pursuing, climbing, achieving, conquering, or cornering some goal or object. 5

My energy is spent in encouraging, supporting, consoling, and praising my children. In teaching, the inner rewards come from without. On any given day, quite apart from teaching reading and spelling, I bandage a cut, dry a tear, erase a frown, tape a torn doll, and locate a long-lost boot. The day is really won through matters of the heart. As my students groan, laugh, shudder, cry, exult,[3] and wonder, I do too. I have to be soft around the edges. 6

1. flukes: the two divided ends of a whale's tail; also, strokes of luck or random accidents
2. singular: related to one thing; also, exceptional
3. exult: rejoice

A few years ago, when I was interviewing for an elementary-school teaching position, every principal told me with confidence that, as a male, I had an advantage over female applicants because of the lack of male teachers. But in the next breath, they asked with a hint of suspicion why I chose to work with young children. I told them that I wanted to observe and contribute to the intellectual growth of a maturing mind. What I really felt like saying, but didn't, was that I loved helping a child learn to write her name for the first time, finding someone a new friend, or sharing in the hilarity of reading about Winnie the Pooh getting so stuck in a hole that only his head and rear show. 7

I gave that answer to those principals, who were mostly male, because I thought they wanted a "male" response. This meant talking about intellectual matters. If I had taken a different course and talked about my interest in helping children in their emotional development, it would have been seen as closer to a "female" answer. I even altered my language, not once mentioning the word "love" to describe what I do indeed love about teaching. My answer worked; every principal nodded approvingly. 8

Some of the principals also asked what I saw myself doing later in my career. They wanted to know if I eventually wanted to go into educational administration. Becoming a dean of students or a principal has never been one of my goals, but they seemed to expect me, as a male, to want to climb higher on the career stepladder. So I mentioned that, at some point, I would be interested in working with teachers as a curriculum coordinator. Again, they nodded approvingly. 9

If those principals had been female instead of male, I wonder whether their questions, and my answers, would have been different. My guess is that they would have been. 10

At other times, when I'm at a party or a dinner and tell someone that I teach young children, I've found that men and women respond differently. Most men ask about the subjects I teach and the courses I took in my training. Then, unless they bring up an issue such as merit pay, the conversation stops. Most women, on the other hand, begin the conversation on a more immediate and personal level. They say things like "those kids must love having a male teacher" or "that age is just wonderful, you must love it." Then, more often than not, they'll talk about their own kids or ask me specific questions about what I do. We're then off and talking shop. 11

Possibly, men would have more to say to me, and I to them, if my job had more of the trappings and benefits of more traditional male jobs. But my job has no bonuses or promotions. No complimentary box seats at the ball park. No cab fare home. No drinking buddies after work. No briefcase. No suit. (Ties get stuck in paint jars.) No power lunches. (I eat peanut butter and jelly, chips, milk, and cookies with the kids.) No taking clients out for cocktails. The only place I take my kids is to the playground. 12

Although I could have pursued a career in law or business, as several of my friends did, I chose teaching instead. My job has benefits all its own. I'm able to bake cookies without getting them stuck together as they cool, buy cheap sewing materials, take out splinters, and search just the right trash cans for useful odds and ends. I'm sometimes called "Daddy" and even "Mommy" by my students, and if there's ever a lull in the conversation at a dinner party, I can always ask those assembled if they've heard the latest riddle about why the turkey crossed the road. (He thought he was a chicken.) 13

Discussion and Writing Questions

1. What, besides reading, writing, and 'rithmetic, is Meier teaching his first graders?

2. Why do so few men teach in elementary schools? What reasons does the author seem to offer?

3. Meier confesses that during job interviews he "even altered [his] language" (paragraph 8). What does he mean? Why did he do that?
4. In paragraph 11, the author observes that outside of school "men and women respond differently" to him. In what ways? How does Meier account for the differences?

Writing Assignments

1. Write a letter to the school principal nominating Meier for Teacher of the Year, or nominate a teacher from your own school history. In either case, discuss what you think makes a good teacher.
2. Do you have any experience in a nontraditional role—perhaps in a club, on a team, or on a job? What prompted you to cross traditional boundaries? How did the experience differ from your expectations? Write about your experience. Conclude with a reflection on how the experience changed, or didn't change, your views on traditional roles.
3. Meier suggests that work, to be rewarding, must provide benefits other than status and salary. Agree or disagree, using examples from your own experience.

Another Road Hog with Too Much Oink

DAVE BARRY

Dave Barry writes a Pulitzer Prize–winning humor column that appears in more than 500 newspapers. The author of twenty-one books, he admits that not one contains useful information. In his spare time, Barry is a candidate for president of the United States; if elected, he promises to seek the death penalty for whoever made Americans install low-flow toilets. In this essay, he takes on America's love of gigantic sport utility vehicles (SUVs).

If there's one thing this nation needs, it's bigger cars. That's why I'm excited that Ford is coming out with a new mound o' metal that will offer consumers even more total road-squatting mass than the current leader in the humongous[1]-car category, the popular Chevrolet Suburban Subdivision—the first passenger automobile designed to be, right off the assembly line, visible from the Moon. 1

I don't know what the new Ford will be called. Probably something like the "Ford Untamed Wilderness Adventure." In the TV commercials, it will be shown splashing through rivers, charging up rocky mountainsides, swinging on vines, diving off cliffs, racing through the surf, and fighting giant sharks hundreds of feet beneath the ocean surface—all the daredevil things that cars do in Sport Utility Vehicle Commercial World, where nobody ever drives on an actual road. In fact, the interstate highways in Sport Utility Vehicle Commercial World, having been abandoned by humans, are teeming[2] with deer, squirrels, birds, and other wildlife species that have fled from the forest to avoid being run over by nature-seekers in multi-ton vehicles barreling through the underbrush at 50 miles per hour. 2

"In the real world, of course, nobody drives a sport utility vehicle in the forest, because the last thing you want is squirrels pooping on it."

In the real world, of course, nobody drives sport utility vehicles in the forest, because when you have paid upward of $40,000 for a transportation investment, 3

1. humongous: huge
2. teeming: filled

"We're not certain why they disappeared, but archeologists speculate that it may have had something to do with their size."

the last thing you want is squirrels pooping on it. No, if you want a practical "off-road" vehicle, you get yourself a 1973 American Motors Gremlin, which combines the advantage of not being worth worrying about with the advantage of being so ugly that poisonous snakes flee from it in terror.

In the real world, what people mainly do with their sport utility vehicles, as far as I can tell, is try to maneuver[3] them into and out of parking spaces. I base this statement on my local supermarket, where many of the upscale patrons drive Chevrolet Subdivisions. I've noticed that these people often purchase just a couple of items—maybe a bottle of diet water and a two-ounce package of low-fat dried carrot shreds—which they put into the back of their Subdivisions, which have approximately the same cargo capacity, in cubic feet, as Finland. This means there is plenty of room left over back there in case, on the way home, these people decide to pick up something else, such as a herd of bison. 4

Then comes the scary part: getting the Subdivision out of the parking space. This is a challenge, because the driver apparently cannot, while sitting in the driver's seat, see all the way to either end of the vehicle. I drive a compact car, and on a number of occasions I have found myself trapped behind a Subdivision backing directly toward me, its massive metal butt looming[4] high over my head, making me feel like a Tokyo pedestrian looking up at Godzilla.[5] 5

I've tried honking my horn, but the Subdivision drivers can't hear me, because they're always talking on cellular phones the size of Chiclets ("The Bigger Your Car, the Smaller Your Phone," that is their motto). I don't know who they're talking to. Maybe they're negotiating with their bison suppliers. Or maybe they're trying to contact somebody in the same area code as the rear ends of their cars, so they can find out what's going on back there. All I know is, I'm thinking of carrying marine flares, so I can fire them into the air as a warning to Subdivision drivers that they're about to run me over. Although frankly I'm not sure they'd care 6

3. maneuver: move skillfully
4. looming: appearing to be huge and towering
5. Godzilla: a fictional monster that menaced cities in Japanese films

if they did. A big reason why they bought a sport utility vehicle is "safety," in the sense of, "you, personally, will be safe, although every now and then you may have to clean the remains of other motorists out of your wheel wells."

Anyway, now we have the new Ford, which will be *even larger* than the Subdivision, which I imagine means it will have separate decks for the various classes of passengers, and possibly, way up in front by the hood ornament, Leonardo DiCaprio showing Kate Winslet[6] how to fly. I can't wait until one of these babies wheels into my supermarket parking lot. Other motorists and pedestrians will try to flee in terror, but they'll be sucked in by the Ford's powerful gravitational field and become stuck to its massive sides like so many refrigerator magnets. They won't be noticed, however, by the Ford's driver, who will be busy whacking at the side of his or her head, trying to dislodge[7] his or her new cell phone, which is the size of a single grain of rice and has fallen deep into his or her ear canal. 7

And it will not stop there. This is America, darn it, and Chevrolet is not about to just sit by and watch Ford walk away with the coveted title of Least Sane Motor Vehicle. No, cars will keep getting bigger: I see a time, not too far from now, when upscale suburbanites will haul their overdue movies back to the video-rental store in full-size, 18-wheel tractor-trailers with names like The Vagabond.[8] It will be a proud time for all Americans, a time for us to cheer for our country. We should cheer loud, because we'll be hard to hear, inside the wheel wells. 8

Discussion and Writing Questions

1. What is Barry's point of view about huge sport utility vehicles (paragraph 1)? What lines tell you this? Barry often exaggerates to get a laugh and to make a point. Can you point to examples of this technique?
2. What passages or details in the essay do you find particularly funny? Look for experiences to which you relate, vivid word use, exaggerations, or lines that create humorous mental pictures.
3. In paragraph 6, Barry says that safety is a big reason why people claim to buy SUVs. Do you agree with their reasoning? What are some other reasons why so many Americans choose to drive giant vehicles?
4. Barry ends his essay with a prediction that American vehicles will get even bigger (paragraph 8). What does he predict will soon happen? Although the essay is humorous, it makes a serious point. Does the last line underscore this point?

Writing Assignments

1. Fill in the blank in this sentence: "If there's one thing this nation needs, it's ______________." Then take a stand, perhaps humorous, as Barry has, about something else Americans crave: fancy cell phones, brand-name clothing, even plastic surgery. Or try a serious approach, arguing for more youth centers, "hybrid" automobiles, or some other goal.
2. Write a response to Dave Barry's criticisms of SUVs and their owners. Defend these vehicles by giving reasons why people *should* drive them. Take a humorous or serious approach, as you wish.
3. Barry suggests that we Americans like our possessions big. What are some other things, besides vehicles, that we continue to super-size? What do you think this trend reveals about Americans?

---

6. Leonardo DiCaprio, Kate Winslet: stars of the film *Titanic*
7. dislodge: remove something stuck
8. vagabond: a wandering person

You Can Take This Job and . . . Well, It Might Surprise You

Ana Veciana-Suarez

If you won a lottery jackpot, what would you do? Buy a house? Take a trip? Quit your job? Not so fast, cautions Ana Veciana-Suarez. According to this *Miami Herald* columnist, there are some very good reasons to keep right on working.

Have you heard about the part-time letter carrier who won the $183 million jackpot in Maryland? She will collect more than $76 million after state and federal taxes, making her one of the largest individual winners in U.S. lottery history. 1

And she bought the ticket on a *whim.*[1] 2

I read about Bernadette Gietka's good fortune just as I was about to begin a grueling[2] workday that consisted of catching up from vacation while juggling new assignments. She reminded me of all the other lottery winners I had heard about, lucky people made suddenly wealthy (and confused) by happenstance.[3] There was the California software consultant who had a $7 million winning ticket stuffed in her purse for two months. And one Nebraska couple who ended up buying the jackpot after the wife had had a bad day at work. 3

"For better or for worse, work provides structure, imposes routine. It gives us an identity."

As my mother used to say *"La suerte es loca y a cualquiera le toca."* Luck is crazy and it can touch anybody. (Believe me, it sounds better in Spanish.) 4

I'm not much of a player, and gambling, in one form or another, holds little attraction. Life itself, with its tribulations[4] and surprises, is risky enough for me. But belief in steady nose-to-the-grindstone economic growth has never stopped me from daydreaming. So in a biting moment of anxiety, I schlepped[5] on over to the grocery store to buy a lottery ticket for the next drawing. You never know; you just never know. 5

Like most people, my friends and I entertain ourselves by coming up with ways to spend money we don't have. (And money we do have.) It is one of those futile[6] exercises that, done right and not too flippantly,[7] can help you focus on priorities, what truly matters to you when money is taken out of the equation. 6

What would I do with a sudden windfall?[8] Take a trip. Buy a house on the beach. Make sure my family is well taken care of. You know, the usual. I don't know if I would quit my job, however. 7

You would? Well, don't be so sure. Gietka, for one, plans to continue making her rounds. 8

We complain about work, curse our bosses, practice Oscar-winning monologues[9] to deliver when we finally walk out of the sweatshop, but most of us would keep punching that time clock. According to a recent Opinion Research Corporation poll, 70 percent of us would go right on working even if the fiscal gods smiled on us. In fact, we're so wedded to our jobs that only 5 percent would go on a vacation and 3 percent would actually splurge on shopping. I think I know why. 9

1. whim: sudden impulse
2. grueling: difficult, exhausting
3. happenstance: accident or twist of fate
4. tribulations: troubles
5. schlepped: dragged or moved clumsily
6. futile: useless
7. flippantly: without much thought or care
8. windfall: unexpected good fortune
9. monologues: long speeches made by one person

For better or for worse, work provides structure, imposes routine. It gives us an 10
identity. How many party conversations, after all, start with: "What do you do for a living?" Work is often social, the place we share stories about spouses and children and each other. Boardroom, factory or cubicle, it is the prime venue[10] and source of juicy gossip.

But there's something more, too. Though we think we never have enough of it, 11
we also suspect, somewhere in the deep recesses[11] of our conniving,[12] greedy little hearts, that money, lots and lots of it, isn't all that it's cracked up to be. We nod knowingly when we hear about co-workers who sue each other over lottery winnings. We tsk-tsk when news reports tell us about a couple splitting up over the winning numbers. And we recognize, if only momentarily, that a weekly paycheck is paradoxically[13] both enslaving and liberating. Just ask your unemployed neighbor.

My mother was right: Crazy, fickle luck. It arrives in many guises[14] and some- 12
times in the shape of a pay stub.

Discussion and Writing Questions

1. Veciana-Suarez begins this article with three examples of recent lottery winners (paragraphs 1–3). Who are they? Do you think these winners' stories sum up the statement "Luck is crazy and it can touch anybody"?

2. Have you ever dreamed of winning the lottery? What would you do if you won 10 million dollars? Explain why you would—or would not—quit your job.

3. What benefits of working, besides a paycheck, does the author discuss (paragraph 10)? Can you think of other benefits that a job provides? Do all jobs offer such benefits, or do only some jobs?

4. In paragraph 6, Veciana-Suarez says that daydreaming about how to spend lottery winnings "can help you focus on priorities, what truly matters to you when money is taken out of the equation." Is this true? List the three most important things you would do if you won 10 million dollars. Does this list help you understand what truly matters to you?

Writing Assignments

1. The odds of winning a multimillion-dollar lottery are about one in 13.98 million, yet millions of people exchange their hard-earned cash for lottery tickets every week. Discuss the reasons why so many people play when the odds are so much against them. Use examples from your own or a friend's experience.

2. The author writes that "we suspect, somewhere in the deep recesses of our conniving, greedy little hearts, that money, lots and lots of it, isn't all that it's cracked up to be" (paragraph 11). What is more important than money? Write a composition in which you answer this question.

3. Describe three or four of the most important *benefits* of being employed. Draw on your own experiences or the experiences of people you know for examples or stories that support your points.

---

10. venue: setting
11. recesses: interior spaces
12. conniving: scheming
13. paradoxically: seeming to go against common sense, yet true
14. guises: forms

A Homemade Education

MALCOLM X

Sometimes a book can change a person's life. In this selection, Malcolm X, the influential and controversial black leader who was assassinated in 1965, describes how, while he was in prison, a dictionary set him free.

1 It was because of my letters that I happened to stumble upon starting to acquire some kind of homemade education.

2 I became increasingly frustrated at not being able to express what I wanted to convey in letters that I wrote, especially those to Mr. Elijah Muhammad.[1] In the street, I had been the most articulate hustler out there—I had commanded attention when I said something. But now, trying to write simple English, I not only wasn't articulate, I wasn't even functional. How would I sound writing in slang, the way I would *say* it, something such as, "Look, daddy, let me pull your coat about a cat. Elijah Muhammad—"

3 Many who today hear me somewhere in person, or on television, or those who read something I've said, will think I went to school far beyond the eighth grade. This impression is due entirely to my prison studies.

4 It had really begun back in the Charlestown Prison, when Bimbi first made me feel envy of his stock of knowledge. Bimbi had always taken charge of any conversation he was in, and I had tried to emulate[2] him. But every book I picked up had few sentences which didn't contain anywhere from one to nearly all of the words that might as well have been in Chinese. When I just skipped those words, of course, I really ended up with little idea of what the book said. So I had come to the Norfolk Prison Colony still going through only book-reading motions. Pretty soon, I would have quit even these motions, unless I had received the motivation that I did.

"I saw that the best thing I could do was get hold of a dictionary—to study, to learn some words."

5 I saw that the best thing I could do was get hold of a dictionary—to study, to learn some words. I was lucky enough to reason also that I should try to improve my penmanship. It was sad. I couldn't even write in a straight line. It was both ideas together that moved me to request a dictionary along with some tablets and pencils from the Norfolk Prison Colony school.

6 I spent two days just riffling[3] uncertainly through the dictionary's pages. I'd never realized so many words existed! I didn't know *which* words I needed to learn. Finally, just to start some kind of action, I began copying.

7 In my slow, painstaking, ragged handwriting, I copied into my tablet everything printed on that first page, down to the punctuation marks.

8 I believe it took me a day. Then, aloud, I read back, to myself, everything I'd written on the tablet. Over and over, aloud, to myself, I read my own handwriting.

9 I woke up the next morning, thinking about those words—immensely proud to realize that not only had I written so much at one time, but I'd written words that I never knew were in the world. Moreover, with a little effort, I also could remember what many of these words meant. I reviewed the words whose meanings I didn't remember. Funny thing, from the dictionary first page right now, that "aardvark" springs to my mind. The dictionary had a picture of it, a long-tailed, long-eared burrowing African mammal, which lives off termites caught by sticking out its tongue as an anteater does for ants.

---

1. Elijah Muhammad: founder of the Muslim sect Nation of Islam
2. emulate: copy
3. riffling: thumbing through

Malcolm X giving one of his many speeches
©Bettman/CORBIS

I was so fascinated that I went on—I copied the dictionary's next page. And the 10
same experience came when I studied that. With every succeeding page, I also learned of people and places and events from history. Actually the dictionary is like a miniature encyclopedia. Finally, the dictionary's A section had filled a whole tablet—and I went on into the B's. That was the way I started copying what eventually became the entire dictionary. It went a lot faster after so much practice helped me pick up handwriting speed. Between what I wrote in my tablet, and writing letters, during the rest of my time in prison I would guess I wrote a million words.

I suppose it was inevitable that as my word-base broadened, I could for the
first time pick up a book and read and now begin to understand what the book 11
was saying. Anyone who has read a great deal can imagine the new world that opened. Let me tell you something: from then until I left that prison, in every free moment I had, if I was not reading in the library, I was reading on my bunk. You couldn't have gotten me out of books with a wedge. Between Mr. Muhammad's teachings, my correspondence, my visitors—usually Ella and Reginald—and my reading of books, months passed without my even thinking about being imprisoned. In fact, up to then, I never had been so truly free in my life.

Discussion and Writing Questions

1. Malcolm X says that in the streets he had been the "most articulate hustler" of all, but that in writing English he "not only wasn't articulate, [he] wasn't even functional" (paragraph 2). What does he mean?
2. What motivated Malcolm X to start copying the dictionary? What benefits did he gain from doing this?
3. What does Malcolm X mean when he says that until he went to prison, he "never had been so truly free in [his] life" (paragraph 11)?
4. Have you ever seen the 1992 film *Malcolm X*? If so, do you think the film's prison scenes showed how strongly Malcolm X was changed by improving his writing skills?

Writing Assignments

1. Choose three entries on a dictionary page and copy them. Then describe your experience. What did you learn? Can you imagine copying the entire dictionary? How do you feel about what Malcolm X accomplished? Where do you think he got the motivation to finish the task?

2. Malcolm X's inner life changed completely because of the dictionary he copied. Write about a time when a book, a story, a person, or an experience changed your life.

3. Have you ever wished that you had a better vocabulary? Learning new words is a process that pays off quickly if you keep at it. For one week, learn and practice a new word every day, perhaps using the following useful vocabulary website with a year's worth of great words. Then write an evaluation of your experiment to share with the class. Go to **<http://www.ccc.commnet.edu/grammar/definition_list.htm>.**

Barbie at 35

ANNA QUINDLEN

The Barbie doll is the world's best-selling toy. To what extent is Barbie responsible for the poor self-image that afflicts so many women? Anna Quindlen—novelist, Pulitzer Prize–winning journalist, and mother—thinks that there is more to Barbie than meets a child's eye.

My theory is that to get rid of Barbie you'd have to drive a silver stake through 1
her plastic heart. Or a silver lamé[1] stake, the sort of thing that might accompany Barbie's Dream Tent.

This is not simply because the original Barbie, launched lo these 35 years ago[2], 2
was more than a little vampiric[3] in appearance, more Natasha of "Rocky and Bullwinkle" than the "ultimate girl next door" Mattel described in her press kit.

It's not only that Barbie, like Dracula, can appear in guises that mask her essen- 3
tial nature: Surgeon, Astronaut, UNICEF Ambassador. Or that she is untouched by time, still the same parody[4] of the female form she's been since 1959. She's said by her manufacturers to be "eleven and one-half stylish inches" tall. If she were a real live woman she would not have enough body fat to menstruate regularly. Which may be why there's no PMS Barbie.

"Barbie—the issue, not the doll—simply will not be put to rest."

The silver stake is necessary because Barbie—the issue, not the doll—simply 4
will not be put to rest.

"Mama, why can't I have Barbie?" 5

"Because I hate Barbie. She gives little girls the message that the only thing 6
that's important is being tall and thin and having a big chest and lots of clothes. She's a terrible role model."

"Oh, Mama, don't be silly. She's just a toy." 7

It's an excellent comeback; if only it were accurate. But consider the recent 8
study at the University of Arizona investigating the attitudes of white and black teen-age girls toward body image.

---

1. lamé: shiny fabric with metallic threads
2. Barbie was 45 in 2004.
3. vampiric: bloodsucking, in the manner of a vampire
4. parody: ridiculous imitation

A girl longing to have—or look like—Barbie
AP/Wide World

9 The attitudes of the white girls were a nightmare. Ninety percent expressed dissatisfaction with their own bodies and many said they saw dieting as a kind of all-purpose panacea.[5] "I think the reason I would diet would be to gain self-confidence," said one. "I'd feel like it was a way of getting control," said another.

10 And they were curiously united in their description of the perfect girl. She's 5 feet 7 inches, weighs just over 100 pounds, has long legs and flowing hair. The researchers concluded: "The ideal girl was a living manifestation of the Barbie doll."

11 While the white girls described an impossible ideal, black teenagers talked about appearance in terms of style, attitude, pride and personality. White respondents talked "thin," black ones "shapely." Seventy percent of the black teenagers said they were satisfied with their weight, and there was little emphasis on dieting. "We're all brought up and taught to be realistic about life," said one, "and we don't look at things the way we want them to be. We look at them the way they are."

12 There's a quiet irony in that. While black women correctly complain that they are not sufficiently represented in advertisements, commercials, movies, even dolls, perhaps the scarcity of those idealized and unrealistic models may help in some fashion to liberate black teenagers from ridiculous standards of appearance. When the black teenagers were asked about the ideal woman, many asked: Whose ideal? The perfect girl projected by the white world simply didn't apply to them or their community, which set beauty standards from within. "White girls," one black participant in the Arizona study wrote, "have to look like Barbie dolls."

13 There are lots of reasons teenage girls have such a distorted fun-house mirror image of their own bodies, so distorted that one study found that 83 percent wanted to lose weight, although 62 percent were in the normal range. Fashion designers still showcase anorexia chic; last year the supermodel Kate Moss was reduced to insisting that, yes, she did eat.

---

5. panacea: cure-all; remedy for everything

But long before Kate and Ultra Slimfast came along, hanging over the life of every little girl born in the second half of the twentieth century was the impossibly curvy shadow (40-18-32 in life-size terms) of Barbie. That preposterous physique, we learn as kids, is what a woman looks like with her clothes off. "Two Barbie dolls are sold every second," says Barbie's résumé, which is more extensive than that of Hillary Rodham Clinton. "Barbie doll has had more than a billion pairs of shoes . . . has had over 500 professional makeovers . . . has become the most popular toy ever created." 14

Has been single-handedly responsible for the popularity of the silicone implant? 15

Maybe, as my daughter suggests while she whines in her Barbie-free zone, that's too much weight to put on something that's just a toy. Maybe not. Happy birthday, Babs. Have a piece of cake. Have two. 16

Discussion and Writing Questions

1. According to the author, why is it necessary to drive a silver stake through Barbie's heart? Why does Quindlen change her wording to "a silver lamé stake" (paragraph 1)?
2. Why does the author consider her daughter's argument that Barbie is "just a toy" (paragraph 7) a false statement?
3. What is the difference between the attitudes of white and black teenage girls toward body image, according to the University of Arizona study? In your experience or opinion, are the conclusions of the study still accurate? What about girls of other races?
4. "Happy birthday, Babs. Have a piece of cake. Have two." What is the significance of these concluding lines of Quindlen's essay?

Writing Assignments

1. Quindlen believes that the fashion industry contributes to white girls' distorted body image (paragraph 13). Write a profile of a model, designer, or celebrity who contributes to this distortion. Alternatively, choose a model, designer, or celebrity who does not distort the female body. Use specific examples of fashions and body types to develop your paper.
2. Have you (or has someone you know well) ever dieted? Were the reasons for dieting similar to those described by the white girls in the Arizona study (to gain self-confidence, control, and so on)? Describe the experience. Include such details as when you dieted, how, why, for how long, and your success rate, both in terms of weight loss or gain and of maintaining the goal weight.
3. Has a Barbie doll or some other toy ever been important to you or to someone you know? What was the toy, and what did it mean personally? Discuss the toy's importance and effects, good or bad, upon the person. If the person is now an adult, mention whether or not the toy influenced this person's adult self.

Papa, the Teacher

LEO BUSCAGLIA

Leo Buscaglia was the youngest of four children of Italian immigrants. In this selection, he describes how a father with only a fifth-grade education taught his children to respect—and even love—learning.

"The greatest sin was to go to bed at night as ignorant as we had been when we awakened that day."

Papa had natural wisdom. He wasn't educated in the formal sense. When he was growing up at the turn of the century in a very small village in rural northern Italy, education was for the rich. Papa was the son of a dirt-poor farmer. He used to tell us that he never remembered a single day of his life when he wasn't working. The concept of doing nothing was never a part of his life. In fact, he couldn't fathom[1] it. How could one do nothing? 1

He was taken from school when he was in the fifth grade, over the protestations[2] of his teacher and the village priest, both of whom saw him as a young person with great potential for formal learning. Papa went to work in a factory in a nearby village, the very same village where, years later, he met Mama. 2

For Papa, the world became his school. He was interested in everything. He read all the books, magazines, and newspapers he could lay his hands on. He loved to gather with people and listen to the town elders and learn about "the world beyond" this tiny, insular[3] region that was home to generations of Buscaglias before him. Papa's great respect for learning and his sense of wonder about the outside world were carried across the sea with him and later passed on to his family. He was determined that none of his children would be denied an education if he could help it. 3

Papa believed that the greatest sin of which we were capable was to go to bed at night as ignorant as we had been when we awakened that day. The credo[4] was repeated so often that none of us could fail to be affected by it. "There is so much to learn," he'd remind us. "Though we're born stupid, only the stupid remain that way." To ensure that none of his children ever fell into the trap of complacency,[5] he insisted that we learn at least one new thing each day. He felt that there could be no fact too insignificant, that each bit of learning made us more of a person and insured us against boredom and stagnation. 4

So Papa devised a ritual. Since dinnertime was family time and everyone came to dinner unless they were dying of malaria, it seemed the perfect forum for sharing what new things we had learned that day. Of course, as children we thought this was perfectly crazy. There was no doubt, when we compared such paternal[6] concerns with other children's fathers, Papa was weird. 5

It would never have occurred to us to deny Papa a request. So when my brother and sisters and I congregated in the bathroom to clean up for dinner, the inevitable question was, "What did *you* learn today?" If the answer was "Nothing," we didn't dare sit at the table without first finding a fact in our much-used encyclopedia. "The population of Nepal is . . . ," etc. 6

Now, thoroughly clean and armed with our fact for the day, we were ready for dinner. I can still see the table piled high with mountains of food. So large were the mounds of pasta that as a boy I was often unable to see my sister sitting across from me. (The pungent[7] aromas were such that, over a half century later, even in memory they cause me to salivate.) 7

Dinner was a noisy time of clattering dishes and endless activity. It was also a time to review the activities of the day. Our animated conversations were always conducted in Piedmontese dialect[8] since Mama didn't speak English. The events we recounted, no matter how insignificant, were never taken lightly. Mama and Papa always listened carefully and were ready with some comment, often profound and analytical, always right to the point. 8

---

1. fathom: understand; get to the bottom of
2. protestations: objections
3. insular: like an island; isolated
4. credo: a statement of belief
5. complacency: a feeling of satisfaction or smugness
6. paternal: having to do with fathers
7. pungent: sharp, spicy
8. Piedmontese dialect: the language spoken in the Piedmont region of northwestern Italy

9 "That was the smart thing to do." "*Stupido,* how could you be so dumb?" "*Cosi sia,*[9] you deserved it." "*E allora,*[10] no one is perfect." "*Testa dura* ('hardhead'), you should have known better. Didn't we teach you anything?" "Oh, that's nice." One dialogue ended and immediately another began. Silent moments were rare at our table.

10 Then came the grand finale to every meal, the moment we dreaded most—the time to share the day's new learning. The mental imprint of those sessions still runs before me like a familiar film clip, vital and vivid.

11 Papa, at the head of the table, would push his chair back slightly, a gesture that signified the end of the eating and suggested that there would be a new activity. He would pour a small glass of red wine, light up a thin, potent Italian cigar, inhale deeply, exhale, then take stock of his family.

12 For some reason this always had a slightly unsettling effect on us as we stared back at Papa, waiting for him to say something. Every so often he would explain why he did this. He told us that if he didn't take time to look at us, we would soon be grown and he would have missed us. So he'd stare at us, one after the other.

13 Finally, his attention would settle upon one of us. "*Felice,*"[11] he would say to me, "tell me what you learned today."

14 "I learned that the population of Nepal is . . ."

15 Silence.

16 It always amazed me, and reinforced my belief that Papa was a little crazy, that nothing I ever said was considered too trivial for him. First, he'd think about what was said as if the salvation of the world depended upon it.

17 "The population of Nepal. Hmmm. Well."

18 He would then look down the table at Mama, who would be ritualistically fixing her favorite fruit in a bit of leftover wine. "Mama, did you know that?"

19 Mama's responses were always astonishing and seemed to lighten the otherwise reverential atmosphere. "Nepal," she'd say. "Nepal? Not only don't I know the population of Nepal, I don't know where in God's world it is!" Of course, this was only playing into Papa's hands.

20 "*Felice,*" he'd say. "Get the atlas so we can show Mama where Nepal is." And the search began. The whole family went on a search for Nepal. This same experience was repeated until each family member had a turn. No dinner at our house ever ended without our having been enlightened by at least a half dozen such facts.

21 As children, we thought very little about these educational wonders and even less about how we were being enriched. We couldn't have cared less. We were too impatient to have dinner end so we could join our less-educated friends in a rip-roaring game of kick the can.

22 In retrospect, after years of studying how people learn, I realize what a dynamic educational technique Papa was offering us, reinforcing the value of continual learning. Without being aware of it, our family was growing together, sharing experiences, and participating in one another's education. Papa was, without knowing it, giving us an education in the most real sense.

23 By looking at us, listening to us, hearing us, respecting our opinions, affirming our value, giving us a sense of dignity, he was unquestionably our most influential teacher.

---

9. *Cosi sia:* Italian for "so be it"
10. *E allora:* Italian for "oh, well"
11. *Felice: Felice* is Buscaglia's real first name. The name *Leo* was taken from his middle name, *Leonardo.*

Discussion and Writing Questions

1. What does Buscaglia mean when he says that his father "wasn't educated in the formal sense" (paragraph 1)? In what way *was* his father educated?
2. How did Buscaglia's father and mother react to information that the children reported at dinnertime? How did their reaction affect Buscaglia as a child? As an adult?
3. Years later, Buscaglia realized that his father had offered the family "a dynamic educational technique" (paragraph 22). What does he mean?
4. What point does the author make by using the population of Nepal as an example in paragraph 14? Is it useful to know the population of Nepal? Why or why not?

Writing Assignments

1. Describe a typical dinnertime in your family as you were growing up. Was dinnertime a time for sharing? Fighting? Eating alone? What effect did this have on you? If you now live away from your birth family, are dinnertimes different?
2. Discuss your attitude toward education. Who or what shaped your point of view? Has your attitude changed since childhood? Why is education important?
3. Did *you* learn anything new today? If so, describe what you learned. If not, what got in the way of your learning?

My English

JULIA ALVAREZ

When her family moved to the United States from the Dominican Republic, ten-year-old Julia Alvarez was uprooted from both her homeland and her native language, Spanish. In this essay, she discusses her childhood struggle to make English her own. Today, Alvarez is a gifted writer of poetry, fiction, and nonfiction—in English.

Mami and Papi used to speak it when they had a secret they wanted to keep 1
from us children. We lived then in the Dominican Republic, and the family as a whole spoke only Spanish at home, until my sisters and I started attending the Carol Morgan School, and we became a bilingual family. Spanish had its many tongues as well. There was the castellano[1] of Padre Joaquín from Spain, whose lisp[2] we all loved to imitate. Then the educated español my parents' families spoke, aunts and uncles who were always correcting us children, for we spent most of the day with the maids and so had picked up their "bad Spanish." Campesinas,[3] they spoke a lilting,[4] animated campuno,[5] *ss* swallowed, endings chopped off, funny turns of phrases.

1. *castellano:* Castilian, the formal Spanish of Spain
2. lisp: a speech flaw (in English) in which the sounds "s" and "z" are pronounced *th*
3. *Campesinas:* peasants (Spanish)
4. lilting: lively and cheerful
5. *campuno:* Spanish with a peasant's accent, rural accent

2 Besides all these versions of Spanish, every once in a while another strange tongue emerged from my papi's mouth or my mami's lips. What I first recognized was not a language, but a tone of voice, serious, urgent, something important and top secret being said, some uncle in trouble, someone divorcing, someone dead. *Say it in English so the children won't understand.* I would listen, straining to understand, thinking that this was not a different language but just another and harder version of Spanish. *Say it in English so the children won't understand.* From the beginning, English was the sound of worry and secrets, the sound of being left out.

3 Soon, I began to learn more English, at the Carol Morgan School. That is, when I had stopped gawking. The teacher and some of the American children had the strangest coloration: light hair, light eyes, light skin, as if Ursulina had soaked them in bleach too long, to' deteñio.[6] I did have some blond cousins, but they had deeply tanned skin, and as they grew older, their hair darkened, so their earlier paleness seemed a phase of their acquiring normal color. Just as strange was the little girl in my reader who had a *cat* and a *dog*, that looked just like un gatito y un perrito.[7] Her mami was *Mother* and her papi *Father*. Why have a whole new language for school and for books with a teacher who could speak it teaching you double the amount of words you really needed?

4 *Butter, butter, butter, butter.* All day, one English word that had particularly struck me would go round and round in my mouth and weave through all the Spanish in my head until by the end of the day, the word did sound like just another Spanish word. And so I would say, "Mami, please pass la mantequilla."[8] She would scowl and say in English, "I'm sorry, I don't understand. But would you be needing some butter on your bread?"

"See you later, alligator. ***How wonderful to call someone an alligator and not be scolded for being disrespectful."***

5 Why my parents didn't first educate us in our native language by enrolling us in a Dominican school, I don't know. Part of it was that Mami's family had a tradition of sending the boys to the States to boarding school and college, and she had been one of the first girls to be allowed to join her brothers. At Abbot Academy, whose school song was our lullaby as babies ("Although Columbus and Cabot never heard of Abbot, it's quite the place for you and me"), she had become quite Americanized. It was very important, she kept saying, that we learn our English. She always used the possessive pronoun: *your* English, an inheritance we had come into and must wisely use. Unfortunately, my English became all mixed up with our Spanish.

6 Mix-up, or what's now called Spanglish, was the language we spoke for several years. There wasn't a sentence that wasn't colonized[9] by an English word. At school, a Spanish word would suddenly slide into my English like someone butting into line. Teacher, whose face I was learning to read as minutely[10] as my mother's, would scowl but no smile played on her lips. Her pale skin made her strange countenance[11] hard to read, so that I often misjudged how much I could get away with. Whenever I made a mistake, Teacher would shake her head slowly, "In English, YU-LEE-AH, there's no such word as *columpio*. Do you mean a *swing*?"

7 I would bow my head, humiliated by the smiles and snickers of the American children around me. I grew insecure about Spanish. My native tongue was not quite as good as English, as if words like *columpio* were illegal immigrants trying to cross a border into another language. But Teacher's discerning[12] grammar-and-vocabulary-patrol ears could tell and send them back.

---

6. *to' deteñio:* all faded, discolored
7. *un gatito y un perrito:* a kitten and a small dog (Spanish)
8. *mantequilla:* butter (Spanish)
9. colonized: inhabited by settlers from elsewhere
10. minutely: carefully, in great detail
11. countenance: facial expression
12. discerning: perceptive

Soon I was talking up an English storm. "Did you eat an English parrot?" my grandfather asked one Sunday. I had just enlisted yet one more patient servant to listen to my rendition of "Peter Piper picked a peck of pickled peppers" at breakneck pace. "Huh?" I asked impolitely in English, putting him in his place. *Cat got your tongue? No big deal! So there! Take that! Holy Toledo!* (Our teacher's favorite "curse word.") *Go jump in the lake! Really dumb. Golly. Gosh.* Slang, clichés, sayings, hot-shot language that our teacher called, ponderously,[13] idiomatic[14] expressions. Riddles, jokes, puns,[15] conundrums.[16] *What is yellow and goes click-click? Why did the chicken cross the road? See you later, alligator.* How wonderful to call someone an alligator and not be scolded for being disrespectful. In fact, they were supposed to say back, *In a while, crocodile.* 8

When we arrived in New York, I was shocked. A country where everyone spoke English! These people must be smarter, I thought. Maids, waiters, taxi drivers, doormen, bums on the street, all spoke this difficult language. It took some time before I understood that Americans were not necessarily a smarter, superior race. It was as natural for them to learn their mother tongue as it was for a little Dominican baby to learn Spanish. It came with "mother's milk," my mother explained, and for a while I thought a mother tongue was a mother tongue because you got it from your mother's breast, along with proteins and vitamins. 9

But at the foot of those towering New York skyscrapers, I began to understand more and more—not less and less—English. In sixth grade, I had one of the first in a lucky line of great English teachers who began to nurture in me a love of language, a love that had been there since my childhood of listening closely to words. Sister Maria Generosa did not make our class interminably[17] diagram sentences from a workbook or learn a catechism[18] of grammar rules. Instead, she asked us to write little stories imagining we were snowflakes, birds, pianos, a stone in the pavement, a star in the sky. What would it feel like to be a flower with roots in the ground? If the clouds could talk, what would they say? She had an expressive, dreamy look that was accentuated by the wimple[19] that framed her face. 10

Supposing, just supposing . . . My mind would take off, soaring into possibilities, a flower with roots, a star in the sky, a cloud full of sad, sad tears, a piano crying out each time its back was tapped, music only to our ears. 11

Sister Maria stood at the chalkboard. Her chalk was always snapping in two because she wrote with such energy, her whole habit shaking with the swing of her arm, her hand tap-tap-tapping on the board. "Here's a simple sentence: 'The snow fell.' " Sister pointed with her chalk, her eyebrows lifted, her wimple poked up. Sometimes I could see wisps of gray hair that strayed from under her headdress. "But watch what happens if we put an adverb at the beginning and a prepositional phrase at the end: 'Gently, the snow fell on the bare hills.'" 12

I thought about the snow. I saw how it might fall on the hills, tapping lightly on the bare branches of trees. Softly, it would fall on the cold, bare fields. On toys children had left out in the yard, and on cars and on little birds and on people out late walking on the streets. Sister Marie filled the chalkboard with snowy print, on and on, handling and shaping and moving the language, scribbling all over the board until English, those verbal gadgets, those tricks and turns of phrases, those little fixed units and counters, became a charged, fluid mass that carried me in its great fluent waves, rolling and moving onward, to deposit me on the shores of my new homeland. I was no longer a foreigner with no ground to stand on. I had landed in the English language. 13

13. ponderously: heavy, awkward
14. idiomatic: peculiar to a particular language
15. puns: plays on words
16. conundrums: riddles or problems with no clear solution
17. interminably: endlessly
18. catechism: a group of basic rules or beliefs
19. wimple: stiff cloth that is part of a nun's headwear

Discussion and Writing Questions

1. What was the author's first childhood experience of the English language (paragraphs 1 and 2)? How did her perceptions change over time as she learned more English and moved to the United States?

2. Alvarez describes several different versions of Spanish. Do you speak more than one version of English? Describe any ways in which your language changes, depending on the situation or the people you are with. For example, do you speak differently with your friends at home than you do in a college class?

3. Why does the author believe that Sister Maria Generosa was a great English teacher (paragraph 10)? Do you agree with her opinion? Have you ever had a teacher who awakened your passion for a subject? What were some of that teacher's special qualities or methods?

4. If your native language is not English, how was your experience of learning English like or unlike that of Julia Alvarez? Alvarez loved certain English words. Did certain English expressions fascinate you, confuse you, or make you laugh?

Writing Assignments

1. Write a paragraph or essay called "My __________" (for example, "My Style," "My Excellent Study Habits," and so on) in which you discuss the process by which you mastered something and made it your own. You might describe how you learned to lose weight, conduct Internet searches, decorate a room, or master a difficult subject.

2. Do you think it's more (or less) important to be bilingual today than it was in the past? Write a composition in which you argue for (or against) learning a second language in addition to knowing English.

3. Do you (or does a member of your family, living or dead) have an interesting or humorous immigrant story? Tell that story, focusing, perhaps, on the journey to the United States or the months just after arrival. Prewrite to gather your best facts and details, and organize before you write. Consider submitting your work for publication on this website: <**http://www.immigrantjourneys.com/**>.

Montgomery, Alabama, 1955

ROSA PARKS

A refusal to give up her seat in a segregated bus pushed Rosa Parks into the spotlight of the civil rights movement. In this excerpt from *Rosa Parks: My Story*, the Medal of Freedom winner tells what really happened.

When I got off from work that evening of December 1, I went to Court Square as usual to catch the Cleveland Avenue bus home.[1] I didn't look to see who was driving when I got on, and by the time I recognized him, I had already paid my fare. It was the same driver who had put me off the bus back in 1943, twelve years earlier. He was still tall and heavy, with red, rough-looking skin. And he was still mean-looking. I didn't know if he had been on that route before—they switched 1

1. home: Parks lived in Montgomery, the capital of Alabama, when racial segregation was legal.

the drivers around sometimes. I do know that most of the time if I saw him on a bus, I wouldn't get on it.

I saw a vacant seat in the middle section of the bus and took it. I didn't even question why there was a vacant seat even though there were quite a few people standing in the back. If I had thought about it at all, I would probably have figured maybe someone saw me get on and did not take the seat but left it vacant for me. There was a man sitting next to the window and two women across the aisle. 2

The next stop was the Empire Theater, and some whites got on. They filled up the white seats, and one man was left standing. The driver looked back and noticed the man standing. Then he looked back at us. He said, "Let me have those front seats," because they were the front seats of the black section. Didn't anybody move. We just sat right where we were, the four of us. Then he spoke a second time: "Y'all better make it light on yourselves and let me have those seats." 3

The man in the window seat next to me stood up, and I moved to let him pass by me, and then I looked across the aisle and saw that the two women were also standing. I moved over to the window seat. I could not see how standing up was going to "make it light" for me. The more we gave in and complied,[2] the worse they treated us. 4

"The only tired I was, was tired of giving in."

I thought back to the time when I used to sit up all night and didn't sleep and my grandfather would have his gun right by the fireplace, or if he had his one-horse wagon going anywhere, he always had his gun in the back of the wagon. People always say that I didn't give up my seat because I was tired, but that isn't true. I was not tired physically, or no more tired than I usually was at the end of a working day. I was not old, although some people have an image of me as being old then. I was forty-two. No, the only tired I was, was tired of giving in. 5

The driver of the bus saw me still sitting there, and he asked was I going to stand up. I said, "No." He said, "Well, I'm going to have you arrested." Then I said, "You may do that." These were the only words we said to each other. I didn't even know his name, which was James Blake, until we were in court together. He got out of the bus and stayed outside for a few minutes, waiting for the police. 6

As I sat there, I tried not to think about what might happen. I knew that anything was possible. I could be manhandled or beaten. I could be arrested. People have asked me if it occurred to me then that I could be the test case the NAACP[3] had been looking for. I did not think about that at all. In fact if I had let myself think too deeply about what might happen to me, I might have gotten off the bus. But I chose to remain. 7

Discussion and Writing Questions

1. How had Parks been treated on buses before this particular bus incident? How had she reacted before?
2. What does the bus driver mean by "make it light on yourselves" (paragraph 3)? What does Parks think about her seatmates' decision to stand up?
3. Paragraph 5 describes the actual moment of deliberation when Parks is deciding whether to stand up. What determined her decision? What factors were not important?
4. Why does the author conclude, "In fact if I had let myself think too deeply about what might happen to me, I might have gotten off the bus" (paragraph 7)? Parks takes full responsibility for her action, however. What two words indicate that?

2. complied: acted in accordance with the rules
3. NAACP: National Association for the Advancement of Colored People

Writing Assignments

1. Have you known someone who protested an injustice? What were the circumstances? Describe the circumstances, along with your reaction. Then discuss how your view of the event has changed (or not changed) over time.
2. Parks maintains that the public's understanding of her motivation (she was old and tired) is simply not true. She thus draws attention to the difference between how others may see us and how we see ourselves. Have you ever acted in a specific way, only to have others describe your actions differently? Write about your experience.
3. Do you have a complaint about college life? In a letter to your school newspaper, try to imitate Parks' low-key style as you describe the problem and suggest a solution.

The Importance of Childhood Memories*

NORMAN M. LOBSENZ

What childhood events or moments do you remember best? According to author Norman M. Lobsenz, these memories may explain a great deal about the person you have become today.

Some years ago, when my young wife became desperately ill, I wondered how I would be able to cope with the physical and emotional burdens of caring for her. One night, when I was drained of strength and endurance, a long-forgotten incident came to mind. I was about ten years old at the time and my mother was seriously ill. I had gotten up in the middle of the night to get a drink of water. As I passed my parents' bedroom, I saw the light on. I looked inside. My father was sitting in a chair in his bathrobe next to Mother's bed, doing nothing. She was asleep. I rushed into the room. 1

"What's wrong?" I cried. "Why aren't you asleep?" 2

Dad soothed me. "Nothing's wrong. I'm just watching over her." 3

I can't say exactly how, but the memory of that long-ago incident gave me the strength to take up my own burden again. The remembered light and warmth from my parents' room were curiously powerful and my father's words haunted me: "I'm just watching over her." The role I now assumed seemed somehow more bearable, as if a resource had been called from the past or from within. 4

In moments of psychological jeopardy[1], such childhood memories often turn out to be the ultimate resources of personality, dark prisms[2] which focus our basic feeling about life. As Sir James Barrie once wrote, "God gives us memory so that we may have roses in December." 5

No parent can ever really know which memory, planted in childhood, will grow to a rose. Often our most vivid and enduring remembrances are of apparently simple, even trivial[3] things. I did not discover this myself until one bright, leaf-budding spring day when my son Jim and I were putting a fresh coat of paint on the porch railing. We were talking about plans to celebrate his approaching 6

1. jeopardy: danger
2. prisms: crystal objects that split light into many colors
3. trivial: unimportant

fifteenth birthday, and I found myself thinking how quickly his childhood had passed.

"What do you remember best?" I asked him. 7

He answered without a moment's hesitation. "The night we were driving 8
somewhere, just you and me, on a dark road, and you stopped the car and helped me catch fireflies."

Fireflies? I could have thought of a dozen incidents, both pleasant and unpleas- 9
ant, that might have remained vivid in his mind. But fireflies? I searched my memory—and eventually it came back to me. I'd been driving cross-country, traveling late to meet a rather tight schedule. I had stopped to clean the windshield, when all at once a cloud of fireflies surrounded us. Jim, who was five years old then, was tremendously excited. He wanted to catch one. I was tired and tense, and anxious to get on to our destination. I was about to tell him that we didn't have time to waste when something changed my mind. In the trunk of the car I found an empty glass jar. Into it we scooped dozens of the insects. And while Jim watched them glow, I told him of the mysterious cold light they carried in their bodies. Finally, we uncapped the jar and let the fireflies blink away into the night.

"What to a grown-up might seem a casual word or action often is, to a child, the kernel of a significant memory on which he will build."

"Why do you remember that?" I asked. "It doesn't seem terribly important." 10

"I don't know," he said. "I didn't even know I did remember it until just now." 11
Then a few moments later: "Maybe I do know why. Maybe it was because I didn't think you were going to stop and catch any with me—and you did."

Since that day I have asked many friends to reach back into their childhoods 12
and tell me what they recall with greatest clarity. Almost always they mention similar moments—experiences or incidents not of any great importance. Not crises or trauma or triumphs, but things which although small in themselves carry sharp sensations of warmth and joy, or sometimes pain.

One friend I spoke with was the son of an executive who was often away from 13
home. "Do you know what I remember best?" he said to me. "It was the day of the annual school picnic when my usually very dignified father appeared in his shirtsleeves, sat on the grass with me, ate a box lunch, and then made the longest hit in our softball game. I found out later that he postponed a business trip to Europe to be there." My friend is a man who experiences the world as a busy, serious place but who basically feels all right about it and about himself. His favorite childhood memory is both clue to and cause of his fundamental soundness.

Clearly, the power parents have to shape the memories of their children in- 14
volves an awesome responsibility. In this respect nothing is trivial. What to a grown-up might seem a casual word or action often is, to a child, the kernel[4] of a significant memory on which he will build. As grownups, we draw on these memories as sources of strength or weakness. Author Willa Cather saw this clearly. "There are those early memories," she wrote. "One cannot get another set; one has only those."

Not long ago, I talked with a woman who has married a young and struggling 15
sculptor. She cheerfully accepted their temporary poverty. "I grew up during the depression," she said. "My dad scrambled from one job to another. But I remembered that each time a job ended, my mother would scrape together enough money to make us an especially good dinner. She used to call them our 'trouble meals.' I know now that they were her way of showing Dad she believed in him, in his ability to fight back. I learned that loving someone was far more important than having something."

If childhood memories are so important, what can parents do to help supply 16
their children with a healthy set?

- For one thing, parents should be aware of the importance of the memory- 17
building process. In our adult preoccupation,[5] we tend to think that the "im-

---

4. kernel: seed
5. preoccupation: mental focus on something other than the present

portant" experiences our children will have are still in their future. We forget that, to them, childhood is reality rather than merely a preparation for reality. We forget that childhood memories form the adult personality. "What we describe as 'character,'" wrote Sigmund Freud[6] "is based on the memory traces of our earliest youth."

- Parents can try to find the extra energy, time, or enthusiasm to carry out the small and "insignificant" plan that is so important to a child. The simple act of baking that special batch of cookies or helping to build that model car, even though you are tired or harried,[7] may make an important memory for your youngster. 18

Conversely,[8] parents can try to guard against the casual disillusionments and needless disappointments which they often unthinkingly inflict[9] on children. I would venture[10] that almost everyone has a memory of an outing cancelled or a promise broken without a reason or an explanation. "My father always used to say, 'we'll see,'" one man told me. "I soon learned that what that meant was 'no,' but without any definite reason." 19

- Parents can keep up family traditions and rituals.[11] Simple observations that may not seem terribly important to a grownup can be enormously meaningful to a child. A ritual walk in the woods on the first day of spring, a family dinner on someone's birthday, these are often significant to a youngster long past the time we might think he or she stopped caring about them. 20
- Parents can think back to their own childhoods and call up their own memories. By remembering the incidents that made important impressions on them, parents can find guideposts to ways in which they can shape the future memories of their own youngsters. 21
- Finally, parents can by their own actions and words communicate emotions as well as experiences to their children. We can give them a memory of courage rather than fear; of strength rather than weakness; of an appetite for adventure rather than a shrinking from new people and places; of warmth and affection rather than rigidity[12] and coldness. In just such memories are rooted the attitudes and feelings that characterize a person's entire approach to life. 22

Discussion and Writing Questions

1. In your own words, what is the thesis, or main point, of this essay? Do you agree with the author that important childhood experiences help shape a person in later life?
2. Lobsenz develops his essay with examples from his own and other people's experiences (the author's son catching fireflies, the father who attended his son's picnic, the mother who made "trouble meals"). Choose one example that moved you and explain what lesson that experience probably taught the child.
3. The author lists five ways in which parents can help give their children a healthy set of memories. What are they? Describe a time (from your own

6. Sigmund Freud: considered the father of modern psychology; stressed the importance of the unconscious mind
7. harried: overworked, rushing
8. conversely: on the other hand
9. inflict: force upon
10. venture: guess or assume
11. rituals: special ceremonies
12. rigidity: stiffness or inflexibility

experience or from your observation) when a parent applied—or failed to apply—one of these principles.

4. Read the final paragraph aloud. Lobsenz uses a strong series of parallel ideas: "courage rather than fear, strength rather than weakness," and so on. How effective is this conclusion?

Writing Assignments

1. Describe a key memory from your childhood, one that you believe is a source of strength or weakness for you today. In the first paragraph, recreate your experience, using specific details and vivid language. In the second paragraph, tell what effects, positive or negative, this experience had on your later life.

2. It is difficult for parents today to spend relaxed, enjoyable times with their children. Some are single parents; many work at least one job and perhaps also go to school. What advice would you give these harried parents, who truly want the best for their children? Refer to one or more of Lobsenz's points if you wish.

3. Study this painting of a positive childhood memory by Carmen Lomas Garza—called *Cama Para Suenos*, or "Bed for Dreams." First, describe the painting for someone who has not seen it, using space order to arrange important details. What is the mother doing downstairs? The children? How many "beds for dreams" do you see? Now, guess what the children might be dreaming of. Do you think the mother has dreams, too? Visit <**http://www.carmenlomasgarza.com/artwork.html#paintings**> to see more of Garza's memories.

Cama Para Sueños (Bed for Dreams) by Carmen Lomas Garza

Artwork © 1985 Carmen Lomas Garza

The Gift*

COURTLAND MILLOY

Help sometimes comes from unexpected places. This newspaper story describes the generosity of a friend whose gift saved someone's life—and baffled most people who knew him. As you read, ask yourself how you would have acted in his place.

When Jermaine Washington entered the barbershop, heads turned and clippers 1
fell silent. Customers waved and nodded, out of sheer respect. With his hands in the pockets of his knee-length, black leather coat, Washington acknowledged them with a faint smile and quietly took a seat.

"You know who that is?" barber Anthony Clyburn asked in a tone reserved for 2
the most awesome neighborhood characters, such as ball players and ex-cons.

A year and a half ago, Washington did something that still amazes those who 3
know him. He became a kidney donor, giving a vital organ to a woman he described as "just a friend."

"They had a platonic[1] relationship," said Clyburn, who works at Jake's Barber 4
Shop in Northeast Washington. "I could see maybe giving one to my mother, but just a girl I know? I don't think so."

"'I had been on the kidney donor waiting list for 12 months and I had lost all hope. One day, I just called to cry on his shoulder.'"

Washington, who is 25, met Michelle Stevens six years ago when they worked 5
for the D.C. Department of Employment Services. They used to have lunch together in the department cafeteria and chitchat on the telephone during their breaks.

"It was nothing serious, romance-wise," said Stevens, who is 23. "He was 6
somebody I could talk to. I had been on the kidney donor waiting list for 12 months and I had lost all hope. One day, I just called to cry on his shoulder."

Stevens told Washington how depressing it was to spend three days a week, 7
three hours a day, on a kidney dialysis machine.[2] She said she suffered from chronic fatigue and blackouts and was losing her balance and her sight. He could already see that she had lost her smile.

"I saw my friend dying before my eyes," Washington recalled. "What was I 8
supposed to do? Sit back and watch her die?"

Stevens's mother was found to be suffering from hypertension[3] and was ineli- 9
gible to donate a kidney. Her 14-year-old sister offered to become a donor, but doctors concluded that she was too young.

Stevens's two brothers, 25 and 31, would most likely have made ideal donors 10
because of their relatively young ages and status as family members. But both of them said no.

So did Stevens's boyfriend, who gave her two diamond rings with his apology. 11

"I understood," Stevens said. "They said they loved me very much, but they 12
were just too afraid."

Joyce Washington, Jermaine's mother, was not exactly in favor of the idea, ei- 13
ther. But after being convinced that her son was not being coerced,[4] she supported his decision.

*From Courtland Milloy, "Giving Up a Kidney for a Friend," *The Washington Post*, 12/23/92, p. D1, Metro Section. Copyright © 1992, The Washington Post, reprinted with permission.

---

1. platonic: nonromantic
2. kidney dialysis machine: a machine that filters waste material from the blood when the kidneys fail
3. hypertension: high blood pressure
4. coerced: pressured into doing something

The transplant operation took four hours. It occurred in April 1991, and began with a painful X-ray procedure in which doctors inserted a metal rod into Washington's kidney and shot it with red dye. An incision nearly 20 inches long was made from his groin to the back of his shoulder. After the surgery he remained hospitalized for five days. 14

Today, both Stevens and Washington are fully recovered. Stevens, a graduate of Eastern High School, is studying medicine at the National Educational Center. Washington still works for D.C. Employment Services as a job counselor. 15

"I jog and work out with weights," Washington said. "Boxing and football are out, but I never played those anyway." 16

A spokesman for Washington Hospital Center said the Washington-to-Stevens gift was the hospital's first "friend-to-friend" transplant. Usually, it's wife to husband, or parent to child. But there is a shortage of even those kinds of transplants. Today, more than 300 patients are in need of kidneys in the Washington area. 17

"A woman came up to me in a movie line not long ago and hugged me," Washington said. "She thanked me for doing what I did because no one had come forth when her daughter needed a kidney, and the child died." 18

About twice a month, Stevens and Washington get together for what they call a gratitude lunch. Since the operation, she has broken up with her boyfriend. Seven months ago, Washington got a girlfriend. Despite occasional pressure by friends, a romantic relationship is not what they want. 19

"We are thankful for the beautiful relationship that we have," Stevens said. "We don't want to mess up a good thing." 20

To this day, people wonder why Washington did it. To some of the men gathered at Jake's Barber Shop not long ago, Washington's heroics were cause for questions about his sanity. Surely he could not have been in his right mind, they said. 21

One customer asked Washington where he had found the courage to give away a kidney. His answer quelled[5] most skeptics[6] and inspired even more awe. 22

"I prayed for it," Washington replied. "I asked God for guidance and that's what I got." 23

Discussion and Writing Questions

1. A year and a half after Jermaine Washington donated a kidney to Michelle Stevens, his friends are still amazed by what he did. Why do they find his action so surprising?
2. Washington says, "What was I supposed to do? Sit back and watch her die?" (paragraph 8). Yet Stevens' brothers and her boyfriend did not offer to donate a kidney. Do you blame them? Do you understand them?
3. In what ways has Stevens' life changed because of Washington's gift? Consider her physical status, her social life, her choice of profession, her "gratitude lunches" with Washington, and so on.
4. According to Washington, where did he find the courage to donate a kidney? How did his action affect his standing in the community? How did it affect other aspects of his life?

Writing Assignments

1. Have you ever been unusually generous—or do you know someone who was? Describe that act of generosity. Why did you—or the other person—do it? How did your friends or family react?
2. Do you have or does anyone you know have a serious medical condition? Describe the situation. How do or how can friends help? Can strangers help in any way?

5. quelled: quieted
6. skeptics: people who doubt or question

3. Stevens and Washington do not have or want a romantic relationship. "We don't want to mess up a good thing," Stevens says (paragraph 20). Does romance "mess things up"? Write about a time when a relationship changed—either for better or for worse—because romance entered the picture.

Anonymity Brings Out Our Dark Sides

LEONARD PITTS JR.

In 2004, Leonard Pitts Jr. of the *Miami Herald* won the Pulitzer Prize for his articles about American society. Here, Pitts tries to make sense of a recent news story with disturbing echoes of a famous crime. The 1964 murder of Kitty Genovese in New York City is still discussed today because dozens of neighbors watched from their windows and did nothing to help. The scene of the crime that Pitts discusses, however, was not a city street but the Internet.

"Under cover of anonymity, in places where no one knows our names, we tend to drop our masks and expose sides of ourselves even we never knew were there."

It's been three weeks since Ripper died, but it didn't make the news until a few days ago. 1

At first, his death seemed depressingly mundane.[1] Phoenix woman goes into her son's room one afternoon to wake him for work. Finds him dead of an overdose of prescription drugs, marijuana and alcohol. It wasn't until days later that his family turned on his computer and discovered the really troubling thing about Ripper's death, which is that he died in a room full of his friends who watched him kill himself while some egged him on. 2

The transcript from their Internet chat room reads like the script from a bad stoner[2] movie. "I got a grip[3] of drugs," Ripper said. To which "%Pnutbot" responded with approving enthusiasm: "Ripper is a gangster!!!" 3

In the privacy of their chat room, in the anonymity of their Internet names, in the darkness of predawn, they watched via a camera hooked up to his computer as he popped pills, drank rum, smoked pot. One friend encouraged him to pass out on camera. Another wanted to see his head smack against the wall. 4

Ripper gave them his cellphone number. "Call if I look dead," he said. 5

Just another day in the virtual community. You remember the virtual community[4]. It's the one we were promised at the dawn of the Internet Age, the one that would link all humankind in brotherhood, sisterhood, enlightenment. 6

Of course, similar promises were made on behalf of the telegraph, the radio and the telephone. But the flaw in all the promises was the same. They depended upon our understanding of the social covenant,[5] our ability to recognize that each of us owes something to the rest of us. That's a notoriously[6] fickle[7] thing in which to place one's trust. 7

So who can be surprised that a virtual community failed Ripper? We've seen the same failure in communities of bricks and mortar[8] for years. 8

I won't be the first to find in Ripper's suicide an echo of Kitty Genovese's murder. She was killed long before the Internet reached the masses, killed 39 years ago on a quiet, tree-lined street in Queens, N.Y. Thirty-seven people watched from 9

1. mundane: ordinary
2. stoner: person who smokes marijuana frequently
3. grip: slang for "a large amount"
4. virtual community: people who communicate with others via the Internet
5. social covenant: unspoken agreement among people
6. notoriously: well-known for wrongdoing
7. fickle: unstable, changeable
8. bricks and mortar: the real world, as opposed to the virtual world

their apartment windows. Thirty-seven people heard her cry for help as a deranged[9] man with a knife spent half an hour killing her.

10 Nobody came to her aid. Nobody even called the police. And afterward, the nation gasped in shock, wondering how such a thing could happen. Wondering how people could be so callous,[10] so cowardly and so cold.

11 The answer was the same then as it is now. We are different in darkness than we are in light. Under cover of anonymity,[11] in places where no one knows our names, we tend to drop our masks and expose sides of ourselves even we never knew were there. We forget to strive toward what we imagine ourselves to be. Forget those duties of basic compassion and simple courage that each owes to all.

12 There's something chilling in the transcript of Ripper's slide into demise.[12] It's as if, for the people watching, he has become something less than real, a video game character performing on command. And when he passes out, some of them have as much compassion as they would for something one-dimensional that existed only on screen.

13 "He's dead," says "Oea."

14 "Happy trails," says "Hast."

15 The panic builds only slowly. Ripper's virtual friends begin to debate calling authorities. At one point, "Oea" does dial 911, asking the room, "Is this the right choice?"

16 "TheKat" types, "No" 10 times.

17 Oea laughs and reports, "Okay. I talked my way out of it. Didn't give them any info."

18 "Whatever," says theKat.

19 Not that it would have made a difference if they had called for help. Ripper's "friends" didn't know who he was. They stood witness to his suicide and didn't even know his name.

20 Brandon Veda was 21.

Discussion and Writing Questions

1. Did Ripper intend to commit suicide? How do you know? What role did drugs and alcohol play in his death?

2. What do paragraphs 12 to 17 reveal about Ripper's online "friends"? Why didn't they alert authorities after Ripper lost consciousness?

3. Did the Internet play a role in Ripper's death? Pitts thinks that Internet and Web-cam viewers lose compassion for the people they watch, who become "one-dimensional," like video-game characters (paragraph 12), to them. Explain why you agree or disagree with Pitts.

4. Pitts concludes his article with a one-sentence paragraph: "Brandon Veda was 21." Why does the author state the young man's real name and age for the first time here? How effective is this conclusion?

Writing Assignments

1. Rewrite Ripper's story, describing changes that might have saved his life. Who could have behaved differently—a parent, friend, coworker, or chat-room "friend"? Describe one, two, or three acts or conversations that could have al-

---

9. deranged: insane
10. callous: unfeeling
11. anonymity: state of being nameless or unknown
12. demise: death

tered Ripper's fate. For ideas, you might explore a suicide prevention site like **<http://www.save.org/>**.

2. Why do some people choose not to get involved when someone clearly needs help (for example, if he or she is under attack)? Are people who don't reach out to others cold and heartless, or do other reasons explain their behavior?
3. The Internet has grown to be a powerful communication tool with both benefits and dangers. Write about some *positive* uses of the Internet. Write from your own experience or visit **<http://www.networkforgood.org>**, a site dedicated to using the Web for good.

Hot Dogs and Wild Geese

FIROOZEH DUMAS

More than 31 million people who live in the United States were born in other countries, and most of them did not speak English very well—or at all—when they first came here. As Iranian-born writer Firoozeh Dumas illustrates with her family's story, learning English is not only confusing but often downright hilarious. This essay appears in her recent book, *Funny in Farsi*.

Moving to America was both exciting and frightening, but we found great comfort in knowing that my father spoke English. Having spent years regaling[1] us with stories about his graduate years in America, he had left us with the distinct impression that America was his second home. My mother and I planned to stick close to him, letting him guide us through the exotic American landscape that he knew so well. We counted on him not only to translate the language but also to translate the culture, to be a link to this most foreign of lands. He was to be our own private Rosetta stone.[2] 1

Once we reached America, we wondered whether perhaps my father had confused his life in America with someone else's. Judging from the bewildered looks of store cashiers, gas station attendants, and waiters, my father spoke a version of English not yet shared with the rest of America. His attempts to find a "vater closet"[3] in a department store would usually lead us to the drinking fountain or the home furnishings section. Asking my father to ask the waitress the definition of "sloppy Joe" or "Tater Tots" was no problem. His translations, however, were highly suspect. Waitresses would spend several minutes responding to my father's questions, and these responses, in turn, would be translated as "She doesn't know." Thanks to my father's translations, we stayed away from hot dogs, catfish, and hush puppies, and no amount of caviar[4] in the sea would have convinced us to try mud pie. 2

We wondered how my father had managed to spend several years attending school in America yet remain so utterly befuddled[5] by Americans. We soon discovered that his college years had been spent mainly in the library, where he had managed to avoid contact with all Americans except his engineering professors. As long as the conversation was limited to vectors,[6] surface tension, and fluid 3

1. regaling: entertaining
2. Rosetta stone: carved stone tablet, the key to translating ancient Egyptian writing
3. "vater closet": *water closet*, the British term for *bathroom*
4. caviar: fancy fish eggs
5. befuddled: confused
6. vectors: mathematical quantities

mechanics, my father was Fred Astaire[7] with words. But one step outside the scintillating[8] world of petroleum engineering and he had two left tongues.

4 My father's only other regular contact in college had been his roommate, a Pakistani who spent his days preparing curry. Since neither spoke English but both liked curries, they got along splendidly. The person who had assigned them together had probably hoped they would either learn English or invent a common language for the occasion. Neither happened.

5 My father's inability to understand spoken English was matched only by his efforts to deny the problem. His constant attempts at communicating with Americans seemed at first noble and adventurous, then annoying. Somewhere between his thick Persian accent and his use of vocabulary found in pre–World War II British textbooks, my father spoke a private language. That nobody understood him hurt his pride, so what he lacked in speaking ability, he made up for by reading. He was the only person who actually read each and every document before he signed it. Buying a washing machine from Sears might take the average American thirty minutes, but by the time my father had finished reading the warranties, terms of contracts, and credit information, the store was closing and the janitor was asking us to please step aside so he could finish mopping the floor.

"After searching fruitlessly for elbow grease, I asked the salesclerk for help."

6 My mother's approach to learning English consisted of daily lessons with Monty Hall and Bob Barker.[9] Her devotion to *Let's Make a Deal* and *The Price Is Right*[10] was evident in her newfound ability to recite useless information. After a few months of television viewing, she could correctly tell us whether a coffeemaker cost more or less than $19.99. How many boxes of Hamburger Helper, Swanson's TV dinners, or Turtle Wax could one buy without spending a penny more than twenty dollars? She knew that, too. Strolling down the grocery aisle, she rejoiced in her celebrity sightings—Lipton tea! Campbell's tomato soup! Betty Crocker Rich & Creamy Frosting! Every day, she would tell us the day's wins and losses on the game shows. "He almost won the boat, but the wife picked curtain number two and they ended up with a six-foot chicken statue." The bad prizes on *Let's Make a Deal* sounded far more intriguing than the good ones. Who would want the matching La-Z-Boy recliners when they could have the adult-size crib and high-chair set?

7 My mother soon decided that the easiest way for her to communicate with Americans was to use me as an interpreter. My brother Farshid, with his schedule full of soccer, wrestling, and karate, was too busy to be recruited for this dubious[11] honor. At an age when most parents are guiding their kids toward independence, my mother was hanging on to me for dear life. I had to accompany her to the grocery store, the hairdresser, the doctor, and every place else that a kid wouldn't want to go. My reward for doing this was the constant praise of every American we encountered. Hearing a seven-year-old translate Persian into English and vice versa made quite an impression on everyone. People lavished[12] compliments on me. "You must be very, very smart, a genius maybe." I always responded by assuring them that if they ever moved to another country, they, too, would learn the language. (What I wanted to say was that I wished I could be at home watching *The Brady Bunch*[13] instead of translating the qualities of various facial moisturizers.) My mother had her own response to the compliments: "Americans are easily impressed."

---

7. Fred Astaire: American dancer and film star of the 1930s, 1940s, and 1950s
8. scintillating: sparkling, brilliant
9. Monty Hall and Bob Barker: early television game show hosts
10. *Let's Make a Deal* and *The Price is Right*: television game shows of the 1960s and 1970s
11. dubious: doubtful, questionable
12. lavished: heaped or poured
13. *The Brady Bunch*: an early 1970s television sit-com

I always encouraged my mother to learn English, but her talents lay elsewhere. Since she had never learned English in school, she had no idea of its grammar. She would speak entire paragraphs without using any verbs. She referred to everyone and everything as "it," leaving the listener wondering whether she was talking about her husband or the kitchen table. Even if she did speak a sentence more or less correctly, her accent made it incomprehensible. "W" and "th" gave her the most difficulty. As if God were playing a linguistic[14] joke on us, we lived in "Vee-tee-er" (Whittier), we shopped at "Veetvood" (Whitwood) Plaza, I attended "Leff-ingvell" School, and our neighbor was none other than "Valter Villiams." 8

Despite little progress on my mother's part, I continually encouraged her. Rather than teach her English vocabulary and grammar, I eventually decided to teach her entire sentences to repeat. I assumed that once she got used to speaking correctly, I could be removed, like training wheels, and she would continue coasting. I was wrong. 9

Noticing some insects in our house one day, my mother asked me to call the exterminator. I looked up the number, then told my mother to call and say, "We have silverfish in our house." My mother grumbled, dialed the number, and said, "Please come rrright a-vay. Goldfeeesh all over dee house." The exterminator told her he'd be over as soon as he found his fishing pole. 10

A few weeks later, our washing machine broke. A repairman was summoned and the leaky pipe was quickly replaced. My mother wanted to know how to remove the black stain left by the leak. "Y'all are gonna hafta use some elbow grease," he said. I thanked him and paid him and walked with my mother to the hardware store. After searching fruitlessly[15] for elbow grease, I asked the salesclerk for help. "It removes stains," I added. The manager was called. 11

Once the manager finished laughing, he gave us the disappointing explanation. My mother and I walked home empty-handed. That, I later learned, is what Americans call a wild-goose chase. 12

Now that my parents have lived in America for thirty years, their English has improved somewhat, but not as much as one would hope. It's not entirely their fault; English is a confusing language. When my father paid his friend's daughter the compliment of calling her homely, he meant she would be a great housewife. When he complained about horny drivers, he was referring to their tendency to honk. And my parents still don't understand why teenagers want to be cool so they can be hot. 13

I no longer encourage my parents to learn English. I've given up. Instead, I'm grateful for the wave of immigration that has brought Iranian television, newspapers, and supermarkets to America. Now, when my mother wants to ask the grocer whether he has any more eggplants in the back that are a little darker and more firm, because the ones he has out aren't right for *khoresht bademjun*, she can do so in Persian, all by herself. And for that, I say hallelujah, a word that needs no translation. 14

Discussion and Writing Questions

1. Why was Dumas so sure that her father would guide the family easily through the mysteries of American life (paragraph 1)? Why was he, in fact, so little help (paragraph 2)? How do you guess that he translated the words *hot dogs, catfish, hush puppies*, and *mud pie* so that his family refused to eat these foods?

2. The author humorously describes the weird skills her mother learned by watching so much American television. What did the mother learn?

3. In paragraph 7, Dumas writes, "At an age when most parents are guiding their kids toward independence, my mother was hanging on to me for dear life." If a

14. linguistic: relating to language.
15. fruitlessly: without success

child of immigrants must serve as a translator for his or her parents, parent-child roles sometimes can be reversed. Is this a problem?

4. Dumas uses funny examples to show how confusing English can be. If English was not your first language, what words or aspects of American culture especially confused you? What was funniest (or most frustrating)?

Writing Assignments

1. Does your town have ethnic shops, markets, restaurants, or neighborhoods that you have never explored? Choose one place that you would like to learn more about and visit there, chat with people, and perhaps have something to eat. Take notes on the sights, sounds, smells, and details; then write a vivid account of your adventure.

A shopper in New York City's Chinatown

(8/10/99) Marilynn K. Yee/The New York Times

2. The United States, with its many races and ethnic groups, has been called a "melting pot." In a group with several classmates, decide whether the United States is more like a *melting pot* (a place where various ingredients melt together into one soup or goo), a *salad* (when different ingredients are tossed together but keep their separate flavors), or a *grocery store shelf* (where many foods in sealed containers do not mix). Write a paper presenting your own ideas.

3. Have you ever found yourself in a place where you did not understand the "rules"? This place might be a new country, a new school, a new job, or the dinner table of your future in-laws. Describe the challenges you faced in this strange new world and tell how you dealt with them. Use humor if you wish.

In This Arranged Marriage, Love Came Later

Shoba Narayan

Although arranged marriages are common in many parts of the world, most Americans believe that the best marriages start with falling in love. In this essay, an American-educated journalist from India discusses her decision to let her family find her a husband.

We sat around the dining table, my family and I, replete[1] from yet another 1
home-cooked South Indian dinner. It was my younger brother, Shaam, who asked the question.

"Shoba, why don't you stay back here for a few months? So we can try to get 2
you married."

Three pairs of eyes stared at me across the expanse of the table. I sighed. Here I 3
was, at the tail end of my vacation after graduate school. I had an airplane ticket to New York from Madras, India, in ten days. I had accepted a job at an artists' colony in Johnson, Vermont. My car, and most of my possessions, were with friends in Memphis.

"It's not that simple," I said. "What about my car . . . ?" 4

"We could find you someone in America," my dad replied. "You could go back 5
to the States."

They had thought it all out. This was a plot. I glared at my parents accusingly. 6

Oh, another part of me rationalized, why not give this arranged-marriage thing 7
a shot? It wasn't as if I had a lot to go back to in the States. Besides, I could always get a divorce.

Stupid and dangerous as it seems in retrospect,[2] I went into my marriage at 8
twenty-five without being in love. Three years later, I find myself relishing my relationship with this brilliant, prickly man who talks about the yield curve and derivatives,[3] who prays when I drive, and who tries valiantly to remember names like Giacometti, Munch, Kandinsky.[4]

My enthusiasm for arranged marriages is that of a recent convert. True, I grew 9
up in India, where arranged marriages are common. My parents' marriage was arranged, as were those of my aunts, cousins and friends. But I always thought I was different. I blossomed as a foreign fellow in Mount Holyoke College where individualism was expected and feminism encouraged. As I experimented with being an American, I bought into the American value system.

I was determined to fall in love and marry someone who was not Indian. Yet, 10
somehow, I could never manage to. Oh, falling in love was easy. Sustaining it was the hard part.

Arranged marriages in India begin with matching the horoscopes of the man 11
and the woman. Astrologers look for balance . . . so that the woman's strengths balance the man's weaknesses and vice versa. Once the horoscopes match, the two families meet and decide whether they are compatible. It is assumed that they are of the same religion, caste[5] and social stratum.[6]

1. replete: filled to satisfaction
2. in retrospect: looking back
3. yield curve and derivatives: technical terms from finance
4. Giacometti, Munch, Kandinsky: great twentieth-century artists
5. caste: one of four social classes in India
6. stratum: level

12 While this eliminates risk and promotes homogeneity,[7] the rationale is that the personalities of the couple provide enough differences for a marriage to thrive. Whether or not this is true, the high statistical success rate of arranged marriages in different cultures—90 percent in Iran, 95 percent in India, and a similar high percentage among Hasidic Jews in Brooklyn, and among Turkish and Afghan Muslims—gives one pause.

13 Although our families met through a mutual friend, many Indian families meet through advertisements placed in national newspapers.

> ***"Stupid and dangerous as it seems in retrospect, I went into my marriage at twenty-five without being in love."***

14 My parents made a formal visit to my future husband's house to see whether Ram's family would treat me well. My mother insists that "you can tell a lot about the family just from the way they serve coffee." The house had a lovely flower garden. The family liked gardening. Good.

15 Ram's mother had worked for the United Nations on women's-rights issues. She also wrote humorous columns for Indian magazines. She would be supportive. She served strong South Indian coffee in the traditional stainless steel tumblers instead of china; she would be a balancing influence on my youthful radicalism.

16 Ram's father had supported his wife's career even though he belonged to a generation of Indian men who expected their wives to stay home. Ram had a good role model. His sister was a pediatrician in Fort Myers. Perhaps that meant he was used to strong, achieving women.

17 November 20, 1992. Someone shouted, "They're here!" My cousin Sheela gently nudged me out of the bedroom into the living room.

18 "Why don't you sit down?" a voice said.

19 I looked up and saw a square face and smiling eyes anxious to put me at ease. He pointed me to a chair. Somehow I liked that. The guy was sensitive and self-confident.

20 He looked all right. Could stand to lose a few pounds. I liked the way his lips curved to meet his eyes. Curly hair, commanding voice, unrestrained laugh. To my surprise, the conversation flowed easily. We had a great deal in common, but his profession was very different from mine. He had an MBA from the University of Michigan and had worked on Wall Street before joining a financial consulting firm.

21 Two hours later, Ram said, "I'd like to get to know you better. Unfortunately, I have to be back at my job in Connecticut, but I could call you every other day. No strings attached, and both of us can decide where this goes, if anywhere."

22 I didn't dislike him.

23 He called ten days later. We talked about our goals, dreams and anxieties.

24 "What do you want out of life?" he asked me one day. "Come up with five words, maybe, of what you want to do with your life." His question intrigued me. "Courage, wisdom, change," I said, flippantly.[8] "What about you?"

25 "Curiosity, contribution, balance, family and fun," he said. In spite of myself, I was impressed.

26 One month later, he proposed and I accepted. Our extended honeymoon in Connecticut was wonderful. On weekends, we took trips to Mount Holyoke, where I showed him my old art studio, and to Franconia Notch in New Hampshire, where we hiked and camped.

27 It was in Taos, New Mexico, that we had our first fight. Ram had arranged for a surprise visit to the children's summer camp where I used to work as a counselor. We visited my old colleagues with their Greenpeace T-shirts and New Age commune mentality. Ram, with his clipped accent, neatly pressed clothes and pleasant

---

7. homogeneity: sameness, similarity
8. flippantly: lightly, thoughtlessly

manners, was so different. What was I doing with this guy? On the car trip to the airport, I was silent. "I think, perhaps, we might have made a mistake," I said slowly. The air changed.

"Your friends may be idealistic, but they are escaping their lives, as are you," he said. "We are married. Accept it. Grow up!" 28

He had never spoken to me this harshly before, and it hurt. I didn't talk to him during the entire trip back to New York. 29

That fight set the pattern of our lives for the next several months. In the evening, when Ram came home, I would ignore him or blame him for bringing me to Connecticut. 30

Two years into our marriage, something happened. I was ashamed to realize that while I had treated Ram with veiled dislike, he had always tried to improve our relationship. I was admitted to the journalism program at Columbia, where, at Ram's insistence, I had applied. 31

Falling in love, for me, began with small changes. I found myself relishing a South Indian dish that I disliked, mostly because I knew how much he loved it. I realized that the first thing I wanted to do when I heard some good news was to share it with him. Somewhere along the way, the "I love you, too" that I had politely parroted[9] in response to his endearments had become sincere. 32

My friends are appalled[10] that I let my parents decide my life partner; yet, the older they get the more intrigued they are. I am convinced that our successful relationship has to do with two words: tolerance and trust. In a country that emphasizes individual choice, arranged marriages require a familial web for them to work. For many Americans, that web doesn't exist. 33

As my friend Karen said, "How can I get my parents to pick out my spouse when they don't even talk to each other?" 34

Discussion and Writing Questions

1. Why did the author agree to an arranged marriage?
2. What factors did her family consider as they matched her with a husband? Which of these factors do you think are important predictors of success in marriage? Which, if any, seem unimportant?
3. How did Shoba Narayan know, after two years, that she was falling in love? If you have ever fallen in love, how was your experience similar or different?
4. What might be the disadvantages, or even risks, of an arranged marriage?

Writing Assignments

1. Soon after they met, Ram asked Shoba what words she would choose to express what she wanted in life. She said, "Courage, wisdom, change." Ram chose "curiosity, contribution, balance, family and fun." What three to five words would you select in answer to Ram's question? Choose your words carefully; then explain why each one is important to you.
2. Marriage in the United States usually occurs after two people "fall in love." Of course, more than 50 percent of marriages in this country end in divorce. Discuss three reasons why marriage that is based on first falling in love is or is not a good idea.
3. Would you consider letting your relatives pick your marriage partner? Take a stand, presenting the two or three most important reasons why you would or would not consider such a move.

9. parroted: repeated mindlessly
10. appalled: shocked

The Hidden Life of Bottled Water

LIZA GROSS

Consumers buy more bottled water than ever, believing that they are satisfying their thirst with something healthy. In fact, they might be better off just turning on the tap, according to this writer for *Sierra,* a magazine devoted to conservation and the environment.

Americans used to turn on their faucets when they craved a drink of clear, cool water. Today, concerned about the safety of water supplies, they're turning to the bottle. Consumers spent more than $4 billion on bottled water last year, establishing the fount[1] of all life as a certifiably hot commodity. But is bottled really better? 1

You might think a mountain stream on the label offers some clue to the contents. But sometimes, to paraphrase Freud, a bottle is just a bottle. "Mountain water could be anything," warns Connie Crawley, a health and nutrition specialist at the University of Georgia. "Unless the label says it comes from a specific source, when the manufacturer says 'bottled at the source,' the source could be the tap." 2

"Consumers spent more than $4 billion on bottled water last year, but is bottled really better?"

Yosemite brand water comes not from a bucolic[2] mountain spring but from deep wells in the undeniably less picturesque Los Angeles suburbs, and Everest sells water drawn from a municipal source in Corpus Christi, Texas—a far cry from the pristine[3] glacial peaks suggested by its name. As long as producers meet the FDA's[4] standards for "distilled" or "purified" water, they don't have to disclose the source. 3

Even if the water does come from a spring, what's in that portable potable[5] may be *less* safe than what comes out of your tap. Bottled water must meet the same safety standards as municipal-system water. But while the EPA[6] mandates daily monitoring of public drinking water for many chemical contaminants, the FDA requires less comprehensive testing only once a year for bottled water. Beyond that, says Crawley, the FDA "usually inspects only if there's a complaint. Yet sources of bottled water are just as vulnerable to surface contamination as sources of tap water. If the spring is near a cattle farm, it's going to be contaminated." 4

Let's assume your store-bought water meets all the safety standards. What about the bottle? Because containers that sit for weeks or months at room temperature are ideal breeding grounds for bacteria, a bottle that met federal safety standards when it left the plant might have unsafe bacteria levels by the time you buy it. And because manufacturers aren't required to put expiration dates on bottles, there's no telling how long they've spent on a loading dock or on store shelves. (Bacteria also thrive on the wet, warm rim of an unrefrigerated bottle, so avoid letting a bottle sit around for too long.) But even more troubling is what may be leaching[7] from the plastic containers. Scientists at the FDA found traces of bisphe- 5

1. fount: source
2. bucolic: rural
3. pristine: pure
4. FDA's: Food and Drug Administration's
5. potable: a beverage that is safe to drink
6. EPA: Environmental Protection Agency
7. leaching: dissolving, draining away

nol A—an endocrine[8] disruptor that can alter the reproductive development of animals—after 39 weeks in water held at room temperature in large polycarbonate containers (like that carboy[9] atop your office water cooler).

Wherever you get your water, *caveat emptor*[10] should be the watchword. If you're simply worried about chlorine or can't abide its taste, fill an uncapped container with tap water and leave it in the refrigerator overnight; most of the chlorine will vaporize. If you know your municipal water is contaminated, bottled water can provide a safe alternative. But shop around. The National Sanitation Foundation (NSF) independently tests bottled water and certifies producers that meet FDA regulations and pass unannounced plant, source, and container inspections. And opt for glass bottles—they don't impart the taste and risks of chemical agents and they aren't made from petrochemicals.[11] 6

To get information on bottled-water standards—or to find out what's in the water you buy—contact the Food and Drug Administration, (888) INFO-FDA, **<http://www.fda.gov/>**. For information on your tap water, called the EPA's Safe Drinking Water Hotline, (800) 426-4791, **<http://www.epa.gov/safewater>.** 7

Discussion and Writing Questions

1. Why might tap water be safer than bottled water?
2. Even if bottled water meets all safety standards, what other problems can affect its quality?
3. According to the author, how can consumers ensure that the bottled water they buy is, in fact, safe spring water?
4. What is the author suggesting about the American public and bottled water? What is she trying to accomplish by writing this article? Does she succeed?

Writing Assignments

1. Check a campus location that sells bottled water (vending machine, cafeteria, campus store). Which brand of bottled water is sold? Contact the Food and Drug Administration (see Gross's last paragraph) to find out what information the federal government has collected on that brand. Is it spring water? Tap water from another location? Safe to drink? What ingredients does it contain? Have any problems been associated with it? Report your findings in a letter to the campus newspaper.
2. Study the contents label of one of your favorite snacks. What are the ingredients? Consult a dictionary to "translate" those ingredients. Does your appetite diminish as a result? Describe the snack, including what you thought its ingredients were and what the ingredients really are. Conclude with a recommendation for other consumers.
3. Gross suggests that perhaps the public has been fooled by the bottled-water industry. What other products do people buy without really needing them? Find an ad for one such product and describe how it works —how it creates a need where there is none. Attach the ad to your description.

8. endocrine: hormonal
9. carboy: oversized bottle
10. *caveat emptor*: a warning in Latin meaning "buyer beware"
11. petrochemicals: compounds derived from petroleum or natural gas

Four Directions

AMY TAN

Have you ever possessed a certain skill or strength, and then, as you grew, lost it? Amy Tan, a Chinese-American novelist who lives in San Francisco, writes about a young chess player who seemed unbeatable—at age ten.

I was ten years old. Even though I was young, I knew my ability to play chess 1
was a gift. It was effortless, so easy. I could see things on the chessboard that other people could not. I could create barriers to protect myself that were invisible to my opponents. And this gift gave me supreme confidence. I knew at exactly what point their faces would fall when my seemingly simple and childlike strategy would reveal itself as a devastating and irrevocable[1] course. I loved to win.

And my mother loved to show me off, like one of my many trophies she pol- 2
ished. She used to discuss my games as if she had devised the strategies.

"I told my daughter, Use your horses to run over the enemy," she informed one 3
shopkeeper. "She won very quickly this way." And of course, she had said this before the game—that and a hundred other useless things that had nothing to do with my winning.

"It was as though I had lost my magic armor."

To our family friends who visited she would confide, "You don't have to be so 4
smart to win chess. It is just tricks. You blow from the North, South, East, and West. The other person becomes confused. They don't know which way to run."

I hated the way she tried to take all the credit. And one day I told her so, shout- 5
ing at her on Stockton Street, in the middle of a crowd of people. I told her she didn't know anything, so she shouldn't show off. She should shut up. Words to that effect.

That evening and the next day she wouldn't speak to me. She would say stiff 6
words to my father and brothers, as if I had become invisible and she was talking about a rotten fish she had thrown away but which had left behind its bad smell.

I knew this strategy, the sneaky way to get someone to pounce back in anger and 7
fall into a trap. So I ignored her. I refused to speak and waited for her to come to me.

After many days had gone by in silence, I sat in my room, staring at the sixty- 8
four squares of my chessboard, trying to think of another way. And that's when I decided to quit playing chess.

Of course I didn't mean to quit forever. At most, just for a few days. And I 9
made a show of it. Instead of practicing in my room every night, as I always did, I marched into the living room and sat down in front of the television with my brothers, who stared at me, an unwelcome intruder. I used my brothers to further my plan; I cracked my knuckles to annoy them.

"Ma!" they shouted. "Make her stop. Make her go away." 10

But my mother did not say anything. 11

Still I was not worried. But I could see I would have to make a stronger move. I 12
decided to sacrifice a tournament that was coming up in one week. I would refuse to play in it. And my mother would certainly have to speak to me about this. Because the sponsors and the benevolent associations[2] would start calling her, asking, shouting, pleading to make me play again.

And then the tournament came and went. And she did not come to me, crying, 13
"Why are you not playing chess?" But I was crying inside, because I learned that a boy whom I had easily defeated on two other occasions had won.

1. irrevocable: impossible to cancel or halt
2. benevolent associations: charities

I realized my mother knew more tricks than I had thought. But now I was tired 14
of her game. I wanted to start practicing for the next tournament. So I decided to pretend to let her win. I would be the one to speak first.

"I am ready to play chess again," I announced to her. I had imagined she 15
would smile and then ask me what special thing I wanted to eat.

But instead, she gathered her face into a frown and stared into my eyes, as if 16
she could force some kind of truth out of me.

"Why do you tell me this?" she finally said in sharp tones. "You think it is so 17
easy. One day quit, next day play. Everything for you is this way. So smart, so easy, so fast."

"I said I'll play," I whined. 18

"No!" she shouted, and I almost jumped out of my scalp. "It is not so easy any- 19
more."

I was quivering, stunned by what she said, in not knowing what she meant. 20
And then I went back to my room. I stared at my chessboard, its sixty-four squares, to figure out how to undo this terrible mess. And after staring like this for many hours, I actually believed that I had made the white squares black and the black squares white, and everything would be all right.

And sure enough, I won her back. That night I developed a high fever, and she 21
sat next to my bed, scolding me for going to school without my sweater. In the morning she was there as well, feeding me rice porridge flavored with chicken broth she had strained herself. She said she was feeding me this because I had the chicken pox and one chicken knew how to fight another. And in the afternoon, she sat in a chair in my room, knitting me a pink sweater while telling me about a sweater that Auntie Suyuan had knit for her daughter June, and how it was most unattractive and of the worst yarn. I was so happy that she had become her usual self.

But after I got well, I discovered that, really, my mother had changed. She no 22
longer hovered over[3] me as I practiced different chess games. She did not polish my trophies every day. She did not cut out the small newspaper item that mentioned my name. It was as if she had erected[4] an invisible wall and I was secretly groping each day to see how high and how wide it was.

At my next tournment, while I had done well overall, in the end the points 23
were not enough. I lost. And what was worse, my mother said nothing. She seemed to walk around with this satisfied look, as if it had happened because she had devised this strategy.

I was horrified. I spent many hours every day going over in my mind what I 24
had lost. I knew it was not just the last tournament. I examined every move, every piece, every square. And I could no longer see the secret weapons of each piece, the magic within the intersection of each square. I could see only my mistakes, my weaknesses. It was as though I had lost my magic armor. And everybody could see this, where it was easy to attack me.

Over the next few weeks and later months and years, I continued to play, but 25
never with that same feeling of supreme confidence. I fought hard, with fear and desperation. When I won, I was grateful, relieved. And when I lost, I was filled with growing dread, and then terror that I was no longer a prodigy,[5] that I had lost the gift and had turned into someone quite ordinary.

When I lost twice to the boy whom I had defeated so easily a few years before, 26
I stopped playing chess altogether. And nobody protested. I was fourteen.

3. hovered over: paid close attention to
4. erected: built
5. prodigy: a person with enormous talents in a particular area

Discussion and Writing Questions

1. Why did the child and her mother fight? Do you think the mother really wanted "all the credit" for herself (paragraph 5)? Why did she refuse to speak to the child after their argument?
2. The mother and daughter almost seem locked in a chess match of their own after their argument. What do you think is happening between them? Does the daughter's age—adolescence—have anything to do with it?
3. Why do you suppose the author says she had lost more than the last tournament, she had lost her "magic armor" (paragraph 24)?
4. The author says that "nobody protested" when she gave up chess permanently at age fourteen (paragraph 26). Do you think people might have protested if she were a boy? Why or why not?

Writing Assignments

1. Did you possess a talent or strength as a young person that you later lost? What happened? What caused you to change?
2. Adolescence is for most people a time of enormous change, and change often produces great anxiety. Was there an incident in your adolescence that caused you such anxiety—because you or your surroundings were somehow changing? Describe this incident.
3. Research suggests that once they reach adolescence, many girls give up asserting themselves—in sports, in class, and in student government, for example—because they feel pressure to be "feminine." Do you think this is true? Discuss why or why not, using yourself or a young woman you know as an example.

Emotional Intelligence

DANIEL GOLEMAN

How important to a person's success is I.Q.—that is, his or her score on an intelligence test? According to a widely read recent book, other personality traits and skills are even more important than I.Q. The author, Daniel Goleman, calls these traits and skills *emotional intelligence.* How would you rate your emotional I.Q.?

It was a steamy afternoon in New York City, the kind of day that makes people sullen[1] with discomfort. I was heading to my hotel, and as I stepped onto a bus, I was greeted by the driver, a middle-aged man with an enthusiastic smile. 1

"Hi! How're you doing?" he said. He greeted each rider in the same way. 2

As the bus crawled uptown through gridlocked traffic, the driver gave a lively commentary: there was a terrific sale at that store . . . a wonderful exhibit at this museum . . . had we heard about the movie that just opened down the block? By the time people got off, they had shaken off their sullen shells. When the driver called out, "So long, have a great day!" each of us gave a smiling response. 3

That memory has stayed with me for close to twenty years. I consider the bus driver a man who was truly successful at what he did. 4

1. sullen: gloomy

5 Contrast him with Jason, a straight-A student at a Florida high school who was fixated[2] on getting into Harvard Medical School. When a physics teacher gave Jason an 80 on a quiz, the boy believed his dream was in jeopardy.[3] He took a butcher knife to school, and in a struggle the teacher was stabbed in the collarbone.

6 How could someone of obvious intelligence do something so irrational? The answer is that high I.Q. does not necessarily predict who will succeed in life. Psychologists agree that I.Q. contributes only about 20 percent of the factors that determine success. A full 80 percent comes from other factors, including what I call *emotional intelligence.*

7 Following are some of the major qualities that make up emotional intelligence, and how they can be developed:

8 **1. Self-awareness.** The ability to recognize a feeling as it happens is the keystone of emotional intelligence. People with greater certainty about their emotions are better pilots of their lives.

"How could someone of obvious intelligence do something so irrational?"

9 Developing self-awareness requires tuning in to . . . gut feelings. Gut feelings can occur without a person being consciously aware of them. For example, when people who fear snakes are shown a picture of a snake, sensors on their skin will detect sweat, a sign of anxiety, even though the people say they do not feel fear. The sweat shows up even when a picture is presented so rapidly that the subject has no conscious awareness of seeing it.

10 Through deliberate effort we can become more aware of our gut feelings. Take someone who is annoyed by a rude encounter for hours after it occurred. He may be oblivious[4] to his irritability and surprised when someone calls attention to it. But if he evaluates his feelings, he can change them.

11 Emotional self-awareness is the building block of the next fundamental of emotional intelligence: being able to shake off a bad mood.

12 **2. Mood Management.** Bad as well as good moods spice life and build character. The key is balance.

13 We often have little control over *when* we are swept by emotion. But we can have some say in *how long* that emotion will last. Psychologist Dianne Tice of Case Western Reserve University asked more than 400 men and women about their strategies for escaping foul moods. Her research, along with that of other psychologists, provides valuable information on how to change a bad mood.

14 Of all the moods that people want to escape, rage seems to be the hardest to deal with. When someone in another car cuts you off on the highway, your reflexive[5] thought may be, *That jerk! He could have hit me! I can't let him get away with that!* The more you stew, the angrier you get. Such is the stuff of hypertension and reckless driving.

15 What should you do to relieve rage? One myth is that ventilating[6] will make you feel better. In fact, researchers have found that's one of the worst strategies. Outbursts of rage pump up the brain's arousal system, leaving you more angry, not less.

16 A more effective technique is "reframing," which means consciously reinterpreting a situation in a more positive light. In the case of the driver who cuts you off, you might tell yourself: *Maybe he had some emergency.* This is one of the most potent ways, Tice found, to put anger to rest.

17 Going off alone to cool down is also an effective way to defuse anger, especially if you can't think clearly. Tice found that a large proportion of men cool down by

2. fixated: rigidly focused
3. jeopardy: danger
4. oblivious: totally unaware
5. reflexive: automatic
6. ventilating: "letting off steam," raving

going for a drive—a finding that inspired her to drive more defensively. A safer alternative is exercise, such as taking a long walk. Whatever you do, don't waste the time pursuing your train of angry thoughts. Your aim should be to distract yourself.

The techniques of reframing and distraction can alleviate[7] depression and anx- 18
iety as well as anger. Add to them such relaxation techniques as deep breathing and meditation and you have an arsenal of weapons against bad moods. "Praying," Dianne Tice also says, "works for all moods."

3. Self-motivation. Positive motivation—the marshaling[8] of feelings of enthu- 19
siasm, zeal and confidence—is paramount for achievement. Studies of Olympic athletes, world-class musicians and chess grandmasters[9] show that their common trait is the ability to motivate themselves to pursue relentless training routines.

To motivate yourself for any achievement requires clear goals and an opti- 20
mistic, can-do attitude. Psychologist Martin Seligman of the University of Pennsylvania advised the MetLife insurance company to hire a special group of job applicants who tested high on optimism, although they had failed the normal aptitude test. Compared with salesmen who passed the aptitude test but scored high in pessimism, this group made 21 percent more sales in their first year and 57 percent more in their second.

A pessimist is likely to interpret rejection as meaning *I'm a failure; I'll never make* 21
a sale. Optimists tell themselves, *I'm using the wrong approach,* or *That customer was in a bad mood.* By blaming failure on the situation, not themselves, optimists are motivated to make that next call.

Your . . . positive or negative outlook may be inborn, but with effort and prac- 22
tice, pessimists can learn to think more hopefully. Psychologists have documented that if you can catch negative, self-defeating thoughts as they occur, you can reframe the situation in less catastrophic terms.

4. Impulse Control. The essence of emotional self-regulation is the ability to 23
delay impulse in the service of a goal. The importance of this trait to success was shown in an experiment begun in the 1960s by psychologist Walter Mischel at a preschool on the Stanford University campus.

Children were told that they could have a single treat, such as a marshmallow, 24
right now. However, if they would wait while the experimenter ran an errand, they could have two marshmallows. Some preschoolers grabbed the marshmallow immediately, but others were able to wait what, for them, must have seemed an endless twenty minutes. To sustain themselves in their struggle, they covered their eyes so they wouldn't see the temptation, rested their heads on their arms, talked to themselves, sang, even tried to sleep. These plucky kids got the two-marshmallow reward.

The interesting part of this experiment came in the follow-up. The children 25
who as four-year-olds had been able to wait for the two marshmallows were, as adolescents, still able to delay gratification in pursuing their goals. They were more socially competent and self-assertive, and better able to cope with life's frustrations. In contrast, the kids who grabbed the one marshmallow were, as adolescents, more likely to be stubborn, indecisive and stressed.

The ability to resist impulse can be developed through practice. When you're 26
faced with an immediate temptation, remind yourself of your long-term goals—whether they be losing weight or getting a medical degree. You'll find it easier, then, to keep from settling for the single marshmallow.

5. People Skills. The capacity to know how another feels is important on the 27
job, in romance and friendships, and in the family. We transmit and catch moods from each other on a subtle, almost imperceptible level. The way someone says

7. alleviate: reduce, make better
8. marshaling: gathering together, using
9. chess grandmasters: experts at the game of chess

thank you, for instance, can leave us feeling dismissed, patronized or genuinely appreciated. The more adroit[10] we are at discerning the feelings behind other people's signals, the better we control the signals we send.

The importance of good interpersonal skills was demonstrated by psychologists Robert Kelley of Carnegie-Mellon University and Janet Caplan in a study at Bell Labs in Naperville, Ill. The labs are staffed by engineers and scientists who are all at the apex[11] of academic I.Q. tests. But some still emerged as stars while others languished.[12] 28

What accounted for the difference? The standout performers had a network with a wide range of people. When a non-star encountered a technical problem, Kelley observed, "he called various technical gurus and then waited, wasting time while his calls went unreturned. Star performers rarely faced such situations because they built reliable networks *before* they needed them. So when the stars called someone, they almost always got a faster answer." 29

No matter what their I.Q., once again it was emotional intelligence that separated the stars from the average performers. 30

Discussion and Writing Questions

1. Goleman names five qualities that contribute to emotional intelligence. What are they?
2. Describe someone you observed recently who showed a high level of emotional intelligence in a particular situation. Then describe someone who showed a low level of emotional intelligence in a particular situation. Which of the five qualities did each person display or lack?
3. Did it surprise you to read that "ventilating" is one of the worst ways to handle rage? Instead, experts suggest several techniques. Suppose you are in the following situation, and your first reaction is anger: *You ask a salesperson for help in choosing a CD player. As she walks right past you, she tells you that the boxes and labels will give you all the information you need.* What might you do to calm yourself down?
4. In paragraphs 24 and 25, Goleman discusses a now-famous study of children and marshmallows. What was the point of this study? Why does Goleman say that the most interesting part of the study came later, when the children reached adolescence?

Writing Assignments

1. Write a detailed portrait of a person whom you consider an "emotional genius." Develop your paper with specific examples of his or her skills.
2. Daniel Goleman claims that weak emotional qualities can be strengthened with practice. Choose one of the five qualities (self-awareness, people skills, and so forth) and recommend specific ways for a person to improve in that area. Your audience is people who wish to improve their emotional intelligence; your purpose is to help them do so.
3. Review or read "The Gift" on page 409, and evaluate the emotional intelligence of Jermaine Washington. Washington saved a friend's life by giving her one of his kidneys after her two brothers and her boyfriend refused to be donors. Most people in their town still think Washington was "crazy" to make this decision. What do you think? Does he have a high level of emotional intelligence? A low level? Why?

10. adroit: skilled
11. apex: top, topmost point
12. languished: stayed in one place

Quotation Bank

This collection of wise and humorous statements has been assembled for you to read, enjoy, and use in a variety of ways as you write. You might choose some quotations that you particularly agree or disagree with and use them as the basis of journal entries and writing assignments. When you write a paragraph or an essay, you may find it useful to include a quotation to support a point you are making. You may simply want to read through these quotations for ideas and for fun. As you come across other intriguing statements by writers, add them to the list—or write some of your own.

Writing

Writing, like life itself, is a voyage of discovery.
—HENRY MILLER

9/06 Writing is the hardest work in the world not involving heavy lifting.
—PETE HAMILL

I think best with a pencil in my hand.
—ANNE MORROW LINDBERGH

A sentence should contain no unnecessary words, a paragraph no unnecessary sentences, for the same reason that a drawing should have no unnecessary lines and a machine no unnecessary parts.
—WILLIAM STRUNK

To me, the greatest pleasure of writing is not what it's about, but the inner music that words make.
—TRUMAN CAPOTE

Writing is the only thing that when I do it, I don't feel I should be doing something else.
—GLORIA STEINEM

I never travel without my diary. One should always have something sensational to read on the train.
—OSCAR WILDE

Write something to suit yourself and many people will like it; write something to suit everybody and scarcely anyone will care for it.
—JESSE STUART

A professional writer is an amateur who didn't quit.
—RICHARD BACH

Learning

Teachers open the door, but you must enter by yourself.
—CHINESE PROVERB

The "silly question" is the first intimation [hint] of some totally new development.
—ALFRED NORTH WHITEHEAD

The mind is a mansion, but most of the time we are content to live in the lobby.
—William Michaels

Education is . . . hanging around until you've caught on.
—Robert Frost

Prejudices, it is well known, are most difficult to eradicate [remove] from the heart whose soil has never been loosened or fertilized by education; they grow there, firm as weeds among stones.
—Charlotte Brontë

Many receive advice; few profit from it.
—Publius

Pay attention to what they tell you to forget.
—Muriel Rukeyser

Education is what you have left over after you have forgotten everything you have learned.
—Anonymous

Only the educated are free.
—Epictetus

The basic purpose of a liberal arts education is to liberate the human being to exercise his or her potential to the fullest.
—Barbara M. White

Love

We can only learn to love by loving.
—Iris Murdoch

To love and to be loved is to feel the sun from both sides.
—David Viscott

So often when we say "I love you," we say it with a huge "I" and a small "you."
—Archbishop Antony

Choose your life's mate carefully. From this one decision will come 90 percent of all your happiness or misery.
—H. Jackson Browne Jr.

Marriage is our last, best chance to grow up.
—Joseph Barth

A divorce is like an amputation; you survive, but there's less of you.
—Margaret Atwood

No partner in a love relationship should feel that she [or he] has to give up an essential part of herself [or himself] to make it viable [workable].
—May Sarton

I can't mate in captivity.
—Gloria Steinem

Gold and love affairs are difficult to hide.
—Spanish proverb

Love doesn't just sit there, like a stone; it has to be made, like bread, remade all the time, made new.
—Ursula K. Le Guin

To be loved, be lovable.
—Ovid

Work and Success

The best career advice to give the young is, find out what you like doing best and get someone to pay you for doing it.
—Katherine Whilehaen

Measure a thousand times and cut once.
—Turkish proverb

There are two things to aim at in life: first, to get what you want and, after that, to enjoy it. Only the wisest . . . achieve the second.
—Logan Pearsall Smith

Money is like manure. If you spread it around, it does a lot of good, but if you pile it up in one place, it stinks like hell.
—Clint W. Murchison

If you have built castles in the air, your work need not be lost; that is where they should be. Now put foundations under them.
—Henry David Thoreau

It is never too late to be what you might have been.
—George Eliot

A celebrity is a person who works hard all his [or her] life to become well known, then wears dark glasses to avoid being recognized.
—Fred Allen

I think most of us are looking for a calling, not a job. Most of us, like the assembly line worker, have had jobs that are too small for our spirit.
—Nora Watson

I am a marvelous housekeeper. Every time I leave a man I keep his house.
—Zsa Zsa Gabor

A good reputation is more valuable than money.
—Publius

If you aren't fired with enthusiasm, you will be fired with enthusiasm.
—Vince Lombardi

Very little is needed to make a happy life.
—Marcus Aurelius Antoninus

When you reach for the stars, you may not quite get one, but you won't come up with a handful of mud.
—Leo Burnett

Family and Friendship

Making the decision to have a child—it's momentous. It is to decide forever to have your heart go walking around outside your body.
—ELIZABETH STONE

Any mother could perform the jobs of several air-traffic controllers with ease.
—LISA ALTHER

Familiarity breeds contempt.—AESOP;

—and children.—MARK TWAIN

It takes a village to raise a child.
—AFRICAN PROVERB

Nobody who has not been in the interior of a family can say what the difficulties of any individual of that family may be.
—JANE AUSTEN

You know the only people who are *always* sure about the proper way to raise children? Those who've never had any.
—BILL COSBY

Insanity is hereditary—you get it from your children.
—SAM LEVENSON

Govern a family as you would fry small fish—gently.
—CHINESE PROVERB

Everything that irritates us about others can lead us to an understanding of ourselves.
—MORTON HUNT

The meeting of two personalities is like the contact of two chemical substances: if there is any reaction, both are transformed.
—CARL JUNG

The only way to have a friend is to be one.
—RALPH WALDO EMERSON

Wisdom for Living

It is not easy to find happiness in ourselves, and it is not possible to find it elsewhere.
—AGNES REPPLIER

Seize the day; put no trust in the morrow.
—HORACE

Don't be afraid your life will end; be afraid that it will never begin.
—GRACE HANSEN

My life, my *real* life, was in danger, and not from anything other people might do but from the hatred I carried in my own heart.
—JAMES BALDWIN

No one can make you feel inferior without your consent.
—ELEANOR ROOSEVELT

Too much of a good thing can be wonderful.
—MAE WEST

What we anticipate seldom occurs; what we least expect generally happens.
—BENJAMIN DISRAELI

Take your life in your own hands and what happens? A terrible thing: no one to blame.
—ERICA JONG

Regret is an appalling waste of energy: you can't build on it; it is good only for wallowing in.
—KATHERINE MANSFIELD

It is good to have an end to journey toward; but it is the journey that matters, in the end.
—URSULA K. LE GUIN

Flowers grow out of dark moments.
—CORITA KENT

Lying is done with words and also with silence.
—ADRIENNE RICH

Pick battles big enough to matter, small enough to win.
—JONATHAN KOZOL

You can't hold a man [or a woman] down without staying down with him [or her].
—BOOKER T. WASHINGTON

A fanatic is one who can't change his [or her] mind and won't change the subject.
—WINSTON CHURCHILL

Nobody cares if you can't dance well. Just get up and dance.
—DAVE BARRY

Time wounds all heels.
—JANE ACE

When you come to a fork in the road, take it.
—YOGI BERRA

APPENDIX 1

Parts of Speech Review

A knowledge of basic grammar terms will make your study of English easier. Throughout this book, these key terms are explained as needed and are accompanied by ample practice. For your convenience and reference, the following is a short review of the eight parts of speech.

Nouns

Nouns are the names of persons, places, things, animals, activities, and ideas.*

Persons:	Ms. Caulfield, Mike, secretaries
Places:	Puerto Rico, Vermont, gas station
Things:	sandwich, Sears, eyelash
Animals:	whale, ants, Lassie
Activities:	running, discussion, tennis
Ideas:	freedom, intelligence, humor

Pronouns

Pronouns replace or refer to nouns or other pronouns. The word that a pronoun replaces is called its *antecedent*.**

My partner succeeded; *she* built a better mousetrap!

These computers are amazing; *they* alphabetize and index.

Everyone should do *his* or *her* best.

All students should do *their* best.

*For more work on nouns, see Chapter 19.

**For more work on pronouns, see Chapter 20.

Pronouns take different forms, depending on how they are used in a sentence. They can be the subjects of sentences *(I, you, he, she, it, we, they)* or the objects of verbs and prepositions *(me, you, him, her, it, us, them).* They also can show possession *(my, mine, your, yours, his, her, hers, its, our, ours, their, theirs).*

Subject:	You had better finish on time.
	Did *someone* leave a laptop on the chair?
Object of verb:	Robert saw *her* on Thursday.
Object of preposition:	That VCR is for *her.*
Possessive:	Did Tom leave *his* sweater on the dresser?

Verbs

Verbs can be either action verbs or linking verbs. Verbs can be single words or groups of words.*

Action verbs show what action the subject of the sentence performs.

Leila *bought* a French dictionary.

Jack *has opened* the letter.

Linking verbs link the subject of a sentence with a descriptive word or words. Common linking verbs are *be, act, appear, become, feel, get, look, remain, seem, smell, sound,* and *taste.*

This report *seems* well organized and complete.

You *have been* quiet this morning.

The **present participle** of a verb is its *-ing* form. The present participle can be combined with some form of the verb *to be* to create the progressive tenses, or it can be used as an adjective or a noun.

Geraldo *was waiting* for the report.	*(past progressive tense)*
The *waiting* taxis lined up at the curb.	*(adjective)*
Waiting for trains bores me.	*(noun)*

The **past participle** of a verb can be combined with helping verbs to create different tenses, it can be combined with forms of *to be* to create the passive voice, or it can be used as an adjective. Past participles regularly end in *-d* or *-ed,* but irregular verbs take other forms *(seen, known, taken).*

*For more work on verbs, see Unit 3.

He *has edited* many articles for us. *(present perfect tense)*
This report *was edited* by the committee. *(passive voice)*
The *edited* report reads well. *(adjective)*

Every verb can be written as an *infinitive: to* plus the *simple form* of the verb.

She was surprised *to meet* him at the bus stop.

Adjectives

Adjectives describe or modify nouns or pronouns. Adjectives can precede or follow the words they describe.*

Several green chairs arrived today.
Collins Lake is *dangerous* and *deep.*

Adverbs

Adverbs describe or modify verbs, adjectives, or other adverbs.**

Brandy reads *carefully*. *(adverb describes verb)*
She is *extremely* tired. *(adverb describes adjective)*
He wants a promotion *very* badly. *(adverb describes adverb)*

Prepositions

A **preposition** begins a *prepositional phrase.* A **prepositional phrase** contains a preposition (a word such as *at, in, of,* or *with*), its object (a noun or pronoun), and any adjectives modifying the object.†

Preposition	Object
after	*work*
on	the blue *table*
under	the broken *stairs*

*For more work on adjectives, see Chapter 21.
**For more work on adverbs, see Chapter 21.
†For more work on prepositions, see Chapter 22.

Conjunctions

Conjunctions are connector words.

Coordinating conjunctions *(and, but, for, nor, or, so, yet)* join two equal words or groups of words.*

James is quiet *but* sharp.

Ms. Chin *and* Mr. Warburton attended the Ice Capades.

He printed out the report, *and* Ms. Helfman faxed it immediately.

She will go to Norfolk Community College, *but* she will also continue working at the shoe store.

Subordinating conjunctions (*after, because, if, since, unless,* and so on) join an independent idea with a dependent idea.

Whenever Ken comes to visit, he takes the family out to dinner.

I haven't been sleeping well *because* I've been drinking too much coffee.

Interjections

Interjections are words such as *ouch* and *hooray* that express strong feeling. They are rarely used in formal writing.

If the interjection is the entire sentence, it is followed by an exclamation point. If the interjection is attached to a sentence, it is followed by a comma.

Hey! You left your wallet in the phone booth.

Oh, she forgot to send in her tax return.

A Reminder

REMEMBER: The same word may be used as a different part of speech.

Harry *thought* about the problem. *(verb)*

Your *thought* is a good one. *(noun)*

*For more work on conjunctions, see Chapters 13 and 14.

APPENDIX 2

Some Guidelines for Students of English as a Second Language

Count and Noncount Nouns

Count nouns refer to people, places, or things that are separate units. You can often point to them, and you can always count them.

Count Noun	Sample Sentence
computer	The writing lab has four *computers*.
dime	There are two *dimes* under your chair.
professor	All of my *professors* are at a conference today.
notebook	I carry three *notebooks* in my backpack.
child	Why is your *child* jumping on the table?

Noncount nouns refer to things that are wholes. You cannot count them separately. Noncount nouns may refer to ideas, feelings, and other things that you cannot see or touch. Noncount nouns may refer to food or beverages.

Noncount Noun	Sample Sentence
courage	It takes *courage* to study a new language.
equipment	The company sells office *equipment*.
happiness	We wish the bride and groom much *happiness*.
bread	Who will slice this loaf of *bread*?
meat	Do you eat *meat*, or are you a vegetarian?
coffee	The *coffee* turned cold as we talked.

Plurals of Count and Noncount Nouns

Most count nouns form the plural by adding *-s* or *-es*. Some count nouns have irregular plurals.*

Plurals of Count Nouns	
ship/ships	newspaper/newspapers
flower/flowers	nurse/nurses
library/libraries	knife/knives
child/children	woman/women

Noncount nouns do not usually form the plural at all. It is incorrect to say *homeworks, equipments,* or *happinesses.*

PRACTICE 1

Write the plural for every count noun. If the noun is a noncount noun, write *no plural.*

1. mountain	mountains	6. man	men
2. wealth	no plural	7. assignment	assignments
3. forgiveness	no plural	8. homework	no plural
4. student	students	9. knowledge	no plural
5. generosity	no plural	10. bravery	no plural

Some nouns have both a count meaning and a noncount meaning. Usually, the count meaning is concrete and specific. Usually, the noncount meaning is abstract and general.

Count meaning: All the *lights* in the classroom went out.
Noncount meaning: What is the speed of *light*?

Count meaning: Odd *sounds* came from the basement.
Noncount meaning: The speed of *sound* is slower than the speed of light.

Food and beverages, which are usually noncount nouns, may also have a count meaning.

Count meaning: This store sells *fruits, pies,* and *teas* from different countries.
Noncount meaning: Would you like some more *fruit, pie,* or *tea?*

Articles with Count and Noncount Nouns

Indefinite Articles

The words *a* and *an* are **indefinite articles.** They refer to one *nonspecific* (indefinite) thing. For example, "a man" refers to *any* man, not to a specific, particular man. **The article *a* or *an* is used before a singular count noun.****

*For work on singular and plural nouns, see Chapter 19.
**For when to use *an* instead of *a*, see Chapter 32.

Singular Count Noun	With Indefinite Article
question	a question
textbook	a textbook
elephant	an elephant
umbrella	an umbrella

The indefinite article *a* or *an* is never used before a noncount noun.

Noncount Noun	Sample Sentence
music	*Incorrect:* I enjoy a music.
	Correct: I enjoy music.
health	*Incorrect:* Her father is in a poor health.
	Correct: Her father is in poor health.
patients	*Incorrect:* Good teachers have a patience.
	Correct: Good teachers have patience.
freedom	*Incorrect:* We have a freedom to choose our courses.
	Correct: We have freedom to choose our courses.

PRACTICE 2

The indefinite article *a* or *an* is italicized in each sentence. Cross out *a* or *an* if it is used incorrectly. If the sentence is correct, write *correct* on the line provided.

1. My friends give me ~~*a*~~ help when I need it. __________
2. He is in ~~*a*~~ love with that singer. __________
3. H ~~*An*~~ honesty is the best policy. __________
4. We have *an* answer to your question. correct
5. They have ~~*an*~~ information for us. __________

Definite Articles

The word *the* is a **definite article.** It refers to one (or more) *specific* (definite) thing (or things). For example, "the man" refers not to *any* man but to a specific, particular man. "The men" (plural) refers to specific, particular men. **The article *the* is used before singular and plural count nouns.**

Definite (*The*) and Indefinite Articles (*A/An*) with Count Nouns

I saw *the* film. (singular; refers to a specific film)

I saw *the* films. (plural; refers to more than one specific film)

I saw *a* film. (refers to any film; nonspecific)

I enjoy seeing *a* good film. (refers to any good film; nonspecific)

I like *a* film that has an important message. (refers to any film that has an important message; nonspecific)

The film that I saw last night had an important message. (refers to a specific film)

The definite article *the* is used before a noncount noun only if the noun is specifically identified.

Noncount Noun	Sample Sentence
fitness	*Incorrect:* He has *the* fitness. (not identified) *Correct:* He has *the* fitness of a person half his age. (identified) *Incorrect:* *The* fitness is a goal for many people. (not identified) *Correct:* Fitness is a goal for many people. (not identified, so no *the*)
art	*Incorrect:* I do not understand *the* art. (not identified) *Correct:* I do not understand *the* art in this show. (identified) *Correct:* I do not understand *the* art that you have created. (identified) *Incorrect:* *The* art touches our hearts and minds. (not identified) *Correct:* Art touches our hearts and minds. (not identified, so no *the*)

PRACTICE 3

The definite article *the* is italicized whenever it appears below. Cross it out if it is used incorrectly. If the sentence is correct, write *correct* on the line provided.

1. She dresses with ~~*the*~~ style. __________
2. *The* beauty of this building surprises me. correct
3. This building has *the* beauty of a work of art. correct
4. ~~*The*~~ courage is an important quality. __________
5. Alex has ~~*the*~~ wealth but not ~~*the*~~ happiness. __________

Verb + Gerund

A **gerund** is a noun that is made up of a verb plus *-ing*. The italicized words below are gerunds.

> *Playing* solitaire on the computer helps some students relax.
>
> I enjoy *hiking* in high mountains.

In the first sentence, the gerund *playing* is the simple subject of the sentence.* In the second sentence the gerund *hiking* is the object of the verb enjoy.** Some common verbs are often followed by gerunds.

---

*For more on simple subjects, see Chapter 6, Part A.

**For more on objects of verbs, see Chapter 20, Part F, "Pronouns as Objects."

Some Common Verbs That Can Be Followed by a Gerund

Verb	Sample Sentence with Gerund
consider	Would you *consider* ***taking*** a course in accounting?
discuss	Let's *discuss* ***buying*** a fax machine.
enjoy	I *enjoy* ***jogging*** in the morning before work.
finish	Sue *finished* ***studying*** for her nursing exam.
keep	*Keep* ***trying*** and you will succeed.
postpone	The Brookses *postponed* ***visiting*** their grandchildren.
quit	Three of my friends *quit* ***smoking*** this year.

The verbs listed above are *never* followed by an infinitive (*to* + the simple form of the verb)*

Incorrect: Would you consider *to take* a course in journalism?

Incorrect: Let's discuss *to buy* a fax machine.

Incorrect: I enjoy *to jog* in the morning before work.

PRACTICE 4

Write a gerund after each verb in the blank space provided. Sample answers

1. Dave enjoys ___watching___ television in the evening.
2. Have you finished ___studying___ for tomorrow's exam?
3. Pat is considering ___flying___ to Mexico next month.
4. I have postponed ___celebrating___ until I receive the results of the test.
5. We are discussing ___leasing___ a car.

Preposition + Gerund

A preposition** may be followed by a gerund.

I forgive you *for* ***stepping*** on my toe.

Alice believes *in* ***pushing*** herself to her limits.

We made the flight *by* ***running*** from one terminal to another.

A preposition is *never* followed by an infinitive (*to* + the simple form of the verb.)

Incorrect: I forgive you *for* ***to step*** on my toe.

Incorrect: Alice believes *in* ***to push*** herself to her limits.

Incorrect: We made the flight *by* ***to run*** from one terminal to another.

*For more on infinitives, see Chapter 12, Part E.

**For more on prepositions, see Chapter 22.

PRACTICE 5

Write a gerund after the preposition in each blank space provided. Sample answers

1. We have succeeding in ___finding___ the CD you wanted.
2. You can get there by ___turning___ left at the next corner.
3. Thank you for ___buying___ those striped socks for me.
4. I enjoy sports like ___canoeing___ and ___kayaking___ .
5. Between ___going___ to school and ___working___, I have little time for ___relaxing___ .

Verb + Infinitive

Many verbs are followed by the **infinitive** (*to* + the simple form of the verb).

Some Common Verbs That Can Be Followed by an Infinitive

Verb	Sample Sentence
afford	Carla can *afford* ***to buy*** a new outfit whenever she wants.
agree	I *agree* ***to marry*** you a year from today.
appear	He *appears* ***to be*** inspired by his new job.
decide	Will they *decide* ***to drive*** across the country?
expect	Jamal *expects* ***to graduate*** next year.
forget	Please do not *forget* ***to cash*** the check.
hope	My nephews *hope* ***to visit*** Santa Fe this year.
intend	I *intend* ***to study*** harder this semester than I did last semester.
mean	Did Frank *mean* ***to leave*** his lunch on the kitchen table?
need	Do you *need* ***to stop*** for a break now?
plan	Justin *plans* ***to go*** into advertising.
promise	Sharon has *promised* ***to paint*** this wall green.
offer	Did they really *offer* ***to babysit*** for a month?
refuse	Sean *refuses* ***to walk*** another step.
try	Let's *try* ***to set*** up this tent before dark.
wait	On the other hand, we could *wait* ***to camp*** out until tomorrow.

PRACTICE 6

Write an infinitive after the verb in each blank space provided. Sample answers

1. The plumber promised ___to fix___ the sink today.
2. My son plans ___to take___ a course in electrical engineering.
3. We do not want ___to be___ late for the meeting again.
4. They refused ___to begin___ before everyone was ready.
5. I expect ___to see___ Jim next week.

Verb + Either Gerund or Infinitive

Some verbs can be followed by *either* a gerund or an infinitive.

Some Common Verbs That Can Be Followed by a Gerund or an Infinitive

Verb	Sample Sentence
begin	They *began* ***to laugh.*** (infinitive)
	They *began* ***laughing.*** (gerund)
continue	Fran *continued* ***to speak.*** (infinitive)
	Fran *continued* ***speaking.*** (gerund)
hate	Juan *hates* ***to drive*** in the snow. (infinitive)
	Juan *hates* ***driving*** in the snow. (gerund)
like	My daughter *likes* ***to surf*** the Net. (infinitive)
	My daughter *likes* ***surfing*** the Net. (gerund)
love	Phil *loves* ***to watch*** soccer games. (infinitive)
	Phil *loves* ***watching*** soccer games. (gerund)
start	Will you *start* ***to write*** the paper tomorrow? (infinitive)
	Will you *start* ***writing*** the paper tomorrow? (gerund)

PRACTICE 7

For each pair of sentences, first write an infinitive in the space provided. Then write a gerund. Sample answers

1. a. (infinitive) Sue hates __to wait__ in long lines.
   b. (gerund) Sue hates __waiting__ in long lines.
2. a. (infinitive) When will we begin __to cook__ dinner?
   b. (gerund) When will we begin __cooking__ dinner?
3. a. (infinitive) Carmen loves __to sing__ in the rain.
   b. (gerund) Carmen loves __singing__ in the rain.
4. a. (infinitive) The motor continued __to rumble__ noisily.
   b. (gerund) The motor continued __rumbling__ noisily.
5. a. (infinitive) Suddenly, the people started __to clap__.
   b. (gerund) Suddenly, the people started __clapping__.

Acknowledgments

Page 376–377: Colman McCarthy, "Needed: Teaching Peace Literacy by Numbers," *National Catholic Reporter,* December 25, 1992, vol. 29, no. 9, p. 14. Reprinted by permission.

Page 380–381: Jack Riemer, "Playing a Violin with Three Strings," *Houston Chronicle,* February 10, 2001. Reprinted by permission of Rabbi Jack Riemer.

Pages 382–385: "Mrs. Flowers" copyright © 1969 and renewed 1997 by Maya Angelou, from *I Know Why the Caged Bird Sings* by Maya Angelou. Used by permission of Random House, Inc.

Pages 386–387: "One Man's Kids" from Daniel Meier, "About Men: One Man's Kids," *The New York Times,* November 1, 1987. Copyright © 1987 Daniel Meier. Reprinted by permission.

Pages 388–390: "Another Road Hog with Too Much Oink," copyright © 2000 by Dave Barry, from *Dave Barry Is Not Taking This Sitting Down* by Dave Barry. Used by permission of Crown Publishers, a division of Random House, Inc.

Pages 391–392: "You Can Take This Job and . . . Well, It Might Surprise You," by Ana Veciana-Suarez. Copyright 2003 by *Miami Herald.* Reproduced with permission of MIAMI HERALD in the format Textbook via Copyright Clearance Center.

Pages 393–394: "A Homemade Education," copyright © 1964 by Alex Haley and Malcom X. Copyright © 1965 by Alex Haley and Betty Shabazz. From *The Autobiography of Malcolm X* by Malcolm X and Alex Haley. Used by permission of Random House, Inc.

Pages 395–397: "Barbie at 35" by Anna Quindlen. *The New York Times,* September 10, 1994. Copyright © 1994, The New York Times Company. Reprinted by permission.

Pages 397–399: "Papa, The Teacher" from *Papa, My Father* by Leo Buscaglia. Copyright © 1989 Leo F. Buscaglia. Reprinted by permission.

Pages 400–402: "My English" copyright © 1982, 1998 by Julia Alvarez. Published in a slightly different form in *Something to Declare,* Algonquin Books of Chapel Hill, 1998. Reprinted by permission of Susan Bergholz Literary Services, New York. All rights reserved.

Pages 403–404: "Montgomery, Alabama, 1955" from *Rosa Parks: My Story* by Rosa Parks with Jim Haskins, copyright © 1992 by Rosa Parks. Used by permission of Dial Books for Young Readers, A Division of Penguin Young Readers Group, A Member of Penguin Group (USA) Inc., 345 Hudson Street, New York, NY 10014. All rights reserved.

Pages 411–412: "Anonymity Brings Out Our Dark Sides," from *The Miami Herald* by Leonard Pitts, Jr. Copyright 2003 by MIAMI HERALD. Reproduced with permission of MIAMI HERALD in the format Textbook via Copyright Clearance Center.

Pages 413–415: "Hot Dogs and Wild Geese," from *Funny in Farsi* by Firoozeh Dumas, copyright © 2003 by Firoozeh Dumas. Used by permission of Villard Books, a division of Random House, Inc.

Pages 417–419: "In This Arranged Marriage, Love Came Later" by Shoba Narayan. Reprinted by permission of the Ellen Levine Literary Agency. Copyright © by Shoba Narayan.

Page 420–421: "The Hidden Life of Bottled Water," by Liza Gross. Reprinted by permission of Sierra.

Pages 422–423: "Four Directions" from *The Joy Luck Club* by Amy Tan. Copyright © 1989 by Amy Tan. Used by permission of G. P. Putnam's Sons, a division of Penguin Putnam Inc.

Pages 424–427: "Emotional Intelligence" from *Emotional Intelligence* by Daniel Goleman, copyright © 1995 by Daniel Goleman. Used by permission of Bantam Books, a division of Random House, Inc.

Index

Index of Rhetorical Modes

This index classifies paragraphs and essays in this text according to rhetorical mode. Very little writing containing errors is listed. The exceptions are four Writers' Workshops and two other passages—marked *with errors*—in which otherwise excellent writing warrants inclusion.

Index to the Readings

Rhetorical Index to the Readings